Enduring Issues in Special Education

Enduring Issues in Special Education is aimed at any course in the undergraduate or graduate special education curriculum that is wholly or partly devoted to a critical examination of current issues in special education. The book organizes 28 chapters into seven sections using familiar structuring principles—what, who, where, how, when, why, and whither. Each section begins with an introduction that provides historical, legal, and theoretical background information and organizing commentary for the chapters that follow. The book's objective, in addition to informing the readers about the issues, is to develop critical thinking skills in the context of special education. Key features include the following:

Dialectic Format—Each of the 28 chapters presents compelling reasons for addressing the issue at hand and specific ways to do so. Because each issue is written from different perspectives and focuses on a variety of aspects, readers are encouraged to weigh the arguments, seek additional information, and come up with synthesized positions of their own.

Organizing Framework—The book's seven sections have been arranged according to a scheme that is the essence of most investigative reporting and provides a coherent, easy-to-understand framework for readers.

Expertise—All chapters are written by leading scholars who are highly regarded experts in their fields and conclude with suggested readings and discussion questions for additional study.

Barbara Bateman is a consultant in special education law and Professor Emerita at the University of Oregon.

John Wills Lloyd is Professor of Education and Coordinator for the Program in Special Education at the University of Virginia, Curry School of Education.

Melody Tankersley is Professor of Special Education and Associate Provost for Academic Affairs at Kent State University.

Enduring Issues in Special Education

Personal Perspectives

Edited by Barbara Bateman
John Wills Lloyd
Melody Tankersley

Routledge
Taylor & Francis Group

NEW YORK AND LONDON

First published 2015
by Routledge
711 Third Avenue, New York, NY 10017

and by Routledge
2 Park Square, Milton Park, Abingdon, Oxon OX14 4RN

Routledge is an imprint of the Taylor & Francis Group, an informa business

Library of Congress Cataloging-in-Publication Data

Enduring issues in special education : personal perspectives / edited by
  Barbara Bateman, John W. Lloyd, Melody Tankersley.
    pages cm
  Includes bibliographical references and index.
  1. Special education.   I. Bateman, Barbara.
  LC3965.E53 2015
  371.9—dc23
  2014027560

ISBN: 978-0-415-53917-3 (hbk)
ISBN: 978-0-415-53918-0 (pbk)
ISBN: 978-0-203-10848-2 (ebk)

Typeset in Minion
by Apex CoVantage, LLC

Printed and bound in the United States of America
by Edwards Brothers Malloy

CONTENTS

David J. Chard		xi
Foreword		xiii
Preface		xvii

Chapter 1	Introduction: Does Special Education Have Issues?	4

JOHN WILLS LLOYD, MELODY TANKERSLEY, & BARBARA BATEMAN

Section I	**What is Special Education?**	9

Chapter 2	What is Special Education?	11

BARBARA BATEMAN, JOHN WILLS LLOYD, MELODY TANKERSLEY,
& TIARA SAUFLEY BROWN

Chapter 3	What Makes Special Education Special?	22

THOMAS E. SCRUGGS & MARGO A. MASTROPIERI

Chapter 4	What is Special Education Instruction?	37

PAIGE C. PULLEN & DANIEL P. HALLAHAN

Chapter 5	What Should We Teach Students with Moderate and Severe Developmental Disabilities?	52

DIANE M. BROWDER

Chapter 6	Special Education as "Specially Designed Instruction": Ode to the Architecture of Information and the Message	74

EDWARD J. KAME'ENUI

Section II	**Who Should Receive and Provide Special Education?**	93
Chapter 7	Who Should Receive and Provide Special Education? BARBARA BATEMAN, JOHN WILLS LLOYD, MELODY TANKERSLEY, & MELISSA K. DRIVER	95
Chapter 8	Cultural and Linguistic Diversity in Special Education JANETTE KLINGNER, BROOKE MOORE, ANNE O. DAVIDSON, AMY BOELÉ, ALISON BOARDMAN, ROBERTO FIGUEROA, SUBINI ANCY ANNAMMA, & NICOLE SAGER	110
Chapter 9	Who Should Receive Special Education Services and How Should Educators Identify Which Students are to Receive Special Education Services? ERICA S. LEMBKE	133
Chapter 10	Co-teaching: Not All Special Educators Should Dance MARGARET P. WEISS	155
Chapter 11	Who Makes a Difference! Next Generation Special Education Workforce Renewal MARCIA L. ROCK & BONNIE S. BILLINGSLEY	168
Section III	**Where Should Special Education Happen?**	187
Chapter 12	Where Should Special Education Take Place? BARBARA BATEMAN, MELODY TANKERSLEY, JOHN WILLS LLOYD, & KAT D. ALVES	189
Chapter 13	*Where* Should Students with Disabilities Receive Their Education? NAOMI ZIGMOND	198
Chapter 14	Placements for Special Education Students: The Promise and the Peril DIXIE SNOW HUEFNER	215
Chapter 15	Place Values: What Moral Psychology Can Tell Us About the Full Inclusion Debate in Special Education ANDREW L. WILEY	232
Section IV	**How Should Special Education be Practiced?**	251
Chapter 16	How is Special Education Practiced? JOHN WILLS LLOYD, MELODY TANKERSLEY, BARBARA BATEMAN, & SHANNA EISNER HIRSCH	253
Chapter 17	How Should Evidence-Based Practices be Determined? BRYAN G. COOK	266

Chapter 18   The Connection Between Assessment and Intervention:
How Can Screening Lead to Better Interventions?   285
KATHLEEN LYNNE LANE & HILL M. WALKER

Chapter 19   How Should Learning Environments (Schools and Classrooms)
be Structured for Best Learner Outcomes?   303
CHARLES R. GREENWOOD

Chapter 20   How Should We Evaluate Whether Special Education Works?   323
MARTHA L. THURLOW

Section V   When Should Special Education Begin and End?   341

Chapter 21   When Should Special Education Start and End?   343
BARBARA BATEMAN, JOHN WILLS LLOYD, MELODY TANKERSLEY, &
SARAH E. DILLON

Chapter 22   Children Should be Identified and Receive Special Education
Services in Early Childhood   351
JUDITH J. CARTA

Chapter 23   When Does Special Education End?   367
MICHAEL WEHMEYER

Section VI   Why Do We Have Special Education?   383

Chapter 24   Why Should We Have Special Education?   385
JOHN WILLS LLOYD, MELODY TANKERSLEY, & BARBARA BATEMAN

Chapter 25   Why We Should Have Special Education   398
JAMES M. KAUFFMAN

Chapter 26   How Should We Pay for Special Education?   410
THOMAS PARRISH

Chapter 27   Science Matters in Special Education   429
TIMOTHY J. LANDRUM

Section VII   Whither Special Education?   441

Chapter 28   Whither Special Education?   444
JOHN WILLS LLOYD, MELODY TANKERSLEY, BARBARA BATEMAN,
CHRISTINE BALAN, & PATRICIA A. LLOYD

Index   465

ABOUT DAVID J. CHARD

We are pleased to have David Chard provide the foreword for this volume. Professor Chard became dean at the Annette Caldwell Simmons School of Education and Human Development at Southern Methodist University in 2007 after holding faculty positions at Boston University, the University of Texas at Austin, and the University of Oregon. After completing undergraduate studies at Central Michigan University, he taught in California public schools and served as an educator in the Peace Corps. He then completed requirements for a Ph.D. at the University of Oregon.

We were fortunate that Professor Chard could interrupt his intense schedule of academic and policy activities to contribute to this volume. In addition to conducting extensive research on early reading and mathematics, Professor Chard has been a member of the Board of Directors for Education Sciences, the advisory group that oversees the U.S. Institute for Education Sciences, and in 2014 he was elected by fellow members of that board as its chair.

FOREWORD

For special education professionals and everyone concerned personally or professionally with children and adults with disabilities, understanding the history of our field is very important. As we near the 40th anniversary of the legislation that defined special education, it is important to understand the dramatic changes that have occurred in schools both as a result of special education and, in some cases, in spite of it. Early thinking about students with disabilities, even thinking that pre-dated special education, focused on the intra-individual characteristics of children, trying to pinpoint the deviation in their cognitive and social behavior. Presumably, the idea was to identify the biological basis of disability so that it might be altered or fixed. As students with disabilities were given access to public schools, emphasis shifted more to the services (i.e., curriculum and related services) schools could provide. For decades, we searched for methods to improve the programmatic support students received including the types of activities that would provide them the benefit they were guaranteed under the law. Subsequently, however, trends shifted again as parents and advocates became more focused on where and with whom students with disabilities received their education rather than on the specific programs and services rendered. Moreover, the push for greater inclusion didn't stop with place but also included access to the general education curriculum and inclusion in state systems of accountability.

Each new generation comes to our field with a sense of the landscape of special education as it is, but not understanding where it came from, what contributions have been made, and with little vision of where it should be going to avoid making repeated mistakes or employing practices that are not effective. Unfortunately, today there is scant knowledge of the hard fought civil rights battles in the 1970s to get children with disabilities guaranteed access to a public education. In the past few years, schools across the country have been working to implement multi-tiered systems of support that include students who are eligible for special education services. Very few new teachers or school leaders know about the Regular Education Initiative or its relationship to the full inclusion movement.

In fact, newer professionals in our field probably do not fully understand the significance of special education legislation in terms of its detailed guidance on implementation and what that has meant to our development. I recall a course on special education law I took nearly 20 years ago from Dr. Barbara Bateman. She told a wet-behind-the-ears audience of graduate students that although P.L. 94-142, the Education for all Handicapped Children Act, was not a perfect piece of legislation, the regulations were thoughtfully crafted to enable schools to provide education programming and related services that students with disabilities would need in order to benefit from their public school experience. These regulations are very unique because they represent a federal law requiring that schools implement a system for referral and identification, education planning and instruction, placement decision-making, and evaluation. These regulations raised the stakes with regard to our expectations of schools to be both efficacious in their practice as well as accommodating to the broadest range of learners. Additionally, the regulations offered a framework that led to an evaluation culture for schools that had not existed earlier.

Perhaps as important as folks being knowledgeable of these large movements in our field is their awareness of specific research and clinical contributions that have been made to our schools as a result of research and innovation in the name of special education. Advances in early reading instruction, positive behavioral supports, curriculum-based measurement, self-determination, and transition are just a few of the many areas that have not only helped children and adults with disabilities in their learning and development, but they have also enhanced the quality of education for all children. This volume offers the reader insight into persistently challenging topics for which significant contributions have been made to our understanding of special education over the past several decades. The editors of this volume, Bateman, Lloyd, and Tankersley, represent three generations of special education scholars and teachers. In turn, they have assembled chapters from some of special education's most prominent research scholars. Their expertise spans developmental levels, theoretical frameworks, disability areas, and domains of academic development. Each author or set of authors was thoughtfully recruited to develop a chapter on their particular expertise and related to fundamental questions; questions that were asked when special education was conceived and are still being asked today. In many ways, these questions are timeless. As our understanding of children advances and our instructional practices are refined based on accumulating evidence, we will likely find ourselves returning to the same questions in another 20 years.

A second feature that I appreciated about the chapters in this volume is that the authors were encouraged to reflect on their personal connections to their work. Some authors describe how their work has dramatically changed their academic expectations for students with disabilities, and others passionately describe how uniquely designed instruction is the cornerstone to effective special education. Others offer extensive reviews of literature on the effectiveness of specific practices that persist in our field sometimes with little evidence of their impact on student outcomes. These personal reflections are sometimes whimsical and sometimes very personal. But, above all else, they illustrate the authors' commitment to special education and to improving the quality of education and life for students with disabilities.

As a parent of two children who have received special education services, this volume also represents a community that produces knowledge that has changed my children's lives. Our two children who have received special education services are nearly a generation apart in age. Our understanding of effective instructional practices, related services, and assessments has changed dramatically in 15 years. The contributions represented in these chapters come from a community of scholars that have deepened the knowledge and skills of teachers, related service personnel, and parents on how to provide for our children with disabilities. Readers should be aware that these contributions are practical and should be at the fingertips of all special education professionals.

Enduring Issues in Special Education: Personal Perspectives is ultimately about improving the futures of children with disabilities. It offers teachers, scholars, university students, and even parents a view of the many dimensions that are part of special education. It also reveals how special education teachers-turned-scholars have worked to answer questions that they have been asking for decades and how those answers affect today's practice. The chapters also tell a story about the power that effective policy can have in improving people's lives; why special education practice and research is fundamental to meeting the needs of individuals with disabilities as well as other children who attend school with them. Above all, this book makes clear why advocacy, knowledge, and improved practice are vital.

David J. Chard
Leon Simmons Dean
SMU Simmons School of Education
and Human Development

PREFACE

We three editors share an interest in discussing issues of special education. In our behavioral moments, we might say that we find it reinforcing to exchange opinions and questions about current topics that our colleagues and we discuss. In lay terms, we'd just say that it's fun to yammer about stuff like identification, inclusion, and implementation of effective practices. That's one explanation for why you are reading this book.

Another explanation is that we wanted to organize the discussion of issues in special education in a coherent, accessible way. In our experience, discussions of issues in special education are usually chaotic or, at best, inchoate. They are simply ill-organized. We think that makes them especially difficult to understand for professionals who are relatively new to the business of special education. It might seem like standing in the center of a sphere with arrows coming at one from multiple—if not all—directions. So, we hatched a plan to use a familiar structure—Kipling's six honest serving-men: *who, what, when, where, how,* and *why*—to organize the discussion of issues. You will have a more complete introduction to this organization when you read our introduction in just a few pages.

Another reason you are reading this book is that special education is a discipline or sub-discipline that is rife with argument. We do have issues (see the introduction)! Special educators are passionate about them. We care about what we do. We squabble. We bicker. We make up names for our colleagues (Segregationists! Inclusionistas! Well, not really . . .). Even if it's not a good idea to call those with whom we disagree names, it's a good idea to talk with each other about these issues, to listen to differing views about them. This book doesn't pretend to present a fully balanced view of all perspectives, but it gives the reader different views. That's one of the reasons we've edited it. We want you to hear other professionals' personal perspectives.

And that helps to highlight another important reason for the existence of this book: There are 20 chapters here contributed by 32 authors (as well eight chapters by we three editors and our six collaborators). This book represents the input of many accomplished special educators. Readers will come to know leaders in special education simply by having completed this book. We are indebted to the contributing authors and our collaborators for their work on this book. They endured our (and especially JohnL's) irregular and last-minute requests for materials. They produced excellent content. They are the reason for the good qualities of this tome. All they get in return is an additional entry on their already hefty curriculum vitae and, perhaps, a free beverage of their choice whenever they see one of the editors near a watering hole.

Yet another explanation for why you are reading this book is that we had editors who believed in the concept and supported us. We are grateful to Alex Masulis for his patience and help in making this project come to fruition. Production schedules that allowed this to work—"it's going to be tight"—probably will rarely again be matched, but we are glad he was willing to push them for us, and to Abigail Stanley for actually making it happen. And, we are especially appreciative of the support of Lane Akers. One of us (John) has worked with Lane for decades and the relationship has always been collegial. It was Lane who really encouraged us to create this book, who took an active interest years before we even sketched a table of contents. Lane has done many fine books. We don't know if this will stand as Lane's last book, but wherever it is in his long list of titles, we hope it is one in which he can take some pride.

Of course, you wouldn't be reading this book if it weren't for the people with whom we live at home. We want to thank our families for tolerating our schedules (i.e., absences) and other misbehavior during our work on this book. They've gotten to see us excited about having such an all-star line-up of contributors, fretting about getting content from a few stragglers, bleary-eyed from editing manuscripts, and dingy after long hours associated with generating our own parts of the book. Although we dedicated the book to our mentors, our families deserve special thanks for sticking by us.

Getting to Know John Wills Lloyd

After volunteering to teach blind kids swimming during junior high, I began working in special schools as a teacher's aide for students with many different types of disabilities—autism, emotional and behavioral disorders, learning disabilities, and intellectual disabilities—ranging from kindergarten to high school when I was in college in the mid- and late-1960s. I learned teaching skills from some very good teachers—and some really challenging students.

Later Pat Lloyd and I were teaching parents for four children who had been living in a state hospital. Although we were in our early 20s, we had children ranging from 7 to 15 living with us. We fixed their meals, did their laundry, taught them manners, took them to school and the fair, and helped them adapt to living in the community.

I went back to teaching—before our modern laws—in very heterogeneous classes of students. Just about every one of the students was intriguing and even delightful in her or his own way. Pat and I even taught together some of the time. I have fond memories of many of them even though that was the 1970s.

I learned how to manage behavior from those very good teachers and those students with whom I worked. I also read the *Journal of Applied Behavior Analysis* and would say to myself, "Oh, I could use that."

I could get my students to sit at their desks, follow directions, and work industriously. I'd read lots of books and journals; I thought I knew a lot. But I didn't know how to structure academic instruction effectively; other than DISTAR, all I really could do was give students graduated sequences of worksheets. So, I went to graduate school to learn about instruction.

The night of my first class in graduate school at Oregon, I listened to Barb Bateman give a three-hour lecture that re-captured and reinterpreted nearly everything I'd read, made me reflect anew on lots of what I'd experienced, challenged me to reconsider my assumptions, and directed me to a path of critical thinking that I hope I've upheld and I know I've never regretted following. And then, after class, in a private moment, she told me that if I wanted to know about teaching, I should go talk to Zig. To my benefit, I followed that advice.

I went home late that night and told Pat Lloyd all about that first class. It was transformative for me. Thanks, Barb.

Getting to Know Melody Tankersley

As far back as I can remember I wanted to be a teacher. My mother recounts the days I would run into the house from kindergarten and first grade and drag my younger brother into my bedroom to teach him what I had just learned in school. My mother likes to talk about all of the admonishments of, *"No, Chuck! Do it this way!"* yelled from my room. By the time he entered kindergarten, he no longer enjoyed "playing" school, so I had to line up my dolls and kittens to be my students (kittens do not take direction very well).

Although I knew I wanted to teach, I did not know who I wanted to teach until I began my practicum experience in my undergraduate program at Winthrop College (now Winthrop University). I was captivated and motivated by my students with emotional and behavioral disorders and knew that I had found my career. My first job was as a special education teacher in a small-town high school in South Carolina where the students had previously been taught in alternative placements. We set up class in the high school basement (colloquially referred to as the dungeon) in the old ROTC room (rumored to have guns in the locked cabinets). Certainly, it was not what I expected my first classroom to look like. It was a new experience for me and also for my students, all of whom had been away from their general education peers for many years. We learned a lot together—and not always lessons that my students or I expected to learn. But my first group of students inspired me to continue looking for answers and approaches that would enhance their learning, interactions, and outcomes.

Eventually, I completed my Masters degree in special education and began teaching students with severe emotional and behavioral disorders in a residential treatment facility in Charlotte, North Carolina. The full array of services brought to bear upon the children, including family, psychological, medical, educational, and agency programming, helped me to understand the pervasive and long-term needs of my students. This experience started me thinking about how we equip teachers and other professionals with the skills, experiences, and fortitude necessary to work most effectively with children and youths with emotional and behavioral disorders.

So, back to school I went. I entered my doctoral program at the University of Virginia with the good fortune of having John Lloyd as my advisor. John encouraged me to keep asking questions and looking at research to provide answers to the most effective practices for students with disabilities. This remains my quest today—to find instructional approaches that have the best likelihood of positively influencing the learning and interactions of children and youths with disabilities, and to make those approaches widely available to their teachers, service providers, and family members.

Getting to Know Barbara Bateman

On a cold wintery night almost 60 years ago I walked up the steps of a state school for the blind to begin a job for which my preparation was a one-hour lecture in my first year of graduate school. I taught six blind children, ages 6–13, who also had emotional–behavioral issues. I had no idea what I was doing, but I fell in love with doing it. After another term in graduate school I did an internship in a state hospital for mentally retarded adults and children and then began doctoral study. After a year Dr. Sam Kirk suggested I should spend a couple of years in public schools doing remedial reading, speech therapy, psychological testing, parent counseling, and more. We were still almost 20 years away from IDEA being passed and many children with disabilities were excluded from school. Those who did attend were often taught by folks as ill prepared as I was.

After finishing my doctorate, I went into college teaching and stayed there, even while going to law school. I graduated from Oregon's law school the year after IDEA (then P.L. 94-142) was passed (near the time John Lloyd graduated from Oregon's special education doctoral program) and since then have stood with one foot each in law and special education. I have thoroughly enjoyed teaching special education law to graduate students, serving as a hearing officer, expert witness, and consultant to attorneys in special education cases, as well as conducting in-service training for special education and related service personnel.

Now that I am 80 and almost retired I spend time birding, writing, and thinking about contentious issues in special education, especially the widespread misunderstanding of LRE and the reluctance of some educators to base decisions on data. And I still ponder how a learning disability ought to be identified.

1

INTRODUCTION:
DOES SPECIAL EDUCATION HAVE ISSUES?

John Wills Lloyd, Melody Tankersley, & Barbara Bateman

Contemporary special education regularly makes headlines for its high costs, perceived inequity in discipline, associations with bullying, and other matters that grab lay public attention and spark controversy. Throughout its history, special education has been wracked by contentious issues. As long ago as the early 1800s, according to Rubinstein (1948), the famous physician Benjamin Rush discussed issues in treatment of children with emotional and behavioral disorders. As the nineteenth century turned into the twentieth century, Bernard Sachs (1895, 1905) published two editions of a 500-page text about "the nervous diseases of children" that covered everything from spina bifida to idiocy and imbecility and insanity, with comments about a controversy over whether masturbation caused the last of these (1905, p. 522).

Current controversies may seem less far-fetched, but one only needs consider suggestions from relatively recent times to find recommendations that make one pause. Special education in the 2000s is only a few decades removed from having children learn to creep and crawl by special patterns or sit in chairs that spin them about as if they were in a carnival ride. So, even if few special educators today need to be prepared to discuss masturbation as a cause for emotional and behavioral disorders, they clearly need to be ready to discuss other issues that are difficult to confront. For example, doesn't special education give preferential treatment to some children and isn't that inherently unfair, even un-American? Special educators cannot shy away from hard topics, whether the topic is fairness or sham therapies.

IN CONSIDERATION OF ISSUES

Today, special education is a well-established part of a public education in the United States and in many parts of the developed and developing world (see, e.g., Lloyd, Keller, & Hung, 2007). However, it is not necessarily a well-understood or well-accepted aspect of public education. Issues of special education's access, costs, protections, instructional methods, teacher preparation, and outcomes seem as prevalent today as they did prior to the establishment of the Education for All Handicapped Children Act in 1975. This is not to say that the field of special education has not established a substantial body of knowledge about the issues; indeed, the scholarship of researchers and theorists in special education is vast, meaningful, and sound. However, issues persist.

Over the past several decades, writings on issues in special education have been categorized as "critical" (Sorrells, Rieth, & Sindelar, 2004; Ysseldyke, Algozzine, & Thurlow, 1992), "controversial" (Byrnes, 2002; Hornby, Atkinson, & Howard, 1997; Stainback & Stainback, 1992), and "contemporary" (Kauffman, 1981; Schmid & Nagata, 1983). Over 50 years ago, Maynard Reynolds (1962) identified segregation (e.g., placement), responsibility of the school (e.g., wrap-around services), financial aid (e.g., funding), and methods of classifying children (for purposes of placement) as current issues in special education. Certainly, these issues seem current today, as well.

It is not worrisome to us that issues are the same over the years. It would be alarming if the issues of more than 50 years ago were exactly the same, though. That is, although access is still an issue, the focus of the issue has evolved from one of access to any sort of instruction, to access into a building, to access to the general education classroom, to access to the general education curriculum. Likewise, teaching technologies also continue to be an issue of debate.

Over the past three decades, research has produced a significant and meaningful knowledge base of instructional techniques, moving the debate from the general question of what to do to the current question of which practices have a trustworthy and comprehensive set of empirical data that identify them as evidence-based. Although we may not have put to rest all issues surrounding access to instruction, place, or content, there are significant changes in the focus of them.

Perhaps many of the issues are the same today as they were in the past because families, students, teachers, taxpayers, and the educational enterprise as a whole continue to need many of the same things—e.g., a place for learning, instructional methods and content that are appropriate for the learner, professional development of the workforce, resources, evidence of effectiveness—yet our knowledge base and the social structure upon which schooling resides continues to change. Research consistently informs us of better ways to teach our students and how to advance our practices. Legislation refines, and often redefines, our processes. Society expects different outcomes from schools and families want new opportunities for their learners. We still have issues, and many of the same issues, because we continue to grow and develop.

Decidedly, special education has issues. And people adopt different views on issues. Perceptions of fairness, individuals' experiences and attributions, research results, and public opinion all may contribute to one's view of an issue. But as a field, it seems that special educators are often susceptible to the adaptation of untried and ineffective interventions. A vexing question related to the credibility of the field is why, historically, ineffective interventions persist and appear with cyclical regularity.

Perhaps one way to reduce adaptation of questionable interventions is to place more emphasis in our professional culture on the history of special education, specifically the history of effective and ineffective interventions. Educators more familiar with the history of special education's effective interventions and how they were developed and used may be better prepared to discriminate effective from ineffective interventions in their current work.

CONSIDERING ENDURING ISSUES

Our goal in preparing this book was to help prepare special educators to discuss difficult issues in special education not by presenting answers to issues, but by presenting intelligent, informed discussion of the issues from the perspectives of leading thinkers in contemporary special education. We have identified clusters of related issues that represent the most important enduring concerns in special education and have eminent special educators discuss them from their perspectives and their experiences in addressing them. These issues recur and the experts who discuss them in this book have either seen them ebb and flow personally during their careers or have studied their histories and are able to place them in perspective.

The enduring issues in special education have to do with ensuring that students with disabilities receive a free and appropriate public education. It is this last phrase—free and appropriate public education—that has characterized the conversation over the last 30 years of the twentieth century and the first 15 years of the twenty-first century. For example, issues of what constitutes a free and appropriate public education are concerned with securing access to educational services for students with disabilities, are focused on the substantial cost of paying for the education of students with disabilities, address the topic of assessing students for eligibility and results, and center around alternative methods for providing educational services for students.

Conceptualizing the issues in special education in this manner puts an extraordinary emphasis on legal aspects of special education. Although this is an appropriate emphasis, especially given that it was not until 1975 that students with disabilities were guaranteed access to public education, the issues that connect to the question of a free and appropriate public education are much more detailed than is captured by that simple phrase. In contemporary terms, the issues include prevention, eligibility and labeling, curriculum and methods, service delivery models, and outcomes.

ORDERING ISSUES CONCEPTUALLY

In this volume we have assembled a collection of statements by eminent authorities on various issues in special education. The collection of statements is organized around a familiar set of questions that we think provide a broad conceptual base for understanding the structure and complexity of issues in special education. The questions will be recognizable to those who have even a passing acquaintance with journalism as "the six *w*s" (who, what, where, when, why, and how), or "the five **w**s and an **h**," or as the six honest serving-men who taught Rudyard Kipling all he needed to know (from *The Elephant's Child*, in *Just So Stories*, 1940).

   What?—What is Special Education?
   Who?—Who Should Receive and Provide Special Education?
   Where?—Where Should Special Education Happen?
   How?—How Should Special Education be Practiced?
   When?—When Should Special Education Begin and End?
   Why?—Why do we Have Special Education?

To round out our discussion, we have added an additional *w* to the list: **Whither?**—Whither Special Education? We've added this seventh **w** to conclude our book as both a summary and question for the future. Whither is the field of special education bound?

This organizing principle is informed by and draws on the structure described in an article by Barbara Bateman (1994) published in a retrospective examination of the legacy of famous papers by Lloyd Dunn (1968; "Special Education for the Mildly Retarded—Is Much of it Justifiable?") and Evelyn Deno (1970; "Special Education as Developmental Capital"). The title of Bateman's article—"Who, How, and Where: Special Education's Issues in Perpetuity"—includes three of the *ws* sections that we use to structure this book. Yet, to cover the breadth of issues in special education, we actually included discussions of all six of the honest serving-men.

We chose this structure in part for what we see as a pedagogical heuristic. We hope that it will help readers to structure their thinking about these discussions. To place the individual chapters into context, each section opens with a brief chapter by the editors and other contributors that discusses some of the issues subsumed by the topic. So, for example, the introduction to the *who* section discusses not only who receives special education (i.e., students), but also who delivers it (i.e., co-teaching) and how teachers are prepared.

We are fortunate that such distinguished scholars agreed to share their experiences, knowledge, and thoughts in this book. We owe them our gratitude. Authors have provided brief personal statements about how they became involved in special education prior to their chapter and supplied a list of some writings that they wanted to share with readers. We believe that such a comprehensive view of the issues, from the perspectives of scholars who have helped shape the discussions of these issues, will benefit readers as they make their own informed decisions about the enduring issues of special education.

JOHN WILLS LLOYD'S SUGGESTIONS
FOR FURTHER READING

Bateman, B. D. (2004). Elements of teaching: A best practice guide for beginning teachers. Verona, WI: Attainment.

Engelmann, S., & Steely, D. (2004). Inferred functions of performance and learning. Mahwah, NJ: Erlbaum.

Lloyd, J. W. (2005). *About teach effectively*. [Web log message]. Retrieved from *http://teacheffectively.com/about-teach-effectively*.

Lloyd, J. W., & Hallahan, D. P. (2005). Going forward: How the field of learning disabilities has and will contribute to education. *Learning Disability Quarterly, 28*, 133–136.

Lloyd, J. W., Kame'enui, E. J., & Chard, D. (Eds.), (1997). *Special education: Issues in identification, assessment, instruction, and policy*. Hillsdale, NJ: Erlbaum.

Lloyd, J. W., Singh, N. N., & Repp, A. C. (Eds.), (1991). *The regular education initiative: Alternative perspectives on concepts, issues, and models*. Sycamore IL: Sycamore.

Patterson, G. R., Reid, J. B., & Dishion, T. J. (1992). *Antisocial boys*. Eugene, OR: Castalia.

MELODY TANKERSLEY'S SUGGESTIONS
FOR FURTHER READING

Cook, B. G. & Tankersley, M. (Eds.), (2013). *Research-based practices in special education*. Upper Saddle River, NJ: Pearson.

Heward, W. L. (2003). Ten faulty notions about teaching and learning that hinder the effectiveness of special education. *The Journal of Special Education, 36*(4), 186–205.

Kauffman, J. M., & Hallahan, D. P. (Eds.), (2011). *Handbook of special education*. New York: Taylor & Francis.

Kazdin, A. E. (1982). *Single-case research designs: Methods for clinical and applied settings*. New York: Oxford University Press.

Landrum, T. J., & Tankersley, M. (2004). Science at the schoolhouse: An uninvited guest. *Journal of Learning Disabilities, 37*, 207–212.

Lloyd, J. W., Forness, S. R., & Kavale, K. A. (1998). Some methods are more effective than others. *Intervention in School and Clinic, 33*(1), 195–200.

Peacock Hill Working Group (Kauffman, J. M., Lloyd, J. W., Cook, L., Cullinan, D., Epstein, M. H., Forness, S. R., Hallahan, D. P., Nelson, C. M., Polsgrove, L., Sabornie, E. J., Strain, P. S., & Walker, H. M.). (1991). Problems and promises in special education and related services for children and youth with emotional or behavioral disorders. *Behavioral Disorders, 16*, 299–313.

Tankersley, M., Niesz, T., Cook, B. G., & Woods, W. (2007). The unintended and unexpected side effects of inclusion of students with learning disabilities: The perspectives of special education teachers. *Learning Disabilities: A Multidisciplinary Journal, 14*, 135–144.

Walker, H. M., Ramsey, E., & Gresham, F. M. (2004). *Antisocial behavior in school: Evidence-based practices* (2nd ed.). Belmont, CA: Wadsworth.

BARBARA BATEMAN'S SUGGESTIONS
FOR FURTHER READING

Bateman, B. (1967). Three approaches to diagnosis and educational planning for children with learning disabilities. *Academic Therapy Quarterly, 2*, 215–222.

Bateman, B. D. (1994). Who, how, and where special education's issues in perpetuity. *The Journal of Special Education, 27*(4), 509–520.

Bateman, B. D. (2011). Individual education programs for children with disabilities. In J. M. Kauffman & D. P. Hallahan (Eds.), *Handbook of special education* (pp. 91–106). New York: Routledge.

Bateman, B. D., & Linden, M. A. (1998). *Better IEPs: How to develop legally correct and educationally useful programs.* Longmont, CO: Sopris West.

Engelmann, S. (1971). *Conceptual learning.* Belmont, CA: Feron.

Kirk, S. A., & Bateman, B. (1962). Diagnosis and remediation of learning disabilities. *Exceptional Children, 29*, 73–78.

REFERENCES

Bateman, B. D. (1994). Who, how, and where: Special education's issues in perpetuity. *The Journal of Special Education, 27*(4), 509–520.

Byrnes, M. (2002). *Taking sides: Clashing views on controversial issues in special education.* Boston: McGraw-Hill.

Deno, E. (1970). Forum: Special education as developmental capital. *Exceptional Children, 37*(3), 229–237.

Dunn, L. M. (1968). Special education for the mildly retarded—Is much of it justifiable? *Exceptional Children, 35*(1), 5–22.

Hornby, G., Howard, J., & Atkinson, M. (1997). *Controversial issues in special education.* New York, NY: Routledge.

Kauffman, J. M. (1981). Historical trends and contemporary issues in special education in the United States. In J. M. Kauffman & D. P. Hallahan (Eds.), *Handbook of special education* (pp. 3–23). New York: Routledge.

Kipling, R. (1940). *Rudyard Kipling's verse.* New York: Doubleday.

Lloyd, J. W., Keller, C., & Hung, L. (2007). International perspectives on learning disabilities. *Learning Disabilities Research & Practice, 22*(3).

Reynolds, M. C. (1962). A framework for considering some issues in special education. *Exceptional Children, 18*, 367–370.

Rubinstein, E. A. (1948). Childhood mental disease in America: A review of the literature before 1900. *American Journal of Orthopsychiatry, 18*(2), 314.

Sachs, B. (1895). *A treatise on the nervous diseases of children: For physicians and students.* New York, NY: William Wood.

Sachs, B. (1905). *A treatise on the nervous diseases of children.* New York, NY: William Wood.

Schmid, R. E., & Nagata, L. M. (1983). *Contemporary issues in special education.* Monterey, CA: McGraw-Hill.

Sorrells, A. M., Rieth, H. J., & Sindelar, P. T. (2004). *Critical issues in special education: Access, diversity, and accountability.* Upper Saddle River, NJ: Pearson.

Stainback, W. C., & Stainback, S. B. (1992). *Controversial issues confronting special education: Divergent perspectives.* Needham Heights, MA: Allyn & Bacon.

Ysseldyke, J. E., Algozzine, R., & Thurlow, M. L. (1992). *Critical issues in special education.* Boston, MA: Houghton Mifflin.

Section I

WHAT IS SPECIAL EDUCATION?

Special education is not general or regular education. It is something different. But, what is that difference? To many people, this is the fundamental issue in special education. People have very different answers to this question. What is it that makes special education special? It is what special educators do that makes special education special. Consider some of the following questions about the *what* question.

- What are the differences between special education and general education?
- How would you know special education if you saw a teacher practicing it?
- What would special education teachers do that general education teachers would not do?
- What are the research bases of the practices of special education?
- What professional knowledge do special educators have that they can use in helping students with disabilities?
- Is there anything to special education other than special teaching?

Getting to Know Tiara Saufley Brown

After I complained to my fourth grade music teacher that her songs were "boring," she suggested I help her with the special education class to learn "new" songs. At the time, I would have preferred she just change the musical selection to Green Day, but coincidentally this is where my love for special education began. I became particularly fascinated with the adaptive instruments and, at 10 years old, remembered thinking, "These kids aren't slow. They just need a different way to do things."

Fast-forward a few years. I received an economics degree from Virginia Tech and a Master's in Sports Administration from Florida State University. I went to work for the Special Olympics and later became the Program Coordinator for the Arc, a day support program for adults with disabilities. Although I enjoyed my job, I quickly realized I wanted to have an impact earlier on in people's lives.

I decided to go to Mary Baldwin College and received a second Master's in special education. I taught for four years in a classroom of students who had moderate to severe disabilities. I thought teaching would be perfect but quickly became aware I needed more instructional knowledge. What were the best practices for students with autism and low-incidence disabilities, and how did I make materials *adaptable* or teach in *different* ways?

My curiosity, coupled with my desire to continue attending every ACC school (free football tickets), led me to the University of Virginia. I am currently a Ph.D. student studying special education with research interests in early childhood interventions, international special education, and autism. I probably will not develop a new musical instrument, but, just as I discovered in fourth grade, I hope to study, and perhaps come up with, *adaptable* and effective ways for *different* students to learn.

2

WHAT IS SPECIAL EDUCATION?

*Barbara Bateman, John Wills Lloyd, Melody Tankersley,
& Tiara Saufley Brown*

Historically, special education was whatever education was provided to children who had disabilities. It simply was whatever "those kids" got. Now the Individuals with Disabilities Education Act of 2004 (IDEA) defines special education as "specially designed instruction . . . to meet the unique needs of a child who has a disability" (see Box 2.1 for the complete U.S. legal definition of "special education"). According to the dictionary definition, "specially" designed instruction means instruction that is different from the ordinary or usual instruction and "unique" needs are those that are singular and unparalleled, having no like or equal. So, bearing in mind those definitions, IDEA tells us that special education is recognizable by two criteria: (a) it is education that is different from the conventional general education and (b) it addresses unusual needs that not many children have.

Box 2.1 The IDEA Definition of "Special Education"

Special education means specially designed instruction, at no cost to the parents, to meet the unique needs of a child with a disability, including

Instruction conducted in the classroom, in the home, in hospitals and institutions, and in other settings; and

Instruction in physical education.

Special education includes each of the following, if the services otherwise meet the requirements of paragraph (a)(1) of this section

Speech-language pathology services, or any other related service, if the service is considered special education rather than a related service under State standards;

Travel training; and

Vocational education

Source: 34 C.F.R. 300.39

Some examples of teaching or instructing are readily identifiable as special education. For example, Anne Sullivan's work teaching Helen Keller (Keller, 1904) certainly qualifies as special education. Someone teaching a blind student to read braille, a speech-language pathologist retraining basic language patterns of a child who had a brain injury, or a behavior management specialist systematically rewarding approximations of a young child's dressing are special education, as are many related services such as physical therapy, occupational therapy, play therapy, and much more. Of course, professionals in physical or occupational therapy, or similar fields, do not typically classify themselves as special educators, preferring to keep their own disciplinary designations. But in the context of IDEA, if a child with a disability needs a related service in order to benefit from special education, it is legally required under the special education umbrella. Some special education is conducted by non-professionals under supervision by professionals, such as an aide collecting data on how many trials it takes Jake to distinguish *b* from *d* consistently or noting how often Jane initiates peer interaction during a 15-minute recess.

In each instance the learner has a unique or uncommon need—to communicate by tactile-kinesthetic means, to read without print, to relearn basic language patterns, to learn how to dress oneself, to discriminate one letter from another, or to initiate interaction with a peer. Most children either learn these behaviors without direct, systematic teaching or have no need to learn them at all. In our examples, the learners have not acquired these skills by the time the skills are needed, so they have educational needs that are different from their peers. Therefore the "unique educational need" portion—the first criterion—of IDEA's definition of special education is met.

The second criterion of IDEA's definition of special education is that the instruction needed is not the ordinary or usual instruction found in general education. Special education is usually much more intensive and individualized than general education. General education is designed to meet the typical and common needs of a group of learners of a given age, whereas special education is designed precisely and systematically to meet the atypical and uncommon needs of a specific learner. The key question in knowing what is and is not special education is whether most students need that type of instruction at a particular time—if they do, it is not special education; it is general education. Most of the foregoing examples obviously differ from general education. Few would advocate teaching braille to everyone, of course. However, people differ about whether students with disabilities should have a different curriculum than their non-disabled peers and the extent to which general and special education should be different.

SHOULD SPECIAL EDUCATION INSTRUCTION DIFFER FROM GENERAL EDUCATION?

Should general education and special education be different from each other? Do they, in fact, differ significantly? Until about 1975 when IDEA became law, the answers were obvious. They were necessarily quite different from each other. The teachers' training and backgrounds were different, the methods and techniques of instruction were different, and even the classrooms or entire school buildings where instruction occurred were different. One of the editors of this book taught special education in the 1950s, usually to small groups of one to three children, in a storage closet, on a stage, in the nurse's room, the boys' locker room, the cafeteria, or the janitor's closet in the furnace room.

The available equipment and curriculum included a tiny portable chalkboard and a box of well-used flash cards.

Doubts about special education have been around for a long time. In the 1970s, even before IDEA was passed, some professionals questioned the need for education that was different from general education (e.g., Budoff, 1972; Kraft, 1972). In the years after IDEA was enacted, others recommended minimizing the differences between special education and general education and even encouraged merging the two—doing away completely with special education's separate purposes, administration, budget, and personnel preparation (Gartner & Lipsky, 1987; Will, 1986). Much of the early impetus for this recommendation—then known as the regular education initiative (Lloyd, Singh, & Repp, 1991) and now called full inclusion (Kauffman & Hallahan, 2005)—came from the Civil Rights movement, which emphasized equality and abolishing racial discrimination, and the deinstitutionalization movement, which took individuals with intellectual disabilities and mental illness out of hospital settings and relocated them within their communities (Lloyd & Gambatese, 1991). Around this same time period, the Rehabilitation Act of 1973 (including Section 504, which is of special interest to schools) was enacted to prevent discrimination based solely on disability. With these movements and legal decisions as a backdrop, and the much earlier case of *Brown v. Board of Education* (1954) banning segregation in public education based on race, special education began to be read by some as illegal segregation based on disability. Although this erroneous interpretation has been explicitly refuted by the U.S. Supreme Court (*Cleburne v. Cleburne Living Center,* 1985), the moral issue of segregating students with disabilities has remained.

The more recent standards-based reform movement, including its emphasis on assessing all children and holding them all to the same high academic standards has also been cited as supporting the full inclusionists' belief that all children should be placed in the general education curriculum. Organizations and advocates of inclusion advance ideas similar to those of 1950s, 1960s, and 1970s, whether for specific groups of children with disabilities (e.g., the National Center on Learning Disabilities; Kaloi, 2010) or as a way of changing entire school systems (e.g., Sailor & Roger, 2005). IDEA itself now requires that the individualized educational program (IEP) of every eligible student contain goals and services "to enable the child to be involved in and make progress in the general education curriculum" (34 CFR 300.320). Undeniably, special education is being pushed more and more toward general education, to the point that we hear people suggesting inclusion is mandated in law (it is not). Although ongoing technological advances, improved teacher preparation, and professional development in the future may lessen the need for some special education services (e.g., accessible formats of printed materials, mobility devices), at the present time, special education is arguably very important for millions of children who have unique educational needs and for the society which hopes to educate them appropriately.

People who advocate the merger of general and special education or the dissolution of special education may prevail in the short term, but unless all children can be made substantially more like each other than they are now, special education will most likely survive or be reborn, perhaps with a different name. Some children need to be taught different things, in different ways, at different paces, or at different times than the great majority. It is also important to note, these instructional differences benefit all exceptional learners including students who are gifted (Tomlinson, 1995). Increasing the pace and intensity of instruction for a student who excels in math, is an example of specialized instruction. Contrastingly, decreasing the pace or implementing a method of explicit instruction for a struggling math learner is also specialized instruction. So, no matter the learner, the quantity and quality of instruction are specialized. Is this perhaps the truly defining feature of special education?

WHAT SHOULD BE THE FOCUS OF SPECIAL EDUCATION?

IDEA (2004) was passed with a goal of preparing children who have disabilities for further education, employment, and independent living. In the long term, that focus must guide special education. However, knowing the destination is not the same as having a map of the route. Although both are essential for a successful journey, how do we, or should we, decide on the best paths to reach our special education goal?

At least two tug-a-wars pull educators in different directions as they decide on the focus of instructional programming for students with disabilities. One tension is between (a) teaching at a broader, more global, indirect level in hopes of getting more "bang for the buck" or (b) teaching only those essential and specific needed competencies and skills and concepts that students must have to succeed at an agreed-upon minimum level. Do we want to ensure that students can get the right answers on one particular test or do we want to ensure that they know the broader concepts so that they can get the answers on just about any test? Another tension is what Zigmond, Kloo, and Volonino (2009) called a historical "tension between teaching students with disabilities 'special stuff' and teaching them what everyone else in their grade and school is being taught" (2009, p. 193). These conflicts of level and "stuff" of special and general curriculum can overlap—some special education programming, for example, can be the same "stuff" as taught to all in a grade, but at a different level of attainment than required by age-mates. As we will see in the upcoming chapters, special education professionals have differing opinions on these conflicts.

In the past (and in some countries still), special education focused heavily on training a person with disabilities for supported employment in sheltered workshops or on providing training in the manual arts, and on practical daily life skills such as simple cooking, cleaning, sewing, or other household chores. In one example of the focus on supported employment, during the 1960s researchers studied how incentives affected the rate of work and the behavior of workers who had intellectual disabilities and were learning work skills in specialized facilities (Teasdale & Joynt, 1967). Concern about supported employment continues today; in Germany researchers are finding that special education services are not preparing students with disabilities for work and that even an additional year of training following high school may be insufficient, as well (Gebhardt, Tretter, Schwab, & Gasteiger-Klicpera, 2011).

During the 1960s and 1970s much of special education emphasized teaching or remediating what were thought of as "basic psychological processes" such as visual memory, auditory sequencing, auditory-vocal association, visual-motor integration, balance, sensory integration, and so on (Mann, 1979). These processes were thought to undergird academic performance and, if deficits in them were patched up, students' learning in other areas such as reading would subsequently improve. As questions were raised about the academic achievement levels of students with mild intellectual disabilities (then known as educable mentally retarded students), most of whom were in special classes, many special education programs began putting more emphasis on teaching these basic academic skills (i.e., the general curriculum). However, for students with severe intellectual disabilities, the primary focus remained on the functional skills of everyday life. This "hidden curriculum" is a hot-spot supported and contested by professionals across the field. But, you will read that Browder recommends teaching demanding content to individuals who require lots of supports.

Today's emphasis on standards-based IEPs and formal academic assessment of all students' performance on state standards is resulting in increased efforts to teach the general education curriculum to more and more special education students (Nolet & McLaughlin, 2005). At the same time there is also an increased focus on teaching transition (to life after secondary school), skills in employment, community living (e.g., transportation, recreation, social group participation), and further education (Bambara, Wilson, & McKenzie, 2007; Kiernan, Hoff, Freeze, & Mank, 2011). Further education for students with intellectual disabilities or severe learning or language disabilities is often in a vocational, technical, or community college setting. More and more students with hearing or vision impairments, orthopedic disabilities, high-functioning autism, learning disabilities, and mental health concerns are attending four-year colleges (Hart, Mele-McCarthy, Pasternack, Zimbrich, & Parker, 2004; Neubert, Moon, Grigal, & Redd, 2001). But this dual focus highlights the issue of whether there is room in the school day of our elementary and secondary schools to emphasize both academic and functional life skills. Is there, in your view? This begs a weighty question because, like many issues in special education, opinions may change over time with research and educational advancements, even for prominent figures in the field (as you will see in Browder's upcoming chapter).

WHAT INSTRUCTIONAL APPROACHES SHOULD BE EMPLOYED BY SPECIAL EDUCATORS?

A major point of agreement among professional special educators in recent years is that the instructional practices used in special education should be based on research and have evidence to support them. IDEA requires that the special education and related services on the child's IEP must be "based on peer-reviewed research to the extent practicable" (34 CFR 320(a)(4)).

Beyond the legal mandate, it seems only sensible that teachers would want to start with practices that have been proven to be effective. Faced with a choice among practices that (a) have been validated, (b) have not been tested, or (c) have been tested and found to be ineffective, why would educators want to start with either (b) or (c)?

However, exactly what constitutes a sufficient research or evidence base is not as clear as is the mandate that the field use programs and practices that have that base. Nor is a solid body of research available for all programs, practices or approaches, including some that are widely used. As a practical matter, educators cannot afford to wait for each and every technique, practice, procedure, or method to be tested rigorously before it is implemented with students; the principal cannot stand at the schoolhouse door and turn the buses away, saying "Sorry, send these students home. We haven't proven every method we're going to use yet."

Almost all commercially available programs now claim to be evidence-based or research-based. Sometimes these claims are based on the "Grandmother's Brownies" fallacy. Suppose your grandmother absolutely, for sure, made the best brownies in the state. After she passed away you carelessly lost her recipe for brownies but not your determination to replicate them. So, you looked at dozens of brownie recipes and found they all included chocolate, sugar, and butter, among other things. Then you said that since you lacked the real recipe you would just toss together some amount of each of the known major ingredients and see what happened. You then baked the concoction for some unknown amount of time—until they looked done through the oven window. What would likely be the result? Would you replicate Grandmother's brownies? Not likely.

This is precisely what some publishers do when they recognize some ingredients of an evidence-based practice, but do not replicate the recipe. For example, some publishers' instructional materials may recognize that successful early reading programs have been found to teach phonemic awareness, phonics, fluency, vocabulary, and comprehension strategies, in certain proportions, at certain times, and employing very specific techniques—just as the National Reading Panel recommended in its report (National Institute of Child Health and Human Development, 2000). To say, as publishers do, that their newest program contains phonemic awareness, phonics, fluency, vocabulary, and comprehension strategy instruction, and therefore is *the* correct recipe for early reading success is as wrong as for you to claim you have now recreated Grandmother's Brownies.

A similar problem educators face is that sometimes educational practices may appear similar, but the similarities are only superficial. As illustrated in Box 2.2, there is a critical difference between direct instruction ("little di") and Direct Instruction ("big DI"). In fact, that difference appears specific to the instructional programming (and field-testing) in our illustration, but that difference is quite substantial. In fact, it is so substantial that Engelmann and Colvin (2006) provided a detailed rubric to guide consumers in distinguishing between authentic and ersatz DI programs.

Box 2.2 Comparison of *Direct Instruction* and *direct instruction*

People use the term "direct instruction" in many different ways. To reduce confusion about two influential versions of direct instruction, people sometimes say "big DI" and "little di," referring to the capitalization of Direct Instruction, as it was used in *Direct Instruction Systems for Teaching Arithmetic and Reading* or DISTAR.

As the accompanying table shows, DI and di share many characteristics, especially with regard to teacher-presentation actions. They differ primarily on the content and structure of the lessons. A good way to understand this difference is to review a big-DI program, following a specific instructional activity across many lessons (perhaps as many as 20–30) to see how it changes gradually: Examine the examples used across the different days and the gradual reduction in teacher supports ("scaffolding"); then observe a teacher using little di and teaching something similar for many lessons. The instructional design differences will probably become obvious.

Another important contrast, however, is not between big DI and little di. It is between these two versions of direct instruction and what some other educators might call "direct instruction." Suppose you heard an educator say, "Oh yes, we use DI. We have intensive lectures where we tell the students just what they need to know, and we have weekly quizzes." To which of the two versions shown in the table—big DI or little di—would you think the speaker was referring? We would answer the question with one word: "Neither."

Feature	Direct Instruction	direct instruction
Lesson Delivery	• Teacher-directed lessons delivered in • Small, homogeneous groups with • Frequent questions and • Lots of practice. • Teachers monitor progress, provide • Praise plus • Corrective feedback, and • Adjust instruction based on performance.	• Teacher-directed lessons delivered in • Small, homogeneous groups with • Frequent questions and • Lots of practice. • Teachers monitor progress, provide • Praise plus • Corrective feedback, and • Adjust instruction based on performance.
Instructional Programming	• Conspicuous strategies throughout. • Scaffolding to insure student independence. • Teacher wording, selection and sequencing of examples, and similar details predicated on principles derived from concept-learning and related literature (e.g., Engelmann & Carnine, 1982, 2011).	• Strategies might be included. • Scaffolding might be provided. • Some learning theories might be incorporated.
Field Testing Prior to Publication	• Extensive.	• Possible.

School district personnel who make curriculum decisions often have difficulties beyond recognizing a "not really Grandmother's Brownies" evidence-based approach and distinguishing it from the original, research-validated program (and di and DI programs). The difficulties of recognizing evidence-based instructional approaches are then followed by the difficulties of implementing evidence-based instructional approaches. Implementing an evidence-based approach, which has been proven effective, requires faithful implementation, often over a significant period of time. But implementing a program with fidelity entails costs—materials, staff training, perhaps additional personnel, possibly new technology, a certain amount of student and teacher time, additional teacher prep time, and more. On the plus side are possible academic or other gains which must be carefully evaluated for educational significance (not the same as statistical significance), possible savings of instructional time, improvements in staff morale, and other intangibles that add up to improved services. And into this already complex mixture are added political and public relations factors urging improvement in test scores, making the recipe even more difficult to follow. Certainly this kind of cost-benefit analysis is necessary when considering what to teach in special education, but it is not easy. Perhaps this fact coupled with other problems, such as the need for meticulous monitoring for fidelity of implementation, helps explain why there has not been a rush to adopt evidence-based programs, methods, practices, and more.

Special education has a recognized history of supporting, engaging in, and attending to research findings to a notably greater extent than general education. This is not to say that all special education practices are solidly grounded in research, but many are.

More importantly, when research has found a practice wanting, which has happened a good deal, it is slowly but surely dropped by special education. For example, in the 1960s and 1970s, many special educators had their students practice walking on rails, making angels in the snow, and engaging in similar motor activities in the hope that these actions would improve learning processes underlying the students' academic difficulties and, hence, allow the students to learn better. When research proved that the practices were not beneficial, the use of such practices became far less common in special education. For example, most special educators abandoned using perceptual-motor exercises as a means of enhancing academic readiness (Kavale & Matson, 1983) or basing reading instruction on "learning styles" once research showed them to be ineffective (Kavale & Forness, 1987; Pashler, McDaniel, Rohre, & Bjork, 2008).

One of the concerns some special educators have is that the more the two disciplines of general and special education are merged into one entity, the less value may be placed on rigorous research and the implementation of its findings. To illustrate, think of the popularity of *Brain Gym*® and other similar perceptual-motor programs; if the rationale for employing such programs is as simple as promoting physical exercise, then it may be warranted; but if it is to promote academic readiness, then the evidence is not yet available (Spaulding, Mostert, & Beam, 2010). Encouragingly, political and social forces are clearly pushing for improvements in education and this pressure may continue to increase the value given to research findings and to evidence-based practices.

In the chapters that follow, experts in the field discuss their experiences and views of the essential elements of special education. Tom Scruggs and Margo Mastropieri use real-life examples to illuminate important concepts like "inclusion" and the "hidden curriculum." Paige Pullen and Dan Hallahan point out critical components and decipher key terms used in the field. Diane Browder uses her life experiences and current research to examine what to teach students with moderate or severe disabilities. Finally, Ed Kame'enui makes a pitch for the central importance of specially designed instruction, referring to scientists, philosophers, examples, and his own personal experience.

So just what exactly is special education? Should special education instruction differ from general education instruction? What should be the focus of special education instruction—addressing underlying process issues, strengthening academic skills, providing accommodations, or tackling functional and daily-living tasks (for students with moderate or severe disabilities)? What instructional approaches should be employed by special educators? How should special educators decide what instructional practices or procedures are appropriate? And, finally should teachers' instructional decisions be constant or are they subject to change over time? These questions are different facets, and *only some* of the facets, of one of the most substantial questions special educators must confront.

Box 2.3 What is an "Instructional Approach?"

Even a casual perusal of current special education literature reveals that the terminology of instructional approaches or practices can be most confusing. Instructional "strategies," "techniques," "methods," "practices," and "approaches" are all used. Some writers distinguish sharply among strategies, methods, and techniques (but rarely between approaches, practices, and any of the others) but others use them interchangeably. Furthermore, a practice such as problem solving is variously known as a strategy, a technique, or a method.

We might be tempted to order these terms. For example, a technique is a lower-order phenomenon than a strategy or practice that, in turn, are lower-order phenomena than methods or approaches. So, a cognitive approach would be composed of multiple cognitive strategies and those cognitive strategies would include many cognitive techniques. The same would be true for the behavioral approach.

Is this just a matter of a "rose by any other name," or does it make a difference?

TIARA SAUFLEY BROWN'S SUGGESTIONS FOR FURTHER READING

Gantos, J. (2011). *Joey Pigza loses control.* New York, NY: Square Fish.

Guiliani, G. A. (2012). *The comprehensive guide to special education law: Over 400 frequently asked questions and answers every educator needs to know about the legal rights of exceptional children and their parents.* Philadelphia, PA: Jessica Kingsley.

Grandin, T., & Panek, R. (2013). *The autistic brain: Thinking across the spectrum.* Boston, MA: Houghton Mifflin Harcourt.

Myles, B. S. (2004). *The hidden curriculum: Practical solutions for understanding unstated rules in social situations.* Overland Park, KS: Autism Asperger.

Notbohm, E. (2005). *Ten things every child with autism wishes you knew.* Arlington, TX: Future Horizons.

Pierangelo, R. (2004). *The special educator's survival guide.* San Fransisco, CA: Jossey-Bass.

REFERENCES

Bambara, L. M., Wilson, B. A., & McKenzie, M. (2007). Transition and quality of life. In S. L. Odom, R. H. Horner, M. E. Snell, & J. Blacher (Eds.), *Handbook of developmental disabilities* (pp. 371–389). New York: Guilford Press.

Budoff, M. (1972). Providing special education without special classes. *Journal of School Psychology, 10*, 199–205.

Cleburne v. Cleburne Living Center, 473 U.S. 432 (1985).

Engelmann, S., & Carnine, D. (1982). *Theory of instruction.* New York: Irvington.

Engelmann, S., & Carnine, D. (2011). *Could John Stuart Mill have saved our schools?* Verona, WI: Attainment.

Engelmann, S., & Colvin, G. (2006). *Rubric for identifying authentic DI programs.* Retrieved from http://zigsite. com/RubricPro.htm.

Gartner, A., Lipsky, D. K. (1987). Beyond special education: Toward a quality system for all students. *Harvard Educational Review, 57*, 367–395.

Gebhardt, M., Tretter, T., Schwab, S., & Gasteiger-Klicpera, B. (2011). The transition from school to the workplace for students with learning disabilities: Status quo and the efficiency of pre-vocational and vocational training schemes. *European Journal of Special Needs Education, 26*, 443–459.

Hart, D., Mele-McCarthy, J., Pasternack, R. H., Zimbrich, K., & Parker, D. R. (2004). Community college: A pathway to success for youth with learning, cognitive, and intellectual disabilities in secondary settings. *Education and Training in Developmental Disabilities, 39*, 54–66.

Individuals with Disabilities Education Improvement Act of 2004, 20 U.S.C. §§ 1400.

Kaloi, L. (2010). Expecting LD students to succeed! New state standards in reading and math released. *LD.org.* Retrieved 6 July 2012 from http://www.ncld.org/ld-insights/entry/1/39.

Kauffman, J. M., & Hallahan, D. P. (Eds.), (2005). *The illusion of full inclusion* (2nd ed.). Austin, TX: Pro-ed.

Kavale, K. A., & Forness, S. R. (1987). Substance over style: A quantitative synthesis assessing the efficacy of modality testing and teaching. *Exceptional Children, 54*, 228–234.

Kavale, K. A., & Matson, P. D. (1983). "One jumped off the balance beam": Meta-analysis of perceptual-motor training. *Journal of Learning Disabilities, 16*, 165–173.

Keller, H. (1904). *The story of my life; with her letters (1887–1901) and a supplementary account of her education, including passages from the reports and letters of her teacher, Anne Mansfield Sullivan, by John Albert Macy.* New York: Doubleday, Page.

Kiernan, W. E., Hoff, D., Freeze, S., & Mank, D. M. (2011). Employment first: A beginning not an end. *Intellectual and Developmental Disabilities, 49,* 300–304.

Kraft, A. (1972). Down with (most) special education classes. *Academic Therapy, 8,* 207–216.

Lloyd, J. W., & Gambatese, C. (1991). Reforming the relationships between regular and special education: Background and issues. In J. W. Lloyd, N. N. Singh, & A. C. Repp, (Eds.), *The regular education initiative: Alternative perspectives on concepts, issues, and models* (pp. 3–13). Sycamore, IL: Sycamore.

Lloyd, J. W., Singh, N. N., & Repp, A. C. (Eds.). (1991). *The regular education initiative: Alternative perspectives on concepts, issues, and models.* Sycamore, IL: Sycamore.

Mann, L. (1979). *On the trail of process: A historical perspective on cognitive process and their training.* New York: Grune and Stratton.

National Institute of Child Health and Human Development. (2000). *Report of the National Reading Panel. Teaching children to read: an evidence-based assessment of the scientific research literature on reading and its implications for reading instruction: Reports of the subgroups* (NIH Publication No. 00-4754). Washington, DC: U.S. Government Printing Office.

Neubert, D. A., Moon, M. S., Grigal, M., & Redd, V. (2001). Post-secondary educational practices for individuals with mental retardation and other significant disabilities: A review of the literature. *Journal of Vocational Rehabilitation, 16,* 155–168.

Nolet, V., & McLaughlin, M. (2005). *Accessing the general curriculum: Including students with disabilities in standards-based reform* (2nd ed.). Thousand Oaks, CA: Corwin Press.

Pashler, H., McDaniel, Rohre, D., & Bjork, R. (2008). Learning styles: Concepts and evidence. *Psychological Science in the Public Interest, 9,* 105–119.

Sailor, W., & Roger, B. (2005). Rethinking inclusion: Schoolwide applications. *Phi Delta Kappan, 86,* 503–509.

Spaulding, L. S., Mostert, M. P., & Beam, A. P. (2010). Is Brain gym® an effective educational intervention? *Exceptionality, 18,* 18–30.

Teasdale, R., & Joynt, D. (1967). Some effects of incentives on the behaviour of adolescent retardates. *American Journal of Mental Deficiency, 71,* 925–930.

Tomlinson, C. (1995). Deciding to differentiate instruction in middle school: One school's journey. *Gifted Child Quarterly, 39,* 77–87.

Will, M. C. (1986). Educating children with learning problems: A shared responsibility. *Exceptional Children, 52,* 411–416.

Zigmond, N., Kloo, A., & Volonino, V. (2009). What, where, and how? Special education in the climate of full inclusion. *Exceptionality, 17,* 189–204.

Getting to Know Thomas E. Scruggs and Margo A. Mastropieri

 Tom Scruggs and Margo Mastropieri have worked for over 40 years in the field of special education as teachers of students with disabilities in public schools, as researchers, and as professors of special education. Tom began his career teaching guitar lessons to students with learning and behavioral disabilities at a special school in Cambridge, Massachusetts. He earned his Master's degree and continued to teach students with special needs at the elementary and secondary levels. He then enrolled as a full-time Ph.D. student at Arizona State, where he met Margo. Also while in Arizona, he taught gifted students and students with special needs in an American Indian community, and he worked at two preschools for students with disabilities.

Margo was a swimming instructor during the summers through high school and college when she volunteered to teach swimming to students with disabilities who were not allowed to enroll in swimming lessons with the "typical" children. During her undergraduate studies she became extremely interested in studying and working with children who experienced challenges learning. Following her B.A. at UMass Amherst, she began her career as a Diagnostic Remediator at the Mt. Holyoke College Learning Disabilities Center. At this position she assessed students with learning difficulties and recommended academic programs to help remediate difficulties learning in school. Subsequently she was a high school resource teacher in Massachusetts where she also was a field hockey coach and class advisor, and later an elementary special education teacher in Arizona prior to enrolling full-time in a Ph.D. program at Arizona State University. Since their ASU collaboration, Margo and Tom have continued to research, teach, and study ways to improve the school success of students with special needs. They have worked at Utah State University, Purdue University, and George Mason University.

3

WHAT MAKES SPECIAL EDUCATION SPECIAL?

Thomas E. Scruggs & Margo A. Mastropieri

Late in the summer before this chapter was due to the editors, Margo had a serious bicycle accident, resulting in multiple arm fractures, dislocation of her wrist, and damage to several teeth. After surgery, including placement of seven screws, a rod, and a metal plate, she lost use of her right arm for an unknown period of time while she went through healing and rehabilitation. As a result, she initially lost her ability to undertake, without assistance, daily living tasks, self-help skills, driving abilities, and work-related tasks requiring the use of a computer with both hands. We had to assess what tasks had to be completed and then figure out how to adapt and modify, so that Margo could successfully do these things without use of her right hand and arm. During this rehabilitation process, we needed to make adaptations to the environment, materials, and tasks for completing even the simplest of everyday jobs. Adaptations included (a) using peer assistance for driving, for cooking, cleaning, and daily living tasks; (b) using assistive technologies such as sticky keys on the computers; and speech-to-text programs, to assist with completing word processing tasks such as email communications, class preparations, manuscript preparation, and other job requirements; (c) requesting reductions and time extensions for work-related tasks and deadlines (including this chapter) because she was unable to work at all initially following the accident, and later required more time to complete the simplest of tasks; and (d) participating in meetings via Skype or telephone conference calls when transportation could not be arranged to be physically present at meetings. But even more importantly, participation in individually designed and tailor-made physical therapy sessions and practice activities were crucial to help rehabilitate her injuries. The physical therapist assessed her hand and arm functioning levels and prescribed very specific exercises, beginning with very simple exercises but increasing in difficulty when more simple movements were mastered. Throughout the extended rehabilitation process, Margo frequently became very frustrated because she was unable to do so many things, everything she did took much longer than normal, and she progressed much more slowly than she wanted. She expressed her frustrations to her physical therapist one day who said to increase the number of times completing the practice exercises at home, and to try not to be frustrated but instead focus on making

22

progress in the right direction. Although temporary (we hope) in nature, this example illustrates the serious need, when appropriate, for modifications, adaptations, and special training, such as found in special education and related services for individuals with all types of disabilities.

In this chapter, we examine the question, "What is special education?" Rather than provide a simple definition, we chose to examine a number of issues relevant to this question. These issues include teaching things that are not commonly part of the general education curriculum, and how special education often includes teaching things that are not directly taught in the general education curriculum but that students are expected to figure out on their own. We also discuss examples of how special education includes teaching things that must be learned differently from the ways that other students learn things, and how special education also includes teaching things that cannot be learned at the level of pace and intensity typically found in general education classrooms. Next, we discuss whether special education treatments need be ineffective for more typical learners, and present research-based examples of effective treatments. Finally, we present the goals and components of special education.

WHAT IS TAUGHT IN SPECIAL EDUCATION?
Special Education Includes Teaching Things That Are Not Commonly Part of the General Education Curriculum

As broad as the general education curriculum is, it presumes that individual students possess a number of abilities and skills needed to succeed in school. It is also assumed that, over the years, individuals will continue to develop in a number of ways commensurate with increasing demands of schooling. Although this is a reasonable expectation for a majority of students, a significant number do not possess or develop many of these skills and abilities, and therefore specialized techniques are needed.

Skills that children are normally expected to bring with them when they first enter school include age-appropriate language, social behavior, affect, and toileting skills. Unfortunately, many students do not bring these skills to school, and therefore new objectives, and means for realizing these objectives, are necessary before general education curriculum objectives can be considered. Without specialized education programs, schools would have little to offer these students. For example, an Arizona teacher once wondered if a preschooler with autism could hear normally, since he never appeared to attend to sound. In order for an audiometric evaluation to be conducted, however, this little boy first needed to learn to sit in a chair at a table, to wear headphones, and to respond by pushing a button when he heard a sound, and another button when he did not. Although these skills were successfully trained, the procedures required several weeks to develop and execute; these procedures would not be at all necessary as part of a general education curriculum (Scruggs, Prieto, & Zucker, 1981).

Although reading is a significant component of elementary grade instruction, it is not explicitly taught in middle and high school, because it is taken for granted that students learning secondary curriculum will be able to read and comprehend relevant texts. Nevertheless, the great majority of students with identified disabilities read well below grade level, and therefore must receive some reading instruction, as well as additional technological and other strategies for coping with difficult text. During Margo's first year as a high school teacher in the late 1970s, she had a high school senior who

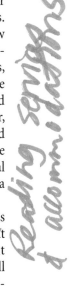

Reading services & accommodations

couldn't read anything. When she started to try to teach him sound-letter associations and simple words he said something that essentially meant, "Please don't try to teach me to read. Teachers throughout my entire schooling have tried to teach me and no one has been successful. I cannot learn to read, I don't want anyone to try to teach me any more. I can do my schoolwork without having to read." As a young first-year teacher, she was astounded at the young man's attitude and strong desire to not have anyone try to teach him anything, because he knew that she would be a failure at teaching him reading. This young man had developed the ability and social skills to be pleasant in classes, get along with his teachers and peers, have text books and tests read to him, and was allowed to dictate his responses to someone. He was able to "get by" because he was a nice student. His teachers graded him in his courses with "circle C"s which essentially indicated that he was a nice boy who tried hard but didn't really learn sufficiently to warrant an ABC grade. This clearly represents a case of someone who desperately needed additional specialized instruction that general education students did not require, but more importantly that had not been provided to him during his many years for public schooling.

Special Education Includes Teaching Things That Are Not Directly Taught in the General Education Curriculum, but That Students Are Expected to "Figure Out" on Their Own

These aspects of schooling, sometimes referred to as the "hidden curriculum," can refer to the complex and subtle interpersonal skills that students are expected to demonstrate (Myles, Trautman, & Schelvan, 2004), but can also refer to a variety of study skills, organizational skills, and test-taking skills that students are expected to use on academic tasks, but that are rarely directly taught. For example, while developing a research intervention, we interviewed middle school students with mild disabilities in Indiana about their textbook studying skills, and they commonly reported simply that they "looked at" their books—meaning just that, they looked at text without any strategy for active text processing. These text processing and study skills are commonly exhibited by other students, but often are expected to be learned spontaneously, leaving many students sadly lacking in appropriate skills. When we interviewed students about how they approached tests, students with learning disabilities commonly indicated they simply chose the first answer that "seemed right." Other students, meanwhile, applied a wealth of active test-taking strategies, such as eliminating answers known to be incorrect, re-checking the reading selection when appropriate, looking for cues in the question stem, and applying prior knowledge (e.g., Scruggs & Mastropieri, 1988).

When Margo was high school teacher of students with special needs, it became obvious that the majority of those high school students did not possess study and organizational skills. For example, some students would come to class carrying backpacks containing books, notebooks, and crumpled papers. When asked to retrieve certain books, materials, or homework, they would proceed to empty everything from their backpacks, but be unable to

"Unfortunately, many students do not bring these skills to school, and therefore new objectives, and means for realizing these objectives, are necessary before general education curriculum objectives can be considered. Without specialized education programs, schools would have little to offer these students."

locate the required materials. When they were able to retrieve something, the papers were tattered, torn, and crossed out in numerous places. Many of the students would have started the assignment, but it was clear that they became lost and were unable to complete it because of lack of understanding. Other students had simply not even attempted the assignments because they had forgotten about it. This was a clear indication that many students had very limited skill in organizing themselves with homework assignments and studying outside of school. Other general education students also had not been explicitly taught these skills, but nevertheless had learned how to apply them on their own.

Why are these appropriate skills not commonly taught in general education? Our conclusion is that teachers have many demands on their time, and do not wish to spend time practicing skills that most students already know, or can acquire on their own. Another possible reason is there is little tradition of academic strategies actively being taught systematically in schools, and no doubt many teachers feel it is helpful for students to develop these on their own. Regardless of the reason, many students who do not acquire these skills must be taught them directly, if they are to succeed.

Special Education Includes Teaching Things That Must Be Learned Differently From Other Students

In some cases, students can learn, but not in the same way that other students learn. The most obvious examples of this are found with students with sensory or physical disabilities, but these are not the only cases. In Illinois, a blind student was included in a general education class that was beginning a science unit involving the study of small things using a microscope. The teachers first advised against including this student, feeling that she may feel left out and unsuccessful; however, with the assistance of special education teachers, they were able to develop physical models and specific techniques to make the lessons meaningful for her (Scruggs & Mastropieri, 1994). In some cases, adapting instruction for special needs can help teachers focus on the most important part of lessons, and teach in ways that may benefit many students. In many cases, however, it is necessary to develop alternate means of teaching. In the same class, a student with learning disabilities experienced considerable difficulties staining specimens for microscope slides, damaging specimens, slides, and slide covers in the process. This difficulty opened the question of the relative importance of the unit, that is, the study of small things such as cellular structure, or the development of laboratory skills. For the former, pre-prepared slides could be used. For the latter, additional time must be found to provide additional appropriate instruction and practice in slide preparation. These are issues particularly suited to special education.

In a series of investigations, we interviewed children with intellectual disabilities about their understanding of scientific concepts, and were sometimes surprised with the responses we received. In one example, we asked elementary grade students with intellectual disabilities what they knew about air:

Interviewer: What is air? What do you know about air?
Martin: Umm . . . It's cold . . . It's winny.
Int: It's what? Windy?
Martin: It's cold and windy outside.

(Scruggs, Mastropieri, & Wolfe, 1994–1995, p. 227)

In another example, Bill provided an unexpected explanation:

Bill: You can make air.
Int: How can you make air?
Bill: With wind and sand.
Int: What?
Bill: With sand.
Int: You mean like wind blowing on sand?
Bill: Yeah.

(Scruggs et al., 1994–1995, p. 228)

Another student said air came into the school through holes in the ceiling. When asked where the air came from, she said, "There's an air place" (Scruggs et al., 1994–1995, p. 229). At first, these answers seem puzzling. However, the literature on children's developing scientific "preconceptions" suggests that preschool age children do not conceptualize air as a material substance, but instead think of air as existing when experienced as cold or a draft. This preschool level of understanding was not dissimilar to the 8–10 year olds in our example, who would certainly be at a disadvantage to their peers in a general science class on this subject (see Driver, Asoko, Leach, Mortimer, & Scott, 1994).

Adaptations are also of considerable importance in addressing social behavior. We remember hearing one teacher telling us her behavior management plan was not working for one student because, as she put it, "If I put him in time-out, he eats his socks!" This represents another instance of the kind of problem we have rarely observed in general education.

It was also clear to us during one research project that teachers could either escalate or de-escalate potentially volatile behavior in classes. For example, in one instance the teacher asked all students to come to the front of the classroom and sit in a circle while she was going to show the students an iguana. All of the students moved quietly towards the front of the room and sat on the floor except for one student with emotional disabilities, who often reacted emotionally and unpredictably to different situations. This teacher had an option at that point of forcing the student with emotional disabilities to come forward with the rest of the class or allowing the child to sit at his own chair and desk. One example would cause a confrontation and power struggle between the teacher and student which would end with the student being sent out of the classroom to the principal's office. The other option might enable the child to participate in the class. Encountering and attempting to solve problems such as this one are characteristic of special education.

"In some cases, students can learn, but not in the same way that other students learn."

Special Education Includes Teaching Things That Cannot Be Learned at the Level of Pace and Intensity Typically Found in General Education Classrooms

In many instances, students with disabilities benefit from instruction that is not dissimilar to that provided to nondisabled students, but may differ markedly in instructional variables such as *pace* and *intensity* (Mastropieri & Scruggs, 2014). Tom, for example, remembers teaching a self-contained class of students with intellectual disabilities. He worked to integrate his students into general education settings whenever possible, and in one case arranged inclusive placement of his small class within a general education art class. After several class meetings, however, it was clear that his students were gaining little from the experience. They were able to learn much of the content and skills, but at nothing like the seemingly relentless pace of instruction through many different tasks in the class. He removed his students from this class and introduced an arts period in his own class, where students practiced art including local desert landscape paintings. They learned and practiced (with considerable redundancy), horizon, converging parallels, vanishing point, lightening tone in the distance, and consistent direction of sunlight in creating shading and shadows. His students were very capable of learning these things, and took considerable pride in their products; however, they could not succeed in a situation where the pace and intensity of instruction was inappropriate.

In a recent investigation, we implemented an intervention to improve the persuasive writing skills of students with significant learning and behavioral disorders using a Self Regulated Strategy Development (SRSD) strategy (Harris, Graham, Mason, & Friedlander, 2008). This intervention was successful, in that students greatly improved their persuasive writing skills. However, a very extensive amount of instruction was necessary, dramatically different from students in the general education curriculum. That is, the general education curriculum in that state allowed three–five days for instruction of persuasive writing—in our case, students required 55 days of instruction to master these same skills. The amount of needed instructional time in this instance might fairly raise the issue of how much time *can* be appropriately allocated to specific learning skills, and whether decisions must be made regarding which skills or content may be reduced in order to allow for the extra time necessary to teach content considered more important.

In addition to the different pace of instruction, special education can also differ substantially with respect to the level of intensity needed to maintain attending to task and providing sufficient practice. Following is a recent response from one student in this same investigation when first asked to write, indicating that affective elements of learning can also significantly impact intensity and pace:

I hate writing.
Writing and me have nothing in common.
I am not writing.

(Mastropieri et al., 2010, p. 316)

In addition to significant learning problems, in this investigation we encountered many challenges keeping students engaged on task. One example of the efforts sometimes required to keep students on task is the following:

MAM (approaching student):	Hi Maria, do you need some help getting started with your essay?
Maria (looking right at MAM):	Something smells.
MAM:	Oh?? Well, let's look at your paper . . .
Maria (still looking right at MAM):	No, I mean something really smells. Real bad.
MAM:	Well, anyway, what is your topic sentence . . .
Maria:	Don't you get it? Smells.

(Mastropieri et al., 2010, p. 316)

Nevertheless, using specialized SRSD strategies and specialized teaching and behavior management techniques, all students made very significant gains in persuasive writing, from an average of about 80 words per essay to over 230 words, with comparable gains in number of paragraphs, essay elements, transition words, and essay quality. It can also be said that learning persuasive skills to represent one's views is of significant importance to a population more likely to use less appropriate means for influencing others. These important learning gains, however, were realized at the cost of a significant amount of instructional time, far beyond that provided in the general education curriculum.

Must Special Education Treatments be Ineffective for More Typical Learners?

In the early years of special education, views of the nature of special education were informed in part by ideas about aptitude-treatment interactions (e.g., Tobias, 1976). For example, Ysseldyke (1973) expressed the orientation of many researchers of the time when he argued,

> The very existence of "special" education is literally dependent on the identification of specific disordinal interactions between learning characteristics (specific personological variables) and the relative educational payoff of differential educational curricula or approaches.
>
> (p. 1)

Disordinal interactions refer to those differential outcomes in which different treatments benefit some groups of learners, but inhibit learning of others. Although disordinal aptitude-treatment interactions were rarely identified over the years (although ordinal interactions have frequently been observed), the concept of disordinal interactions suggested that special education treatments must be qualitatively different in order to be valid.

This has not proven to be the case—disordinal interactions have rarely been reported in education. But should ordinal interactions be an expectation for special education treatments? That is, must students with special learning needs benefit differentially from a specific intervention for it to be considered "special education?"

It would seem reasonable to suggest that interventions that benefit special education and general education students similarly may not qualify as "special education." Yet even in this case, there may be some differential benefit. That is, an intervention that benefits all students similarly (e.g., an effect size of .30 for all groups of learners), may still benefit special education students differentially, if it raises a higher proportion beyond a minimal or passing criterion.

Are mnemonics "special education" strategies?

In other cases, we may expect students with special needs to benefit differentially from a particular strategy intervention, if simply because many general education students spontaneously employ many study and elaborative learning strategies similar to those being trained; or do not exhibit the limitations in, e.g., prior knowledge, attention, semantic memory, or working memory, that many learning strategies are intended to address (e.g., Swanson & Saez, 2003). For example, mnemonic (memory-enhancing) strategy instruction has long been seen to facilitate substantial gains in memory for school-related content among students with special needs, such as learning disabilities, emotional or behavioral disabilities, and mild intellectual disabilities (Scruggs & Mastropieri,

2000). These strategies have been very helpful in a variety of contexts, including English and foreign language learning, reading vocabulary, science, and social studies. However, mnemonic strategies have also been seen to improve the memory of typically achieving, or even gifted students (e.g., Scruggs, Mastropieri, Jorgensen, & Monson, 1986). Nevertheless, mnemonic strategies have had a special role in special education, because they address areas of particular concern for these populations, and because they address the learning characteristics of many students with disabilities in facilitative ways.

As an example, consider the scientific term *ranidae*, which refers to the family of common frogs. Using the mnemonic keyword, the unfamiliar term is first converted to an acoustically similar keyword, that is easy to picture. In this case, "rain" (or, "rainy day"), would be a good keyword for *ranidae*, because it sounds like "rain" and is easily pictured. Then, the meaning is shown in an illustration interacting with the keyword. In the present example, a frog (meaning of *ranidae*) is shown sitting in the rain (keyword for *ranidae*). After studying this illustration and the mnemonic strategy, when learners are asked for the meaning of *ranidae*, they first think of the keyword, rain, think of the illustration of the rain, remember a frog is sitting in the rain, and provide the answer, frog. Mnemonic strategies have been associated with some of the highest effect sizes in the special education literature (Scruggs, Mastropieri, Berkeley, & Graetz, 2010.

Mnemonics such as the keyword method are of particular value in special education because they minimize relative weaknesses of learners (e.g., spontaneous strategy production, verbal fluency, semantic memory), while maximizing their relative strengths (e.g., memory for pictures, memory for semantically or phonetically elaborated information; see Scruggs, Mastropieri, Berkeley, & Marshak,

"Mnemonic strategies have had a special role in special education, because they address areas of particular concern for these populations, and because they address the learning characteristics of many students with disabilities in facilitative ways."

2010). To this extent, mnemonic strategies can be considered valuable special education interventions, even though they also may be beneficial to other learners, who may be able to rely on alternate resources to enhance their learning.

In Indiana, we worked with a student with learning disabilities who needed to learn all 50 states and capitals as a condition for passing into eighth grade, and he was struggling to meet this standard, having failed this test several times previously. We showed him relevant keyword strategies to improve his memory for this information. For example, to remember that Tallahassee is the capital of Florida, we showed a picture of a *flower* (keyword for Florida) on top of a *television* (keyword for Tallahassee). We practiced with him the keywords for each state and capital, and said, for example, "When I ask for the capital of Florida, think of the keyword, 'flower,' remember the flower was on top of a television, remember 'television' is the keyword for Tallahassee. Tallahassee is the capital of Florida" retrieving the correct answer. This strategy is complicated because it includes two keywords; nevertheless this student with significant learning problems learned how to use it and learned all his states and capitals. So when he took the test the last time, he earned 100 percent correct. Unfortunately, we heard later that the teacher had given him an "F," reasoning that he couldn't possibly learn this well in such a short time! Fortunately, we were able to convince the teacher that the student's learning gains were real, and he was able to advance to eighth grade. This example highlights how special learning strategies can be employed to address particular difficulty areas, and the seemingly impossible learning gains that are sometimes realized.

Explicit instruction

Special educational intervention techniques may not always refer to specific learning strategies. We (Mastropieri & Scruggs, 2002; 2014) described many of the effective teacher presentation techniques as the SCREAM variables (structure, clarity, redundancy, enthusiasm, appropriate rate, maximized engagement). Collectively, these presentation techniques address many commonly observed characteristics of students with disabilities, such as sustained attention, distractibility, memory, cognitive organization, social behavior, affect, and motivation (e.g., Mastropieri & Scruggs, 2014). And although such techniques have been shown to facilitate learning in more typical learners (Mastropieri & Scruggs, 2004), these variables may be mandatory for learning to take place for students with disabilities.

Differential effectiveness

Beyond the issue of whether special learning techniques are more necessary for students with disabilities, are these techniques demonstrably more effective for students with disabilities than for more typical learners? The answer to this is unclear, although some evidence is available to inform the issue. Scruggs, Mastropieri, Berkeley, and Graetz (2010) summarized available literature on secondary content area learning for students with disabilities, and identified an overall mean effect size of 1.00, a large effect indicating the average student in the treatment group would be at about the 84th percentile of the comparison group. These treatments included peer tutoring, hands-on learning, spatial learning, study and learning strategies, mnemonic instruction, and explicit instruction, all of which appeared to address specific characteristics of exceptional learners.

Over the past decade or so, we and our colleagues conducted 10 investigations of particular relevance to the "differential facilitation" issue. These studies, which included 1128 students, 283 of whom had special needs, employed multiple specialized intervention techniques, including peer tutoring with self-monitoring, explicit teaching, tiered activities with peer mediation, and mnemonic instruction, with and without peer mediation. In these studies, which were carried out in inclusive settings, effects were calculated for both general education and special education students. Most of these investigations were conducted over a period between 8 and 18 weeks duration. Although these are not exhaustive of inclusive content-area investigations, they nevertheless comprise a consistent and coherent subset of available research literature in this area. Across all studies, effect sizes were a substantial .63 for general education students, but a much larger 1.40 for students with special needs (Scruggs, 2012). Students with disabilities scored 1.03 standard deviations lower than general education students in control conditions, but in the experimental conditions, scored overall only .26 standard deviations lower.

Implementation issues

These findings of differential effectiveness support the notion that, when students can profitably be included with general education classrooms, specialized instructional techniques, at least in some cases, can be expected to narrow the achievement gap between general education students and students with disabilities. Unfortunately, however, it is less likely that these techniques will be implemented in today's inclusive classrooms. In

1996, and more recently in 2011, we (Scruggs & Mastropieri, 1996; Scruggs, Leins, & Mastropieri, 2011) summarized all available survey research on teacher attitudes toward inclusion, and noted that teacher attitudes seemed to have changed very little over the years. While a majority of teachers supported at least some form of inclusion of students with disabilities, only small minorities agreed they had the time, training, or support needed to implement inclusion effectively. These findings suggest that teachers believe they lack the means to teach students with disabilities effectively in inclusive classes.

Another discouraging finding on contemporary practice was reported by Scruggs, Mastropieri, and McDuffie (2007). We integrated and summarized 32 qualitative investigations of co-teaching in inclusive classrooms. These studies included a total of 453 co-teachers, 142 students, and 42 administrators, and employed procedures such as extended classroom observations with field notes, interviews, and examination of classroom products. Although teachers reported generally favorable attitudes toward co-teaching, specialized instructional or learning strategies were almost never observed. Zigmond and Matta (2004) reported in their investigation of co-teachers: "none of what we saw would make it more likely that the students with disabilities in the class would master the material . . . We virtually never saw the special education teacher provide explicit strategic instruction to facilitate learning or memory of the content material" (p. 73).

Reviewing the findings of all 32 investigations, we concluded:

> Classroom instruction has generally continued as whole class and lecture driven, and special education co-teachers have generally attempted to fit within this model to deliver assistance to students in need. Practices known to be effective and frequently recommended—such as peer mediation, strategy instruction, mnemonics, study skills training, organizational skills training, hands-on curriculum materials, test-taking skills training, comprehension training, self-advocacy skills training, self-monitoring, or even general principles of effective instruction—were only rarely observed.
>
> (Scruggs, Mastropieri, & McDuffie, 2007, p. 412)

Overall, it can be concluded that many specialized treatments exist that are particularly appropriate—and, at least in some cases, differentially effective—for students with disabilities. However, survey and observational data suggest reluctance on the part of general education teachers to implement these treatments. The reason for this is not known, but perhaps has to do with limited time, training, or support for general education teachers; or because of teacher reluctance to implement strategies perceived to be of particular utility for only a small number of students in the class. In either case, it will be important to increase the implementation of these techniques in general education classes in order to promote success in inclusive classrooms.

THE GOALS OF SPECIAL EDUCATION

With the passage and implementation of the No Child Left Behind Act, the goals of special education seem to have been integrated within the general education curriculum standards. And, on one hand, it seems very appropriate to set this high standard as accessible to all learners. But is success in the general education curriculum really the only goal for special education? Many of us who have worked in special education are aware that, although general education curriculum standards may be attainable for some special education students, for many others, this is simply not a realistic standard. Certainly, many students with more severe disabilities, for example those with very limited language or communication skills, will not meet these standards; but also many students with "mild" or "moderate" disabilities may encounter great difficulties. Several years ago, for example, we worked in a mid-western inner-city middle school with eighth graders who had learning and intellectual disabilities and who were able to read at about the third or fourth grade level. Although these students were clearly able to learn many things, it would have been unrealistic to have assumed they would have been able to meet all age-appropriate curriculum standards.

Clearly, special education cannot restore sight to the blind, hearing to the deaf, or motor control to those with permanent physical disabilities. And in these cases, there is little expectation that it will do so. Often, however, we hear an implication that the "mild disabilities" are malleable, and that special education cannot be considered successful until students with emotional or behavioral disorders, intellectual or learning disabilities, are essentially "cured" of these challenges. In our view, disability identification should not be undertaken lightly, and those identified appropriately as having a disability are likely to be challenged by this disability for much of their lives. Certainly, limitations in vision, hearing, and physical disability can in some cases be restored; some individuals with specific cognitive or emotional challenges can learn to overcome these. But in very many cases—and relevant data bear this out—disability is an extensive, long-term issue, and many affected students will need substantial support to pass through the grades successfully and gain important academic and life skills.

> "These findings of differential effectiveness support the notion that, when students can profitably be included with general educational classrooms, specialized instructional techniques, at least in some cases, can be expected to narrow the achievement gap between general education students and students with disabilities."

Does this mean schools should give up on certain students who seem unlikely to meet general education academic expectations? Certainly not. For many students, more important and realistic objectives include learning to read and appreciate basic text independently (or recognize emergency words); exhibit appropriate interpersonal skills; make purchases, maintain bank accounts, and budget money; learn marketable career or technical skills; and participate in our democracy. Such goals and skills may in many cases easily be as significant and important as, for example, mastering a foreign language or learning trigonometry, and especially so when these latter goals are unlikely to be attained. We prefer the wisdom of the original IDEA provisions, which established teams of professionals and parents, and often students themselves, planning objectives that seem to be in the best interest of the individual student, and revisiting these objectives periodically. This to us seems to be at the heart of the intent of special education.

WHAT ARE THE COMPONENTS OF SPECIAL EDUCATION?

Special education should focus primarily on keeping identified students in school, and promoting systematic progress on specific need areas, as identified by a multidisciplinary team, parents, and the student. Although we have often heard about remediating weaknesses vs. building on relative strengths—and certainly our own research considers these issues—special educators should use all means at their disposal to realize the best outcomes for their students. They should improve areas of social or academic limitation, where such improvement is realistic; actively address broader areas of generalized functioning; and develop and implement accommodations to allow students to access relative strength areas to address relative limitations. They should continually implement appropriate techniques with the ultimate goal of maximizing independence.

We included our view on important and necessary components of special education in our book, *The Inclusive Classroom: Strategies for Effective Differentiated Instruction* (Mastropieri & Scruggs, 5th ed., 2014). Although directed toward general education teachers in inclusive classes, we included information of particular importance for special educators. This includes important knowledge areas (knowledge of laws, regulations, and issues; knowledge of the characteristics of exceptionality); and effective specialized teaching skills (task analysis; evaluation and assessment; explicit instruction; use of classroom peers; addressing significant psycho-educational challenges, such as attention, memory, organizational skills, motivation, and affect; and managing social behavior). In addition, special education teachers employ specialized adaptations and learning strategies specific to all areas of academic functioning, such as literacy, mathematics, science, and social studies. Many of these areas are not specifically addressed in many existing response-to-intervention (RTI) models, which appear to address best the needs of those who really do not belong in special education programs.

A final, and critically important, component of special education is advocacy. Special education teachers very often serve as a buffer between the student with special needs, and teachers, administrators, and staff who may on occasion seem uninformed, unsympathetic, or even hostile to an individual student. Comments such as "I won't spoon-feed these students," or, "They have to learn to survive in the real world," are commonly heard, and data from attitude surveys bear out these sentiments (Scruggs et al., 2011). However, skilled advocacy strategies on the part of special education teachers, including problem solving, provision of appropriate supports and alternatives, and mediating conflicts, can play an invaluable role in student success.

"But in very many cases—and relevant data bear this out—disability is an extensive, long-term issue, and many affected students will need substantial supports to pass through the grades successfully and gain important academic life skills."

CONCLUSION

We have seen many changes in policy, organization, structure, and intervention strategies over the years; yet one thing we have noticed is that the students entering school in need of specialized assistance each year has been a constant. Our years in the profession have shown us that special educators fulfill a critically important need area.

Just as accidents such as Margo's can happen at any time, to anyone, there will always be students who require some type of special education and/or related services in order to be successful in school. The special education services need to be tailor-made to the individual in order to meet particular students' needs. This will always result in a need for specialized training of professionals to work with students and their families. We hope the field will continue to expand and have professionals work together to identify the best research-based practices to help students meet their educational needs.

Discussion Questions

1. Think of subjects and skills not explicitly taught at higher grade levels (i.e., after students enter middle school). Using some of your examples, explain how the lack of explicit instruction in these subjects may affect the achievement of students with disabilities.
2. What is your opinion of the "hidden curriculum" (i.e., should teachers focus on organizational and study skills)? Why or why not?
3. What is an example of teaching a student to learn something differently than other students (think of the example of blindness and braille)? What are ways this makes instruction and instructional planning challenging for the teacher?
4. Should students with disabilities be treated differently when it comes to classroom discipline? Why or why not?
5. Give an example of how a teacher could alter an assignment by pace and intensity.
6. Explain the significance of the following statement:

    The very existence of "special" education is literally dependent on the identification of specific disordinal interactions between learning characteristics (specific personological variables) and the relative educational payoff of different educational curricula or approaches.

7. Do you think mnemonics are beneficial as both special education and general education strategies?
8. Why do you think today's inclusive classroom limits the use of specialized instructional techniques, and how may this impact achievement?
9. Why may a general education teacher be reluctant to implement specialized treatments?
10. Discuss the importance of advocacy for special education students. Who are their best advocates?

TOM SCRUGGS'S AND MARGO MASTROPIERI'S SUGGESTIONS FOR FURTHER READING

Mastropieri, M. A., & Scruggs, T. E. (2014). *The inclusive classroom: Strategies for effective differentiated instruction* (5th ed.). Upper Saddle River, NJ: Prentice Hall.

Mastropieri, M. A., Scruggs, T. E., Guckert, M., Thompson, C. G., & Weiss, M. P. (2013). Inclusion and learning disabilities: Will the past be prologue? In J. P. Bakken, F. E. Obiakor, & A. F. Rotatori (Eds.), *Advances in Special Education: Learning disabilities: Practice concerns and students with LD* (vol. 25, pp. 1–17). Brighton, England: Emerald Group.

Mastropieri, M. A., Scruggs, T. E., & Mills, S. (2011). Special education teacher preparation. In J. M. Kauffman & D. P. Hallahan (Eds.), *Handbook of special education* (pp. 47–58). New York: Routledge.

Scruggs, T. E., Mastropieri, M. A., & Marshak, L. (2011). Science and social studies. In J. M. Kauffman & D. P. Hallahan (Eds.), *Handbook of special education* (pp. 445–455). New York: Routledge.

Scruggs, T. E., & Mastropieri, M. A. (2012). Teaching students with high-incidence disabilities. In R. A. McWilliam, B. G. Cook, & M. Tankersley (Eds.), *Research-based practices for improving outcomes for targeted groups of learners* (pp. 14–24). Upper Saddle River, NJ: Pearson.

Scruggs, T. E., & Wong, B. Y. L. (Eds.), (1990). *Intervention research in learning disabilities.* New York: Springer.

REFERENCES

Driver, R., Asoko, H., Leach, J., Mortimer, E., & Scott, P. (1994). Constructing scientific knowledge in the classroom. *Educational Researcher, 23*(7), 5–12.

Harris, K. R., Graham, S., Mason, L. H., & Friedlander, B. (2008). *Powerful writing strategies for all students.* Baltimore: Brookes.

Mastropieri, M. A., & Scruggs, T. E. (2002). *Effective instruction for special education* (3rd ed.). Austin, TX: Pro-Ed.

Mastropieri, M. A., & Scruggs, T. E. (2004). Effective classroom instruction. In C. Spielberger (Ed.), *Encyclopedia of applied psychology* (pp. 687–691). Oxford, UK: Elsevier.

Mastropieri, M. A., & Scruggs, T. E. (2010). The study of human exceptionality: How it informs our knowledge of learning and cognition. In T. E. Scruggs & M. A. Mastropieri (Eds.), *Literacy and learning: Advances in learning and behavioral disabilities* (vol. 23, pp. 303–319). Bingley, UK: Emerald.

Mastropieri, M. A., & Scruggs, T. E. (2014). *The inclusive classroom: Strategies for effective differentiated instruction* (5th ed.). Upper Saddle River, NJ: Prentice Hall.

Mastropieri, M. A., Scruggs, T. E., Cuenca-Sanchez, Y., Irby, N., Mills, S., Mason, L., & Kubina, R. (2010). Persuading students with emotional disabilities to write: A design study. In T. E. Scruggs & M. A. Mastropieri (Eds.), *Literacy and learning: Advances in learning and behavioral disabilities* (vol. 23, pp. 237–268). Bingley, UK: Emerald.

Myles, B. S., Trautman, M. L., & Schelvan, R. L. (2004). *The hidden curriculum: Practical solutions for understanding unstated rules in social situations.* Shawnee, KS: AAPC.

Scruggs, T. E. (2012). Differential facilitation of learning outcomes: What does it tell us about learning disabilities and instructional programming? *International Journal for Research in Learning Disabilities.*

Scruggs, T. E., Bennion, K., & Lifson, S. (1985a). An analysis of children's strategy use on reading achievement tests. *The Elementary School Journal, 85,* 479–484.

Scruggs, T. E., Bennion, K., & Lifson, S. (1985b). Learning disabled students' spontaneous use of test-taking skills on reading achievement tests. *Learning Disability Quarterly, 8,* 205–210.

Scruggs, T. E., Leins, P., & Mastropieri, M. A. (2011, April). *Teacher attitudes towards inclusion: A synthesis of survey, comparative, and qualitative research, 1958–2010.* Paper presented at the annual meeting of the Council for Exceptional Children, Washington, DC.

Scruggs, T. E., & Mastropieri, M. A. (1988). Are learning disabled students "test-wise"?: A review of recent research. *Learning Disabilities Focus, 3,* 87–97.

Scruggs, T. E., & Mastropieri, M. A. (1994). Successful mainstreaming in elementary science classes: A qualitative investigation of three reputational cases. *American Educational Research Journal, 31,* 785–811.

Scruggs, T. E., & Mastropieri, M. A. (1996). Teacher perceptions of mainstreaming/inclusion, 1958–1995: A research synthesis. *Exceptional Children, 63,* 59–74.

Scruggs, T. E., & Mastropieri, M. A. (2000). The effectiveness of mnemonic instruction for students with learning and behavior problems: An update and research synthesis. *Journal of Behavioral Education, 10,* 163–173.

Scruggs, T. E., Mastropieri, M. A., Berkeley, S., & Graetz, J. (2010). Do special education interventions improve learning of secondary content? A meta-analysis. *Remedial and Special Education, 36,* 437–449.

Scruggs, T. E., Mastropieri, M. A., Berkeley, S., & Marshak, L. (2010). Mnemonic strategies: Evidence-based practice and practice-based evidence. *Intervention in School and Clinic, 46,* 79–86.

Scruggs, T. E., Mastropieri, M. A., Jorgensen, C., & Monson, J. A. (1986). Effective mnemonic strategies for gifted learners. *Journal for the Education of the Gifted, 9,* 105–121.

Scruggs, T. E., Mastropieri, M. A., & McDuffie, K. A. (2007). Co-teaching in inclusive classrooms: A meta-synthesis of qualitative research. *Exceptional Children, 73,* 392–416.

Scruggs, T.E., Mastropieri, M.A., & Wolfe, S. (1994–1995). Scientific reasoning of students with mental retardation: Investigating preconceptions and conceptual change. *Exceptionality, 5,* 223–244.

Scruggs, T. E., Prieto, A. G., & Zucker, S. H. (1981). Classroom hearing assessment: An operant training procedure for the non-verbal, autistic child. *Monographs in Behavior Disorders, 4,* 89–95.

Swanson, H. L., & Saez, L. (2003). Memory difficulties in children and adults with learning disabilities. In H. L. Swanson, K. Harris, & S. Graham (Eds.), *Handbook of learning disabilities* (pp. 182–198). New York: Guilford.

Tobias, S. (1976). Achievement treatment interactions. *Review of Educational Research, 46,* 61–74.

Ysseldyke, J. E. (1973, February). *Aptitude treatment interaction research with learning disabled children* Paper presented at the annual meeting of the American Educational Research Association, New Orleans. (ERIC Document Reproduction Service No. ED 074 101).

Zigmond, N., & Matta, D. (2004). Value added of the special education teacher on secondary school co-taught classes. In T. E. Scruggs & M. A. Mastropieri (Eds.), *Research in secondary schools: Advances in learning and behavioral disabilities* (vol. 17, pp. 55–76). Oxford, UK: Elsevier.

Getting to Know Paige C. Pullen

I began my career as an elementary teacher. In my first few years most of my students learned to read beyond my expectations in spite of my inexperience. Seeking more challenge, I took a position in a Title 1 resource room for students at increased risk for reading failure. It was obvious there was a high percentage of children who needed better reading instruction from me as well as my fellow teachers.

Seeking to discover the elements of exemplary reading instruction, I enrolled in the Ph.D. program in reading at the University of Florida. I also enrolled in a doctoral seminar in special education taught by Cecil Mercer. I realized then that I needed to be in special education, where the focus was on explicit and systematic instruction. I owe much to Cecil, not only for making it obvious I should switch to the special education program, but also for helping me take a position at the University of Virginia, which happened to be where he had attained his Ph.D.

Getting to Know Daniel P. Hallahan

Reflecting on how or why I ended up a professor of special education, the "butterfly effect" comes to mind. But here are a few events and circumstances that might have contributed in some way: (1) growing up in a blue/white collar neighborhood in Detroit (*appreciation for individual differences in cognitive and behavioral abilities*), being a fan of the Detroit Tigers (*penchant to root for underdogs*), (3) attending a Jesuit High School (*inculcation in social justice values and recognition of power of systematic instruction*), (4) caddying at Detroit Golf Club (*tolerance for arrogance*), (5) bartending on Mackinac Island (*tolerance for ambiguity*), (6) having superb academic mentors—as an undergrad, John Hagen; as a graduate student, William Cruickshank (*direction and guidance*); and collaborating with superb special education colleagues at UVA (*e.g., Jim Kauffman, John Lloyd, Rebecca Kneedler, and Paige Pullen*).

4

WHAT IS SPECIAL EDUCATION INSTRUCTION?

Paige C. Pullen & Daniel P. Hallahan

Although there are certainly those who don't "believe" in special education, i.e., they think it is not needed in schools because all students can be educated within the general education system, for those who do believe in the need for special education, there is little disagreement on the definition of "special education." Most adhere to the following elements of the federal definition of special education:

> Special education means specially designed instruction . . . to meet the unique needs of a child with a disability. . . .
>
> Specially designed instruction means adapting, as appropriate to the needs of an eligible child under this part, the content, methodology, or delivery of instruction—
>
> . . . To address the unique needs of the child that result from the child's disability. . . .
>
> (Sec. 300.39 Special Education, http://idea.ed.gov)

INDIVIDUALIZED INSTRUCTION

To deliver *specially designed instruction* to meet students' *unique needs*, IDEA further specifies that students with disabilities must be provided an *individualized* educational program (IEP). To our way of thinking, it's individualization that is the *sine qua non* of special education instruction. The singular adjective that describes special education is that it is *individualized.* Without individualization, special education just doesn't exist. As Fred Weintraub, one of the key players in the creation of the original law (P.L. 94-142) establishing the status of the IEP, has recently said:

> The cornerstone of special education policy for the past four decades has been individualization. IDEA was and remains unique in educational policy in that it prescribes no truth in what is appropriate for children with disabilities. Rather, it provides for a process whereby the individualized educational program (IEP) team that knows the child determines what is appropriate for the child. (Weintraub, 2012, p. 53)

ACHIEVING INDIVIDUALIZED INSTRUCTION: A LEXICON OF CRITICAL COMPONENTS OF SPECIAL EDUCATION INSTRUCTION

It's hard to debate that students with disabilities need instruction tailored to their needs. Pinning down what constitutes specially designed instruction is more challenging. Just what does it mean to adapt content, methodology, and delivery of instruction? Can special education instruction be further explicated?

Admittedly, in the case of some disabilities, such as deafness and blindness, there are clear instructional differences—sign language and braille being the most obvious—which make distinguishing special from general education easy. Our focus in this chapter, therefore, is on those oft-referred-to high incidence disabilities characterized by deficits in learning—learning disabilities and intellectual disabilities, especially the former. These are the areas of special education that are most often criticized as not needing instruction from special educators. This is not to say, however, that much of what we discuss doesn't also apply to other disabilities to some extent.

"The cornerstone of special education policy for the past four decades has been individualization."

In preparation for writing this chapter, we were struck by how much overlap exists in various researchers' listings of the elements that characterize special education instruction. Although far from a scientific survey, some of the concepts/terms we encountered the most were, in no particular order: direct, explicit, systematic, goal-directed, intense, iterative, relentless, well-paced, low pupil–teacher ratio, attention to curriculum, frequent assessment and monitoring of performance, distributed and cumulative practice, guided practice, scaffolding, careful sequencing, carefully designed.

At the same time as there was consensus on the critical components of special education instruction, definitions of these elements were often absent, differed from each other, or overlapped with each other. Therefore, we propose a lexicon of critical components that differentiate special education from general education.

Explicit and Systematic Instruction

The phrase, "explicit and systematic instruction," has become so commonplace that it can almost be considered a cliché. As a field, we talk about students in special education needing explicit and systematic instruction, yet in discussions with general educators, we rarely, if ever, explain effectively what those terms mean. What does explicit and systematic instruction look like in practice? Is explicit instruction necessarily systematic? If instruction is systematic, is it necessarily explicit? We believe that explicit instruction and systematic instruction are critical to special education, but we define them and consider them separately in our lexicon.

Explicit instruction

According to the Collins COBUILD Advanced Dictionary of American English (Harper Collins, 2012), "something that is *explicit* is expressed or shown clearly and openly, without any attempt to hide anything." Thus explicit teaching requires the teacher to explain skills and concepts in a clear and direct manner. If instruction is explicit, the teacher provides a clear explanation or model of the skill or concept (Mercer & Pullen, 2009).

Systematic instruction

Harper Collins (2012) defines *systematic* as "something that is done according to a fixed plan, in a thorough and efficient way." A teacher who uses systematized instruction adheres to a "fixed plan" by using an optimal order for introducing new information—easy skills precede more difficult skills, pre-skills of a strategy are taught before the strategy is presented. Systematic instruction is efficient in that high utility skills are taught before less useful ones. It is iterative in that teachers require students to repeat skills or skill sequences until they are ready to move on to more difficult skills. Additionally, a teacher separates strategies and information that students are likely to confuse (Carnine, Silbert, Kame'enui, Tarver, & Jungjohann, 2006).

Systematic instruction also requires that the teaching be *structured*, another term that is often used to describe special education instruction. In other words, the teacher needs to arrange instruction "in a careful, organized pattern or system" (Harper Collins, 2012). To our way of thinking, structured also means that the nature of the instruction is predictable for the student. He or she knows in advance what to expect within a lesson.

Intensive Instruction

"*Intensive* activity involves concentrating a lot of effort or people on one particular task in order to achieve a lot in a short time." One goal of special education should be to accelerate student learning. The achievement gap between students with and without disabilities will increase or remain constant unless special education instruction accelerates student learning. That is, students with disabilities need to make more than one year's progress in one year's time. For this to occur, instruction must be intensive.

Few would argue that in order to accelerate student learning requires intensive instruction; however, little agreement exists as to *how* to best intensify instruction. This topic has become particularly important as schools and districts attempt to define the tiers of instruction in a response to intervention programs. Several terms in our lexicon help to elucidate intensive instruction.

Pacing

Two usages of the word pace are important in considering pacing of instruction. First, "the *pace* of something is the speed at which it happens or is done," and second, "if you *pace* yourself when doing something, you do it at a steady rate." Both explanations of the term "pace" from the COBUILD dictionary, "speed and steady rate," help to determine appropriate pacing of instruction. To intensify the pace of instruction, a teacher maintains a steady and relentless pace. The speed of instruction is based on two defined terms—systematic and mastery. Teaching adheres to a set order and does not proceed until the student has mastered a particular skill.

Group Size

When group size is included as intensifying instruction, teachers typically think of whole-group, small-group, or one-on-one instruction. What is the number of students in a small group that allows for optimal teaching (i.e., intensified instruction)? Is one-on-one instruction always better than small group instruction?

Research is unclear as to the ideal group size for intervention effectiveness. In general, one-on-one interventions for students with learning disabilities result in high effect sizes (Wanzek & Kent, 2012). In a study comparing one-on-one instruction to various sized small groups, results favored one-on-one instruction. No statistical differences were found

"The achievement gap between students with and without disabilities will increase or remain constant until special education instruction accelerates student learning."

among the small groups (2, 3, 4, or 5 students), however, the trend in the data suggested that intervention effectiveness decreased as the group size increased.

Research also supports the effectiveness of small-group interventions (Rashotte, MacPhee, & Torgesen, 2001). In a study across first through sixth grades comparing explicit, small-group reading and whole-class instruction, the low performers receiving small-group instruction (three–five students) performed significantly better than their matched controls in whole-group instruction. More recently, guidelines for RTI in elementary and middle school mathematics suggest that small groups should be homogenous with three to five students (Gersten et al., 2009).

Duration and frequency

Intensity of instruction is increased when the instruction happens more often (frequency) and for a longer period of time (duration). The amount of time in a school day is a limited resource, thus decisions may need to be made regarding the priorities of instruction (Zigmond & Pullen, 2012). In order to intensify the instruction in one area (e.g., reading or mathematics), more time will need to be devoted to the intervention and something else may receive less attention. Gersten et al. (2009) recommend that interventions in general education classrooms for students below grade level should be implemented three to five times per week for 20 to 40 minutes per session. Students with learning disabilities may require interventions to be more frequent and for a longer duration. Increasing duration is not limited to the number of minutes per day of instruction. Interventions may need to be implemented over multiple years (Vaughn et al., 2010).

Corrective Feedback

Several research syntheses have captured the rich history of the positive effects of corrective feedback in teaching students with learning disabilities. These syntheses have concentrated on language arts and literacy, e.g., reading fluency (Chard, Vaughn, & Tyler, 2012; Eckert, Dunn, & Ardoin, 2006), reading word recognition (Heubusch & Lloyd, 1998), reading comprehension (Heubusch & Lloyd, 1998; Kouri, Selle, & Riley, 2006), and spelling (Wanzek et al., 2006). Evidence also exists for corrective feedback's value in teaching math facts (addition, subtraction, multiplication, and division; Brosvic, Dihoff, Epstein, & Cook, 2006).

There might be several reasons why corrective feedback is so important for students with learning disabilities. For example, the idea of making frequent errors is inherent in being identified as having learning disabilities. Without correction, the likelihood of repeating the same mistakes increases. And the longer one goes making the same mistakes, the more difficult it becomes to rectify them.

Several definitions of corrective feedback and several different kinds of corrective feedback have been proposed and researched. Space here doesn't allow us to discuss all the nuances associated with corrective feedback; however, we think a couple particulars are worth mention. First, the more immediate the correction, the better the results (Brosvic et al., 2006; Heubusch & Lloyd, 1998; Wanzek et al., 2006). For example, if asked to compute a list of math problems, it's more effective to correct the student immediately after he makes an error than to wait to provide the feedback after the list is completed (Brosvic et al., 2006).

Second, the more explicit the corrective feedback, the better the results. For example, Kouri et al. compared two types of corrective feedback during guided reading instruction—"graphophonemic word decoding" and "meaning-based." When the students made an error, the former, which was more effective, involved cueing the student with respect to letter-phoneme correspondence. The latter, in the whole-language tradition, involved asking the students to "find the problem" in the sentence read, to re-read the sentence, or to do both.

Corrective feedback is often paired with the teacher modeling the correct response and other instructional actions. The following serves as a prototype of what we envision of how corrective feedback should be typically executed: "The correction procedure for incorrect responses during small-group [language] instruction is directed toward the whole group and consists of as many as five steps: model, lead, test, firm up, and delayed test" (Carnine, Silbert, Kame'enui, Tarver, & Jungjohann, 2006). The teacher models the correct response. (S)he "leads," if necessary, by saying the correct sound or word along with the group. She "tests" by asking the group to say the sound or word again. "Firming up" involves the teacher repeating the few sounds or words that had already been presented up to the sound or word that had been corrected before moving on to new material. Then, later in the lesson, the teacher might deliver a "delayed test," in which the student making the error or the group is directed to say the sound or word again.

Reinforcement

Reinforcement, a component that at one time was practically synonymous with special education instruction, seems in recent years to have been relegated to the status of a forgotten stepchild. Although admittedly highly anecdotal,[1] we find it telling that it is missing in the entry to the indices of the 57-chapter, 787-page *Handbook of Special Education* (Kauffman & Hallahan, 2011); the highly praised (with good reason) *Explicit instruction: Effective and Efficient Teaching* (Archer & Hughes, 2011); the first edition of the current book, *Handbook of Learning Disabilities* (Swanson, Harris, & Graham, 2003); and only warranted four pages in the popular *Teaching Students with Learning Problems* (Mercer, Mercer, & Pullen, 2011). Whether it's been shunned because of its original association with operant conditioning, or it's now simply taken for granted as a necessary component is hard to say. However, its absence in mainstream discussions of special education instruction is curious.

In any case, we think reinforcement is clearly deserving of mention as a critical component of special education instruction. We recognize the important role of intrinsic reinforcement, such as a *student's feeling* positive because of having completed a task or of having straightforwardly been given feedback on, for example, the number of problems solved correctly. However, for our purposes we focus more on extrinsic reinforcement—*teacher behaviors* associated with reinforcement. And we consider extrinsic reinforcement as being on a continuum from more to less overtly extrinsic, e.g., free time on playground, tokens that can be used to "buy" free time on the playground, social praise.

HOW IS SPECIAL EDUCATION INSTRUCTION DIFFERENT FROM GENERAL EDUCATION INSTRUCTION?

Having addressed the critical components of special education instruction, we believe it important to tackle the longstanding claim that special and general education should be viewed as synonymous because (a) *good* general education teaching mimics *good* special education teaching and (b) the very popular notion in general education that providing "differentiated instruction" can meet the needs of all students in the classroom regardless of whether they have a learning disability. In other words, adopting a differentiated instruction model satisfies the legal mandate of individualizing instruction.

ARE SPECIAL EDUCATION INSTRUCTION AND GOOD GENERAL EDUCATION INSTRUCTION EQUIVALENT? QUANTITATIVE AND QUALITATIVE CONSIDERATIONS

We wish we had a dollar[2] for every time we've heard someone say, "Good general education is simply good special education," or vice-versa, "Good special education is simply good general education." As one prominent special education researcher put it, "Good teaching is good teaching" (Algozzine & White, 2007).

As with any pronouncement that reaches the virtual status of an aphorism, there's a certain degree of truth to this assertion. Another, and perhaps better, way to phrase the question is, "Is special education instruction quantitatively or qualitatively different from general education?" In other words, is special education instruction merely a matter of doing more of the same thing that's done in general education? Or is special education instruction somehow a different entity, with its own identity?

"Reinforcement, a component that at one time was practically synonymous with special education instruction, seems in recent years to have been relegated to the status of a forgotten stepchild."

In our opinion, when it comes to learning disabilities, it's both—special education instruction doesn't include any techniques that can't, and aren't, used by good general education instructors.[3] However, there is a difference in the quantity of these techniques, with respect to the degree to which they're used, the regularity of their use, and how many different techniques are used. And it's the greater *quantity* that makes special education differ from general education; it's what makes special education qualitatively different from general education; it's what gives special education its own identity; it's what makes special education *special*.

The notion of special education being both quantitatively and qualitatively different from general education is similar to how many psychological and medical conditions are determined. For example, a person's feelings of self-worth, hopelessness, lethargy, and so forth can vary on continua. Considering the range and severity of these symptoms, the psychologist or psychiatrist makes a clinical judgment about whether the individual is clinically depressed. And a person's weight can vary along a continuum. If the weight reaches a certain point on that continuum, the person is considered to exhibit obesity. In each of these examples, it takes a certain quantity of a variable or variables before the person is considered to be qualitatively different, e.g., clinically depressed or obese. Similarly, once a student reaches a certain level or amount of critical components of special education instruction, the IEP team makes the judgment that he or she is best served by being considered learning disabled or intellectually disabled.

Instruction on Continua

A useful way to think about the terms in our lexicon of instructional techniques is that we can place each of them on a continuum of quantity (Kauffman & Hallahan, 2005). For example, a teacher's approach to teaching a student to read can vary with respect to how much it's explicit, intense, and systematic, and how corrective feedback and reinforcement are used.

We hypothesize that there's a limit to the quantity or degree to which we can reasonably expect each of these techniques to be used by general education teachers. These limitations can be due to a variety of factors, e.g., the teacher's preparation, ability, teaching philosophy, the amount of support provided by the principal, class size, the characteristics of the students, etc.

Consider four hypothetical second-grade students—Jamal, who is reading on or above grade level, Carter, who is reading ½ standard deviation below grade level, and Lisa and Andre, each of whom is reading 1½ standard deviations below grade level. We posit that each of these students needs a certain quantity of the five critical components noted above in order to have the best opportunity of achieving at grade level: explicitness, intensive, systematic instruction, with corrective feedback and reinforcement. Figure 4.1 compares the quantity of the five components each student needs to the level we can expect of general education teachers.

In Figure 4.1, we see that Jamal does not require high levels of explicit,[4] intense instruction, and corrective feedback. In addition, he requires a relatively average amount of systematic instruction, but a bit more than average amount of reinforcement. For Carter the picture is more mixed. He requires slightly higher degrees of explicit, intensive, and systematic instruction, an average amount of corrective feedback, and a relatively low level of reinforcement. Lisa needs high levels of explicit and systematic instruction and a bit higher than average amounts of intensive instruction and corrective feedback. The degree of reinforcement she needs is slightly lower than average. Andre needs very high levels of all five instructional practices.

Where is the line between general and special education? In our proposed paradigm for special education, the further out on the continua in Figure 4.1 the teacher needs to go in order for the student to learn at grade- or age-level,[5] the greater the student needs

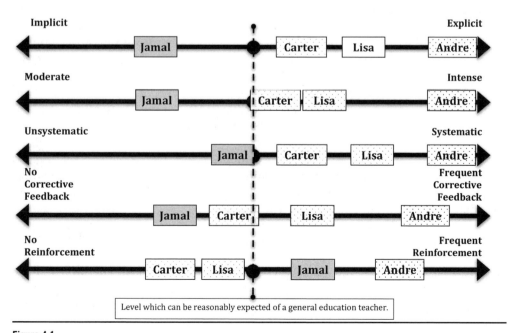

Figure 4.1

instruction by a special education teacher. The special educator differs from the general educator in the quantity of explicit, intensive, and systematic instruction and corrective feedback and reinforcement she or he is prepared to deliver. These quantitative instructional differences between general and special education teachers are due to a matter of preparation, as well as efficiency. By applying higher levels of these instructional techniques to a smaller number of students, the general education teacher is freed up to deliver lesser degrees of these same instructional techniques to the benefit of the much larger number of students without disabilities.

The importance of a continuum of placements. Several researchers and practitioners have asserted that special education is about instruction and not placement. This is true in the sense that what's best instructionally for a student should determine his or her placement and not vice versa, as is all too often the case in IEP meetings (Bateman & Linden, 2012). In other words, instructional needs must drive placement needs. The IEP prescribes the level of explicitness and systematization, the frequency and duration of instruction, the frequency of progress monitoring, the required level of mastery, and so on. Based on these determinations, a placement is selected that will allow the student to receive this instruction from a highly trained special education professional.

Because of the myriad possible profiles of instructional demands exhibited by students, the need to offer several placement options is obvious. Generally, the wider the margin between the quantity of instructional practices (such as those depicted in Figure 4.1) the typical general education teacher is able to deliver and what the student needs, the greater the need for, not only a special education teacher, but also a separate setting. We posit that even a highly trained special education teacher is constrained by the realities of the degree to which students differ from the norm with respect to their instructional needs.

Our analysis re-affirms Evelyn Deno's (1970) time-honored conceptualization of special education placement as falling along a continuum from inclusive to more separate settings. The following metaphor tells the story:

> General education is like the train system—it goes between point x and point y. You get on the train and get off at the train's destination. Special education's values are more like trucking. Depending on the need, we provide different types of trucks and deliver the product to the destination it requires. . . . What worries me most is the tendency to make special education into a train taking all the students to one designated point, regardless of their individual differences.
>
> (Weintraub, 2012, p. 52)

Like Weintraub, we are also concerned about the bastardization of special individualization, not only by general educators, but by special educators, as well. In considering what's best for a student, it's critical that the determination of placement be made based on a finer grained analysis of the student's needs than is typically the case. All too often results from a standardized achievement test and an IQ test (if an IQ-achievement discrepancy is being used) are all that are used to determine special education eligibility and placement.

"The special educator differs from the general educator in the quantity of explicit, intensive, and systematic instruction and corrective feedback and reinforcement she or he is prepared to deliver."

Returning to our four hypothetical students, we can conjecture what placements each student should be in. We hypothesize that:

- Jamal, who is reading on or above grade level, is in the general education receiving the standard curriculum from the general education teacher.
- Carter, who is reading ½ standard deviation below grade level, is receiving Tier 2 instruction (in a group with four other students at about his reading level) in order to improve his reading and to try to ensure that he doesn't fall further behind such that he might be evaluated for special education identification.
- Lisa, who is reading 1 and ½ standard deviations below grade level and has been previously identified for special education, is receiving supplemental reading instruction from a special education teacher 1 hour per day, 3 days per week in a group of four other students who are also struggling with reading.
- Andre, who is reading 1 and ½ standard deviations below grade level and has been previously identified for special education, is receiving supplemental reading instruction from a special education teacher 1 hour per day, 5 days per week.

It's important to point out that, even though Lisa and Andre are both reading on the same level (1 and ½ standard deviations below grade level), as measured by a standardized reading test, their placements are different. We stress this because it's important that placement decisions be based on a finer-grained analysis of student needs than one score on a standardized achievement test. Figure 4.1 shows that Andre is much further from the norm than Lisa with respect to the teacher's need to emphasize the five critical components. Based on this, as well as perhaps some other factors, Andre needs a less inclusive setting than Lisa.

INDIVIDUALIZED INSTRUCTION AS A MEANS TO AN END: MASTERY

Having spent the majority of the chapter focusing on the *process* of individualizing instruction, we'd be remiss if we didn't address the desired *outcome* of this instruction. In other words, although individualization may be at the heart of special education *instruction*, this begs the question of individualized instruction for what? We propose that the *what*—the outcome—should be *mastery*: "If you show *mastery* of a particular skill or language, you show that you have learned or understood it completely and have no difficulty using it" (HarperCollins, 2012). A major reason for focusing on mastery is that special education students often have difficulties in maintaining what they have learned, on generalizing it to other learning situations, or both acquiring the knowledge and skills and applying them in new situations. They need a firm understanding of the skill or concept being taught before moving on to the next skill or concept. Popularized by Benjamin Bloom in the 1960s and 1970s, the notion of mastery learning has historical roots in the behaviorist learning tradition:

The concept of mastery learning can be attributed to the behaviorism principles of operant conditioning. According to operant conditioning theory, learning occurs when an association is formed between a stimulus and response (Skinner, 1984). In line with the behavior theory, mastery learning focuses on overt behaviors that can be observed and measured (Baum, 2005). The material that will be taught to mastery is broken down into small discrete lessons that follow a logical progression. In order to demonstrate mastery over each lesson, students must be able to overtly show evidence of understanding of the material before moving to the next lesson (Anderson, 2000). (Mastery Learning, 2012)

FREQUENT ASSESSMENT AND PROGRESS MONITORING

As with mastery, we would be remiss if we did not emphasize the role of frequent assessment and progress monitoring in special education instruction. In fact, frequent assessment and progress monitoring go hand-in-hand with teaching for mastery—they are a way to determine whether the individualized instruction is leading to mastery. Based on these frequent assessments, the teacher can further individualize the instruction by making adjustments with respect to the relative emphases on the critical components—degree of explicitness, systematization, intensity, corrective feedback, and reinforcement. Frequent assessment and progress monitoring that leads to databased, instructional decisions is a hallmark of special education.

Curriculum-based measurement (CBM) is a commonly used means of measuring student progress in order to guide instruction. CBM involves assessing students' skills on materials closely linked to the curriculum (e.g., 1-minute sample of oral reading fluency). CBM is a more robust measure of academic skills than typical standardized achievement tests because the behaviors measured are directly linked to the abilities targeted for improvement.

IN CONCLUSION

Putting it all together, it's clear that special education is both qualitatively and quantitatively different than general education. First and foremost, we aver that special education instruction is individualized and that it leads to mastery. With the aim of reaching mastery through individualized instruction, we also contend that this instruction is not always possible in the general education setting thus, instruction and environment cannot be considered as entirely separate qualifiers of special education.

Why can't students receive individualized instruction in the general education classroom? Consider the students' needs in Figure 4.1. Is it possible for one teacher to meet all of these students' needs in the context of a typical school day? We present here a lexicon of instructional components that are necessary to individualize instruction. It's unrealistic to assume that the additive nature of these characteristics of instruction that many students with disabilities need can be implemented effectively in general education.

"Frequent assessment and progress monitoring that leads to data-based, instructional decisions, is a hallmark of special education."

As we mention earlier many educators and researchers use the terms we present in our lexicon, as well as others that we have not included. This is not to say that the other terms (e.g., relentless, iterative) are not important. We have selected those obligatory characteristics without which instruction could not be specialized.

We also provide a paradigm in Figure 4.2 that explains special education instruction. First, special education instruction begins with screening and diagnosis. Screening measures are administered to determine who in a group is likely to excel and who is likely to need additional support and/or more comprehensive assessment. Assessment instruments for the purpose of diagnosis identify a student's strengths and weaknesses. Educators (i.e., classroom teacher, special education teacher, and others from a multidisciplinary team) and parents use the diagnostic measures to determine the degree to which the student needs the critical components that define special education, step two in our paradigm. The third step in the paradigm includes both frequent progress monitoring and individualized (explicit, systematic, corrective, reinforced, intense) instruction. The frequent progress monitoring allows the teacher to determine when mastery has been reached, or if instruction needs to be altered because a student is not reaching mastery (step 4). If a student is not reaching mastery, the level of intensity, explicitness, or any of the other components may need to be increased. Likewise, if a student is excelling and reaching mastery ahead of schedule, the level of these components may be lessened. Finally, outcome measures confirm student mastery. It's important to note that assessment begins the special education process, is critical throughout instruction, and ends the special education cycle for a given goal. The outcome measures are important to document progress on goals identified in the individualized education program (IEP).

Our paradigm and lexicon simplifies an extremely complex issue: Students with disabilities need special education. Although we may not have covered every term and addressed all of the issues within special education instruction, we hope that we have given the field the beginning of a lexicon that we may use to continue to advocate for the

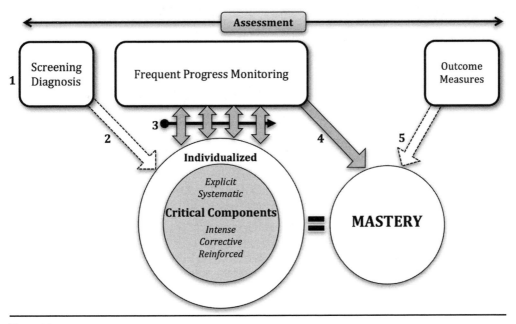

Figure 4.2

distinct needs of students with disabilities. If we speak in a unified voice on the significance of specialized instruction, we may be able to help future generations of students with disabilities reach their potential.

Discussion Questions

1. The authors note an overlap in "various researchers' listings of the elements that characterize special education instruction." What are some possible explanations for this?
2. The authors created a "lexicon" of critical components to separate special education from general education. What were their reasons for doing this and what did this help?
3. What do you see as the major difference between explicit and systematic instruction? How will these differences be used in your current or future classroom instruction (list some examples)?
4. Describe how pacing, group size, and duration/frequency help to elucidate intensive instruction.
5. Why do you think corrective feedback is so important when working with students with learning disabilities?
6. Do you think intrinsic or extrinsic reinforcement is more beneficial for students with disabilities? Why (use examples)?
7. Describe examples of special education instruction using the continua described in this chapter.
8. Do you agree or disagree with the idea that instructional needs drive placement needs? Why or why not?
9. The authors compare general education to a train and special education to trucking. Devise another metaphor to compare general and special education. Explain the metaphor using concepts you learned from this chapter.
10. Overall, how are general education and special education qualitatively and quantitatively different? How do these differences affect your career in education when working with many types of students?

NOTES

1. We readily recognize that indices are often prepared by freelancers and may not be completely accurate.
2. With all due respect to Hank Williams and his song, "I Wish I Had a Nickel," we felt a need to adjust for inflation.
3. At the same time, we can't ignore the fact that many instructional techniques used in general education were *first* introduced, researched, and adopted by special educators.
4. We recognize that the modifiers (e.g., low, nearly average, slightly higher) we use in describing Figure 4.1 are far from precise. This fits with our view that there is inherent subjectivity in judging the levels or degrees of these critical components.
5. We include age-level here, because even though we are focusing in this chapter on learning disabilities, our model might also be applicable to teaching students with emotional/behavioral disorders.

PAIGE C. PULLEN'S AND DANIEL P. HALLAHAN'S SUGGESTIONS FOR FURTHER READING

Hallahan, D. P., Kauffman, J. M., & Pullen, P. C. (2015). *Exceptional learners: Introduction to special education.* (13th ed.). Upper Saddle River, NJ: Pearson.

Kauffman, J. M., & Hallahan, D. P. (2005). *Special education: What it is and why we need it.* Boston: Allyn & Bacon.

Kauffman, J. M., & Hallahan, D. P. (Eds.), (2011). *The handbook of special education.* New York: Routledge.

Mercer, C. D., Mercer, A., & Pullen, P. C. (2011). *Teaching students with learning problems* (8th ed.). Upper Saddle River, NJ: Pearson.

Pullen, P. C., & Cash, D. (2011). Reading. In J. M. Kauffman & D. P. Hallahan (Eds), *Handbook of Special Education* (pp. 409–421) New York: Routledge.

Pullen, P. C., Tuckwiller, E. D., Maynard, K., Konold, T. R., & Coyne, M. (2010). A response to intervention model for vocabulary instruction: The effects of tiered instruction for students at risk for reading disability. *Learning Disabilities Research and Practice, 25,* 110–122.

REFERENCES

Alogozzine, B., & White, R. (2007, October 12). *School-wide academic and behavior support.* Presentation for Forum for Change School-Wide Positive Behavior Support Planning for Systems Change: Ideas That Work. Washington D.C.: U. S. Department of Education.

Anderson, J. R. (2000). *Learning and memory: An integrated approach* (2nd ed.). New York: John Wiley and Sons, Inc.

Archer, A. L., & Hughes, C. A. (2011). *Explicit instruction: Effective and efficient teaching.* New York, NY: The Guilford Press.

Bateman, B. D., & Linden, M. (2012). *Better IEPs: How to develop legally correct and educationally useful programs* (5th edition). Verona, WI: Attainment Company.

Baum, W. M. (2005). *Understanding behaviorism: Behavior, culture and evolution.* Malden, MA: Blackwell Publishing.

Brosvic, G. M., Dihoff, R. E., Epstein, M. L., & Cook, M. L. (2006). Feedback facilitates the acquisition and retention of numerical fact series by elementary school students with mathematics learning disabilities. *The Psychological Record, 56,* 35–54.

Carnine, D. W., Silbert, J., Kame'enui, E. J., Tarver, S. G., & Jungjohann, K. (2006). *Teaching struggling and at-risk readers: A direct instruction approach.* Upper Saddle River, NJ: Pearson.

Chard, D. J., Vaughn, S., & Tyler, B.-J. (2012). A synthesis of research on effective interventions for building reading fluency with elementary students with learning disabilities. *Journal of Learning Disabilities, 35,* 386–406.

Deno, E. (1970). Special education as developmental capital. *Exceptional Children, 37,* 229–237.

Eckert, T. L., Dunn, E. K., & Ardoin, S. P. (2006). *Journal of Behavioral Education, 15,* 149–162. doi: 10.1007/s10864-006-9018-6.

Gersten, R., Beckmann, S., Clarke, B., Foegen, A., Marsh, L., Star, J. R., & Witzel, B. (2009). *Assisting students struggling with mathematics: Response to Intervention (RtI) for elementary and middle schools* (NCEE 2009–4060). Washington, DC: National Center for Education Evaluation and Regional Assistance, Institute of Education Sciences, U.S. Department of Education. Retrieved http://ies.ed.gov/ncee/wwc/pdf/practiceguides/rti_math_pg_042109.pdf.

Harper Collins (2012). Collins COBUILD dictionary of advanced American English. In *Dictionary for iPhone/iPad (1.0.1).* Japan: Monokakido Co. Ltd.

Heubusch, J. D., & Lloyd, J. W. (1998). Corrective feedback in oral reading. *Journal of Behavioral Education, 8,* 63–79.

Kauffman, J. M., & Hallahan, D. P. (2005). *Special education: What it is and why we need it.* Upper Saddle River, NJ: Pearson.

Kauffman, J. M., & Hallahan, D. P. (2011). *Handbook of special education.* New York: Routledge.

Kouri, T. A., Selle, C. A., & Riley, S. A. (2006). Comparison of meaning and graphophonemic feedback strategies for guided reading instruction of children with language delays. *American Journal of Speech-Language Pathology, 15,* 236–246.

Mastery Learning. (2012, October). In *Wikipedia.* Retrieved November 3, 2012, from http://en.wikipedia.org/wiki/Mastery_learning.

Mercer, C. D., & Pullen, P. C. (2009). *Students with learning disabilities* (7th ed.). Upper Saddle River, NJ: Merrill-Prentice Hall.

Mercer, C. D., Mercer, A., & Pullen, P. C. (2011). *Teaching students with learning problems* (8th ed.). Upper Saddle River, NJ: Pearson.

Rashotte, C. A., MacPhee, K., & Torgesen, J. K. (2001). The effectiveness of a group reading instruction program with poor readers in multiple grades. *Learning Disability Quarterly, 24*, 119–134.

Skinner, B. F. (1984). The evolution of behavior. *Journal of Experimental Analysis of Behavior, 41*, 217–221.

Swanson, H. L., Harris, K. R., & Graham, S. (Eds.), (2003). *Handbook of learning disabilities.* New York, NY: The Guilford Press.

Vaughn, S., Wanzek, J., Wexler, J., Barth, A., Cirino, P. T., Fletcher, J. M., . . . Francis, D. J. (2010). The relative effects of group size on reading progress of older students with reading difficulties. *Reading and Writing: An Interdisciplinary Journal, 23*, 931–956.

Wanzek, J., & Kent, S. C. (2012). Reading interventions for students with learning disabilities in the upper elementary grades. *Learning Disabilities: A Contemporary Journal, 10*(1), 5–16.

Wanzek, J., Vaughn, S., Wexler, J., Swanson, E. A., Edmonds, M., & Kim, A.-E. (2006). A synthesis of spelling and reading interventions and their effects on spelling outcomes of students with LD. *Journal of Learning Disabilities, 39*, 528–543.

Weintraub, F. J. (2012). A half century of special education: What we have achieved and the challenges we face. *Teaching Exceptional Children, 45*, 50–53.

Zigmond, N., & Pullen, P. C. (2012, February). *Does RTI meet the needs of students with learning disabilities?* Paper presented at the annual meeting of the Learning Disabilities Association of America, Chicago, IL.

Getting to Know Diane M. Browder

 In the sixth grade, I volunteered in one of the first special education classrooms in Henrico County, Virginia. The teacher was a remarkable woman who expected more than I thought possible for students with disabilities. In high school, I had a positive experience as a summer camp counselor with children with intellectual disabilities. One of the parents encouraged me to explore special education as a career choice. A summer job in an institution for individuals with intellectual disabilities was an important epiphany. I realized that I wanted to have a career working with individuals with disabilities, but not in an institutional setting.

When I applied for teaching jobs, there were not yet any public school programs for students with severe disabilities. I accepted a job in the mountains of Virginia teaching everyone who came to school with disability who was in the third through fifth grades. Later the students in my class received a variety of classifications— mild or moderate mental retardation (the term at that time), learning disabilities, behavior disorders, autism. I was excited to be part of a project on inclusion (called "mainstreaming" at the time).

When I matriculated for my doctoral program, I was able to be part of one of the first personnel preparation grants in severe disabilities with Dr. Martha Snell. In my first university position, I was able to continue to contribute to services for individuals with disabilities. Part of my job was to help found and consult in a program for children with autism spectrum disorders. A few years later, I was able to help found some community and job services for adults with severe disabilities leaving institutions. To this day, my favorite times are those I spend with students with disabilities and their teachers.

5

WHAT SHOULD WE TEACH STUDENTS WITH MODERATE AND SEVERE DEVELOPMENTAL DISABILITIES?

Diane M. Browder

One day in the spring of 2004, I went to visit a special education teacher in a classroom for students with moderate/severe intellectual disability in the urban school system that surrounds the university where I teach in Charlotte. The teacher was a participant in a study I was conducting on teaching literacy. The night before I visited the classroom, I began to worry about asking teachers to try a literacy lesson that involved a read aloud and comprehension questions. After spending 20 years convincing teachers of the importance of teaching skills directly referenced to home and community activities, I felt I might be leading these teachers astray. What would happen to the students who lacked basic self-care if their teacher devoted so much effort to the comprehension of books?

When I arrived, the teacher began to provide some background on the lesson she would show us. Then a loud siren began to sound, the signal for a school lock down. Not sure if this was a drill or actual lock down in this inner city school, the teacher locked her classroom door and ushered us all into the classroom bathroom as instructed in the school's policy for this class. Fortunately, the bathroom was large enough to hold 10 students, a paraprofessional, the teacher and me. The adults were the only ones anxious about the event; the students thought it delightful to be "hiding" together in the bathroom. One student decided she had to use the toilet and proudly showed the group her new independence. When the next siren sounded, we exited the bathroom and learned it was only a drill. Two students with intellectual disability, who should have been in their general education classrooms during the drill, came bursting through the door with the assistant principal. The teacher found out later that when the siren sounded, the students' general education teacher sent the students back to their special education classroom assuming inclusion did not apply to lock downs. This left the students stranded in a hall with all classroom doors locked where they were found by an angry assistant principal. Fortunately the lock down was only a drill, giving the special education teacher an opportunity to help the general education teacher realize these were "her students" in an emergency.

Needless to say, the excitement created and time lost for the lock down, made it impossible to observe the literacy lesson that day. I did get to meet the student for whom it was planned. She was six years old and her IEP had no goals in literacy. Instead, the goals set by her prior teacher focused on skills related to daily functioning like toileting, eating, and communicating basic needs (e.g., eat, toilet). Like many of the families served in this school system, she came from a family who had recently immigrated to the United States. I wondered as I drove home that day whether the kind of literacy instruction I had envisioned could ever be achieved in this context. Not only was there the issue of incorporating this instruction into an already-full schedule, but the teachers also faced the challenges that come with the daily realities of life in public schools, like lock downs, fragile inclusion, and students who come from widely diverse backgrounds. As you may know from my research, something happened that convinced me to push forward to promote literacy and other academic instruction for students with moderate and severe disabilities. Let me explain what led me to believe more academic learning might be possible.

I relocated to the University of North Carolina at Charlotte in 1998 after 17 years at Lehigh University where I focused on research on teaching functional life skills to students and adults with moderate and severe intellectual disability or autism spectrum disorders. The academic content I targeted in my research was "functional academics" because it focused primarily on the activity (e.g., grocery shopping, cooking, making a purchase), and secondarily on the academic response (e.g., grocery sight words, recipe words, using a dollar). When I was in my doctoral program in the late 1970s, teaching students to engage in activities typical of peers of the same chronological age to prepare them for a future of increased independence in the community was a new idea proposed by experts like Lou Brown (Brown et al., 1979). I was fortunate to study with one of the leaders in severe disabilities, Marti Snell, who developed one of the earliest textbooks in this specialty (Snell, 1978). I built my early research career being one of many to discover that teaching community-referenced skills was not only an ideal, but one that could be demonstrated through using principles of applied behavior analysis. I promoted teaching functional life skills in my writing (e.g., Browder, 2001) and even proposed a decision model for when *not* to teach academics to students with severe disabilities (Browder & Snell, 1993; p. 443). As I tell my students, I no longer agree with the Browder of 1993 who recommended some students bypass academic learning.

In 1998, the 1997 Amendments of IDEA (P. L. 105-17) had recently been passed. These amendments included requiring students to have access to general curriculum and to offer an alternate assessment for students unable to participate in state's general assessments with accommodations. On one of my trips to a conference, I happened to sit by a special education director from a large school system in a nearby state. She recognized me and was eager to get my impression about testing students with severe disabilities on state academic content standards. I was so entrenched in my research on functional life skills at the time that I could not even absorb what she meant. I thought she had misinterpreted IDEA 1997, but her question piqued my interest about the newly emerging alternate assessments. Because I had a longstanding interest in how to assess students with severe disabilities, I attended a session at the international CEC conference that year on alternate assessments. I quickly realized states were still making decisions about how to assess this population. Being eager to join the conversation and having devoted some writing to the topic of assessment of students with severe disabilities (e.g., Browder, 1987; 2001), I began to do research on alternate assessment.

In summarizing the research with my colleagues, it became clear there were many questions about both what and how to assess students with the more severe disabilities (Browder, Fallin, Davis, & Karvonen 2003). One of the best early models was a portfolio assessment developed in Kentucky (Kleinert & Kearns, 1999). North Carolina developed a similar portfolio of student classroom work. I became a proponent of using data to show progress on this work and illustrated with a research team how training teachers in data-based decisions improved student outcomes on the alternate assessment (Browder, Karvonen, Davis, Fallin, & Courtade-Little, 2005). Although the portfolios focused on language arts and math, we were still primarily showing teachers ways to incorporate functional academics. For example, one sample lesson plan we developed for teachers focused on recognizing numbers while making a smoothie in a blender. In another, students learned to read the sight words that made up their daily schedule. Each set of skills was important, but they did not address the academic content standards typical of math and language arts for the students' assigned grade.

Two things radically altered my thinking about how much academics might be taught. First, our research teams began to conduct content analyses of several states' alternate assessments (Browder et al., 2004; Flowers, Browder, & Ahlgrim-Delzell, 2006). I thought we would find that the assessments contained functional life skills dressed in various ways to be called math and reading (e.g., counting items to pass out a snack; reading a restroom sign). I sometimes referred to our content analyses as the "Emperor's New Clothes" based on the children's book by this name. Like the emperor who is convinced to have a suit made from invisible cloth, I thought we would discover a lack of substance in the academic content in these assessments. Some assessment items were what I predicted—daily living skills with very minor academic links. Some items failed to be either functional or academics by trying too hard to be both (e.g., measuring growth of fingernails during a manicure). To my surprise, some items reflected skills with much higher academic content than I had ever seen taught, but operationalized in ways that seemed teachable. These skills especially intrigued me because they modeled a way to gain entry into the grade-level content for students beginning with lower numeracy and literacy skills. For example, students could count tiles to indicate the surface area of a rectangle in square inches. By doing so, students could apply emerging counting skills while having a "hands-on" experience with the concept of surface area. A second example was to have students indicate the plot of a story by placing three pictures in sequence. Using pictures to retell a story sequence also seemed doable for many students with moderate and severe disabilities if the text were read aloud and understandable. Both types of skills were opening the door to meaningful participation in grade-level content.

> "I became a proponent of using data to show progress on this work and illustrated with a research team how training teachers in data-based decisions improved student outcomes on the alternate assessment."

After this research discovery that came from close inspection of some of the best alternate assessments states were developing, the second event that shaped my thinking was the passage of No Child Left Behind (NCLB, 2001) requiring schools to "count" students with significant cognitive disabilities in school accountability systems using the outcomes of these alternate assessments. NCLB also required that alternate assessments be aligned with the state academic content standards, even if based on alternate achievement standards. The stakes were now high for schools to provide academic content instruction for students with severe disabilities and to use scientifically based interventions.

I wondered what evidence existed on teaching academic content to students with moderate and severe developmental disabilities and worked with teams at our university to conduct some comprehensive reviews of the experimental research literature. We discovered research on reading was primarily focused on sight word instruction (Browder, Wakeman, Spooner, Ahlgrim-Delzell, & Algozzine, 2006) and mathematics on money and simple computation (Browder, Spooner, Ahlgrim-Delzell, Harris, & Wakeman, 2008). We could not find any research on science until we included daily living skills studies with some science link (Spooner, Knight, Browder, Jimenez, & DiBiase, 2011). Although these reviews provided evidence students with moderate and severe disabilities might learn academic content, there were no models for teaching content that aligned with grade-level content standards in the experimental research. There also was minimal guidance in the textbooks on teaching academics for students with severe disabilities at that time. There were some early models in the literature. For example, Ryndak and Alper (1996) described how to blend content from the general curriculum and functional life skills in planning IEPs. Downing and Demchak (1996) offered suggestions for adapting general curriculum content to be inclusive of students with severe disabilities. Some qualitative researchers had observed how students with moderate and severe intellectual disabilities made transitions into independent reading (Kliewer, 1998; Ryndak, Morrison, & Sommerstein, 1999). I found this descriptive and qualitative literature provided excellent foundations for thinking more about how to design experimental research on grade-aligned academic instruction. For example, I was convinced of the importance of all students having access to the literature of their grade level. As an experimental researcher, I also was eager to build on these descriptions to demonstrate a causal relationship between a defined intervention and student learning.

Although we continued to study alternate assessment as part of the National Alternate Assessment Center (e.g., Flowers, Wakeman, Browder, & Karvonen, 2009), I became absorbed with finding out if students with moderate and severe developmental disabilities could meet the increased academic content expectation reflected in NCLB (2001). How could policy require schools to be accountable for students with severe disabilities learning academic content with such a limited evidence base? Our research team began with literacy. I found my first ideas by considering early childhood resources on using interactive read alouds (e.g., Ezell & Justice, 2005) and some of the ways shared stories had been adapted in case studies with students with severe disabilities (e.g., Koppenhaver, Erickson, & Skotko, 2001). Our team brainstormed how to make these read alouds age and grade appropriate. We would encourage teachers to use literature typically read by the students' same age peers and add the types of supports found in younger literature. For example, books for preschoolers often use repetition of a key phrase. We decided any book could be augmented by repetition of the main idea at the end of each page. Sometimes books for young readers are made of cardboard for easy page turning. We discovered several ways to make the books easy to manipulate. In an interactive read aloud, the student typically takes multiples turns engaging with the content as pages are read. We created multiple ideas for these turns like locating a picture or key word, answering a simple recall question, or helping to read the repeated story line using a voice output communication device. We also noted that books could be shortened for brief attention spans by skipping some sentences and pages without losing the plot. We recruited teachers for this first study on literacy. We gave the teachers a general format for a lesson that began with some vocabulary instruction, then a read aloud of a story, followed by comprehension questions, and finally an activity using the topic of the story (e.g., artwork). This takes me back to my visit to the classroom in Charlotte.

Despite the prior lock down experience, the teacher still wanted me to observe the literacy lesson she had developed for our research. When I went back to see the student, the teacher had chosen to read aloud a book based on the Disney movie *Toy Story* because the student had a high preference for this topic. The teacher showed me the communication board she had made with symbols for the book *Toy Story* such as robot, cowboy, birthday cake, etc. The board had nine abstract symbols; none were pictures from the book. The last communication symbols I had seen for this student were "eat" and "toilet" so the board seemed far too complex to me. I was not expecting much as the teacher began to read the story aloud and paused to ask comprehension questions.

She asked, "Who was the favorite toy first?" To my surprise, the girl pointed to the symbol for cowboy.

"Who was the new toy?" She pointed to the robot. Now I was really shocked.

"When did the boy get the new toy?" The girl leaned over the picture of the birthday cake and began to blow as if blowing out the candles. I was truly amazed!

Six months before, it seemed appropriate simply to target a few communication symbols for this student to communicate basic needs. Through literacy instruction, it became evident this student could communicate much more if we gave her materials about which to communicate (e.g., a story) and an adequate range of symbols. As I drove home that day, the magnitude of what I had seen began to capture my imagination. If this student could learn these symbols so quickly when the teacher had a procedure to follow and the student had motivational materials, how much more could she learn? Would she be able to comprehend more advanced text read aloud? Would she be able to learn to read? In fact, in the years to come, this student did learn to read. She mastered decoding and learned to read simple passages (first through second-grade level), with comprehension of what she read. What if the teacher had spent that first year only focused on pointing to the picture symbols for the restroom, to eat, and to take breaks? What if in future years the girl only had been given the chance to learn lists of everyday sight words? How could we have discovered that she had the potential to learn to read except by teaching her to read? Her IQ, which was well below 55, did not predict her success. Her lack of early literacy skills or even a communication system did not predict her success. What promoted her success was the opportunity to learn with skills broken into small steps taught with systematic prompting and feedback. While learning early literacy skills, and later to read, she also learned to request bathroom breaks and to take care of her personal needs. These did not seem like such large achievements when her teachers were focused on milestones in reading.

> "If this student could learn these symbols so quickly when the teacher had a procedure to follow and the student had motivational materials, how much more could she learn?"

This student was one of the first participants in Project RAISE (Browder & Flowers, 2005), an IES-funded project focused on developing a method to teach early literacy and reading to students with IQs below 55. Students made important gains in phonological awareness which we measured using a nonverbal assessment because so many of the participants relied on argumentative and assistive communication (AAC) (Browder, Ahlgrim-Delzell, Flowers, & Baker, 2012). While almost 100 students participated in Project RAISE, and most made literacy gains, this student was one of the stars who not only mastered all of the levels of the early literacy program, but graduated into a beginning reading program. As we were making our discoveries, other researchers were also demonstrating that students with intellectual disability could learn to read (e.g., Allor, Mathes, Roberts, Jones, & Champlin, 2010; Al Otaiba & Hosp, 2004; Bradford, Shippen, Alberto, Houchins, & Flores, 2006).

For older students who continued to be nonreaders, we developed the interactive read aloud to be focused on a summary of a novel from the students' grade level (Browder, Trela, & Jimenez, 2007). To create this adapted text, we asked reading experts to help us select high quality novels that were the most frequently taught in the students' grade band (e.g., middle school). We then rewrote the novel into short chapter summaries and added features like a repeating story line. (For an example of a text summary, see Figure 5.1.) We also found we were able to teach comprehension responses using the story format to students with the most severe disabilities (Browder, Lee, & Mims, 2011; Mims, Browder, Baker, Lee, & Spooner, 2009). In a few years, shared story reading became an evidence-based practice teachers could use to promote comprehension of a variety of text (Hudson & Test, 2011) and was replicated by other researchers (Shurr & Taber-Doughty, 2012). When we did the original review on reading, it was disturbing to discover how few of the studies had any measure of comprehension (Browder, Wakeman, Spooner, Ahlgrim-Delzell, & Algozzine, 2006). We have continued to build strategies to teach comprehension in our research on interactive read alouds (e.g., Mims, Hudson, & Browder, 2012). One of our teams also developed a conceptual model for literacy for students with severe disabilities (Browder, Gibbs, et al., 2008). In this model, we propose giving all students the opportunity to learn to read and to make this instruction a high priority in the elementary years. We also propose teaching all students to comprehend text through the use of interactive read alouds. This ensures students build comprehension even if independent reading is slow to progress or not attained.

Having increased comprehension of text opens opportunities for students with moderate and severe disabilities. Understanding the content of text is not only crucial to overall academic success, but to many activities of daily life. Reading may be one of the most "functional" skills students can learn as it prepares them to be able to use the vast resources of the internet, to enjoy literature, to read job manuals, and to learn about current events. Given the increasing evidence that students with moderate and severe disabilities can learn to read (Allor et al., 2010) or at least to comprehend text read aloud (Hudson & Test, 2011), I would propose that literacy be at the top of the list for what to teach students with moderate and severe disabilities (I use the term "literacy" instead of reading to be inclusive of students who "read" through alternative means of accessing text). As Katims (2000) described, historically, literacy has not been the priority for students with intellectual disability. Even the term "trainable" was applied to designate students who needed training in skills of daily living versus those academically "educable." To make literacy a priority does not require forgoing teaching skills of daily living which can be addressed during their naturally occurring routines (e.g., eating with a spoon during lunch; putting on a coat before going outside; washing hands after toileting). Other skills might be taught during a specific class time devoted to life skills (e.g., cooking, budgeting) and used to help students generalize emerging academic competence (e.g., read aloud of a recipe or job ad). What must change from prior years is spending

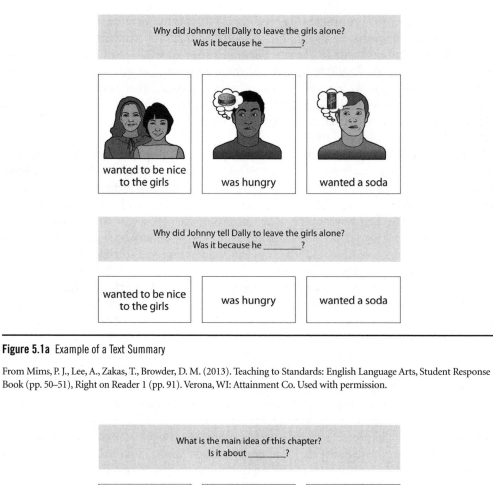

Figure 5.1a Example of a Text Summary

From Mims, P. J., Lee, A., Zakas, T., Browder, D. M. (2013). Teaching to Standards: English Language Arts, Student Response Book (pp. 50–51), Right on Reader 1 (pp. 91). Verona, WI: Attainment Co. Used with permission.

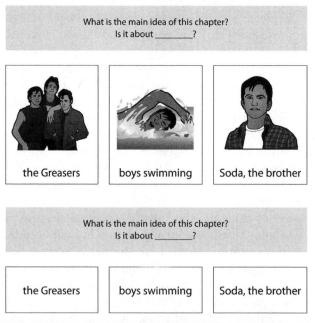

Figure 5.1b Example of a Text Summary

From Mims, P. J., Lee, A., Zakas, T., Browder, D. M. (2013). Teaching to Standards: English Language Arts, Student Response Book (pp. 50–51), Right on Reader 1 (pp. 91). Verona, WI: Attainment Co. Used with permission.

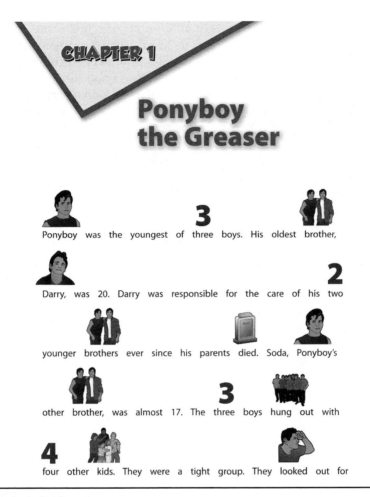

Figure 5.1c Example of a Text Summary

From Mims, P. J., Lee, A., Zakas, T., Browder, D. M. (2013). Teaching to Standards: English Language Arts, Student Response Book (pp. 50–51), Right on Reader 1 (pp. 91). Verona, WI: Attainment Co. Used with permission.

the entire day *only* teaching these life skills. For students with moderate and severe disabilities to acquire independence in accessing and comprehending text, a sustained focus on literacy every day and every year will be needed.

Some of these literacy skills will not have immediate functional use (e.g., blending sounds), but will be essential to optimal performance in reading.

"I would propose that literacy be at the top of the list for what to teach students with moderate and severe disabilities."

Given that schools were also required to show student outcomes in math and science under NCLB (2001), and the research in these areas was even more limited than reading (Browder et al., 2008; Spooner et al., 2011), we began to explore what was possible in these other content areas. In mathematics, we found two strategies to be especially effective. One was to task analyze the math operation and teach each step using systematic prompting (Jimenez, Browder, & Courtade, 2008). The other was to turn the math problem into an interactive read aloud building on what we had learned in literacy

(Browder, Jimenez, & Trela, 2012). (For an example of a math story, see Figure 5.2.) When we used the math stories, we also included a graphic organizer for summarizing the numerical facts known and task analyzed the steps to complete the problem. We found this strategy could be applied to a large array of the math standards for the grade level in which the student was placed based on chronological age (Browder, Trela, et al., 2012). Horner et al. (2005) recommend at least five studies across three research teams with a minimum of 20 participants to identify a practice as evidence-based. Our collection of studies using math stories with graphic organizers and task analyses included more than 20 students with IQs below 55, but more studies with replication by other research teams is needed to build an evidence base.

In considering the rationale to teach mathematics, we discovered that many of the real life applications we could include in the math story problems were job-related or community-referenced activities. In the past we would focus on the activity (e.g., going to the mall) and insert a small amount of functional academics as critically needed (e.g., paying for an item with cash). Instead we began thinking about the standards of the students' assigned grade level based on their chronological age. I called this "grade-aligned" instruction. By thinking about the math concepts first, we began to discover more of the demands for mathematics in job and community contexts. Often the real life activity in which the skill would be applied could be lifted and adapted from the general education textbook word problems. Other times, we found the applications in thinking about the school or community experiences the students encountered. For example, one math lesson focused on planning how much paint would need to be purchased to create signs for a pep rally. Another focused on how machinists trace the surface area of a part and included an internet video clip of this real life application. The students seem to know that this was a new and high expectation. In the first study on algebra, the high school students would ask to go into the hall to show other students their materials. They wanted to take them home to show brothers and sisters they could do real math. One of Horner et al.'s (2005) criteria for indicating the quality of a study that contributes to an evidence base is to provide evidence of the social validity of the outcomes. Our teams have often asked the teachers, and if possible the students, if they liked the intervention. This preference for the content seems important in deciding to focus on more math instruction. In contrast, preference is only one way the importance of teaching skills like mathematics might be documented. The ability to apply the skills in the actual activity (e.g., using real materials), generalization of problem solving to new contexts, and incidental learning (e.g., of literacy during math read alouds) might be additional ways to evaluate the impact of math instruction.

In science, we discovered that a variety of grade-aligned content was teachable if we used a standard format for directed inquiry (Browder, Trela, et al., 2012). Students learned about a concept by engaging in an experiment (e.g., how a solution is formed or why it rains) and acquired new vocabulary to express what they had learned (e.g., solvent, solute, solution). (For an example of science, see Figure 5.3.) A series of studies followed in which our research teams focused on teaching science concepts (e.g., Knight, Spooner, Browder, & Smith, 2012; Jimenez, Browder, Spooner & DiBiase, 2012). We found students not only learned to state the concept, but they could generalize the concept to untrained materials (Jimenez, Browder, & Courtade, 2009). Science was probably the most fun of all the academic content areas to teach. Students had the opportunity to explore materials to see a concept come to life. They learned critical safety rules like

Student government elections

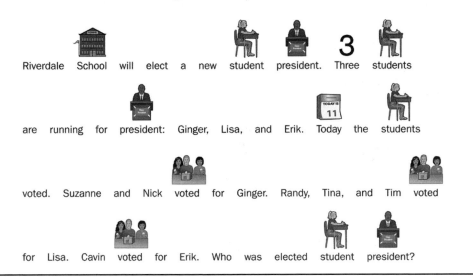

Riverdale School will elect a new student president. Three students are running for president: Ginger, Lisa, and Erik. Today the students voted. Suzanne and Nick voted for Ginger. Randy, Tina, and Tim voted for Lisa. Cavin voted for Erik. Who was elected student president?

Figure 5.2a Example of a Math Story and Task Analysis

From Trela, K., Jimenez, B., & Browder, D. (2008). MathWork. Verona, WI: Attainment Co. (pp. 90–91). Used with permission.

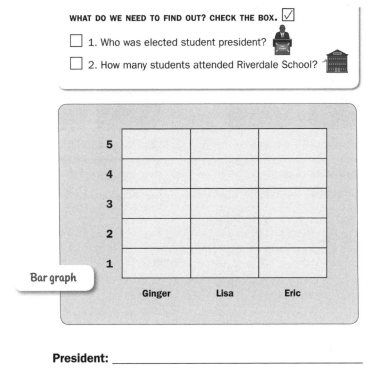

WHAT DO WE NEED TO FIND OUT? CHECK THE BOX. ☑

☐ 1. Who was elected student president?

☐ 2. How many students attended Riverdale School?

Bar graph

	Ginger	Lisa	Eric
5			
4			
3			
2			
1			

President: _____

Figure 5.2b Example of a Math Story and Task Analysis

From Trela, K., Jimenez, B., & Browder, D. (2008). MathWork. Verona, WI: Attainment Co. (pp. 90–91). Used with permission.

Student Report

1 Find soil.

2 Circle two soils that are different.

Figure 5.3a Example of Science Concept

From Jimenez, B., Knight, V., Browder, D. (2012). Early Science, My Science Log. Verona, WI: Attainment Co. (pp. 44–46). Used with permission.

3 This picture shows _____ .

land	soil	tree	cat

4 Soil is made of _____ things.

different	no
change	the same

Figure 5.3b Example of Science Concept

From Jimenez, B., Knight, V., Browder, D. (2012). Early Science, My Science Log. Verona, WI: Attainment Co. (pp. 44–46). Used with permission.

3

5 Name three things you might find in soil.

_____

_____

_____ .

Figure 5.3c Example of Science Concept

From Jimenez, B., Knight, V., Browder, D. (2012). Early Science, My Science Log. Verona, WI: Attainment Co. (pp. 44–46). Used with permission.

not eating unknown materials and not mixing mysterious liquids. They looked through microscopes and saw the difference between a living leaf and a silk leaf. They learned what causes an earthquake and what makes it rain. I was visiting a classroom one day and asked a student what he was learning in science.

"Earth," he said pointing to a model of the earth.
"What about the earth?" I asked.
"It's big. It's round." He replied.
"What else?" I queried.
"I stand on it. Bigger than Charlotte. Bigger than the school."
"Anything else?" I asked.
"Don't eat it," he said applying a rule of thumb the teacher had given him for being safe during science.

Critics like Ayres, Lowrey, Douglas, and Sievers (2011) have noted that even though educators *can* teach skills aligned with grade level standards to students with severe disabilities, that does not mean that they *should* do so, especially if it comes at the cost of not acquiring essential life skills. In a recent publication, a team of us offered seven reasons why we think it is important to teach the state academic content standards (Courtade, Spooner, Browder, & Jimenez, 2012) which I review briefly here. First, students with severe disabilities should have the right to a full educational opportunity. Curricular priorities for students with severe disabilities have evolved in the last three decades with each milestone reflecting increased expectations. We have discovered that these students: (a) can learn in public schools, (b) can learn skills relevant to their communities, (c) can benefit from opportunities to learn with their peers who are nondisabled, and (d) can learn state standards adapted for alternate achievement. Second, all of the Common Core State Standards (http://www.corestandards.org) now adopted by most states, were developed to prepare students for the real-life demands of adulthood. In teaching the standards, educators are teaching students to be ready for future careers and other life demands. A third reason is that educators do not yet know the potential of students with severe disabilities. Students have only received a limited range of functional academics in the past. The surprise of the current era is that students may be able to learn algebra, science concepts, and reading. It is just as important to allow students with severe disabilities to pursue their academic potential as it is for all students. A fourth reason teaching state standards is justifiable, is that functional skills are not a prerequisite to academic learning. The double standard that has been applied to students with severe disabilities is to require mastering nearly all life skills before getting opportunities to learn reading, math, and other content. What would happen if educators applied the same criteria to all students? Rather than being considered "college ready," many students who currently have strong academic histories would still be learning to clean their rooms. A fifth reason is that academic and functional life skills can be taught concurrently. Students with severe disabilities continue to need instruction in community, home, and job skills. These need not dominate the entire school day, but as mentioned previously can be taught during school routines and in classes specifically focused on life skills. Sixth, functioning as an adult without academic learning fosters dependency and limits job opportunities. Finally, students themselves are creating the changing expectations. When students demonstrate that they can learn more, it is difficult to justify teaching less.

Hunt, McDonnell, and Crocket (2012) have proposed that all decision making about what to teach students with severe disabilities be framed within an ecological curricular framework. An ecological curricular framework is one that begins with a student-focused approach. After defining quality of life goals with the student and family, the IEP team considers how to make prioritized state academic standards meaningful for the individual student. Individual objectives related to the standards are also addressed across multiple activities and contexts so that the student learns how to apply new academic contexts. As Hunt et al. conclude, when educators frame what to teach students of severe disabilities as an either/or debate between state standards and functional life skills, they miss the opportunity to discover new ways to address both.

> "When students demonstrate that they can learn more, it is difficult to justify teaching less."

RECOMMENDATIONS FOR MOVING FORWARD IN DETERMINING WHAT TO TEACH

The curricular expectations for students with severe disabilities are changing rapidly as states adopt the Common Core State Standards for all students including those who participate in alternate assessments. Educators do not yet have the science to know how to teach most of these standards to students with moderate and severe developmental disabilities. There are some emerging directions like using interactive read alouds for comprehension of text, teaching science concepts, and using task analyses with real life applications to teach math processes. However, until more research emerges, there is a need to proceed with caution as well as expectation. I would like to offer several recommendations for moving forward.

Use Research-based Practices

How much individuals with moderate and severe disabilities will learn will depend on how well they are taught. Providing many opportunities to respond with systematic prompting and feedback used to shape correct responding has been a powerful strategy for teaching academic content to students with moderate and severe disabilities. For example, Jameson, McDonnell, Polychronis, & Riesen (2008) taught middle school peer tutors to provide instruction on key vocabulary in general education classes to students with moderate intellectual disability. The peers learned to embed trials using time delay for near errorless learning. In a study by Collins, Branson, Hall, & Rankin (2001), students with moderate intellectual disability learned letter writing components in twelfth grade composition through a task analysis and system of least intrusive prompting provided by peers. In Mims et al. (2009), students with severe intellectual disability, who were also legally blind, learned to answer comprehension questions during a read aloud through a system of least intrusive prompting. For students to have the optimal context for learning academic content, special education teachers need to master the application of systematic instruction strategies with fidelity. Unfortunately, sometimes teachers learn to use the terms (e.g., time delay), but not to apply the practice. Student teaching, internships, and professional development need to give teachers the opportunity to demonstrate that they can effectively deliver systematic instruction.

Provide Templates and Resources

Teachers often simply do not have time to "cook from scratch" in creating plans to teach general curriculum content. One option is to provide a template for instruction that can be applied across a wide range of standards. In Browder, Trela et al. (2012), we used a prescribed intervention across multiple math standards (math story + graphic organizer + task analysis of process) and across science standards (inquiry task analysis + concept statement + experiment). By training teachers in the format, they could generate lessons for additional standards (Browder, Jimenez et al., 2012). Our research teams also have translated several of our studies into commercial curricula with Attainment Company that include scripted lesson plans (making systematic instruction accessible to all teachers) and student materials (reducing preparation time). I encourage other researchers to find ways to make interventions commercially available. One way to shorten the distance between research and practice is to translate an intervention into a teacher-friendly format (e.g., something that can be displayed and purchased in a conference exhibit).

Produce Models of Blended Practice

The difficult current challenge for teachers is providing instruction on challenging academic standards that is meaningful to students while retaining the integrity of the content. Skills needed for independence in home, community, and job settings continue to be critical to achieving optimal post-school outcomes, but may be overlooked with the current strong focus on teaching to the standards. What teachers need are models of blended practice that offer examples of high quality academic instruction and community-referenced instruction. For example, the NSTTAC website (www.NSTTAC.org) offers examples of addressing content standards and transition goals concurrently for older students. A blended practice does not mean every lesson must be both academic and community-referenced. Sometimes the priority of a lesson may be to master the academic concept. Sometimes the priority of a lesson may be a specific activity of daily living with no academic focus (e.g., hand-washing).

Revisit Expectations for Achievement as New Research Emerges

At the present time little is known about how much academic content students with moderate and severe disabilities can learn. The research on teaching grade level standards and reading suggests that it is much more than what was once thought possible. Most would agree, the goal probably is some form of alternate, rather than grade level, achievement. That is, the student will learn some specific skills in geometry that are typical of what all fifth graders learn, but not the entire set of skills and possibly in ways that are adapted (e.g., demonstrated with manipulatives only). This alternate achievement also must take into consideration gaps in past learning. Students with severe disabilities progress across grade levels based on their chronological age rather than by passing end of grade testing. Alternate assessments have school accountability, but not student accountability. That is, students do not have to "pass" an alternate assessment to move forward to the next grade. An eighth grader with severe disabilities may not have mastered the seventh grade math

> "At the present time, little is known about how much academic content students with moderate and severe disabilities can learn."

objectives set for her. This eighth grader also may or may not have had any math instruction in the elementary grades. In contrast, another student in the eighth grade may have had years of instruction in math and performed well on objectives set for seventh grade. This variable context makes it difficult to set standards for alternate assessments and teacher effectiveness. As more research emerges, and students have access to general curriculum content across their school careers, it may become easier to establish benchmarks for what to expect across grades or grade bands for students with severe disabilities.

Evaluate Long-term Outcomes

The adult outcomes for students with moderate and severe disabilities often have been disappointing with only a small percent gaining employment. For example, only about a third of students with all levels of intellectual disability gain employment (NLTS2); the number is likely lower for those with more severe disabilities. Improving adult service options, like increased access to supports for employment and community living, will certainly be critical to enhanced outcomes. What is not yet clear is if promoting increased academic competence will help students gain access to these supports and enhance their overall functioning as adults. The Common Core State Standards were developed to help all students become college and career ready. What is not yet known is if teaching to these standards will help more students with moderate and severe disabilities enter careers and participate in college programs for students with intellectual disabilities.

SUMMARY

In this chapter I have shared how after investing 20 years in research on teaching daily living, and functional academic skills, I shifted my focus to promoting academic learning for students with moderate and severe disabilities. My shift began with seeing the creative thinking some state teams had done in developing their alternate assessments and then fully evolved as I saw actual students perform academic skills once considered unreachable because of the severity of their disability. Although I have been one of the advocates for making literacy the top priority of instruction and providing instruction of state standards for all students, I continue to encourage educators to use a blended approach that includes promoting real life applications for all skills and continuing to teach important life skills that have no academic link. One of the most frequent emails I receive from educators asks, "Should an IEP include some functional life skills? Must these be aligned with the state's academic content standards?" My answer is that I believe the IEP is where the blending begins. All students should have IEPs that promote learning the general curriculum content of their assigned grade level, but also contain the other unique needs the student has for specially designed instruction in self-care, social skills, and related therapies. Trying to link all of these other skills to the state academic standards is neither necessary nor feasible.

I have written this chapter to share the journey of how my thinking and research related to general curriculum access for students with severe disabilities evolved. I encourage the reader to engage other experts in severe disabilities to consider their perspectives about what should be taught. I also welcome your thinking and feedback. One of the principles of scientific inquiry is to disclose research to encourage professional scrutiny and critique (National Research Council, 2002). I hope that by sharing not only my research, but also the evolution of my thinking about what to teach students with severe disabilities, I have encouraged you to articulate your own perspective. I look forward to hearing what you have to say and anticipate my own thinking will continue to develop. If you read this book several years from its original publication date, please realize I may have gained a new perspective.

Discussion Questions

1. What reactions do you have, as someone interested in the field of education, to the "lock down" story?
2. Describe the factors that contributed to Browder's changing vision of what to teach students with severe disabilities. Do you agree that visions should change as time goes on, or do you feel educational standpoints should be unwavering?
3. After reading the chapter, what are your views on assessment for children with moderate to severe disabilities (i.e. standardized by the state, different than general education assessments, focusing on academic or functional tasks)?
4. Do you think it is more important to teach content subjects (math and reading) or functional skills to this population?
5. Do you think reading is a purely academic skill, or can it be a functional skill? Explain this in relation to students with moderate or severe disabilities.
6. What are your feelings on "grade-aligned" instruction? What are some benefits and negatives with this type of instruction for students with more severe disabilities?
7. Browder and her colleagues suggest seven reasons why it is important to teach the state academic content standards. Which of these reasons do you agree with? Disagree with?
8. Browder gives recommendations for "what" to teach students with severe disabilities. Name these reasons and discuss how they could be used in the classroom.
9. Do you agree or disagree with the following statement? Explain.

   The research on teaching grade-level standards and reading suggests that it is much more than what was once thought possible. Most would agree, the goal probably is some form of alternate, rather than grade level, achievement.

10. Explain how the IEP is where blending instructional content and standards begins.

DIANE M. BROWDER'S SUGGESTIONS
FOR FURTHER READING

Browder, D. M., Ahlgrim-Delzell, L., Flowers, C., & Baker, J. N. (2012). An evaluation of a multicomponent early literacy program for students with severe developmental disabilities. *Remedial and Special Education, 33,* 237–246.

Browder, D. M., & Courtade, G. (2011). *Aligning IEPs to common core standards for students with moderate and severe disabilities.* Verona, WI: IEP Resources Attainment Company.

Browder, D. M., & Spooner, F. (2011). *Teaching students with moderate and severe disabilities.* New York: Guilford Press.

Hudson, M. E., Browder, D. M., & Wakeman, S. Y. (2013). How to adapt and teach comprehension of grade-level text to early readers and nonreaders with moderate and severe intellectual disability. *Teaching Exceptional Children, 45*(3), 14–23.

Saunders, A., Bethune, K. S., Spooner, F., & Browder, D. B. (2013). Solving the Common Core equation: An approach to teaching Common Core Mathematics Standards to students with moderate and severe disabilities. *Teaching Exceptional Children, 45*(3), 24–33.

Smith, B. R., Spooner, F., Jimenez, B., & Browder, D. M. (2013). Using an early science curriculum to teach science vocabulary and concepts to students with severe developmental disabilities. *Education & Treatment of Children, 36*, 1–31.

REFERENCES

Allor, J. H., Mathes, P. G., Roberts, J. K., Jones, F. G., & Champlin, T. M. (2010). Teaching students with moderate intellectual disabilities to read: An experimental examination of a comprehensive reading intervention. *Education and Training in Autism and Developmental Disabilities, 45*, 3–22.

Al Otaiba, S., & Hosp, M. K. (2004). Providing literacy instruction to students with Down Syndrome. *Teaching Exceptional Children, 36*, 28–35.

Ayres, K. M., Lowrey, K. A., Douglas, K. H., & Sievers, C. (2011). I can identify Saturn but I can't brush my teeth: What happens when the curricular focus for students with severe disabilities shifts. *Education and Training in Autism and Developmental Disabilities, 46*, 11–21.

Bradford, S., Shippen, M. E., Alberto, P., Houchins, D. E., & Flores, M. (2006). Using systematic instruction to teach decoding skills to middle school students with moderate intellectual disabilities. *Education and Training in Developmental Disabilities, 41*, 333–343.

Browder, D. M. (1987). *Assessment of individuals with severe handicaps: A behavioral life skills approach.* Baltimore, MD: Paul H. Brookes.

Browder, D. M. (2001). *Curriculum and assessment for students with moderate and severe disabilities.* NY: Guilford Press.

Browder, D. M., Ahlgrim-Delzell, L., Flowers, C., & Baker, J. N. (2012). An evaluation of a multicomponent early literacy program for students with severe developmental disabilities. *Remedial and Special Education, 33*, 237–246.

Browder, D. M., Fallin, K., Davis, S., & Karvonen, M. (2003). A consideration of what may influence student outcomes on alternate assessment. *Education and Training in Mental Retardation and Developmental Disabilities, 38*, 255–270.

Browder, D. M., & Flowers, C. (2005). *Project RAISE: Reading Accommodations and Interventions for Students with Emergent Literacy.* U.S. Department of Education. Institute of Education Sciences Research Grant. ($600,000 per year for 5 years).

Browder, D. M., Flowers, C., Ahlgrim-Delzell, L, Karvonen, M., Spooner, F., & Algozzine, R. (2004). The alignment of alternate assessment content to academic and functional curricula. *The Journal of Special Education, 37*, 211–224.

Browder, D. M., Gibbs, S. L., Ahlgrim-Delzell, L., Courtade, G., Mraz, M., & Flowers, C. (2008). Literacy for students with severe developmental disabilities: What should we teach and what should we hope to achieve? *Remedial and Special Education, 30*, 269–282.

Browder, D. M., Jimenez, B., Mims, P., Knight, V., Spooner, F., Lee, A., & Flowers, C. (2012). The effects of a "Tell-Show-Try-Apply" professional development package on teachers of students with severe developmental disabilities. *Teacher Education and Special Education, 35*, 212–227.

Browder, D. M., Jimenez, B., & Trela, K. (2012). Grade-aligned math instruction for secondary students with moderate intellectual disabilities. *Education and Training in Autism and Developmental Disabilities, 47*, 373–388.

Browder, D. M., Karvonen, M., Davis, S., Fallin, K., & Courtade-Little, C. (2005). The impact of teacher training on state alternate assessment scores. *Exceptional Children, 71*, 267–282.

Browder, D. M., Lee, A., & Mims, P. J. (2011). Using shared stories and individual response modes to promote comprehension and engagement in literacy for students with multiple, severe disabilities. *Education and Training in Autism and Developmental Disabilities, 46*, 339–351.

Browder, D. M., & Snell, M. E. (1993). Functional academics. In M.E. Snell (Ed.), *Instruction of students with severe disabilities* (pp. 442–479). New York: MacMillan Publishing Co.

Browder, D. M., Spooner, F., Ahlgrim-Delzell, L., Harris, A., & Wakeman, S. (2008). A meta-analysis on teaching mathematics to students with significant cognitive disabilities. *Exceptional Children, 74*, 407–432.

Browder, D. M., Trela, K., Courtade, G. R., Jimenez, B. A., Knight. V., & Flowers, C. (2012). Teaching mathematics and science standards to students with moderate and severe developmental disabilities. *The Journal of Special Education, 46*, 26–35.

Browder, D. M., Trela, K., & Jimenez, B. A. (2007). Training teachers to follow a task analysis to engage middle school students with moderate and severe developmental disabilities in grade-appropriate literature. *Focus on Autism and Other Developmental Disabilities, 22*, 206–219.

Browder, D. M., Wakeman, S. Y., Spooner, F., Ahlgrim-Delzell, L., & Algozzine, B. (2006). Research on reading instruction for individuals with significant cognitive disabilities. *Exceptional Children, 72*, 392–408.

Brown, L., Branston, M. B., Hamre-Nietupski, S., Pumpian, I., Certo, N., & Gruenwald, L. (1979). A strategy for developing chronological age-appropriate and functional curriculum content for severely handicapped adolescents and young adults. *The Journal of Special Education, 13*, 81–90.

Collins, B. C., Branson, T. A., Hall, M., & Rankin, S. W. (2001). Teaching secondary students with moderate disabilities in an inclusive academic classroom setting. *Journal of Development and Physical Disabilities, 13*, 41–59.

Courtade, G., Spooner, F., Browder, D. M., & Jimenez, B. (2012). Seven reasons to promote standards-based instruction for students with severe disabilities. *Education and Training in Autism and Developmental Disabilities, 47*, 3–13.

Downing, J.E., & Demchak, M. (1996). First steps: determining individual abilities and how best to support students. In J.E. Downing, *Including students with severe and multiple disabilities in typical classrooms: practical strategies for teachers* (pp. 35–61). Baltimore: Paul H. Brookes.

Ezell, H. K., & Justice, L.M. (2005). *Shared storybook reading*. Baltimore, MD: Paul H. Brookes.

Flowers, C., Browder, D. M., & Ahlgrim-Delzell, L. (2006). An analysis of three states' alignment between language arts and math standards and alternate assessment. *Exceptional Children, 72*, 201–215.

Flowers, C., Wakeman, S., Browder, D., & Karvonen, M. (2009). An alignment protocol for alternate assessments based on alternate achievement standards. *Educational Measurements: Issues and Practice, 28* (1), 25–37.

Horner, R. H., Carr, E. G., Halle, J., McGee, G., Odom, S., & Wolery, M. (2005). The use of single-subject research to identify evidence-based practice in special education. *Exceptional Children, 71*, 165–179.

Hudson, M. E., & Test, D. W. (2011). Evaluating the evidence base for using shared story reading to promote literacy for students with extensive support needs. *Research and Practice for Persons with Severe Disabilities, 36*, 34–45.

Hunt, P., McDonnell, J., & Crocket, M. A. (2012). Reconciling an ecological curricular framework focusing on quality of life outcomes with development and instruction of standard-based academic goals. *Research and Practice for Persons with Severe Disabilities, 37*(3), 139–152.

Individuals with Disabilities Education Act Amendments (IDEA) of 1997, PL 105-17, 20. U.S.C. 1400 §§ *et seq.*

Jameson, J. M., McDonnell, J., Polychronis, S., & Riesen, T. (2008). Embedded, constant time delay instruction by peers without disabilities in general education classrooms. *Intellectual and Developmental Disabilities, 46*, 346–363.

Jimenez, B. A, Browder, D. M, & Courtade, G. R. (2008). Teaching algebra to students with moderate cognitive disabilities. *Education and Training in Developmental Disabilities, 43*, 266–274.

Jimenez, B. A., Browder, D. M., & Courtade, G. R. (2009). An exploratory study of self-directed science concept learning by students with moderate intellectual disabilities. *Research and Practice for Persons with Severe Disabilities, 34*(2), 1–14.

Jimenez, B., Browder, D., Spooner, F., & DiBiase, W. (2012). Inclusive inquiry science using peer-mediated embedded instruction for students with moderate intellectual disability. *Exceptional Children, 78*, 301–317.

Katims, D. S. (2000). Literacy instruction for people with mental retardation: Historical highlights and contemporary analysis. *Education and Training in Mental Retardation & Developmental Disabilities, 35*, 3–15.

Kleinert, H., & Kearns, J. (1999). A validation of the performance indicators and learner outcomes in Kentucky's alternate assessment for student with significant disabilities. *Journal of the Association for Persons with Severe Handicaps, 24*, 100–110.

Kliewer, C. (1998). Citizenship in the literate community: An ethnography of children with Down syndrome and the written word. *Exceptional Children, 64*, 167–180.

Knight, V., Spooner, F., Browder, D. M., & Smith, B. R. (2012). Teaching science concepts using graphic organizers to students with autism spectrum disorder. *Journal of Autism and Developmental Disabilities, 42*, 378–389.

Koppenhaver, D. A., Erickson, K. A., & Skotko, B. G. (2001). Supporting communication of girls with Rett syndrome and their mothers in storybook reading. *International Journal of Disability, Development and Education, 48*, 395–410.

Mims, P., Browder, D., Baker, J., Lee, A., & Spooner, F. (2009). Increasing comprehension of students with significant intellectual disabilities and visual impairments during shared stories. *Education and Treatment in Developmental Disabilities, 44*, 409–420.

Mims, P., Hudson, M., & Browder, D. (2012). Using read alouds of grade-level biographies and systematic prompting to promote comprehension for students with moderate and severe developmental disabilities. *Focus on Autism and Developmental Disabilities, 27*, 65–78.

National Longitudinal Transition Study-*2* (NLST2). (2009).*NLST 2 Wave 3 2005 Parent/Youth Survey: Employment of youth out-of-secondary school a year or more.* http://www.nlts2.org.

National Research Council (2002). *Scientific research in education.* Washington, DC: National Academy Press. pp. 50–80.

No Child Left Behind Act of 2001, 20 U.S.C. §§ 6301 *et seq.* (2002).

Ryndak, D. L., & Alper, S. (1996). *Curriculum and assessment for students with significant disabilities in inclusive settings.* Boston: Allyn and Bacon.

Ryndak, D. L., Morrison, A. P., & Sommerstein, L. (1999). Literacy before and after inclusion in general education settings: A case study. *Journal of the Association for Persons with Severe Handicaps, 24*, 5–22.

Shurr, J., & Taber-Doughty, T. (2012). Increasing comprehension for middle school students with moderate intellectual disability on age-appropriate texts. *Education and Training in Developmental Disabilities, 47*, 359–372.

Snell, M. E. (1978). *Systematic instruction of the moderately and severely handicapped.* Columbus, OH: Charles E. Merrill.

Spooner, F., Knight, V., Browder, D.M., Jimenez, B., & DiBiase, W. (2011). Evaluating evidence-based practice in teaching science content to students with severe developmental disabilities. *Research and Practice in Severe Disabilities, 36*, 62–75.

Getting to Know Edward J. Kame'enui

I had no intention of becoming a teacher. In fact, as an English literature major who studied writers like Camus, O'Neill, and Euripides, I harbored a snobbish disdain for "education" as a discipline or area of study. I could not fathom what there was to really study—education, really? Then the fiscal realities of leveraging an English literature degree in the marketplace in 1970 exacted their toll, and Brenda Kame'enui and I found our way, albeit serendipitously, to a residential treatment center for children identified at the time as "emotionally disturbed." We served as house-parents, then teachers at a residential center in Wisconsin. I realized very quickly though that although I genuinely enjoyed kids, especially kids who struggled mightily in their young lives, the very topic that I once disdained, teaching, had me flummoxed.

With this chapter, I conclude my career as an educator who has been passionate about education for 45 years, especially the technical aspects of instruction and the need for more rigorous educational research. In doing so, I cannot help but reflect on the privileges the field that I once disdained has given me. There are many, including my mentors—*Doug Carnine, Wes Becker, Zig Engelmann, Jerry Silbert, Herb Prehm, Andy Halpern, Barbara Bateman*, and *John Wills Lloyd*. I have also had the supreme privilege of mentoring (one-by-one) and learning from a wonderful group of doctoral students (listed chronologically): *Deb Simmons, Cyndy Griffin, Asha Jitendra, Shirley Dickson, David Chard, Carrie Thomas Beck, Dae-Sik Lee, Sister Mary Karen Oudeans, Mike Coyne, Sarah McDonaugh, Kristen MacConnell*, and *Darci Burns*. Finally, I have enjoyed the singular privilege of working with incredible colleagues at the University of Montana, Purdue University, the Office of Special Education Programs (OSEP), the National Center for Special Education Research (NCSER) in the Institute of Education Sciences (IES), and particularly the University of Oregon and the Center on Teaching and Learning (CTL). To all, I am sincerely indebted. Thank you for the privilege.

6

SPECIAL EDUCATION AS "SPECIALLY DESIGNED INSTRUCTION": ODE TO THE ARCHITECTURE OF INFORMATION AND THE MESSAGE

Edward J. Kame'enui

In their gracious and personalized letter inviting me to contribute a chapter to this book, the Editors asserted rather boldly that they had "hatched a plan." Fair enough as an attention getter and cautiously intriguing, as edited book writing invitations go. Now, "plans" however "hatched," are a necessary part to any successful endeavor involving an edited book with multiple authors, but here's the "hatched" part of the plan: The editors proposed to "take a unique approach" to the topic of *special education*—one that would "... be both pedagogically informative and inspirational to special education students, as well as fun for the authors and editors to create" (Letter dated 7 April 2012). For readers who are uninitiated in the potentially tedious art of book writing (or merely *writing*), the phrase "unique approach" (Note: Remember, *unique* for the Editors means that the chapter authors must deliver *content* that is "both pedagogically informative and inspirational to special education students") and the word "fun" are not frequently associated with *writing*, at least not professional academic or scientific writing, including writing on such a topic as *special education*. In fact, I am very confident (99 percent confidence level) that if *any* academic scholar in a discipline outside of education read John and Melody's invitational letter invoking the words "unique approach" and "fun" in the writing of a scholarly chapter, they would report it to Congress (*and* no doubt the *Daily Show*) as compelling evidence of the continuing arrested development and scientific immaturity of the field of special education. I jest, of course, but writing is generally serious business, and rarely fun, especially for those of us in the "Academy" who ostensibly *write* for a living. Well, the proposed hatched plan got my attention, despite the high standards of creating pedagogically informative and inspirational content, and persuaded me to agree to contribute a chapter—a fun chapter, that is, but you'll be the severe and unapologetic judge of that, won't you? Oh, what fun!

For the record and before the real *fun* begins, I feel compelled to set Editors Bateman, Lloyd, and Tankersly straight about the fun of writing, and recommend that they dust off and revisit the works of Hunter S. Thompson, who asserted rather acerbically (my acerbic inference, because I don't know that he did, but his writing and life portends nothing less), "Writing is the flip side of sex—it's good only when it's over." Writing even for a prolific writer like Thompson was clearly "funner" for the reader, because "Uncle Duke" could be quite raw and unpredictable much of the time, which one could assume (again, my inference) was related in part to his distaste for writing (and life). I doubt that Barbara, John, and Melody are looking for Gonzo Journalism in this scholarly effort, but it's darn tempting especially because it would be *fun* and certainly *unique*. However, because I know Barbara and John fairly well—after all, they were my unmerciful "mentors" when I was a student in the Master's and Doctoral programs in special education at the University of Oregon from 1975 to 1980—I'm going to take them at their word, and will happily embrace their unwitting charge to have "fun" in the writing of this chapter. In doing so, however, I will certainly mount a serious effort to deliver content that is "both pedagogically informative and inspirational to special education students." Wish me luck, but I must confess, I can't wait until it's over.

IN THE BEGINNING . . .

I was not born an educator or a teacher, or for that matter, a thinker and therefore, a writer (all writing, as notable writers have noted, is revealed thinking); far from it. In fact, my adopted Hawaiian parents thought I was "retarded," because, as they reasoned at the time and continuously thereafter, I apparently had a "big head." Naturally for them, I simply had to be retarded. After all, I was adopted, born prematurely with a big head, and was the second member of fraternal twins to divine air when first entering the world in 1948. After all, there was no other explanation for such deviations in cranial structure (or as Franz Joseph Gall called it, phrenology—the "pseudoscience" of determining one's intelligence and character by actually measuring the size of one's head), at least none that a Hawaiian culture steeped in joyous superstition would permit at the time. Thus, I grew up in a household in which my twin brother, John, who, according to parental folklore, was at least 2 minutes older than me, was called affectionately, "Palakiko," the Hawaiian word for rascal—and he was and continues to be. In contrast, my father, William (Bill) Kapuke Kame'enui, a misanthropic man of pure Hawaiian descent, who we both feared and admired mightily, called me "Big Head." Upon reflection now as a well-practiced adult, I must have had a really big head to warrant such a notable moniker. Clearly, this was not necessarily a good start for a kid growing up in the rough neighborhood of Kalihi, outside of Honolulu on the Island of Oahu, and whose greatest ambition was to become a Honolulu Police officer, like his tall, tough, and handsome Uncle Andrew. But it makes for a great narrative tinged with irony, especially for someone who serendipitously became a special education teacher, researcher, administrator, Dean-Knight Professor of Education at the University of Oregon, and the first Commissioner of the National Center for Special Education Research (NCSER) in the Institute of Education Sciences (IES), the research, evaluation, and statistical arm of the U. S. Department of Education (and, of course, former student of Editors Barbara Bateman and John Wills Lloyd).

Naturally, in retrospect—but only the kind that comes with a sizeable bite of adult years (as Ralph Waldo Emerson once observed, "The years teach much which the days never knew," or as Daniel Webster lamented, "Wisdom begins in the end")—I cannot fault my parents, even slightly, for considering me *retarded,* after all, they knew only what their high school diplomas permitted, constrained unforgivingly by the natural geological and cultural edges of a series of islands pounded out of volcanic rock and debris in the middle of the vast Pacific Ocean. Importantly, they weren't the first to get it wrong, certainly there were many, many highly respected, and "educated" individuals before them who advanced more spectacularly preposterous ideas of "FLKs" (i.e., according to InternetSlang.com, FLK stands for "Funny Looking Kids"). Thomas Willis, for example, was a founding member of the Royal Society and pioneer on brain anatomy (aka "Circle of Willis" or the cerebral arterial circle, a circle of arteries that supply blood to the brain and surrounding structures; http://en.wikipedia.org/wiki/Circle_of_Willis); coined the term, *neurology*; and provided the first description of intellectual disabilities as a "disease" (http://en.wikipedia.org/wiki/Thomas_Willis). Long, long before Willis, Hippocrates, the father of Western medicine and founder of the Hippocratic School of Medicine, thought that mental retardation was caused by an imbalance of the "four humors in the brain," which I think is perhaps the best explanation for my so-called "big head." After all, it only stands to reason that one had to have a generous dose of *humors* to endure "big headedness" in the streets of Kalihi in particular, and in Kalihi Valley in general, and to gain entrance in kindergarten to the widely envied (at least by native Hawaiians) Kamehameha Schools, a school reserved entirely and exclusively for *children of Hawaiian ancestry*, apparently big headed and other normal headed individuals alike.

Upon reflection, perhaps I should have been more grateful that my parents didn't call me "Cretin," "idiot" or "imbecile," all popular labels in the twentieth century for someone identified as retarded. As a biographical aside, they could have called me those names, but I'm sure my Grandma Simeona would not have permitted it, especially because, as the family folklore goes, she cared for the preemie twins and massaged their limbs in the dark of night and into the early, crisp and breezy Hawaiian mornings. On another personal note, I should also probably be thankful that my parents didn't invoke their paternalistic instincts to ship me off to a segregated institution on the Island of Molokai to join the lepers (see Jack London's article in the January 1908 issue of the *Woman's Home Companion* magazine entitled, "The Lepers of Molokai," for a compassionate view of leprosy, another supremely misunderstood "disease"; http://carl-bell2.baylor. edu/~bellc/JL/TheLepersOfMolokai.html). The colorful history of special education, as most readers of this text should know, has a rather "black" history of institutionalization; that is, that of "warehousing" individuals identified with disabilities (see YouTube video entitled, "Suffer the Little Children, Pennsylvania Pennhurst, Home for Disabled Children, Child Abuse by State Social Services," a 1968 NBC exposé at www.youtube.com/watch?v=YG33HvIKOgQ).

So, one could argue and be technically and historically accurate, that I sort of knew "special education," at least tacitly and experientially from the time I was a young child, not only because my parents labeled me "retarded" and called me "Big Head," but also because they found it necessary to tell *all* the neighbors about my condition and associated behaviors, especially my peculiar behavior of stripping brown crust from slices of bread, rolling the soft, white part of the bread into little balls, then hiding them in silent corners of the house. Of course, the rolled bread balls only confirmed my parents' diagnosis of me as retarded. In addition, when my twin brother, John, and I were fairly young, perhaps seven or eight years old, my adopted mother became deaf after she suffered a stroke, and for much of our adolescent and young adult life, the entire family, my father included, were severely challenged to communicate with her through lip reading antics, highly animated hand gestures and, when all else failed, written notes. Not surprisingly, written communications were invoked incidentally and in unbridled desperation. These feeble strategies of communication were made necessary because my mother, Jeanette, shunned all efforts to learn sign language or any form of communication that called attention to her newly acquired "disability." Contrary to my mom's intent to not call attention to herself, one can only imagine how we looked as a family—the twins, the little sister named Kismet, the husband, Bill—all gesturing frantically and impatiently in public to get Jeanette's attention or to plead a case at the Kamehameha Shopping Center that another night of tripe stew for dinner was simply not acceptable. It wasn't pretty, believe me, and most of our communications were simply dysfunctional and only incited greater family tension.

The retrospective truth about my personal and familial experience with special education and disabilities is rather obvious; I really didn't *know* special education then. Whatever I knew at the time represented only a gratuitous conceit of most "knowing" that passes as knowledge and experience in the early, developmental years. Such knowing certainly doesn't represent the coercive foundation of research and disciplinary knowledge that services special education as a field today and which the Editors of this book seek as the fundamental concepts and principles that warrant explication for its readers. Arguably, what ostensibly passed as my parents' uninformed notions of special education or a perceived disability was probably par for the course in the 1950s and through the time span when Public Law 94-142, the *Education for All Handicapped Children Act* became the law of the land in 1975, the year I started my Master's program in Special Education at the University of Oregon. In general, one could argue that the general public at the time was supremely uninformed, perhaps even *clueless*, about special education or a disability. But why would one expect the public *not* to be clueless about these matters? After all, the enlightenment era of Special Education and disabilities was not advanced officially until the federal legislation of 1975.

So, it seems an appropriate and necessary rejoinder to ask, "Well, are we still clueless about special education and disabilities today, especially on the more fundamental constructs that actually define special education"? Or pitched with a more positive spin, "Are we any more informed about Special Education and disabilities today, almost four decades after the passage of P.L. 94-142, than we were in the past?"

> "Are we any more informed about special education and disabilities today, almost four decades after the passage of P.L. 94-142, than we were in the past?"

WHAT IS SPECIAL EDUCATION?

As a title of a chapter in this book, the Editors, Barb, John, and Melody, posed a simple but more delicately phrased foundational question, "What is special education?" From my perspective, the first paragraph of their chapter reveals the basic principles that serve as the foundation for any analysis of the fundamental constructs and organic canons of special education:

> Historically, special education was whatever education was provided to children who had disabilities. It simply was whatever "those kids" got. Now the Individuals with Disabilities Education Act of 2004 (IDEA) defines special education as "specially designed instruction . . . to meet the unique needs of a child who has a disability

.... According to the dictionary definition, "specially" designed instruction means instruction that is different from the ordinary or usual instruction and "unique" needs are those that are singular and unparalleled, having no like or equal. So, bearing in mind those definitions, IDEA tells us that special education is recognizable by two criteria: (a) it is education that is different from the conventional general education and (b) it addresses unusual needs that not many children have.

From Chapter 2, this volume, p. 11.

Since P.L. 94-142 was established as law, the definition of special education has not changed, period. In fact, the definition remains exactly the same, and as the Editors note, is defined as "specially designed instruction . . . to meet the unique needs of a child who has a disability." What is provocative about this federal definition is what the definition is not, but could have been. In other words, contrary to popular belief, definitions are imprecise and inelegant linguistic vehicles for "defining" (i.e., "making definite, distinct or clear") things with cold precision, especially complex entities with multiple meanings and semantic nuances. For example, take a minute to look up the definition of the word, "siphon." What you will invariably discover is a statement or definition similar to the following—siphon: "*A pipe or tube in the form of an upside-down U, filled with liquid and arranged so that the pressure of the atmosphere forces liquid to flow upward from a container through the tube, over a barrier, and into a lower container.*" Are you persuaded? Instead of relying on a definition of a word, an actual demonstration involving material examples of "siphon" would probably work better, and for the more advanced in brain and cranial development, perhaps the same concrete examples coupled with the definition.

Thus, it is curious to speculate out loud, why the crafters of P.L. 94-142 chose the three highly specified words, "specially designed instruction" to define *special education*, instead of other words that were arguably more common in educational parlance and practice at the time and more closely associated with the class of individuals known to the public nominally as "retarded" (*and* who required something "different" than what was typically in place in schools for *all* the *other* kids). For example, the crafters could have defined special education as a "special curriculum" or "special practices," or "special procedures" appropriate to children with "special" needs. They could have pitched a range of other constructs that had as its primary feature "accommodation," modification, or alternatives to what was in the general school milieu at the time. However, the record is sufficiently clear that the crafters of the law didn't. Moreover, the original codified definition of special education has not changed a stitch in almost four decades.

What is profound about the definition of special education in the original law is that the crafters chose explicitly and one should assume, purposively, the words, "specially designed instruction." Thus, the crafters had an idea of a central and highly specified construct they wanted to communicate to the public (and the education profession writ large) about special education. In doing so, they employed very specific language (i.e., words) that gave special emphasis to the construct of *instruction* (*not* curriculum, *not* teaching, *not* practice, *not* place or accommodation). Moreover, they also turned and introduced a phrase, *specially designed* "instruction" as if to force singular attention on the "design" of what schools, teachers, publishers, or others in the educational marketplace would purposively craft as the kind of instruction *necessary* for children requiring special education. That the crafters of this language—that is, the words, *specially designed instruction*—sought intentionally to privilege the *design* of the *instruction* is, to me, noteworthy, especially for students who consider themselves special education professionals. Why do I take the words so seriously and assign them such high purpose and meaning? Well, the words in almost all things matter, and the right words matter a lot. As Mark Twain noted, "The difference between the almost right word and the right word is really a large matter—it's the difference between the lightning bug and the lightning."

Thus, at the generous invitation of the Editors, I offer my variation on the purpose of special education with particular reference to *instruction*. After all, as I have noted thus far, special education gives special privilege to instruction and in particular, to *specially designed instruction*. So, exactly what does that mean?

AFTER THE BEGINNING . . .

I got my start in special education at a residential treatment center located in Neillsville, Wisconsin, but it wasn't my first choice. It was a default start, as starts go, because it was not where I had envisioned the beginning of a professional career as an English Literature major would begin. Instead of teaching selected works of Keats, Faulkner, and Hemingway, or the sonnets and tragedies of Shakespeare to gifted (and perhaps wealthy) young men and women in a private school, I ended up serving as a houseparent (and breaking in a new marriage to boot) to eight young adolescent males ranging in age from 13 to 17 at a private, residential facility in the middle of Wisconsin where the winters are nothing less than what Jack London penned in "To Build a Fire." In doing so, I also ended up intimately embracing as a life theme the essence of the following lines in Shakespeare's *Hamlet*:

> Not a whit. We defy augury. There's a special providence in the fall of a sparrow. If it be now, 'tis not to come. If it be not to come, it will be now. If it be not now, yet it will come—the readiness is all. (Act 5, Scene 2).

I was certainly not "ready" for the long Wisconsin winters (remember, I was born and raised on a warm, tropical "rock"). Nor was I "ready" for the thoroughly demanding work, emotionally and psychologically, that a residential center had in stock for me. Candidly, to this day, I am persuaded that nothing other than the raw, hands-on, in-your-face experience of working at a residential treatment center and directly with children identified, at least in 1970s, as "seriously emotionally disturbed," could ready anyone for such an experience. *Nothing*. It was simply "trial by fire" and nothing less than the blistering heat of actual experience would do in forging one's experience and outlook. It was very difficult work even for someone who had worked at very demanding physical jobs that included, for example, pulling lumber off a "dry chain" during the grave yard shift at a lumber mill in Montana, emptying 50 gallon barrels of waste at Dole's pineapple factory in Honolulu, and picking up garbage at 4 a.m. in Forest Grove, Oregon. A houseparent is ostensibly charged with "parenting" (i.e., caring, feeding, preparing meals, medicating, managing, guiding) *other* people's children within what always struck me as an unforgiving and brutal schedule of care—24 hours a day, five days a week with two days off. Of course, as we became veterans, we became immensely fond of our charges, who, if they are still alive at this writing, are settling well into the upper end of their middle-age years—it's *very* hard to believe.

After a year of house-parenting more than a dozen or so young men through puberty, including the excessive use of "hair oil" and other adolescent transitional experiences in Hiawatha (the name of the house in which we served as house-parents), I had the opportunity to become a "teacher" at the same residential treatment center, *and* mind you, without any "formal" special education training or official special education certification. "What other training do I need?" I thought. After all, I had survived and experienced first hand the insidious stability of the "extinction curve," placed adolescent young men (and women) in monitored time-out rooms on countless occasions, endured the "mouthing" of daily doses of medication that, because they were not consumed, triggered behaviors that were potentially harmful, both physically and emotionally, and weathered enough personal verbal assaults to last a lifetime. Importantly, however, I knew how to "manage" and control highly disruptive and highly charged volatile behaviors. What more experience, pedagogy, and "felt need" (Thomas Dewey's words) could possibly be required or needed to serve as a *teacher* in a residential treatment center for children with serious emotional problems? Furthermore, if actual "teaching expertise" was necessary in addition to managing behavior, well, it would simply come *naturally*, so I thought. After all, adults were *born* teachers. Weren't they?

As a teacher for four years at Sunburst Youth Homes (formerly Winnebago Children's Home) in Neillsville, Wisconsin, I learned one unassailable lesson—I could manage the "problem" behaviors of students (any problem behavior, no matter how hostile, physically or verbally) and do so with ample confidence and proficiency and in a highly proactive manner. However, it became clear to me from the very beginning of my teaching experience that I did not have a clue about how to *teach*, period. More poignantly, my inability to teach did not improve over time and with more "hands-on" experience.

Oh, please don't misunderstand my personal and professional confession—I certainly "caused my kids to know something" (e.g., taught them a skill) and kept them engaged in what I considered to be important tasks. Importantly, I also increased their performance on standardized achievement measures and based on their infrequent testimonies, I even "caused" my kids to feel good about themselves in the face of untenable odds that were not in their favor, especially as young adults at ages 13 through 17.

> "However, it became clear to me from the very beginning of my teaching experience that I did not have a clue about how to *teach*, period. More poignantly, my inability to teach did not improve over time and with more 'hands-on' experience."

What I realized then and with unfettered clarity and conviction now, is that I was thoroughly unprepared and clueless about providing "specially designed instruction" in ways that would meet the unique needs of the individual students in my classroom of eight students. In other words, I was haunted by an intuitive sense that there simply had to be a better way—that is, more efficient, more effective, more systematic, more explicit and direct, and more parsimonious and punctuated techniques designed to "accelerate" the flow and intake of information—to teach those kids than what I was employing in what struck me as a rather haphazard and piecemeal approach.

The other observation I held at the time about these kids under my charge in the residential treatment center was that in almost every case with perhaps one or two exceptions, children identified with serious behavior or emotional problems who were made "wards of the state," removed from their homes, parents, brothers and sisters, and sent to a residential treatment facility were invariably and substantially behind their same-age peers in almost *all* basic skills and content knowledge. I didn't have the "technical" language to characterize this apparent "gap" in psychometric terms at the time, but I knew they were substantially (and depressingly) behind their same-age peers, and experienced persistent problems acquiring new information and holding on to things that were deemed "sufficiently taught" already. Finally, it became clear to me at the time that the academic, school-based learning problems gave cause in dramatic ways to the physical and verbal cycles of problem behaviors. I know now that those kids were being as smart as they could be when they responded with physical and verbal threats to the presentation or introduction of difficult academic tasks (see Kame'enui & Darch, 1995; Darch & Kame'enui, 2004). After all, they had been taught to practice those threatening behaviors with repeated and incremental perfection and with unchecked results that were immediate and definitive in permitting them to get what they desired.

So, the assertion that the Editors offer about "specially designed instruction" as ". . . instruction that is different from the ordinary or usual instruction" and that the "unique" needs of the individual who receives this instruction ". . . are those that are singular and unparalleled, having no like or equal . . ." strike me as a reasonable interpretation of the general boundaries of "specially designed instruction." But, what is this thing called specially designed instruction? What does it mean? Why and how does it apply uniquely to children who have needs that are "singular and unparalleled?"

The "Design" of Specially Designed Instruction

As noted previously, I have assigned high and almost transcendent purpose to the term *specially designed instruction*. I am clearly persuaded that the crafters of P.L. 94-142 were singularly calculating and intentional in their selection and use of the terms "specially designed instruction." Moreover, I am persuaded (but with less vigor) that the use of the term was not capricious or cursory in intent or form, in part because of the research literature on the "design of instruction" that lurked in the experimental psychology at the time, as well as the "instruction set architecture" literature that was persuasive in computer science and engineering (Goldstine, 1972), also lurking around the same time period. Both of these literatures, albeit from different disciplines that are cosmically beyond education or special education borders, could have served as the disciplinary and empirical basis to this newly coined phrase, specially designed instruction. Given this phrase, it only stands to reason that the crafters "had" to have derived it from the extant research literature. Admittedly, this would represent extraordinary, if not prescient insight on the part of the crafters of the law, but it's not an unreasonable historical inference given the general elegance of the law, from a legal, civil rights perspective, and now arguably, from a pedagogical and instructional perspective.

As I see it, the key words in the phrase, *specially designed instruction*, are the words "designed instruction," which is a short, underhand stone's throw, at least semantically, to the terms, "design of instruction," and thus, the resulting empirical linkage to the research on the design of instruction (Engelmann & Carnine, 1982; Gagne, Briggs, & Wager, 1992; Tennyson & Cocchiarella, 1986). The key words are also related to "instruction set architecture," which is more of a skipping stone's throw across the lake to the language of computer science and engineering (Goldstine, 1972)—I would include in this wide-range of literature the lectures on computation by the 1965 Nobel Laureate in Physics, Richard P. Feynman (Hey & Allen, 1996), and specifically his lectures on "Coding and Information Theory" (see Chapter Four in Hey & Allen, 1996). Both of these genres of instructional design literature are related in principle to a single, common conceptual and theoretical construct—that of *information*—and to information theory and associated constructs.

Information? Information Theory? Really? What does *information* have to do with specially designed instruction and students identified with disabilities who have unique individual instructional needs? Well, from my well-worn perch, not everything; that is, information and information theory do not represent the whole "kit and caboodle" of what is nominally delineated in the federal law (currently, P.L. 108-446, *The Individuals with Disabilities Education Improvement Act of 2004*) and defined as special education and related services. However, when instruction is part of the special education equation, which it is given, the definition of special education as "specially designed instruction," then information and information theory have a heck of a lot to do with special education!

Let me explain and in doing so, let me invoke—that is, take cover and gain protection from—the words of others who have given the theory of information more muscular thought than I have. I'll continue to take blame for extending information theory to specially designed instruction and thus, special education (see Kame'enui, 1991; Kame'enui, Fien, & Korgesaar, 2013). In *Grammatical Man: Information, Entropy, Language and Life*, Jeremy Campbell (1982) poses the following series of questions:

> What do the codes used for sending messages back from spacecraft have in common with genes on a molecule of DNA? How is it that the second law of thermodynamics, a physicist's discovery, is related to communication, so that we can speak of the "entropy" of a musical score, or a page of text, or a conversation? Why are knotty problems in the mathematical theory of probability connected with the way we express ourselves in speech and writing?
>
> (p. 15)

Given the priming offered previously, it should not be a surprise that Campbell answers these questions with one word: *information*. He elaborates:

> The very fact that a single concept can link so many diverse ideas is an indication of its great generality and power . . . In its most familiar sense today, information is news, intelligence, facts and ideas that are acquired and passed on as knowledge . . . the word was used also with a more active, constructive meaning, as something which gives a certain form or character to matter, or to the mind; a force which shapes conduct, trains, instructs, inspires or guides.
>
> (p. 15)

Campbell traces the origins of information theory to Claude Shannon of Bell Telephone Laboratories and the design of early-learning radar systems, color television transmission (Yes, color TV!) and the recovery of intact messages from distant spacecraft. Shannon published two papers in the *Bell System Technical Journal* in July and October 1948 in which he specified a set of theorems of sending messages from one place to another "quickly, economically and efficiently" (Campbell, 1982, p. 17). What Shannon offered the field of radio and telephone engineering at the time was a formal logic and mathematical framework for thinking about information as communication—laws of information that characterized common constructs including "order and disorder, error and control of error, possibilities and the actualizing of possibilities, uncertainty and the limits of uncertainty" (p. 18). (Question: Now, doesn't "order and disorder, error and control of error" have an instructional ring to it?) In short, what Shannon provided was a scientific analogy of sorts, between the motion of energy (e.g., pollen grains suspended in water and their unpredictable paths; aka Brownian motion and "entropy") and information, ostensibly arguing that the communication or the sending of messages was analogous to the Brownian motion of pollen grains—motions that appear to be random but instead could be determined and predicted mathematically. As Campbell (1982) notes:

> A message, like the track of a particle of pollen, is a sequence of events spread out in time. These events are not known completely in advance. The price of a share as it moves up or down in the course of a day's trading on the stock market is a series of the same kind ... In somewhat the same way, a sentence of English prose is a series of letters and words obeying certain statistical rules. It is internally consistent, so that if a person knows the rules, the sequence is not completely unpredictable. Given the first half of the sentence, it may be possible to guess the second half, or come near to guessing it, or at least to predict the next letter. But the whole point of a message, the whole point of writing the next sentence in a book, is that it should contain something new, something unexpected. Otherwise there would be no reason to write it in the first place.

> Only the probable track of a pollen grain suspended in water, only probable fluctuations in the price of a share of IBM, only the probable arrangement of letters and words on a page of print, can be predicted. In making such a prediction, a mathematician considers not one future, but a multiplicity of simultaneous futures, all of which can be said to coexist in an abstract sense. Statistics can do nothing with a single piece of data. An isolated event has no meaning. It needs to be part of a pattern of many possible events, each with a certain likelihood of being realized.

"Thus, it seems reasonable to assert that special designed instruction should at the very least, be 'designed' in a way that makes one message more probable than another message and certainly more probable than 'noise'."

(p. 28)

The probable path of a message communicated in space from one point to another like the movement of a grain of pollen, or the path of a missile from a German airplane (which preoccupied Shannon and his colleagues, Norbert Weiner, J. R. Pierce, Bertrand Russell, and G. H. Hardy, at the time) was Shannon's primary focus and he was interested in the task of separating the probability of the receipt of the target message from other "noise" in the communication. Let's pause here momentarily. Now, doesn't the probable path of a message communicated in the natural space from a teacher to students resemble the path that preoccupied Dr. Shannon? I think so. As Campbell states:

> In an ordinary conversation, information is conveyed when the speaker says something that changes the listener's knowledge. This means that the listener is in a state of uncertainty as to what message he will actually hear. We say "uncertainty" rather than complete ignorance because he does know, at least, that the message will be one of a range of possible messages. It may be highly improbable, and therefore very hard to predict, or it may be extremely probable, in which case the listener could have

predicted it with ease. But the message will not be impossible, in the sense that it violates grossly the rules of grammar or meaning; otherwise, it could not be called information at all. In the listener's mind, as in the statistician's charts and tables, are a number of possibilities or contingencies, some more probable than others. When the speaker sends his message, he makes one these possibilities actual, excluding the others and resolving the listener's uncertainty.

(p. 29)

If we paraphrase and apply Campbell's words in terms of "specially designed instruction," we could readily pose the following question: Is specially designed instruction akin to charging the Teacher with the responsibility of making his or her intended message more "actual" (that is, more probable) in "resolving the listener's uncertainty?" Thus, it seems reasonable to assert that specially designed instruction should at the very least, be "designed" in a way that makes one message more probable than another message and certainly more probable than "noise."

The Message of Specially Designed Instruction

In any kind of instruction, the logic is rather straightforward: The *Teacher* (T) is in essence charged (either as part of the implied public trust or as part of an explicit contractual and fiscal agreement and arrangement) with sending a message (i.e., a new concept or bit of information that is not yet known or only partially known) to the *Student* (S) who is the receiver and primary "target" of the information. Of course, this relation of Teacher (T or in this case, X) to Student (S or in this case, Y) can be represented statistically in a total effect, two-variable (*x* causes *y*) path diagram model with accompanying equations (associated error term and all) in a regression model (e.g., $Y = i_1 + cX + e^1$). The primary assumption of this model is that the Teacher (T) is one variable and the *independent variable* (X) that directly *causes* the Student (S), the other variable and the *dependent variable* (Y), to gain the *information* or the new "actual" message (*c*) that Student (S) did not have in its cognitive grasp or learning experience before. Thus, the outcome is that the Student (S) is determined via some form of evaluation or assessment to have demonstrated the acquisition (or not) of the new information or the new message that it gained primarily, if not exclusively from the Teacher (T).

Naturally, the teaching equation is supremely more complex than a simple, two-variable, *direct* path effect model in which "everything," "noise" and all, can be accounted for in the simple, direct interaction between the Teacher (T) and Student (S). Other variables must obviously be considered in the "teaching equation," such as the lesson, the curriculum, the teacher's ability and experience, the student's prior knowledge about the target content, the classroom environment, the average socio-economic status of students in the school, mother's education, and so forth—the direct or indirect variables that could be under consideration are infinite. In fact, it is more appropriate to think of a "mediated" model with multiple variables for the teaching and learning process than a simple, total effects, two-variable model. However, for purposes of conceptual clarity in understanding *specially designed instruction* at a molecular level, our primary focus is on the *information* that the T (Teacher) communicates directly to the S (Student). The design of instruction, like Claude Shannon's focus on information theory and the potential communication of a message explicitly and purposively, is on the probability or certainty that the information or message will be communicated clearly and unambiguously to the receiver, and that the receiver will apprehend and understand the communication.

The jacket cover (yes, the jacket cover!) to *Grammatical Man: Information, Entropy, Language and Life* asserts:

> *Grammatical Man* is the first book to tell the story of information theory, how it arose with the development of radar during World War II, and how it evolved ... Just as physics made sense of the mysteries of earth, air, fire and water, it can be said that this new science of information enriches and unifies an amazing diversity of modern sciences from physics and mathematics to biology and linguistics.

As book-jacket marketing goes, this is a reasonably concise and accurate summary of Campbell's treatise. Whether information theory "unifies" a diverse body of the modern sciences is perhaps arguable. It is certainly not arguable that information theory has yet to find its way, in any substantive form, into special education or perhaps even education writ large. However, the theoretical and conceptual principles and tenets that serve as the underpinnings of information theory can be found in some of the same general principles, concepts, and tenets of the *design of instruction* or *instructional design* research literature, which has been applied to special education and to children identified with disabilities.

The *design of instruction* or *instructional design* has a particular meaning and one that makes transparent its alignment with special education as "specially designed instruction." For example, according to Smith and Ragan (1999) the design of instruction refers to "a systematic process of translating principles of learning and instruction into plans for instructional materials and activities" (p. 3). I extend this definition to also include "initially preparing instruction that (a) has *a high probability of preventing learner errors and/or misconceptions and misrules*" (Tennyson & Christensen, 1986, p. 4, emphasis added). Thus, like information theory, definitions of instructional design have a common feature, that is, the reliance on a probabilistic model (i.e., knowing the probability of preventing learner errors) and a focus on the prescription of instructional procedures "to achieve particular changes in learner behaviour" (Moore, 1986, p. 202). In information theory, achieving a particular change in a learner's behavior is akin to "resolving the listener's uncertainty."

Bruner (cited in Moore, 1986) elevates the province of instructional design to an instructional "systems" level that includes the following four critical features:

a. a description of the experiences necessary for learning,
b. an analysis of the structure and forms of knowledge,
c. a specification of teaching sequences in which to present the materials to be learned, and
d. a system for monitoring and rewarding student performance during the instructional process (Kame'enui et al., 1995).

These four features of instructional design represent a fairly comprehensive system of instruction beginning with the "pre-requisite skills" a learner must know as a precondition for instruction and for achieving a change in his or her learning behavior. It also includes a rather esoteric and abstract feature—the analysis of the *structure* and *forms* of the knowledge. Hmmm.

So, let's pause here for a moment and revisit the Editors' "hatched plan" for the writing of this chapter. Well, if you read the charge carefully, the editors proposed to "take a unique approach" to the topic of *special education*—one that would "be both pedagogically informative and inspirational to special education students, as well as fun for the authors and editors to create." Sorry readers, the Editors'

> "That is, the structure (Think: Shape, form, architecture) of the information or content dictates, in part, how the information is to be taught, communicated, sent or delivered to the receiver or learner of the content. Thus, 'the *what*' that is to be taught determines, in part, *how* it should be taught."

charge was for *me* to have fun. So, here's where the "real fun" begins—at least, for me. From my perspective, this "structure of knowledge" stuff is the "what" or content to be taught to the students. Put simply, the analysis of the "structure and forms of knowledge" includes the full, unadulterated spectrum of knowledge or *information* that is known to schooling and referred most recently as the "Common Core State Standards" (CCSS) that the teacher is required to teach. In Campbell's terms, this is the stuff that teachers or publishers must initially prepare for instruction or communicate as messages, but in ways that increase the "probability of preventing learner errors and/or misconceptions and misrules" (Tennyson & Christensen, 1986, p. 4).

Bruner's analysis also includes a detailed "specification of teaching sequences" which also warrants explication. A specified teaching sequence represents, at least from my perspective, a string of actionable teacher-delivered activities—the Teacher enacts a specified plan that encapsulates and transmits the "message" (stuff, content or material) to the learner. Such a plan is typically constructed or designed ahead of time (*before* the instruction is delivered) so that ample consideration is given to maximizing the odds (or certainty) and minimizing the uncertainty that the intended message will be communicated clearly and with little to no error. The design or architecture of information (or content) is predicated on the somewhat haughty assumption that the structure of the information to be taught is of paramount importance in communicating the content or information to the learner, especially to students with unique individual needs. That is, the structure (Think: Shape, form, architecture) of the information or content dictates, in part, how the information is to be taught, communicated, sent or delivered to the receiver or learner of the content. Thus, "the *what*" that is to be taught determines, in part, *how* it should be taught. For example, if the *what* to be taught is a fairly uncomplicated concept, like *under* (e.g., "The ball is under the table"), that has reasonably clear definitional boundaries, then it might be best, at least initially, to teach the concept of *under* using concrete materials (e.g., a ball, table) and a specified sequence of positive (i.e., The ball placed under the table) and negative examples (The ball placed outside the edges of the table) of the concept. The Teacher would model the specified teaching sequence and in doing so, place the ball under the table in a range of locations with each placement representing a range of positive examples of *under* and associated teacher wording ("The ball is under the table"). In that same teaching sequence, the Teacher would juxtapose negative examples of the concept (e.g., The Teacher places the ball just outside the vertical plane of the edges of the table so that the ball is *not* under the table, with some "negative" examples placed a few inches outside the edges of the table and other negative examples placed a foot or more outside the edges of the table) and employ the following statement, "The ball is *not* under the table").

Now, if the structure of *what* needs to be taught is a fairly complex if-then rule relationship (e.g., "When the dog is *under* the table, it is safe from small falling objects"), then it might be best to use the same set of concrete examples previously noted but paired with a statement of the if-then rule relationship and a series of highly specified if-then questions to facilitate the acquisition of the rule and its application, and so forth. This kind of teaching will require significant prerequisite knowledge on the part of the learner (e.g., knows concept of *dog*, *table*, and what it means to be *safe*), a highly specified set of examples and teaching language (e.g., the number and sequence of the examples and descriptions the teacher presents to the learner). It is obviously more complex than teaching a single-dimension concept like *under*, and is certainly more complex with many moving parts. Nonetheless, like the teaching of the concept of *under*, the information to be communicated requires careful design, scaffolding, and packaging before it is delivered.

Now, the teaching analysis and description of *under* I provided in the previous paragraph represents what I have learned from two individuals at the University of Oregon, and their lifetime of work in special education—Siegfried Engelmann and Douglas W. Carnine. In their book, *Theory of Instruction* (1982), and more recently in *Could John Stuart Mill Have Saved Our Schools?* (2011), Engelmann and Carnine offer a compelling case for how their instructional design analysis of cognitive learning aligns with Bruner's theory and analysis, as well as other prominent instructional design theorists and architects (Bruner, 1966; Gagne, 1985; Markle & Tiemann, 1969; Tennyson & Christensen, 1986; Tennyson & Cochiarella, 1986; Tennyson & Park, 1984), including, I would argue, Shannon's theory of information.

Engelmann and Carnine (1982; 2011) employ what they characterize as a "logico-empirical approach to instruction" which has tenets similar to those of information and communication theory (Campbell, 1982). Like Campbell, Engelmann and Carnine too believe that, "In communications parlance, noise is anything which corrupts the integrity of a message: static in a radio set, garbling in a printed text, distortion of the picture on a television screen" (Campbell, 1982, p. 26). In information and communications theory, for a signal (or message) to be received clearly and unambiguously, the signal (or message) must be clearly communicated and without distortion or disruption. Engelmann and Carnine's trenchant focus over the years has been on "*transforming the structure of information* in a way that the intended message is communicated clearly, unambiguously, and efficiently" (Kame'enui, 1991 p. 254, italics original). They employ two general analyses: (a) the logic of communicating information through examples (induction); (b) empirical considerations based on observations of the learner's behavior or responses to the particular communication. According to Engelmann and Carnine (2011):

> In broad terms, the first and primary analysis is logical. Questions of clarity are approached first from a logical perspective, then from an empirical perspective. Is the presentation clear in terms of what we show and the discriminations we teach? In practice, the answer is never definitively yes, but rather, apparently, yes, until the empirical analysis renders the final decision of clarity.
>
> (p. 125)

Interestingly, Engelmann and Carnine (2011) identified and described in ambitious detail five principles from Mill's work, *A System of Logic* (1843) (*direct method of agreement, method of difference, joint method of agreement and difference, method of residues, and method of concomitant variations*) they argue could "provide something of a blueprint for instruction" (p. 19). An example of one of Mill's methods warrants consideration to appreciate the character and validity of Engelmann and Carnine's (2011) assertion that Mill's work could be of value in designing instruction. For example, Mill's method of agreement asserts:

> If two or more instances of the phenomenon under investigation have only one circumstance in common, the circumstance in which alone all the instances agree is the cause (or effect) of the given phenomenon.
>
> (Engelmann & Carnine, 2011, p. 20)

In explaining Mill's first principle, Engelmann and Carnine (2011) observed:

> The "circumstance" is a feature or detail. This method indicates that only one feature is shared by all the examples. By changing a few words, this principle becomes a technical principle for demonstrating to students how things are the same. Stated in more causal terms, the teacher will identify some things with the same label or submit them to the same operation. *If the examples in the teaching set share only one feature, that single feature can be the only cause of why the teacher treats instances in the same way.*
>
> For example, we want to teach a perfectly naïve learner the meaning of the word *blue*. We create a set of six blue objects (book, table, pillow, bird, sky and lake). The only feature the examples have in common is the blueness. Note that the examples are greatly different from each other. The sky is not an object like a bird, and a bird is greatly different from a pillow, a table, or a lake.
>
> The teacher points to each example and says, "This is blue ... this is blue ... this is blue...." The same label signals that the same feature appears in all the examples. Stated differently: What caused the teacher to call each example blue? The only common featured shared by the examples is the color. Therefore, the color logically is the only possible cause or basis for the teacher indicating that each example is "blue." The label is the same because the single feature is the same across examples.
>
> (p. 20)

Interestingly, Engelmann and Carnine (2011) did not discover the "parallels" between their seminal work on the "design" or architecture of instruction entitled *Theory of Instruction* (Engelmann & Carnine, 1982) and Mill's *A System of Logic* (1843), until after they "had finished writing the bulk" of their book and only when they were "writing a chapter on theoretical issues" (p. 39). As the authors noted, "In their search for literature relevant to their philosophical orientation, they came across Mill's work and were shocked to discover that they had independently identified all the major patterns that Mills had articulated. *Theory of Instruction* even had parallel principles to the methods in *A System of Logic*" (p. 39).

"If the field of special education is really serious about *specially designed instruction*, then significant focus on *instruction and the communication of information* is substantially warranted."

In *Theory of Instruction*, a book that Engelmann and Carnine (1982) published almost 30 years ago and a creation that took them 10 years to write, the authors delineated an expansive set of "juxtaposition" principles, rules, procedures, and examples for teaching or "communicating" a full range of content beginning with "single dimension" concepts (e.g., teaching concepts such as the orientation of objects in space, such as *under*) to multi-dimensional noun concepts (e.g., concepts such as *animal, cup, chair*), to if-then rule relationships (e.g., "If two things happened together, it doesn't necessarily mean that one causes the other"), to "cognitive routines" (e.g., operation of the solar system). The application of the design of instruction is predicated on the logico-empirical analysis that Engelmann and Carnine argue is important to "causing" learning to happen (see *Theory of Instruction* for a complete theoretical treatment of Direct Instruction). Many of the juxtaposition principles and procedures for designing instruction that Engelmann and Carnine (1982) delineated in the *Theory of Instruction* are consistent with much of the experimental research on concept teaching and learning, as well as the disciplinary knowledge and research on *instructional design*.

IN CONCLUSION

Like most, if not all, pieces of writing designed to provoke thinking (and fun), I trust I have raised as many questions as I have answered about the nature and role of instruction in special education as *specially designed instruction*. As I have argued, a very important and often concealed feature of specially designed instruction is the architecture of the instruction—the structure and form of the information (the content and "the what" that the teacher teaches and attempts to communicate to the student). I also offered a larger theoretical and disciplinary canvas for thinking about specially designed instruction—a canvas that includes *information theory* and the *theory of instructional design*. Special education as a discipline has enjoyed generous and unfiltered historical influences from a wide range of disciplines including medicine, psychology, neurology, optometry, anthropology, and the like. If the field of special education is really serious about *specially designed instruction*, then significant focus on *instruction as the communication of information* is substantially warranted, as Shannon, Campbell, Feynman, Mills, Engelmann and Carnine, and others, appear to argue. Naturally, there is much that I did not cover in this chapter, including the empirical basis for the design of instruction, especially rigorous (the randomized control trials kind) research on the extent to which the manipulation of the design of instruction can accelerate and advance special education students' academic and social growth. But that's a topic for another *fun* chapter.

> *Discussion Questions*
> 1. After reading Kame'enui's childhood experiences, what is your opinion on the following statement? Compare some of his past examples to today.
> "Are we anymore informed about Special Education and disabilities today, almost four decades after the passage of P.L. 94-142, than we were in the past?"
> 2. The author speculates why the crafters of P.L. 94-142 chose the words "specially designed instruction." Why do you think these words are meaningful?
> 3. Many teacher educators assert that "hands-on" experience is the most beneficial in preparing new teachers. Kame'enui may disagree with this statement. Which side do you take? Why?

4. After reading this chapter, how can you use "specially designed instruction" for a variety of learners (i.e., students with different abilities)?
5. Do you think information and information theory has a place in special education? Why or why not?
6. Explain how you view the interplay between the teacher, student, and message delivery. In what ways is this similar to the ideas in this chapter (i.e., the regression equation on page 84) and in what ways is it different?
7. What did you take away from the argument about the "architecture of instruction?" Explain the *what* and how this may impact your teaching.
8. Review the following statement. What do you see as the main needs of special education instruction in the future?

"If the field of special education is really serious about *specially designed instruction*, then significant focus on *instruction and the communication of information* is substantially warranted."

EDWARD J. KAME'ENUI'S SUGGESTIONS FOR FURTHER READING

Feynman, R. P. (1999). *The pleasure of finding things out.* Cambridge, MA: Perseus Publishing.
Gawande, A. (2002). *Complications: A surgeon's notes on an imperfect science.* NY: Metropolitan Books.
Kahneman, D. (2011). *Thinking, fast and slow.* NY. Farrar, Straus and Giroux.
Kuhn. T. (1962). *The structure of scientific revolutions.* Chicago: University of Chicago Press.
Pinker, S. (1995). *The language instinct: How the mind creates language.* New York: HarperCollins. (First Harper Perennial Modern Classic edition published 2007.)
Searle, J. R. (1995). *The social construction of reality.* New York: The Free Press.

REFERENCES

Bruner, J. S. (1966). *Toward a theory of instruction.* Cambridge, MA: Belknap Press of Harvard University.
Campbell, J. (1982). *Grammatical man: Information, entropy, language and life.* New York: Simon and Schuster.
Darch, C. B., & Kaméenui, E. J. (2004). *Instructional classroom management: A proactive approach to behavior management* (2nd ed.). Upper Saddle River, NJ: Prentice Hall.
Engelmann, S., & Carnine, D. (1982). *Theory of instruction: Principles and applications.* New York, NY: Irvington Publishers.
Engelmann, S., & Carnine, D. (2011). *Could John Stuart Mill have saved our schools?* Verona, WI: Attainment Company.
Goldstine, H. H. (1972). *The Computer: From Pascal to von Neumann.* Princeton, New Jersey: Princeton University Press.
Gagne, R. M. (1985). *The conditions of learning and theory of instruction* (4th ed.). New York: Holt, Rinehart & Winston.
Gagne, R., Briggs, L., & Wager, W. (1992). *Principles of instructional design* (4th ed.). Fort Worth, TX: HBJ College Publishers.
Hey, J. G., & Allen, R. W. (1996). *Feynman lectures on computation.* Reading, Mass: Addison-Wesley.
Kame'enui, E. J. (1991). Toward a scientific pedagogy: A sameness in the message. *Journal of Learning Disabilities, 24,* 364–372.
Kameenui, E. J., & Darch, C. (1995). *Instructional classroom management: Proactive approach to behavior management.* White Plains, NY: Longman, Inc.
Kame'enui, E. J., Jitendra, A. K., & Darch, C. B. (1995). Direct instruction reading as contronym and eonomine. *Reading & Writing Quarterly: Overcoming Learning Difficulties, 11*(1), 3–17.
Kame'enui, E. J., Fien, H., & Korgesaar, J. (2013). Direct instruction as *Eo nomine* and *Contronym*: Why the right words and the details matter. In L. Swanson, K. Harris, & S. Graham (Eds.). *Handbook on learning disabilities* (2nd ed.; pp 489–506). Baltimore, MD: Brookes.

Markle, S. M., & Tiemann, P. W. (1969). *Scripts for really understanding concepts or in frumious pursuit of the Jabberwock*. Chicago, IL: Tiemann Associates.

Mill, J. S. (1843). *A system of logic, ratiocinative and inductive: Being a connected view of the principles of evidence, and the methods of scientific investigation.* (Vol. 1). London, UK. John W. Parker.

Moore, J. (1986). Direct instruction: A model of instructional design. *Educational Psychology*, 6, 201–229.

Smith, P. L., & Ragan, T. J. (1999). *Instructional design* (2nd ed.). Upper Saddle River, NJ: Merrill.

Tennyson, R., & Christensen, D. (1986, April). *Memory theory and design of intelligent learning systems.* Paper presented at the American Educational Research Association, San Francisco, CA.

Tennyson, R. D., & Cochiarella, M. J. (1986). An empirically based instructional design theory for teaching concepts. *Review of Educational Research*, 56, 40–71.

Tennyson, R., & Park, O. (1984). Computer-based adaptive instructional systems: A review of empirically based models. *Machine-Mediated Learning*, 1(2), 129–153.

Section II

WHO SHOULD RECEIVE AND PROVIDE SPECIAL EDUCATION?

It is, of course, immediately obvious that a foremost part of the answer to the question about who is involved in special education is, "the students." Special educators care about their students. Are they the right students, though? Another really important component is the teachers and prospective teachers who provide services for those students (and their families). In addition, there are many other people and professionals—school administrators, psychologists, speech-language pathologists, and more—involved in special education. In this section, we can only discuss some of the issues related to *who*. Here are some of the questions one ought to consider in thinking about the *who* issue.

- Who should be eligible for special education?
- How should eligibility be determined?
- How do educators ensure that students with disabilities who have cultural or linguistic differences get appropriate services?
- How do educators make sure that cultural or linguistic differences do not mistakenly cause students to be identified as having disabilities?
- What specialized knowledge and skills are needed to provide special education? Can all teachers be expected to be capable of serving students who need special education?
- What specialized training should be required of teachers who plan to teach students with disabilities?

Getting to Know Melissa K. Driver

 My first job working in a school setting was not as a teacher. After Hurricane Katrina I worked with Americorps as a disaster relief volunteer, reopening schools throughout the New Orleans Recovery School District. This experience exposed me to our country's achievement gap, as well as the critical shortage of classroom teachers in Louisiana. I entered the teaching profession through Teach For America (TFA), and was assigned to teach special education at an over-age middle school program in Baton Rouge, LA. My students had all been retained in school at least twice, and had horrifyingly low reading levels. A typical student of mine was 16 years old, in eighth grade, and reading on a third grade level. I'm still trying to wrap my head around how so many students fell, and continue to fall, through the cracks of our public school systems.

In my first year of teaching I assumed the role of the special education school site facilitator, worked collaboratively with general educators and administrators, struggled tremendously, and fell in love with teaching literacy. During my time in the classroom, I witnessed the inequity students experienced that fell along stark lines of race, socio-economic status, and disability labels. These experiences led me to work as an instructional coach, supporting teachers during their first two years with a focus on elementary and special education.

After two years coaching teachers, I felt I needed to learn more about evidence-based practices and effective school models. This desire brought me to graduate school, where I am studying as a Ph.D. student in special education. I am very interested in teacher preparation and ongoing support, particularly in preparing teachers to work with students who have disabilities, racially and culturally diverse populations, in low-income communities, and in chronically low-performing schools.

7

WHO SHOULD RECEIVE AND PROVIDE
SPECIAL EDUCATION?

Barbara Bateman, John Wills Lloyd, Melody Tankersley, & Melissa K. Driver

Who should receive special education? Three answers are possible: all children, no children, or some children. If the premise is that some children should receive special education, then these questions shift to: Who are the children being served? Who is deciding if and how they should be served? Who should serve them, and in what capacity?

Questions about "who" are central to the field of special education and are closely connected to questions about the what, where, and how of service delivery. In this introduction we briefly address core issues associated with "who" in special education that are discussed further and expanded on in the subsequent chapters. First, we provide a brief overview of the criteria used to identify students for special education. Then, we give a historical perspective on disability terminology. Next, we call attention to issues of disproportionality and the overrepresentation of culturally and linguistically diverse students in special education. Finally, we highlight the ongoing discussion over who is qualified to deliver services and instruction to students with disabilities.

ELIGIBILITY AND IDENTIFICATION:
THE PROBLEM OF CRITERIA

When considering "who" should receive special education services, we first ponder the criteria used to identify individuals with a disability. Definitions and eligibility criteria are commonly used to determine the eligibility for services. One position people take on this matter is to promote "full inclusion." Full inclusion refers to a service delivery model in which students with disabilities receive all of their instruction in general education settings. Some advocates consider general education settings to be the Least Restrictive Environment (LRE) for students with disabilities. Some advocates of full inclusion and others also suggest that labeling of children is neither necessary nor appropriate (e.g., Lauchlan & Boyle, 2007).

An alternative perspective is that "all children are special," and everyone should receive special education. To advocate special education for all children is to focus on the undeniable desirability of program individualization. An education tailored to fit each child's unique needs might be ideal, yet the realities of school environments are often not conducive to this notion.

Some who believe special education should be abolished altogether may not intend that no child should ever receive special education, but rather that special education as a "separate entity" which may be stigmatizing needs to become part of, not apart from, general education. Arguably, the most tenable and pragmatic position is that some children need special education (cf. Reynolds, 1991). The question is how should we decide which children ought to receive special education services. What ought the criteria be?

Given that no system for identifying the children to be served by special education will be perfect, should we err on the side of over- or under-identification? Is it better to risk stigmatizing a child or failing to provide a needed service? Is it possible to provide special education with no risk of stigma or other harm to the student? Is it legitimate to ask, as part of the identification process, what would be the consequence to the child of not providing special education?

CRITERIA

In disability related areas we find different definitions and criteria are employed for different purposes. For example, Section 504 of the Rehabilitation Act of 1973 and the Americans with Disabilities Act are intended to protect certain people from discrimination based on disability. For the purpose of protecting people from discrimination, a disabled person is defined as one who "has a mental or physical impairment which substantially limits one or more major life activities" (IDEA, 34 C.F.R. 104.3(j)(2)(i)). The definition of children eligible to receive a free appropriate public education (FAPE) under the Individuals with Disabilities Education Act (IDEA) is significantly different as we discuss later.

Another criterion which some have suggested is that to receive special education a child must be able to benefit from the services (see Garda, 2004, for a discussion). Do you believe that is a reasonable requirement? Because that requirement is not in IDEA, courts will not employ it. Should schools be required to provide services in the absence of evidence the student can benefit from the services?

SHIFTING CRITERIA

Special education costs more per child to provide than does general education. In times of financial stress school districts face difficult budget choices and special education is a tempting target. Pressure increases to reduce the numbers of students in special education. This can happen either by explicitly changing the criteria or by applying existing criteria more restrictively. Reducing the amount or type of services a child is deemed to need is another way to reduce per capita costs, as is increasing the caseloads of professionals. Do you believe it is fair and appropriate for budget problems to result in fewer children being identified as disabled or fewer services being provided to those who are identified?

Another force that can change criteria, definitions, and even the terminology of disability is political correctness. When a term acquires a negative connotation it is often replaced. A recent example is that mental retardation has now become intellectual disability. In 2010, federal legislation made this change in U.S. law, and President Barack Obama signed the documents in the presence of Rosa Marcellino, a youngster who has Down Syndrome and after whom the law had been named because she had championed the efforts to enact the changes in her home state of Maryland (Diament, 2010). As discussed later, some criteria have also shifted, along with terminology. Is it appropriate that we try to use increasingly positive language in the context of disability? Or does the effort itself seem demeaning or derogatory?

A BRIEF HISTORY OF "WHO" TERMINOLOGY

Over the last century significant changes have occurred in the terminology and the criteria used to diagnose disabilities. For example, until recently an intellectual disability was called mental retardation and before that, mental deficiency and feeble-mindedness, among other terms. As recently as the 1960s an IQ of 85 or below was considered indicative of mental retardation. The definition has since evolved to one with more emphasis on functional behaviors and the environmental context. Less emphasis is placed on IQ now and, when it is used, only IQs below 70–75 are considered to be significantly low. Clinical judgment plays a larger role than earlier.

The term "specific learning disability" has also undergone recent change. Initially, IDEA defined it primarily by a severe discrepancy between estimated intellectual potential and achievement. Most states further defined discrepancy as a 15–22 point standard score difference and some (e.g., New York and Hawai'i) used that as the sole criterion. The courts have ruled such reliance is improper. IDEA now allows data from response-to-intervention or instruction (RTI) as a factor in diagnosing specific learning disabilities. In her chapter, Lembke provides insight on how student data are collected and used in RTI to make decisions about educational services and disability classification.

A revised definition of autism was proposed for the newest version of the Diagnostic and Statistical Manual of the American Psychiatric Association (DSM-5). The proposed definition of Autism Spectrum Disorder encompasses previously separated diagnosis of autistic disorder, Asperger's disorder, childhood disintegrative disorder, and pervasive developmental disorder not otherwise specified. These conditions are now considered to be part of the same spectrum, with different degrees of severity in social communication and repetitive behaviors (American Psychiatric Association, 2013). Some say the change will reduce the number of people diagnosed on the autism spectrum and therefore eligible for services. The evidence is mixed with some researchers (e.g., Huerta, Bishop, Duncan, Hus, & Lord, 2012) saying only small reductions occur and others (e.g., Neal, Matson, & Hattier, 2012) reporting many children may no longer be identified as having autism under DSM-V. Would such a reduction affect IDEA eligibility rates and, if it were to occur, would it be a desirable outcome?

A cautionary statement in DSM-IV, the previous guide that specifies the diagnostic criteria for recognized mental disorders, notes that the inclusion of a diagnostic category in the DSM-IV does not mean that it meets legal or other non-medical criteria for what constitutes a mental disorder or disability. "To each his own" discipline can well be said of definitions of disability. So, it is not surprising that IDEA has its own definitions and criteria for eligibility for special education. Nor is it surprising that the definitions have engendered controversy. The overall eligibility requirement of IDEA is that the child must have a qualifying disability (as defined in IDEA) and as a result of the disability "must need special education and related services" (34 CFR 300.8 (a) (1)).

Few would argue that special education should be provided to children who do not need it. But what does it mean to "need special education?" The IDEA definitions of the specific disabilities that qualify (except for learning disabilities and multiple disabilities) also add that the disability must "adversely affect the child's educational performance." Is "adverse effect on educational performance" to be understood as explanatory of "needs special education" or is it an additional requirement that must be met for eligibility? The adverse effect requirement has been used in many cases to deny IDEA eligibility and services to a child whose academic grades, test scores, or teacher's observations suggested that educational performance was not negatively affected, even though the child had a qualifying disability. This happens especially with students who have emotional disturbance and those who have Asperger's Syndrome (which is presently on the autism spectrum but is slated for possible removal). These students may have serious social, behavioral, and emotional issues while performing reasonably well academically. Is it appropriate to deny eligibility and services to them?

The term "educational performance" has different meanings to different people. Some believe it encompasses anything that contributes to living a productive and fulfilling life, but others believe that only academics are "educational performance." The Federal Second Circuit Court of Appeals, for example, is adamant that educational performance is strictly limited to academic progress and that adverse effect on any other areas is irrelevant to IDEA eligibility (see, e.g., *C.B. v. Dept. of Education of the City of New York, 52 IDELR 121 [2nd Cir. 2009]*).

Garda (2004) provided an extensive legal analysis (72 pp., 739 footnotes) of the terms "adverse effect," "educational performance," and "needs special education and related services." He concluded, contrary to the Second Circuit, that: (1) "adverse effect" means any adverse effect, however slight; (2) "educational performance" means any area addressed by the state curriculum or tracked by the state, such as attendance or behavior; and (3) "needs special education" means that a child's performance in any area in the curriculum or tracked by the state is failing, poor, or below average (p. 512). If Garda's analyses were accepted by hearing officers and courts, substantially more children would be found eligible under IDEA than is the case now. Would this be desirable?

Eligibility controversies exist within certain disability categories as well as across the general eligibility criteria. Under U.S. law, three categories of disability have proven to be most problematic: specific learning disabilities, emotional disturbance, and other health impaired (viz., ADHD). These disabilities are less visible and more subjective than others, hence more readily subject to dispute and to change.

DISPROPORTIONALITY—RACE-ETHNICITY AND GENDER IN SPECIAL EDUCATION

Should action be taken to insure that the proportion of various sub-groups of the special education population to be proportionate to their numbers in the general population? A numerically disproportionate relationship between a sub-group in relation to the population to which the sub-group belongs is common in our society. White males, for example, have held a hugely disproportionate number of seats on the U.S. Supreme Court. The gender balance of many occupations is disproportionate. Racial disproportion is rampant in athletics, and so forth.

The 30th Annual Report to Congress reports on disproportions in disability categories for the year 2006. Compared to all other racial-ethnic groups combined (1) American Indians and Alaska natives are twice as likely to be labeled deaf-blind; (2) African Americans are more than twice (2.28) as likely to be labeled emotionally disturbed and almost three times (2.75) more likely to be labeled intellectually disabled; (3) Whites are one and a half times (1.47) more likely to be labeled other health impaired (probably ADHD-related); and (4) Asian Americans and Pacific Islanders are only one half (.51) as likely as all others to be identified as disabled.

Should we be disturbed by evidence of such disproportionality? Should we be disturbed by some findings of disproportionality but not by others? These are among the questions that Klingner, Moore, Davidson, Boelé, Boardman, Figueroa, Annamma, and Sager consider in Chapter 8. Special educators have long been aware of disproportionate numbers of some racial and ethnic groups in special education. The disproportion of males to females served by special education has also long been noted. However, this gender disparity has raised little concern among parents or professionals, especially when compared to the concern over racial-ethnic disproportions.

Racial disproportion in athletics is well known and accepted. However, the situation in special education is different. The under-representation of Asian Americans in programs for intellectual disabilities and learning disabilities is not generally considered problematic, but the over-representation of African Americans, American Indians, and others in these programs and in those for students with emotional and behavioral disorders is viewed with substantial concern. Is this difference as simple as we view athletics favorably and special education less so? If, in fact, special education is viewed negatively, why are we seemingly indifferent to the gender disproportion in special education, where males outnumber females by 2 or 3:1? In the categories of learning disabilities and emotional disturbance about 75 percent of the students are male. If special education is truly viewed as negative, how likely is it that we would ignore this disproportion?

Does whether disproportion is viewed positively, neutrally, or negatively depend upon how the activity or service itself is viewed? Does it depend on possible different needs of the sub-group? Or on other contributing factors such as historical, cultural, sociological, or inherent causes of the disproportion? On what bases do we, and should we, determine whether differential treatment of disparate groups is or is not equitable?

Perhaps the most important and provocative question of all is what actions should be taken if and when it is determined that gender and racial-ethnic disproportionality should be abolished and proportionality established? What issues would be raised by these actions? Should schools adhere to strict limits—quotas—on how many students of each gender or ethnic group may receive special education for students with, for example, emotional and behavioral disorders?

WHO SHOULD PROVIDE SPECIAL EDUCATION?

In an ideal world we would have a constant and adequate supply of qualified, effective special education providers for the 6 million children who receive special education services each year. What factors are operative in the effectiveness of a provider? Billingsley (2011) described three interactive factors that influence special education teacher quality and effectiveness: (1) professional knowledge and skills (initial preparation, induction, in-service professional development); (2) conditions of service (work context and assignment) and (3) shortage-surplus (demand, supply, and retention).

Economists Chetty, Friedman, and Rockoff (2011) conducted a longitudinal study of the long-term effects of teachers on 2.5 million children. They asked whether teachers' impact on students' test scores was a valid measure of teacher effectiveness as measured by the relationship between student test gain scores and their adult outcomes. They found that students who had at least one teacher between fourth and eighth grades who raised test scores significantly were more likely to attend college, earned higher salaries, lived in higher SES areas, and saved more for retirement than those who did not have such a teacher. They concluded that effective teachers create significant economic value and the teacher's impact on student test scores is a non-biased and useful measure of teacher effectiveness. If this study were replicated using special education students and teachers do you believe the student adult outcomes would be similarly related to test score gains or to teacher effectiveness?

Measuring the effectiveness and the impact of special education teachers may be different and more difficult than doing so with general education teachers. Few evaluation systems have the capacity to differentiate among specific types of teachers, such as special education teachers. More than half of school districts use their own evaluations. The majority of districts have contractual agreements that prevent them from modifying the evaluation process for special education teachers, even though half of them believe the process should be different (Holdheide, Goe, Craft, & Reschly, 2010). How should special education teachers be evaluated?

In what they described as the first quantitative study of the relationship between teacher training and disabled students' achievement, Feng and Sass (2010) reported that: (1) in-service professional development was not related to increased student achievement; (2) student test score gains increase over the first few years of special education teachers' careers; (3) special education teachers who have advanced degrees produce larger student gains, especially in reading; and (4) extensive pre-service training for special education reading teachers is effective.

The last finding is consistent with a synthesis by Darling-Hammond and Ducommon (2000) of research on teacher quality and student achievement which found the strongest correlates of student reading and math achievement are teacher preparation and certification. Some available research suggests that graduates of extensive special education preparation programs are more likely to promote student achievement than are fast track and alternative certification preparation programs (see, e.g., Nougaret, Scruggs, & Mastropieri, 2005). The latter programs can actually result in higher teacher attrition and lower student achievement.

Special education is faced with an acute and continuing teacher shortage and at the same time with the desirability of having highly trained and experienced teachers. Resolving the dilemma poses difficult challenges and choices in the future. Some suggest that all special education students can and should be educated in general education classes. What does this position suggest about preparation of teachers?

CONCLUSION

A central component of special education is that each student receives a free appropriate education, one that is individualized to support his or her unique strengths and needs. To ensure we are providing the highest quality education to students with disabilities, we must continue to ask: Who are the children being served? Who is deciding if and how they should be served? Who should serve them, and in what capacity? The subsequent chapters are dedicated to addressing these questions.

MELISSA K. DRIVER'S SUGGESTIONS
FOR FURTHER READING

Boe, E. E., Shin, S., & Cook, L. H. (2007). Does teacher preparation matter for beginning teachers in either special or general education? *The Journal of Special Education, 41*, 158–170.

Brownell, M. T., Sindelar, P. T., Kiely, M. T., & Danielson, L. C. (2010). Special education teacher quality and preparation: Exposing foundations, constructing a new model. *Exceptional Children, 76*, 357–377.

Shealey, M., McHatton, P., & Wilson, V. (2011). Moving beyond disproportionality: The role of Culturally Responsive Teaching in special education. *Teaching Education, 22*, 377–396.

Sindelar, P. T., Brownell, M. T., & Billingsley, B. (2010). Special education teacher education research: Current status and future directions. *Teacher Education and Special Education, 33*, 8–24.

Sullivan, A. L. (2011). Disproportionality in special education identification and placement of English Language Learners. *Exceptional Children, 77*, 317–334.

REFERENCES

American Psychiatric Association (2013). *Highlights of changes from DSM-IV-TR to DSM 5.* 1–19. American Psychiatric Publishing.

Billingsley, B. S. (2011). Factors in influencing special education teacher quality and effectiveness. In J. M. Kauffman & D. P. Hallahan (Eds.), *Handbook of special education* (pp. 391–405). New York: Routledge.

Chetty, R., Friedman, J. N., & Rockoff, J. E. (Dec. 2011). *The long-term impacts of teachers: Teacher value-added and student outcomes in adulthood.* Retrieved from http://abso.r.c.fas.harvard.edu/chetty/value_added.pdf.

Darling-Hammond, L., & Ducommon, C. E. (2000). Teacher quality and student achievement: A review of state policy evidence. *Education policy analysis archives, 8*(1), 1–44.

Diament, M. (2010). Obama signs bill replacing "mental retardation" with "intellectual disability" [Web log message]. Retrieved from http://www.disabilityscoop.com/2010/10/05/obama-signs-rosas-law/10547.

Feng, L., & Sass, T. R. (2010). What makes special-education teachers special? *Calder Working Paper 49.* Retrieved from http://www.urban.org/publications/1001435.html.

Garda, R. A. (2004). Untangling eligibility requirements under the individuals with disabilities education act. *Missouri Law Review, 69*, 441–512.

Holdheide, L. R., Goe, L., Croft, A. & Reschly, D. J. (2010). Challenges in evaluating special education teachers and English language learner specialists. *National Comprehensive Center for Teacher Quality.* Retrieved from http://www.tq.source.org/publications/July2010Brief.pdf.

Huerta, M., Bishop, S. L., Duncan, A., Hus, V., & Lord, C. (2012). Application of DSM-5 criteria for autism spectrum disorder to three samples of children with DSM-IV diagnoses of pervasive developmental disorders. *The American Journal of Psychiatry, 169*, 1056–1064.

Individuals with Disabilities Education Act of 2000, 34 C.F.R. 104.3(j)(2)(i).

Lauchlan, F., & Boyle, C. (2007). Is the use of labels in special education helpful? *Support for Learning, 22*, 36–42.

Neal, D., Matson, J. L., & Hattier, M. A. (2012). A comparison of diagnostic criteria on the Autism Spectrum Disorder Observation for Children (ASD-OC). *Developmental Neurorehabilitation, 15*, 329–335.

Nougaret, A., Scruggs, T. E., & Mastropieri, M. (2005). Does teacher education produce better special education teachers? *Exceptional Children, 71*, 217–229.

Reynolds, M. C. (1991). Classification and labeling. In J. W. Lloyd, N. N. Singh, & A. C. Repp (Eds.), *The regular education initiative: Alternative perspectives on concepts, issues, and* models (pp. 29–41). Sycamore, IL: Sycamore.

Getting to Know Janette Klingner, in memoriam

 Janette Klingner was the oldest of five siblings and began her career as an educator holding "nursery school" for her brothers and the other kids in their California neighborhood. She spent 10 years as a special education teacher before becoming a professor of bilingual special education. As a professor, Janette prided herself on being a mentor, touching the lives of her students through her dedication and support. Her mother noted that Janette "just gave herself to everyone, in everything that she did." For those of us who were lucky enough to be close to Janette, we saw how she lived her unending passion to address the inequities in education. Janette passed away in 2014 after a battle with cancer. She was a generous friend, mentor, and researcher whose legacy will continue to inform teachers and researchers for years to come.

Getting to Know Brooke Moore

My mother was a teacher, so it may seem logical that I, too, went into education. But my plan was to be a thriving artist. After several years working long hours with low pay as a graphic designer, my mother quietly suggested that I consider teaching. I enrolled in an alternative program, and selected special education. At the time, I believed it would be rewarding, and after what I had been doing, I felt a strong desire to make a difference. I was not disappointed. During my 12 years as a public school, elementary and middle school special education teacher in Texas and Utah, I was rewarded in my work. And, I hope that I did make a difference in the lives of my students. Of course, I made some mistakes and learned a lot along the way, but I also cherish the amazing experiences I have gained from being a special educator.

Getting to Know Anne O. Davidson

As a child, my mother led by example, teaching me that everyone is a capable individual regardless of traits others may perceive as limitations or disabilities. My interest in educational advocacy expanded during my years as a special education teacher, when I saw how extensively schools labeled and segregated students perceived as having a disability or learning difference. I continue to follow the example of equity and respect I was raised with by advocating for the students who are continually marginalized in schools, and the best practices for supporting the learning needs of all students in inclusive classrooms.

Getting to Know Amy Boelé

In my sophomore year of college, I was contemplating my education and career options. Toggling back and forth between elementary education and a degree in psychology/counseling, I found myself wanting to take another route. In a conversation with my mother, a kindergarten teacher, she suggested special education. I took her advice and continued on to earn my undergraduate degree with a double major in K-12 special education and elementary education. Throughout college, I worked as a caretaker for adults and children with developmental disabilities, assisting them with daily living skills and activities. After graduating, I taught high school students with learning disabilities, emotional and behavioral disorders, and autism for three years. I then relocated to a different state and secured a position teaching elementary students with special needs. In my work now, I strive to work toward valuing the voices and experiences of students with special needs.

Getting to Know Alison Boardman

A family friend was a special education teacher at my elementary school. I would visit her classroom and her students, amazed by the colorful displays of books, letters, and the sand trays she used to teach reading. It struck me that I never saw her students in my own class. I didn't know to ask why. But, later, in my own special education classroom, I couldn't stop asking why my students weren't more involved in their general education classrooms and why some seemed invisible to their classroom teachers. I continue to work towards increasing awareness, relationships, and the implementation of sound instructional strategies that will allow all students to succeed in whatever learning environment is the best fit for them.

Getting to Know Roberto Figueroa

I began my career in Oaxaca, Mexico during college, teaching English to child criminal offenders. After graduating, I taught in a bilingual preschool program, where I became the lead teacher after a few months. After that year, I faced a decision between going into special education or school psychology. I went with special education because it would allow me to forge meaningful connections with a diverse range of students over the course of an entire year. I worked in middle schools in Los Angeles and Seattle, collaborating with teachers on all core subjects for general and special education students. Because I was able to work in inclusion schools, I was able to collaborate with general education teachers, parents, and students to make sure that every student of mine found success. Each year brought a new appreciation of the work that teachers and students are capable of.

Getting to Know Subini Ancy Annamma

 Working with students with learning, emotional, and behavioral disabilities is something I have always loved. Using pedagogy rooted in their lives, I found that these students were bright and savvy, and they taught me much about resilience in the face of inequities. When I worked in a large, urban high school and juvenile incarceration settings, I realized that most of my classroom was made up of students of color and began to wonder why. When I entered the academy, I committed to studying the relationship between race and disability status in urban education, collaborating with teachers and students to identify exemplary educational practices. All of my work focuses on increasing access to equitable education for historically marginalized students, particularly children identified with disabilities.

Getting to Know Nicole Sager

I entered kindergarten in the U.S. after having lived in South America for three years. After hearing me speak English with a heavy Spanish accent, my teachers placed me in the "slow" group. Spoken and unspoken messages led me to quickly wipe out my accent and my childhood consisted of multiple series of Spanish attrition and revitalization. As an adult who loves languages I am extremely grateful for my childhood bilingualism and am passionate about encouraging parents, educators, and children to take pride in and maintain their linguistic and cultural heritage.

8

CULTURAL AND LINGUISTIC DIVERSITY
IN SPECIAL EDUCATION

Janette Klingner, Brooke Moore, Anne O. Davidson, Amy Boelé,
Alison Boardman, Roberto Figueroa, Subini Ancy Annamma, & Nicole Sager

The numbers of culturally and linguistically diverse students in schools continue to grow (Aud et al., 2011). Culturally and linguistically diverse students are more likely to attend segregated schools than in the past and more likely to attend high-poverty schools. They are also more likely to be overrepresented in special education placements (Artiles & Bal, 2008) and in disciplinary actions (Skiba et al., 2011). This is especially true of African-American males.

English Language Learners (ELLs)[1] are the fastest growing student population in the United States (National Clearinghouse on English Language Acquisition, 2011). Approximately 7.6 percent of the ELLs across the U.S. have a disability label (National Center for Education Statistics, 2009), although placement rates vary a great deal within and across districts (Artiles, Rueda, Salazar, & Higareda, 2005; Sullivan, 2011). The eligibility process for determining whether an ELL has a disability must establish that the difficulties the student is experiencing are *not* primarily due to language acquisition. Yet, figuring this out is challenging. Some ELLs are erroneously identified as having a learning disability (LD) and misplaced in special education while others are overlooked and do not receive the special education support that could benefit them.

> "Culturally and linguistically diverse students are more likely to attend segregated schools than in the past and more likely to attend high-poverty schools. They are also more likely to be overrepresented in special education placements and in disciplinary actions. This is especially true of African-American males."

In this chapter, we present eight case studies, each drawn from our first-hand experiences as special education teachers. The cases reflect a variety of disability categories, ages, grade levels, ethnicities, and situations. Some are ELLs; others are not. Each case conveys an important lesson learned by the author; we report them in first person, so watch as the first person pronoun changes (indicated by our initials) in each case from one of us to another. These lessons have had a profound impact on us and affected our practice to this day. We hope that they will influence your understanding of the complexity and importance of cultural and linguistic diversity factors in special education.

GERARDO: FROM SILENCE TO "SCIENTIFIC GURU"

Gerardo was entering third grade when I (BM) first met him. Though initially very quiet, I soon came to know a chatty, enthusiastic young man over the three years he was part of my pull-out special education reading-language arts classes. Gerardo was identified as an ELL and classified through special education with a specific LD in reading-writing. Gerardo's family was from the Coahuila region of Mexico, but lived locally on a dairy where his father had a steady but low-paying job that qualified Gerardo for free or reduced lunch status at school. While Gerardo's father spoke English fluently, his mother predominantly spoke Spanish. Gerardo's English language acquisition was at the intermediate stage. He communicated well verbally, yet he continued to struggle with literacy in both English and Spanish.

Gerardo attended Jasper Intermediate School, where I taught, which housed all third through fifth grade students of a mid-sized town located in a rural, agrarian county in central Texas. Of the 525 students at Jasper Intermediate, 70 percent were classified as White, 26 percent as Hispanic, and 4 percent as other. Forty-nine percent of students qualified for free or reduced lunch, 32 percent were identified as English language learners and 21 percent as at-risk or in need of special education services.

For the three years I served as Gerardo's special education teacher in a pull-out resource classroom, I used a variety of "evidence-based" reading-writing interventions and programs to focus on word study (Wilson Language Training, Words Their Way), oral reading fluency (Read Naturally, Six-Minute Solutions), reading comprehension (Collaborative Strategic Reading, PALs), and writing (Self-Regulated Strategy Development, 6-Trait Writing Instruction). On the Dynamic Indicators of Basic Early Literacy Skills (DIBELS) oral reading fluency measure, Gerardo demonstrated a growth of 51 words per minute over the three years in my class and on the Woodcock Johnson Reading Mastery (WJRM) test, he improved his word identification by 26 words and his word attack (sounding out nonsense words) by four words. Gerardo's growth on these measures did not indicate a significant gain in reading skills. However, his spirit was strong and he remained persistent throughout his time with me, working diligently to improve his literacy skills.

Although I was Gerardo's teacher, it was Gerardo who taught me an incredible lesson in his fifth grade year. When Gerardo came to Jasper Intermediate, he came with needs that his third and fourth grade general education teachers were either not able or not willing to address. According to Berry (2006) such teachers are "pathognomonic," as they consider a student's disability to be a stable characteristic that is better served in a setting removed from the general education classroom. In such classrooms, Gerardo had the ability to disappear. He was incredibly silent and seemed to dissolve into his chair. Rarely did he participate and often quietly asked to go to his ELL or special education classrooms for help—places where he felt safe and could be himself. Gerardo's perceived "problems," as defined by his general education teachers, were too profound to attend to in the general education setting. Gerardo was at Tier 3 in the school's RTI system: he came to me for the language arts block, one and a half hours of intensive remedial support. Yet, Gerardo was destined to meet Mrs. Patterson, his fifth grade home-room teacher.

After two years of quality time spent intensively exploring phonemes, digraphs, roots, affixes, and anomalies of the English language, I also learned a few idiosyncrasies about Gerardo. Gerardo loved animals. He knew the most obscure facts about any animal you could imagine. I capitalized on that knowledge, bringing in any text I could find that might hold his interest for deeper word study analysis and repeated readings. Being predominately monolingual, I searched for cognate lists and pestered his ELL teacher to help me find ways to connect his interest in animals with learning to read in English. Mrs. Patterson, and Gerardo's dad, found that connection—and Gerardo's lesson—when she introduced a unit on mammals in science.

Mammal in Spanish is *mamífero*, but more importantly, a mammal has mammary glands which produce milk. Dairy cows produce milk; so do mothers—mommies (*Mamí*). The dairy industry is acutely focused on bovine mammary glands, considering that the glands produce the milk that also provides income. And, Gerardo was keenly interested in dairy cows, particularly newborn calves, given that his father often had Gerardo help him take care of the newborn calves on the dairy where he worked. Gerardo's lesson to teach us all resided within the word *mammal*.

Mrs. Patterson was a believer in reciprocal teaching. She was also what Berry (2006) described as an "interventionist" teacher, one who believes a disability to be a barrier to learning but also believes the child can be successful in the regular classroom. She grouped students heterogeneously when she taught science or social studies. To support heterogeneous groups, Mrs. Patterson did not allow her students to be pulled out during science and social studies. She needed them all—and she was determined to teach them all. In early February, her fifth graders were to learn all about mammals. On that day in class, she assigned a reading to groups where they read together and then discussed in small groups what they learned. Suddenly, the quietest student in the class—the voice of one who never participated—emerged in the discussion. In a conversation later described by Mrs. Patterson, Gerardo's knowledge of dairy cows (*mamífero*), his ability to break words apart to study them, his experience with English/Spanish cognates, and his passion for the topic took his group's conversation to a new depth which then spread throughout the class. First, as Gerardo's peers in his group read the passage aloud (Gerardo never volunteered to read aloud), he heard words that captured his attention. In the text, he recognized word parts—"mam"— that connected to his understanding of what his peers were saying—mammals produce milk. He became alert—they were talking about something he knew. Gerardo spoke—he shared—he started to push back. "No, mammals are like mothers— *mamífero*—they produce food for their young. They do not have to find it for them." Mrs. Patterson recognized Gerardo's expertise and brought in readings that would capitalize on his knowledge. In class he pointed out cognates—gestation or *gestación*. He taught his classmates how to break words apart to understand them: circulatory system—a system in the mammalian body that circulates the blood. He attacked the word "lactate," determined that breaking it apart would provide insight when Mrs. Patterson initially thought it best just to explain it. Instead, she agreed and allowed Gerardo to lead a class lesson on what it could mean. With her help, they looked up the suffix "ate"—to make a word into verb (not particularly helpful). They looked up the root "lact"—it means milk. Added together, the word lactate means the action (verb) of producing milk. Gerardo was right—you could break a word apart and study it to figure out its meaning.

At the end of the mammalian unit, Gerardo's status in his class had changed. No longer was he the silent Hispanic kid who quietly left whenever he could. He was Gerardo, a scientific guru among fifth graders with knowledge that awed and amazed. Not only did he know science stuff, but he knew big words and what they meant and he knew words in another language. How cool was that? Gerardo's diverse ways of knowing became recognized beyond just his peer level. Mrs. Patterson shared what she gleaned from Gerardo with *her* peers. By contributing knowledge to his peer group, Gerardo gained status as an equal (Cohen & Lotan, 1995). His peers benefitted from his knowledge and his participation was seen as valuable and not as interference to the group process (Slavin, 1996; 2011).

The lesson Gerardo taught us was simple. Diversity is not something to be remediated: It is to be valued and recognized (Annamma, Boelé, Moore, & Klingner, 2013). Even though Gerardo was still struggling to learn the English language in all its intricacies alongside having a reading disability, he brought to the classroom an amazing set of tools that enhanced his own learning as well as the learning of his peers. What was gained was immeasurable. We must include diversity in classrooms by capitalizing on unique ways of knowing and different ways of thinking. What we gain can be profound.

AMEENA: THE VALUE OF RECIPROCAL RELATIONSHIPS WITH PARENTS

Ameena, a third grade student in my (AD) small, mixed-grade elementary class of seven students, had a bright, magnetic personality with a jovial demeanor. If she recognized you passing by, she would look up, smile, clasp her hands and open her small arms to invite a hug or blow a kiss, or try to make you laugh, making it difficult to walk by without engaging. From Nepal, her parents spoke Nepali with Ameena at home and fluent English at school while Ameena was learning English and American Sign Language in school. Ameena was identified with a moderate cognitive delay, a hearing impairment in one ear, and a speech impairment. She also had a worsening muscle condition that presented significant physical challenges when she attempted to use her walker. Yet she remained one of the most active, well-liked, and charismatic students in the school. She loved to engage everyone using all of her language modalities, verbal, sign and gesture, and her new digital communication device.

> "Diversity is not something to be remediated: it is to be valued and recognized."

Our self-contained school provided specialized support for students in kindergarten to age 21 with significant cognitive, physical, and medical needs. In a large public school district, our school had 16 mixed-grade classrooms and extensive staff to support every student in the building. School events and therapies were integrated with regular lessons and activities. If Ameena was inexpressive or unexcitable, it was generally a sign that she was not feeling well. She could make a sad face and point to what hurt to let us know if she was feeling ill. The only other time Ameena didn't seem to be excited and eager to engage was when she was using her walker to move around the school.

Due to her medical condition, the muscles in her legs were getting tighter as she grew, making walking increasingly difficult. Ameena's parents reported she often crawled to get around the house and said that their goal was for Ameena to walk. The IEP team responded by including this as a learning goal. Ameena's family traveled home to Nepal annually, spending a week or more at a specialized clinic focused on walking. Although Ameena's family highly valued walking as an essential skill, Ameena did not want to walk. She would smile, focus on her talker and work her hardest to request "music class," but her walker was met with a grimace, crossed arms and a "NO!" In her walker, a 200 yard transition would take 10 or 15 minutes, every step slow and difficult, every person an engaging distraction.

By the time Ameena got to "specials" (i.e., music, art, physical education, etc.), she had missed a significant portion of learning time. Class time was traded for walking time but the task was so difficult that she was too tired to focus when she arrived. Though she transitioned around 10 times a day, spending upwards of 2 hours walking, I saw no improvement in her resistance. Ameena's therapists reported that her walking would continue to regress as she encountered each new growth spurt. As her special education teacher, I had legal and ethical obligations to support her progress towards achieving the physical, cognitive, and mental goals on her IEP, including building independence. I was concerned that the challenge of walking was presenting a barrier to her accomplishing other goals. She was not building independence with her walking because of her worsening physical condition and she was missing extensive learning time each day.

As an advocate for all of Ameena's needs, I had to contemplate how to address this dilemma in a collaborative conversation with her parents. During previous years, Ameena's parents had been resistant to the idea of even discussing a wheelchair because walking was their focus. I explored Ameena's goals, successes, and challenges with her IEP team. We discussed Ameena's goals in reading, writing, and math, speech using her digital device, and independent life skills in addition to the goal of walking, and how walking was cutting into Ameena's energy and time needed to focus on her other goals. Clearly walking was important but Ameena needed an alternative for some transitions that would preserve the time and energy needed to progress on her other goals as well.

I prepared documentation on Ameena's progress, or lack thereof, on her many goals as well as an alternative support that would maintain the walking practice that had been such an essential value for her parents. By understanding how important the idea of walking and the annual trips to Nepal were for Ameena's family and the history of the context within the school, I was able to facilitate a collaborative conversation among the whole team, including Ameena's parents. Instead of suggesting that Ameena switch to a wheelchair, we discussed the purposes of her goals, of which walking was only one, and the other goals the parents wanted to prioritize.

By discussing Ameena's goals and progress and examining time and energy barriers, the conversation naturally led the team to explore when walking was purposeful and when possible alternatives might be preferable. If Ameena left one class earlier to begin her transition, she would have more time in the next class but at the expense of lost time in the first, and she would still be tired. The wheelchair idea came out of a collaborative conversation of strategic support for success rather than as a sacrifice of the walking goal that Ameena's parents valued as essential. Using the wheelchair strategically, Ameena would recover her class time and arrive with the energy needed to access her instructional opportunities, and could still use her walker at other times during the day. The whole team was on board with seven walking transitions and six that could be better supported with a wheelchair; and Ameena's parents agreed.

Soon a little blue wheelchair came into Ameena's world. Her jovial antics and tendency to engage everyone did not change, but her reluctance during transitions and progress on her many other goals did change, significantly. With more time and energy in classes, Ameena began to read full sentences instead of just words, type words instead of just finding letters, and even construct multi-word sentences on her digital talker. She was not only increasing her reading and writing skills, she was increasing her expressive communication. Ameena's parents spoke English in school and Nepali at home, and learning to use a complicated, high-tech digital communication device had proven to be a challenge because of Ameena's language learning needs in addition to her physical needs. Now, she was telling us what she learned in class, how she felt or what she wanted with accurate detail on her talker, using words and complex sentences she had never been able to construct before.

As Ameena grew more comfortable with the wheelchair, regaining energy, she began to build strength and to propel herself. For the first time, she was able to transition and navigate around the school independently. While she still focused on walking during certain transitions and therapies, resistance to walking during transitions had turned into eager requests for her wheelchair. Long, slow transitions turned into quick, independent transitions when Ameena would push herself with speed and ease, and fully participate with her class, even when she used her walker for therapeutic activities.

At the end of the year, Ameena's father came in one Friday to pick her up for a doctor's appointment preparing for their trip to Nepal. I walked to the front of the school, Ameena pushing her wheelchair next to me and her father greeted us at the front door. "Can we bring this back on Monday?" he asked. He wanted to take the wheelchair home so they could show the doctor the significant progress Ameena had made. "It's amazing what you have done for her," he told me, recalling how resistant they had been to the idea of a wheelchair in the past. He shared how essential it had been to discuss Ameena's goals to help him understand that a wheelchair could be a strategic support rather than a devaluing of the values and efforts they contributed as parents.

Parents of children with disabilities have rights, of course. They also have feelings and dreams for their children (Harry & Harry, 2010). Our task as special educators is to collaborate, to understand, and to build an educational program that is supportive of achievement, but also valuing of the individual child.

MARTA: LANGUAGE ACQUISITION OR LEARNING DISABILITY?

Marta was tested, identified as having LD, and placed in my (JK) LD class before the beginning of third grade. Her second-grade teacher had referred her for a special education evaluation because of her lack of academic progress. Marta especially struggled with reading. She seemed to know words one day and not the next and to have limited understanding of what she read. Based on the results of their battery of tests, the district's multi-disciplinary team considered Marta to be low in both her home language (Spanish) and English. They believed that she had auditory processing deficits and showed a significant discrepancy between her potential (especially as demonstrated by her non-verbal IQ score of 108 and Woodcock-Johnson Reading Score of 85).

"Our task as special educators is to collaborate, to understand, and to build an educational program that is supportive of achievement, but also valuing of the individual child."

Marta's educational history was mixed. She had been in a bilingual program and received instruction in Spanish in kindergarten, but then her family had moved to a school in the same district without a bilingual program and she had been instructed in English only in first and second grades. Spanish was Marta's stronger language and the language she spoke almost exclusively at home. She had progressed to an intermediate level of English proficiency and could converse in English with her peers. Marta's parents described her as intelligent and very helpful at home with her younger siblings. They said she was motivated to do her homework, but that because they spoke little English, they were unable to provide much assistance. They were concerned that she was not doing better in school, and trusted the school's judgment that Marta needed special education.

When Marta became my student in September, I assessed her in both Spanish and English using the Brigance and made the decision (in collaboration with her family and others) to provide her with Spanish literacy instruction (as well as intensive oral English language instruction). I used the Language Experience Approach with Marta. She dictated stories to me in Spanish that she then learned to read. The words from her stories became the basis for sound and word study. She "took off," so to speak, gaining two grade levels in Spanish reading in just a few months. She expressed a strong interest in also reading in English, and so in February I began English literacy instruction. I continued to use the Language Experience Approach. I also used Direct Instruction System for Teaching Arithmetic and Reading (DISTAR), plus thematic units based on interest. Like all of my students, Marta wrote a lot and "published" her own little books that she shared with others and even displayed in the school's library. By June she was on grade level in English and above grade level in Spanish. We reassessed her eligibility for special education and found that she no longer qualified. She was exited from the program and continued to thrive in fourth grade.

Marta in many ways was like other students I taught, ELLs who had not received consistently strong, appropriate instruction, whose language needs had not been understood, and who had been misdiagnosed as having LD (Klingner, Artiles, & Barletta, 2006). The extent of her progress was unusual, but not her profile. Because so many of my ELLs responded quite favorably to the instruction they received in my special education class, when I had a student who did not respond, I could confidently say that there must be something more going on with that student. This is an important principle that we have learned from our work with diverse students—when most ELLs in a class are thriving and only a few similar peers are struggling, it is the few who stand out as not making progress who are most likely to truly have LD (Artiles & Klingner, 2006; McMaster, Fuchs, & Compton, 2005).

"THEY JUST DON'T CARE ABOUT SCHOOL."

I (Amy B) was in my fourth year of teaching when I started at Truman Elementary School as a special education teacher. My special education teaching partner and I split the caseload of students so that I worked with second, fourth, and sixth graders, and she had the odd grade levels. We shared the kindergarten students between us.

The Hernández family had four children who attended Truman at the time, all of whom were diagnosed with LD: Maria, fourth grade; Antonio, third grade; Ezekiel, second grade; and José, kindergarten. Their father is Latino and their mother is White, and both were in special education while in school. Upon seeing Maria and Ezekiel on my list of students, with their Hispanic sounding last name, I initially assumed that they must be ELLs. Of course, this assumption was made out of my naïveté, or more bluntly, ignorance. They were not in fact ELLs, but were monolingual English speakers. Their father told us of how he had come to the United States as a young boy and had received instruction only in English, to the detriment of his Spanish development, not to mention his personal relationships with his very own family members.

Maria had just been placed in special education at the end of her third grade year. As is the case with many students her age, learning to read grew increasingly difficult as instruction became less about oral reading fluency and more about comprehension. A skilled decoder, Maria struggled with vocabulary and overall comprehension. Math and writing were additional areas requiring support. Despite her academic challenges, Maria played a very important role at school among her siblings. As the eldest of the four, Maria was her brothers' keeper. She ensured that each went to his spot in line before the start of the school day and could be found rounding up her brothers before heading home, making sure that each one had his appropriate materials.

Although I did not work with Antonio my first year, I had heard that he was becoming aware of his LD label, as he became increasingly able to position himself among the ranks of his third grade classmates. Receiving extra time on tests and assignments, being placed in the lowest ability group for all subjects, and frequently calling out "wrong" answers, inadvertently singled him out as one who didn't quite do school the way it is supposed to be done.

Ezekiel, too, was becoming aware of his struggles in second grade. He frequently became overwhelmed. For example, when encouraged to use his knowledge of letters and sounds when writing words he didn't know how to spell, he would revert to drawing pictures or would place his pencil down to cover his eyes and cry. He wanted to get it right, and there were just too many words he didn't know.

José, a kindergartener, was a happy-go-lucky learner with bottomless energy. He had trouble with counting objects and identifying numbers and letters, but he was playful and social, and often very impulsive and inattentive. His teacher frequently reprimanded him for not following her directions. All three of his older siblings would meet him in his kindergarten class at the end of the school day to guide him out.

The Hernández parents were no strangers to the school. Within the first few months of my teaching experience at Truman, Mrs. Hernández had written a letter to the school principal after an incident involving Antonio and another boy in his class. It was handwritten with large, bulky writing and rife with spelling and grammatical errors. She expressed that it seemed as though the teacher had not fully understood the situation, that Antonio should not have been disciplined because he was being bullied and was only sticking up for himself by shoving his classmate. She wrote that the teacher was playing favorites and picking on her son.

Between parent–teacher conferences scheduled at the end of each trimester, along with four IEP meetings to attend throughout the school year, not to mention other classroom and school-wide events, Mr. and Mrs. Hernández had regular appointments at the school. On occasion, they were late or did not show up at all. As a result, the Hernández parents were often the subject of disparaging talk in the teacher's lounge. Negative teacher talk, often occurring informally in the teachers' lounge or hallway, works pervasively to reinforce teachers' beliefs about students and families (Horn & Little, 2010).

I learned that during an initial evaluation meeting one year, Mr. Hernández had expressed his deep concern about placing his child in special education. Both he and his wife had been educated separately from their peers in a secluded section of their respective schools, only having contact with other students with special needs, most of whom had severe needs. Upon moving to the United States during his elementary school years, Mr. Hernández was just learning English. His teachers mistook his second language development process as a disability, and they assumed that in special education, at least he would be getting help. However, his struggles only worsened throughout his schooling career. Mrs. Hernández had been diagnosed with LD and was teased on a daily basis about being "dumb." Thus, these parents did not want history to repeat itself for their four children.

At Truman, Mrs. Hernández was perhaps most infamous for regularly pulling all four children out of school when only one child needed to leave early, perhaps for a doctor's appointment or when becoming ill at school. One staff member shook her head as she said to me, "I don't understand why when one leaves, they all have to leave. They just don't care about school."

They just don't care about school. That was a sentiment that I regrettably allowed to sink, unchallenged, into my subconscious. The cultural bias that I held about what parent involvement entails was discolored by my largely White, middle-class schooling experience, which is pervasive in schools across the nation (Sleeter, 2001). I thought that involved parents come to every meeting. Involved parents support teachers' decisions. Involved parents read with their children at home. Involved parents are invested in homework. Involved parents ensure that their children are at school at all costs.

Everything changed when I visited their home. I am not sure what I expected as I drove up to their house, probably chaos and dysfunction. As I parked the car, Maria and Ezekiel came running out to greet me. They cheerfully escorted me into their house, where I met their mother and brothers. Mrs. Hernández offered me some lemonade, and we sat on the couch in their front room, chatting informally, with all four children chiming in. I looked around and couldn't help but notice how clean and orderly the house was. I learned that each of the kids had daily chores they fulfilled, and each had a special place at the table to complete homework. Maria brought me some children's books from her room and excitedly told me that these were books she read to her brothers. While telling me about her husband's job, Mrs. Hernández explained that the two of them shared one vehicle and had to plan out their respective days so that he could get to his job and she could take the kids to and from school.

A realization came over me, "Of course this family cares about school! How could I have been so presumptuous to think otherwise?" Although they may not have appeared to be the culturally prescribed "involved" parents that I had shallowly expected out of all parents, they were certainly involved in their children's education. Perhaps more importantly, they were involved in supporting each other. It became clear to me that each had a commitment to the family. Their cultural practice was to take care of one another, both in and out of school.

"... taking the time to learn about family strengths and finding ways to build on those strengths as an asset can make an important difference in the lives of all students."

This experience reflects what I came to realize as a challenge to my mainstream cultural expectations of parent and family involvement in schools. It worked to help me to better understand my own vulnerabilities in blindly accepting colleagues' perceptions of families' desires, intents, and attitudes toward school (Harry & Klingner, 2014). Under the surface, this was a family that encountered many barriers in the school setting, from the father's difficulties in learning English to all six family members' academic and social struggles. On top of that, the parents' work demands and financial means prevented them from having full-time availability to attend meetings and events scheduled at the school's discretion. These parents certainly did not need erroneous assumptions that they didn't care about school; nor did they deserve the lack of respect that went along with this mistaken belief. Clearly, they cared, and desired the best educational experiences possible for their children. As Harry and Klingner (2014) noted in their work, taking the time to learn about family strengths and finding ways to build on those strengths as an asset can make an important difference in the lives of all students.

DARNELL: REACHING OUT TO OTHER TEACHERS AS AN ADVOCATE FOR STUDENTS WITH LD

Lakeside Middle school is ethnically diverse and about 90 percent of the students qualify for free or reduced price lunch. Most students are African American, with large Latino and Asian populations. Almost half of the students are ELLs. A few impressions might strike a visitor to Lakeside Middle School. First, the school is run down, carpeting is dingy and frayed and hallways are bare of student work. A garbage can in the hallway is blackened, suggesting that at one time or another a match was tossed in and singed the papers within. Inside classrooms, students share limited materials and many struggle with basic reading, writing, and mathematics.

Students' opportunities to learn are inconsistent. Open one door and you might find students engaged in lively discussions, behind another door you may see a teacher leading an animated discussion on probability and filling the board with complex math symbols while students are attentive and taking notes. Open several other doors and you are met by students chatting with one another, as if their teachers were nothing more than a mild distraction from more interesting aspects of teen life. Teacher turnover is high and each year begins with a roster of several first-year teachers, many on emergency credentials or from alternative certification programs.

This is a case of diversity but the real story is about the inequity of under-resourced schools. Special education classes, particularly in racially diverse settings, often have even fewer supplies than general education classrooms (Parrish, 2002). When I (Alison B) arrived at my classroom in a portable far from the main school building as a special education teacher, there were no supplies. Nothing. I walked back to the main office on that first day and inquired. I returned with three items: A roll of tape, a package of colored construction paper, and a box of chalk. I stood my ground. I insisted on the grade-level texts for the subject areas I was assigned to teach. I asked for the curricula. It took months but slowly the textbooks arrived. But what about teaching reading? I bought a few books and combed garage sales on weekends but it wasn't enough. I soon discovered a school district warehouse with out-of-adoption books. I called it the Old Book House. It was dark and dusty but it was filled with books. I scavenged. If it looked like it could be used to teach reading, I took it. I filled a bookshelf with books. Many of them were written in the 1950s and 1960s and featured young white children playing in tree-lined suburbs . . . it wasn't much. But it was a start.

As a special education teacher for students with mild to moderate disabilities, I taught classes of between 12 and 15 students. According to their IEPs, students received some combination of special education language arts, math, social studies, and possibly a period to catch up on work from general education classes. I also consulted with teachers and provided support in general education classes. My position had been held by a revolving door of substitutes, I had a large caseload of students, and I arrived as one of those un-credentialed first-year teachers, eager, but inexperienced.

I met Darnell as a tall, African-American, 13-year-old, seventh-grader with an unmistakable chip on his shoulder and a strong presence. He excelled in math but was close to failing all other general education subjects. He had LD, with goals for reading, writing, and behavior. Many teachers were challenged by Darnell. He was intimidating and he could be confrontational. He was often removed from class for talking back to teachers, refusing to do work, and occasionally for being physically disruptive. For example, he had recently knocked over a desk in frustration and it had banged into the teacher's desk and broken a picture frame. In my class, he could be defiant or endearing, engaged or enraged. Research indicates that the response of school personnel is to remove African-American males more frequently from general education classroom settings than their White peers based on perceptions of problem behaviors (Lewis, Butler, Bonner, Fred, & Joubert, 2010; Skiba et al., 2011). Removal from the classroom, unfortunately, negatively impacts their academic achievement. As a special education teacher, I saw Darnell outside of the large mainstream classes and I had the time to get to know him. A colleague once said that you can't teach beyond your relationship, and that was never more true than with Darnell. He challenged me to teach him and teach him well and we quickly built a relationship. I spoke frequently with his mother, a busy nurse's assistant, and my room became a safe haven for him. Issues of fairness were important to Darnell. He hated being in "special ed" and he complained of being singled out by teachers. Often, after being removed from one class or another, we would argue at first. The following dialogue was a common one:

Me: You cannot tell Mr. Smart that his breath stinks. Even if it's true.
Darnell: But he is always disrespecting me Miss. All the kids are messing around and he comes up to me and tells me to get to work. Nobody is working in that class.
Me: Let's look at the assignment together. Be a student and do the work.
Darnell: Okay, but it's not fair that he is up in my face all the time, calling me out in front of everyone. I can't stand that X?%$!
Me: Darnell, you are right. It's not fair to be the only one to get in trouble when other kids are also not working. But you need to show him with your work not with your mouth. You can do this.

We would then work through the assignment—typically reading a textbook section together, which was not easy for Darnell, and then answering questions, which was easy for him. There would be more negotiation before Darnell would agree to return to the class to hand in his assignment.

Darnell knew what he needed and he asked for it from me. "Miss B., I am not reading these baby books. You better get some better books in your class so I can read!" He was right. He was reading at a second-grade reading level and he didn't want to read books that looked like they were for second graders. I was thrilled when I went to the Old Book House to find a fresh set of high-interest, low-level chapter books that were still wrapped in plastic. Perfect! With Darnell's help and the reading courses I was taking at night, I learned to teach reading and Darnell learned to read.

Perhaps one of the greatest successes was Darnell's experience in Ms. Dean's class. Ms. Dean was tough. She had high expectations, a relevant curriculum, and above all, she taught her students to be writers. Darnell respected Ms. Dean and she seemed to connect with him. And then one day, he stormed into my room when he should have been in Ms. Dean's English class.

Darnell: How can she do that? I did my work. I spent days working on this critique of *Hamlet*. And this is good. Read it! You read it!

He shoved the paper at me. It was wrinkled, with many erasures and the writing was messy. It was difficult to read because there were so many misspellings, but it was indeed an original critique of *Hamlet* and contained complex ideas that showed he understood the text. On the top was his grade in red: 13 out of 20 with a note. *Darnell, there are some great ideas but you need to spend more time on your work. Please proofread your writing and check your spelling. Sloppy work sends a message that you don't care. See me after school to discuss.*

Up until this point, I had not worked with Ms. Dean. Only a few of my students were in general education English classes, and her reputation was so strong that I had taken for granted that she understood how to make accommodations and modifications for students with disabilities. In fact, Darnell's IEP stated that he should not be graded on his spelling and that he should be allowed to type written assignments on the computer. How could I have missed this? And I worried because this was a teacher whom Darnell trusted. He attended class and had tried to succeed, but was met with what he perceived to be unfair treatment once again. I talked with Ms. Dean. We reviewed Darnell's IEP and we discussed ways to collaborate. We talked with Darnell. Together, we worked to provide him with the instruction and the accommodations he needed to be successful in his general education class. Setting high expectations, yet remaining culturally responsive and cognizant of a student's need for modifications creates the potential for learning to occur (Gay, 2010).

Darnell was positioned in school as a difficult-to-teach student who fit into an easy stereotype of the troubled African-American youth (Lewis et al., 2010; Skiba et al., 2011). Darnell could be both his best advocate and his worst enemy. He needed to connect with his teachers and he needed high-quality instruction and accommodations for his disability. The constraints placed on teachers with large classes and limited resources did not work in Darnell's favor. With Darnell's help, I learned to initiate conversations with general education teachers, to facilitate some of those relationships, and to offer suggestions for accommodations and collaboration. As was the case in Ms. Dean's English class, Darnell had the potential to excel academically, but needed a coordinated program of supports in order to succeed and teachers who could look beyond his attitude and his disability to see his strengths. As Delpit (2003) noted, "we can educate all children if we truly want to. To do so, we must first stop attempting to determine their capacity. We must be convinced of their inherent intellectual capability, humanity, and spiritual character" (p. 20). Our lesson learned from Darnell is that we must see each student as teachable, work with our colleagues to share that vision, and use the resources we have available, even though they may be limited.

MISTAKES

She moved the pencil on her desktop aimlessly. The design grew and grew, and her work remained untouched on the side of the desk. I (RF) saw it immediately, but waited to say something. She had done so well recently, especially for someone in a class for students with emotional and behavioral difficulties. Her attitude and work had been extremely impressive. She asked questions in class and seemed to care about doing well. Even though her skills were far below grade level, she seemed focused. Being in my second year as a middle school special education teacher, I thought that a few weeks of this behavior signified a lasting change. In that moment, I forgot to consider who Maria was, and everything she might be going through. But I couldn't let drawing on the desk go, right? I had to say something, right? So I told her, "Please, Maria, no drawing on the desk. You'll have to clean that up after class." She refused. I pushed, saying she must. She swore at me and walked out. That was the last time she attended my class.

Soon after this, she would unleash a wave of curses at me in front of a class she did not even attend. She heard me telling her friend that I would not excuse being late for anyone. Maria pulled open the door, and screamed at me. I did my best not to listen, knowing there was nothing I could do. Yelling back would get us nowhere, and even listening would be flustering and embarrassing. I focused on every sound other than her voice, the dial tone, the voice of the secretary, even my own breath. She left after yelling for a full minute, and I turned to a usually talkative class who sat in stunned, jaw-dropped silence. It would be the last time Maria and I talked, if you could call that talking.

At this point, it seemed as though the story would end. But I knew a little bit about Maria's life. She lived in foster care after being horrifically abused by family and after being the abuser of family. She had to miss school to go to court every so often, and each time she would return angry at everyone and everything. She seemed to be a student without a place at home or at school. I wondered, as I found out this information, how our final two interactions must have seemed from her perspective, or what possibly could have happened outside of my knowledge. She had been working so well, and here was this teacher trying to tell her she had to stay and clean tables. Had she just been told she could not see her birth mother anymore? Or that she would be moving foster homes? On the day she entered the class to yell at me, did she think that this teacher was not giving her friend a break just for being a couple minutes late? Barr (2011) noted the importance of developing empathy for students: the ability to better understand and relate appropriately to students. I realized that I had no idea the amount of pain she went through on a daily basis, but I also thought that if I tried to talk to her, our emotions could possibly take over. So I wrote a letter.

My handwriting is notoriously bad, but I handwrote the letter. It had been several months after she had yelled at me in class. Since then, we had barely seen each other. She cursed at me under her breath as we passed in the hall, but that was the extent of our interactions. She refused to come to my special education math class, and nothing her behavior specialist teacher did could change Maria's mind. I cannot remember why I decided to write her the letter. I was busy, as every teacher is, and my most recent memories of her were not exactly pleasant. But one day, I pulled out a piece of lined paper and wrote her a two-page letter in my chicken scratch handwriting. I hoped that hand writing the letter would make me less likely to edit, and to speak from the heart.

I put a lot in that letter. I apologized for the initial incident with drawing on the desk, and told her that I had not been a good teacher in that moment. I told her about myself and my thoughts on how I should have been a better teacher. I told her that I admired her loyalty to her friend, even if it did not go so well. It was one of the most personal letters I have ever written. I did not make a copy of the letter, because I was convinced that I would not get a response. I hoped that it would show her that I was not just some authority figure who did not care about her. I sealed the letter in an envelope and gave it to the behavior specialist to give to her.

A few weeks later, Maria's teacher gave me her response. I read it, and immediately wrote back. She would send one more letter after mine. By this time, the school year had come to an end. Maria had finished the eighth grade, and would not return. We would not talk in person. We only sent two letters apiece before school ended. In the end, I never got to see if I had actually done anything meaningful. In my ignorance, I had not taken into account just how different her life was than mine, and I allowed myself to be pushed away. A letter? After months of silence? It was a gesture that did not offer enough, though in her letters she was appreciative.

> "The teacher must understand the diversity of his students, not just in terms of race, culture or language, but every part of a student's life that affects them."

As educators, we may not always get it right in our relationships with students. We mis-perceive the complex issues with which they are dealing, we mis-diagnosis learning problems, our navigation of social relations may be faulty. However, we must also always remind ourselves that every action made by a student does not exist in a vacuum. Nor does it exist because of us, the educators. The home and outside lives of students can be stressful, supportive, traumatizing, or encouraging. The culture of a student can bring positives, and in the absence or separation from culture there is the possibility that the student has little to no support. The teacher must understand the diversity of his students, not just in terms of race, culture or language, but every part of a student's life that affects them (Gay, 2010; Harry & Klingner, 2014). When this is understood, then mistakes we make as educators may be avoided, and learning opportunities can emerge.

ASHLEY: UNDERSTANDING STUDENTS' LIVES OUTSIDE OF SCHOOL

When I (SAA) met Ashley she was a 17-year-old African American with an emotional disability label, with whom several teachers and staff had had run-ins during middle and high school. She would often come sauntering in late and want teachers to help her catch up. Teachers often described her as loud and bossy. She would show up with a tank top that was too small, teachers would demand that she change and she would refuse. In general, her teachers found her frustrating and she was suspended many times. Ashley's attitude did not endear her to teachers and staff. School staff complained that "it was always something" and they discussed how they shouldn't have to spend time helping her catch up when "she had been out having fun with her friends." Ashley and I talked at length and eventually she told me why she was always late.

Ashley: I always missed a lot of (middle) school. I always helped out with sisters and brothers.

SAA: Do you remember the kind of things you had to do for your siblings?

Ashley: Like help them with food, showers, brushing teeth, getting ready for school . . . I would cook and clean up and my mom was on bed rest from a car accident and back surgery. And I missed so many days to help all my brothers and sisters get ready. I had to go grocery shopping, get everyone to school, go to my siblings' teacher's conferences . . . . So I like regret missing so much school but I had to help out my mom so I just said forget school . . . I was taking care of my family but then, I would tell my mom I was going to school. Cuz I had to put my sisters and brothers in school so then I would already be late and then they'd be tripping on me because I was late.

The original reasons Ashley was late had nothing to do with hanging out with friends but instead taking care of her family. When she arrived late to her own school, Ashley would be reprimanded with lectures, detention, or even suspension. The school response of punishing Ashley for truancy exacerbated problems instead of alleviating them. Ashley was punished for breaking a rule without the school considering the context of her life. Therefore, she was punished not just for truancy, but also for taking care of her family.

Additionally, when Ashley did attend school, she felt harassed. She noted that many teachers complained about the way she was dressed. She later told me that her family didn't have the money to buy new clothes since her mom was on disability and therefore she had to wear things that were too small for her. Her socioeconomic status meant that Ashley struggled to meet the standard dress code her school had set. So when she got to school, not only did teachers and school staff badger her about being late, but they also harangued her about the way she was dressed. She often wondered out loud to me why she was constantly bothered about these small details when she was trying to get her education while juggling a multitude of family issues. The mismatch in perceptions between what teachers at the school believed and what was the reality for Ashley perpetuated Ashley's disengagement from school (Annamma, 2014; Harry & Klingner, 2014).

Ashley also noted that teachers often told her she was too bossy and demanding. She told me of the need to tell her siblings what to do in a loud, firm voice in order to get their attention and command their respect. She had learned quickly that if she asked, she often did not get what she needed at home or school and the only way to get a response was a directive. At 14, Ashley was living as a grown woman, being a caretaker for her mother and siblings. She often acted like an adult at school because she had to act like one everywhere else in her life.

Ashley's need to support her family, taking the place of her mother at times, caused her to miss long stretches of school. Eventually, Ashley noted she was withdrawn from the school she attended without anyone ever checking up on why she was missing school.

SAA: Do you remember any of your teachers at that school?

Ashley: Um, I don't remember anybody. I wasn't even there enough. That's why I ended up in trouble, they just withdraw me after so many days, they just withdraw me.

SAA: That's why you ended up leaving that school?

Ashley: Um hm.

SAA: So where did you go after that?

Ashley: I didn't go to school. Then in ninth I restarted and didn't go to school.

SAA: So do you feel like when you began getting suspended a lot more in eighth grade, did that have an effect on whether you wanted to go back to that school?

Ashley: Yeah, like I was unwanted and I didn't want to go to school . . . because I had tried. In middle school, I was like, they done gave up on me, that's the way I felt, like how are you going to kick me out of school? If you guys had any idea what I go through at home, you wouldn't kick me out of school . . . especially when I'm trying to go to school.

Ashley's removal from school as punitive discipline caused her to lose access to an education. She had to wait for her mother to get strong enough to take her to a new school, enroll her and then figure out new transportation for both herself and her siblings. During this additional time out of school, Ashley lost learning opportunities along with a chance to build a positive relationship with school.

When Ashley attended a new school, she struggled with a teacher complaining about her behavior without understanding her circumstances.

Ashley: Yeah, I had this math teacher and I missed like three months straight and she's like, if you're going to come here, you need to start coming more often because I don't appreciate you missing this much of class and then you just want to drop in. And then I never went back to her class anymore.

Ashley missed many days of school in order to support her ill mother and to care for her siblings; therefore this teacher's frustration was misplaced. When the teacher suggested Ashley just wanted to drop in, the implication was that Ashley did not take school seriously. However, from her descriptions above, it was clear that Ashley did take school seriously but that the basic needs of her family overruled her opportunity for an education. Teachers did not take Ashley's home life into account. As Ashley's quote illustrated, this lack of concern for what she faced outside of school had a direct impact on her physical and emotional connection with school.

> "As educators, it is our job to understand the complexities of life our students experience, both in and out of school, and to foster collaborative learning environments that are more supportive of the diverse ways of knowing and learning that our students bring with them to school daily."

When I asked Ashley why she did not just tell school staff the reasons for her tardiness and refusal to follow the dress code, her answer was disarmingly simple. "No one ever asked. They were too busy yelling at me for not following rules."

What we learned from this experience was that Ashley's struggles were real but could easily be interpreted as disinterest in school and outright defiance (Annamma, 2014).

However, simply talking to Ashley revealed that her life was much more complicated than school staff and teachers guessed. As educators, it is our job to understand the complexities of life our students experience, both in and out of school, and to foster collaborative learning environments that are more supportive of the diverse ways of knowing and learning that our students bring with them to school daily (Baglieri & Knopf, 2004).

TINA: A FORMER ELL GROWN UP

Meet Tina. Tina works as a teaching assistant in a public preschool and she uses Spanish and English every day in her work in a classroom comprised of a mixture of Anglo and Latino children. Although one of her main roles is to support instruction of the children in Spanish, she feels more comfortable reading to children in English. She finds herself asking another aide how to say certain vocabulary in Spanish or using circumlocution to get her ideas across in Spanish. The language model she provides the children in Spanish does not move beyond the colloquial level.

Tina was born in a small, rural town in Colorado to parents who immigrated to the United States from Mexico. Tina lives with her parents, her younger brother, and her four-year-old son. She told me (NS) that in her home they currently speak a mixture of Spanish and English. Her 20-year-old brother has "lost" most of his Spanish and Tina finds herself being the interpreter for her brother and her parents. Her parents speak to her brother in Spanish and he answers them in English.

The language use at home wasn't always such a mixture of languages, however. Growing up, Tina heard only Spanish spoken in the home. When she began kindergarten she was a monolingual Spanish speaker and was placed in an English only classroom. She remembers feeling shy and out of place initially, but by second grade she was comfortable and academically thriving in an all-English classroom environment. Though pleased with her progress in English, her parents were concerned when they saw increasing evidence that Tina's Spanish language skills were waning. Not only did they think she was "losing" her Spanish, but she was also losing her interest in speaking Spanish. Thus her parents made the decision to enroll her in a bilingual program in the third grade.

According to Tina, this program was far from bilingual. In fact, she characterized it as all Spanish. She noted that all the gains she had made in her emerging English literacy skills were suddenly not being put to use. She had to start trying to survive in an all-Spanish third grade classroom without having literacy skills in Spanish. She continued to struggle to develop academic skills in third, fourth, and fifth grades in all-Spanish classrooms. When it was time to enter sixth grade, the "bilingual" program was no longer an option and for the remainder of her education, Tina was placed in all-English (sink or swim) classes.

From the sixth grade until she graduated from high school Tina had an IEP and was placed in special education classes. She remembers her diagnosis mentioning a disability related to language-processing but she never really understood what that meant and no one ever explained to her the nature of her "disability." In the end she simply assumed it meant that she just wasn't very smart. This is a self-perception that she carries with her to this day. This self-perception is described by scholars as stigmatic—labeling that draws attention to difference in ways that marginalize and dehumanize (Brantlinger, 2001; Macedo & Martí, 2010).

Though detrimental to her self-esteem, Tina feels that her placement in special education at least enabled her to get by. She was put in smaller classes where she could get more individual attention and help. Unfortunately, this "help" consisted of teachers helping her "get her work done" without teaching her academic skills she needed to go further in her education. After graduating from high school, Tina attempted studying at community college. She abandoned her studies after one semester. She felt overwhelmed and could not pass several of her courses. She feels she lacks "the basics" needed to succeed in academics. She states, "I have no idea how to write. I just can't do it." In addition to lacking confidence in her writing ability, she struggles with reading comprehension and must read very slowly to understand academic English. Tina even noted that it can be difficult for her to understand spoken English if the scope goes much beyond the simple, everyday conversational level. (It is interesting to note that for all Tina feels her academic literacy skills in English are lacking, they exceed her Spanish academic literacy skills).

So does Tina actually have LD? At this point, it would be a challenge to try to tease apart whether her diagnosis was due to: (1) interrupted and incomplete language acquisition resulting from the various discontinuities in her education, (2) language processing challenges due to a learning difference inherent to Tina, or (3) some combination of 1 and 2 (Klingner et al. 2006). Though it would be difficult to say the precise cause of her difficulties it would be safe to say that the various shifts in language environment in her education and her experiences in special education have had an impact on her abilities and sense of agency when it comes to academics. If Tina remains convinced of her inability to succeed, she is unlikely to attempt community college again. This has a profound impact on her career options. Not being able to get an Associate's or a Bachelor's degree limits her capacity to advance in her work and to get promoted to lead teacher. Such missed opportunities in school, propelled by negative self-perceptions, can ultimately lead to the potential for future economic hardships as students with disabilities struggle to find jobs in competitive markets (Erevelles, 2000).

Important issues that Tina's story raised for us as educators and scholars revolve around educational discontinuity and school systems' infrastructure (or lack thereof) to understand and address linguistic diversity. As for educational discontinuity, it exists in many forms and for various reasons. It can be particularly acute when it comes to "bilingual" education which has multiple instructional models and implementations. As long as such discontinuities exist, teachers and parents need to be aware of how it can impact learning. Teachers need to find out the educational history of their students, *especially* the struggling ones. Even the brightest of students could appear to have a disability if their prior educational experiences were extremely disjointed as in the case of Tina.

As for schools knowing how to address student diversity, it is possible that Tina was given an IEP and placed in special education because teachers simply did not know what to do with her. Maybe they did not understand how she could have such gaps in her English skills. Or if they did understand, perhaps the school lacked sheltered English classes or teachers skilled at differentiating instruction so as to make content accessible to Tina. Students ought not to be placed in special education by default; however schools at times lack the resources to understand and address the linguistic diversity of their student population. Although identification and placement into special education may be beneficial and necessary for children with true disabilities, it can be stigmatizing and lead to inequitable educational opportunities for students who are mis-identified and placed into special education (Donovan & Cross, 2002; Gándara & Bial, 2001).

CONCLUSION

Cultural and linguistic diversity in special education is a given fact. The lessons we have learned along the way, as educators and as scholars, have provided us valuable insight. The case studies presented here are real stories, but stories that many special educators share in common. The themes that are woven through these stories teach us valuable lessons.

First, our experiences teach us the importance of *knowing*: knowing our students, knowing the difference between a disability and a language difference, and knowing our own beliefs and perceptions. Special educators must have empathy toward their students' self-perceptions, as Tina taught us, while also setting high expectations for student success, as we learned from Darnell. Nirje (1994) suggested that a key principle of special education should be "normalization." The "normalization principle" is not meant to help students pass as normal, but to guide educators to seek equality through the acceptance of individuals with disabilities and an assured quality of life and recognition of human rights (Wolfensberger & Tullman, 1982). As we work toward this principle, our task is also to understand the difference between a disability and a learning difference better, as in the case of Gerardo, Marta, and Tina. Finally, we must know ourselves. We have all made mistakes along the way, but learning from them is the key to effective practice. Special educators must engage in "inquiry as stance," or critical reflection, of their own knowledge and beliefs about students and about their families (Cochran-Smith & Lytle, 1999; Mezirow, 2003). Through reflection on our beliefs, we stand to gain knowledge that can work toward supporting diverse students in more engaging ways.

Second, collaboration with colleagues and parents is a key tenet of successful special education programming. Coupled with knowing about students, special educators must know about the complexities in their lives. As Ashley, Maria, and the Hernández family taught us, the lives of our students can be challenging and have an impact on their learning (Lareau, 2011). Ameena reminded us that parents love and value their children, and have dreams and expectations, too. We need to recognize those perspectives and experiences and work together to validate them and integrate them into our learning environments (González, Moll, & Amanti, 2005). We also need to collaborate with colleagues—pathognomic and interventionist alike (Berry, 2006)—so more students can see successes like Gerardo's.

Finally, we must recognize and value diversity, and do our part to share that with our colleagues in schools. Each of our stories celebrated the diverse ways of knowing and learning that our students brought with them to school (Heath, 1982). Without Gerardo's *mamífero*, or Darnell pushing his teachers to challenge him academically, or Ashley's persistence to continue school despite the cards stacked against her, we may have missed valuable opportunities to embrace diversity as a means toward a more positive and equitable future for all.

Discussion Questions

1. How might the case studies' learners' characteristics be erroneously identified as a learning disability or overlooked as an indicator of a disability?
2. What lessons do the cases point out about who receives and does not receive special education services?
3. What are some consistencies among the cases regarding effective instruction?
4. Identification for special education is complicated. How do the cases demonstrate the need to consider cultural and linguistic diversity when identifying students?
5. How have the cases illustrated the conclusion that "we must recognize and value diversity" that Klingner et al. assert? How was diversity recognized? How was diversity valued?

NOTE

1.   We use the term *ELLs* (ELLs) to refer to those students who speak one or more languages other than English and who are in the process of acquiring English but are not yet considered fluent. We prefer the term *emerging bilinguals* because it better represents students' linguistic strengths and potential for bilingualism, but use ELLs as the more common term.

JANETTE KLINGNER'S SUGGESTIONS FOR FURTHER READING

Annamma, S., Boelé, A., Moore, B., Klingner, J. (2013). Challenging the ideology of normal in schools. *International Journal of Inclusive Education, 17*, 1278–1294.

Haager, D., Klingner, J. K., & Jiménez, T. (2010). *How to teach English language learners: Effective strategies from outstanding educators.* San Francisco, CA: Jossey Bass.

Harry, B., & Klingner, J. K. (2014). *Why are so many minority students in special education? Understanding race and disability in schools, Second Edition.* New York: Teachers College Press.

Harry, B. & Klingner, J. K. (2007). Discarding the deficit model. *Educational Leadership, 64*(5), 16–21.

Hoover, J., Klingner, J. K., Baca, L., & Patton, J. (2007). *Methods for teaching culturally and linguistically diverse exceptional learners.* Upper Saddle River, NJ: Merrill/Prentice Hall.

Klingner, J. K., Boardman, A. G., & McMaster, K. (2013). What does it take to scale up and sustain evidence-based practices? *Exceptional Children, 79*, 195–211.

Klingner, J. K., & Eppolito, A. M. (2014). *English language learners: Differentiating between language acquisition and learning disabilities.* Arlington, VA: Council for Exceptional Children.

Klingner, J. K., Vaughn, S., & Boardman, A., & Swanson, E. (2012). *Now we get it! Boosting comprehension with Collaborative Strategic Reading.* San Francisco, CA: Jossey Bass.

REFERENCES

Annamma, S. A. (2014). Disabling juvenile justice: Engaging the stories of incarcerated young women of color with disabilities. *Remedial and Special Education, 35*, 313–324.

Annamma, S., Boelé, A., Moore, B., & Klingner, J. K. (2013). Challenging the ideology of normal in schools. *International Journal of Inclusive Education, 17*, 1278–1294.

Artiles, A. J., & Bal, A. (2008). The next generation of disproportionality research: Toward a comparative model in the study of equity in ability differences. *Journal of Special Education, 42*, 4–14.

Artiles, A., & Klingner, J. (2006). Forging a knowledge base on English language learners with special needs: Theoretical, population, and technical issues. *The Teachers College Record, 108*, 2187–2194.

Artiles, A. J., Rueda, R., Salazar, J., & Higareda, I. (2005). Within-group diversity in minority disproportionate representation: ELLs in urban school districts. *Exceptional Children, 71*, 283–300.

Aud, S., Hussar, W., Kena, G., Bianco, K., Frohlich, L., Kemp, J., & Tahan, K. (2011). *The condition of education 2011* (NCES 2011-033). U.S. Department of Education, National Center for Education Statistics. Washington, DC: U.S. Government Printing Office.

Baglieri, S. & Knopf, J. H. (2004). Normalizing difference in inclusive teaching. *Journal of Learning Disabilities, 37*, 525–529.

Barr, J. J. (2011). The relationship between teachers' empathy and perceptions of school culture. *Educational Studies, 37*, 365–369.

Berry, R.A. (2006). Beyond strategies: Teacher beliefs and writing instruction in two primary classrooms. *Journal of Learning Disabilities, 39*, 11–24.

Brantlinger, E. (2001). Poverty, class, and disability: A historical, social and political perspective. *Focus on Exceptional Children, 33*, 1–19.

Cochran-Smith, M. & Lytle, S. L. (1999). Relationships of knowledge and practice: Teacher learning in communities. *Review of Research in Education, 24*, 249–305.

Cohen, E. G., & Lotan, R. A. (1995). Producing equal-status interaction in the heterogeneous classroom. *American Educational Research Journal, 32*, 99–120.

Delpit, L. (2003). Educators as "seed people" growing a new future. *Educational Researcher, 32*, 14–21.

Donovan, S., & Cross, C. T. (2002). *Minority students in special and gifted education.* Washington, D.C.: National Academy Press.

Erevelles, N. (2000). Educating unruly bodies: Critical pedagogy, disability studies, and the politics of schooling. *Educational Theory, 50*, 25–47.

Gándara, P., & Bial, D. (2001). *Paving the way to postsecondary education: K-12 intervention programs for underrepresented youth.* Washington, D.C.: National Center for Education Statistics, Office of Educational Research and Improvement, U.S. Dept. of Education.

Gay, G. (2010). *Culturally responsive teaching: Theory, research, and practice.* New York: Teachers College Press.

González, N., Moll, L. C., & Amanti, C. (Eds.), (2005). *Funds of knowledge: Theorizing practices in households, communities, and classrooms.* Mahwah, NJ: Lawrence Erlbaum Associates.

Harry, B., & Harry, M. (2010). *Melanie, bird with a broken wing: A mother's story.* Bloomington, IN: Xlibris.

Harry, B. & Klingner, J. (2014). The construction of family identity: Stereotypes and cultural capital. In B. Harry & J. Klingner (Eds.), *Why are so many minority students in special education? Understanding race and disability in schools, Second Edition* (pp. 78–98). New York: Teachers College Press.

Heath, S. B. (1982). What no bedtime story means: Narrative skills at home and school. *Language and Society, 2*, 49–76.

Horn, I. S. & Little, J. W. (2010). Attending to problems of practice: Routines and resources for professional learning in teachers' workplace interactions. *American Educational Research Journal, 47*, 181–217.

Klingner, J. K., Artiles, A. J., & Barletta, L. M. (2006). English Language Learners Who Struggle With Reading Language Acquisition or LD? *Journal of Learning Disabilities, 39*, 108–128.

Lareau, A. (2011). *Unequal childhoods: Class, race, and family life.* Berkeley, CA: University of California Press.

Lewis, C. W., Butler, B. R., Bonner, I. I., Fred, A., & Joubert, M. (2010). African American male discipline patterns and school district responses resulting impact on academic achievement: Implications for urban educators and policy makers. *Journal of African American Males in Education, 1*(1), 7–25.

Macedo, D., & Martí, T. S. (2010). Situating labeling within an ideological framework. In. C. Dudley-Marling & A. Gurn (Eds.), *The myth of the normal curve* (pp. 53–70). New York: Peter Lang.

McMaster, K. L., Fuchs, L. S., & Compton, D. L. (2005). Responding to nonresponders: An experimental field trial of identification and intervention methods. *Exceptional Children, 71*, 445–463.

Mezirow, J. (2003). Transformative learning as discourse. *Journal of Transformative Education, 1*, 58–63.

National Center for Education Statistics. (2009). *Table A-6-1. Number and percentage distribution of 3- to 21-year olds served under the Individuals with Disabilities Education Act (IDEA), Part B, and number served as a percentage of total public school enrollment, by type of disability: Selected school years, 1976–77 through 2007–08.* Washington, DC: Institute of Education Sciences, U.S. Department of Education. Retrieved from http://nces.ed.gov/programs/coe/2010/section1/table-cwd-1.asp.

National Clearinghouse on English Language Acquisition (2011, February). *The growing numbers of English learner students, 1998/99–2008/09.* Retrieved on February 13, 2012 from http://www.ncela.gwu.edu/publications.

Nirje, B. (1994).The normalization principle and its human management implications. *The International Social Role Valorization Journal, 1*(2), 19–23.

Parrish, T. (2002). Racial disparities in the identification, funding, and provision of special education. In D. J. Losen & G. Orfield (Eds.), *Racial inequity in special education* (pp. 15–37). Cambridge: Harvard Education Press.

Skiba, R. J., Horner, R. H., Chung, C. G., Rausch, M. K., May, S. L., & Tobin, T. (2011). Race is not neutral: A national investigation of African American and Latino disproportionality in school discipline. *School Psychology Review, 40*, 85–107.

Slavin, R. E. (1996). Research on cooperative learning and achievement: What we know, what we need to know. *Contemporary Educational Psychology, 21*, 43–69.

Slavin, R. E. (2011). Instruction based on cooperative learning. In R. E. Mayer & P. A. Alexander (Eds.), *Handbook of Research on Learning and Instruction* (pp. 344–360). New York: Routledge.

Sleeter, C. E. (2001). Preparing teachers for culturally diverse schools research and the overwhelming presence of whiteness. *Journal of Teacher Education, 52*, 94–106.

Sullivan, A. (2011). Disproportionality in special education identification and placement of ELLs. *Exceptional Children, 71*, 317–334.

Wolfensberger, W., & Tullman, S. (1982). A brief outline of the principle of normalization. *Rehabilitation Psychology, 27*, 131–145.

Getting to Know Erica S. Lembke

 My parents were teachers when I was growing up (Dad teaching high school mathematics and science and Mom teaching special education) so that was part of my formative experience. Given the amount of time and effort teaching takes, I have to admit that I was not always sure that would be my career path. However, visiting my mom's special education classroom over the years and volunteering for Special Olympics as a coach for my mom's class really resonated with me and, when I went to college, special education seemed like a natural career path.

Once I was in the program, I was hooked! After graduating with my degree in special education, I taught in Iowa for six years in a small, rural district. I was the only teacher who had a focus on mild intellectual and behavior disorders, so I taught students in grades K–5. It was challenging and extremely rewarding. I learned a lot about myself and how to be a better communicator, collaborator, and facilitator.

Now that I've moved on to train pre-service teachers and to consult with in-service teachers, all of the experiences that I participated in early in my career benefit me immensely. My goal is that the research and training I do to help support students with disabilities is multiplicative in that I train future teachers who work with hundreds of students during their careers. I feel like I'm on my way to making that impact, particularly given the work I do to help support not only special educators, but general educators as well!

9

WHO SHOULD RECEIVE SPECIAL EDUCATION SERVICES AND HOW SHOULD EDUCATORS IDENTIFY WHICH STUDENTS ARE TO RECEIVE SPECIAL EDUCATION SERVICES?

Erica S. Lembke

INTRODUCTION

In graduate school we were asked to read Dunn (1968) and Deno (1970) prior to reading several articles from a special issue of *The Journal of Special Education* (1994, volume 27, issue 4). That special issue addressed the legacy of special education 25 years after Lloyd Dunn's article, "Special Education for the Mildly Retarded—Is Much of it Justifiable?" and Evelyn Deno's article, "Special Education as Developmental Capital." In the special issue (1994), several authors revisited issues raised in the seminal articles by Dunn and Deno, with a primary discussion surrounding where we stood as a field 25 years after their publications. In the introduction to the special issue, Hallahan and Kauffman comment that "many are questioning the very existence of special education by asking such things as whether separate special education settings are necessary and whether special education teachers engage in teaching behaviors different from their general education peers" (p. 373).

As my students and I read these articles again this semester in my doctoral level seminar on trends in special education, it was again apparent how much the field remains the same with respect to the questions we still have regarding who should be served in special education. The students in my doctoral seminar and I reflected on the statements made by Dunn and Deno over 40 years ago and authors of the special issue almost 20 years ago. We came to the same realization. The more things change, the more they stay the same. I asked my students to develop titles for what their article would be about if they were to reflect on Dunn and Deno and where we are currently as a field. Their titles largely referred to hope for greater collaboration between general and special education, "State of the Union: Current Collaboration Efforts Among General and Special Education in America;" "44 Years After Dunn and Deno: Moving Towards a Shared Responsibility;" "44 Years After Dunn & Deno, Re-Visioning Special Education & the Role of Special Educators—Embracing Collaborative Partnerships Between General and Special Educators to Promote the Success of SWDs and Struggling Learners in the General Education Classroom."

However, we were all struck by the statements made by Dunn and Deno over 40 years ago and how relevant those statements still are today. Some might say, "How disappointing that we haven't done more as a field." Others might say, "We have tried methods and learned lessons and how can we move forward?" It is important to build upon the past, reflecting on historical lessons, but to also be progressive and innovative as we move forward. It is at this intersection that we stand today with respect to identification for special education. We want to capitalize on all that we have learned as a field regarding the best and most accurate methods to identify students for special education services, while incorporating current innovation.

Response-to-Intervention (RTI) identification methods provide a good example of how the intersection can be approached. As researchers and teachers, we want to be certain that we are using the best methods to identify students early, but also to identify the correct students—students who have disabilities that adversely affect their educational performance—not students who are struggling because of transiency, lack of exposure to content or expectations, or inadequate instruction. There are advantages and disadvantages to using RTI as a model for identification. In the next section, we will discuss some of those advantages and disadvantages and move closer to answering one of the questions that this chapter poses: how should educators identify which students should receive special education services? However, prior to that, a more thorough discussion of how, when, and who should receive special education services is in order.

FIRST: THE HOW AND WHEN

When P.L.-94-142 was put into law in 1975, teachers, researchers, parents, and advocacy groups celebrated for students who would now be recognized and provided special services and dollars to back up those services. Unfortunately, while the services remained, the dollars to support those services have never been realized (see Pardini, 2002, for example) creating a deficit for the districts that serve students with special needs from the very beginning. Following ratification of P.L.-94-142, criteria were established for how to identify students with disabilities and these criteria have remained largely unchanged until the recent addition of RTI to the learning disabilities section in 2004. In this chapter, I'll primarily address criteria for students with learning disabilities, as this is the area that has changed most radically in the past ten years and the area that is probably most controversial.

> "As researchers and teachers, we want to be certain that we are using the best methods to identify students early but also to identify the correct students—students who have disabilities that adversely affect their educational performance—not students who are struggling because of transiency, lack of exposure to content or expectations, or inadequate instruction."

Overall, I believe that school districts, school child find teams, and individual educators make valiant attempts to identify students who are struggling and to provide them the support that they need. *How* and *when* to identify students for specialized instruction are primary questions in this process. In relation to *how,* multiple measures that districts and teachers can be confident in, and that provide reliable and valid information about students as early as preschool and into high school need to be utilized. Measures need to be administered and data collected several times per year for all students in primary academic subjects like reading and mathematics. Data need to be collected more often for students who are deemed at risk. These data need to be utilized through an effective problem-solving team process that capitalizes on all members' knowledge for determining evidence-based interventions that can be feasibly implemented by classroom teachers prior to referral for special education. The multiple, standardized measures that are collected over time are used to determine whether a student is responding to intervention.

When to identify students for specialized instruction is a critical question with a less specific answer. The generic answer would be "as early as possible." However, educators want to make sure that they have given classroom instruction a chance to work before referring a student for additional intervention. Target students too early, and they may be receiving intervention needlessly, in that they are actually not students at risk but just have not had enough time to profit from instruction (false positives). Target students too late and you have lost precious time that could have been dedicated to early intervention (false negatives). Of course, the question of when to identify students for intervention is separate from when to identify students for special education.

RTI FOR INTERVENTION AND IDENTIFICATION

As an example of *when to identify students for intervention*, consider a school that just collected schoolwide screening data. Following a review of the screening data and other standardized data by each grade level team, students are placed in three tiers to receive enrichment (Tier 1), or strategic or intensive intervention (Tier 2 and Tier 3). For students at risk, evidence-based intervention is provided for a minimum of 30–45 minutes daily and progress is monitored using a Curriculum Based Measurement (CBM) tool once per week or every other week. After at least six weeks of instruction, the grade level team meets to examine each student's data, to make sure that student placement is flexible, and tiered membership is based on data.

The team utilizes a decision-making rule like the 4-point rule or the trend-line rule (see Appendix B for an example) to make decisions about who should continue in intervention, who might need additional or enhanced intervention, and who might not need intervention any more. For instance, if the last four consecutive data points or the trend of current performance is: (1) below the goal line, make an instructional change; (2) both above and below the goal line (in the case of data points) or about the same as the goal line (in the case of the trend line), continue with the same instructional routine; (3) above the goal line, raise the goal or consider moving the student to a less intensive tier. In addition, for students for whom the team is considering making a change to a more intensive tier, the team considers the intensity of instruction provided (frequency of occurrence and length of time instruction) and the fidelity of implementation of the instruction before moving the student to a more intensive tier.

When RTI was proposed as an alternative identification method to the discrepancy model (determination of eligibility by the evidence of a meaningful discrepancy between scores on measures of intelligence and achievement) for students with learning disabilities in the 2004 revision of IDEA, many researchers in both special education and school psychology (e.g., Fuchs & Fuchs, 2006; VanDerHeyden, Witt, & Gilbertson, 2007) lauded this new method for identification, citing weaknesses of use of the discrepancy model. Criticisms of the discrepancy model included: (1) students waiting to fail, meaning that students were not provided services until they had already failed, which sometimes was not until second or third grade, and (2) identification almost solely based upon scores from standardized achievement and intelligence tests. In addition, criticisms of the prevalent referral and testing model at that time suggested that an alternative framework for defining underachievement was needed that eliminated poor instructional quality as an explanation for learning problems. RTI researchers (Fuchs & Fuchs 2006; Vaughn, Wanzek, & Fletcher, 2007) suggested that unresponsiveness could be defined as a dual discrepancy, with students' level and rate of performance considered prior to referral for more specialized services, thereby making RTI a process for identification of students with learning disabilities.

RTI as a model for *identification* has not been implemented nearly as frequently as RTI as a model for how to structure *intervention delivery* and data-based decision making for all students in a building—particularly at the elementary level (Vaughn, Wanzek, Woodruff, & Linan-Thompson, 2006). Legislation regarding RTI prompted schools to formalize their procedures for identifying and providing enrichment and intervention to all students, accompanied by schoolwide screening and ongoing progress monitoring of performance. This RTI legislation followed on the heels of the end of the Reading First funding (see http://www2.ed.gov/programs/readingfirst/index.html) for many buildings, and with the parallels between the two initiatives, schools embraced the opportunity to continue to embed the same structures that they had as part of Reading First. In addition, and perhaps more widespread across grades, states, and time, were the parallels between RTI and the problem-solving model (Deno, 2005). First articulated by Deno in his 1985 paper, the problem-solving model provided a framework for schools to create a cycle of identification of low achieving students through the use of screening mechanisms, work with a grade level or schoolwide problem-solving team to determine which students needed intervention and what that intervention was, implementation of the intervention accompanied by ongoing progress monitoring (data collection), and a review of the data on a frequent (e.g., monthly) and regular basis to determine whether intervention or goal changes were necessary. For individual teachers, buildings, and districts that had been using the problem-solving model for some time, the RTI model was a reframing or a different way to articulate what they had already been doing. In some cases, districts had been using the problem-solving model since as early as the early 1990s.

For example, Minneapolis Public Schools received a waiver from the state of Minnesota to use an alternative identification system for learning disabilities in the early 1990s (Marston, Muyskens, Lau, & Canter, 2003). The district developed and tested their own screening and progress monitoring measures, established decision-making rules for qualification for the disability, and used a non-categorical system (i.e., Student in Need of Alternative Programming, SNAP) as an alternative to using a discrepancy model to identify students with learning needs. Other states such as Ohio and Iowa also adopted alternative identification systems similar to RTI (Tilly, 2002) prior to RTI being conceptualized as an alternative for identification.

MORE SPECIFICS ON WHO: DECISION-MAKING RULES

Early implementers of the problem-solving model grappled with what implementers of RTI now have to address as well—what are the data decision rules for "qualifying" a student for special education services? The RTI model suggests that students who have learning needs are those who do not respond to otherwise effective instruction. Defining non-responsiveness and quantifying and qualifying "otherwise effective instruction" has been an evolving process. Researchers in school psychology (Burns, Riley-Tilman, & VanDerHeyden, 2013; Ardoin & Christ, 2009; Francis et al., 2008; Hintze & Christ, 2004;

Petscher, Cummings, Biancarosa, & Fien, 2013) and special education (Fuchs, Fuchs, & Compton, 2004; McMaster, Fuchs, Fuchs, & Compton, 2005) have led the way in using advanced statistical modeling and high-quality methodological studies to determine more precise cut scores on screening and progress-monitoring measures as well more fine-tuned fidelity measures for instruction.

In the case of Minneapolis Public Schools and the state of Iowa, CBM played an integral part in developing effective decision-making rules. CBMs are quick to administer, reliable, and valid indicators of academic performance and progress were initially developed to assist special education teachers in determining if their students were making progress as a result of the instruction or intervention that was being implemented. Later, CBM measures were implemented as part of the use of the problem-solving model for identification in districts like Minneapolis Public Schools and regions like Heartland Education Agency in Iowa who used CBM measures and established decision-making rules to identify students who were in need of services. For example, when using reliable and valid measures administered two times per week, if the trend of student performance is below the goal that is set for the student after a minimum of four weeks of instruction, make a change in instruction. If after eight weeks of instruction, the trend is still below the goal line, consider referring for an abbreviated special education evaluation. Usually, this evaluation would entail only those assessments that were deemed necessary to rule out behavior disorders or intellectual disability, but would not routinely utilize achievement and intelligence measures (see Fuchs, Fuchs, Hintze, & Lembke, 2007). However, some in the field would suggest that the established rules and measures utilized are no better or no more accurate than the measures and rules used in the discrepancy model (see the white paper from the Learning Disabilities Association of America, http://www.ldanatl.org/pdf/LDA%20White%20Paper%20on%20IDEA%20Evaluation%20Criteria%20for%20SLD.pdf and a response from the Consortium on Evidence Based Practices—http://www.rtinetwork.org/images/content/articles/learn_about_RTI/LDAResponsefinal.pdf).

There are some key differences in the use of the RTI model for identification as compared to the discrepancy model. In an RTI model, the provision of high-quality interventions to all students who are in need is provided early in a child's career and throughout the time the student continues to be identified as in need of support. In addition, screening measures are utilized for all students at least three times per year and progress monitoring measures are utilized for all students who are in intervention as often as weekly. This is juxtaposed with the discrepancy model where students in need might not be identified until they are severely at risk and where students may have little to no progress monitoring data to support a case for extended services.

"When RTI was proposed as an alternative identification method to the discrepancy model (determination of eligibility by the evidence of a meaningful discrepancy between scores on measures of intelligence and achievement) and for students with learning disabilities in the 2004 revision of IDEA, many researchers embraced the RTI model as an alternative to what they felt was a flawed model (discrepancy)."

THE NEED FOR GREATER SPECIFICITY FOR DECISION MAKING

Even with the benefit of enhanced supports early in the process as part of the RTI model, there is still the need for more specific criteria for decision making for identification. Discussion in the literature and on websites (Barth et al., 2008; Reynolds & Shaywitz,

2009; rtinetwork.org; Hughes & Dexter, 2011) suggests that there is concern related to four primary factors that are part of RTI decision making: (1) the measures that are utilized for screening and progress monitoring and whether these measures are of sufficient reliability and validity to be utilized for high stakes decision making; (2) how goals are set for students who are low achieving; (3) the evidence base that supports core instruction and any intervention that the student is receiving, along with fidelity of implementation; and (4) the number of data points that need to be collected, weeks of instruction implemented prior to implementing decision-making rules, and cut points utilized for risk or disability status.

First, a brief discussion of the measures that are utilized as part of decision making. As mentioned previously, CBM is one of the primary data collection systems in RTI models. National technical assistance centers such as the National Center on Student Progress Monitoring (studentprogress.org), the National Center on RTI (rti4success.org), and the National Center on Intensive Intervention (NCII; intensiveintervention.org) have created mechanisms for expert review of CBM measures. These reviews are provided in easy-to-read "Consumer-Reports" style tables that can be sorted by the grade level, topic, or technical feature that is being examined. For the NCII tables, data are categorized by general psychometric standards (reliability and validity of the performance level score and of the slope), including whether disaggregated data are available; by progress monitoring standards (alternate forms, sensitivity to student improvement, end of year benchmarks, and rates of improvement); and by data-based individualization standards (decision rules for increasing goals or changing instruction, and data on whether progress monitoring using the specified CBM measures leads to better student achievement or improved teacher planning).

Publishers of CBM products submit their tools for review and experts provide an indication of the level of evidence that might support each of the aforementioned areas: convincing evidence, partially convincing evidence, unconvincing evidence, or data not available. Data from studies are summarized and made available to the user by simply clicking on the particular psychometric standard of interest for the measure of interest. So the question of "which measures to use for decision making" becomes more straightforward when district or school teams have information that they can readily access on technical qualities of measures. However, issues related to measure selection might still arise if the measure that a school is hoping to use has not yet been reviewed, if studies have not been completed on certain aspects of the measure, or if teachers cannot interpret the information provided. If studies have not yet been completed, districts should utilize measures that are already vetted. To alleviate the concern regarding interpretation of technical information, a data-leader or school psychologist in the building can be utilized.

Determining how goals are set for students who are low achieving. The National Center for Intensive Intervention (intensiveintervention.org) describes three potential methods for goal setting for students at risk or who are on IEPs: using national norms or benchmarks, using weekly rates of improvement (ROIs), or using an intra-individual framework. Each has its strengths and weaknesses for instructional and decision-making purposes. Setting goals using national norms or benchmarks allows a teacher to compare the performance of a student(s) to the performance of other students at that grade level who were part of the norming group. Norms provide a stable indication of how students might compare to benchmarks at critical points during the year, which can support a rationale for a student needing increased academic support. However, these grade-level norms can be difficult to use in instructional decision making if students are performing several grades below their actual grade level, thus making goals unreachable. Out-of-grade-level measures can be utilized, but goals set using out-of-grade-level norms will only help the student grow to that grade-level norm and may not "push" the student enough. In addition, goals set using out-of-grade-level norms cannot provide the peer-comparison data that might eventually be needed to support a rationale for referral for special education services.

For students with disabilities, it may be better to set progress monitoring goals using weekly Rates of Improvement (ROIs). Similar to norms or benchmarks, these rates of improvement are calculated utilizing grade-level data collected from the norming group. In the literature, ROIs have been calculated most precisely using slope data from measures administered weekly, but have also been calculated by subtracting the initial benchmark score from the final benchmark score and dividing by the number of weeks. ROIs may be preferential to use with students who are at risk or identified with learning disabilities because weekly growth rates can be multiplied by the number of weeks the student will be progress monitored to create a more specific goal. In addition, ROIs can be easily "boosted" if a teacher wants to challenge a student more. For instance, if the weekly ROI for a particular measure is a one word increase per week, setting the ROI at 1.5 words per week for a particular student might challenge the student to rise to meet expectations and also might challenge the teacher to keep refining instruction to help the student meet the goal.

> "For students with disabilities, it may be better to set progress monitoring goals using weekly ROIs."

The final method for setting goals that is specified by the NCII is the use of an intra-individual framework. When using this framework, student progress monitoring begins at the student's grade level or as close as possible to grade level. The goal for a student is based on multiplying the slope (ROI) from at least 8 data points by 1.5 to raise expectations, and then adding the result to the average of the baseline starting point (baseline + (slope × 1.5)). This method utilizes student scores, making it ideal for monitoring the progress of students with learning disabilities, but does not utilize existing norms or benchmarks, so comparisons to grade level may not be embedded. In an RTI model, data-based decision making is key, so the ability to make high-quality decisions using student data that are at an accurate level would be a strength for the intra-individual framework.

In summary, goal setting is critical in an RTI model, whether the teacher is simply monitoring progress for instructional decision making or is using the data to make high-stakes decisions about student placement in special education. The use of grade level, normed data in goal setting would be important for making high stakes decisions, but for some students it is not possible to monitor progress at grade level. In cases where out-of-grade-level measures need to be used, teachers should consider using the ROI for the student's instructional level multiplied by 1.5 or an increment that provides a higher goal-level expectation.

Number of data points, weeks of instruction, and cut points for risk. A third important factor when making decisions about student progress in an RTI model is the number of data points that have been collected, over how many weeks, and what the cut point will be to indicate risk status for students. When students at risk are being progress monitored, teachers should give the intervention or instruction enough time to cause the desired positive change in academic improvement. Devote too little time to the intervention, and a teacher might move to something else too quickly, before the intervention has had time to work. In addition, the number of data points collected during intervention implementation is crucial to lay a solid foundation for decision making in RTI, particularly if the decisions being made are those regarding potential disability status. Although I remember being told as a pre-service special education teacher that two interventions implemented for two weeks each was enough for pre-referral intervention, the field has become much more sophisticated at decision making and two weeks is simply not long enough for an academic intervention.

For instance, in an effective RTI model, data teams meet to discuss student data after the student has at least 6 to 8 data points. Examining the graphed data, the team considers how many weeks of instruction or intervention—and especially importantly, fidelity of instruction during this time (discussed next)—have occured. Next, the team utilizes decision-making cut points to determine whether to continue the current instructional routine or to make a change. If data are being utilized to assess potential disability risk status, a dual discrepancy model might be utilized where both level and rate of progress data is examined (Fuchs & Fuchs, 1998; Fuchs & Deshler, 2007). Examples of decision-making rules might be the 4-point rule, the trend line rule, or an examination of level and rate of data (see Appendix B or case study below for example). Making the most accurate decisions based on the student data is important, but making data accessible and understandable is also important. If data are being used for instructional decision making, and calculating a trend line is not immediately feasible, examining the most recent four consecutive data points as compared to the goal line can provide information about how effective instruction is for the student. If all 4 points are above the goal line, consider raising the goal, if all 4 are the same as the goal line, continue with the same instruction, and if all 4 are below the goal line, implement an instructional change. Using the trend of data is more accurate, because trend takes into account all data, not just the most recent 4 points. Examining trend line versus goal line, similar decisions as those made in the 4-point rule can be applied: if trend is steeper than the goal line, raise the goal; if trend is the same as the goal line, continue with the same instruction; and if the trend line is less steep than the goal line, make a teaching change.

When using progress monitoring data for decision making that has higher stakes (i.e., decisions about special education referral), a dual discrepancy approach might be utilized where both level and rate of student progress data is examined. In this case, after 6 to 8 data points are collected, the level and rate of student progress is examined as compared to the goal level and rate. More on this in the next section where I provide a case example of the use of level and rate for disability decision making.

Examining the evidence base that supports core instruction and intervention and fidelity of implementation. The final area that is critical as we enhance specificity of decision making in an RTI model is an examination of core instruction and intervention, including duration, intensity, and perhaps most importantly, fidelity. In an RTI model, the core academic instruction that is in place (including the curriculum, materials, and delivery of instruction) serves as a universal for all students in the school. If this core instruction is not research-based or if it is not delivered with fidelity, students are at risk of being instructionally disabled and it is difficult to tease out whether there is a true disability until curriculum and teaching effectiveness is addressed. Schools engaging in an RTI process understand that an examination of core instruction is paramount, and many buildings choose to focus on Tier 1 instruction prior to, or at least in tandem with, implementation of individualized interventions. Leaders in buildings use tools such as Compelling Conversations (Piercy, 2007) to meet with teachers and conference about how they are meeting the needs of all of their students. These conversations rely on data that the teacher brings for a class or individual student, and outcomes might include more mentoring for the teacher, brainstorming of ideas for further intervention, or resources or support provided. These conversations are one piece of an examination of how universals are functioning in a building, but fidelity checks also need to be completed, either in the form of self-checks, colleague checks, or administrator checks. Many curricula include fidelity checklists, or people can develop their own.

Observational and fidelity data that are collected have to be discussed with the teacher, rather than put in the teacher's mailbox or sent via email. The discussion and ideas that arise as these data are discussed help advance teaching practices for all students. If fidelity of instruction is not checked, the underlying cause of a child's difficulties cannot be determined, as these difficulties may be a result of delivery or composition of core instruction.

> "If this core instruction is not research-based or if it is not delivered with fidelity, students are at risk of being instructionally disabled and it is difficult to tease out whether there is a true disability until curriculum and/or teaching effectiveness is addressed."

In addition to a thorough examination of core instruction, evidence-based interventions need to be selected and these interventions must be delivered with fidelity as well. The criteria used to determine if an intervention is evidence-based must include information about the effect size of the intervention following controlled studies, the number of participants in the studies that examined the intervention, whether the intervention has been published in peer-reviewed journals, the replicability of the procedures, and the number of studies that have been conducted on the intervention. Charts like those available on the National Centers for RTI (rti4success.org) and Intensive Intervention (intensiveintervention.org) can be utilized to determine which interventions have been vetted by experts and results of the vetting process. If interventions are not well-chosen and fidelity of implementation is not assessed on a frequent basis, the ability to say that a student is a non-responder might be in question. If interventions are evidence-based and a commitment is made to selecting and implementing a fidelity plan along with the intervention, teachers can feel more confident that in combination with the data that they are collecting, they have a clear picture of student progress with the selected intervention.

An applied example. Implementation of each of the pieces of the RTI model leads to an examination, selection, and further refinement of evidence-based practices in education. So by implementing the components of RTI, districts are enhancing their use of what we know to be high quality practices in education. Zirkel and Thomas (2010) provide information suggesting that all but seven states at the time of the study either recommended or required implementation of the critical RTI components. However, only nine states at the time of the study address the critical RTI components with respect to legal requirements. So how does the implementation of the critical components lead to making high quality decisions about special education status? Zirkel and Thomas reveal that only six states at the time of their study have specific standards for moving from RTI to special education referral and evaluation. If states are going to implement all of the components of RTI with fidelity and if they have been collecting ongoing data about the effectiveness of instruction and intervention, it makes sense for them to be able to use this information as they make decisions about referral and evaluation for special education.

As an example of the process of using data collected as part of an RTI process for decision making for referral for special education and within a special education evaluation, consider the case of the local school district I work with in Missouri. Some buildings in the district have been engaging in RTI processes for a while (building-wide), but others have limited their use of practices like screening and progress monitoring just to special education. Due to the number of buildings that are already using RTI in some manner and the frequent use of a screening and progress monitoring system (in the case of this district, Aimsweb; http://www.aimsweb.com), the district chose to develop and implement a plan for the use of their RTI data in decision making for eligibility. They needed to attend to Missouri state guidelines for eligibility decision making and also wanted to be as specific as possible about criteria that they would use to determine if students should move forward to eligibility decision making. Initially, the district limited the use of the process with just a few buildings. School psychologists serve in a critical role, providing input on the criteria, bringing cases forward to apply the process to, and continuing to refer back to the literature and to expert feedback. I was invited to be a part of the process of developing the criteria and we continued to refine as we explored how the criteria were working with student cases. The results of this work include the process along with checklists you see in Appendices C and D.

Initially, for step 1 of the process, *Screening,* the school-wide or grade level problem-solving team examines screening data from school-wide benchmarking measures to determine if the student falls below the 10th percentile compared to national norms for the suggested measure for the student's grade level. If the student is below the 10th percentile, other standardized measures (such as state or district test scores) are also examined to make certain that multiple measures indicate that the student is at risk. Use of standardized, non-subjective data is critical at this point, and for this district, they use data from Aimsweb or STAR, the Missouri state assessment, and other standardized test data that are available. Due to the high-stakes decision that is being made (eligibility determination), if screening data indicate that the student is below the 10th percentile, the next step is *Evaluation.* For this step, a standardized achievement test is administered in the area of concern or suspected disability for the student in order to verify low level of performance, which has to be a standard score of 80 or below (corresponding to below the 10th percentile). This *low level* of performance is then verified as part of the dual discrepancy.

If the student's low level of performance is verified in the *Evaluation* step, the third step, *Intervention,* begins if it has not already been put into place. A moderately intensive intervention that would be replicable in the general education setting is begun, attempting to emulate the conditions under which the implemented intervention could persist if it is effective. The intervention has to be evidenced-based and delivered with at least 80 percent fidelity for at least 12 sessions (see Appendix D for the fidelity sheet that the local district utilizes). To aid in monitoring, an intervention attendance record is kept. Prior to initiating an intervention, a goal is set for the student (*1st goal setting*) with the goal rate of improvement (ROI) set at the 50th percentile based on Aimsweb norms at current grade placement. As opposed to goal setting when students are receiving intervention in RTI and eligibility determination is not in question, goal setting for progress monitoring when eligibility determination is being determined needs to be at grade level to show the discrepancy between the student and peer norms. *Progress monitoring* is conducted as the intervention is being implemented to determine whether the student responds to that intervention and whether the intervention is effective. At least 6 progress monitoring data points are needed to make a decision. For the *1st decision* the student is progressing at a *slow rate* if the trend ROI is below the goal ROI. As an example, if the student is in fourth grade and is being progress monitored with oral reading fluency, the problem-solving team would compare the student's ROI from his/her progress monitoring data to the fourth grade ROI norm. If the student's trend ROI is .5 words per week and the fourth grade ROI norm for oral reading is .8 words per week, then the student's ROI would be determined to be at a *slower rate* than the norm.

If the student's ROI is not the same as the norm for his/her grade level, an *instructional change* is made to make instruction more intensive and an *updated goal* is set. The student's baseline for intervention round #2 is the median of the last 3 data points from intervention round #1. The goal rate of improvement (ROI) is set at the 50th percentile based on Aimsweb norms at the current grade placement. As with the initial intervention, an evidenced-based intervention is delivered with at least 80 percent fidelity for at least 12 sessions. An attendance record is kept to track implementation and progress monitoring is conducted, with at least 6 progress monitoring data points needed to make a decision. Once again, the team determines that the student is growing at a *slow rate* if the trend ROI is below the goal ROI. With respect to *eligibility determination*, the student may be identified as having a specific learning disability if both rate of progress is slow and overall level is low at the end of two rounds of interventions. Observations in the general education setting are conducted in area(s) of suspected disability and exclusionary factors apply.

How is this method of identification better than the traditional discrepancy method? First, students are identified early and are receiving intervention throughout the process. Second, ongoing data are collected on how the student is responding to existing instruction, providing a better assessment-curriculum link. Third, as opposed to some existing models using RTI, the criteria are well articulated. Fourth, decisions are made based on the results from standardized, technically adequate measures and the student's own progress data.

OPTIMAL METHODS FOR IDENTIFICATION

So for teachers and teams and schools and districts that are trying to make the best decisions they can about which students should receive special education services, what are the optimal ways to determine which students should receive special education services? Are schools employing appropriate practices? Readers can probably sense my bias towards a Response-to-Intervention model for identification. As noted in the applied example from a school district, the RTI model can be supported by abbreviated versions of standardized assessments to rule out behavior disorders or intellectual disabilities, and to collect more data in the area of suspected disability. Why should RTI be used as the primary method for special education identification? I believe there are several reasons. First and foremost, RTI identification makes use of existing

"While teachers and schools might have been collecting data and implementing interventions in the past, RTI provides a framework for implementation of these important elements."

student data. When using the discrepancy model, a chief complaint is that the data collected do not mirror the type of assessment that is conducted in the classroom. The content does not match, the assessment methods do not match, and therefore the data are not as accurate as they might be if they were more closely aligned with the curriculum and assessments given in the classroom. A second reason why RTI might be a preferred method for identification is that intervention and data collection are ongoing, even prior to pre-referral. So prior to any indication that the student might be referred for special education services, data are collected and examined and interventions are implemented and adjusted. Although teachers and schools might have been collecting data and implementing interventions in the past, RTI provides a framework for implementation of these important elements. In addition, if a decision is made for referral, the interventions and data that have been collected can be used to support a case for services. So pre-referral interventions will have already been implemented and tested, to some extent.

Are schools employing effective practices? Although almost every state has an RTI model (see rti4success.org, state guidelines), most states continue to use a combination of data from RTI and standardized assessments for identification. Zirkel and Thomas (2010) indicated that at the time the article was published, 12 states required RTI in some combination with standardized assessments. For all other states, use of RTI for identification is a choice. Ideally, as teams meet to discuss potential disability status, the following would be in place: (1) rule out poor classroom instruction as a cause for disability by using evidence-based core instruction and core principles of effective teaching; (2) frequent, reliable, and valid data collected and graphed for the student's areas of need (i.e., reading, mathematics); (3) intervention implemented as needed to provide remediation or enhancement of particular skill deficits as identified through diagnostic assessments; (4) frequent fidelity checks of both classroom instruction and intervention; and (5) decision-making rules employed on a frequent and scheduled basis to examine student progress or lack thereof. Although each of these is really best practice in schools, it becomes complicated to employ all steps.

This complication leads to the potential obstacles for the use of RTI for identification. Much earlier in the chapter I discussed potential problems with the use of the discrepancy model for identification, but what are the potential problems with the use of the RTI model for identification? They are directly related to the pieces that teams must have in place. First, poor classroom instruction must be ruled out as a cause. If schools are not using an evidence-based core curriculum, or individual teachers are not implementing it with fidelity, instruction can be compromised. If a large portion of students in a building are in Tiers 2 and 3, building staff must first look to universal classroom instruction to determine that it is meeting the needs of the majority of the students in the school. Each teacher needs to be implementing the chosen curriculum with fidelity and checks need to be scheduled on a frequent basis. These fidelity checks can be self-checks, peer checks, or administrator or specialist checks. Most importantly, discussion of the results of the fidelity checks is crucial, as this aids in identifying areas where support is needed and also highlights areas that are strengths. These teaching strengths might even be modeled for other teachers.

A second obstacle for the use of RTI for identification is that data must be collected frequently on reliable and valid measures in the subject area you are assessing. The frequency with which data are collected and graphed has been debated, with a balance sought between the number of data points that provide the greatest technical adequacy and making decisions quickly enough so that student intervention or referral is not delayed.

Third, interventions implemented must be specific to student need and must be evidence-based. It should be noted that if RTI is being used as a model for eligibility, the interventions implemented cannot be so significant, specialized, and time consuming that they will not be able to be sustained. For instance, some buildings actually have special education teachers pulling students not on IEPs for 30- to 45-minute intervention sessions. Although this may be wonderful for the student at the time, sustaining this type of intervention may be difficult and the school may actually be unknowingly delaying needed services for students. Finally, problem-solving teams comprised of either grade-level, content-level, or school-wide staff need to meet together on a regular and scheduled basis to examine graphed, objective data to make decisions about student progress and effectiveness of intervention.

So what would Deno and Dunn say about the status of special education now? Hopefully they would say that in the changes to the law for learning disabilities, for instance, we are trying to identify and provide services to those students who need it most. Hopefully they would say that schools are providing a service to students when they use an RTI model prior to and during the eligibility determination process, rather than waiting for students to fail. Hopefully they would say that decision making by teachers and teachers' use of data has drastically improved as a result of providing an infrastructure in schools where data are expected and data team meetings are regularly scheduled. Most importantly, hopefully they would say that while RTI is in varying degrees of implementation, schools, districts, and states are attempting to refine the model for identification so that decisions are more precise, more specific, are made as soon as possible, and intervention and important data are being collected along the way. For schools that are implementing or considering implementation, please see the resources in Appendix E.

Appendix A.   Sample fidelity checklist for comprehension*

Self-monitoring—to be completed (circle one):
Weekly   Bi-monthly   Monthly

Topic: Comprehension strategies

The following comprehension strategy is being implemented at this time (i.e. prediction, summarization, brainstorming, etc.): _____

Place a check next to each step as you complete it for a given lesson.

_____ Provide an objective for the lesson in concrete and measureable terms.

_____ Provide students a rationale for the strategy that you will be teaching them.

_____ Introduce the strategy through modeling.

_____ Use the strategy with the students on a short piece of text (guided practice).

_____ Have the students repeat back the steps in the strategy.

_____ Have students work independently or in pairs to implement the strategy as they read some text.

_____ Teach for generalization.

_____ Teach for maintenance.

On a scale from 1–10, I implemented the lesson with this degree of fidelity (defined as implementing the lesson utilizing the given steps or sequence):

1   2   3   4   5   6   7   8   9   10
Low fidelity   High fidelity

* Use only if the curriculum or program you are using does not already have a fidelity checklist

Appendix B. Sample decision-making framework

Decision-making rubric—to be implemented at least every six weeks

Three questions to guide discussion on data at problem-solving team meetings:

1) What is the student's goal? Current level?
2) What decision-making rule are we using (4-point; Trend; Other)? Can we apply that now?
3) If a change needs to be made, what do we do?

FIRST, to make a decision on movement/non-movement between tiers, the following rubric should be applied:

Student should move to a more intensive tier	Student should stay in a tier and an instructional change should be made	Student should stay in a tier with no changes	Student should be moved to a less intensive tier
Trend of data or last 4 consecutive data points are below the goal line for the past 6 weeks, AND when the student was checked 6 weeks prior	Trend of data or last 4 consecutive data points are below the goal line for the past 6 weeks	Trend of data or last 4 consecutive data points are even with the goal line	Trend of data or last 4 consecutive data points are above the goal line AND when the student was checked 6 weeks prior

SECOND, if a change needs to be made, the team questions:

1. Has the instruction/intervention been as **intense** as it could be?
   a. T/S ratio, curriculum used, time engaged.
2. Has the instruction/intervention been delivered with **fidelity**?
   a. Implementation reports are provided by the teacher or someone has observed implementation.
3. Is the instruction/intervention **evidence-based**?
   a. References are provided or someone has checked on this.
4. Has the **duration** of the instruction been lengthy enough?
   a. Does the team feel that lack of results is due to not having the intervention in place long enough?

Appendix C.   Special education eligibility plan using RTI, Missouri

Response to Intervention & Special Education Eligibility

State department guidelines require at least 24 intervention sessions over two structured, planned interventions before proceeding with an eligibility determination for a specific learning disability using a response to intervention model. Important guidelines to consider:

- *Interventions have to be research- or evidence-based.*
- *At least 12 sessions have to be provided to the student (per intervention).*
- *Progress monitoring data needs to be systematically collected at least once per week.*
- *Fidelity checks needs to be conducted with a score of 80 percent or higher.*
- *Parents need to be notified of the nature of the interventions, their student's lack of progress, and their right to request an evaluation.*

Eligibility Process for Special Education

Screening & Evaluation Period

- See *Eligibility Determination using Response to Intervention* document (p. 149) for screening guidelines and data decision rules.
- A standardized achievement test is conducted in the area(s) of suspected academic disability at the beginning of the evaluation period. *Note:* This is not required if sufficient progress monitoring data is documented (3+ months) upon re-evaluation.
- If not already done, targeted interventions are written into the *Evaluation Plan* and implemented as part of the comprehensive evaluation after data decision rules are met.
- Observations are conducted in the regular education setting in area(s) of suspected disability.

Evidence-Based/Research-Based Interventions
- *Round #1 (Tier 2/moderate intensity):*
  - Minimum of 12 sessions.
  - No more than 1 session per day.
  - At least 20 minutes per session.
  - At least 6 data points are needed to make decisions.

- *Round #2 (Tier 3/strong intensity):*
  - Minimum of 12 sessions.
  - No more than 1 session per day.
  - At least 20 minutes per session.
  - At least 6 data points are needed to make decisions.

Eligibility
- A lack of responsiveness to two increasingly intensive interventions is used to initially identify students in need of special education and related services under the category of SLD.
- A lack of progress is defined by *slow rate of improvement* (using data trend) **and** *low level of performance* (based on benchmark data and standardized achievement scores).
- Upon re-evaluation, progress monitoring data collected during special education service delivery may be used to support continued evidence of a disability.
- All SLD exclusionary factors apply including lack of instruction in reading and math.

Note. *Special education timelines and notice/consent requirements begin with the referral for evaluation.*
Note. *A written agreement to extend timelines is permissible if parents and the team decide additional time is needed to ensure that sufficient intervention data are collected to make an appropriate decision.*

Columbia Public Schools
Eligibility Determination using Response to Intervention

Screening
- Benchmark student in area(s) of concern. If scores fall *below the 10th percentile* based on AIMSweb norms, proceed with Review of Existing Data and Evaluation Plan if all other screening information warrants suspicion of a disability.

Evaluation
- Immediately after obtaining consent to test, administer a standardized achievement test in the area(s) of suspected disability in order to verify **low level of performance**. A standard score of *80 or below* (corresponding to below the 10th percentile) will verify low level of performance.

Need for Diagnostic Intervention
- If the student's low level of performance is verified, begin a moderately intensive intervention.
- Chosen intervention should be replicable in the general education setting.

1st Goal Setting
- Goal rate of improvement (ROI) is set at the 50th percentile based on AIMSweb norms at current grade placement.

1st Intervention & Progress Monitoring
- Evidenced-based intervention delivered with at least 80% fidelity for at least 12 sessions.
- Intervention attendance record is kept.
- At least 6 progress monitoring data points are needed to make a decision.

1st Decision Rule
- Student progressing at **slow rate** if the trend ROI is below the goal ROI.
- Norms used (school year is 36 weeks): Fall = week 1 through 12; Winter = week 13 through 24; Spring = week 25 through 36.

2nd Goal Setting
- If student is progressing at a slow rate, change intervention to be more intensive and set new goal.
- Student's baseline for intervention round #2 is the median of the last 3 data points from intervention round #1.
- Goal rate of improvement (ROI) is set at the 50th percentile based on AIMSweb norms at current grade placement.

2nd Intervention & Progress Monitoring
- Evidenced-based intervention delivered with at least 80% fidelity for at least 12 sessions.
- Intervention attendance record is kept.
- At least 6 progress monitoring data points are needed to make a decision.

2nd Decision Rule
- Student progressing at **slow rate** if the trend ROI is below the goal ROI.

Eligibility Determination
- The student may be identified as having a specific learning disability if **both** rate of progress is slow and overall level is low at the end of two rounds of interventions.
- Observations in the general education setting are conducted in area(s) of suspected disability.
- Exclusionary factors apply.

Appendix D.   Intervention Fidelity Checklist: General

Intervention name: _____   Date: _____

Interventionist: _____   Checklist completed by: _____

BEFORE (Check boxes when observed)

☐ 1. Has the correct student and teacher materials (i.e., teacher guide and word cards)
☐ 2. Starts intervention ON TIME
➤ All students are present (not checklist item)
  ○ If not, list students absent:

_____

_____

DURING

☐ 3. Follows curriculum and uses appropriate materials at appropriate times
☐ 4. Teacher is actively teaching intervention components
☐ 5. Answers students' relevant questions accurately and appropriately
☐ 6. When teacher instructs students to participate, ALL STUDENTS PARTICIPATE
☐ 7. Does not allow students to leave instruction unless necessary
☐ 8. Intervention lasts the whole time period it is supposed to
☐ 9. Provides students ample opportunities to respond
☐ 10. If students do not understand concept, teacher works with them to ensure they comprehend materials
➤ Offers more positives than redirects (with ultimate goal being approx. 4:1) (not checklist item). *Yes* _____ *No* _____

FIDELITY CHECK:

of boxes checked = _____   # of boxes total = **10**
Percent intervention completed with fidelity = _____
Goal = at least **80%**   Goal Met (check one)?   Yes _____   No _____

Comments:

_____

_____

_____

Appendix E.   Selected Resources for RTI and interventions

Selected RTI Resources

- National Center on RTI—rti4success.org.
- RTI Action Network—rtinetwork.org.
- National Center on Intensive Intervention—intensiveintervention.org.
- National Center on Learning Disabilities—ncld.org.
- Center on Positive Behavioral Interventions and Supports—pbis.org.
- National Center on Student Progress Monitoring—studentprogress.org.

- Research Institute on Progress Monitoring—progressmonitoring.org.
- Institute on Education Sciences Practice guides—http://ies.ed.gov/ncee/wwc/Publications_Reviews.aspx?f=All%20Publication%20and%20Review%20Types,3;#pubsearch.
- Fuchs, D., & Fuchs, L.S. (2006). Introduction to responsiveness-to-intervention: What,
  why, and how valid is it? *Reading Research Quarterly, 41*, 92–99.
- National Association of School Psychologists (NASP, 2010). *Interventions for achievement and behavior problems in a three-tier model including RTI.* Shinn, M.R. and Walker, H.M., Eds. NASP: Bethesda, MD.
- National Center on Response to Intervention (March 2010). *Essential components of RTI— A closer look at response to intervention.* Washington, DC: U.S. Department of Education, Office of Special Education Programs, National Center on Response to Intervention.

Selected Reading Intervention Resources

- Florida Center on Reading Research—fcrr.org.
- Intervention Central—www.interventioncentral.org.
- STEEP—http://www.gosbr.net/.
- IRIS center—http://iris.peabody.vanderbilt.edu/resources.html.

Selected Mathematics Intervention Resources

- Evidence-based Intervention Network—ebi.missouri.edu.
- Helping your child learn mathematics: http://www.ed.gov/parents/academic/help/math/math.pdf.
- Mathematics curriculum focal points (NCTM): http://nctm.org/standards/focalpoints.aspx?id=298.
- Lesson plans on illuminations.nctm.org.
- IRIS center (http://iris.peabody.vanderbilt.edu/resources.html).

Discussion Questions

1. Describe the pros and cons of RTI and the traditional discrepancy model used to identify students with learning disabilities.
2. What should be considered when setting goals and determining the duration of interventions?
3. Why does the quality of instruction, use of evidence-based practices, and fidelity of implementation matter in the decision-making process?
4. What are the implications of inaccurately identifying a child with or without a learning disability? How might this affect students, teachers, and schools?
5. What should teachers and schools consider for English Language Learners (ELLs) in the RTI process?

6. Do you see RTI as a sustainable model for intervention and identification in schools? Why or why not?
7. Who are the people who should be involved in making decisions about a students' eligibility for special education services? Should they be different if the student is being considered for different categories of special education (e.g., autism versus learning disability)? Should different people be involved at different stages of an RTI process?

ERICA LEMBKE'S SUGGESTIONS FOR FURTHER READING

Selected RTI Resources

- National Center on RTI—http://rti4success.org.
- Center on Positive Behavioral Interventions and Supports—http://pbis.org.
- National Center on Student Progress Monitoring—http://studentprogress.org.
- Research Institute on Progress Monitoring—http://progressmonitoring.org.
- National Center on Intensive Intervention—intensiveintervention.org.
- National Center on Learning Disabilities—ncld.org.

Selected Reading Intervention Resources

- Florida Center on Reading Research—http://fcrr.org.
- Intervention Central—http://www.interventioncentral.org.

Selected Mathematics Intervention Resources

- Evidence Based Intervention Network—ebi.missouri.edu.
- National Council for Teachers of Mathematics Illuminations—illuminations.nctm.org.

REFERENCES

Ardoin, S. P., & Christ, T. J. (2009). Curriculum based measurement of oral reading: Estimates of standard error when monitoring progress using alternate passage sets. *School Psychology Review, 38,* 266–283.

Barth, A. E., Stuebing, K. K., Anthony, J. L., Denton, C. A., Mathes, P. G., Fletcher, J. M., & Francis, D. J. (2008). Agreement among response to intervention criteria for identifying responder status. *Learning and Individual Differences, 18,* 296–307.

Burns, M. K., Riley-Tillman, T. C., & VanDerHeyden, A. M. (2013). *Advanced RTI applications: Intervention design and implementation.* New York: Guilford.

Deno, E. (1970). Special education as developmental capital. *Exceptional Children, 37,* 229–237.

Deno, S. L. (1985). Curriculum-based measurement: The emerging alternative. *Exceptional Children, 52,* 219–232.

Deno, S. L. (2005). Problem-solving assessment. In R. Brown-Chidsey (Ed.), *Assessment for intervention: A problem-solving approach* (pp. 10–40). New York, NY: Guilford Press.

Dunn, L M. (1968). Special education for the mildly retarded: Is much of it justifiable? *Exceptional Children, 35,* 5–22.

Francis, D. J., Santi, K. S., Barr, C., Fletcher, J. M., Varisco, A., & Foorman, B. R. (2008). Form effects on the estimation of students' oral reading fluency using DIBELS. *Journal of School Psychology, 46,* 315–342.

Fuchs, D., & Deshler, D.D. (2007). What we need to know about responsiveness to intervention (and shouldn't be afraid to ask*). Learning Disabilities Research & Practice, 22,* 129–136.

Fuchs, L. S., & Fuchs, D. (1998). Treatment validity: A unifying concept for reconceptualizing the identification of learning disabilities. *Learning Disabilities Research & Practice, 13,* 204–219.

Fuchs, D., & Fuchs, L.S. (2006). Introduction to response to intervention: What, why, and how valid is it? *Reading Research Quarterly, 41,* 93–99.

Fuchs, D., Fuchs, L., & Compton, D. (2004). Identifying reading disabilities by responsiveness-to-instruction: Specifying measures and criteria. *Learning Disability Quarterly, 27,* 216–227.

Fuchs, D., Fuchs, L. S., Hintze, J., & Lembke, E. (2007). *Using curriculum-based measurement to determine response to intervention (RTI).* Retrieved on 13 April 2013, from http://www.studentprogress.org/summer_institute/default.asp#RTI.

Hintze, J. M., & Christ, T. J. (2004). An examination of variability as a function of passage variance in CBM progress monitoring. *School Psychology Review, 33,* 204–217.

Hughes, C. A., & Dexter, D. D. (2011). Response to intervention: A research-based summary. *Theory into Practice, 50,* 4–11.

Marston, D., Muyskens, P., Lau, M., & Canter, A. (2003). Problem-solving model for decision making and high-incidence disabilities: The Minneapolis experience. *Learning Disabilities Research & Practice, 18,* 187–200.

McMaster, K. L., Fuchs, D., Fuchs, L. S., & Compton, D. L. (2005). Responding to nonresponders: An experimental field trial of identification and intervention methods. *Exceptional Children, 71*(4), 445–463.

NCS Pearson Inc. (2011). Aimsweb. Accessed on 29 January, 2015 http://www.aimsweb.com/.

Pardini, P. (2002). The history of special education. *Rethinking Schools, 16.* Retrieved from http://www.rethinking-schools.org/restrict.asp?path=archive/16_03/Hist163.shtml, 4/21/13.

Petscher, Y., Cummings, K., Biancarosa, G., & Fien, H. (2013). Advanced measurement applications of curriculum-based measurement in reading. *Assessment for Effective Intervention, 38,* 71–75.

Piercy, T. (2007). *Compelling conversations: Connecting leadership to achievement.* Englewood, CO: Lead and Learn Press.

Reynolds, C. R. Shaywitz, S. E. (2009) Response to intervention: Ready or not? Or, from wait-to-fail to watch-them-fail. School Psychology Quarterly, *24*(2), 130–145.

The Journal of Special Education (1994). *Special Issue 27*(4), 373–551.

Tilly W. D. III. (2002). Best practices in school psychology as a problem-solving enterprise. In A. Thomas & J. Grimes (Eds.), *Best practices in school psychology,* 4th ed. (pp. 21–36). Bethesda, MD: National Association of School Psychologists.

VanDerHeyden AM, Witt JC, Gilbertson D. (2007). A multi-year evaluation of the effects of a response to intervention (RTI) model on identification of children for special education. *Journal of School Psychology, 45,* 225–256.

Vaughn S, Wanzek J, Fletcher JM. (2007). Multiple tiers of intervention: A framework for prevention and identification of students with reading/learning disabilities. In B. M. Taylor, J. Ysseldyke, (Eds.), *Educational interventions for struggling readers* (pp. 173–196). New York: Teacher's College Press.

Vaughn, S. R., Wanzek, J., Woodruff, A. L., S. Linan-Thompson (2006). A three-tier model for preventing reading difficulties and early identification of students with reading disabilities. In D. H. Haager, S. Vaughn, J. K. Klingner, (Eds.), *Validated reading practices for three tiers of intervention* (pp. 11–28). Baltimore, MD: Brookes.

Zirkel, P. A., & Thomas, L B. (2010). State laws and guidelines for implementing RTI. *Teaching Exceptional Children, 430,* 60–73.

Getting to Know Margaret P. Weiss (Peggy)

 I am an Assistant Professor at George Mason University, where I teach courses in secondary methods and collaboration. I began my career as a secondary social studies teacher. I was surprised by the fact that many very capable students in my class were not able to read the textbook. So, I had to find out more. I learned that these students had various learning disabilities (LD) and I was hooked on figuring out the puzzles they presented. I tutored and taught students with LD until I decided to get my license to teach in the public schools. I completed my Masters' and eventually taught students with LD in middle and high schools and at the college level.

I first encountered co-teaching in a middle school. Neither of us knew what we were doing but we were both social studies people, so it worked. Then I began teaching with teachers in other content areas, some worked well and some did not. As a Ph.D. student, I never forgot the fundamental shift necessary to go from teaching by myself to teaching with someone else. As I studied co-teaching, I realized that there were many different ways to do it, and there was so much more we needed to know. I remember telling my advisor that I did not want to be defined by my dissertation topic of co-teaching. However, with the increasing number of students with LD who are in co-taught classrooms, finding ways to do it well is critical to their success. And so, I now study it, teach it, and, obviously, write about it.

10

CO-TEACHING: NOT ALL SPECIAL EDUCATORS SHOULD DANCE

Margaret P. Weiss

The Individuals with Disabilities Education Act (IDEA) guarantees a free, appropriate public education to students with disabilities and aligns with the No Child Left Behind Act (NCLB) of 2001 in its focus on providing students with access to the general education curriculum, scientifically based instruction, and subsequent assessments of performance. This focus is frequently interpreted to mean that students with disabilities are to be placed in general education classrooms for instruction (Deshler et al., 2001). For example, in 1990–91, approximately 33 percent of students with disabilities spent more than 80 percent of their day in general education classrooms. In 2009–10, that had risen to 59 percent (U. S. Department of Education, 2011). One way that schools have met the need for service delivery options in the general education classroom is through co-teaching. Though co-teaching has evolved for some time, there are many questions that remain about its implementation and effectiveness. The question of who should co-teach, specifically which special educators should co-teach, is one of the critical questions that has not been adequately addressed. In this chapter, I suggest that the teachers who implement co-teaching must have specific characteristics in order to provide the instruction necessary to meet the unique needs of students with disabilities.

DEFINING CO-TEACHING

The concept of team teaching has a history in general education, however, team teaching as a service delivery model in special education evolved in the 1990s from significant work by Marilyn Friend and Lynne Cook. In their book, *Interactions: Collaboration Skills for School Professionals*, Friend and Cook (2010) state that co-teaching

> is a service delivery option for providing special education or related services to students with disabilities or other special needs while they remain in their general education class. Co-teaching occurs when two or more professionals jointly deliver substantive instruction to a diverse, blended group of students in a single physical space.
>
> (p. 109)

Friend and Cook (2010) continue to define co-teaching as occurring when the following conditions are met: (a) it involves at least two appropriately credentialed professionals (not para-educators), (b) the two contribute to the planning and delivery of substantively different instruction (that which cannot be done by an individual teacher), (c) the classroom includes a diverse variety of students and instructional needs, and (d) teachers share a common classroom space.

As one reads about co-teaching, it becomes clear that the purpose of co-teaching is to provide qualitatively different instruction to meet the needs of students with disabilities in a general education classroom instead of in a separate space. Two fully credentialed professionals work to bring their expertise together, not to change one another, to provide both access to the general education curriculum and intensive, individualized instruction as outlined in students' individualized education plans. These big ideas and defining characteristics are critical to the current discussion of whether co-teaching is an effective service delivery model and how best to implement it.

"One way that schools have met the need for service delivery options in the general education classroom is through co-teaching."

In addition to defining co-teaching, Friend and Cook (2010) also describe the conditions necessary to make co-teaching successful. These include volunteering to participate, common planning time, clear role definitions and ideas about co-teaching, administrative support, and professional development. Given these conditions and the basic principles described above, advocates argue that co-teaching will provide what is necessary for students with disabilities to access the general curriculum and have their unique needs met.

CO-TEACHING RESEARCH: HOW MAKING ASSUMPTIONS DISTRACTS

The focus of many articles and much research on co-teaching has been on the format of this classroom, including models of co-teaching (e.g., Walther-Thomas, Korinek, McLaughlin, & Williams, 2000), relationships between co-teachers (e.g., Trent, 1998), and administrative contexts (e.g., Weiss & Lloyd, 2003) with few studies that focus on the instruction taking place. These descriptions and discussions of co-teaching—the prodding, poking, critiquing, and lauding—have focused on it as a singular entity. It is a "collaboration," "marriage," or "dance" (e.g., Howard & Potts, 2009), discussed with the assumption that, perhaps if the marriage or dance is working, there must be good things happening for students with disabilities. For those of us old enough to remember, Walter Matthau, as the coach of the Bad News Bears, made the point that "when you ASSUME, you make an ASS out of U and Me!"[1] In the book, *Seven Secrets for How to Think like a Rocket Scientist* (2004), James Longuski refers to this scene and makes the elegantly simple statement that "it's the hidden assumptions that can get us into so much trouble" (p. 81). The implementation of co-teaching is an example of how many different assumptions about a model can cause an almost chaotic approach to its implementation.

RECENT REVIEWS

Several reviews of the research on co-teaching have been published in the last 15 years. In a narrative review, Weiss and Brigham (2000) concluded that:

- Authors omitted vital information about their measures,
- Almost all research reported on "successful" co-teaching pairs,

- Teachers said the major variable was personality,
- Neither general educators nor special educators had a clear definition of collaboration or co-teaching,
- Behavioral and grade changes were described qualitatively, and
- There were few descriptions of instructional actions.

In a subsequent narrative review, Scruggs, Mastropieri, and McDuffie (2007) found that the benefits for co-teachers included professional growth; those for students without disabilities included cooperation, extra teacher attention, and social modeling; and for students with disabilities, benefits included achievement success and increased teacher attention, as long as they had a minimum skill level. The authors also noted that the "one teach, one assist" model was most often used and special educators spent most of their time supporting the traditional role of the general educator. Finally, teachers stated that they needed administrative support, planning time, training, and compatibility to make things work (Scruggs et al., 2007).

In a quantitative review, Murawski and Swanson (2001) found an overall effective size of 0.40 for co-teaching in general education classrooms. Unfortunately, out of the 89 articles they found, only six studies met their inclusion criteria and three of these studies were ERIC documents and not published in peer-reviewed journals. The authors reiterated the findings of Weiss and Brigham (2000) and emphasized the fact that little was described about the instructional actions of the teachers in these classrooms. They stated, "Of greater concern to us, however, is that none of the studies reported explicit measures of treatment integrity" (p. 265).

> "The implementation of co-teaching is an example of how many different assumptions about a model can cause an almost chaotic approach to its implementation."

Early on in the co-teaching literature, several authors examined what was happening in instruction in co-taught classrooms. In a series of case studies in the early 1990s, Zigmond (1995a,b) and Baker (1995a,b) observed students with special needs in co-taught classrooms. They found that there was little special education taking place in these classrooms. In Boudah, Schumaker, and Deshler (1997), the researchers trained teachers to work together using the Collaborative Instruction Model and evaluated what the teachers were actually doing during instruction. They found that, after training, teachers spent a greater percentage of time mediating instruction and exchanging roles and a lesser percentage of time presenting content, circulating, and engaging in non-instructional behaviors. Unfortunately, this did not result in improved achievement for the students with learning disabilities in the classrooms (Boudah et al., 1997). In middle and high school co-taught classrooms, Weiss and Lloyd (2002) found that the instructional actions of special educators were distinctly different when they participated in instruction in both co-taught and special education classrooms than when they were assistants in the one teach, one assist model. In this qualitative study, teachers stated that they participated in the one teach, one assist role because they did not feel accepted by the general educator, they lacked content knowledge, they lacked suitable planning time, or because both teachers defined co-teaching this way.

In a study of middle school co-taught and singly taught classrooms, Magiera and Zigmond (2005) found only two significant differences for students with disabilities. First, students in co-taught classrooms had individual instructional interactions 2.2 percent of the time versus 1 percent of the time in singly taught classrooms. In singly taught classrooms, general education teachers interacted with students with special needs 62 percent of the time but only 45 percent of the time in co-taught classrooms. Unfortunately, there was no significant difference in the total number of student–teacher interactions across classrooms. The authors concluded "on the surface, our results fail to identify substantial additive effects stemming from having a special education teacher assigned to co-teach with a general education teacher" (p. 84). None of the teachers in this study had received training in co-teaching in the previous three years, only two pairs had common planning time, but all teachers were certified in their content areas.

Finally, in Harbort et al. (2007), researchers videotaped two teacher teams and used momentary time sampling to identify teaching behaviors in secondary biology and physical science. They found that, in most situations, the teachers used the one teach, one assist model, even though all teachers were experienced and licensed. General education teachers presented information to the group 30 percent of the intervals, the special educator less than 1 percent. The general educator responded to students 22 percent of the intervals, the special educator 30 percent of the intervals. Teachers were observed to work with small groups about 11 percent of the intervals "with the regular education teachers surprisingly observed in this type of interaction about twice as often as the special education teachers" (p. 21). Again, these teachers did not have common planning time and had some experience co-teaching but no specific training was listed.

In these studies and reviews of co-teaching, it is clear that little attention has focused on the fidelity of the implementation of the model as described by Friend and Cook (2010). Many of the co-teachers in these studies defaulted to the one teach, one assist model of instruction with little change in the instructional actions of the classroom. Few had common planning time, professional development, similar philosophies or definitions of co-teaching, or other forms of administrative support. If the research mirrors what is happening in schools, what does this mean for determining who should co-teach?

FINALLY, WHO SHOULD CO-TEACH?

When one examines co-teaching from the practitioner's perspective, the issues of implementation and assumptions about instruction can no longer be ignored. Co-teachers look the student in the eye and know he cannot read on grade level but needs to understand Shakespeare or Voltaire; they identify a student's working and long-term memory issues but realize she needs to know and apply 15 new vocabulary words related to rocks and continental drift in two days; and they understand the student is not fluent in basic math facts but must independently use the Pythagorean Theorem. Though there are ideas and lists of professional and personal characteristics for co-teachers (e.g., professionalism, collaborative skills, and punctuality) in descriptive papers, there is no concrete evidence about who makes co-teaching work. Is every special educator a good candidate? Is every special educator in every context a good candidate? Is the success of co-teaching as a service delivery model dependent upon the personalities of the teachers involved?

There are perhaps infinite variables involved in the implementation of a successful co-teaching service delivery model. However, if one is focused on what special educators could make it work, I would answer "no" to all of the questions posed previously. As Rock and Billingsley discuss in their chapter in this book, there are so many responsibilities pulling special educators in many different directions and the role of the special educator is ever changing. Each special educator reacts to these conditions in different ways. For example, as a new special educator, fresh from graduate school with no experience or instruction in co-teaching, I walked into the main office of my new middle school bright-eyed and bushy-tailed on the first day. I was almost run over by a teacher on her way out. She was shouting, "I did not ask for this. I don't want to do this. I do fine with the sped kids on my own." SLAM. When I finally got into the office area and asked what was going on, the assistant principal sheepishly told me that she had just broken the news to that teacher that I would be co-teaching with her. By the end of the first month, we were finishing each other's sentences and integrating strategy instruction with concepts related to American government.

Given my experience, the teachers I have worked with, and the research summarized above, my hypothesis is that there are two fundamental factors that are necessary but not sufficient for special educators to implement co-teaching successfully. First, the special educator must be a teacher with expert knowledge of the instructional actions necessary to meet the unique needs of the students with disabilities in that classroom. In other words, the special educator must know her special education instructional stuff. Second, the successful special educator must have a sense of agency and ownership in her position; a belief that she has some control or power in determining critical aspects of that co-teaching situation. She cannot be satisfied to take the position of a pawn in the classroom or collaborative relationship.

Being a Special Education Expert

There is a great deal of literature about what makes an expert different from a novice (e.g., Lyon & Weiser, 2009; Tsui, 2009). One of the major characteristics is a deep knowledge of the topic. This means knowing more than terms or superficial concepts. It means an ability to analyze, synthesize, and apply one's knowledge to novel situations. For a special educator in a co-taught classroom, it means being able to understand the curriculum of the course and the needs of the students with disabilities to a level where one can then synthesize the two and provide the necessary instruction. According to Brownell et al. (2010) this means

> that special education teachers must have well-integrated knowledge bases, including an understanding of (a) content and how to teach it, (b) specific problems that students with disabilities may experience in a particular content area, (c) the role of technology in circumventing learning issues or supporting access to more sophisticated learning, and (d) the role of specific interventions and assessments in providing more intensive, explicit instruction within a broader curricular context.
>
> (p. 369)

This does not simply mean to provide accommodation but, rather, to provide qualitatively different instruction. Instruction, not accommodation, is the heart of a free appropriate public education. Students with disabilities need to learn skills such as strategic approaches to learning the content on which they will be evaluated. They need multiple practice opportunities. They need distributed review. They need explicit, systematic instruction. They need intensity in instruction. Students with disabilities need special educators who can make the necessary instruction happen in general education, co-taught classrooms. Special educators on provisional licenses or those who do not have this expert knowledge cannot do this in separate settings, let alone when combined as a "peer" with expert content teachers. This is a difficult problem to overcome, given the long-standing issues of retention and shortages in special education (Billingsley, 2004; McLeskey & Billingsley, 2008). However, we must not let that deter us. We must, as a field, demand that only those who are fully qualified *and* expert special educators be put in a co-teaching situation with fully qualified and expert general educators. Otherwise, special educators will continue to be the assist in one teach, one assist and instruction for students with disabilities will not be any different from regular instruction.

> "For a special educator in a co-taught classroom, it means being able to understand the curriculum of the course and the needs of the students with disabilities to a level where one can then synthesize the two and provide the necessary instruction."

Having Ownership and Agency

When special educators have this expert knowledge and skill set, they are better able to advocate for conditions and instruction necessary for their students to succeed. However, having the skills is helpful but not always the best way to make things happen in schools. Underlying the shift of greater numbers of students with disabilities into the general education classroom and, therefore, great numbers of teachers' participation in co-teaching is the notion that the role of the special educator must change. This change in role has been somewhat forced upon special educators by changes in the systems within which they work. An example is a quote from a recent article, "Once practices have been identified, schools are faced with the challenge of implementing multiple evidence-based practices that often compete for limited resources. In response, *researchers* and *policy makers* have proposed three-tier schoolwide prevention models for academic and social behavior support" (Simonsen et al., 2010; italics added). The premise of this article was that special educators should redefine their roles as interventionists, working within a three-tiered response to intervention (RTI) model (Simonsen et al., 2010). This premise is echoed in many articles in the literature (e.g., Wasburn-Moses, 2005). And, though it has been around a bit longer than RTI, co-teaching is part of this changing role of special educators and should be considered in light of the research known about change and innovation in schools.

There is much written about change and acceptance of innovation so I want to focus on several ideas that seem particularly pertinent in co-teaching, as evidenced by the default of many special educators to the assist position in the "one teach, one assist" model of co-teaching. These ideas are part of a conceptual framework outlined by Ketelaar, Beijaard, Boshuizen, and Den Brok (2012). In this conceptual framework, there are three major components to a teacher's acceptance and participation in an educational innovation. These include ownership, sense-making, and agency. According to Spillane, Reiser, and Reimer (2002) and Vähäsantane and Eteläpelto (2009) (as cited in Ketelaar, Beijaard, Boshuizen, & Den Brok, 2012), "it is not a matter of simply accepting or rejecting what is being imposed: teachers actively position themselves in relation to an innovation" (p. 273).

This positioning is related to teachers' identities and their ownership, sense-making, and agency related to the innovation.

Ownership is "understood as a mental or psychological state of feeling owner of an innovation, which develops through the teacher's mental and/or physical investment in it" (Ketelaar et al., 2012, p. 274). Sense-making is

> an active cognitive and emotional process in which a person attempts to fit the new information into existing knowledge and beliefs. . . . Assimilation, which means that the teacher uses his or her own frame of reference in the sense-making process and adapts the new ideas in such a way that they fit into the existing frame. . . . Accommodation, in which the teacher transforms his or her own frame of reference in such a way that it fits in with the situational demands. . . . Toleration, whereby the teacher accepts the new situational demands but at the same time maintains his or her own frame of reference, which results in different perceptions with the teacher. . . . Distantiation, where the teacher totally rejects the situational demands and continues to use his or her initial frame of reference."
>
> (Ketelaar et al., 2012, p. 274–75)

Finally, agency

> is the extent to which someone feels in control of his or her own actions {. . .}. Teachers who experience agency within their work feel in control of the choices they make within their work and that these choices are based upon their own goals, interest, and motivations {. . .}. The degree to which teachers experience agency within their work will probably influence their response to the innovation.
>
> (Ketelaar et al., 2012, p. 275)

In a small-scale study by Ketelaar et al. (2012), researchers conducted semi-structured interviews and video-stimulated interviews of 11 teachers who were implementing a new vocational coaching program. This program differed from their usual teaching in that it required the teachers to stop whole class lessons and allow students to work independently to achieve goals. Results indicated that teachers fell along continuums of high to low in ownership and agency and fit into each subgroup of sense-making. Teachers with a high level of ownership said "the coaching role seemed to belong to their teacher identity" (p. 278) and they placed a great deal of importance on it. Teachers who assimilated the coaching role found it "as a continuous, ever-present role," unlike those who tolerated the role. Finally, teachers with a high level of agency played an active role in creating their own sense and program as they saw fit. Agency, in this study, seemed to work in two different directions. Teachers who experienced high levels of ownership and agency worked hard to make the innovation work for them. Teachers who experienced low levels of ownership but high levels of agency worked to make the innovation fail (Ketelaar et al., 2012).

This study provides a recent example of variables outside of content expertise that must be considered when determining who should co-teach in order to make the situation successful for students and teachers. Special educators who should co-teach will own co-teaching as part of their professional identities. This goes back to Friend and Cook's (2010) ideas that special educators will believe that co-teaching is two professionals working together to deliver instruction. The teachers who have a high level of ownership of co-teaching will understand that they are peers of their general educators who are in the general education classroom to provide qualitatively different and effective instruction for students with disabilities. They have expertise and they see it as their role to use their expertise to provide quality instruction. Those who do not have a high level of ownership will probably not participate in instruction in the same way.

Special educators who should co-teach will make sense of co-teaching by assimilating it, bringing the responsibilities, roles, and functions into their own frame of reference. In this, these special educators will bring the ideas of instruction in a co-taught classroom into their knowledge and understanding of effective instruction for students with disabilities. They will analyze the classroom, the needs, and the demands in order to synthesize how best to deliver the needed instruction and accommodation. They will then work to make that instruction happen, not just adjust to the situation.

"Special educators who should co-teach will own co-teaching as part of their professional identities."

Finally, and in my view, most important, special educators who should co-teach will have a high sense of agency. This means that when they are put into situations that do not allow them to implement what they own and make sense of, they take action. These teachers do not sit back in the classroom and say, "I'm not the content expert." They read the textbooks, the content standards, and the scope and sequence. They talk with their general education co-teachers so that they can learn. Or they work to get into co-taught classrooms where they do know the content better. These teachers also do not become martyrs for their students or the administration. They do not agree to co-teach in seven classrooms (on a block schedule with four periods) with no planning period with their co-teachers. These are the special educators who understand that, in order for the innovation (co-teaching) to work, it must be implemented with fidelity, and they do everything they can to make that happen.

CONCLUSIONS

It would be wishful thinking to believe that we could only put special educators with the right combination of expertise and thinking into every co-taught classroom. The complexities of schools and the demands of students make it difficult to meet current needs. As Rock and Billingsley discuss in their chapter, there are a host of issues related to having a well-prepared workforce. However, there are many things we, as a field, can do to attempt to get as close to the ideal as possible. First, we must determine how to identify the special educators who fit these two criteria reliably. That will require a great deal of work and more fully operationalizing the concepts of ownership, sense making, and agency. We could use the research lines from general education and earlier work in special education teacher efficacy to begin to define ownership and agency. As Rock and Billingsley also state, special education is still trying to work out how to prepare highly qualified teachers. Second, how can we get those who do not fit the criteria closer to fitting them? Alternatively, do we want to? Just as not everyone wants to be a parent or a veterinarian, not every special educator should be forced to be a co-teacher. Third, do we see differences in instruction when teachers with these criteria are in the co-taught classroom? Fourth, if we see differences, are we also seeing differences in the learning of students with disabilities? These final two questions are at the foundation of the co-teaching service delivery model. Advocates might think co-teaching is the greatest idea in the world; however, if research indicates that it requires a tremendous amount of resources and energy with little effect on learning when implemented under the best conditions, we must find better alternatives. My hypothesis is that if, as a field, we could find and place a special educator with the content expertise and professional agency described in this chapter into the co-taught classroom, we would be able to make great changes in instruction and, therefore, in achievement for students with disabilities. The co-teaching "dance" would be realized and those special educators who are not quite right for this cha cha could sit it out.

Discussion Questions

1. What are the pros and cons of being in an inclusion classroom from a special education teacher's perspective? From a general education teacher's perspective?
2. How does the concept of being an instructional expert relate to Rock & Billingsley's chapter (Chapter 11)?
3. What should school administrators consider when deciding co-teaching partners and classrooms?
4. Do you think you can make the argument that collaborative co-teaching has supportive evidence? Why?
5. In your opinion, what does agency and ownership look like in an inclusive classroom?
6. What should teacher-training programs take into account when preparing special and general education teachers for inclusive classrooms?

NOTE

1. I recognize that many others (Felix Unger in *The Odd Couple* and Oscar Wilde, unless that's another assumption) have used this aphorism, too.

MARGARET P. WEISS'S SUGGESTIONS FOR FURTHER READING

Weiss, M. P. (1999). The actions of secondary special educators in cotaught and special education settings (Doctoral dissertation. Retrieved from ProQuest. (9935032)

Weiss, M. P., & Brigham, F. J. (2000). Co-teaching and the model of shared responsibility: What does the research support? In T. E. Scruggs & M. A. Mastropieri (Eds.), *Advances in Learning and Behavioral Disabilities: Educational Interventions* (pp. 217–246.). Stamford, CT: JAI Press.

Weiss, M. P. & Lloyd, J. W. (2002). Congruence between roles and actions of secondary special educators in co-taught and special education settings. *The Journal of Special Education, 36,* 58–68.

Weiss, M. P., & Lloyd, J. W. (2003). Conditions for co-teaching: Lessons from a case study. *Teacher Education and Special Education, 26*, 27–41.

Weiss, M. P. (2004). Co-teaching as science in the schoolhouse: More questions than answers. *Journal of Learning Disabilities, 37*, 218–223.

REFERENCES

Baker, J. (1995a). Inclusion in Virginia: Educational experiences of students with learning disabilities in one elementary school. *The Journal of Special Education, 29*, 116–123.

Baker, J. (1995b). Inclusion in Minnesota: Educational experiences of students with learning disabilities in two elementary schools. *The Journal of Special Education, 29*, 133–143.

Billingsley, B. S. (2004). Promoting teacher quality and retention in special education. *Journal of Learning Disabilities, 37*, 370–376.

Boudah, D. J., Schumaker, J. B., & Deshler, D. D. (1997). Collaborative instruction: Is it an effective option for inclusion in secondary classrooms? *Journal of Learning Disabilities, 20*, 293–316.

Brownell, M. T., Sindelar, P. T., Kiely, M. T., & Danielson, L. C. (2010). Special education teacher quality and preparation: Exposing foundations, constructing a new model. *Exceptional Children, 76*, 357–377.

Deshler, D. D., Schumaker, J. B., Lenz, B. K., Bulgren, J. A., Hock, M. F., Knight, J., & Ehren, B. J. (2001). Ensuring content-area learning by secondary students with learning disabilities. *Learning Disabilities Research and Practice, 16*, 96–108.

Friend, M., & Cook. L. (2010). *Interactions: Collaboration skills for school professionals.* Boston: Pearson.

Harbort, G., Gunter, P. L., Hull, K., Brown, Q., Venn, M. L., Wiley, L. P., & Wiley, E. W. (2007). Behaviors of teachers in co-taught classes in a secondary school. *Teacher Education and Special Education, 30*, 13–23.

Howard, L., & Potts, E. A. (2009). Using co-planning time: Strategies for a successful co-teaching marriage. *Teaching Exceptional Children Plus, 5*(4), article 2.

Ketelaar, E., Beijaard, D., Boshuizen, H. P. A., & Den Brok, P. J. (2012). Teachers' positioning towards an educational innovation in the light of ownership, sense-making, and agency. *Teaching and Teacher Education, 28*, 273–282.

Longuski, J. (2004). *The seven secrets of how to think like a rocket scientist.* New York: Copernicus.

Lyon, G. R., & Weiser, B. (2009). Teacher knowledge, instructional expertise, and the development of reading proficiency. *Journal of Learning Disabilities, 42*, 475–485.

McLeskey, J., & Billingsley, B. S. (2008). How does the quality and stability of the teaching force influence the research-to-practice gap? A perspective on the teacher shortage in special education. *Remedial and Special Education, 29*, 293–305.

Magiera, K., & Zigmond, N. (2005). Co-teaching in middle school classrooms under routine conditions: Does the instructional experience differ for students with disabilities in co-taught and solo-taught classes? *Learning Disabilities Research and Practice, 20*, 79–85.

Murawski, W. W., & Swanson. H. L. (2001). A meta-analysis of co-teaching research: Where are the data? *Remedial and Special Education, 22*, 258–267.

Scruggs, T. E., Mastropieri, M. A., & McDuffie, K. A. (2007). Co-teaching in inclusive classrooms: A metasynthesis of qualitative research. *Exceptional Children, 73*, 392–416.

Simonsen, B., Shaw, S. F., Faggella-Luby, M., Sugai, G., Coyne, M. D., Rhein, B., . . . Alfano, M. (2010). A schoolwide model for service delivery: Redefining special educators as interventionists. *Remedial and Special Education, 31*, 17–23.

Trent, S. C. (1998). False starts and other dilemmas of a secondary general education collaborative teacher: A case study. *Journal of Learning Disabilities, 31*, 503–513.

Tsui, A. B. M. (2009). Distinctive qualities of expert teachers. *Teachers and Teaching: Theory and Practice, 15*, 421–439.

U. S. Department of Education (2011). *The condition of education.* Washington, DC: Author.

Walther-Thomas, C., Korinek, L., McLaughlin, V. L., & Williams, B. T. (2000). *Collaboration for inclusive education: Developing successful programs.* Needham, Heights, MA: Allyn & Bacon.

Wasburn-Moses, L. (2005). Roles and responsibilities of secondary special education teachers in an age of reform. *Remedial and Special Education, 26*, 151–158.

Weiss, M. P., & Brigham, F. J. (2000). Co-teaching and the model of shared responsibility: What does the research support? In T. E. Scruggs & M. A. Mastropieri (Eds.), *Advances in learning and behavioral disabilities: Educational interventions* (pp. 217–246.). Stamford, CT: JAI Press.

Weiss, M. P., & Lloyd, J. W. (2002). Congruence between roles and actions of secondary special educators in co-taught and special education settings. *The Journal of Special Education, 36,* 58–68.

Weiss, M. P., & Lloyd, J. W. (2003). Conditions for co-teaching: Lessons from a case study. *Teacher Education and Special Education, 26,* 27–41.

Zigmond, N. (1995a). Inclusion in Pennsylvania: Educational experiences of students with learning disabilities in one elementary school. *The Journal of Special Education, 29,* 124–132.

Zigmond, N. (1995b). Inclusion in Kansas: Educational experiences of students with learning disabilities in one elementary school. *The Journal of Special Education, 29,* 144–154.

Getting to Know Marcia L. Rock

 Growing up in a large family, my two favorite pastimes were teaching school with my dolls and playing Star Trek with my brothers. As the only girl, I was often the outsider—the one who saw, thought, and behaved differently than my five brothers. Through those childhood experiences, I learned that advocacy matters and became an ardent fighter for the underdog!

Fast forward to my first semester as a college freshman, sitting in Psychology 101. When we got to Chapter 4, "Basic Principles of Learning," in the Bourne and Ekstrand (1979) text, our professor used a movie to demonstrate how behavioral principles could be used to teach a student with Down Syndrome. Intuitively, I understood the "art" of teaching, but the "science" was new to me. I was hooked. And the rest, as they say, is history . . .

Getting to Know Bonnie S. Billingsley

Growing up I spent years playing the violin, so it wasn't surprising that I began a career in music. However, in my first year of college, I met a woman, Myra, who was enrolled in a Ph.D. program in music therapy. She introduced me to a preschool girl with autism and I was involved in her care and education for several years. I also helped Myra collect data for her dissertation, in an institution for children with emotional disorders.

I entered a special education program in 1975, the year P.L. 94-142 became law. It was an exciting time in the field, as so many changes were taking place, including deinstitutionalization. My years working in public schools as a teacher and administrator fueled my interests in special education teachers and their work contexts.

11

WHO MAKES A DIFFERENCE! NEXT GENERATION SPECIAL EDUCATION WORKFORCE RENEWAL

Marcia L. Rock & Bonnie S. Billingsley

In my (BB) first week as a special education supervisor, the personnel director asked the second author, "why are our special education teachers leaving in droves?" Having just arrived, I couldn't answer her question, but it didn't take long to identify some of the challenges: It was an urban district with a high percentage of students from high-poverty households; the surrounding suburban districts offered higher salaries; and our district hired more out-of-field teachers than the surrounding districts, a risk factor for leaving. Like many districts, our system struggled to find, develop, and keep qualified special educators.

Similarly, in my (MLR) initial week of teaching in a self-contained classroom, I thought of leaving the profession more than once. Although I was trained as a special educator, to say I was ill prepared for the many workplace challenges I faced would be an understatement. Teaching students with emotional behavioral disorders, in a high needs elementary school, I had no para-educator, no curriculum or instructional materials, no crisis team support, and no mentor. Before week's end, I was injured by one of the students I was working tirelessly to teach. Not unlike many beginning teachers, I wondered whether I had made the right career choice. My options were clear: stay, leave, or transfer.

An underlying assumption in the quest for recruiting, developing, and retaining effective teachers is that *who teaches our students matters a great deal*. Students taught by the most effective teachers make greater achievement gains than those taught by less effective teachers (Hanushek, Rivkin, & Kain, 2005). Some evidence in special education suggests that teachers with more extensive preparation use effective practices more than those on emergency certificates (Nougaret, Scruggs & Mastropieri, 2005). Using value-added analyses, Feng and Sass (2010) reported that specific teacher preparation factors (e.g., special education degrees, more hours of coursework, certification in special education) were related to the achievement gains of students with disabilities. Clearly, all students with disabilities need and deserve highly qualified teachers.

Even though there is broad consensus that teachers matter, the field of special education has not been able to solve the perplexing problem of creating a qualified workforce for all students with disabilities. The purpose of this chapter is to consider the challenges school districts face in finding, developing, and keeping expert teachers (*We've Got Issues*); why we need to look beyond the teachers themselves to assure that teachers have opportunities to be effective (*All Things Considered*); and possible solutions for making sure that students with disabilities have opportunities to be taught by qualified and effective teachers (*Fresh Air*).

WE'VE GOT ISSUES

In the U.S. we do not have enough qualified and willing special education teachers to fill new and vacant positions each year. To address the lack of qualified teachers, state educational agencies grant waivers that allow districts to hire individuals who aren't prepared for their jobs. Waivers are a poor solution and clearly a threat to student achievement. We might ask how many people would consider going to a physician, counselor, or even a hair stylist who hadn't completed or even begun their preparation? Unprepared individuals in these fields are not permitted to provide these services.

"An underlying assumption in the quest for recruiting, developing, and retaining effective teachers is that who teaches our students matters a great deal."

Unfortunately, special education teachers are listed as among the highest areas of teacher need in the U.S. (American Association for Employment in Education [AAEE], 2011). The shortage of special education teachers is usually defined as the percentage of individuals hired who are not fully qualified for their positions. This has ranged from about 7 to 12 percent over the last two decades (Billingsley, 2011; Boe et al., 2013). Even though the vast majority of special education teachers are qualified for their positions, thousands of students with disabilities continue to be taught by unqualified teachers. For example, in 2007–8, there was a shortage of approximately 34,000 teachers (U.S. Department of Education, 2010). Given the average caseload of 17 students for each special education teacher (McLeskey, Tyler & Flippin, 2004), a rough estimate is that about 578,000 students were taught by special education teachers who were not fully qualified. Although there is some evidence that the shortage of special education teachers has lessened since the economic downturn of 2008 (Boe et al., 2013), there are still considerable shortages in special education (AAEE, 2011).

It is tragic that students in high-poverty schools bear the brunt of the shortage. In a study of early career teachers, 24 percent of teachers in high-poverty districts were on emergency certificates, compared to 2 percent in districts in low-poverty districts (Fall & Billingsley, 2008). In addition, early-career special education teachers in high-poverty schools had significantly fewer credentials on quality indicators such as certification, advanced degrees, graduation from selective institutions, performance on teacher tests, and time spent in student teaching, than their counterparts in low-poverty schools (Fall & Billingsley, 2008). Special educators in high-poverty schools also had poorer work conditions (Fall & Billingsley, 2011). The higher rates of turnover among teachers in high-poverty schools (Guarino, Santibanez, & Daley, 2006) mean that students are often subjected to one unqualified teacher after another.

Unfortunately, we have observed first-hand the poor teaching practices of woefully unprepared teachers as they struggled to get through each teaching day. No doubt these teachers need intensive support and training to become effective and these unprepared special education teachers are also a group that is at-risk of leaving (Billingsley, 2004). As a former special education supervisor (BB), I often thought a newly identified student would be better off in general education without any special education services than taught by a long-term substitute or a special educator with only an emergency certificate.

Reducing the shortage of special educators won't happen with quick fixes. Many policy-makers and educators have promoted so called "fast routes" with a course or a summer program as the only requirement for beginning a teaching career. However, these fast routes are unlikely to remedy the problem, as teachers with minimal preparation are not as ready for the demands of teaching and are also perhaps less committed than their more extensively prepared colleagues (Sindelar, Brownell & Billingsley, 2010).

ALL THINGS CONSIDERED: IT'S COMPLICATED

In the previous sections we focused on areas of shortage in the special education teaching workforce. However, simply hiring highly qualified teachers is not sufficient for improving teacher effectiveness and student outcomes. As Ladson-Billings (2009) noted, teachers require *opportunities to teach* to be effective—they need to be able to use their expertise in an environment that is "conducive to teaching and learning" (p. 207). A problem interfering with special education teachers' effectiveness is expanding and unrealistic expectations—leaving them unable to address their most important role—that of providing instruction.

Highly Qualified or Highly Unrealistic?

At the same time that districts struggle to find qualified special educators, expectations for their work have never been higher. The Individuals with Disabilities Education Act (IDEA) (2004) confirmed the expectation of No Child Left Behind (NCLB) (2001) that all special education teachers be highly qualified. Special educators are expected to hold state certification in special education and also demonstrate content expertise for the subjects they teach. The underlying rationale is fairly straightforward—all students deserve to be instructed by those with a strong grasp of the content being taught and their success in learning and in passing tests required for graduation depends on adequate educational opportunities.

Yet content knowledge requirements create daunting challenges as special education teachers may need knowledge in teaching early reading or adolescent literature, elementary mathematics or algebra, science, and social studies. Early career special education teachers indicate content expectations are among the most challenging aspects of their jobs, and some indicate that they learn the content as they teach it, which leaves less time for instructional planning (Billingsley, Griffin, Smith, Kamman & Israel, 2009). Moreover, special education teachers need to have knowledge about positive behavior supports, social skills development, special education law, Response-to-Intervention (RTI), and if in secondary settings, how to facilitate the transition of students from high school to post-secondary settings.

"A problem interfering with special education teachers' effectiveness is expanding unrealistic expectations—leaving them unable to address their most important role—that of providing instruction."

Perhaps the content requirement would not be as daunting if teachers were prepared to teach in either elementary or secondary settings. However, most state education agencies require special education teachers to be certified to teach kindergarten (or first grade) through high school (Geiger, Crutchfield, & Mainzer, 2003). Requiring teacher preparation programs to prepare special education teachers to teach grades K–12 presents a substantial challenge both for teacher preparation programs and the prospective teachers. Given this expectation, special education teachers must learn about the specific developmental needs of students across this wide age range and develop an understanding of extensive and complex curricula. The new curriculum requirements under the Common Core Standards are more complex than those of some state standards, requiring even higher levels of expertise for special teachers.

In addition to requiring extensive content knowledge, special education teachers also need to be well versed in evidence-based instructional practices, particularly in literacy, mathematics, and behavioral interventions. IDEA 2004 requires Individualized Education Program teams to select academic and behavioral interventions that are supported by peer-reviewed research. Special education teachers need to be knowledgeable about these practices, not only to meet IDEA requirements, but also because these practices are most likely to make a difference in their students' achievement. Mastering evidence-based practices is a complex endeavor and special education teachers need specific guidance and feedback to master these practices. Unfortunately, new special education teachers are also less likely to receive mentoring assistance than general educators (Billingsley, Carlson & Klein, 2004; Washburn-Moses, 2010), leaving many without adequate instructional guidance.

In addition to becoming content and instructional experts, special educators need to have in-depth knowledge across a range of exceptionality areas. Because noncategorical programs are the norm in many districts, special education teachers must be prepared to teach students with widely varying needs. Evidence from the largest sample of special education teachers studied suggests that many special educators teach multiple groups of students, with a quarter teaching students from four different exceptionality groups (Carlson, Brauen, Klein, Schroll, & Willig, 2002). Moreover, these teachers may work in varied instructional arrangements, requiring different types of skills for specific roles, such as co-teaching (see Weiss, this volume).

Instruction Isn't Necessarily the Main Thing

Given the complex world of special education teaching, it isn't surprising that special education teachers express concern about their jobs. Special educators report they are overloaded with work, do not have sufficient time to do their jobs well, and lack opportunities to collaborate with general educators (Billingsley, 2004). Some special education teachers report that they do not have a clear understanding about what their jobs should be (Billingsley et al., 2009), and over half indicate routine duties and paperwork interfered with their teaching to a great extent (Paperwork in Special Education, 2003).

Until recently, we had had few data on how special education teachers actually spend their time. However, an observational study of 36 special education teachers at work for 2,200 hours presents a bleak picture. Vannest and Hagan-Burke (2010) reported that special education teachers spent their time in the following ways: teaching academics (15.6 percent), instructional support (14.6 percent), paperwork (12.1 percent), personal time (9.4 percent), consulting/

"In addition to becoming content and instructional experts, special educators need to have in-depth knowledge across a range of exceptionality areas."

collaboration (8.6 percent), "other responsibilities (7.9 percent), supervision (7.2 percent), discipline (7.0 percent), and planning (5.4 percent)" (p. 138). Special education teachers spent less than 5 percent of their time on assessment and nonacademic instruction. These findings suggest that special education teachers spend their time in fragmented ways, with non-instructional activities taking far more time than instruction.

In summary, special education teachers' work has grown more complex over the past decades. Today's new special educator may be expected to: (1) teach almost any grade/age/exceptional student group; (2) instruct in multiple content areas; (3) demonstrate expertise in a wide range of evidence-based practices; (4) work effectively and collaboratively across varied instructional arrangements; and (5) manage a wide range of non-instructional tasks. Although the field needs special education teachers who are able to meet students' needs in a range of contexts, one could easily argue that we are setting them up for expectations that are difficult, if not impossible to meet. At what point will their contributions be so diluted that we question the need for these teachers?

In addition, there is evidence that these challenges (e.g., role overload, non-teaching demands, and lack of supports) lead to dissatisfaction and turnover (Billingsley, 2004). Boe, Cook and Sunderland (2007) reported that across all types of turnover (moving to other positions, transfer to general education teaching, attrition from teaching), rates increased from 18.8 percent in 1991–92 to 28.7 percent in 2004–5. More special education teachers left to "escape teaching" than general education teachers, 36.7 percent and 23.8 percent, respectively (Boe, Cook, and Sunderland, 2008). We can expect that special education teachers will continue to leave their jobs if they are structured in ways that keep them from doing their main work—that of teaching students.

FRESH AIR: FROM ORDINARY TO EXTRAORDINARY

As we contemplate how these issues impact special education teachers and students, it is easy to allow pessimism and anxiety to cloud our forecast about the future of special education. Without expert special education teachers and the teaching conditions that allow them to teach effectively, students with disabilities will have fewer opportunities to achieve important educational outcomes. How do we reverse such troubling trends? How do we ensure special education teachers and the students they serve a brighter future?

The complexity of problems outlined above suggests the need for multi-faceted solutions. For nearly a decade strategies such as the following have been proposed to improve the supply of qualified teachers: (1) offering forgivable loans that are repaid by service over time; (2) increasing the capacity of Institutes of Higher Education (IHEs) to prepare teachers in key shortage areas; and (3) incentivizing "grow your own" programs that allow districts and IHEs to develop partnership programs to serve high-need schools (Darling-Hammond & Sykes, 2003). However, efforts to decrease the shortage of special educators have been piecemeal and insufficient to remedy the problem. Keeping special education teachers in the field also reduces the need to hire additional teachers, so improving retention needs to be part of the solution.

Recognizing the need to further develop solutions, as academics, we intuitively turn to solutions with a theoretical knowledge base. In recent years, value added approaches, which are also intended to strengthen the teacher workforce and improve student outcomes have relied on economic principles. Considering current criticisms, like Jabbar's (2011), we wonder whether economics have been applied too narrowly and concur that broader conceptions, such as those derived from behavioral economics, are needed.

Although scholarly definitions of behavioral economics abound (see Etzioni, 2011), we think Sutherland offers the most practical in his 2011 TEDx Talk, entitled *"Perspective is Everything."* With powerful delivery and profound pragmatism, he describes behavioral economics as an interdisciplinary intellectual framework for understanding how people actually behave and make decisions, rather than how theoretical models predict they should. Theoretically sound, practical solutions, Sutherland insists, can only be achieved when researchers consider the roles played by economics, technology, and psychology.

Using Sutherland's (2011) framework to target the range of factors that influence the quality and efficacy of the special education workforce (see Carlson & Billingsley, 2010) we crafted a plan for action. In what follows, guided by four overarching priorities, we describe key activities and spotlight supporting elements (see also Table 11.1), the latter of which illustrate how technological, psychological, sociological, and economic principles intertwine to create what Charlie Munger refers to as a robust latticework model (Kaufman, 2008). Although by no means comprehensive and definitive, we think these solutions hold promise.

More specifically, the model we describe in Table 11.1 and the sections that follow includes four major components: (a) transforming workforce conditions, (b) engineering greater workforce capacity, (c) advocating for reform of personnel development policy, and (d) modernizing recruitment, preparation, and induction practices. The initial

Table 11.1 TEAM: Strategic Solutions and Research Priorities for Special Education Workforce Renewal

Priorities	Strategic Actions	Technology Tools and Interface
Transform Workforce Conditions	Increase Opportunities to Teach	• DATA TO KNOWLEDGE http://d2k.tamu.edu/ (Vannest & Adiguzel, 2012)
	Increase Opportunities to Learn	• My Instructional Learning Opportunities Guidance System (*MyiLogs*) http://www.myilogs.com/ Kurz et al., 2010; Kurz et al., 2012; Roach et al., 2009
	Understand Teacher Time Use	• Teacher Time Use Studies (Vannest & Hagan-Burke, 2010)
	Determine reasonable workload	• Workload studies (Dahlstrom & Nahlinder, 2009; Zheng, et al., 2012)
	Support SETs through mentoring, job embedded PD, and learning communities	• Professionally mediated outlets for blogging (http://www.cecreality101.org/) • Blended and virtual professional learning communities, e-mentoring, and virtual coaching (Rock et al., 2011)
	Assess new SETs workplace conditions	• Online career communities that evaluate workplace conditions http://www.glassdoor.com
	Track SET and SET faculty workplace needs and satisfaction and develop responsive solutions	• Web-based tools http://www.qualtrics.com http://www.surveymonkey.com http://www.cgu.edu/sefna (Special Education Faculty Needs Assessment)

(Continued)

Table 11.1 (Continued)

Priorities	Strategic Actions	Technology Tools and Interface
Engineer Sound Workforce Planning and Analysis Tactics	Expand capabilities for capturing the scope and complexity of education workforce supply data	• More interface among local, state, national, and international education workforce databases • School & Staffing Surveys (National Center for Education Research) and state data (http://nces.ed.gov/surveys/sass/index.asp) • A new database of representative groups of SETs that provides more information about the SET workforce • Sites for workforce data and/or findings to be deposited, accessed, and shared • Life course perspective for collecting and analyzing workforce data (Marshall et al., 2009)
Advocate For Workforce Policy Reform	Increase SET advocacy	• Internet and social media to expand communities and reach constituents: CEC Legislative Action Center (http://capwiz.com/cek/home) CEC Teacher Education Division (TED) PALS/GALS Wiki (http://tedpal.pbworks.com) AACTE Advocacy Toolkit (http://advocacy.aacte.org) CEC *Policy Insider* E-newsletter and blog (http://cecblog.typepad.com/policy) U.S. Department of Education *Homeroom* blog (http://www.ed.gov/blog), Education Week *On Special Education* blog (http://blogs.edweek.org/edweek/speced) TASH blog *Advocacy & Issues* tab (http://tash.org/advocacy-issues). • Apps (e.g., *i*Advocate) (http://itunes.apple.com/us/app/iadvocate/id427814325?mt=8)
	Determine effective advocacy methods and measure impact	• Impact charting and power mapping (http://www.moveon.org/organize/campaigns/powermap.html; http://www.chartingimpact.org/)
Modernize Workforce Recruitment, Preparation & Induction Practices	Provide increased opportunities for training and feedback under varied conditions	• Range of technology tools to support teacher development such as: Virtual worlds http://secondlife.com Simulation training (Dieker et al., 2008) (http://mclserver.eecs.ucf.edu/teachlive/index.php) e-Coaching (Rock et al., 2009; Rock et al., 2012) Web-based mentoring (http://www.newteachercenter.org/) Online video conferencing (Israel et al., 2009) Online learning modules (IRIS Center http://iris.peabody.vanderbilt.edu/, eLearning *Design Lab* http://elearndesign.org, www.specialconnections.ku.edu)
	Bridge traditional knowledge to practice gaps and learn to talk within communities, rather than about them	• Adopt technology that fosters situated learning (Lave & Wenger, 1991). For example, use Swivls (www.swivl.com), or online video conferencing, such as Skype (www.skype.com), for remote observation, coaching, collaboration, dialogue, and reflection.

letters of each form the acronym *TEAM*, a concept we think is important in conceptualizing the "Who" as well as the relationships that are needed in twenty-first-century special and general education.

Transform Workforce Conditions

As described previously, today's special and general education teachers work under less than ideal conditions; and now more than ever, teachers are dissatisfied (*MetLife Survey of the American Teacher*, 2011). One approach to improving workforce conditions involves ameliorating factors associated with dissatisfaction. Most malcontent, researchers say, stems from a variety of factors—chief among them ever-changing role expectations. This has led some (Vannest and Hagan-Burke, 2010) to suggest that many special education teachers are in the throes of what psychologists commonly refer to as an identity crisis (see Whitbourne, 2010).

The special education teacher identity crisis may be further fueled by the demands associated with performing a multitude of responsibilities each day. When high caseloads and minimal support compound, the "too many tasks, too little time" phenomenon often results in role conflict and overload. Notions about resolving this dilemma any time soon would be Pollyannaish, to say the least. Does that mean we should throw up our hands in frustration and surrender to the complexities change inevitably brings? We think not. Like Vannest and Hagan-Burke (2010), we view teacher time use (TTU) as a finite resource—a valuable economic commodity. And we think it's a good place to begin optimizing special education teachers' *opportunities to teach*, which, in turn, could go a long way toward resolving their identity crisis and improving workplace conditions.

Although preliminary, the research conducted by Vannest and colleagues (see Vannest & Hagan-Burke, 2010; Vannest & Parker, 2009; Vannest, Soares, Harrison, Brown, & Parker, 2010), sheds new light not only on understanding how special education teachers spend time, but also on considering how their day might be altered. The supporting logic is straightforward: Decreases in the amount of time special education teachers spend on nonteaching-related responsibilities each day yield increases in the amount of time they can provide instruction (i.e., opportunities to teach). To help practitioners do just that, Vannest and Adiguzel (2012) have turned to the power of the Internet. Project DATA TO KNOWLEDGE includes a web-based portal where special education teachers can access tools for making data-informed decisions about TTU, academics, and behavior.

> "And we think it's a good place to begin optimizing special education teachers' opportunities to teach, which in turn, could go a long way toward resolving their identity crisis and improving workplace conditions."

Similarly, members of another research team, headed by Alexander Kurz and Stephen Elliott, have also explored how special education teachers and general education teachers use time—albeit from a slightly different perspective—*opportunities to learn* (see Kurz, Elliott, Wehby, & Smithson, 2010; Kurz, Talapatra, & Roach, 2012; Roach, Chilungu, LaSalle, Talapatra, Vignieri, & Kurz, 2009). Kurz and his colleagues define opportunities to learn as the amount of time teachers engage in evidence-based practices that are not only differentiated to meet students' unique needs, but that are also aligned with prescribed standards. Harnessing the power of web-based technology, they too have developed a platform, My Instructional Learning Opportunities Guidance System (*MyiLogs*), where teachers and researchers can access electronic logs for planning, communicating, and monitoring instruction aimed at enhancing students' academic outcomes.

Clearly, we think reconfiguring special education teachers' time use by increasing their opportunities to teach and opportunities to learn is a good start; however, we caution against stopping there. Using block-entry regression analysis, Hughes (2012) found that work *over*load was a significant predictor of attrition. A challenge for the field is to determine what constitutes a *reasonable* workload. One method for doing so involves conducting mental workload studies. Vasile (2010) defines mental workload as "an interaction between task requirements and human capabilities or resources" (p.133). Evaluating mental workload usually involves a combination of objective observations, physiological measures (e.g., ECG, EOG, EEG), and subjective assessments. The results are then used to optimize human wellbeing *and* system performance. Typically reserved for those professionals who work under constant strain in difficult conditions, most of the mental workload studies, to date, have been conducted with airline pilots and surgeons (Dahlstrom & Nahlinder, 2009; Zheng et al., 2012). Like Vasile, we think there is immeasurable value in carrying out a series of well-orchestrated workload studies in classroom environments to determine the *middle* ground of mental workload wherein performance is optimized for teachers and learners.

Also, we need researchers to launch studies that lead to a more in-depth understanding of TTU. An underlying premise supporting Vannest et al's. work is that the more time special education teachers spend on instruction the better. Do we have sufficient data to support that notion? Perhaps. Nonetheless, we need to know more. We need to know how quantity *and* quality affect TTU. In other words, what matters most under what conditions and with whom? Is it the amount of time a special educator engages in individualized instruction or the quality of the time spent that yields more desirable student outcomes? Answering these and other questions will help us resolve the identity crisis among special educators by determining which roles and responsibilities special education teachers should engage in and to what extent. When we have these data in hand, we can also more accurately and convincingly claim the value added by special education teachers, a topic that remains hotly debated and largely undetermined in the current era of accountability.

We hope, too, that professionally mediated outlets for blogging, such as the Council for Exceptional Children's Reality 101 Blog, continue to expand. Web-based outlets like this not only give special education teachers and other education personnel a voice, but also a public platform for sharing the joys and challenges they face in the trenches. Another benefit is that blogs provide a rich data source for qualitative researchers interested in learning more about identity issues and workload conditions.

Other online career and workplace communities such as Glassdoor.com help job seekers evaluate working climate and conditions. Such sites provide special education teachers, general education teachers, and other education personnel with an opportunity to preview anonymously posted school district ratings prior to interviewing or accepting a position. Let's face it: Special education can be a problem-saturated profession (Rock, Thead, Gable, Hardman, & VanAcker, 2006). More often than not, for example, special education teachers find themselves working with students who are the most difficult to reach and teach within an educational system that fails to provide sufficient resources and support. Rather than simply restructuring special education teachers' time use or showering them with the latest stress-busting strategies, we also need to equip them with a better understanding of the work they are required to perform *and* the school conditions in which they are expected to do so. Sites like Glassdoor.com may help us do the latter.

We have focused much of our discussion about workplace improvement on resolving the special education teacher identity crisis by applying economic and psychological principles, and suggesting a series of strategic empirical pursuits. Still, we recognize that special education teachers and other education personnel need practical support, namely authentic ongoing professional development. Realizing the shortcomings of traditional "one shot" or workshop-driven approaches, more recent professional development (PD) efforts have tapped into the power technology. Through blended or virtual professional learning communities (PLCs) (Duncan-Howell, 2010), e-Mentoring (Gareis & Nussbaum-Beach, 2008), and e-Coaching (Rock, Zigmond, Gregg, & Gable, 2011), special and general education teachers and other education personnel receive increased support through job-embedded PD. And through national non-profits in the U.S., like the New Teacher Center, not only can novice special education teachers access a variety of supports, but also researchers, administrators, education leaders, and policymakers can work collaboratively to address important beginning teacher issues. Equipping practitioners in the workplace with the most up-to-date knowledge and skills rests on advancing efforts like these.

> "Rather than simply restructuring special education teachers' time use or showering them with the latest stress-busting strategies, we also need to equip them with a better understanding of the work they are required to perform *and* the school conditions in which they are expected to do so."

Given the complexities of real world practice, there is little doubt that transforming workforce conditions and increasing satisfaction requires a multifaceted approach. Proffering only a handful of possibilities, the approaches we have emphasized hold broad utility. How will we know whether these and other efforts are effective? Keeping a pulse on satisfaction in the education workplace has never been easier. Web-based tools, such as Qualtrics or Survey Monkey, ease burdens typically associated with survey administration, data collection, and analysis. PD providers, researchers, or administrators should survey workplace satisfaction approximately every six to twelve months, a timeframe deemed sufficient for capturing small changes in satisfaction, while also allowing for timely turnaround efforts should satisfaction dwindle.

Engineer Sound Workforce Planning and Analysis Tactics

Improving workplace conditions is a necessary first step toward ensuring a brighter future for special education teachers and the students with disabilities they teach. But such tactics alone will not suffice. We must also guarantee the continued viability of the special education teacher workforce. In other words, goals aimed at enhancing workforce quality and efficacy cannot be fully achieved until we create an human resource pool of special educators that is adequate not only in size, but also in composition.

Although some efforts have been undertaken to address the workforce shortage, in our view, there is still much to do. First, we should expand current capabilities for capturing the scope and complexity of education workforce supply data. Second, we should adopt a proven framework for analyzing education workforce data. And we must undertake both with a sense of urgency. But how?

Influenced by research in industrial and organizational (I/O) psychology, we think workforce planning and analysis tactics, which also have economic underpinnings, offer a sensible solution. The U.S. Department of Health & Human Services (1999) defines workplace planning and analysis as a strategic approach for getting "the right number of people with the right skills, experiences, and competencies in the right jobs at the right time." This approach, according to Emmerichs, Marcum, and Robbert (2004), emphasizes the importance of investing in human capital, an undeniably invaluable commodity when it comes to strengthening the special education teacher workforce.

In "Avoiding the Crunch at Crunch Time," Sloan (2008) echoes the need for accurate and robust workforce data. The good news is advances in technology have made large-scale web-based education personnel data systems possible. For over a decade, the U.S. Department of Education's Institute for Education Sciences (IES) has housed the Schools and Staffing Survey (SASS) system. Researchers, practitioners, and policy analysts can access the SASS dataset through the IES web portal; however, which data they can access is differentiated by non-restricted use and restricted use. Although the SASS database is currently linked to the National Center for Education Statistics' (NCES) Common Core of Data (CCD), ongoing issues with timely release and small sample of special educators limit its utility. Consequently, we think more interface and openness among local, state, national, and international education workforce databases is desirable. Weller (2011), author of *The Digital Scholar: How Technology is Transforming Scholarly Practice*, enumerates the benefits of large, open datasets and calls for the creation of more combined datasets. Intrigued by this notion, we think one example he mentioned has great practical utility in our field. RealClimate, a commentary site, developed and maintained by climate scientists, also includes a catalogue of selected data and code sources specific to climate change. We envision a similar site wherein de-identified special education teachers, general education teachers, and other education workforce data and findings can be deposited, accessed, and shared. Developing such a site through an established center like the University of Florida's National Center to Inform Policy and Practice in Special Education (NCIPP) might be a step toward making this a reality. No doubt, researchers face many issues before undertaking such an endeavor, and protecting participants' confidentiality is chief among them. Given the IES requirement that Goal Four applicants include data sharing plans, we maintain reason for optimism.

Sloan (2008) also reminds us that workforce planning and analysis involves more than just counting heads. When considering special education workforce data, our analysis should account for *supply*, *demand*, and *need*. The latter is especially relevant in addressing issues of diversity and leadership. As we mentioned previously, current supply data confirm longstanding shortages that have plagued the field for decades are reaching epidemic proportions. Compounding the issue of shortages in the number of special education teachers available in the workforce is the limited supply of future faculty who prepare them (Smith, Pion, Tyler, Sindelar & Rosenberg, 2001; Smith, Robb, West & Tyler, 2010; West & Hardman, 2012).

Faced with a similar predicament in the field of Library and Information Sciences (LIS), Marshall, Rathbun-Grubb, and Marshall (2009) adopted a *life course perspective* for collecting and analyzing workforce data. Life course perspective has been used for over five decades, across a variety of social science disciplines, as a framework for examining someone's experiences over time (Marshall et al., 2009; Solomon & Rathbun-Grubb, 2009). Characterized by two dimensions, the life course perspective allows researchers to study not only special education teachers' biographical information, but also the contexts (i.e., the political, economic, and historical changes) that have influenced it.

Advocate for Workforce Policy Reform

Unlike general education, the U.S. government plays a unique and vital role in special education personnel development. Although federal funding has supported development of the special education teacher workforce for over 40 years (Kleinhammer-Trammill, Tramill, & Brace, 2010), along the way more than a few policy issues not only shifted priority allocations, but also endangered investment expenditures. The onslaught as of 2013, which includes sequestration, negotiated rule making, and Elementary and Secondary Education Act (ESEA) and IDEA reauthorization, poses an unprecedented threat that would only further diminish an already fragile workforce. Examining these attacks, from a psychological standpoint, leads us to conclude that today's teacher workforce suffers from a public image problem. Much like resolving an identity crisis, overcoming an image problem requires a thoughtful, well-coordinated campaign.

How then can members of the special education workforce, who represent a minority point of view, gain support from the overwhelming majority for their cause? We think Dr. Seuss offers an instructive allegory. In *Horton Hears a Who*, the Whos, in order to avoid being boiled in "Beezelnut Oil," must make their voices known to the jungle folk who cannot seem to hear or see them. Weathering more than a few failed attempts, the Whos finally succeed by ensuring *all* members of their society contribute to the noise that must reach the majority with whom their fate rests. In extending this metaphor to contemporary special educators' political action efforts, we also see the vital roles technology, psychology, and economics play.

Today's technology tools offer a vast, almost seamless conduit for transmitting the voice and vision of special education teacher advocacy to the masses. Social media, such as Facebook, Twitter, Tumblr, and Pinterest, provide web-based outlets for informing others, rallying the troops, and achieving impact. We applaud the members of our special education teacher community who are currently making use of these tools and encourage others to follow suit.

The technology tools included in Table 11.1, although by no means exhaustive, demonstrate how we can use technology to transform individual networks into collective entities that enable faster, easier, and wider distribution (Weller, 2011). But is faster, easier, and wider better when it comes to advocacy? We need more research, using techniques such as *impact charting* and *power mapping*, to answer that question. Fortunately, online tools are available to assist with those pursuits, too.

Based on a review of political, sociological, and psychological literature, Weerts, Cabrera, and Sanford (2009) examined factors that motivate and shape an individual's involvement in political action activities. Interestingly, they reported that involvement hinges on several factors, including past participation, current capacity, present availability, and network proximity. These findings enable us to more strategically cultivate the next generation of special education workforce advocates.

From an economic frame of reference, when it comes to political advocacy, the capital at stake is both human and monetary. Failing to educate and persuade others about the value of special education teacher workforce policy reform trickles down to adversely affect a small but vulnerable portion of the P–12 student population (Kleinhammer-Trammill, Tramill, & Brace, 2010). Unfortunately, for over 30 years, the goal of achieving full funding for IDEA has remained elusive. In short, we have accepted less than what was promised. Although there is undeniable merit in embracing the "some is better than none" logic, we have to wonder what outcomes have been sacrificed.

A closer examination of Part D funding patterns reveals the level of support has decreased annually when controlled for inflation (Kleinhammer-Trammill, Trammill, & Brace, 2010). Accordingly, in Fiscal Year 2012 alone, the Council for Exceptional Children (CEC) recommended a $239,192 increase for Part D funding (Council for Exceptional Children, 2012). Just one example, this leads us to question the cumulative effect. In other words, how many students with disabilities would have had access to a well-trained, effective special education teacher workforce if funding revenues had been preserved? One thing is clear: if we want to improve outcomes for students with disabilities, we must ensure continued funding that supports development of a capable special education teacher workforce. One that is characterized by special educators who are reflective, resourceful, and resilient in their advocacy endeavors—all of which are known characteristics affiliated with those who remain in the field (Gehrke & Murri, 2006).

> "From an economic frame of reference, when it comes to political advocacy, the capital at stake is both human and monetary."

Modernize Workforce Recruitment, Preparation, and Induction Practices

According to Maxwell, author of *The 17 Irrefutable Laws of Teamwork* (2001), "the single biggest way to impact an organization is to focus on leadership development. There is almost no limit to the potential of an organization that recruits good people, raises them up as leaders and continually develops them" (p. 185). With this in mind, we believe the path to creating a brighter future for the special education teacher workforce and students with disabilities is paved in part by undertaking a series of new generation workforce development (e.g., recruitment, preparation, and induction) activities. Bringing workforce development into the twenty-first century will not be easy. Mired by skepticism, many will resist the upgrades made possible through progressive and innovative practices. Nevertheless, we must stay the course; the future of our field depends on it.

Attrition data and changing demographics confirm we need a strong focus on diversity as well as smarter and more sustainable workforce development strategies. No doubt technology plays an integral role in helping us achieve both. For instance, traditional recruitment barriers imposed by time and distance are nearly eliminated not only by web-based social networking tools, such as Facebook, Twitter, and LinkedIn, but also through blogs (e.g., SpedPro.org) and websites (e.g., Higher Education Consortium for Special Education [hecse.net]). Such options allow us to extend recruitment outreach nationally and globally.

How well we prepare special education teachers for the profession matters, too. Given the increased diversity of the school-age population, the constant shifts in service provision models, and the ever-changing roles and responsibilities of special education teachers, tomorrow's workforce must be better prepared than ever before. That means teacher educators must focus not only on preparing special education teachers to provide relentless, intensive, and individualized instruction, but also to do so when the conditions they encounter are less than ideal. Technology can aid in these efforts. Whether online or on campus, a small number of today's more innovative preparation programs provide special and general education teacher candidates with increased *opportunities for training and feedback* under varied conditions through virtual worlds (e.g., Second Life), simulation training (TeachLivE [Dieker, Hynes, Hughes, & Smith, 2008; Dieker, Rodriguez,

Lignugaris/Kraft, Hynes, & Hughes, 2014]), eCoaching (Rock et al., 2009; Rock et al., 2012; Rock et al., 2014), web-based mentoring (Peña & Almaguer, 2007), and online video conferencing for remote supervision (Israel, Knowlton, Griswold, & Rowland, 2009). We would like to see these become the norm—especially in light of findings produced by Billingsley and Scheuermann's (2014) review of the literature, which spotlight the promise technology holds for improving clinical field experiences. In most programs, across the United States, although once considered cutting edge, online learning courses (e.g., Blackboard), web-based modules (e.g., IRIS Center at Vanderbilt University, the University of Kansas' eLearning Design Lab [eDL], Special Connections), and distance-learning options are nearly commonplace as of 2013. More often than not, teacher educators require candidates to make use of best practice sites (e.g., What Works Clearinghouse, PBIS, CAST, RTI) and video models obtained through YouTube and TeacherTube when preparing instructional content and developing positive behavior interventions and supports. Both illustrate how teacher educators harness technology to ensure that teachers develop a substantive knowledge base in special education.

Contemporary induction practices also benefit from technology. For example, the National Commission on Teaching and America's Future (NCTAF) has partnered with Qualcomm and several IHEs to investigate how mobile devices (e.g., smartphones and tablets) can empower beginning teachers with "just-in-time support" and dissolve the barriers between oft-disparate communities of knowledge and practice.

Technology alone, however, will not suffice. We turn to educational psychology for the theoretical underpinnings that guide next-generation workforce development initiatives. Certainly not new, we see great value in adopting principles of situated learning (SL) (Lave & Wenger, 1991). Doing so ensures special education teacher candidates and future leaders learn to talk *within* communities of practice, rather than *about* them, especially during preparation and induction. We see this dialogue as vital to advancing adoption of evidence-based practices and practice-based evidences. By no means do we imply that when faced with the pressures of real-world practice, special education teachers should abandon what works for students with disabilities. Instead, we suggest that situated learning should be used as a vehicle for novice, mid-career, and veteran education professionals to tackle problems of practice, wrestle with varied complexities, foster collaborative problem solving, and engage in shared decision making.

Economically speaking, we view the outcomes of investments in next-generation workforce development activities as more than financial. Commodities such as learning, time, knowledge, and practice hold untold value in today's global, knowledge-based society. When combined, they form the building blocks of human, intellectual, and cultural capital—all of which create advancement opportunities for systems, markets, individuals, and societies.

CONCLUSIONS

In this chapter, we considered *who makes a difference* for improving outcomes for students with disabilities. We began by calling attention to long-standing dilemmas, which we described from the vantage point of our work in schools. Based on our current roles as teacher education faculty, we argued that achieving a brighter future for individuals with disabilities and their families depends, in large measure, on strengthening the availability of a capable, caring, and committed workforce and the conditions that affect their daily work. Through the lens of behavioral economics, we suggested interdisciplinary solutions aimed at overcoming known challenges that adversely affect the special educator workforce.

Although we focused specifically on special education teachers, everyone in the educational enterprise has a role to play and a responsibility to assume in making a difference. It is general educators who also teach students with disabilities; it is district leaders and principals who can work to assure that special education teachers and general education teachers have opportunities to work together to use evidence-based practices; and it is, of course, an adequate supply of committed special educators, who have the skills to provide intensive and focused instruction for the students who need it most. To underscore our view that special education teachers cannot go it alone, we used the TEAM acronym (see Table 11.1).

Finally, we acknowledged the scope and complexity of recruitment, development, and retention issues in the special education workforce, problems that are shared by other professions and fueled, in part, by the "graying of America." Encouraged by bright and capable individuals who enter teacher preparation programs, as well as the enthusiasm and idealism they bring to teaching, we speculated that there is reason for optimism. To make special education "a career of choice" (Fish & Stephens, 2010), we propose working not only across disciplines but also across generations. Innovative platforms, including knowledge cafés, sometimes known as World Cafés, offer collaborative venues for exchanging ideas, discussing challenges, brainstorming solutions, and sharing insights. No doubt, it will take the collective wisdom and Herculean effort of many to craft and carry out the empirical and practical pursuits needed to advance the efforts of the special education workforce. Why bother? In the U.S. alone, there are six million students with disabilities and counting *who* depend on us.

Discussion Questions

1. What should "highly qualified and highly effective" entail for special education teachers? Should this differ for elementary and secondary teachers?
2. How can teacher preparation programs proactively address special education teacher retention and turnover?
3. How should school administrators proactively recruit and retain effective special education teachers?
4. What are the pros and cons of web-based professional development and support groups?
5. What should the federal government's role be in supporting special education teacher training and development?
6. What do you think would help make special education "a career of choice" (Fish & Stephens, 2010)?

MARCIA ROCK'S AND BONNIE BILLINGSLEY'S SUGGESTIONS FOR FURTHER READING

Billingsley, B. Crockett, J.C., & Kamman, M. (2014). *Recruiting and retaining high quality special education teachers and administrators.* In P. Sindelar, M. Brownell, B. Lignugaris-Kraft, & E. McCray (Eds.), *Handbook for research on special education teacher preparation.* (pp. 94–112). New York: Routledge.
Brownell, M. T., Sindelar, P. T., Kiely, M. T., & Danielson, L. C. (2010). Special education teacher quality and preparation: Exposing foundations, constructing a new model. *Exceptional Children, 76,* 357–377.

Dukes, C., & Darling, S.M. (2014). Special issue: Special education teacher education in the 21st century: Evolving approaches. *Teacher Education and Special Education, 37* (1).

Rock, M.L., & Billingsley, B. (2014). From metaphorically speaking to acting boldly: A commentary on the special issue. *Teacher Education and Special Education, 37,* 71–76.

Rosenberg, M.S., Walther-Thomas, C. (2014). Innovation, policy, and capacity in special education teacher education: Competing demands in challenging times. *Teacher Education and Special Education, 37,* 77–82.

REFERENCES

American Association for Employment in Education (AAEE) (2011). *Teacher Job Outlook: 2011 and Beyond.* Retrieved from www.aaee.org.

Billingsley, B. (2004). Special education teacher retention and attrition: A critical analysis of the research literature. *The Journal of Special Education, 38,* 39–55.

Billingsley, B. (2011). Factors influencing special education teacher quality and effectiveness. In J. M. Kauffman & D. P. Hallahan (Eds.), *Handbook of special education* (pp. 391–405). Routledge, Taylor-Francis: New York, NY.

Billingsley, B., Carlson, E., & Klein, S. (2004). The working conditions and induction support of early career special educators. *Exceptional Children, 70,* 333–347.

Billingsley, B. S., Griffin, C. C., Smith, S. J., Kamman, M., & Israel, M. (2009). *A review of teacher induction in special education: Research, practice, and technology solutions.* (NCIPP Doc. No. RS-1). Retrieved from http://ncipp.org/reports/rs_1.pdf.

Billingsley, G.M., & Scheuermann, B.K. (2014). Using virtual technology to enhance field experiences for pre-service special education teachers. *Teacher Education and Special Education, 37,* 255–272.

Boe, E. E., Cook, L. H., & Sunderland, R. J. (2007). *Trends in the turnover of teachers from 1991 to 2004: Attrition, teaching area transfer, and school migration.* (Data Analysis Report No. 2007-DAR2). Philadelphia: University of Pennsylvania, Graduate School of Education, Center for Research and Evaluation in Social Policy.

Boe, E. E., Cook, L. H., & Sunderland, R. J. (2008). Teacher turnover: Examining exit attrition, teaching area transfer, and school migration. *Exceptional Children, 75,* 7–31.

Boe, E. E., deBettencourt, L. U., Dewey, J. F., Rosenberg, M. S., Sindelar, P. T., & Leko, C. D. (2013). *Variability in demand for special education teachers: Indicators, explanations, and impacts. Exceptionality, 21,* 103–105.

Bourne, L. E., & Ekstrand, B. R. (1979). *Psychology: Its principles and meanings* (3rd ed.). New York: Holt, Rinehart, and Winston.

Carlson, E., & Billingsley, B. (2010). Workforce issues in special education. In B. McGraw, P. Peterson, & E. Baker (Eds.), *International encyclopedia of education* (pp. 886–891). Amsterdam: Elsevier.

Carlson, E., Brauen, M., Klein, S., Schroll, K. & Willig, S. (2002). *Study of personnel needs in special education: Key findings.* Retrieved from http://fer.dig.coe.ful.edu/spense/KeyFindings.pdf.

Council for Exceptional Children (2012). *Federal outlook for exceptional children: Fiscal year 2012.* Arlington, VA: Council for Exceptional Children.

Dahlstrom, N., & Nahlinder, S. (2009). Mental workload in aircraft and simulator during basic civil aviation training. *International Journal of Aviation Psychology, 19,* 309–325.

Darling-Hammond, L., & Sykes, G. (2003). Wanted: A national teacher supply policy for education: The right way to meet the "highly qualified teacher" challenge. *Education Policy Analysis Archives, 11*(33). Retrieved from http://epaa.asu.edu/epaa/v11n33.

Dieker, L. A., Hynes, M., Hughes, C., & Smith, E., (2008). Implications of mixed reality and simulation technologies on special education and teacher preparation. *Focus on Exceptional Children, 40*(5), 1–20.

Dieker, L. A., Rodriguez, J. A., Lignugaris/Kraft, B., Hynes, M. C., Hughes, C. E. (2014). The potential of simulated environments in teacher education: Current and future possibilities. *Teacher Education and Special Education, 37,* 21–33. doi: 10.1177/0888406413512683.

Duncan-Howell, J. (2010). Teachers making connections: Online communities as a source of professional learning. *British Journal of Educational Technology, 41,* 324–340.

Emmerichs, R. M., Marcum, C. Y., Robbert, A. A. (2004). *An operational process of workforce planning.* Santa Monica, CA: RAND Corporation.

Etzioni, A. (2011). Behavioral economics: Toward a new paradigm. *American Behavioral Scientist, 55,* 1099–1119.

Fall, A. M., & Billingsley, B. (2008). Disparities in teacher quality among early career special educators in high and low poverty districts. In T. E. Scruggs & M. A. Mastropieri (Eds.), *Advances in learning and behavioral disabilities: Personnel preparation* (vol. 21, pp. 181–206). Stanford, CT: JAI.

Fall, A. M., & Billingsley, B. (2011). Disparities in work conditions among early career special educators in high- and low-poverty districts, *Remedial and Special Education, 32,* 64–78.

Feng, L., & Sass, T. (2010). *What makes special education teachers special? Teacher training and achievement of students with disabilities.* Calder Urban Institute (Working Paper 49). Retrieved at http://www.caldercenter.org/publications.cfm.

Fish, W., & Stephens, T. L. (2010). Special education: A career choice. *Remedial and Special Education, 31,* 400–407.

Gareis, C., & Nussbaum-Beach, S. L. (2008). Electronically mentoring to develop accomplished professional teachers. *Journal of Personnel Evaluation in Education, 20,* 227–246.

Gehrke, R. S., & Murri, N. (2006) Beginning special educators intent to stay in special education: Why they like it here. *Teacher Education and Special Education, 29,* 179–190.

Geiger, W. L., Crutchfield, M. D., & Mainzer, R. (2003). *The status of licensure of special education teachers in the 21st century.* Retrieved from http://www.coe.uf.edu/copsse/pubfiles/RS-7.pdf.

Guarino, C. M., Santibanez, L., & Daley, G. A. (2006). Teacher recruitment and retention: A review of recent empirical evidence. *Review of Educational Research, 76,* 173–208.

Hanushek, E. A., Rivkin, S. G., & Kain, J. F. (2005). Teachers, schools, and academic achievement. *Econometrica, 73,* 417–458.

Hughes, G. D. (2012). Teacher retention: Teacher characteristics, school characteristics, organizational characteristics, and teacher efficacy. *The Journal of Educational Research, 105,* 245–255.

Israel, M., Knowlton, H. E., Griswold, D., & Rowland, A. (2009). Applications of video conferencing technology in special education teacher preparation. *Journal of Special Education Technology, 24,* 15–25.

Jabbar, H. (2011). The behavioral economics of education: New directions for research. *Educational Researcher, 40,* 446–453.

Kaufman, P. D. (Ed.). (2008). *Poor Charlie's almanack: The wit and wisdom of Charles T. Munger* (Expanded 3rd ed). Virginia Beach, VA: Donning Company.

Kleinhammer-Tramill, J., Tramill, J., & Brace, H. (2010). Contexts, funding history, and implications for evaluating the office of special education program's investment in personnel preparation, *The Journal of Special Education, 43,* 195–205.

Kurz, A., Elliott, S. N., Wehby, J. H., & Smithson, J. L. (2010). Alignment of the intended, planned, and enacted curriculum in general and special education and its relation to student achievement. *The Journal of Special Education, 44,* 131–145.

Kurz, A., Talapatra, D., & Roach, A. T. (2012). Meeting the curricular challenges of inclusive assessment: The role of alignment, opportunity to learn, and student engagement. *International Journal of Disability, Development, and Education, 59,* 37–52.

Ladson-Billings, G. (2009). Opportunity to teach: Teacher quality in context. In D. H. Gitomer (Ed.), *Measurement issues and assessment for teacher quality,* (pp. 206–222). Thousand Oaks, CA, Sage Publications Inc.

Lave, J., & Wenger, E. (1991). *Situated learning: Legitimate peripheral participation.* New York: Cambridge University Press.

Marshall, V., Rathbun-Grubb, S., & Marshall, J. G. (2009). Using the life course perspective to study library and information science careers, *Library Trends, 58,* 127–140.

Maxwell, J. (2001). *The 17 indisputable laws of teamwork.* Nashville, TN: Thomas Nelson, Inc.

McLeskey, J., Tyler, N. C., & Flippin, S. S. (2004). The supply of and demand for special education teachers: A review of research regarding the chronic shortage of special education teachers. *The Journal of Special Education, 38,* 5–21.

MetLife. (2011). *The MetLife survey of the american teacher: Teachers, parents, and the economy.* Retrieved from https://www.metlife.com/.../MetLife-Teacher-Survey-2011.pdf.

Nougaret, A., Scruggs, T., & Mastropieri, M. (2005). Does teacher education produce better special education teachers? *Exceptional Children, 71,* 217–229.

Paperwork in special education (SPeNSE Factsheet). (2003). *SPeNSE Factsheet.* Retrieved from http://ferdig.coe.ufl.edu/spense/Paperwork.doc.

Peña, C. M., & Almaguer, I. (2007). Asking the right questions: Online mentoring of student teachers. *International Journal of Instructional Media, 34,* 105–113.

Roach, A. T., Chilungu, E. N., LaSalle, T. P., Talapatra, D., Vignieri, M. J., & Kurz, A. (2009). Opportunities and options for facilitating and evaluating access to the general curriculum for students with disabilities. *Peabody Journal of Education, 84,* 511–528.

Rock, M. L., Gregg, M., Thead, B. K., Acker, S. E., Gable, R. A., & Zigmond, N, (2009). Can you hear me now? Evaluation of an online wireless technology to provide real-time feedback to special education teachers-in-training. *Teacher Education and Special Education, 32,* 64–82.

Rock, M., Gregg, M., Gable, R., Zigmond, N., Blanks, B., Howard, P., & Bullock, L. (2012). Time after time online: An extended study of virtual coaching during distant clinical practice. *Journal of Technology and Teacher Education, 20,* 277–304.

Rock, M. L., Schumacker, R., Gregg, M., Gable, R. A., Zigmond, N. P., & Howard, P. (2014). How are they now? Longer term effects of virtual coaching through online bug-in-ear technology. *Teacher Education and Special Education. (OnlineFirst)*. 1–21. doi: 10.1177/0888406414525048.

Rock, M. L., Thead, B. K., Gable, R. A., Hardman, M. L., & VanAcker, R. (2006). In pursuit of excellence: The past as prologue to a brighter future for special education. *Focus on Exceptional Children, 38*(8), 1–19.

Rock, M. L., Zigmond, N. P., Gregg, M., & Gable, R. A. (2011). The power of virtual coaching. *Educational Leadership, 69*(2), 42–47.

Sindelar, P. T., Brownell, M. T., & Billingsley, B. (2010). Special education teacher education research: Current status and future directions. *Teacher Education & Special Education, 33*, 8–24.

Sloan, J. (2008). Avoiding the crunch at crunch time. *The Australian Library Journal, 57*(1), 33–38.

Smith, D. D., Pion, G., Tyler, N. C., Sindelar, P., & Rosenberg, M. (2001). *The study of special education leadership personnel with particular attention to the professoriate.* Nashville, TN: Peabody College. Vanderbilt University.

Smith, D. D., Robb, S. M., West, J., & Tyler, N. C. (2010). The changing education landscape: How special education preparation can make a difference for teachers and their students with disabilities. *Teacher Education and Special Education, 33*, 25–43.

Solomon, P., & Rathbun-Grubb, S. (2009). Workforce planning and the school library media specialist. *Library Trends, 58*, 246–262.

Sutherland, R. (2011, December). Rory Sutherland: Perspective is everything. Retrieved from http://www.ted.com/talks/rory_sutherland_perspective_is_everything.html.

U.S. Department of Education (2010). *Individuals with Disabilities Education Act (IDEA) Data.* Retrieved from http://www.ideadata.org

U.S. Department of Health & Human Services (1999). *Major and Management Challenges and Program Risks: A Government wide Perspective* (GAO/OCG-99-1), p. 102.

Vannest, K., & Adiguzel, T. (2012). D2K: Data to Knowledge© [World Wide Web]. College Station, TX: Texas A&M University. Retrieved from http://d2k.tamu.edu.

Vannest, K. J., & Hagan-Burke, S. (2010). Teacher time use in special education. *Remedial and Special Education, 31*, 126–142.

Vannest, K. J., & Parker, R. I. (2009). Measuring time: The stability of special education teacher time use. *The Journal of Special Education, 44*, 94–106.

Vannest, K. J., Soares, D. A., Harrison, J. R., Brown, L., & Parker, R. I. (2010). Changing teacher time. *Preventing School Failure, 54*, 86–98.

Vasile, C. (2010). Mental workload: Cognitive aspects and personality. *Petroleum-Gas University of Ploiesti Bulletin, Educational Sciences Series, 62*, 132–137.

Washburn-Moses, L. (2010) Rethinking mentoring: Comparing policy and practice in special and general education, *Educational Policy Analysis Archives, 18*(32). Retrieved from http://epaa.asu.edu/ojs/article/view/716.

Weerts, D. J., Cabrera, A. F., & Sanford, T. (2009). Beyond giving: Political advocacy and volunteer behaviors of public university alumni. *Research in Higher Education, 51*, 346–365.

Weller, M. (2011). *The digital scholar: How technology is transforming scholarly practice.* New York, NY: Bloomsbury Academic.

West, J. E., & Hardman, M. L. (2012). Averting current and future special education faculty shortages: Policy, implications, and recommendations, *Teacher Education and Special Education, 35*, 154–160.

Whitbourne, S. K. (2010). *The search for fulfillment.* New York: Ballantine Books.

Zheng, B., Rieder, E., Cassera, M., Martinec, D., Lee, G., Panton, O., Park, A., & Swanström, L. (2012). Quantifying mental workloads of surgeons performing natural orifice transluminal endoscopic surgery (NOTES) procedures. *Surgical Endoscopy, 26*, 1352–1358.

Section III
WHERE SHOULD SPECIAL EDUCATION HAPPEN?

The place where special education occurs received increasing emphasis during the last 20 years of the twentieth century. Beginning in the 1980s, some advocates emphasized the "least restrictive environment" clause of U.S. laws. This reflected concerns about deinstitutionalization and its benefits, especially for students with moderate and more substantial disabilities. It is important not to exclude people who have disabilities from participating in the environments of their peers. Some advocates recommended full inclusion—all students should participate in general education all the time. Not everyone agreed, however. Those who disagreed suggested that some students needed to have special learning environments; for some students a general education situation would, in fact, be restrictive. The authors of the chapters in this section discuss *where* special education occurs. Consider these questions to help you think ahead about the *where* topic.

- Should all students with disabilities be in the same classrooms and go to the same schools as their non-disabled peers?
- Is it possible that some students with disabilities will have better outcomes in special settings than general settings?
- Does the place special education services are delivered affect how well they will be delivered? Can special education services be the same, regardless of where they are provided?
- Why does the place question matter more to some advocates than it does to others?

Getting to know Kat D. Alves

I have been involved in horseback riding for most of my life (since elementary school) and it has always been my favorite activity. I was the little girl (and the slightly older girl) with a room full of horse books and horse posters. When I went to college, I had the opportunity to volunteer at a therapeutic horseback riding facility, hoping to share my love of horses with children with disabilities. I quickly became very involved in the riding program and working at this program became an important part of my college experience. Over the next several years, I spent a lot of time supporting students in their lessons and working with them on horse care and other barn activities. Seeing the progress of these students and the joy they felt being successful led me to pursue a career in special education.

While at the University of Virginia, I completed a Bachelor's degree in psychology and a Master's degree in teaching for special education. After graduation, I remained in Charlottesville and ventured out into the classroom. I spent seven years teaching elementary special education, kindergarten through fifth grade, a variety of settings and disabilities. Although I enjoyed my time in the classroom and loved my interactions with students, I felt the desire to reach more students and teachers than I had access to in my classroom or school. With this in mind, I decided to apply to graduate school. At the time I contributed to this book, I was enrolled in the doctoral program at the University of Virginia, focusing on literacy at the upper elementary school level for students with high-incidence disabilities.

12

WHERE SHOULD SPECIAL EDUCATION TAKE PLACE?

Barbara Bateman, Melody Tankersley, John Wills Lloyd, & Kat D. Alves

No issue in special education has been more contentious than placement, i.e., where should special education happen? As these chapters will show, there is no one easy answer. The argument often divides participants into two camps: those who favor full inclusion in all circumstances and those who do not. The chapters in this section will present this argument from a research perspective (Zigmond), a legal perspective (Huefner), and a psychological and moral perspective (Wiley). First, we begin with a discussion about some of the issues that need to be considered when determining placement for special education services.

In education, the discussion of placement begins with thoughts about what happens in the placement. When we plan an activity, what factors are considered in determining where it should happen? The answer depends in part on the nature of the activity. If the activity is swimming, a place with water is essential. But the activity itself is not the only factor that determines where it should be performed. Think of someone swimming in preparation for the Iron-man triathlon compared to someone just learning to swim. They both need a place with water, but the ocean would do nicely for one and poorly for the other. Also, if our swimmer is training to break the world record in the 200 meter freestyle, it would be important to have an Olympic-size pool complete with appropriate timing apparatus. These examples show us that it is important to consider the characteristics of the participants and how they will or can respond within the context when determining where the activity should happen. In addition, the purpose of the activity can also be important in choosing the "where" for it to occur.

In short, where an activity can most profitably and appropriately be conducted depends, at a minimum, on the nature of the activity, the characteristics of the participants, and the purpose of the activity. When examining placement of students for special education services, Zigmond discusses how these issues become important pieces of the decision-making process. For some activities other factors such as cost, legal considerations, or even social values may be important. In education, these other factors, such as costs and legal considerations—as Huefner brings to light—are also crucial to decisions about placement.

In the context of the educational placement of a child who has a disability we need to ask, among other things, "What goes on, or should go on, in that educational placement?" In other words, we need to determine the nature of education, i.e., what does the activity of education require of the place in which it happens? We also need to examine what characteristics of special education students are relevant to their placement, and we must inquire as to the purpose of special education for a child who has a disability.

THE NATURE OF EDUCATION REQUIRES...

One workable description of education is that it is the process in which the teacher(s) attempts to impart knowledge to and enhance the social behavior of the learner(s). To paraphrase President James Garfield, a forest log with a good teacher on one end and the learner on the other, both engaged in extended conversation, is the ideal place for education. Today, that wonderful log may be considered too uncomfortable to be appropriate for more than a brief lesson, perhaps on deforestation or how to tell a pine from a fir tree. For some special education purposes the 1:1 teacher student ratio might be important. However, the idea of small groups of students engaged in meaningful interactions with teachers and other learners is still at the heart of education. As you will read in her chapter, Huefner defines special education as "the delivery of individualized (and therefore special) educational services to children with disabilities." How does this definition relate to the best place for students with disabilities to receive special education services?

Some evidence suggests that a low ratio of students to teacher is likely to be a positive characteristic for a learning environment (e.g., Mosteller, 1995, but note Hanushek, 1999). Other research, however, suggests that within certain limits and age ranges, class size may be only a minor variable in student achievement in comparison with, for example, family background (Akerhielm, 1995). But it must be noted that the bulk of the research on class size and achievement has been done in general education, not in special education settings or with students who have disabilities. Many professionals believe that special education students, on average, have greater needs for individualized instruction than do others. To the extent that this is true, a lower student to teacher ratio might be appropriate. Zigmond provides a discussion about class size in relation to students with disabilities and she concludes that smaller group size can lead to improved outcomes for students with disabilities. She argues that the large number of students in a general education classroom may interfere with the ability to learn for a student with disabilities.

In addition to the number of people involved in the environment, other characteristics of the learning setting are important considerations. Where 2,000-year old Redwoods are being felled by noisy chainsaws, a trio would have some difficulty practicing a lullaby. For some people, a TV at ordinary volume interferes substantially with normal conversation. An audiologist might need a sound-proof room in which to conduct audiometric testing. Interestingly, a half-century before ADHD became the common condition and prevalent diagnosis it is now, many special educators advocated a nearly distraction-free environment for many children with high-incidence disabilities (e.g., Cruickshank, Bentzen, Ratzeburg, & Tannhauser, 1961). In short, the levels of sensory stimuli present may enhance or detract from a learning environment, and more so for some students than others.

At a minimum, an environment conducive to learning must not have an unduly high level of distraction, be it visual, auditory, or other. However, the argument can also be made that the learning environment should mimic the "real world" or the out-of-school environment. The wisdom of this may well depend on such factors as when in the teaching-learning process we are talking about, how much attention is being be given to generalization of the learning, and so on. It can almost, but not quite, go without saying that an adequate learning environment will also have appropriate lighting, ventilation, square footage, furniture, access to restrooms, and any essential specialized equipment. Many of us have recently seen vivid pictures of elementary classrooms in less-priviledged countries where upward of 60 students sit, shoulder-to-shoulder and wall to wall on dirt floors, with their legs extended in front of them. We can be grateful most of our classrooms are much, much closer to adequate, however, there is still an appalling discrepancy between the most and the least suitable classrooms.

LEARNER CHARACTERISTICS

Clearly few if any blanket generalizations can be made about the pertinent characteristics of children who have disabilities. However, many of them learn some things more slowly, require more trials to mastery, and perform lower in some areas than non-disabled children of the same age. Others may have sensory deficits such as vision or hearing impairments, mobility difficulties, speech differences, or emotional and behavioral issues that interfere with learning. Under the Rehabilitation Act of 1973, Section 504, children who have disabilities are entitled to reasonable accommodations in the classroom, the school, on the playground, on the school bus, and anywhere public education takes place. Under the Individuals with Disabilities Education Act (IDEA) learners with disabilities are entitled to a free appropriate public education in the least restrictive environment (LRE). Both Zigmond and Huefner will discuss the importance of the LRE and other important provisions of IDEA when considering placement for students with disabilities. Each child's individualized education plan (IEP) should delineate all the modifications and accommodations required for that child to meet his unique educational needs. The school is responsible for providing all that the IEP requires. Among the most common changes in the learning environment required by IEPs are certain seating, some tests administered one-on-one or in a distraction-free area, scent-free spaces, extra time allowed for assignments, special access to restrooms and quiet areas, and others. IEPs also provide students access to support in the form of a special education teacher, a paraprofessional, or a related service provider. These services can be provided either in a general education classroom or a special education classroom and a big part of the debate is where is the best place for these services? Can they be provided effectively in the general education classroom? Should students be removed to be taught specific content? These questions and more will be addressed in the following chapters.

THE PURPOSES OF SPECIAL EDUCATION

Special education has almost as many purposes and combinations of purposes as there are special education students. For one student the purpose may be to improve articulation, for another to build upper body strength to facilitate transfers in and out of a wheelchair. For many the primary purpose is to improve basic academic skills, but for many others it is to teach age-appropriate social skills. And the list could continue. Students with disabilities may be working on grade-level skills and content, they may be working on content that is below grade level, or they may be working on functional skills. The content being taught should be individualized to meet the needs of students. Zigmond discusses whether or not she believes that this type of specialized instruction can be delivered in a general education classroom.

Special education is not one entity, but rather is a wide range of services with an even wider range of purposes, all depending on the unique needs of each of the six million children it serves each year, ranging in age from birth to 22. The severity and complexity of their disabilities are also unique to each child. It is therefore not surprising that there are many possible and many appropriate places where special education can happen. In fact, IDEA promises the availability of a continuum of services that will be available to meet the needs of a wide range of students. For these reasons, placement is the most hotly disputed issue in special education, as will be seen in these chapters.

IDEA and Placement

Special education today is governed by the federal law known as the IDEA which specifies that the purpose of special education is to provide a free appropriate public education (FAPE) in the least restrictive environment (LRE) in which education can be achieved satisfactorily for a given child. But what is the LRE? Specific IDEA requirements regarding LRE include: (a) Children with disabilities must be educated with non-disabled children to the maximum extent appropriate; (b) Each agency must make available a *continuum of alternative placements* including regular classes, special classes, special schools, home instruction, instruction in hospitals and institutions, and supplemental services such as resource room and itinerant instruction; (c) In selecting the LRE, consideration must be given to any potential harmful effect on the child or on the quality of services; and (d) A child is not removed from the regular classroom solely because of needed modifications to the general education curriculum. Zigmond and Huefner discuss least restrictive environment (LRE) and how this concept plays into placement decisions.

Those who advocate full inclusion of special education students in general education emphasize "with non-disabled children" and "no removal due solely to needed modifications in the general curriculum" requirements of IDEA. Zigmond also states that proponents of full inclusion consider not only access to non-disabled peers, but also access to a general education curriculum, which is assumed to be provided in the general education classroom. Those who advocate more specialized and/or segregated placements focus on the mandated "continuum of placements" and on "the potential harmful effects" of a placement on the student and on the "quality of the needed services" delineated in IDEA. These supporters believe that intensive, individualized instruction might not take place in a general education classroom and that students with disabilities may need to be educated in a separate setting for all or part of the day. These different emphases will be seen in the chapters in this section.

Case law has elaborated two more important points: (a) All placement decisions must be *individualized* and made by a team, not by any one individual; and (b) If a district fails to provide FAPE and a parents' chosen private placement does provide FAPE for that child then the district must pay for the private placement. Should the LRE requirement apply to parents' private placements? Could a school for deaf students, autistic students, or learning disabled students ever be the LRE? This has been a difficult question for the courts. Huefner's chapter will provide a more complete history of important court decisions in special education placements and how these court decisions influence the question of "where."

These legal considerations give us mandatory guidelines for making the placement decision for an IDEA-eligible student. We must decide upon the LRE for that student. But what is the LRE? In general, the LRE is the most normal or ordinary setting or combination of settings from the continuum of alternative placements in which FAPE can be delivered satisfactorily to that student. Underlying most placement disputes over the amount of inclusion with non-disabled students that is appropriate is a disagreement seldom articulated about the primary purpose of special education. Some believe that being with general education students in a general education setting is a fundamental civil right, is inherently good, that it leads to better social development and to friendships, and is conducive to our society becoming ever more accepting of diversity, especially the diversity of disabilities.

Those who favor more specialized settings with peers who also have disabilities value an emphasis on increasing the knowledge and skills levels of each student, on improving areas of weakness, and on directly teaching necessary social and other life skills and doing this in an environment relatively safe from failure, ridicule, and other negative experiences. They question whether general education can provide the intensity, individualization, and specialization of services they believe are necessary for students to reach their potential. They are also concerned that in the general education classroom too much teacher attention and time might necessarily be taken away from the non-disabled children—to the detriment of those learners' educational opportunities. There are also concerns about whether there is sufficient room in the general curriculum for functional life skills instruction.

LRE is second only to FAPE in the number of student-centered cases which progress through hearing and into court. LRE cases typically pose a conflict between placements which differ in the amount of inclusiveness or "mainstreaming" they offer. Many people have analyzed court cases to identify patterns in outcomes (e.g., Lupini & Zirkel, 2003; Newcomer & Zirkel, 1999; Richey, 2003; Zirkel, 2012). The total number of cases in which the courts rule for a more inclusive placement is approximately equal to the number of rulings for less inclusive placements. The striking difference is that parents win slightly more often than districts when they seek a more inclusive placement and when a less inclusive placement is sought, districts win overwhelmingly (about 8:1). However, in all placement cases parents win only about 35 percent of the time. Even so, this is higher than the 27 percent of the time parents win FAPE cases.

Should Public Schools Be Responsible for Private Placements?
Sometimes disputes arise over the desirable amount of inclusion for a given child. One scenario occurs when parents of a child with a learning disability seek a private placement that offers specialized instruction and peers who also have learning disabilities. In these cases the court must determine whether the district provided FAPE and, if not, is the private placement "proper." Embedded in this inquiry is whether LRE applies to private placements. Courts have taken three positions: (1) LRE applies and private placements are too restrictive to be "proper" (e.g., *Lachman v. Illinois St. Bd. of Ed.*, 1988); (2) The benefits of LRE must be weighed against the benefits of specialized instruction with peers who have the same disability (e.g., *Egg Harbor Township Bd. of Ed. v. S. O.*, 1992); or (3) In the 3rd, 6th, and 8th Circuits, LRE does not apply to private placements (e.g., *Cleveland Heights - University Heights City School District v. Boss*, 1998). Whether the public school must pay for the private placement depends on the particular facts and on which analysis the court uses.

A numerically smaller, but equally intense group of disputes arise when parents of deaf children who believe in teaching ASL and belonging to the deaf culture face a public school inclusion program that emphasizes an oral-aural approach in a mainstream setting. Courts are divided on this and related issues involving, e.g., cued speech, finger spelling, signing exact English, and other means of communication. Many courts give great deference to the methodology employed by the district (see, e.g., *Lachman v. Illinois St. Bd. of Ed.*, 1988) but others give more weight to parents' preferences, abilities of the individual child, and cultural factors (e.g., *Visco v. School District of Pittsburgh*, 1988).

As the statistics presented earlier show, about 70 percent of the cases are resolved in favor of the district's placement and program. Perhaps this shows that many districts have heeded Justice Sandra Day O'Connor's advice to districts in the *Carter* case:

> There is no doubt that Congress has imposed a significant financial burden on States and school districts that participate in IDEA. Yet public educational authorities who want to avoid reimbursing parents for the private education of a disabled child can do one of two things: give the child a free appropriate public education in a public setting, or place the child in an appropriate private setting of the State's choice. This is IDEA's mandate, and school officials who conform to it need not worry about reimbursement claims.
>
> (*Florence County School District Four v. Carter*, 1993)

Not everyone agrees that it is appropriate for the public sector ever to be required to pay for the private education chosen by the parents. It should be remembered that IDEA is optional for the states. Today, every U.S. state has opted in to IDEA in exchange for the federal dollars participation yields for each state. The basic contractual arrangement provides that the state, in return for federal money, agrees to make FAPE available to every eligible child with a disability. It is only when a state fails to make FAPE available that it must pay for a private placement. Although it is true this arrangement has occasionally resulted in seemingly outrageous public expenditures on behalf of one child, studies have shown that it is less expensive in the long term for society to provide FAPE than to fail to provide it. Even so, there is still understandable questioning when we hear about particularly expensive cases such as a youngster requiring a $125,000-a-year private placement in New York a few years ago.

A closely related issue is that of what responsibility the public school has for developing the IEP when the child is in a private placement which may be across the country. It also happens sometimes that relationships between the private school and the district are not ideal, further complicating things.

The issues around what makes an appropriate placement for a particular child involve what the child's needs are, i.e., what activities will take place in the setting, the student's unique and relevant characteristics, and the purposes for providing special education to him or her. IDEA mandates a range of placements from which each individualized decision may draw, perhaps suggesting that no one placement is equally appropriate for the six million children who need special education to meet their unique educational needs. Remember, however, that some special educators and parents believe that all learners can and should be educated in general education classes. The chapters in this section shed light on—or fuel the fire about—placement issues.

OVERVIEW

In the following chapters, you will read three different perspectives examining the arguments for and against full inclusion, as well as other issues in making placement decisions. Zigmond presents the results of research examining issues of placement, Huefner presents pivotal court cases that have influenced placement decisions, and Wiley presents a discussion of moral psychology that can be used when considering placement issues.

Zigmond and Huefner both begin with a brief discussion of the history of special education. They discuss how the roots of placement issues begin with early special education that kept students with disabilities segregated and separate from non-disabled peers. Drawing on the seminal court case *Brown v. Board of Education*, parents and advocates began to push for more inclusion for students with disabilities. This has led to a movement of supporters that believe that all students should be included with non-disabled peers at all times. In contrast, opponents to this view argue that the purpose of special education is to provide intense individualized instruction and that this type of instruction can probably not be provided in a general education classroom.

Zigmond and Huefner raise these and other considerations that lead to a common conclusion that perhaps there is not a single answer to the question of "where should students with disabilities be educated?" Instead, we may say that "it depends." It depends on characteristics of the student, characteristics of the setting, and the nature of the instruction and content to be learned. Different students will have different needs and may require different types of placements. In addition, students may be working on grade-level content or they may be working on below-grade-level or functional skills. If they are working below grade level, it may make sense for some or all of their instruction to be provided in a separate placement. Consider what you have read in this introduction and, as you read the following chapters, think about the different pieces that may be pertinent when making placement decisions.

In contrast, Wiley presents a model of moral psychology and explains how this model may be used in arguments about placement decisions. He explains different aspects of the model and how people make moral judgments. In addition, he describes how difficult it can be for people to change their minds once they have made a decision about a moral issue. Wiley presents this model in the hopes that it can help readers understand why advocates and opponents of full inclusion make the arguments that they do and how discussions may proceed in consideration of the social intuitionist model.

As you read the following three chapters, consider the arguments for and against full inclusion. Remember to think about the characteristics of the student and the setting, as well as the type of content being taught in the placement.

KAT ALVES'S SUGGESTIONS FOR FURTHER READING

Gardill, M. C., & Jitendra, A. K. (1999). Advanced story map instruction: Effects on the reading comprehension of students with learning disabilities. *The Journal of Special Education, 33*, 2–17, 28.

Gersten, R., Fuchs, L. S., Williams, J. P., & Baker, S. (2001). Teaching reading comprehension strategies to students with learning disabilities: A review of research. *Review of Educational Research, 71*, 279–320.

Idol, L. (1987). Group story mapping: A comprehension strategy for both skilled and unskilled readers. *Journal of Learning Disabilities, 20*, 196–205.

Idol, L., & Croll, V. J. (1987). Story-mapping training as a means of improving reading comprehension. *Learning Disability Quarterly, 10*, 214–229.

Kintsch, W. (1998). *Comprehension: A paradigm for cognition.* NY: Cambridge University Press.
Kintsch, W., & van Dijk, T. A. (1978). Toward a model of text comprehension and production. *Psychological Review, 85,* 363–394.

REFERENCES

Akerhielm, K. (1995). Does class size matter? *Economics of Education, 14,* 229–241.

Cleveland Heights - University Heights City School District v. Boss, 144 F. 3rd. 391 (6th Cir. 1998).

Cruickshank, W. M., Bentzen, F. A., Ratzeburg, F. H., & Tannhauser, M. T. (1961). *A teaching method for brain injured and hyperactive children: A demonstration pilot study.* Syracuse, NY: Syracuse University Press.

Egg Harbor Township Bd. of Ed. v. S. O., 19 IDELR 15 (D. N.J. 1992).

Florence County School District Four v. Carter, 510 U.S. 7 (1993). Retrieved from https://bulk.resource.org/courts. gov/c/US/510/510.US.7.91-1523.html.

Hanushek, E. A. (1999). Some findings from an independent investigation of the Tennessee STAR experiment and from other investigations of class size effects. *Educational Evaluation and Policy Analysis, 21*(143). Retrieved from http://epa.sagepub.com/content/21/2/143.

Lachman v. Illinois St. Bd. of Ed., 852 F. 2nd 290 (7th Cir. 1988).

Lupini, W. H., & Zirkel, P. A. (2003). An outcomes analysis of education litigation. *Educational Policy, 17,* 257–279.

Mosteller, F. (1995). The Tennessee study of class size in the early school grades. *The Future of Children, 5,* 113–127.

Newcomer, J. R., & Zirkel, P. A. (1999). An analysis of judicial outcomes of special education cases. *Exceptional Children, 65,* 469–480.

Richey, K. (2003). Special education due process hearings: Student characteristics, issues, and decisions. *Journal of Disability Policy Studies, 14,* 46–53.

Visco v. School District of Pittsburgh, 684 F. Supp. 1310 (W.D. Pa. 1988).

Zirkel, P. A. (2012). Judicial appeals for hearing/review officer decisions under idea: An empirical analysis. *Exceptional Children, 78,* 375–384.

Getting to Know Naomi Zigmond

I was sure I would be a ballet dancer. From the time I could walk I wanted to dance. I studied very seriously, long hours, many days a week. I loved the discipline, the control, the practicing, the beauty of it all, but the truth had to be faced: I just wasn't all that good! So I thought I would be a neurosurgeon. My father had been a neurologist. I was fascinated with how the brain worked, and with what might be wrong when it didn't work. But a prerequisite to medical school was chemistry and I hated chemistry! I struggled through it in high school and didn't do well. So, I gave up that dream, too.

I settled on being a detective. That's what you became when you studied with Helmer Myklebust at the Institute for Language Disorders at Northwestern University. Your target was the cognitive processing of a child who was not learning to speak, to understand speech, to read, to write, to do arithmetic, to make sense of the world around him. Your mission was to figure this child out, to understand how he thought, how he listened, how he saw the world, how he processed information, and then, most challenging of all, how he learned!

This early training in Myklebust's teacher-as-detective paradigm has grounded all of my research work, too. I've devoted my career to looking carefully and thinking deeply about kids and schools, about how things are, why they are the way they are, and how to make them better. For nearly 50 years, I have held up a mirror, laid bare some of the problems of special education service delivery, or special education teacher education, and fed my passion to "find out." What my colleagues and I have seen and reported has not always been good news. And changes we have advocated have not always taken hold. But every now and then, one teacher, one school, or one district has used our detective work to improve the delivery of educational services to students with disabilities and that has been truly rewarding.

13

WHERE SHOULD STUDENTS WITH DISABILITIES
RECEIVE THEIR EDUCATION?

Naomi Zigmond

Before there was Federal legislation requiring public education for all students, including those with disabilities, parents of children with cognitive, emotional, or physical disabilities, deafness, blindness or the need for speech therapy had few options other than to educate their children at home, institutionalize them in a state-run facility, or pay for expensive private education. As recently as 1948, only 12 percent of all children with disabilities in the United States were receiving some form of education. By the early 1950s, some public school special education services and programs became available, but because students with disabilities were considered unable to perform academic tasks, these programs were housed in special centers or special schools and focused on learning manual skills such as basket weaving and bead stringing. In most states across the nation, the answer to the question of *where* students with disabilities should be educated was clearly, "Not in my public school!"

To fill the gap in the provision of educational services for their children, family associations began forming in the 1950s and 1960s. One of the first organizations was the American Association on Mental Deficiency. Then came the United Cerebral Palsy Association, the Muscular Dystrophy Association, and John F. Kennedy's Panel on Mental Retardation (what we now call "Intellectual Disability") shown in the accompanying photograph. These parent-run associations each offered separate educational programs for children (by disability), parent support, and advocacy for specially trained teachers who would work in their schools. In response, in the late 1950s, the federal government began to allocate funds to develop methods for working with children with disabilities and passed several pieces of legislation that supported developing and implementing programs and services to meet the needs of those children and their families. Two laws provided training for teachers to work with students with intellectual disability (P. L. 85-926 in 1958 and P. L. 86-158 in 1959). The Teachers of the Deaf Act (P. L. 87-276 in 1961) provided for training of teachers to work with the students who were deaf or hard of hearing. The Elementary and Secondary Education Act (P. L. 89-10) and the State Schools Act (P. L. 89-313), both passed in 1965, granted funds to states to help educate children with disabilities, and in 1968, the Handicapped Children's Early Education Assistance Act of 1968 (P. L. 90-538) funded preschool and early childhood intervention

Figure 13.1 Photograph of President John F. Kennedy meeting "a panel of outstanding scientists, doctors, and others to prescribe a plan of action in the field of mental retardation."

Abbie Rowe, National Park Service/John F. Kennedy Presidential Library and Museum, Boston. Public Domain.

for children with disabilities. Nevertheless, despite these advances in federal financial support for unique special education teacher training programs and some federal dollars to promote educational services to students with disabilities, many states had laws on the books that explicitly excluded children who were blind or deaf, and children labeled "emotionally disturbed" or "mentally retarded" from attending neighborhood public schools (National Council on Disability, 2000). School districts and schools across the nation answered the question of *where* students with disabilities should be educated with a resounding, "Not in the same public schools as students without disabilities!"

In 1954, the Supreme Court of the United States issued a bold decision that forever changed American public schools. In Brown v. Board of Education, the Supreme Court ruled that it was illegal practice under the 14th Amendment of the U.S. Constitution to discriminate arbitrarily against any single group. The Court applied this principle to the schooling of African-American students, holding that a separate education based on race is not an equal education. Building on the *Brown v. Board of Education* ruling, several landmark court decisions (in particular, *Pennsylvania Association for Retarded Citizens (PARC) v. Commonwealth of Pennsylvania* in 1971 and *Mills v. Board of Education of the District of Columbia* in 1972) established new responsibilities for states with regard to the education of children with disabilities. Segregation and exclusion from school of students with disabilities violated the equal opportunity clause under the 14th amendment; if Brown prohibited segregation by race, some argued that schools should not be able to segregate or otherwise discriminate by ability and disability.

Yet by 1975, American public schools still educated only one in five children with disabilities. More than 1 million students were refused access to public schools each year, and another 3.5 million received little or no effective instruction. Then, Congress passed a landmark federal law: The Education for All Handicapped Children Act (EHA P. L. 94-142) (later reauthorized as the Individuals with Disabilities Act [IDEA, 1997] and the Individuals with Disabilities Improvement Act [IDEIA, 2004]) established once and for all a right to public education for *all* children regardless of disability, and required all public schools in states that accept any federal funds for education to provide a *special* education for children with qualifying disabilities. The answer to the question of *where* students with disabilities should receive a free, public education was now, "In the same public schools as everyone else."

The Education of All Handicapped Children Act (EHA, 1975) emphasized two important concepts that dealt with the question of *where*: *continuum of services* on the one hand, and *least restrictive environment* on the other. The continuum of services recognized that, to meet the educational needs of *all* students with disabilities, school district and public agencies would need to establish a broad array of service delivery models. The continuum was exemplified by the Deno (1970) Cascade of Services in which the extent of a student's integration into the general education classroom or the local public school could be increased or decreased systematically to meet the needs of particular students eligible for the protections afforded by P. L. 94-142. Decision making about placement along the continuum was to be tempered by the *least restrictive environment (LRE)* concept that assured

> that, to the maximum extent appropriate, handicapped children . . . are educated with children who are not handicapped and that . . . removal of handicapped children from the regular educational environment occurs only when the nature or severity of that handicap is such that education in regular classes with the use of supplemental aids and services cannot be achieved satisfactorily.
>
> (EHA, 1975, Part B, Section 612(5)(B))

In other words, the LRE provision in the special education federal law required that, given two or more alternative educational settings, children with disabilities should be placed in the least drastic or most normal setting in which education can be achieved satisfactorily.

"The answer to the question of *where* students with disabilities should receive a free, public education was now, 'In the same public schools as everyone else.'"

In the decade following the passage of P. L. 94-142, efforts were made to move services for students with disabilities from separate schools to regular schools, and from special classes in regular schools to more mainstream settings (i.e., general education classrooms) for at least part of the school day. Pull-out, itinerant, resource, or part-time special class special education placements flourished. In the spirit of the 1975 law, a balance was sought between making available to children and families the full continuum of special education services and following the principle of an LRE.

Then, in the mid-1980s, the question of *where* students with disabilities should be educated surfaced again. Essays on the failure of pull-out special education had begun to proliferate. The theme was consistent; fundamental changes in the delivery model for special education were needed to increase the accomplishments of students with disabilities. Even Madeline Will, then Assistant Secretary of Education and head of the Office of Special Education Programs, joined the fray. "Although well intentioned, the so-called 'pull-out' approach to the educational difficulties of students with learning problems has failed in many instances to meet the educational needs of these students," she wrote in 1986 (p. 413). Will and other advocates of a Regular Education Initiative (REI) called for completely integrated educational experiences (i.e., full inclusion) for children with learning problems to achieve "improved educational outcomes" (Will, 1986, p. 413), "academic growth" (Gartner & Lipsky, 1989, p. 21), and "better outcomes" (National Association of State Boards of Education, 1992, p. 4). Model programs of full inclusion were proposed and studied.

Almost simultaneously, in the 1997 reauthorization of IDEA, the definition of restrictiveness shifted. Whereas earlier definitions of "restrictiveness" had focused on *access* of students with disabilities *to nondisabled peers*, the new focus substituted *access to the general education curriculum*. With the additional requirement that students with disabilities participate in (and perform respectably on) statewide assessments and accountability procedures, pressures to favor one kind of placement (inclusion in the general education *classroom*) over any other (providing pull-out services in some other place) mounted. Full inclusion with co-teaching (a general and a special educator sharing the same general education classroom space to teach the same group of diverse students, some of whom had disabilities and were in need of a special education) became the preferred service delivery model for *all* students with disabilities. The push towards full inclusion was strengthened further by the standards-based education and accountability

> "Whereas earlier definitions of 'restrictiveness' had focused on *access* of students with disabilities *to non-disabled peers*, the new focus defined restrictiveness in terms of *access to the general education curriculum*."

provisions written into the No Child Left Behind in 2001 and reiterated in the reauthorization of the Individuals with Disabilities Education Improvement Act in 2004. Students with disabilities were to have access not only to their nondisabled peers and to everything in the general education curriculum, but also to the general education teachers fully qualified to teach that curriculum. For many special education teachers and their students, the answer to the question of *where* appeared to be, "In the general education classroom, and nowhere else!"

CONCLUSIONS ABOUT THE WHERE QUESTION

I have been immersed in the "*where?*" question for more than 30 years. I have searched the research literature for an empirically based answer to that question. I have explored, systematically, the impact on the achievement of students with learning disabilities of fully inclusive models of service delivery with and without co-teaching, as well as variations on pull-out models of instruction. I have written at least seven journal articles (see Zigmond, 1994, 2001, 2003; Zigmond & Baker, 1994, 1995, 1996; Zigmond, Kloo, & Volonino, 2009) and three book chapters (see Zigmond 1997, 2003, 2006) trying to reason through an answer to the question of *where?* And I have come to the following conclusions.

1. Research Evidence on the Relative Efficacy of One Special Education Placement Over Another is Scarce, Methodologically Flawed, and Inconclusive

There have been many attempts by researchers to demonstrate the effectiveness of specific special education services in improving outcomes (academic, social, behavioral, etc.) for students with disabilities. The database is a little sobering, in large part because efficacy research is so very hard to do. In a perfect outcome study, students with comparable levels of ability and disability would be identified for the study. Then, students from that large pool would be randomly selected and assigned to one of two special education programs (i.e., the same special education delivered in two different places). What happened to the students in their special education programs would be carefully scripted and monitored so that we could be sure that all the students in each of the two groups got the prescribed treatment. Then all students would be tested to see if Group 1 (in place 1) did better in the end than Group 2 (in place 2).

Of course, in real life, we seldom have the luxury of randomly assigning students to educational programs. Groups of students are usually not perfectly comparable. And we have very little control over the implementation of an educational program. So, in all of the efficacy research, researchers have had to make compromises and the data have to be examined closely and interpreted carefully. Some studies use control groups, often samples of students experiencing "traditional" programs (sometimes referred to as business-as-usual), in non-experimental schools. In some studies, the researchers manage to achieve random assignment of students to treatments, but use intact groups of students assigned to the teacher or teachers who volunteered to participate in the experimental treatment program. Often the experimental treatment is well described, although degree and fidelity of implementation are not. Descriptions of the control treatment and its degree of implementation (if indeed a control group is used) are rarely provided. Most often, neither treatment is described sufficiently, nor its implementation monitored sufficiently, to make replication possible. So, even if reliable achievement changes are demonstrated in a research study, the difficulty in identifying critical treatment variables makes replicability impossible in virtually all cases. Achievement gains, or lack thereof, cannot be related to replicable interventions. Despite the fact that the efficacy research literature on the *places* in which special education services are provided spans more than three decades, and despite the fact that dozens of studies have been reported in refereed special education journals, the fundamental question of whether *place A* is better than *place B* cannot actually be answered.

The accumulated evidence on *where,* to date, produces only one unequivocal finding. Languishing in a regular education classroom where nothing changes and no one pays you any attention is not as useful to students with mild-moderate learning and behavior disorders as getting some help. All other evidence on whether students with disabilities learn more, academically or socially, and are happier in one school setting or another is at best inconclusive. Resource programs are more effective for some students with disabilities than self-contained special education classes or self-contained general education classes, but they are less effective for other students with similar disabilities. Fully inclusive programs are superior for some students with disabilities on some measures of academic or social skills development, and inferior for other students or on other measures. The empirical research not only does not identify one best place, but also often finds equivalent progress being made by students with disabilities across settings; that is, the research reports non-significant differences in outcomes.

2. *The Question of* **Where** *is Intimately and Inextricably Tied to the Question of* **Who**

Special education has evolved as a means of providing specialized interventions to students with disabilities based on individual student's progress on individualized objectives. The bedrock of special education is instruction focused on *individual* need. The very concept of "one best place" contradicts this commitment to individualization. Furthermore, results of research on how *groups* of students respond to treatment settings does not help the researcher or practitioner make an *individualized* decision for an individual student's plan. A better question to ask, if we dare, is "best for whom?" or, for which individual students with which individual profiles of characteristics and needs is one place better than another? An answer to this question would require that we abandon the rhetoric in which we call for *all* students to do this, or *all* students to learn that, or *all* students be educated in this place or that one.

> "Despite the fact that the efficacy research literature on the *places* in which special education services are provided spans more than three decades, and despite the fact that dozens of studies have been reported in refereed special education journals, the fundamental question of whether *place A* is better than *place B* cannot actually be answered."

Special educators understand about individual differences. Special educators understand that no matter how hard they try or how well they are taught, there are some students who will never be able to learn on the same schedule as most others; there are some students who will take so long to learn some things that, each school year; they will have to forego learning other things; and that there are some students who will need to be taught curricular content not ordinarily taught. Special educators understood this when they fought hard for the legal requirement of an Individualized Educational Plan for children with disabilities, to permit formulation of unique programs of instruction to meet unique individual needs. By continuing to frame the research question as "what's the best place?" we are ignoring what we know.

3. *The Question of* **Where** *is Intimately and Inextricably Tied to the Question of* **What**

Different settings offer different opportunities for teaching and learning. IDEA '97 introduced, and IDEA '04 reiterated, the notion that all students with disabilities should have access to the general education curriculum. These reauthorizations of the federal special education law demand that, whether taught in a general education classroom or in a special self-contained classroom or school, students with disabilities are to be exposed to the same curricular content as students who do not have disabilities (i.e., the curriculum set by state or school district guidelines) and they are to be held to the same achievement standards as students who do not have disabilities. This mandate, coupled with the long-standing commitment to educating students with disabilities in the least restrictive environment, has compelled many school districts to return students with disabilities to their home schools and to regular classrooms (or to not remove them from those environments in the first place) (McLeskey, Hoppey, Williamson, & Rents, 2004).

It makes perfectly good sense. If students with disabilities are to have access to the same content as their nondisabled classmates, they need to be there when that content is taught. The general education classroom allows for access to curricula and textbooks to which most other students are exposed, access to instruction from a general education teacher whose training and expertise are quite different from those of a special education teacher, access to subject matter content taught by a subject matter specialist, access to students who do not have disabilities, and access to all of the stresses and strains associated with the preparation for, taking of, and passing or failing the statewide assessments. In other words, there are very good reasons for students with disabilities to be in regular schools, and in general education elementary or in secondary classes, taught by teachers who are "highly qualified" in the content. If the goal is to have students learn content subject information, or learn how to interact with nondisabled peers, the general education classroom is the place to do that. And a co-teaching service delivery model may be useful in helping teachers accommodate the needs of students with disabilities in their content subject classes.

On the other hand, if the goal is to have students with disabilities learn a unique set of skills, or a set of skills no longer taught in the general education classroom at that grade level, a pull-out setting may be more appropriate. Pull-out settings allow for smaller teacher–student ratios and flexibility in the selection of texts, choice of curricular objectives, pacing of instruction, scheduling of examinations, and the assignment of grades. Special education pull-out settings allow students to be learning different "stuff," in different ways, and on a different schedule. If students need intensive instruction in basic academic skills well below the grade level at which nondisabled peers are learning how to read or do basic mathematics, if students need explicit instruction in controlling behavior or interacting with peers and adults, or if students need to learn anything that is not customarily taught to everyone else, a pull-out special education setting may be the answer.

4. The Question of Where is Intimately and Inextricably Tied to the Question of How

According to Hallahan and Kauffman (1978, p. 4) "special education means specially designed instruction which meets the unique needs of an exceptional child." Delivering that specially designed instruction may require special materials, teaching techniques, equipment, and/or facilities. Early textbooks on educating students with disabilities describe specially designed instruction in terms of ability or process training; behavior modification; developmental and ecological approaches; psychodynamic or psychoeducational teaching strategies; social learning approaches, and task analysis (see Kirk & Gallagher, 1979) or in terms of teaching models—biophysical, psychological, behavioral, or environmental (see; Ysseldyke & Algozzine, 1984). Special education textbooks also describe specially designed instructional strategies particularly suited to certain groups of students, like those with Down syndrome, or hearing impairment, or intellectual disability, or learning disabilities, or multiple and severe disabilities, etc., although more recent texts tend to focus more on strategies differentiated by subject matter or by instructional setting than by disability category (see Culatta, Tompkins, & Werts, 2003; Mastropieri & Scruggs, 2007; Sabornie & deBettencourt, 2009).

Special education differs from ordinary teaching in its emphasis on intensity, on direct instruction, and on systematic, well-scaffolded instructional tasks. Direct instruction has been a long-standing pillar of special education. Intervention research has shown positive effect sizes for the use of systematic, direct instruction, particularly when coupled with explicit strategy instruction with students who have learning and behavioral disabilities (see Gersten, Vaughn, Deshler, & Schiller, 1997; Swanson, Hoskyn, & Lee, 1999; Vaughn, Gersten, & Chard, 2000). Many students benefit from explicit, direct, systematic instruction that is directly linked to their area of instructional need (Vaughn & Linan-Thompson, 2003). However, direct instruction occurs infrequently in whole-class instructional settings, and given the overwhelming favor of whole-group instruction in general education classrooms, one can deduce that skill-focused direct instruction occurs marginally there.

5. Students with Disabilities are Entitled to a Special Education, Not Just a General Education Sprinkled with Accommodations

Not all students are alike. Students in classroom groups differ in background knowledge, readiness to learn, language proficiency, preferences in learning style, interests, and ability to react responsively, and these differences are becoming more and more pronounced. "Differentiated instruction" has been promoted as one solution to this problem. Differentiated instruction is a teaching theory based on the premise that instructional approaches should vary and be adapted in relation to individual and diverse students in classrooms (Hall, 2002). It requires teachers to be flexible in their approach to teaching and to adjust the curriculum and presentation of information to learners rather than to expect students to modify themselves for the curriculum. It encourages teachers to offer students multiple options for taking in information and making sense of ideas. The intent of differentiating instruction is to maximize each student's growth and individual success by meeting each student where he or she is and adjusting instruction to be sensitive to individual differences in readiness levels, interests, and preferred modes of learning. Differentiated instruction provides *multiple approaches* to content, process, and product. Teachers offer different approaches to what students learn, how they learn it, and how they demonstrate what they've learned.

> "Special education differs from ordinary teaching in its emphasis on intensity, on direct instruction, and on systematic, well-scaffolded instructional tasks."

Differentiated instruction is based on the idea that "all learners do not necessarily learn in the same way, and it refers to the practice of ensuring that each learner receives the methods and materials most suitable for that particular learner at that particular place in the curriculum" (Mastropieri & Scruggs, 2007, p. 126). An expansive literature base has explored numerous effective strategies and pedagogies for differentiated instruction designed to help general education teachers meet diverse student needs in their classrooms. Research suggests instructional adaptations such as the use of content enhancement routines, advanced organizers, and cognitive strategy instruction have a positive impact on classroom learning when explicitly, effectively, and thoughtfully implemented (DeLaPaz & MacArthur, 2003; Swanson & Deshler, 2003). However, studies have also shown that differentiated instruction is rarely explicitly, effectively, or thoughtfully applied in actual classroom practice (Fuchs & Fuchs, 1998).

Providing differentiated instruction in a general education classroom is not the same as providing a *special* education. Special education is more explicit, intensive, and supportive than general education can ever be (Torgesen, 1996). Attempts to transport teaching methods developed and validated in special education to general education settings have not been successful. Instructional practices that focus on individual decision making for individual students and improve outcomes of students with severe learning problems are not easily transposed into practices that can survive in a general education classroom. General educators will make instructional adaptations in response to students' persistent failure to learn, but the accommodations are typically oriented to the group, not to the individual, and are relatively minor in substance, with little chance for helping students with chronically poor learning histories (Zigmond & Baker, 1995).

6. In Many Ways, Place is Not the Critical Issue

While most would agree that students with mild and moderate disabilities should spend a large proportion of the school day with peers who do not have disabilities, research does not support the superiority of any one service delivery model over another. Effectiveness appears to depend not only on the characteristics and needs of a particular student but also on the quality of a program's implementation. A poorly run model with limited resources will seldom be superior to a model in which there is a heavy investment of time, energy, and money. Good programs can be developed in any setting; so can bad ones. *Setting is less important than what is going on in the setting* and *place* is not what makes special education "special" or effective. Effective teaching strategies and an individualized approach are the most critical ingredients in special education and neither of these is associated solely with one particular environment.

7. Nevertheless, if Place is Not the Critical Issue, the Office of Special Education Programs (OSEP) is Sending Confusing Messages in its Annual Reports to Congress

As early as 1979, federal monitoring of state programs was put into place not only to guard against too much segregation of students with disabilities but also to guard against "inappropriate mainstreaming" (U.S. Department of Health, Education and Welfare, 1979, p. 39). Annual Reports to Congress, required every year as part of the federal special education legislation (P. L. 94-142, then IDEA), ask for an accounting of *hours spent by students with disabilities outside a general education class*. Historically, these data were requested because of concerns about whether special education services are being provided in the least restrictive environment and about the number of special education students receiving costly services in private day and residential facilities at public expense, diverting scarce resources from other areas of the educational system. The reporting identified how many students with disabilities were served in each of the educational environments along the continuum of placements from regular classes to residential facilities and homebound or hospital placements.

In the first of these *Annual Reports*, issued in 1977, the first year of full implementation of the Education of All Handicapped Act, and in every report since, the Office of Special Education Programs (OSEP) tabulated, among other things, *the settings* in which students with disabilities "receive special education services" (see U.S. Department of Education, 2002, p. III{-}43). OSEP defines *regular class placement* as one in which students with disabilities receive special education and related services outside the regular class for 0 to 20 percent of the school day. *Resource room placements* are those in which students receive special education and related services outside the regular class for 21 to

60 percent of the school day. *Separate class placements* include students who receive special education and related services outside the regular class for more than 60 percent of the school day. In the remaining placement options, students receive their special education and related services in a separate school or facility. Notice that what is being counted and reported here is time outside the regular classroom. Notice also the presumption that it is during this time outside the regular classroom (and only during the time outside the general education classroom) that students with disabilities are receiving their *special* education. This presupposes that special education is not happening in general education classrooms but is happening in a separate place. In fact, this is the only part of each *Annual Report* that tells Congress how much special education students are getting, and it only counts special education delivered outside the general education setting. Services provided inside the general education classroom are not counted. By its own accounting system, OSEP treats special education and related services as a *place*.

8. For Students With Disabilities, Instructional Group Size Matters, and in General Education Classrooms, There are Just Too Many Students

There is some research evidence that typical general education environments are not supportive places in which to implement what are known to be effective teaching instructional strategies for students with disabilities (see Zigmond, 1996). For one thing, with a typical class size of about 25 pupils, the general education teacher has too many children to worry about, and the special education student has too many peers with whom to compete for the teacher's attention and feedback. For at least 20 years, we have known that the number of students in a class has the potential to affect how much is learned (see Mosteller, 1995). For example, class size could affect how students interact with each other and with the teacher, how much noise is produced, how disruptive individual student's behaviors are, and the kinds of activities that can be accomplished. Class size could affect how much time the teacher is able to focus on individual students and their specific needs rather than on the group as a whole. Class size could also affect how much material can be covered, how much feedback can be delivered, how much to use open-ended assignments, or how much to engage in discussions. Research tells us that students in small general education classes (defined as 16 or 17 students) had higher standardized test scores in reading and mathematics than did students in larger classes of 24 to 27.

> "By its own accounting system, OSEP treats special education and related services as a *place*."

But a small class size in special education is not 14 to 16 students but rather small groups of three to five students or one-on-one instruction. In the special education research literature, there are countless studies on the effects of instructional group size on student achievement, and the findings are consistent: Smaller group size is associated with improved outcomes. Smaller groups reduce variability in the instructional needs of students (e.g., Elbaum, Vaughn, Hughes, & Moody, 1999). Group size affects amount and quality of oral language used among students learning English as a second language (e.g., Gersten & Jiménez, 1998). Smaller groups allow reading instruction to be more tailored to students' individual needs (e.g., Rashotte, MacPhee, & Torgesen, 2001). Instruction in small groups or student pairs produces higher effect sizes than whole class instruction, even when the "whole class" is no more than 12-14 students (e.g., Elbaum et al., 1999). Although the optimal group size for special education instruction has yet to be established, research indicates that 1:1 and 3:1 are both better in terms of student achievement than 10:1 (Vaughn et al., 2003). One meta-analysis shows that 1:1 instruction exceeded outcomes for group instruction by an average of .41 standard deviations (Elbaum, Vaughn, Hughes, & Moody, 2000).

9. Inclusion is a Good Thing; Full Inclusion (Zero Time Outside the General Education Classroom) May be Too Much of a Good Thing!

There are many reasons for students with disabilities to be educated in general education classrooms. It gives them access to nondisabled classmates and opportunities for important social interactions. It gives them access to the content taught to their nondisabled classmates and opportunities to develop "cultural literacy." It gives them access to highly qualified content teachers and opportunities to increase their vocabulary and improve listening skills. It changes the climate of a school, making students with disabilities a more integral part of the student body and a shared responsibility of all the general and special educators. Access to the general education classroom and curriculum, education provided alongside general education peers, is an honored tenet and valued goal of special education. However, that "access" should not come at the expense of eliminating opportunities for intense, individualized, and explicit skill/strategy instruction provided by specialists. As my colleague Jan Baker and I wrote in 1996, "We cannot support the elimination of a continuum of services for students with LD. Inclusion is good; full inclusion may be too much of a good thing" (Zigmond & Baker, 1996, p. 33).

10. High-stakes Testing and Accountability Have Become Entangled With Where in Ways That May be to Students' Detriment

Students with disabilities are being placed in general education classrooms in large part because policy makers believe that if they are going to have to take the same accountability tests at the end of the year and meet the same proficiency standards as their nondisabled classmates, they better be in the same classrooms to hear what is going on there. But taking a hard test doesn't make students smarter, and *exposure* or *access* does not lead them to mastery, even if classroom instructional duties are shared between a general education teacher and a special education co-teacher.

Co-teaching is not an *intervention*. It is not a *treatment*. It is a *service delivery model* designed to help students with disabilities get more out of the instruction being provided to classmates in a general education classroom. By teaming a general education content specialist with a special education pedagogy specialist, the lessons being delivered in a general education class could be made more accessible to students who were struggling readers, writers, and mathematicians, or whose cognitive and language skills were poor.

"However, that 'access' should not come at the expense of eliminating opportunities for intense, individualized, and explicit skill/strategy instruction provided by specialists."

Once introduced, co-teaching immediately gained enormous intuitive appeal and was widely implemented in schools across the nation. However, research on the instructional validity of co-teaching and on student outcomes as a result of its implementation is extremely limited. A review of the literature reveals gaps and omissions in the research evidence for the actual contribution of co-teaching to the teaching-learning process (see Weiss, in this volume, as well as Cook, McDuffie-Landrum, Oshita, & Cook, 2011; Zigmond, Magiera, Simmons, & Volonino, 2013).

In an article on the results of a large-scale observational study of co-teaching in secondary school content subject classes, my colleague David Matta and I reported on the value-added of the special education co-teacher in English, math, science, and social studies classes (Zigmond & Matta, 2004). The data were surprising. General and special education students and general education teachers all agreed that the special education co-teacher was a nice addition, an occasional relief for the general education teacher, and allowed for a little more attention to be paid to students with disabilities when class was organized for small group (team) or independent seatwork. But none of what we observed would make it more likely that the students with disabilities in those classes would master the content subject material. We did not hear the special education teachers chime in with carefully worded elaborative explanations. We rarely heard special education teachers rephrase something already said to make the explanation clearer. We virtually never saw the special education teachers provide explicit strategic instruction to facilitate learning or memory of the content material. If students with disabilities were mastering the high school content and earning passing grades in these high school courses, it was not because of something special the special education teacher was doing in their class. If students with disabilities were not mastering the content, and not earning passing grades, the kinds of coaching and team teaching we saw was not likely to make much difference in their academic achievement.

For me, this research raised questions about the purpose of co-teaching. If students with disabilities and their teachers are placed in general education classes to make it possible for the students to be exposed to the curriculum and instruction being delivered by the general education teacher, then the co-teaching in the classes we observed was successful. The general education curriculum was being delivered, the special education teacher was helping out, and the students were being exposed to (and learning or not learning) the material being covered. If, however, the inclusion aimed to provide students with disabilities with opportunities to master essential curriculum content in preparation for full participation in statewide accountability assessments, then there was nothing about the co-teaching going on in those classrooms that would have led students to mastery. The special education teachers we saw shared the instructional burden but did not make a unique contribution. They were around to answer a question or help with a solution, but there was no sustained instruction for students having particular difficulties, no re-teaching of students who had not reached mastery, and no strategic instruction for students who needed explicit instruction in strategies. There was no reason to believe that the extra teacher would make it any more likely that the students with disabilities would end up proficient on the statewide accountability assessments in reading or mathematics at the end of the school year.

THERE IS NO EASY ANSWER

So, what is the answer to the question, "Where should students with disabilities receive their education?" Well, what do we know? We know that what goes on in a place is what makes the difference, not the location itself. We know that some instructional practices are easier to implement and more likely to occur in some settings than in others. We know that general education classrooms are not particularly conducive for providing direct and intensive instruction and that they provide few opportunities for sustained and consistent time on task, immediate and appropriate feedback, sufficient opportunities to practice until mastery, regular and frequent communications about expectations for achievement, and progress monitoring—all building blocks of *special* education. We know that you learn what you spend time on, and that most students with disabilities will not learn to read or to write or to calculate if not explicitly taught. We know that we need more research that asks better and more focused questions about who learns what best where. And we know that a combination of inclusion and pull-out is likely to provide the best access to the general education curriculum and the best opportunities to improve basic skills.

We haven't yet figured out how to organize schooling to provide the most appropriate and productive combination of pull-out and in-class programs possible. There have been virtually no research studies or model demonstration programs focused on how to provide accessible mainstream content *and* intensive direct pull-out instruction in basic skills to a school's special education population. We have not answered a whole slew of questions about the pull-out portion of the equation. For example:

- Pulled out for how long? That is, what is the most efficient, or more importantly, most effective length of an intensive instructional session? If students miss part of a general education instructional period in order to receive pull-out special education services, how will we help them make up for the missing chunks of lessons? And, how many days per week should pull-out services be delivered? If a student missed every other social studies class in order to get direct reading instruction three times per week, how will he or she make sense of the social studies lessons missed?
- Pulled out of what? Does it matter what subjects students miss when we try to schedule intensive pull-out instruction? Torgeson recommends a 90-minute block, every day, for middle or high school students who have significant word-level reading problems plus comprehension problems. What would need to be taken off the students' schedules to accomplish that? If the student is a high schooler, will he or she still be able to accumulate sufficient credits to graduate?
- What is the most effective instructional group size? One-to-one? Three-to-one? Six-to-one? Ten-to-one? Can group size and length of session (both ways of increasing or decreasing the intensity of an intervention) be flexible? What kind of staffing would be needed to make pull out work? Is it practical? Is it affordable? Has co-teaching used up all the special education personnel resources? Has RTI implementation reduced the number of special education students by fully engaging the special education teaching staff in Tier One and Tier Two activities, leaving no teacher resources left to provide Tier Three intervention instead of prevention?
- And what about the need to provide support for the student with disabilities and his or her general education teacher in the general education classrooms? Advocates of co-teaching make a strong case for the usefulness of a second teacher in content classes. Is providing an appropriate special education really a two-person job?

(see Zigmond, 2007)

There are some who claim that arguments about place are moot. Students with disabilities belong in general education classes, full time, period! Some interpretations of law and concerns for equity and social justice support that position. Also supporting that position is the assertion that a special education can be delivered anywhere, because "special education is a service, not a place" (ALL Inclusive, 2001, p. 1). Special educators, expertly trained to meet the individual needs of exceptional students and armed with a comprehensive repertoire of evidenced-based instructional strategies, can deliver a special education anywhere. But, research tells us this is not (and perhaps never has been) the case.

And so, the search for the one best place in which to deliver special education services goes on, and will go on until educators are ready to say that receiving special education services in a particular setting is good for some students with disabilities but not for others; that different educational environments are more conducive to different forms of teaching and learning; that different students need to learn different things taught in different ways; and that a special education is not special if it is the same education everyone else gets, in the same classroom, delivered by same teacher. There is no simple answer to the where question. And debates fueled by passion and principle rather than by reason and rationality will not bring us any closer to finding one.

Discussion Questions

1. How has legislation directed where special education should occur over time?
2. Zigmond distinguishes between the continuum of services and the least restrictive environment. Do you think those distinctions have become blurred? If so, how are they treated similarly and if not, how are they implemented distinctly?
3. Zigmond's conclusions over a 30-year career in asking where special education should be taught included that the question of *where* must be considered in relation to questions of *who*, *what*, and *how*. How might you use her conclusions in discussions with an IEP team regarding a learner's placement?
4. Explain what Zigmond means when she states, "Providing differentiated instruction in a general education classroom is not the same as providing *special* education." When might differentiated instruction in a general education classroom be appropriate?
5. Discuss the implication of the *Annual Reports* from Office of Special Education Programs reporting time out of general education as special education.

NAOMI ZIGMOND'S SUGGESTIONS FOR FURTHER READING

Donne, V., & Zigmond, N. (2008) Engagement during reading instruction for students who are deaf/hard of hearing in public schools. *Communication Disorders Quarterly, 29*, 219–235.

Kloo, A., & Zigmond, N. (2008). Coteaching revisited: Redrawing the blueprint. *Preventing School Failure: Alternative Education for Children and Youth, 52*, 12–20.

Zigmond, N. (2006) Twenty-four months after high school: Paths taken by youth diagnosed with severe emotional and behavioral disorders. *Journal of Emotional and Behavioral Disorders, 14*, 99–107.

Zigmond, N. (2007) Delivering special education is a two-person job: A call for unconventional thinking. In J. B. Crockett, M. M. Gerber, and T. J. Landrum (Eds.), *Radical reform of special education: Essays in honor of James M. Kauffman* (pp. 115–138). Mahwah, NJ: Lawrence Erlbaum.

Zigmond, N. & Baker, J. (1997). A comprehensive examination of an experiment in full inclusion. In T. Scruggs & M. A. Mastropieri (Eds). *Advances in learning and behavioral disabilities* (Vol 11: pp. 101–134), Greenwich, CN: JAI Press, Inc.

Zigmond, N. & Kloo, A. (2011) General and special education are (and should be) different. In J.M. Kauffman & D.P. Hallahan (Eds.), *Handbook of special education* (pp. 160–172). Routledge: New York.

Zigmond, N., Kloo, A., & Volonino, V. (2009). What, where, and how? Special education in the climate of full inclusion. *Exceptionality, 17*, 189–204.

Zigmond, N. & Miller, S.E. (1992). Improving high school programs for students with learning disabilities: A matter of substance as well as form. In F. Rush & L. DeStefano (Eds.), *Special education students in transition* (pp. 17–31). Champaign, IL: Sycamore Press.

REFERENCES

ALL Inclusive, June, 2001. Introductory Issue: Special education is a service—not a place. Maryland Department of Education retrieved December 2014, from http://www.msde.state.md.us/SpecialEducation/AllInclusive.pdf

Brown v. Board of Education, 347 U.S. 483 (1954).

Cook, B. G., McDuffie-Landrum, K. A., Oshita, L., & Cook, L. C. (2011). Co-teaching for students with disabilities: A critical analysis of empirical literature. In J. M. Kauffman & D. P. Hallahan (Eds.), *Handbook of special education* (pp 160–172) New York: Routledge.

Culatta, R. A. Tompkins, J. R., & Werts, M. G. (2003). *Fundamentals of special education: What every teacher needs to know.* Engelwood Cliffs, NJ: Merrill Prentice Hall.

DeLaPaz, S., & MacArthur, C. (2003). Knowing the how and why of history: Expectations for secondary students with and without learning disabilities. *Learning Disability Quarterly, 26*, 142–154.

Deno, E. (1970). Special education as developmental capital. *Exceptional Children, 37*, 229–237.

Education of All Handicapped Children Act (EHA), PL 94-142, Section 612 (5)(B) (1975).

Elbaum, B., Vaughn, S., Hughes, M. T., & Moody, S. W. (1999). Grouping practices and reading outcomes for students with disabilities. *Exceptional Children, 65*, 399–415.

Elbaum, B., Vaughn, S., Hughes, M. T., & Moody, S. W. (2000). How effective are one-to-one tutoring programs in reading for elementary students at risk for reading failure? A meta-analysis of the intervention research. *Journal of Educational Psychology, 92*, 605–619.

Fuchs, L. S., & Fuchs, D. (1998). General educators' instructional adaptation for students with learning disabilities. *Learning Disability Quarterly, 21*, 23–33.

Gartner, A., & Lipsky, D. K. (1989). *The yoke of special education: How to break it.* Washington, DC: National Center on Education and the Economy.

Gersten, R., & Jiménez, R. (1998). Modulating instruction for language minority students. In E. Kaméenui & D. Carnine (Eds.), *Effective teaching strategies that accommodate diverse learners* (pp. 161–178). Upper Saddle River, NJ: Prentice-Hall.

Gersten, R., Vaughn, S., Deshler, D., & Schiller, E. (1997). What we know about using research findings: Implications for improving special education practice. *Journal of Learning Disabilities, 30*, 446–476.

Hall, T. (2002). *Differentiated instruction.* Wakefield, MA: National Center on Accessing the General Curriculum. Retrieved September 28, 2009 from http://www.cast.org/publications/ncac/ncac_diffinstruc.html.

Hallahan, D., & Kauffman, J. (1978). *Exceptional children: Introduction to special education.* Englewood Cliffs, N.J.: Prentice-Hall, Inc.

Individuals With Disabilities Education Act (IDEA) of 2004, 20 U.S.C. 1415 *et seq.*

Individuals with Disabilities Education Act (IDEA) of 1997, PL 107-05, 20 U.S.C. 1400 *et seq.*

Kirk, S., & Gallagher, J. (1979) *Educating exceptional children,* third edition. Boston: Houghton Mifflin Company.

Mastropieri, M., & Scruggs, T. E. (2007). *The inclusive classroom: Strategies for effective instruction* (3rd ed.). Upper Saddle River, N.J.: Pearson.

McLeskey, J., Hoppey, D., Williamson, P., & Rents, T. (2004). Is inclusion an illusion? An examination of national and state trends toward the education of students with learning disabilities in general education classrooms. *Learning Disabilities Research and Practice, 19*, 109–115.

Mills v. Board of Education of the District of Columbia, 348 F. Supp. 866, 880 (1972).

Mosteller, F. (1995). The Tennessee study of class size in the early school grades. *Critical Issues for Chidren and Youths, 5*(2), 113–127.

National Association of State Boards of Education (1992). *Winners all: A call for inclusive schools.* Alexandria, VA: Author.

National Council on Disability (2000) Back to school on civil rights: Advancing the federal commitment to Leave No Child Behind," downloaded 9/24/2012 from http://www.ncd.gov/publications/2000/Jan252000#1.

Pennsylvania Association for Retarded Children v Commonwealth of Pennsylvania, 343 F. Supp. 279, Consent Agreement (1972).

Rashotte, C. A., MacPhee, K., & Torgesen, J. K. (2001). The effectiveness of a group reading instruction program with poor readers in multiple grades. *Learning Disability Quarterly, 24,* 119–134.

Sabornie, E. J., & deBettencourt, L. U. (2009). *Teaching students with mild and high-incidence disabilities at the secondary level* (3rd ed.). Upper Saddle River, N.J.: Pearson Merrill Prentice Hall.

Swanson, H., & Deshler, D. (2003). Instructing adolescents with learning disabilities: Converting a meta-analysis to practice. *Journal of Learning Disabilities, 36,* 124–135.

Swanson, H. L., Hoskyn, M., & Lee, C. (1999). *Interventions for students with learning disabilities.* New York: Guilford Press.

Torgesen, J.K. (1996). Thoughts about intervention research in learning disabilities. *Learning Disabilities: A Multidisciplinary Journal, 7,* 55–58.

U.S. Department of Health Education and Welfare (1979). *Progress toward a free appropriate public education: A report to Congress on the implementation of Public Law 94-142, the Education of All Handicapped Children Act.* Washington, D.C.: U.S. Government Printing Office.

U.S. Department of Education (2002), 24th Annual Report to Congress on the Implementation of the *Individuals with Disabilities Education Act,* 2002, Washington, D.C.: Office of Special Education and Rehabilitative Services downloaded from http://www2.ed.gov/about/reports/annual/osep/2002/index.html, 9/25/2012.

Vaughn, S., Gersten, R., & Chard, D. J. (2000). The underlying message in LD intervention research: Findings from research syntheses. *Exceptional Children, 67,* 99–114.

Vaughn, S., & Linan-Thompson, S. (2003). What is special about special education for students with learning disabilities? *The Journal of Special Education, 37,* 140–147.

Vaughn, S., Linan-Thompson, S., Kousekanani, K., Bryant, D. P., Dickson, S., & Blozis, S. A. (2003). Reading instruction grouping for students with reading difficulties. *Remedial and Special Education, 24,* 301–315.

Will, M. C. (1986). Educating children with learning problems: A shared with learning disabilities. *Educational Leadership, 57*(6), 86–88.

Ysseldyke, J., & Algozzine, B. (1984). *Introduction to special education.* Boston: Houghton Mifflin Company.

Zigmond, N. (1994). Delivering special education services to students with learning disabilities in public schools: Out or in? *Perspectives on Inclusion, 20*(4), 12–14.

Zigmond, N. (1996). Organization and management of general education classrooms. In D. Speece & B. Keogh (Eds.), *Research on classroom ecologies: Implications for inclusion of children with learning disabilities* (pp. 163–190). Hillsdale, NJ: Erlbaum.

Zigmond, N. (1997). Educating students with disabilities: The future of special education. In J. W. Lloyd, E. J. Kameenui & D. Chard (Eds.), Issues in educating students with disabilities (pp. 377–390). Hillsdale, N.J.: Earlbaum Associates.

Zigmond, N. (2001). Special education at a crossroads. *Preventing School Failure, 45,* 70–74.

Zigmond, N. (2003). Where should students with disabilities receive special education services? Is one place better than another? *The Journal of Special Education, 37,* 193–199.

Zigmond, N. (2006). Where should students with disabilities receive special education? Is one place better than another? In B. Cook & B. Shermer (Eds.), *What is special about special education?* (pp 127–136). Austin, TX: Pro-Ed.

Zigmond, N., & Baker, J. (1994). Is the mainstream a more appropriate educational setting for students with learning disabilities: The case of Randy. *Learning Disabilities Research and Practice, 9,* 108–117.

Zigmond, N., & Baker, J. M. (1995). Concluding comments: Current and future practices in inclusive schooling. *The Journal of Special Education, 29,* 245–250.

Zigmond, N., & Baker, J. M. (1996). Full inclusion for students with disabilities: Too much of a good thing? *Theory Into Practice, 31*(1), 26–34.

Zigmond, N., & Kloo, A. (2011). General and special education are (and should be) different. In J. M. Kauffman & D. P. Hallahan (Eds.), *Handbook of Special Education* (pp. 160–172) New York: Routledge.

Zigmond, N., Kloo, A. & Volonino, V. (2009). What, where, and how: Special education in the climate of full inclusion. *Exceptionality, 17,* 189–204.

Zigmond, N., Magiera, K., Simmons, R., & Volonino, V. (2013). Strategies for improving student outcomes in co-taught general education classrooms. In B. G. Cook & M. Tankersley (Eds.), *Research-Based Practices in Special Education* (pp. 116–124), Upper Saddle River, NJ: Pearson.

Zigmond, N. & Matta, D. (2004). Value added of the special education teacher on secondary school co-taught classes. In T. E. Scruggs & M. A. Mastropieri (Eds.), *Research in secondary schools: Advances in learning and behavioral disabilities* (Vol. 17, pp. 55–76). Oxford, UK: Elsevier Science/JAI.

Getting to Know Dixie Snow Huefner

 When I was a senior in high school, the Vice-Principal invited a small group of student body leaders to his home. After listening to something I said at dinner, he suggested that I was cut out to be a teacher. Over 20 years later, I remembered his long-ignored remark after embarking on a teaching career in special education. Prior to my return to graduate school, I had used my undergraduate major in Political Science to engage in volunteer work with the League of Women Voters. An interest in public education had also generated many years of volunteer work in the schools. A son with first grade reading difficulties propelled me into the field of dyslexia and then graduate work in learning disabilities. I became thoroughly fascinated with the combination of education, psychology, neuroscience, and disability history that was reflected in the emerging field of learning disabilities.

After IDEA (then P.L. 94–142) came along in 1975, I became a clinical instructor in the Department of Special Education at the University of Utah, teaching courses in learning disability and parent–professional collaboration. The department wanted to offer a course in special education law, and I was the one who was interested in doing so. I became absorbed in the law and decided to go to law school while continuing to teach. Barbara Bateman was a great role model for this combination. After law school and a judicial clerkship, I received a tenure-track appointment in my department. I taught primarily special education law and disability policy, loving the challenges of integrating special education and law.

As a young woman, I never would have imagined how my career would emerge in mid-life and be so rewarding. Now as a professor emerita, I witness the constant scrutiny given to the field of special education and observe its continuing challenges, but millions of children have benefitted from the work that has been done and continues to be done by skilled and dedicated special educators.

14

PLACEMENTS FOR SPECIAL EDUCATION STUDENTS: THE PROMISE AND THE PERIL

Dixie Snow Huefner

Placement issues in special education have been controversial and problematic for decades. To explore the issues lurking within special education placements, we should at least have a working definition of special education. In basic terms, it has been considered the delivery of individualized (and therefore *special*) educational services to children with disabilities. That definition will suffice for this essay. The key questions that follow are: Can specialized services be delivered in general education settings, and if so, how? Is the place in which those services are delivered also part and parcel of special education?

When I started getting interested in special education in the 1970s, I discovered that, for many decades, special education had been linked with special placements for children with disabilities. Prior to the 1960s and 1970s, children with moderate to severe intellectual disabilities (formerly labeled mental retardation) and physical disabilities (such as cerebral palsy) usually had been separated into institutional settings or separate schools and minimally educated. Some had been placed on waiting lists for private placements that never materialized. Initially, institutional placements were seen as an appropriate community response to the needs of these children. Over time, the placements were seen as increasingly inadequate for the children placed there. Looking back on this period, society has come to realize that these children were being denied an equal opportunity to learn when denied access to the public schools and suitable educational interventions.

The right to education movement of the 1960s and 1970s changed the lack of access and provided for the education of all children with disabilities in public school settings, although frequently self-contained ones. In more recent decades, with the onset of the inclusion movement, special education has become linked with inclusive settings, primarily delivery of special services in general education classrooms. Although placement priorities have changed, in a very real sense special education services are still difficult to separate from debates of one sort or another about placement. I will try to share my sense of where we have been, where we are, and where we might be going in terms of special education placements.

HISTORICAL CONTEXT

Brown *Decision and the Civil Rights Framework*

In many ways, the debate about special education placement can be traced to the U.S. Supreme Court's 1954 decision in *Brown v. Board of Education*. In that historic case, public school segregation of black children and white children was held to be a denial of the equal protection of the laws under the 14th amendment to the U.S. Constitution. In famous language, the Court concluded that separate schools were inherently unequal and created a sense of inferiority among black children, even assuming that the schools were equal in terms of facilities, equipment, and staff. Providing an equal opportunity for an education was seen as an important part of the concept of equal protection of the laws.

The implications of the *Brown* decision for children with disabilities were not lost on advocates for those children. If segregation on the basis of race was unconstitutional, should segregation on the basis of disability also be viewed as unconstitutional or at least as terribly wrong? Less ambitiously, advocates reasoned that if racial *segregation* was unconstitutional, then total *exclusion* of some children with disabilities from all public schooling must clearly be unconstitutional. That was the legal decision in the landmark 1972 case of *Mills v. District of Columbia*, which established a right to education for all children with disabilities in the D.C. public school system, preferably in general education settings, unless a hearing determined that such a setting could not provide suitable educational services.

"Federal courts determined that the right to education meant that children with disabilities must be provided with an equal opportunity to learn, while acknowledging that their instruction requirements might differ from those without disabilities."

The *Mills* case and another 1972 federal district court decision, *PARC v. Pennsylvania*, were catalysts for the 1975 Education for all Handicapped Children Act (Public Law 94-142)—the forerunner of today's Individuals with Disabilities Education Act (IDEA). Those court cases did not hold that children with disabilities had to be educated in the same schools as children without disabilities, but they established several important principles and protections:

1) All children, including children with disabilities, have a right to education.
2) Children with disabilities must be given notice and a hearing before being removed from general education settings.
3) An individualized and adequate education must be provided, regardless of setting.

In other words, these federal courts determined that the right to education meant that children with disabilities must be provided with an equal opportunity to learn, while acknowledging that their instructional requirements might differ from those without disabilities. The decisions did not confront the argument that the children must always be included in general education settings; instead, the setting in which their education was provided should be determined on an individual basis with opportunity for parents to challenge decisions by the public schools to separate their children from mainstream settings.

The Emergence of Least Restrictive Environment in Federal Statutes

As informed readers know, special education across the 50 states and the District of Columbia became largely governed by the 1975 federal statute now known as the Individuals with Disabilities Education Act (IDEA). Throughout its nearly 40 year history, this law has required that special education placements be determined individually and that public school districts make available a placement continuum to meet each child's needs. The continuum includes the general education classroom on one end and home, hospital, and institutional placements on the other end, with resource rooms, separate classrooms, and separate schools along the continuum. At the same time, the law has stated a preference for the education of children with disabilities in the same environment as children without disabilities "to the maximum extent appropriate." This concept has been labelled the "least restrictive environment." It means that the setting must be the environment closest to the general education classroom in which a free appropriate public education (FAPE) can be delivered. If FAPE cannot be delivered in such a setting, that setting is not the LRE. Many individuals have not understood the meaning of LRE and instead have equated it with the general education classroom. I believe that this error has led many parents and school districts astray.

In recent years, IDEA has also required that those who develop a child's individualized education program (IEP) state in the IEP the extent to which the child's education will *not* be alongside children without disabilities. This provision reverses earlier wording that required the IEP to include a statement that described the extent to which the child *would* be educated in general education settings. The newer requirement creates a stronger expectation that inclusion will occur in most cases and that IEP teams must consider and describe (or at least put in writing) any decision to separate a child with disabilities from his or her general education peers. This shift is important and reflects the change in the political winds as inclusion became the darling of the 1990s for special education policy.

Federal regulations to implement IDEA provided criteria to use in determining the least restrictive placement for a child. The current regulations continue to require that placement be determined annually by a team that includes the parents. Further, they require that the placement be based on the IEP, which means that academic, behavioral, and developmental goals and needed services should guide the placement, not vice versa. In other words, the IEP precedes placement, and the child's label must not be the determinant of the appropriate placement. Many school districts have been slow to implement this regulation because they had established self-contained placements for students categorized as ID (MR), LD, ED, and so forth. They would evaluate a student, determine the student's disability classification, and then place the student in the setting established for those students. This may have been bureaucratically efficient but denied the individuality of each student with disabilities, ignoring the need to consider what individualized services were needed and how close to the mainstream they could be delivered.

> "The newer requirement creates a stronger expectation that inclusion will occur in most cases and that IEP teams must consider and describe (or at least put in writing) any decision to separate a child with disabilities from his or her general education peers."

The regulations also state a preference for more inclusive placements in neighborhood schools by reminding placement teams that the placement is to be as close to the child's home as possible and in the school the child would ordinarily attend, unless the IEP requires otherwise. Finally, in selecting the LRE, the team must consider "any potential harmful effect" on the child or the quality of services needed by the child. This provision seems to provide more discretion than the preceding requirements but has often been neglected in placement issues, at least in those decided in court.

ARGUMENTS FOR AND AGAINST INCLUSION

For Inclusion

The inclusion movement of the 1980s and continuing thereafter owes much to the deinstitutionalization and community placement movement that began earlier. Readers may know that the deinstitutionalization movement asserts that adults with intellectual disabilities and psychiatric disabilities were and are isolated and underserved in institutional settings and deserve to be more a part of the community in which they live. Advocates for school children, particularly those with moderate to severe intellectual and physical disabilities, were also concerned that separation was leading "ordinary" children and adults to be fearful and suspicious of many children with disabilities. The children were being denied acceptance by their peers, as well as opportunities to achieve, learn, and work that should be open to all. Parents of children with intellectual disabilities and physical disabilities spearheaded the inclusion movement because their children had suffered the most from exclusion from society and school communities. They asserted the following multiple benefits from inclusion:

1) More inclusive settings would allow children without disabilities and children with disabilities to become friends. Common interests could emerge, and children without disabilities could discover that children with disabilities had talents and, in many ways, were more like them than different. The sense of isolation and strangeness could be dissipated.

2) Children with disabilities would have more typical role models and could learn more readily and behave more appropriately with such models. In general, the behaviors and language skills of children in general education settings are at a more age-appropriate level than are the skills of children with disabilities, and the latter can benefit from the examples set by general education students.

3) Expectations would rise, and children with disabilities would achieve more. Low academic expectations for children with disabilities have plagued many a special education classroom, and the general education classroom with its focus on the general curriculum would be more able to encourage skill development in the general curriculum.

4) Inclusion in general educational settings could spill over into employment and other post-school settings as these children grow up and exit the school system. Transitions from school to post-school environments are difficult for many children with disabilities, and the experience in general education settings could make that transition an easier one if employers, fellow employees, and neighbors had had prior experience with disabilities in school settings.

5) All children have individual needs, and the separation and labels attached to children with disabilities mask their individuality. The lines drawn by labels are arbitrary and unnecessarily stigmatizing. Disability labels obscure the continuum of

abilities and disabilities that are a part of everyone's lives and tend to categorize individuals unnecessarily.

6) Inclusion could reduce the separation of minority students into separate special education settings—settings that reflect discriminatory practices rather than actual need for separation. Statistics gathered over the decades reveal that students from ethnic minorities, especially African Americans and Native American Indian children, are disciplined, suspended, and placed in separate classrooms at a rate far exceeding their proportion in the schools. Among the reasons for this disparity is thought to be the possibility of continuing discrimination by teachers and administrators.

Against Full Inclusion (For Retention of the Continuum)

On the other hand, advocates for retention of the placement continuum assert that although inclusion is appropriate for many children, it is not appropriate for all of them all of the time. The primary advocates for retention of the continuum are parents of children with learning disabilities and parents from the Deaf Community. The mental health community also has a stake in the issue but lacks a strong parent advocacy group and has depended more on professionals to assert their individualized needs. Advocates for retention of the continuum make a number of arguments that differ from those raised by advocates of full inclusion:

1) Special education is a tool to individualize instruction for children whose needs are different in many ways from the needs of other children. Individualization requires individualized placement decisions.

2) General education classroom teachers are not trained to individualize for children with disabilities. They resent being asked to manage children whose behaviors and skill deficits often require far more attention than those of the average child.

3) Many children with disabilities have already failed to succeed in general education classrooms, necessitating the emergence of special education in the first place. Why return to a failed model? This argument has special force in the Deaf Community, whose members insist that their children be taught to learn American Sign Language (ASL) as their first language, a language that is often not able to be taught in a general education classroom. Parents of children with learning disabilities also have concerns about full-day re-integration of their children into classrooms where they have failed in the past. They have watched as schools have neglected to assess their children for reading and math disabilities, especially in grades K-3, delaying much needed assessment and specialized instruction. The fear is that inclusion may well return their children to settings in which their needs for specialized instruction will again be overlooked.

4) For inclusion to succeed, it must be supported—with special educators and paraprofessionals in the general education classroom helping the general education teacher. This requires more resources than are available, and the lack thereof frequently results in "dumping" special education students into general classrooms.

5) Mental and behavioral health issues among children are growing, and general educators are ill equipped to handle moderate to severe behavioral and emotional issues. These children need access to behavioral interventionists and skilled

therapists. Only when their issues are ameliorated are they able to function well in general education classrooms. For instance, the number of children given a diagnosis of autism has been growing at an alarming rate. These children, who have language and social communication disabilities that spill over into behavioral issues, including restrictive, repetitive behaviors, require highly individualized programming and a small student-teacher ratio. Although some of these children with milder symptoms may be able to be managed and challenged in general education classrooms, children with severe classical autism typically need much preparation before being able to be integrated into general education classrooms.

6) When some children with disabilities are prematurely placed in general education classrooms, they often experience bullying, harassment, and social isolation from other children, rather than the sought-for acceptance. In addition, sometimes aides assigned to these children coach them too much and do too much of their work for them so that they can keep up with the class, thereby actually hindering their actual learning. In some cases, paraprofessionals or classroom aides actually function to inhibit interaction among students.

Obviously, there is merit in the arguments both for and against full inclusion. I think that one can see that the arguments are based on the values and experiences of individuals and groups on each side of the argument. Recognizing the merit of both sides should help people understand the complexity of the issues.

INTERPRETATIONS BY THE FEDERAL COURTS

Placement issues have been a focus of a multitude of court cases in the federal courts. In fact, placement cases have dominated the special education caseloads of federal courts. Clearly, plaintiffs have felt that placement of their children has an important impact on how special education can be delivered. The cases have gone in two diametrically different directions: (1) parents seeking private and even residential placements for their children with severe disabilities, and (2) parents seeking the inclusion of their children with milder disabilities in general education classrooms. The nature of these cases itself reveals the differing needs of children and the polarization among parents about the desirability of inclusion as a placement for their special education students.

"Recognizing the merits of both sides should help people understand the complexity of the issue."

In general, court decisions that allow children to be placed in private or residential settings at public expense have been based on findings that FAPE was not available in the public school setting, whether in general or special education classrooms. In contrast, decisions to remove children from separate placements and return them to general education placements have been based on findings that the school had made no or inadequate attempts to deliver special services in general education settings. Several court decisions illustrate these different kinds of cases.

An early residential placement case reveals the challenge of educating children with severe and profound multiple disabilities. *Kruelle v. New Castle County School District*, a

1980 decision upheld in the U.S. Court of Appeals for the Third Circuit, considered the needs of an adolescent with profound retardation and cerebral palsy who could not walk, speak, dress himself, or eat unaided. Under stress he self-induced vomiting. A Delaware school district placed him in a self-contained classroom, and the parents challenged the lack of a residential program. The court determined that 1) the boy required far more consistency than could be provided in a day program, 2) the boy's medical, social, and emotional problems were not segregable from his educational needs, and 3) that full time round-the-clock services were essential to his learning.

In contrast to the residential placement cases, probably the best known inclusion cases are *Daniel R.R. v. State Board of Education*, decided in 1989 by the U.S. Court of Appeals for the Fifth Circuit, and *Sacramento City Unified School District v. Rachel H.*, a 1994 Ninth Circuit decision.

In *Daniel R.R.*, although the court rejected a general education placement for a kindergarten student with Down syndrome, it established a legal standard for inclusion that has been adopted by five other federal appellate circuits across the country. The standard requires a school to attempt to accommodate an included student by providing sufficient supplementary aids and services and program modifications in the general education setting. Then, if the student is not benefitting, both academically and nonacademically, from those accommodations and modifications, the placement is not the LRE. Another factor in determining the LRE includes the student's effect on the general education teacher and classroom students. In other words, a disruptive effect on the classroom militates against the placement. Of special importance is the requirement that the school district not "dump" the student into the mainstream setting but instead provide genuine and appropriate supplementary services and program modifications. In this case, Daniel had received curriculum modifications and extra attention, but his present developmental level would have required changes to virtually the entire curriculum. In addition, he was falling asleep in his class and developing a stutter.

The court in *Daniel R.R.* proceeded to state that if a student could not be accommodated in a general education setting, the public school must mainstream the student in other ways to the maximum extent appropriate, for instance, through social mainstreaming at recess and in the lunchroom. (By the way, after returning to a developmental kindergarten program, Daniel later was able to be mainstreamed in his elementary school classrooms.)

A 1991 Eleventh Circuit case, *Greer v. Rome City School District*, followed the *Daniel R.R.* standard but added a cost factor: If the cost of the regular placement would significantly reduce the money available for the education of other students, the mainstream placement would not be appropriate.

The Ninth Circuit's standard for LRE in the *Rachel H.* case is comparable to *Daniel R.R./ Greer*. In upholding a second-grade general education classroom placement for a young girl with an intellectual disability, the court weighed the educational benefits of that placement (including supplementary aids and services) against special education placement while ascertaining the nonacademic benefits as well. The court determined that the child was receiving both academic and nonacademic benefits. Also relevant was the court's determination that the child's effect on the teacher and other students was not disruptive and that the cost of mainstreaming the student was not substantial. (The Ninth Circuit did not address the second part of the *Daniel R.R.* decision, which required a consideration of other kinds of mainstreaming when inclusion in the general classroom was not appropriate.)

In contrast, one of the best known placement decisions upholding a separate day-school placement in a public setting is the 1994 case of *Clyde K. v. Puyallup School District*, also decided by the Ninth Circuit, using its *Rachel H.* standard. In *Clyde K.*, the parents of a high school student with ADHD and Tourette syndrome sought to keep their son in his junior high school classrooms with a personal aide. The school district sought to remove him to a self-contained placement in a separate school with a more structured environment and more individualized attention. The boy was extremely disruptive in his general education setting, his academic test scores had declined, he was socially ostracized by his peers, and he had regularly harassed his peers and assaulted a teacher. Under these facts, the court determined that the school could properly remove the boy from his general education setting.

NEIGHBORHOOD SCHOOL CASES

A separate but smaller line of cases has concerned neighborhood placements or the lack thereof. A group of cases in the U.S. Court of Appeals for the Fourth, Sixth, and Eighth Circuits has utilized a standard upholding centralized services or facilities in non-neighborhood schools when those services cannot be feasibly provided in a child's neighborhood school. The student plaintiffs in these cases had been seeking decentralization of services so that they could go to school where their friends went to school. The rulings in favor of the school districts were based on the cost savings and more efficient use of scarce resources (such as medical personnel and related service providers) that were possible in centralized settings. The cases reflect sensitivity to the resource limitations on school districts.

Somewhat different cases have been brought by plaintiffs who directly asserted that IDEA required placement in neighborhood schools as a matter of right. Plaintiffs in these cases hoped that court decisions would recognize and advance policy arguments for inclusion. Plaintiffs, however, have lost their argument because IDEA itself (the statute) is silent about neighborhood placements, and the IDEA regulations, while expressing a preference for them, do not require them. The legislation and regulations still reflect the individualized decision making that underlies IDEA and its precursor statute.

It is worth noting in this context that full inclusion, where all students are placed in general education classrooms, would violate IDEA every bit as much as full separation. Blanket placements of either variety violate the whole underlying concept of IDEA as specialized services and individually determined placements.

THE SUPREME COURT'S ROLE

"Full inclusion, where all students are placed in general education classrooms, would violate IDEA every bit as much as full separation. Blanket placements of either variety violate the whole underlying concept of IDEA as specialized services and individually determined placements."

I find it interesting that the U.S. Supreme Court has thus far distanced itself from LRE issues, declining on multiple occasions to hear appeals of LRE rulings in the appellate courts and thereby declining to set a national legal standard for LRE determinations. It is tempting to suggest that the Court may sense that these decisions are best left to individualized fact finding and deference to current congressional legislation that provides for individualized placement decisions based on that fact finding.

When the Supreme Court has addressed placement, it has been to uphold private placements when FAPE has not been provided in the public school. The issue has not been LRE but rather whether public school districts can be held responsible for the tuition costs when parents select a private school for their child. In the 1985 case of *Burlington School Committee v. Massachusetts Department of Education*, the plaintiff school board argued that the law's so-called "stay put" provision meant that parents could not remove their child from the public school setting while a controversy was being resolved by impartial hearing officers or courts. The Supreme Court rejected this argument, stating that parents could not be prevented from removing their child from what they saw as an unsatisfactory school placement. At the same time, however, the Court stated that parents place their child in a private school at their own financial risk: If a determination is made that FAPE was provided at the public school, then the parents are responsible for the private school costs. If FAPE was unavailable, however, and the parents' placement was "proper," then reimbursement would be available. The Court did not define what would be a "proper" placement.

A subsequent Supreme Court case, *Florence County School District Four v. Carter* (1993), went one step further and ruled that parents need not use the same criteria for placement as the school district. Explaining, the Court stated that parents were not a public agency and, therefore, did not have to follow the FAPE and placement criteria found in IDEA. What was at stake, among other things, was whether the private school of the parents' choice had to be on the state's approved list, had to develop an IEP, and had to employ only certified teachers. The Court reiterated its earlier ruling that the private school placement simply must be "proper." (The 2006 federal IDEA regulations echo the Court decisions but substitute the word "appropriate" for "proper" while also stating that "appropriate" does not mean meeting state standards. The term seems to be linked with the notion of acceptable educational progress because the meaning of FAPE has increasingly been linked with measurable progress toward IEP goals.)

The implication of the Supreme Court rulings in these private placement cases is that LRE is not a key factor in ascertaining whether the parental placement is proper or appropriate. Parents should not be held to the same standard as public schools in determining the extent to which a child with disabilities will be educated with general education peers because parents need some discretion in locating what they think will be a suitable placement for their child. For instance, private schools may or may not be special education schools. The choice is essentially the parents' in deciding what the child's primary needs are when a public school has denied FAPE.

Lower courts addressing parental choice of a private school have generally reflected the implications of Supreme Court decisions that parents need some latitude in determining a private placement for their children. Nonetheless, some lower courts have set limits on parental discretion (for instance, geographic ones—as in a case where an in-state private school should have been considered instead of a school in Japan). Several court decisions have held that the availability of some interaction with general education students can be one of the factors in deciding whether a given placement was proper or appropriate.

LOCATION OF THE DELIVERY OF RELATED SERVICES

Less thorny but also important to consider is the location of related services. Related services are those needed to assist a child to benefit from his or her special education. Among the more common related services are physical therapy (PT), occupational therapy (OT), and speech therapy. The IEP now must include a statement of the location of related services. The law does not explain this requirement. If it is to encourage the delivery of related services in the general education classroom, I think it is problematic and often unrealistic. In my view, classroom delivery of IDEA related services is likely to be counterproductive unless the classrooms are already designed and used in ways that allow multiple activities simultaneously. PT and OT sometimes require specialized equipment and exercises; speech therapy requires verbal instruction and response between the therapist and the student. These services can be conspicuous and distracting when delivered in the general education classroom. Other related services, like early identification and assessment, medical services for diagnostic and evaluation purposes, orientation and mobility services, school health services, and counseling and psychological services are more clearly services that require locations outside the general education classroom. To me, delivery of related services in suitable private locations should not be seen as anti-inclusion, although if they are available at the school site where the child is being educated, so much the better.

RELATED SERVICES UNDER SECTION 504

At this point, Section 504 of the Rehabilitation Act deserves a paragraph or two. Section 504 is a broad anti-discrimination statute enacted in 1973 that protects individuals with disabilities from birth to death. Some children with disabilities are not covered by IDEA because their disability does not require special education. These children can receive a 504 plan to ensure that their learning opportunities are as adequate as those of children without disabilities. These children are general education students, and their education is conducted in general education classrooms. They receive classroom accommodations for their disabilities. They are entitled to receive "related services," a term that does not have the same meaning as related services under IDEA because the services are not needed to assist them to benefit from special education. Instead they equate to the accommodations needed to provide appropriate learning opportunities needed in general education settings.

For these children with disabilities, inclusion is already a reality. Typical Section 504 students would include children with diabetes who have special dietary requirements, children with asthma who need to use inhalers when a breathing problem occurs, children with orthopedic impairments who may need special equipment or a service dog in the classroom, children with visual impairments who need large-print books, and children with hearing impairments who use hearing aids and need careful seating in the classroom in full view of the teacher. A larger group of Section 504 students include those with attention deficit hyperactivity disorder (ADHD) who can achieve at or near grade level if given accommodations (such as stand-up desks, reduced length of assignments, opportunities to move while learning) for their distractibility, impulsivity, and hyperactivity.

The kinds of accommodations that are mentioned in the previous paragraph are considered related services under Section 504. Note that these services do not need to be delivered in pullout settings but can be delivered in general education environments, including the school cafeteria. This is entirely appropriate because they do not require services from specialists but feasible changes to the school routine that can be implemented by regular school personnel.

RTI ISSUES

The newest kid on the block is nicknamed RTI. More formally known as Response to Treatment Intervention, RTI refers to a major effort to reduce the number of children with disabilities or potential disabilities, particularly learning disabilities, served under IDEA. A current hypothesis circulating widely is that many children with reading and math problems are being labeled as having learning disabilities (or some other disability) when their problems are primarily due to poor instruction. RTI is an attempt to engage general educators and aides or tutors in earlier individualized interventions in the general classroom to sort out those who respond to more intensive interventions from those who continue to exhibit significant underachievement. In most models, there are two interventions prior to a referral for disability evaluation. The first intervention is likely to be a semi-weekly or more frequent group tutoring session with a trained aide, or even the general education teacher—with slower and more systematic instruction, extra practice, and more feedback. If that intervention is not successful, then a more intensive intervention (e.g., one-on-one, or one-on-two instruction with a trained tutor) may be offered more often and for longer sessions and perhaps with a change of teaching method. Both interventions should be empirically validated, and performance data reflecting the general curriculum should be recorded and evaluated. If both interventions fail to bring a student within normal ranges of achievement for his or her grade level, then it will be appropriate for the teacher to refer the student for more comprehensive assessment and evaluation for a possible disability.

In cases of severe disability, in which multiple intellectual, physical, and behavioral challenges manifest themselves, it will be clear that RTI may well represent a waste of time and resources. It may be far less clear, however, in situations in which academic underachievement is the primary issue. In those situations, it may be worth the effort to explore more intensive instruction prior to referral for special education evaluation, particularly for learning disabilities. Nonetheless, in recognition of the possibility of unjustified and possibly intentional delay, the federal IDEA regulations give parents the right to request a comprehensive evaluation for IDEA eligibility without waiting for RTI results. Although the school district need not consent to the request when it does not have reason to suspect a disability, RTI is not to be used to delay or deny a child's right to a full evaluation when a disability is suspected. Furthermore, a child's nonparticipation in RTI cannot be the basis for a refusal to evaluate. Of course, to exercise their parental right, parents must be aware of it, a different issue altogether.

Because RTI is meant to be delivered in the general education classroom and could result in fewer children being removed from that classroom for resource room support, it is compatible with inclusion goals. It is well motivated and reflects the fact that instruction in many classrooms does not reflect best practices and frequently places too much reliance on basal reading and math series that may not provide for systematic instruction of individual students who are not learning at the same rate as other students. Among other things, the general education teacher may not include opportunities for continuous monitoring of student responses, immediate feedback on correct and incorrect responses, and mastery of content before moving to more difficult content.

RTI has achieved success in some places where training is conducted, best practices implemented, and outcomes monitored. It is difficult to bring RTI to scale, however, just as it is difficult to bring most innovations to scale across the country. It has the potential benefit of allowing more individualization within general education classrooms, encouraging modifications in instruction and methodologies, and thereby enhancing classroom instruction for at-risk children. On the other hand, it can also be used to delay effective and early assessment of children with disabilities and delay the kind of instruction they truly need. Much depends on the model being used, the training provided, the level of administrative support, and the willingness and ability to evaluate outcomes systematically and make decisions based on those outcomes. The tension between RTI and timely evaluation of a disability is real, and the results are still out on RTI.

PLACEMENT TRENDS

What have been placement trends over the past decades? From the inception of the precursor to IDEA in 1975, resource rooms have remained the most popular special education placement. Resource rooms are meant to be just that—a resource to the general classroom. They allow specialized instruction from a special educator in a pullout setting, usually for part of the day, thereby complementing instruction in the general classroom. IDEA views resource rooms as supplementary services that are consistent with the concept of inclusion. Over the past twenty years, the percentage of students placed in resource rooms has grown. Only a very small percentage of children are placed in separate schools or institutional settings. As of fall 2006, the last year, as of this writing, for which figures were available from the U.S. Department of Education in its *30th Annual Report to Congress on the Implementation of IDEA*, the percentage was 5 percent, up a percent from the previous year. (Only 1 percent of students were in institutional or homebound settings.) Most of the 5 percent were children with multiple disabilities or deaf-blindness. Self-contained placements within ordinary public schools remain, but more and more children are spending less and less time there. This is true of children with intellectual and behavioral disabilities as well as other disabilities. Over half of all special education students were being removed from their general education classrooms for less than 21 percent of the school day. Another fourth were spending from 21 to 59 percent of their time in pullout settings, and less than one fifth were spending 60 percent or more in separate classes. In the first two situations, a good deal of both instructional and social mainstreaming is available, and in all three situations, social mainstreaming should be occurring, where special education students are able, at least theoretically, to interact with children without disabilities on the playground, in the lunchroom, and in certain extracurricular activities.

The above placement percentages vary (sometimes considerably) by disability, age group, state, and racial and ethnic background. For instance, between 25–30 percent of children with deaf-blindness and multiple disabilities were in "other" settings outside the regular classroom in the Fall of 2006, compared to 17.5 percent of children with emotional disabilities, 6.9 percent of children with intellectual disabilities, and 2 percent of children with learning disabilities. Moreover, although over 50 percent of students from most ethnic groups (i.e., White, Hispanic, Asian/Pacific Islander, and American Indian/Alaska Native), were spending 80 percent or more of the day in regular classrooms, only 44.9 percent of Black students were doing so. What these variations suggest is not only the continuing use of a continuum of placements for students with differing needs but also the need for more data and more research. What settings are best suited for which children with which kinds of instructional needs? How much of the variation is due to differences among states and geographic regions? Is discrimination accounting for some of the variation?

WHAT'S SPECIAL ENOUGH ABOUT SPECIAL EDUCATION TO REQUIRE PULLOUT PLACEMENTS IN SOME SITUATIONS?

Given the increase in the percentage of children with disabilities being included in general education classrooms, I have pondered when inclusion is inappropriate and when pullout placement is still needed. My answer varies depending on context, but some of the questions affecting my answer include the following:

1) Has the general classroom teacher had effective instruction in handling the instructional and behavioral needs of children with disabilities? Does the teacher have a positive attitude toward children with disabilities?
2) Are trained aides or skilled paraprofessionals available to help in the classroom, if needed? Have they been trained to instruct rather than simply aid the child to perform? In other words, are they helping to ensure the independence of the child whom they are assisting instead of increasing the child's dependence on the aide?
3) Are appropriate kinds of assistive technology available for given students with disabilities? The provision of assistive technology and delivery of assistive technology services are newer aspects of IDEA and hold promise for facilitating inclusion in general education classrooms. For instance, when children with visual impairments, hearing impairments, and orthopedic impairments can use such technology as braille materials, text-to-speech devices, computer instructional software, and computers with adapted keyboards, they can access instructional material that would otherwise be unavailable to them.
4) What is the classroom size? Is it possible for the general education teacher to develop a personal relationship with each student? Research suggests that the individual teacher is the most important factor in a child's learning. The teacher's ability to motivate a child increases when a positive personal relationship is developed. Are smaller student-teacher ratios and more individual attention needed for the child than is possible in the general education classroom?
5) What kind of teamwork exists in the school, and is the special educator able to function as a specialized resource to the general classroom teacher rather than as a classroom aide? Are highly specialized behavioral and instructional methodologies available if needed?
6) Has the special education assessment system been able to accurately identify the current educational performance of the child, and has the IEP team set appropriate goals and recommended appropriate instructional strategies to assist the general educator? Are some of the goals incompatible with implementation in the general classroom?

No doubt there are other important questions as well, but these suggest some of the elements needed for successful inclusion.

THE CHALLENGES OF FULL INCLUSION

Given the current system of public education in this country, I believe that the challenges of full inclusion for all children with disabilities outweigh the potential benefits. The issue of training is quite a profound one. It is not reasonable to expect most general education teachers to provide individualized instruction to special education students, at least not until our entire education system is able to efficiently individualize for all students—something that would represent a radical departure from our current approach to public education. Over and over again, I hear classroom teachers complain about the time away from their other students because of their need to attend to the behaviors and skill needs of the 2 or 3 students with intellectual or behavioral difficulties who have been placed in their classrooms by IEP teams. They typically experience a lack of administrative support and feel that they are left to their own devices.

Lack of resources adds to the burden. Schools do not have the means to provide in each school for children who need access to medical personnel, scarce related service providers, or nursing care. Rural school districts are particularly unable to provide related services in each school for children with multiple needs.

Special educators themselves are in short supply, given current demand. They often have large caseloads and are unable to individualize for the children whom they serve, even if trained to know how to do so.

A pricklier question relates to the human tendency to categorize and classify differences, even when everyone deserves acceptance as part of the large human family. Inclusion is a desirable goal but difficult to achieve, given these human tendencies. Over the years, we have tried to reduce the stigma attached to various labels by changing the labels, and after a while, the latest label also becomes stigmatizing. Sadly, bullying, teasing, and isolating and ignoring children who are seen as different are likely to remain part of school experiences for many children, not solely children with disabilities. I am skeptical that education systems and classroom learning environments can change quickly, although we must continue to try to model kindness and acceptance for our students. Idealistically, it would be wonderful if classrooms were designed to accommodate the individual needs of each child and if we could all learn to accept, cherish, and help one another to grow and develop, regardless of our ability levels and personalities. This can and does happen in great classrooms with excellent teachers. The question is how to create those great classrooms and give every child a good teacher year after year. (Supporting the professional development of teachers, creating nurturing learning environments, and defining what constitutes good instruction are subjects of different chapters in this book.)

> "Given the current system of public education in this country, I believe that the challenges of full inclusion for all children with disabilities outweigh the potential benefits."

Public education financing is in jeopardy across the country. Although money isn't everything, its lack is a severe hindrance to improved education systems. In many, if not most states, the investment of the citizenry in the education of children has been diminishing in the light of reduced tax revenues, economic hard times, and the resultant competing priorities for public money. At the top of the list of competing priorities are the demands of the elderly for health care and retirement income. Children do not have the political power of senior citizens, and the costs of Medicare, Medicaid, and social security (so-called entitlements because the authorizing statutes also determine automatic expenditure levels) are occupying higher and higher percentages of the federal budget at the expense of discretionary education spending to help states with services such as public education. In today's political climate, where many persons and groups are clamoring for states to take over more of our health care, I worry that if states pick up more of the health care costs, those expenditures will be directly competing with the costs of education, which at the moment is one of the largest expenditures in state budgets. If seniors (of which I am one) win out over children's education, what will be the long-term costs to the country as a whole and not just to children with disabilities who are seeking inclusion in their neighborhood schools?

SUMMARY

Here are what I see as justifiable conclusions about approaches to placement decisions accompanying the delivery of appropriate special education to children with disabilities:

- IDEA's placement provisions and regulations are satisfactory, as currently written. They honor the need for individualized placement decisions by a team that includes parents.
- Section 504 should be embraced as an important tool of nondiscrimination, and general education teachers should be trained to understand and implement it as such. Section 504 appropriately allows inclusion for children with disabilities who do not qualify for special education under IDEA.
- RTI needs further refinement and evaluation and needs to be brought to scale, if evaluation merits it. More attention should be paid to what constitutes good instruction for all children, especially in the critical early grades when children decide whether they like school and can succeed in public school settings.
- The evolving role of technology in public education has the potential to facilitate inclusion. At the same time, universal design of evaluation instruments and monitoring the effectiveness of assistive technology devices and services are important to keep costs manageable.
- Until general and special education training is transformed and auxiliary resources are available in each public school, it is not realistic to expect good results from full inclusion for all children with disabilities.
- Finally, inclusion issues cannot be separated from the quality of special education itself and the overall state of public education. Think about it. I repeat: Inclusion issues cannot be separated from the quality of special education itself and the overall state of public education.

Discussion Questions

1. At the beginning of the chapter, Huefner posed two questions: Can specialized services be delivered in general education settings, and if so, how? Is the place in which those services are delivered also part and parcel of special education? How did your thinking about answers to those questions change as you read the chapter?
2. Why do you think many school districts have been slow to implement the "IEP precedes placement" regulation? That is, what are the barriers to allowing the academic, behavioral, and developmental goals determined by the IEP team to guide the placement?

3. In selecting the LRE, Huefner states that the regulations require that IEP teams must consider "any potential harmful effect" on the child or the quality of services needed by the child. Harmful effects of separate placements are often discussed in the literature, but what are some of the potential harmful effects inclusion could have on students' academic, behavioral, and social development?

4. Huefner summarized the two most common directions federal court cases take when the focus is on placement: (a) parents seeking private placements for their children with severe disabilities and (b) parents seeking inclusion of their children with high-incidence disabilities in general classrooms. Under what circumstances might parents of a student with high-incidence disabilities seek a segregated placement for their child?

5. What do you see as the biggest challenges in implementing LRE legally and effectively? General education teacher training? More specially trained teachers? Financial resources? Others?

DIXIE SNOW HUEFNER'S SUGGESTIONS FOR FURTHER READING

Fisher, R. & Ury, W. (1981). *Getting to yes: Negotiating agreement without giving in.* Boston, MA: Houghton Mifflin.
Goodwin, D. K. (2013). *The bully pulpit.* New York: Simon & Schuster.
Huefner, D. S. (2009). Updating the FAPE standard under IDEA. *Journal of Law and Education, 37,* 367–379.
Huefner, D. S. & Herr, C. M. (2012). *Navigating special education law and policy.* Verona, WI: Attainment Co.
Kauffman, J. M. & Hallahan, D. P. (2005). *Special education: What it is and why we need it.* Boston, MA: Pearson Education.
Minow, M. (1990). *Making all the difference: Inclusion, exclusion, and American law.* Ithaca, NY: Cornell University Press

REFERENCES

Brown v. Board of Education, 347 U.S. 483 (1954).
Burlington School Committee v. Massachusetts Department of Education, 471 U.S. 359 (1985).
Clyde K. v. Puyallup School District, 35 F.3d 1396 (9th Cir. 1994).
Daniel R. R. v. State Board of Education, 874 F.2d 1036 (5th Cir. 1989).
Florence County School District Four v. Carter, 510 U.S. 7 (1993).
Greer v. Rome City School District, 950 F.2d 688 (11th Cir. 1991), *op. withdrawn,* 956 F.2d 1025 (1992), *reinstated,* 967 F.2d 470 (1992).
Kruelle v. New Castle County School District, 642 F., 2d 687 (3d Cir. 1981).
Mills v. District of Columbia Board of Education, 348 F. Supp. 866 (D.D.C. 1972).
PARC v. Pennsylvania, 343 F. Supp. 279 (E.D. Pa. 1972).
Sacramento City Unified School District v. Rachel H., 14 F.3d 1398 (9th Cir. 1994).

Getting to Know Andrew L. Wiley

In the late 1970s, when I was almost nine years old, my mom was hired as a speech therapist at a newly opened public school for students with moderate to profound intellectual disabilities. Over the next 12 years, I spent many days and hours at this school, working and playing with the students, volunteering for field days, and (on teacher workdays) racing my brother in wheelchairs up and down the empty hallways. It was an exciting place to be. The teachers worked continuously to find innovative ways to help their students gain independence, and every bit of progress was cause for celebration. This was the place where my love for special education began.

In the early 2000s, I began working as a behavior specialist in the same district that housed "my" school. One day in late August, as I was driving to lunch with my colleagues, we happened to pass the school. One of my colleagues, a new hire and recent graduate from a highly regarded special education program, pointed to the school and asked me if it was a special school for students with intellectual disabilities. When I answered yes, she turned away and said, "Well, those places make me sick!"

I thought often about that moment while writing my chapter for this book. I hope that what I have written will help others think more clearly about moral reasoning and moral judgment in relation to complex moral issues in special education.

15

PLACE VALUES: WHAT MORAL PSYCHOLOGY CAN TELL US ABOUT THE FULL INCLUSION DEBATE IN SPECIAL EDUCATION

Andrew L. Wiley

People differ in their moral judgments of *place* in special education. Some have judged providing special education in places other than the general education classroom to be, in every or almost every instance, morally wrong (e.g., Baglieri & Knopf, 2004; Brantlinger, 1997; Danforth & Rhodes, 1997; Gallagher, 2001; Lipsky & Gartner, 1987, 1996; Reid & Valle, 2004; Sapon-Shevin, 1996; Skrtic, 1991; Slee, 2001; Stainback & Stainback, 1992; Taylor, 1988). According to this perspective, physically separating some students from others for the purpose of special education is a discriminatory practice that both reflects and perpetuates a historical and institutionalized intolerance of individual differences. Thus, proponents of *full inclusion*—the idea that all or very nearly all students should be taught in the same place, regardless of their differences—view the issue as fundamentally moral in nature (Baglieri & Knopf, 2004; Connor & Ferri, 2007; Gallagher, 2001; Obiakor, Harris, Mutua, Ratatori, & Algozzine, 2012). Others have argued that separate and specialized instructional settings are sometimes justified because, in their judgment, the special educational needs of at least some students with disabilities cannot be effectively and appropriately met without them (e.g., Brigham & Kauffman, 1998; Fuchs & Fuchs, 1994; Gliona, Gonzales, & Jacobson, 2005; Kauffman, 2009; Kauffman, Bantz, & McCullough, 2002; Mock & Kauffman, 2005; Zigmond, 2003). In other words, opponents of *full* inclusion worry that eliminating or severely restricting the continuum of placement options would deprive some, if not many, students with disabilities of the opportunity to receive the intensive educational services they need to maximize their achievement and independence.

Which is the correct moral judgment? Is separate special education immoral? Is full inclusion immoral? The answer has profound implications for students with disabilities, their families, and their teachers. Special education practices that devalue and oppress children and youth with disabilities are unacceptable, as are policies that prevent or substantially inhibit the delivery of the services and supports that these students need. Neither side of the debate can be very satisfied with the current state of affairs in special education. On the one hand, a substantial number of students receive services at least partly in separate settings (U.S. Department of Education, 2011). On the other hand, it appears that the special educational needs of a large number of students with disabilities are not being addressed adequately (Morgan, Frisco, Farkas, & Hibel, 2010; Newman et al., 2011). It is difficult to imagine a solution that would simultaneously and meaningfully address the moral concerns of both advocates and opponents of full inclusion.

Observing that people are *morally* divided is usually a good way to stop a discussion, not to start one. This is because debates framed in moral terms—for example, debates about issues like abortion, gay marriage, and capital punishment—are notoriously futile and intractable. People rarely negotiate, compromise, or change deeply held moral beliefs, and discussions that involve even mild challenges to such beliefs tend to elicit strong negative feelings that are not generally conducive to productive dialogue. The hostility and intensity of moral disagreements can make it difficult for undecided third parties to understand and evaluate the arguments for either side. All of this applies to the perpetual and emotionally charged debate over *where* students with disabilities ought to be taught. Conventional wisdom has it that moral divides, like the one that underlies the full inclusion debate, cannot be closed or bridged. The effect this divide has had on the field of special education is unclear. Some might argue that the full inclusion debate has strengthened special education by sharpening its focus on particular moral concerns and forcing stakeholders to address these concerns as fully as possible. A more pessimistic assessment is that the moral divide has done little but swallow up enormous amounts of attention, goodwill, energy, creativity, and intelligence that might have otherwise been devoted to achieving better and more just educational outcomes for students with disabilities.

"Conventional wisdom has it that moral divides, like the one that underlies the full inclusion debate, cannot be closed or bridged."

My purpose is to shed new light on the full inclusion debate in special education and help answer this question: what is the *right place*, in the moral sense, to educate students with disabilities? Instead of directly examining the arguments for and against full inclusion, I analyze the full inclusion debate in relation to current research in moral psychology. Moral psychology is the scientific study of the causes, correlates, and consequences of moral thinking, including moral reasoning and moral judgment. In other words, my focus is on understanding *how moral judgment works* and the psychological processes that contribute to divisive and polarized moral attitudes. I have chosen this approach because I believe that an examination of how moral judgment works can accomplish certain things that are not often observed in the present stage of the debate. It can trigger unexpected insights, create new opportunities for meaningful dialogue, add clarity to moral assessments, and maybe even change a few minds along the way. I also recognize that this approach has significant limitations and potential disadvantages, including the possibility that some of what I say could offend people with strong beliefs about full inclusion. If certain findings from moral psychology are correct, this could cause people to reject the ideas I present, cause people to defend their existing moral beliefs more vigorously, and cause me to lose social status among my peers. As the saying goes, nothing ventured, nothing gained.

This chapter is divided into three sections. In the first, I provide a brief overview of a relatively recent development in moral psychology—the social intuitionist model of moral judgment (Haidt, 2001)—as well as its implications for understanding the full inclusion debate. In the second, I review additional findings from moral psychology suggesting that what divides proponents and opponents of full inclusion is not their moral values but how they hold them. In the third, I present the story of one prominent special education scholar who defied conventional wisdom and changed her deeply held moral beliefs about teaching students with disabilities. I present this story to demonstrate that people do, in fact, cross over moral divides.

Part I—The Social Intuitionist Model of Moral Judgment

If you are like me, the last time you spent more than a few passing moments thinking about the formal psychological study of morality was in an undergraduate introduction to psychology course. You may remember studying Kohlberg's (1969) stage theory of moral development, in which children attain increasingly sophisticated understandings of morality as they mature. Over the past few decades, several new developments in psychology and related disciplines have cast doubt on Kohlberg's rationalist theories of morality. In psychology, the "cognitive revolution" of the 1960s and 1970s was followed in the 1980s and 1990s by increased interest in emotion and evolutionary psychology (Haidt, 2008). One of the most significant outcomes of this increased interest was the accumulation of evidence that our minds are composed of two cognitive processing systems—one that is relatively new, in evolutionary terms, and one that is very old. The newer system is the one that we associate with slow, conscious, verbal reasoning, while the older system is fast, intuitive, and affect-laden (Zajonc, 1980). The fast, affectively primed intuitive system is always "on," always evaluating (good/bad, like/dislike), and always "pushing" us, more or less intensely, toward approach or avoidance (Haidt, 2007). To varying degrees, these affective/intuitive evaluations influence our thinking—from preferences, to judgments, to decision making, and so on (Bargh, 1994; Bargh & Chartrand, 1999). Over time, this research converged with research in primatology (e.g., Flack & de Waal, 2000) and neuroscience[1] (e.g., Greene, Sommerville, Nystrom, Darley, & Cohen, 2001) to suggest that *emotions* (anger, disgust, sympathy, etc.) are the basic building blocks of morality (Haidt, 2007), and that most of the "action" in moral thinking may be in the fast, intuitive processing system, not the slow, deliberative system that we associate with conscious verbal reasoning.

In response to these and other findings, Haidt (2001) formulated the social intuitionist model of moral judgment. Before I provide an overview of the social intuitionist model, two cautions are in order. First, keep in mind that the social intuitionist model is *descriptive*, not *prescriptive*—the purpose of the model is to present an accurate portrayal of how moral judgment typically works, not how it *ought to* work (Haidt, 2001). In this chapter, I explore ways that understanding *how* moral judgment works might inform *how we make* moral judgments (for example, in relation to special education placement), but we must be careful to avoid committing the naturalistic fallacy (mistaking what is natural for what is right or good); or violating the eighteenth-century philosopher David Hume's dictum that one should not derive an *ought* from an *is*. Second, note that the social intuitionist model has been frequently misunderstood and misinterpreted, both in terms of its descriptive claims and its implications (e.g., Haidt, 2004). If you find yourself thinking that the claims of the social intuitionist model are that "morality is just blind instinct, no smarter than lust," or that the model "denies any causal role for moral reasoning . . . or the possibility of moral change" (Haidt & Bjorklund, 2007, p. 181), I suggest that you go directly to the sources I cite before you draw any firm conclusions.[2] Like all scientific models, the social intuitionist model can be, should be, and has been legitimately critiqued (e.g., Pizarro & Bloom, 2003), but such critiques should be based on a sufficient understanding of what the model actually does and does not say.

The difference between the social intuitionist model and rationalist models of moral judgment is primarily a difference in the way that the "ingredients" or psychological processes are arranged, as well as a significant difference in emphasis (i.e., where the "action" is). The central claim of the social intuitionist model is that *in most cases,* intuitive moral judgments cause moral reasoning, not the other way around (Haidt, 2001). The core of the model is composed of four links—the *intuitive judgment* link, the *post-hoc reasoning* link, the *reasoned persuasion* link, and the *social persuasion* link. The first link—intuitive judgment—starts with a *moral intuition,* which is defined as "the sudden appearance in consciousness . . . of an evaluative feeling (like-dislike, good-bad) about the actions or character of a person, without any conscious awareness of having gone through steps of search, weighing evidence, or inferring a conclusion" (Haidt & Bjorklund, 2007, p. 184). Moral intuitions typically (but not inevitably) elicit conscious moral judgments— verbal thoughts of approval or disapproval. Again, the construction of this first link was prompted by evidence for the ever-evaluating mind and for the implicit and automatic nature of social cognition (Bargh & Chartrand, 1999).

In the second link—post-hoc reasoning—intuitive moral judgments are followed, when needed, by slow, deliberate moral reasoning (Haidt, 2001). In other words, moral reasoning is most often deployed in support of an already made intuitive moral judgment. Evidence for the post-hoc nature of moral reasoning comes from research indicating that everyday reasoning is heavily biased toward finding ways to support a preferred, predetermined conclusion (e.g., Ditto & Lopez, 1992). This biased reasoning is also called *motivated* reasoning. There are many types of motives that may predispose us to "discover," through selective attention to some reasons but not others, what we already believe, or what we want to believe. Emotionally primed moral judgments provide an especially powerful motive for post-hoc moral reasoning (Uhlmann, Pizarro, Tannenbaum, & Ditto, 2009). The bias or one-sidedness of everyday reasoning is difficult to understand if you think that verbal reasoning evolved primarily as a means to reach correct conclusions (Haidt & Bjorklund, 2007). It is more likely that our language abilities evolved in response to the demands of living in small, tightly knit webs of social accountability—demands like tracking the reputations of others and protecting and enhancing our own reputations (Dunbar, 1996). While conscious verbal reasoning *can* be deployed, under certain circumstances, to dispassionately seek the truth (the "intuitive scientist" metaphor), it is essential to recognize that language evolved for other purposes, including winning arguments (the "intuitive lawyer" metaphor) and maximizing social status (the "intuitive politician" metaphor; Haidt, 2007).

The third and fourth links (reasoned persuasion, social persuasion) capture the importance of the *social* part of the social intuitionist model—it is through social interaction that moral reasoning is most likely to exert a causal force on moral judgment. Moral discussions, in which we talk about other people and their actions, are ubiquitous in our social lives. These interpersonal exchanges sometimes require us to explain or justify our moral judgments, and we sometimes feel the need to influence or change the moral judgments of others (Haidt, 2001; Haidt & Bjorklund, 2007). In these links, the term "persuasion" refers to attempts to trigger new or different intuitions in others, and this can be accomplished through appeals to logic, emotion, or both. When one or more of the participants in a moral discussion is at least somewhat open to this kind of persuasion, moral reasoning *passed between people* can change moral judgments, often for the better, even when each of the individual discussants is engaging in post-hoc reasoning (see link two). Thus, the social part of the social intuitionist model posits a kind of "distributed reasoning" approach to moral judgment (Haidt & Bjorklund, 2007). Remember that participants are not always open to persuasion. In conflict situations (i.e., the participants openly and ardently identify with opposing moral communities or viewpoints), moral discussions are unlikely to change moral judgments and may, in fact, motivate more intense post hoc reasoning and thereby strengthen the existing moral judgment (e.g., Nyhan & Reifler, 2010).

The full social intuitionist model includes two additional links—the *reasoned judgment* link and the *private reflection* link—that account for the fact that private, non-post-hoc reasoning or private reflection can cause or change moral judgments, although this is hypothesized to be far more the exception than the rule (Haidt, 2001). An existing intuitive moral judgment may be overridden by logic or by a new intuition triggered by role-taking or changing one's perspective on a matter. While the actual occurrence of this sequence of events—private reasoning or reflection causing moral judgment—is believed to be rare, the *perception* that this has happened is common. We are prone to overestimate the extent to which our moral reasoning caused a moral judgment, and to underestimate the extent to which an intuitive judgment caused our reasoning (a voluminous research literature describes the cognitive errors that make us vulnerable to this type of misperception, e.g., Dawes, 2001; Tavris & Aronson, 2008). Haidt (2001) calls this the "wag-the-dog" illusion—the perception that "our own moral judgment (the dog) is driven by our own moral reasoning (the tail)" (p. 823). There is another related illusion that Haidt calls the "wag-the-other-dog's-tail" illusion. This is the belief that, in a moral disagreement, peppering your opponent with reasons and arguments (wagging the other dog's tail) will cause your opponent to change her mind (make the other dog happy). When reasons and arguments do not change your opponent's moral judgment, it is easy to conclude that your opponent must be irrational, unintelligent, or—most problematic—immoral. The belief that one's opponent is not morally motivated promotes a kind of "good vs. evil" thinking that is a major contributor to the futility and self-righteousness that characterize debates that have been framed in moral terms.

A convergence of research findings in psychology and related disciplines prompted the creation of the social intuitionist model of moral judgment, and a substantial body of research has subsequently corroborated many aspects of the model, although important questions remain (Haidt, 2007; Haidt & Kesebir, 2010). There is one more important aspect of the social intuitionist model to discuss, but consider the implications so far. First, if moral reasoning, especially private reasoning, is most typically used to defend an already made intuitive moral judgment, how can we hope to accomplish our objective of advancing the full inclusion debate and moving closer to resolution of this moral controversy? The obvious solution of directly teaching people to reason better and to think critically about divisive social issues like full inclusion remains a worthwhile goal, but the intuitionist approach to morality provides one explanation for why this is such a difficult thing to do (Lillenfeld, Ammirati, & Landfield, 2009). Prior moral beliefs and commitments are such powerful motives for biased reasoning that they can influence more than just our attitudes and opinions. They can impact how we attend to, evaluate, and assimilate factual information (Liu & Ditto, 2013). This creates a real policy problem. If people who disagree morally about a policy also cannot agree about the facts of the matter—for example, the facts related to global warming or the safety of nuclear power—it is unlikely that piling on more facts and fact-based arguments will move stakeholders closer to consensus or compromise (Kahan, Jenkins-Smith, & Braman, 2011). The *way* people hold their moral beliefs and commitments is especially relevant.

The social part of the social intuitionist model offers some hope. Although *private* moral judgments about full inclusion and where students ought to be taught may be, in most cases, based on reasoning that is biased by prior moral judgments, explaining and justifying our judgments to other people can produce less biased moral reasoning. This only happens, however, when the participants in such exchanges perceive themselves to be allies (or at least not enemies). Morality is, in many ways, a "team sport" (Haidt & Kesebir, 2010), and we are more likely to open-mindedly contemplate challenges to our moral judgments if they come from our "teammates." All of this suggests several possibilities for helping people *reason better*—that is, in a less biased way—about the moral implications of issues related to placement in special education. For example, relevant factual information about these issues can be presented in a way that upholds, rather than threatens, prior moral commitments. Factual information can also be disseminated, when possible, by people who represent diverse moral and political viewpoints (Kahan, 2010). The purpose here is not to trick or deceive people into accepting a particular belief about full inclusion—the term we have for that sort of activity is "propaganda."

> "Morality is, in many ways, a 'team sport,' and we are more likely to open-mindedly contemplate challenges to our moral judgments if they come from our 'teammates.'"

The final aspect of the social intuitionist model I discuss is this—what, exactly, are *moral intuitions?* To understand what moral intuitions are, it is essential to realize that our minds are not "blank slates," capable of learning anything we try to teach it with equal ease (Joseph, Graham, & Haidt, 2009). Instead, our minds have certain innate psychological systems, or foundations, that enable us to learn some things more readily than others. Evolution has built into our minds five moral foundations that prepare us to develop a small set of moral intuitions, and "these intuitions then enable and constrain the social construction of virtues and values" (Haidt & Bjorklund, 2007, p. 183; see also Haidt & Joseph, 2004). The five foundations are *harm* (sensitivity to suffering—related to virtues such as compassion and kindness); *reciprocity* (reciprocal altruism—related to virtues such as fairness and justice); *ingroup* (recognizing, trusting, and cooperating with one's co-residing ingroup—related to virtues such as loyalty and patriotism); *hierarchy* (sensitivity to hierarchical social arrangements—related to virtues such as respect, duty, and benevolence); and *purity* (sensitivity to contamination—related to virtues such as sanctity and self-restraint).

If we all have these moral foundations, why do the moral worldviews of people and groups differ? First, note that the five moral foundations, and the moral emotions that are closely tied to them, enable and constrain, but do not dictate, the construction of values and virtues. Values are also shaped by individual and cultural differences (Shweder, 1990). One moral intuition can override another, and moral worldviews differ in the extent to which the "volume" is turned up or down on any of the five moral foundations. This helps explain differences, for example, between the moral worldviews of liberals and conservatives. The moral worldviews of liberals are constructed almost entirely on two of the moral foundations—harm and fairness. Conservatives, on the other hand, have built their moral worldviews on all five foundations (Graham, Haidt, & Nosek,

2009). Haidt and Graham (2007) suggest that it is this difference that is at the heart of the culture war. They argue that conservatives have moral intuitions (ingroup, hierarchy, purity) that are essentially "invisible" to liberals, and that this "blind spot" causes liberals to believe that conservatives, in their opposition to issues that liberals support, are not morally motivated (recall the previous discussion of the "wag-the-other-dog's-tail" illusion). Instead of acknowledging and trying to understand the moral concerns of conservatives, liberals tend to explain them away, often in very unflattering ways. Haidt and Graham contend that this situation has hurt liberals politically. They also suggest that if liberals could step out of their moral comfort zone for just a moment, they might see that the moral concerns of conservatives include many rational ideas that serve a useful purpose in society. Understand that this does not require liberals to abandon their ideals and goals related to social justice—it may actually improve their efforts to achieve them.

The two moral foundations that figure most prominently in the full inclusion debate are *fairness-justice* and *harm-care*, so it is not surprising that most special educators tend to be politically liberal. In the next section I address what might account for the moral schism between advocates and opponents of full inclusion.

Part II—Place Values and How We Hold Them

Advocates of full inclusion in special education focus a great deal of their "moral attention" on concerns related to fairness and justice. Concerns about the fair and just treatment of people with disabilities are rational and justified, not delusional. History is replete with examples of unfair and unjust treatment of people with disabilities, and such injustice continues in different forms around the world. From the "pro" full inclusion perspective, *injustice* is mainly about the *unequal* treatment of students with disabilities in society—as well as the belief that the origin of this unequal treatment is the students themselves, rather than the unfair way society has responded to differences like disability. For supporters of full inclusion, fighting injustice means opposing the unequal treatment inherent in the practice of labeling students as disabled and physically separating them from their peers (Brantlinger, 1997; Lipsky & Gartner, 1987; Gallagher, 2001).[3]

> "Advocates of full inclusion in special education focus a great deal of their 'moral attention' on concerns related to fairness and justice."

The value of fairness and justice for students with disabilities is one that can be identified in the moral worldviews of both advocates and opponents of full inclusion, but there is a critical difference in the way that these two groups *hold* this value. For advocates of full inclusion, fairness and justice (or equal treatment) for students with disabilities is a *protected* value. A protected value is a value that "resists tradeoffs with other values, particularly economic values" (Baron & Spranca, 1997, p. 1). Here, "economic" refers to costs and benefits in a broad sense, not just in relation to money. Protected values reflect deontological rules—rules prohibiting certain actions, regardless of their consequences (Ritov & Baron, 1999). When we say that the "ends do not justify the means," we are drawing a deontological moral conclusion. All of us have values or moral beliefs that would be considered deontological—many think that torture or child labor should be prohibited no matter what benefits (monetary or otherwise) might accrue from such activities.

Proponents of full inclusion have likened separate special education to slavery (Stainback & Stainback, 1987), apartheid (Connor & Gabel, 2013; Lipsky & Gartner, 1987), and segregation (Wang & Walberg, 1988). Labeling students for special education purposes has been compared by supporters of full inclusion to the Nazi practice of pinning yellow stars on Jews and pink triangles on homosexuals (Forest & Pearpoint, 1992). All of these are comparisons to actions that the vast majority of us would judge to be inherently wrong—even the thought of weighing the potential benefits of any of these activities is repugnant to most. Equating separate placements with these types of abhorrent acts is a strong indication that equal treatment for students with disabilities is a protected, or deontological, moral value for supporters of full inclusion. Opponents of full inclusion, in contrast, hold their values related to special education placement in a more *consequentialist* manner. That is, opponents of full inclusion are more willing to weigh the consequences (harms and benefits) of "unequal" (different) treatment, such as teaching students with disabilities in places other than the general education classroom. They are more willing to trade off values that relate to equal treatment with values related to harm and care.

"Opponents of full inclusion, in contrast, hold their values related to special education placement in a more *consequentialist* manner."

Some might object to this analysis and point out—correctly—that full inclusion advocates concede that separate educational placements may be justified under "highly extraordinary circumstances" (Gallagher, 2001, p. 638). Full inclusion advocates do acknowledge that inclusion in general education might be harmful (and unjustified) in a small number of cases involving students with the most severe impairments; they also acknowledge that some students with disabilities (e.g., deafness) and their families might prefer separate educational settings and ought to be allowed to choose them (e.g., Brantlinger, 1997; Gallagher, 2001). However, these very limited exceptions[4] are clearly not the *primary* basis for the moral judgments of full inclusion supporters. If moral judgments in support of full inclusion were principally consequentialist in nature, one would expect proponents of full inclusion to devote far more attention than they do to specifying the conditions under which separate placements are or are not morally acceptable, as well as the consequences (harms and benefits) that ought to be weighed when choosing or rejecting full inclusion. The evidence strongly suggests that moral judgments in favor of full inclusion are *primarily* based on deontic intuitions, or the belief that the practice of labeling and placing students in separate educational settings is wrong in and of itself. For proponents of full inclusion, the value of equal treatment of students with disabilities can rightly be understood to be a protected value because it is *resistant* to tradeoffs with other values, even if it does not absolutely prohibit them.

Researchers in moral psychology and related fields have identified several psychological phenomena associated with protected values. First, and somewhat paradoxically, having protected values affects how people perceive the consequences of these values. By definition, consequences are supposed to be irrelevant to protected values. Nonetheless, the need to justify our protected values (to ourselves and to others) may put pressure on us to defend these values from a *consequentialist* perspective. However, the consequentialist case in support of a protected value is not always as clear-cut as the deontological case. Ditto and Liu (2011) call conflict or tension between deontic intuitions and consequentialist intuitions "deontological dissonance." Deontological dissonance, like other types of cognitive dissonance, must be reduced. The research suggests that the way that we typically reduce deontological dissonance is not by modifying or abandoning a protected value. Instead, we modify our consequentialist beliefs so that they support and align with the protected value. For instance, if we believe that capital punishment is wrong on deontological grounds, we are also likely to conclude that capital punishment does not deter murder, and we are likely to deploy motivated reasoning (selective attention to confirmatory evidence) in support of this conclusion. Put another way, people rarely take a purely principled stand in defense of a protected value—stating that torture, for example, is inherently wrong, while at the same time admitting that torture is an effective method for extracting information that can be used to prevent a terrorist attack. Baron and Spranca (1997) concluded that people use "wishful thinking" about harms and benefits to deny that a protected value requires any kind of consequentialist trade-off at all.

The consequentialist case for or against full inclusion is unclear. Research comparing the educational outcomes experienced by students with disabilities taught in different placements (e.g., inclusion, resource, self-contained) is inconclusive (e.g., Zigmond, 2003). There are several reasons for this inconclusiveness, including the diversity of the population (such that some students may benefit from one place while others will not) and the difficulty associated with designing and conducting research that truly teases out the impact of place on student outcomes. It is also inconclusive because *place* is almost certainly not the critical variable directly impacting student outcomes so much as the nature of the *instruction* provided in those places (Kauffman, 1995; Zigmond, 2003). Place plays an indirect role, because certain physical, professional, and social dimensions of different instructional environments can either inhibit or promote the implementation of effective teaching practices for students with disabilities (Kauffman & Hallahan, 1997). In this regard, there is evidence to suggest that intensive special education practices are not often used in inclusive general education classrooms (e.g., Murawski, 2006; Volonino & Zigmond, 2007; Zigmond, Kloo, & Volonino, 2009). Regardless, consistent with the theory of deontological dissonance, advocates of full inclusion tend to interpret ambiguous or inconclusive research on the educational consequences of placement as favoring the effectiveness of inclusion over separate placements (e.g., Baker, Wang, & Walberg, 1994; Lipsky & Gartner, 1987, 1996; Stainback, 2000; TASH, 2012). Alternatively, many full inclusion advocates dismiss effectiveness research altogether as meaningless and irrelevant to the debate over the best place to teach students with disabilities (e.g., Gallagher, 2001).

Another psychological phenomenon associated with protected values is increased susceptibility to *omission bias*. Omission bias is "the tendency to be less concerned with harms caused by omission than with identical harms caused by action" (Ritov & Baron, 1999, p. 80; see also Baron & Ritov, 2009). Omission here refers to inaction—sometimes harmful consequences are the result of *not* doing something. We are all vulnerable to omission bias, regardless of how we hold a particular value, in part because of the practical difficulty of enforcing ethical rules against inaction (e.g., failing to act to save an endangered species vs. actions directly leading to the extinction of a species). Another example—people oppose policies requiring vaccination when told (hypothetically) that vaccinating will cause five deaths out of 10,000 children, but *not* vaccinating will cause 10 deaths (from disease) out of 10,000 children (Ritov & Baron, 1990). When people or groups have protected values, the omission bias is likely to be magnified. The omission bias of full inclusion supporters is reflected in the belief that, when it comes to considering the consequences (harms and benefits) of educational placement as part of the overall moral calculus, "the onus lies with those who propose to label and place" (Gallagher, 2001, p. 648). What is omitted, from this perspective, is the harm associated with *not* labeling and *not* placing students who may need and benefit from intensive special education. One important harm that is omitted is the possibility that students with disabilities who do not receive the most effective services and instruction will, as a consequence, experience more exclusion throughout their lives (e.g., unemployment, underemployment, incarcer-

> "One important harm that is omitted is the possibility that students with disabilities who do not receive the most effective services and instruction will, as a consequence, experience more exclusion throughout their lives."

ation, reduced opportunities for postsecondary education, difficulty forming and maintaining relationships, limited options for adult services, and so on).

The last psychological phenomenon associated with protected values that I discuss is *anger* at the thought of violations of the value (Baron & Spranca, 1997; Bauman & Skitka, 2009). This anger can best be understood by considering this question—if a protected value is right in principle, and it is right from a consequentialist perspective, what type of person would oppose the value? Graham and Haidt (2011) used quantitative and qualitative methods to examine the social psychological process whereby "strongly held values, in the presence of intergroup conflict or competition, lead to the sacralization of specific people, places, or ideas." "Sacralization" means holding something (like a moral value, or a victim of oppression) to be sacred, and sacralization leads to "an attendant vision of evil as whatever threatens or stands in the way of what's sacred." I do not have examples of full inclusion supporters calling full inclusion opponents *evil*, but many have implied or stated directly that opposition to full inclusion is immoral, or at least not morally motivated. The *anger* is evident in the use of unflattering terms[5] to describe the beliefs of critics of full inclusion, especially when representing these beliefs to third parties (i.e., terms like "disease orientation" and "deficit thinking"; Cochran-Smith & Dudley-Marling, 2012).

Anger is also evident in the practice of moral stereotyping—forming and reinforcing a caricatured portrayal of the beliefs and motives of the "enemy" of the sacred (Graham & Haidt, 2011; Graham, Nosek, & Haidt, 2011). Like all stereotypes, moral stereotypes exaggerate group differences and exacerbate intergroup conflict. Here, I briefly describe four moral stereotypes of critics of full inclusion, and provide a brief rebuttal of the stereotype. My purpose is to provide examples of moral stereotypes and to suggest that, by dispelling these stereotypes, more productive discourse about the moral implications of placement in special education will be possible.

1. Opposition to full inclusion is not morally motivated. Many advocates of full inclusion have directly stated or implied that critics of full inclusion are not morally motivated, and that their work and their concerns fall "outside a social justice perspective" (Cochran-Smith & Dudley-Marling, 2012). The belief that *only* full inclusion supporters approach special education from a social justice perspective is arguably the most damaging moral stereotype of the full inclusion debate. The destructive power of this stereotype comes mainly from the self-righteousness and Manichean, good-vs.-evil thinking it inspires (Haidt, 2012). Stakeholders on both sides of the debate are human, and although they can have secondary motives related to prestige, their careers, monetary gain, and so on, it is unconscionable to claim in the absence of direct and specific evidence that any of these things are the *real* reason behind their moral judgments. The two sides of the full inclusion debate differ in their vision of social justice for students with disabilities and how to achieve it. If either side cannot make its case without stereotyping and demonizing the people who disagree with it, then one has to question whether there is any real case to be made at all.

2. Opponents of full inclusion artificially prop up their arguments with false claims of scientific objectivity. Full inclusion advocates have challenged the legitimacy of the quantitative educational research[6] that full inclusion critics use to examine the tenability or desirability of severely limiting the continuum of placement options. The basic argument is that scientific objectivity in education research is impossible because there is no way to "rise above" our own subjective beliefs, attitudes, experiences, expectations, and goals in order to obtain a "God's eye view" that could be considered truly objective (Gallagher, 1998). The social intuitionist model of moral judgment suggests that subjectivity and bias do, indeed, influence how we perceive and assimilate information, particularly in relation to a divisive and complex social issue.

However, the model also says something about a solution, and it is one that is entirely consistent with scientific research in education. Greater objectivity and less bias are attainable through *other people*, through social or public inquiry. While a "God's eye view" is unattainable, the process of allowing other people to evaluate and challenge our perceptions and beliefs provides us with a view that reaches beyond our own private subjectivity. Science is a type of social inquiry that involves shared standards for knowledge claims, common ownership of information, cultivated disinterestedness, and organized skepticism (Rumrill, Cook, & Wiley, 2011). Groups can make errors, including groups of researchers, but the solution to that problem is more science, not less—more scientists using more rigorous scientific methods to test knowledge claims and reduce bias or error. The problem of subjectivity does not make scientific inquiry impossible, just necessary. The postmodern denial of scientific objectivity is itself the product of a kind of motivated reasoning. If one looks, one will find philosophers who, while acknowledging important limitations, have demonstrated that acquiring objective knowledge through science and other forms of rational inquiry is both possible and, from a social justice perspective, indispensable (e.g., Blackburn, 2005; Stove, 2001).

3. Labeling degrades and devalues students with disabilities. Full inclusion advocates argue that "disability" is socially constructed and that the practice of labeling students in special education arbitrarily assigns an inherently negative and stigmatizing meaning to what are naturally occurring individual differences (e.g., Baglieri & Knopf, 2004; Gallagher, 2001). The idea of "disability" is socially constructed. We can observe any of the individual differences that we associate with disability and assign to them whatever meaning we wish, including no meaning at all. Drawing the line between "disability" and "not disability" is a judgment call. But this judgment is neither *arbitrary* nor *malevolent*, and neither is the social construction of the idea we call "disability." Ideas like "disability" are constructed for a purpose, and, in schools, judgment calls related to disability are made based on what we know about how certain types and degrees of differences impact the educational functioning (and the special educational needs) of the students who exhibit them.

Consider another example. "Obesity" and "anorexia" are also social constructions—they are made-up ideas, diagnosis is based on a judgment call (i.e., there are no completely objective criteria for drawing the line between "obese" and "not obese"), and they are part of a natural range of differences in body weight (i.e., they occur in nature). Diagnosis is a judgment call, but it is not arbitrary. At a certain point, an extreme weight difference is associated with an unacceptably high probability of negative outcomes. Is it automatically degrading to name these conditions, or to try to prevent or treat them in the most efficient and effective manner possible? Are the only negative consequences or negative meanings associated with being anorexic or obese those that society "constructs" about these conditions? Societal attitudes may contribute to the extreme weight differences that we call anorexia and obesity, and those attitudes ought to be addressed. But it does not follow that the people who identify these conditions, or research them, or communicate about them, or try to coordinate resources to treat them, are therefore trying to discriminate against or stigmatize the people who have them. Special educators, families, advocates, and researchers demonstrate every day that is possible to label disabilities and still value and dignify the students who have these disabilities. The claim that the effect or intent of labeling is to oppress or dehumanize students with disabilities is unsubstantiated, and it is part of a moral stereotype that presents a significant obstacle to productive dialogue in the full inclusion debate. Kauffman (2010, 2013) points out that labeling is necessary for communication, that without a label we simply refuse to talk about a phenomenon and that the labeling argument has been used to attribute malice falsely to special education (Kauffman, 2009).

4. *Opponents of full inclusion focus narrowly or entirely on intrinsic, within-student causes of learning and behavior problems.* This moral stereotype follows from the stereotype about labeling for immoral purposes. For example, Cochran-Smith and Dudley-Marling (2012) write that "equating disability with deficits firmly situates learning problems in the minds and bodies of individual students," and that "this gives little reason to consider the role that other factors . . . play in academic failure" (p. 240). This stereotype is breathtaking for its inaccuracy.[7] The "traditional" (i.e., not pro-full inclusion) special education researchers and practitioners at whom this criticism is aimed employ methods that are almost exclusively focused on the *environmental* and *ecological* variables that impact academic and social functioning. Examples of these methods include applied behavior analysis, curriculum-based measurement, direct instruction, and positive behavior support, to name just a few. In addition, the methods that these special educators use are specifically designed to identify and build on student strengths and competencies—the claim that these methods are "deficit driven" is demonstrably false.

ONE QUESTION, MANY ANSWERS

In their investigation of the relationship between sacred values and the social construction of "evil adversaries," Graham and Haidt (2011) quote the philosopher Isaiah Berlin who, in his essay titled "My Intellectual Path," suggests that a major cause of injustice in the world is something that he calls *moral monism*. Berlin defines moral monism as the belief that "to all true questions there must be one true answer and one only, all others being false." The antidote to moral monism is *moral pluralism*, which is the idea that "true questions" can have multiple answers.

"From an ethical perspective, there are many correct answers to the question of *where* students with disabilities ought to be taught, and for this reason we need to maintain and strengthen the continuum of placement options."

Consider the question, "What is the right place, in the moral sense, to educate students with disabilities?" This question is a *true* question in the sense that the *place of instruction* both enables and constrains different special educational activities and (consequently) different outcomes for different students with disabilities. Special education placements, activities, and outcomes ought to be judged based on a plurality of moral values, not just one. From a psychological perspective, moral pluralism provides us with the right answer because there are "many independent sources of moral value," and "moral theories that value one source and set to zero[8] all others are likely to produce psychologically unrealistic [moral] systems" (Haidt & Bjorklund, 2007, p. 212). From an ethical perspective, there are many correct answers to the question of *where* students with disabilities ought to be taught, and for this reason we need to maintain and strengthen the continuum of placement options. The correct answer to the question of *where* in special education will always be the answer based on a "broad enough consequentialism . . . to acknowledge the plurality of sources of value," and that therefore allows us to "set about maximizing the total" of these values (Haidt & Bjorklund, 2007, p. 214). This is not the straightforward answer that some may have hoped for, and it is not an answer that will eliminate disagreement and conflict in special education placement decisions. Acknowledging multiple sources of moral value requires rational and thoughtful analysis, discussion, negotiation, and compromise, all in the pragmatic pursuit of the maximum good for the individual student.

Part III—The Moral of the Story

One prominent special education scholar did what many may think is impossible—she changed her mind about matters of moral importance in special education. Dr. Poplin is a prominent scholar in the area of learning disabilities, instruction, and research methods in special education. She is best known for her critiques of reductive, behaviorist theories of learning, teaching, and learning disabilities (Poplin, 1988a, 1988b). According to Google Scholar, these two publications have been cited well over 200 times each—very impressive numbers in the field of special education. The ideas that Poplin develops in these critiques mirror some of the arguments made in support of full inclusion. In brief, Poplin calls special education to task for assuming that there is a verifiable within-child reality called "learning disability"; for relying on a reductive, measurement-oriented scientific paradigm; for being "deficit driven"; for using instructional practices that demean students and "coerce" them into learning; and for constructing the special education category in an "attempt to segregate students from one another in order to deliver better instruction" (Poplin, 1988a, p. 398; 1988b). Poplin also states that there is "little evidence" that separate, homogeneous grouping (labeled a "reductionist" practice) leads to better learning outcomes (1988a).

Another of Poplin's publications (Poplin & Rogers, 2005) has received far less attention. In this paper, Poplin provides an excellent example of what a *change in moral judgment* looks like and how such changes are most likely to happen. What she writes is an apology for what she sees as errors she made in her critique of "reductionistic" special education ideas and practices. Note that Poplin does not abandon all of her ideals or moral concerns, but she does make substantial modifications to several important moral judgments related to the full inclusion debate. The language Poplin uses in her apology and the events she describes leading up to her change of heart are very much consistent with ideas captured by Haidt's (2001) social intuitionist model of moral judgment—including the "trap" of post-hoc motivated reasoning and the psychological mechanisms that sometimes allow us to escape this trap.

For example, Poplin describes herself as "ideologically enamored" by alternatives to "reductionistic" teaching practices, and she attributes her mistaken judgments to the "error of making ideologies the center [of her thinking] rather than the student" (Poplin & Rogers, 2005, p. 159). Poplin observes that "ideologies are useful theoretically to help us devise diverse strategies and practices, but lethal when they become prisons to our thinking and acting with children" (Poplin & Rogers, 2005, p. 159).[9] How did Poplin escape the "prison" of her own ideologically motivated moral reasoning? She singles out two pivotal events. The first occurred while observing a six-year-old student struggling to spell a word. The student's well-intentioned "non-reductionistic" teacher refrained from providing the student with the correct answer, and the little girl eventually broke down and cried. The experience of *feeling what the student felt* triggered a moral intuition for Poplin, one that suggested that non-reductionist practices may not always be right or good. This closely matches what is described in the *private reflection* link of the social intuitionist model (Haidt, 2001). The second occurred while reading Delpit's (1995) critique of constructivist practices for African-American children living in poverty. Delpit's book provides Poplin with reasons that constructivist teaching practices do not always adequately meet the educational needs of this population of students, and Poplin describes reading Delpit's book as the "final blow" to her "ideological stubbornness" (p. 159). This description resembles the *reasoned judgment* link of the social intuitionist model, in which reasoning overcomes an existing moral intuition.

The changes Poplin made in her moral judgments are substantial. She now believes that "there are situations when behaviorist practices of reducing a skill and teaching it directly works best" (Poplin & Rogers, 2005, p. 159). She still believes that there is a need to do more in special education than teach skills using direct instruction, as do many "traditional" special education researchers (e.g., Scruggs & Mastropieri, 2007). Poplin also concludes that while "to some degree," learning disabilities are a "cultural and sociopolitical invention," it is also true that "children who end up with the label LD also appear to demonstrate some sort of atypical psychological phenomenon that limits their learning to do simple academic tasks as easily as their peers" (pp. 159–60). She notes that "too much postmodernism and critical theory can 'deform' education in all sorts of ways," and that we ought not "lose sight of the fact that reading and math are real and that the ability to perform these skills makes a tremendous difference in a person's life" (p. 160). Poplin says that we can "debate whether this should be so, whether it is a sociopolitical construction, whether it is true in all cultures, and whether it is a right- or left-wing conspiracy, but for our students they are essential skills that will make it more feasible to achieve their own destinies" (p. 160). These statements suggest that Poplin has moved from a deontological moral perspective to a more consequentialist view of special education practices and outcomes.

> "If we agree on only one thing, I hope it is this—we should all try to avoid 'good vs. evil' thinking in our debates about complex social issues, including debates about different conceptions of social justice for students with disabilities."

I believe Poplin has crossed a bridge over the moral divide between proponents and critics of full inclusion in special education. I admire her for doing this, and for showing others that it is possible to change and, from my perspective, improve moral judgments.

I hope that increasing our understanding of how moral judgment (and moral change) works will ultimately help us make better moral judgments in relation to teaching students with disabilities. I know that a highly motivated reader could take much of what I have written and find a way to turn it against many of the points I have made, especially my points critiquing arguments for full inclusion. We should all welcome debate and disagreements that enhance our moral reasoning and moral judgments. If we agree on only one thing, I hope it is this—we should all try to avoid "good vs. evil" thinking in our debates about complex social issues, including debates about different conceptions of social justice for students with disabilities. In other words, whether we decide to cross over any bridges, let's at least agree not to burn them.

NOTES

1. For example, Damasio (1994) studied patients with brain injuries who had sustained damage to the ventromedial area of the prefrontal cortex. These patients maintained their knowledge and reasoning abilities related to social norms and rules, but they lost the flashes of affect that normally accompany making decisions in social contexts. Being "freed" from emotion did not enhance their judgment and decision making, as might be predicted from a Kohlbergian perspective—quite the opposite. These patients showed extreme impairments in their ability to navigate their social environments.

2. One oversimplified assumption is that reason is "smart" and intuition and emotions are "dumb." Reasoning and intuition are two different types of the same thing—cognition—and both have strengths and weaknesses depending on the context. Emotions have been unduly vilified as the enemy of reason, especially in relation to moral judgment. Emotions are critical to morality—moral values do not matter much if people do not care about them and their purpose in society.

3. It is interesting to note that Gallagher, at the end of her reasoned argument in support of full inclusion, uses the kind of "persuasion" (attempting to trigger a moral intuition) that is described in the third link of the social intuitionist model—she writes, "How many students would we label and place if we had to look students squarely in the eye and say to them, 'You are labeled and placed in this special classroom because of the choices we have made. We have constructed a world, a society, schools, and classrooms in which you do not fit; and under the circumstances this seems like the best option.' Most likely, the answer is very few" (Gallagher, 2001, p. 651).

4. Making even minor exceptions (or tradeoffs) to a protected, deontological value is difficult and comes with a psychological cost that sometimes necessitates a restorative gesture, or some other type of "moral cleansing" (Tetlock, Kristel, Elson, Green, & Lerner, 2000). For example, after Brantlinger (1997) concedes that there are "compelling and unavoidable reasons for students to sometimes be in restricted settings," her very next sentence states that "unfortunately . . . when institutions exist, they tend to be used." She then recommends the "substantial dismantling of separated educational structures" (pp. 433, 435). Similarly, immediately after Gallagher (2001) acknowledges that some in the deaf community prefer separate schools and should not be denied the right to choose them, she expresses the concern that "segregation [i.e., separate schools for the deaf] may serve to perpetuate the prejudices that made separate schooling necessary in the first place" (p. 638).

5. An illustrative example from the "culture war" is Newt Gingrich's infamous 1996 GOPAC memo titled "Language: A Key Mechanism of Control." In this memo, Gingrich provides Republican activists and politicians with a list of negative words to use when describing liberal ideas, policies, and politicians. Examples of words include "bureaucracy," "decay," "permissive," "red tape," and many more.

6. Full inclusion advocates may find it easier to dismiss quantitative educational research in part because their moral judgments are more deontological than consequentialist. Consequentialist moral judgment emphasizes measuring and quantifying harms and benefits in a way that deontological moral reasoning does not. Recently, Baglieri, Valle, Connor, and Gallagher (2011) suggested the need for an expansion or greater plurality of perspectives on disability in special education practice and research. Unfortunately, a major portion of their paper was dedicated to invalidating or disqualifying one of those perspectives—quantitative special education research. This is the nature of all morality, not just the morality of the full inclusion movement; morality binds moral communities together, and it blinds those communities to their own self-contradictions (Haidt, 2012).

7. In criticizing the "traditional" special education perspective with which they disagree, Cochran-Smith and Dudley-Marling (2012) add that "from this point of view . . . the poor are poor because they are deficient in

effort and/or ability" (p. 240). I know of no "traditional" special educator who has espoused this belief, and I submit that this is a particularly hurtful (and angry) smear directed at a community of people who are more likely than most to be offended by such a gross oversimplification of the causes of poverty (not to mention the fact that this belief has been falsely attributed to them).

8. The postmodern rejection of quantitative educational research effectively "sets to zero" all consequentialist sources of moral value. Consequentialist concerns literally do not count if we deny the possibility of quantifying and measuring harms and benefits. For more on the moral issues involving disabilities, see Anastasiou and Kauffman (2013).

9. Poplin's description of her own ideologically motivated reasoning calls to mind another widely circulated metaphor for confirmation bias—Morton's demon. Glen Morton (2002), an ex-creationist who initially did not want to believe the scientific evidence for evolution, imagined a little demon guarding the gate to his mind. When the demon saw evidence in support of creationism approaching, he would open the gate. When he saw "contradictory data" approaching, he would close the gate. Morton writes that "in this way, the demon allowed me to believe I was right and to avoid any nasty contradictory data" (p. 1).

ANDREW WILEY'S SUGGESTIONS FOR FURTHER READING

Haidt, J., Graham, J., & Joseph, C. (2009). Above and below left–right: Ideological narratives and moral foundations. *Psychological Inquiry, 20*, 110–119.

Kauffman, J. M. (2000). The special education story: Obituary, accident report, conversion experience, reincarnation, or none of the above? *Exceptionality, 8*, 61–71.

Wiley, A. L., Brigham, F. J., Kauffman, J. M., & Bogan, J. (2013). Disproportionate poverty, conservatism, and disproportionate identification of minority students with EBD. *Education and Treatment of Children, 36*, 29–50.

Wiley, A. L., & Kauffman, J. M. (2014). Conservatism and the under-identification of students with emotional and behavioral disorders in special education. *Exceptionality, 22*, 237–251.

Wiley, A. L., & Siperstein, G. N. (2011). Seeing red, feeling blue: The impact of state political leaning on state identification rates for emotional disturbance. *Behavioral Disorders, 36*, 195–207.

Wiley, A. L., Tankersley, M., & Simms, A. (2012). Teachers' causal attributions for student problem behavior: Implications for school-based behavioral interventions and research. In B. G. Cook, M. Tankersley, & T. J. Landrum (Eds.), *Advances in learning and behavioral disabilities: Classroom behavior, contexts, and interventions* (Vol. 25; pp. 279–300). Bingley, UK: Emerald Publishing Group.

REFERENCES

Anastasiou, D., & Kauffman, J. M. (2013). The social model of disability: Dichotomy between impairment and disability. *Journal of Medicine and Philosophy, 38*(4), 441–459.

Baglieri, S., & Knopf, J. H. (2004). Normalizing difference in inclusive education. *Journal of Learning Disabilities, 37*, 525–529.

Baglieri, S., Valle, J. W., Connor, D. J., & Gallagher (2011). Disability studies in education: The need for a plurality of perspectives on disability. *Remedial and Special Education, 32*, 267–278.

Baker, E. T., Wang, M. C., & Walberg, H. J. (1994). The effects of inclusion on learning. *Educational Leadership, 52*, 33–35.

Bargh, J. A. (1994). The four horsemen of automaticity: Intention, awareness, efficiency, and control as separate issues. In R. S. Wyer, & T. K. Srull (Eds.), *Handbook of social cognition: Vol. 1, Basic processes* (2nd ed., pp. 1–40). Hillsdale, NJ: Erlbaum.

Bargh, J. A., & Chartrand, T. L. (1999). The unbearable automaticity of being. *American Psychologist, 54*, 462–479.

Baron, J., & Ritov, I. (2009). Protected values and omission bias as deontological judgments. *Psychology of learning and motivation, 50*, 133–167.

Baron, J., & Spranca, M. (1997). Protected values. *Organizational behavior and human decision processes, 70*(1), 1–16.

Bauman, C. W., & Skitka, L. J. (2009). In the mind of the perceiver: Psychological implications of moral conviction. *Psychology of Learning and Motivation, 50*, 339–362.

Blackburn, S. (2005). *Truth: A guide.* New York: Oxford University Press.

Brantlinger, E. (1997). Using ideology: Cases of nonrecognition of the politics of research and practice in special education. *Review of Educational Research, 67*, 425–460.

248 • Wiley

Brigham, F. J., & Kauffman, J. M. (1998). Creating supportive environments for students with emotional or behavioral disorders. *Effective School Practices, 17*(2), 25–35.

Cochran-Smith, M., & Dudley-Marling, C. (2012). Diversity in teacher education and special education: The issues that divide. *Journal of Teacher Education, 63,* 237–244.

Connor, D. J., & Ferri, B. A. (2007). The conflict within: Resistance to inclusion and other paradoxes in special education. *Disability & Society, 22,* 63–77.

Connor, D. J., & Gabel, S. L. (2013). 'Cripping' the curriculum through academic activism: Working toward increasing global exchanges to reframe (dis)ability and education. *Equity & Excellence in Education, 46,* 100–118.

Damasio, A. (1994). *Descartes' error: Emotion, reason, and the human brain.* New York: Putnam.

Danforth, S., & Rhodes, W. C. (1997). Deconstructing disability: A philosophy for inclusion. *Remedial & Special Education, 18,* 357–366.

Dawes, R. M. (2001). *Everyday irrationality: How pseudo-scientists, lunatics, and the rest of us systematically fail to think rationally.* Boulder, CO: Westview Press.

Delpit, L. (1995). *Other people's children: Cultural conflict in the classroom.* New York: The New Press.

Ditto, P. H., & Liu, B. (2011). Deontological dissonance and the consequentialist crutch. In P. Shaver & M. Mikulincer (Eds.), *The social psychology of morality: Exploring the causes of good and evil* (pp. 51–70). New York, NY: APA Books.

Ditto, P. H., & Lopez, D. F. (1992). Motivated skepticism: Use of differential decision criteria for preferred and nonpreferred conclusions. *Journal of Personality and Social Psychology, 63,* 568–584.

Dunbar, R. (1996). *Grooming, gossip, and the evolution of language.* Cambridge, MA: Harvard University Press.

Flack, J. C., & de Waal, F. B. M. (2000) "Any animal whatever": Darwinian building blocks of morality in monkeys and apes. *Journal of Consciousness Studies, 7,* 1–29.

Forest, M., & Pearpoint, J. C. (1992). Putting all kids on the MAP. *Educational Leadership, 50* (2), 26–31.

Fuchs, D., & Fuchs, L. S. (1994). Inclusive schools movement and the radicalization of special education reform. *Exceptional Children, 60,* 294–309.

Gallagher, D. J. (1998). The scientific knowledge base of special education: Do we know what we think we know? *Exceptional Children, 64,* 493–502.

Gallagher, D. J. (2001). Neutrality as a moral standpoint, conceptual confusion and the fullinclusion debate. *Disability & Society, 16,* 637–654.

Gliona, M. F., Gonzales, A. K., & Jacobson, E. S. (2005). Dedicated, not segregated: Suggested changes in thinking about instructional environments and in the language of special education. In J. M. Kauffman & D. P. Hallahan (Eds.), *The illusion of full inclusion: A comprehensive critique of a current special education bandwagon* (2nd ed.) (pp. 135–146). Austin, TX: Pro-Ed.

Graham, J., & Haidt, J. (2011). Sacred values and evil adversaries: A moral foundations approach. In P. Shaver & M. Mikulincer (Eds.), *The social psychology of morality: Exploring the causes of good and evil* (pp. 11–14). New York: APA Books.

Graham, J., Haidt, J., & Nosek, B. A. (2009). Liberals and conservatives rely on different sets of moral foundations. *Journal of Personality and Social Psychology, 96,* 1029–1046.

Graham, J., Nosek, B., & Haidt, J. (2011). The moral stereotypes of liberals and conservatives: Exaggeration of differences across the political divide. *Available at SSRN 2027266.*

Greene, J. D., Sommerville, R. B., Nystrom, L. E., Darley, J. M., & Cohen, J. D. (2001). An fMRI study of emotional engagement in moral judgment. *Science, 293,* 2105–2108.

Haidt, J. (2001). The emotional dog and its rational tail: A social intuitionist approach to moral judgment. *Psychological Review, 108,* 814–834.

Haidt, J. (2004). The emotional dog gets mistaken for a possum. *Review of General Psychology, 8,* 283–290.

Haidt, J. (2007). The new synthesis in moral psychology. *Science, 316,* 998–1002.

Haidt, J. (2008). Morality. *Perspectives on Psychological Science, 3,* 65–72.

Haidt, J. (2012). *The righteous mind: Why good people are divided by politics and religion.* New York: Paragon.

Haidt, J., & Bjorklund, F. (2007). Social intuitionists answer six questions about morality. In W. Sinnott-Armstrong (Ed.), *Moral psychology, Vol. 2: The cognitive science of morality* (pp. 181–217). Cambridge, MA: MIT Press.

Haidt, J., & Graham, J. (2007). When morality opposes justice: Conservatives have moral intuitions that liberals may not recognize. *Social Justice Research, 20,* 98–116.

Haidt, J., & Joseph, C. (2004). Intuitive ethics: How innately prepared intuitions generate culturally variable virtues. *Daedalus, 133,* 55–66.

Haidt, J., & Kesebir, S. (2010). Morality. In S. Fiske, D. Gilbert, & G. Lindzey (Eds.), *Handbook of Social Psychology, 5th Edition* (pp. 797–832). Hobeken, NJ: Wiley.

Joseph, C. M., Graham, J., & Haidt, J. (2009). The end of equipotentiality: A moral foundations approach to ideology-attitude links and cognitive complexity. *Psychological Inquiry, 20,* 172–176.

Kahan, D. (2010). Fixing the communications failure. *Nature, 463,* 296–297.

Kahan, D. M., Jenkins-Smith, H., & Braman, D. (2011). Cultural cognition of scientific consensus. *Journal of Risk Research, 14,* 147–174.

Kauffman, J. M. (1995). Why we must celebrate a diversity of restrictive environments. *Learning Disabilities Research and Practice, 10,* 225–232.

Kauffman, J. M. (2009). Attributions of malice to special education policy and practice. In T. E. Scruggs & M. A. Mastropieri (Eds.), *Advances in learning and behavioral disabilities: Vol. 22. Policy and practice* (pp. 33–66). Bingley, UK: Emerald.

Kauffman, J. M. (2010). The problem of early identification. In H. Ricking & G. C. Schulze (Eds.), *Förderbedarf in der emotionalen und sozialen Entwicklung: Prävention, Interdisziplinarität, und Professionalisierung* (pp. 171–177). Bad Heilbrunn, Germany: Klinkhardt.

Kauffman, J. M. (2013). Labeling and categorizing children and youth with emotional and behavioral disorders in the USA: Current practices and conceptual problems. In T. Cole, H. Daniels, & J. Visser (Eds.), *The Routledge international handbook of emotional and behavioural difficulties* (pp. 15–21). London: Routledge.

Kauffman, J. M., Bantz, J., & McCullough, J. (2002). Separate and better: A special public school class for students with emotional and behavioral disorders. *Exceptionality, 10,* 149–170.

Kauffman, J. M., & Hallahan, D. P. (1997). A diversity of restrictive environments: Placement as a problem of social ecology. In J. W. Lloyd, E. J. Kameenui, & D. Chard (Eds.), *Issues in educating students with disabilities* (pp. 325–342). Hillsdale, NJ: Lawrence Erlbaum Associates, Inc.

Kohlberg, L. (1969). Stage and sequence: The cognitive-developmental approach to socialization. In D. A. Goslin (Ed.), *Handbook of socialization theory and research* (pp. 347–480), Chicago: Rand McNally.

Lillenfeld, S. O., Ammirati, R., & Landfield, K. (2009). Giving debiasing away: Can psychological research on correcting cognitive errors promote human welfare? *Perspectives on Psychological Science, 4,* 390–398.

Lipsky, D. K., & Gartner, A. (1996). Inclusion, school restructuring, and the remaking of American society. *Harvard Educational Review, 66,* 762–796.

Lipsky, D. K., & Gartner, A. (1987). Capable of achievement and worthy of respect: Education for handicapped students as if they were full-fledged human beings. *Exceptional Children, 54,* 69–74.

Liu, B., & Ditto, P. H. (2013). What dilemma? Moral evaluation shapes factual belief. *Social Psychological and Personality Science, 4,* 316–323.

Mock, D. R., & Kauffman, J. M. (2005). The delusion of full inclusion. In J. W. Jacobson, R. M. Foxx, & J. A. Mulick (Eds.), *Controversial therapies for developmental disabilities: Fad, fashion and science in professional practice* (pp. 113–128). London: Lawrence Erlbaum Associates, Publishers.

Morgan, P. L., Frisco, M. L., Farkas, G., & Hibel, J. (2010). A propensity of score matching analysis of the effects of special education services. *The Journal of Special Education, 43,* 263–254.

Morton, G. R. (2002). *Morton's demon.* Retrieved from http://www.oldearth.org/mortond.htm.

Murawski, W. (2006). Student outcomes in co-taught secondary English classes: How can we improve? *Reading & Writing Quarterly, 22,* 227–247.

Newman, L., Wagner, M., Knokey, A. M., Marder, C., Nagle, K., Shaver, D., Wei, X., with Cameto, R., Contreras, E., Ferguson, K., Greene, S., & Schwarting, M. (2011). *The post-high school outcomes of young adults with disabilities up to 8 years after high school. A report from the National Longitudinal Transition Study-2 (NLTS2)* (NCSER 2011–3005). Menlo Park, CA: SRI International.

Nyhan, B., & Reifler, J. (2010). When corrections fail: The persistence of political misperceptions. *Political Behavior, 32,* 303–330.

Obiakor, F. E., Harris, M., Mutua, K., Rotatori, A., & Algozzine, B. (2012). Making inclusion work in general education classrooms. *Education and Treatment of Children, 25,* 477–490.

Pizarro, D. A., & Bloom, P. (2003). The intelligence of the moral intuitions: A reply to Haidt (2001). *Psychological Review, 110,* 193–196.

Poplin, M. S. (1988a) The reductionist fallacy in learning disabilities: Replicating the past by reducing the present. *Journal of Learning Disabilities, 21,* 389–400.

Poplin, M. S. (1988b) Holistic/constructivist principles of the teaching and learning process: Implications for the field of learning disabilities, *Journal of Learning Disabilities, 21,* 401–416.

Poplin, M. S., & Rogers, S. M. (2005). Recollections, apologies, and possibilities. *Learning Disabilities Quarterly, 28,* 159–162.

Reid, K., & Valle, J. W. (2004). The discursive practice of learning disability: Implications for instruction and parent-school relations. *Journal of Learning Disabilities, 37,* 466–481.

Ritov, I., & Baron, J. (1999). Protected values and omission bias. *Organizational Behavior and Human Decision Processes, 79,* 79–94.

Ritov, I., & Baron, J. (1990). Reluctance to vaccinate: Omission bias and ambiguity. *Journal of Behavioral Decision Making, 3,* 263–277.

Rumrill P. D., Jr., Cook, B. G., & Wiley, A. L. (2011). *Research in special education: Designs, methods, and applications.* Springfield, IL: Charles C. Thomas.

Sapon-Shevin, M. (1996). Full inclusion as disclosing tablet: Revealing the flaws in our present system. *Theory into Practice, 35,* 35–42.

Scruggs, T. E., & Mastropieri, M. A. (2007). Science learning in special education: The case for constructed versus instructed learning. *Exceptionality, 15*(2), 57–74.

Shweder, R. A. (1990). In defense of moral realism: Reply to Gabennesch. *Child Development, 61,* 2060–2067.

Skrtic, T. M. (1991). The special education paradox: Equity as the way to excellence. *Harvard Educational Review, 61,* 148–206.

Slee, R. (2001). Social justice and the changing directions in educational research: The case of inclusive education. *International Journal of Inclusive Education, 5,* 167–177.

Stainback, S. (2000). The inclusion movement: A goal for restructuring special education. In M. A. Winzer & K. Mazurek (Eds.), *Special education in the 21st century: Issues of inclusion and reform* (pp. 27–40). Washington, DC: Gallaudet University Press.

Stainback, S., & Stainback, W. (1987). Integration versus cooperation: A commentary on "Educating Children with Learning Problems: A Shared Responsibility." *Exceptional Children, 54,* 66–68.

Stainback, S. & Stainback, W. (1992). *Curriculum considerations in inclusive classrooms: Facilitating learning for all students.* Baltimore: Paul H. Brookes.

Stove, D. (2001). *Scientific irrationalism: The origins of a postmodern cult.* London: Transaction.

TASH (2012). *What the research says: Inclusive education achieves results.* Downloaded November 1, 2012, from http://tash.org/advocacy-issues/inclusive-education.

Taylor, S. J. (1988). Caught in the continuum: A critical analysis of the principle of the least restrictive environment. *Journal of the Association for Persons with Severe Handicaps, 13*(1), 1–53.

Tavris, C., & Aronson, E. (2008). *Mistakes were made (but not by me): Why we justify foolish beliefs, bad decisions, and hurtful acts.* New York: Houghton Mifflin Harcourt.

Tetlock, P. E., Kristel, O. V., Elson, S. B., Green, M. C., & Lerner, J. S. (2000). The psychology of the unthinkable: taboo trade-offs, forbidden base rates, and heretical counterfactuals. *Journal of Personality and Social Psychology, 78,* 853–870.

Uhlmann, E. L., Pizarro, D. A., Tannenbaum, D., & Ditto, P. H. (2009). The motivated use of moral principles. *Judgment and Decision Making, 4,* 476–491.

US Department of Education (2011). *30th annual report to Congress on the implementation of the Individuals with Disabilities Education Act, 2008.* Washington, DC: Author.

Volonino, V. & Zigmond, N. (2007). Promoting research-based practices through inclusion? *Theory into Practice, 46,* 291–300.

Wang, M. C., & Walberg, H. J. (1988). Four fallacies of segregationism. *Exceptional Children, 55,* 128–137.

Zajonc, R. B. (1980). Feeling and thinking: Preferences need no inferences. *American Psychologist, 35,* 151–175.

Zigmond, N. (2003). Where should students with disabilities receive special education services? Is one place better than another? *The Journal of Special Education, 37,* 193–199.

Zigmond, N., Kloo, A., & Volonino, V. (2009). What, where, and how? Special education in the climate of full inclusion. *Exceptionality, 17,* 189–204.

Section IV

HOW SHOULD SPECIAL EDUCATION BE PRACTICED?

Special education has been provided in many different ways. One often hears about patience and understanding as necessary characteristics of special educators, but there clearly must be more than patience and understanding alone. What is that "more?" The focus of the chapters in this section is on *how* special education happens, the "more."

- In what way should special education be provided?
- How do we plan special education?
- How does special education work?
- Are some ways of providing special education preferable to other ways?
- How do we know whether special education works?

Getting to Know Shanna Eisner Hirsch

 I spent the first 12 years of my life observing a phenomenal teacher run a demonstration classroom at a local university. The teacher taught using science and passion. I learned early on that teachable moments happen everywhere and as a teacher you must capitalize on them. I saw her wear her heart on her sleeve and do whatever it took for her students to meet their goals. That teacher is my mother, Eileen Eisner. She inspired (and later pushed) me into the field of teaching students with disabilities.

After college I taught at a non-public school for students with autism and co-morbid psychiatric disabilities (e.g., schizophrenia). This experience stimulated and challenged me as a middle school special education teacher. I felt compelled to pursue a Master's in special education with a focus in managing challenging behaviors in the classroom. Vanderbilt University sparked my interests in applied behavior analysis and interventions based on functional assessments. Immediately after receiving my Master's degree, I headed back to the classroom as a resource room teacher and then later as a behavior analyst. When I worked on this book, I was pursuing a Ph.D. in special education with a focus on preventing and reducing challenging behaviors in the classroom through positive behavior interventions and supports.

16

HOW IS SPECIAL EDUCATION PRACTICED?

John Wills Lloyd, Melody Tankersley, Barbara Bateman,
& Shanna Eisner Hirsch

Although *who* and *where* may get a lot of the attention in discussions about special education, the question of *how* we practice special education is clearly very important. Obviously, no one would reasonably advocate doing it poorly, but controversies abound about how to do it well. These are the issues of practice. Some of them are about macro-level concerns—policies regarding assessment, for example: Should students with disabilities be required to take the same tests as their peers who do not have disabilities and take the tests under the same conditions? Other issues of practice are at the micro level—should students with disabilities be asked questions in different ways than their non-disabled peers during lessons?

The authors of chapters in this section discuss some contemporary issues, some of which have already been raised in previous chapters. For example, Lembke (Chapter 9) discussed multi-tiered methods that became popular during the 2000s, and there is more about those methods in some of the following chapters, especially those by Lane and Walker (Chapter 18) and Greenwood (Chapter 19). Cook's topic (Chapter 17), evidence-based practice, has been implicitly considered by many of the previous authors, but Thurlow's (Chapter 20) discussion of assessing outcomes of special education provides different perspectives from what has been presented so far.

Other controversies are not considered in the following chapters, primarily because they are of historic importance (but some still appear to have some currency in contemporary practice). For example, a foundational tenet of special education is that instruction should be adapted to meet individual learners' needs, but there have been variations in the application of this tenet that should not be adopted. For example, in the 1960s and 1970s it was popular to promote differentiation of instruction based on patterns of students' strengths and weaknesses. In an approach variously known as "diagnostic-remedial" or "diagnostic-prescriptive teaching" (Bateman, 1967), educators carefully examined results from batteries of tests that were designed to assess underlying language and perceptual processes and planned instruction to capitalize on students' areas of strength in those processes and to remediate their areas of weakness (see Arter & Jenkins, 1979, for a thorough review). Modalities (visual, auditory, etc.) were frequently considered in this mix, and the idea that auditory learners would benefit more from auditory instruction than visual learners and vice versa caught educators' fancy. In a survey 87 percent of special education teachers in Illinois in the 1970s reported that they knew about the model and 91 percent said that modality should be an important consideration when planning instruction (Arter & Jenkins, 1977). Although critiques of the ideas were available (Mann, 1971) and research evidence was lacking almost from the beginning for the modality-matching hypothesis, both in its specific (e.g., Ysseldyke, 1973) as well as its more general incarnation (Cronbach & Snow, 1977), the idea continues to be popular. For example, after disavowing belief in it, Murawski and Spencer (2011) offer multiple pages of examples about how to teach according to modality-based instruction.

The fact of the matter is that there is virtually no scientific reason for differentiation on the basis of learners' modality (Kavale & Forness, 1987; Landrum & Landrum, 2014; Pashler, McDaniel, Rohrer, & Bjork, 2008). Moreover, there is often little educational reason to differentiate on the basis of variables such as modality or other person-based features (e.g., personality types), because such differentiation often does not show that "different strokes are better for different folks." Usually it is the case that one method is better for just about everyone; alternative methods are just worse for some groups of students (Lloyd, 1984).

Reading instruction for students with disabilities has been another controversial topic. Despite compelling evidence available in the 1960s (e.g., Chall, 1967), the great debate between whole language and phonics instruction occurred throughout the 1980s and 1990s. In 2000, the National Reading Panel identified five essential components of effective reading instruction: phonological awareness training, phonics, instruction, fluency instruction, vocabulary instruction, and comprehension (National Institute of Child Health and Human Development, 2000). Nevertheless, research supporting the use of explicit phonics instruction dates back to the 1970s (Becker, 1977; Carnine, 1976; Williams & Ackerman, 1971) and before (e.g., Garrison & Heard, 1931) and continues more recently (Adams, 1990; Roberts, Torgesen, Boardman, & Scammacca, 2008).

As these examples illustrate, it is important to understand that how special education is practiced should be strongly grounded on empirical evidence. Special education has pursued some false leads. Learning styles is a prime example. But, special educators have righted the ship. In his chapter, Bryan Cook explains how special education research does this.

A MODEL FOR HOW

Bateman (1971; 2007) described a general model of how to teach. She synthesized the main ideas from a diverse range of sources to describe four major components in instruction, as we have summarized in Table 16.1. Bateman's OTTER approach (see the table to decode the acronym) is predicated on a deceptively simple idea: One teaches students to do new things—whether those new things are academic (skills or concepts) or social (interpersonal or self-help)—by making planned, systematic, and repeated changes in the students' environment. Put another way, teaching is the "intentional arranging or manipulating of the environment so that the child will learn what is being taught more efficiently than if he were to learn it incidentally from the world at" (Bateman, 1971, p. 8).

Borrowing from Bateman's OTTER approach, we have structured the introduction for this section around three main aspects of how to teach. After first explaining a few assumptions about our approach, we discuss planning, implementing, and evaluating special education. We think of this as a recipe for a pie, a teaching pie.

Table 16.1 Bateman's OTTER Approach to Teaching

Feature	Description	Example
Objectives (instructional goals)	Formulate specific observable and measurable objectives.	To teach a group of first-grade students to read 60 consonant-vowel-consonant words or more within 1minute with no more than 2 errors.
Task-Analysis (organizing content)	Consistently select and organize content with the abilities of the learner.	What must the students know? • Start at the "left" of text and go "rightwards" (i.e., -->). • Letter-sound relationships. • Blending, including (a) sliding from one sound to the next and (b) collapsing stretched out pronunciations to normal speech rates.
Teaching (content)	Employ instructional practices and strategies to obtain the desired objectives.	• Present letter-sound combinations repeatedly, having students say the sounds for the letters. • Model for students how to sound out words.
Evaluating (results of teaching)	Objectively evaluate instructional outcomes.	Have students read aloud from multi-column lists of regularly pronounced consonant-vowel-consonant words; count the number of correct and incorrect words read in a 1-min period.
Recycle (teach again) or Rejoice (enjoy your success)	Change the antecedents or consequences as needed (recycle), once the evaluation shows that the learner has met the instructional objectives (rejoice).	As the students approach criterion, move to more sophisticated objectives.

ASSUMPTIONS

The *what* and *how* sections are uniquely intertwined, because the principles are integral to special education success. As noted in the previous *what* chapters, special education includes explicit teaching of skills that are not necessarily part of the general education curriculum (Scruggs & Mastropieri, Chapter 3) and that may be similar to but is quantitatively and qualitatively different from general education (Hallahan & Pullen, Chapter 4).

The notion of providing services based purely on a students' special education disability category is a short-sighted view of special education. As special educators we systematically determine a student's strengths and areas in need of improvement. This information is in turn used to create individual plans (often delineated in students' Individual Education Programs). The foundation of the OTTER approach is to design and employ systematic instructional strategies which are specially designed to meet the needs of students. This may include materials and equipment, but mostly it has to do with plain-sense planning and execution.

Environment

Consistent with the multi-tier systems approach, instruction should take place in a situation that is optimal for learning. Thus, the school and classroom environments should be conducive to success. This would probably mean that a school-wide system of positive behavior supports (e.g., Bradshaw, Reinke, Brown, Bevans, & Leaf, 2008) would be in place and the classroom would be structured to optimize learning opportunities; there would be consistent routines, an emphasis on positive consequences, and similar appropriate behavior management procedures (see both the classic recommendations by Becker, Engelmann, & Thomas, 1971, and the more recent treatment by Alberto & Troutman, 2012 for guidance).

Curricula

The overall structure of instruction should be coordinated so that what students learn in one class or at one grade level articulates with what they have learned previously and will learn subsequently. It is often difficult to find a curriculum that is organized well, meets the needs of students with disabilities, has a strong evidence base, and can be implemented broadly (i.e., across virtually all classrooms in a school). At the elementary level in the area of tool skills (e.g., reading, writing, arithmetic), the Direct Instruction (DI) programs have been rigorously field-tested and bolstered with four decades of data (e.g., Becker & Carnine, 1981; Carnine, 1980; Engelmann, 1968; Gersten, Keating, & Becker, 1988). Other curricula that can be implemented broadly such as *Success for All* (e.g., Slavin et al., 1996), have focused more specifically on language arts and also have admirable track records (see Borman et al., 2007).

General Teaching Procedures

In addition to employing powerful curricula, teachers should promote student learning through the use of systematic teaching strategies. Teachers will not have carefully programmed and field-tested curricula for each and every instructional activity; they will need general instructional principles to guide them. Brophy and Good (1986), Rosenshine and Stevens (1986), and Kauffman, Mostert, Trent, and Pullen (2006) all describe beneficial general teaching strategies. These procedures include the following (loosely summarized from Rosenshine & Stevens, 1986):

(a) Review previous learning (activating prior knowledge) at the beginning of an activity or lesson.
(b) State goals clearly so that students know what they are supposed to learn.
(c) Model or demonstrate how students should perform tasks so that they can accomplish tasks successfully; show them how to do it (and peers can show them, too); anticipate where they will have problems and provide extra demonstrations and practice on these segments.
(d) Present new material in small segments.
(e) Provide frequent guided practice opportunities for students; "guided practice" means that the teacher closely monitors students' performance and provides feedback along the way.
(f) Include frequent checks for understanding; this means more than asking students if they "get it"; have them explain concepts or show how to perform operations.
(g) Deliver feedback and corrections. This is fundamental. If teachers are not letting students know when they answered correctly, when they treated fellow students appropriately, when they did well, then the students have no basis for growth. Similarly, if a student makes a mistake, a teacher can kindly and gently provide a correction (e.g., O'Leary & Becker, 1968).
(h) Incorporate independent practice and periodic review; provide the practice opportunities in different situations and with diverse examples.

These procedures should be utilized as a package rather than as individual, stand-alone practices. Systematic instruction can be applied to academic content, social skills, and behavior intervention plans. They need to be integrated into well-planned lessons so that they provide students high levels of success. And as Landrum will argue in the last chapter of this book, they need to be automatic in their implementation.

PLANNING

Planning is the first ingredient in the teaching pie and planning instruction occurs at many different levels. There is planning on the larger scale (e.g., curricula) and on the smaller scale (e.g., discrete trials). Planning includes selecting curricula, which are plans in themselves, as well as structuring time, from the school year to the school day. Of course, there are also lesson plans. And, IEPs are essentially plans.

Contemporary special education usually takes place within the context of multi-tiered models of prevention. These models, as discussed by Lane and Walker in Chapter 18, are developed to prevent problems, identify students who need assistance, and serve students who need even more help (Lane, Menzies, Oakes, & Kalberg, 2012). In these models schools have a system to identify and address students who require targeted interventions. Additionally resources are allocated in an efficient manner, because targeted interventions are costly and time consuming.

The models usually are composed of multiple tiers, namely a primary or universal (Tier 1), targeted (Tier 2), and tertiary (Tier 3). The primary or universal tier (Tier 1) is designed to prevent academic and social-behavioral concerns. The entire school population participates in this level, as Tier 1 is composed of procedures to teach, reinforce, and encourage positive behavior. Tier 1 programs should be designed so that at least 80 percent of students reach mastery by participating in them. Examples of curricula that can be implemented broadly mentioned previously (direct instruction programs in reading, writing, and arithmetic; the *Success for All* literacy program) have good records as Tier 1 academic models; on the behavior side, positive behavior intervention and supports would be a good example of a Tier 1 model.

Universal screening is conducted to determine student and school risk levels in addition to identifying students for targeted interventions. The second tier (Tier 2) is designed to meet the needs of a targeted group of students who may require additional behavioral or learning support beyond what Tier 1 procedures provided. Resources at Tier 2 might include supplemental lessons, self-monitoring of target behavior, and so forth. The services provided at Tier 2 should permit approximately 15 percent of students to reach mastery of objectives.

The tertiary tier (Tier 3) is designed to assist students who require intensive and individualized interventions. It is often equated with special education services. In theory, under the multi-tier systems approach, approximately 5 percent of students would require Tier 3 services. This level of support often consists of targeted interventions based on, for example, functional assessments.

Specifically tertiary supports such as special education encompass specially designed curriculum and educational environments. Direct instruction (DI) programs such as Corrective Reading have proven to be effective (Przychodzin-Havis et al., 2005). DI programs are designed to increase student learning and outcomes (Engelmann, 1979). This is attributed to DI's highly structured format, curriculum design, and scripted presentation, permitting them to incorporate those features listed earlier in this chapter. Furthermore, the integration of key features (e.g., identify the "big ideas" to organize content; teach explicit, generalizable strategies; scaffold instruction, integrate skills and concepts; and provide adequate review) underlies all DI programs and promotes effective teaching practices (Marchand-Martella, Slocum, & Martella, 2004; Stein, Carnine, & Dixon, 1998). The key feature of these materials is that they incorporate advanced instructional programming and design (Engelmann & Carnine, 1982; 2011).

To plan what should happen in special education, think again about the recommendations provided by the authors of the chapters in the *What* section. Let Kame'enui (Chapter 6), Browder (Chapter 5), Hallahan and Pullen (Chapter 4), and Scruggs and Mastropieri (Chapter 3) guide you.

IMPLEMENTING

The question of how educators implement special education might be interpreted to ask about how educational agencies arrange services. Is special education implemented according to a cross-categorical model? The meaning of "implement" (our second ingredient in the teaching pie) to which we limit ourselves here, however, refers to the practice or execution of teaching. Even more specifically, in this section we focus primarily on the act of teaching at the level of individual tasks.

Figure 16.1 presents a simplified model of an instance of teaching. It shows how a teacher presents a specific task, students respond, and the teacher then acts based on the students' responses. Teaching is built of many little acts such as the one described in the figure (relatedly, see Landrum's Chapter 27 for an illustration of the decisions teachers make). Greer (1994; Greer & McDonough, 1999) refers to something similar as "learn units." For people who have experience teaching students with autism, the model looks a lot like a discrete trial training (see Smith, 2001).

Whatever one wants to call it, the brief segment of teaching provides many opportunities for learners to respond and teachers to provide consequences. These are fundamental parts of implementing special education, as Hallahan and Pullen (Chapter 4) noted earlier, and they must be done with fidelity. Those are the topics of the following subsections.

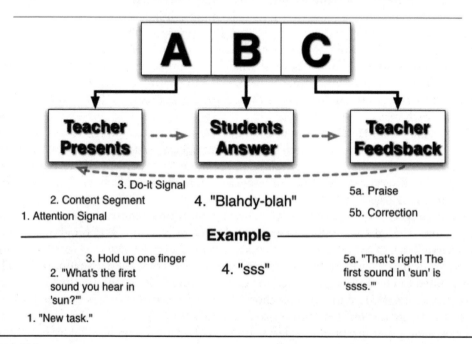

Figure 16.1

Providing Opportunities to Respond

Whether one calls it "active engagement," "practice," or "participation," having students respond during teaching is a critical part of *how* to teach. Opportunities to respond (OTR) are brief instructional probes where a teacher provides a prompt and students respond by sharing their knowledge and understanding of a topic. There are many ways to promote opportunities to respond. Examples of OTRs include answering an individual question, reading aloud, rephrasing a topic, answering by showing response cards, electronic response devices, and choral responding during a lesson.

Programs such as ClassWide Peer Tutoring increase the frequency of peer-to-peer responding. As Greenwood notes (Chapter 19) students who participated in CWPT engaged in conversations around academics and demonstrated higher achievement scores in addition to improved social behavior. Providing frequent opportunities to respond has even been shown to have beneficial side effects on social behavior (for examples, see Hirsch, Lloyd, & Kennedy, 2014). Bowman-Perrott and her colleagues reviewed evidence showing that CWPT has beneficial effects on both academic (Bowman-Perrott et al., 2013) and social-behavioral outcomes (Bowman-Perrott, Burke, Zhang, & Zaini, 2014).

Evaluating Responses

When students respond, teachers immediately have data they can evaluate for accuracy, allowing them to determine whether students are "getting it." In a sense, this is a first, less-formal stage of monitoring progress. Through the use of OTRs teachers can gauge whether students are grasping the topic and adjust their instruction. In addition to providing the teacher with immediate feedback on student performance it also enables the teacher to provide an immediate academic consequence (reinforcement or correction), a topic we return to in the very next subsection.

To evaluate the accuracy of students' answers, one must know the correct answer. For many academic learning activities, correct answers are obvious. However, it is important to note that having unambiguous questions help to make correct answering easier for students. Also, it is important to remember that asking opinion questions requires one to be prepared to accept lots of different answers!

Consequating Responses

Once a student or a group of students has responded and the teacher has evaluated the accuracy of the answer, the time is ripe for consequences. Should we increase the probability of that response recurring? If so, then reinforce it. That is, if a student responds correctly to the teacher prompt, a behavior specific praise statement should be made directly to the student(s). However, if a student does not respond or responds incorrectly, a correction should be made (within seconds).

Providing corrections is a critical part of teaching. When a learner makes a mistake, the teacher has excellent evidence that there is a need for instruction. Corrections do not have to be harsh or discouraging. Indeed, if done well, they empower the student to be able to answer correctly the next time the task is presented. And, a good correction sequence should provide several opportunities to answer the missed item very soon after the correction.

There are two basic kinds of mistakes. One is a fact mistake; the learner does not know an answer or gives the wrong answer. The other is a performance or procedural mistake; the learner does not know how to form a response or how to complete a sequence of steps, for example. Box 16.1 provides illustrations of corrections for each of these two types of mistakes

---

Box 16.1 Corrections

Here is an example of a correction sequence for a fact mistake. In this example, the student is simply learning to say a sound for a given letter:

Teacher: What sound does this letter make (pointing to *s*)?
Student: *No Response*
Teacher: /s/, This letter makes the sound /s/. What sound does this letter make (pointing to *s*)?
Student: ssss.
Teacher: Yes! That's it. /s/!

Here is an example of a correction sequence for a performance mistake. In this example, the student is learning to spread semi-soft foods such as peanut butter or mayonnaise on bread; there are many parts to the task including scooping the appropriate amount from the container, holding the spreader level while moving it to the bread, starting at the edge of the bread, distributing the food evenly while spreading it, and so forth. Because many of these steps involve physical movements, the teacher cannot simply tell the student how to correct an error, but must guide the student manually. Although it is possible to put the food onto the middle of the bread and then spread it, suppose that the protocol indicates that the student should start at the edge of the bread, but the student presses too hard as he applies the spread, causing food to squirt off the edges of the bread:

Teacher: Ooops. Where do you start spreading?
Student: At the edge.
Teacher: Yes! You start at the edge. Touch the edge with your spreader.
Student: [Positions the spreader on the edge of the bread away from his non-dominant hand.]
Teacher: Good positioning. And you spread smoothly [teacher may provide hand-on-hand guidance, demonstrating smooth, slow, even spreading]. Good. Let's do it again [teacher provides guidance only by lightly touching the back of the student's hand]. That was smooooooth spreading. One more time [teacher gently guides from the student's elbow, as student practices smooth, slow, even spreading]. Right! Now, all by yourself. Get a scoop and spread it smoothly.
Student: [Scoops food, positions the spreader on the edge of the bread away from his non-dominant hand, and spreads contents onto the bread.] Like that?
Teacher: Yes! That's the way you do it. That's the way you *spread* food on the *bread*.

Note that there are many ways that a teacher might provide guidance in a situation such as the one described here. The physical prompt (hand-on-hand guidance) might not be the best choice in some circumstances, and the graduated fading illustrated in this correction might have been previously introduced over many practice opportunities. For more about using and fading prompts, consult texts on behavior analysis and management (e.g., Alberto & Troutman, 2012).

EVALUATING

The third ingredient in our teaching pie is evaluating students' learning. Not only should one evaluate individual responses, but there should be evaluation of learning outcomes at a higher level, too. How do students with disabilities participate in evaluations? Some of the ways of evaluating outcomes in education are closely related to teaching. For example, teachers use progress monitoring systems to assess students' learning as it is developing. Also, many students with disabilities participate in the high-stakes testing that has become common in education in the U.S.

Monitoring Progress

The integration of assessment systems into the classroom enables teachers to track student performance systematically to determine if the learner understands the content material. Researchers have developed formative assessment measures that are employed frequently to determine a students' response to instruction (Deno, 1985; Deno & Mirkin, 1977; Hosp, Hosp, & Howell, 2007). Thus, formative assessment can be referred to as "assessment *for* learning" (Torgesen & Miller, 2009) instead of "assessment *of* learning" (Hosp, 2012). Formative assessment occurs at the same time as instruction using general outcome measures (e.g., oral reading fluency). A major benefit of formative assessment is that it does not take a much time away from instruction (Linn & Baker, 1996; Wilson & Sloane, 2000). Curriculum-based measures (CBM) are used to track student progress over the course of a brief period of time (e.g., Deno, 1985; Deno & Mirkin, 1977; Hosp et al., 2007).

Recording data while teaching provides a record of student responses and the instructional approach that was utilized and yields information that can be used to guide future instruction and track educational goals. For students who are receiving targeted interventions such data are required to show progress over time—progress data that are important for the individual education programs (IEPs) for students who receive special education services. Not only does the integration of assessment systems into the classroom enable teachers to track student performance and show progress for instructional decision-making, but such data provide feedback to the students, parents, administrators, or other IEP stakeholders. This integrated approach links instruction directly to progress monitoring variables (Wilson & Sloane, 2000).

Meeting Standards

Since the passage of No Child Left Behind (2002) and the reauthorization of the Individuals with Disabilities Education Act, schools and their students are more engaged with and accountable for high-stakes testing than ever in our history. Previously, students with disabilities were exempted from performance accountability on high-stakes testing; today, most students with disabilities are required to pass the same standards-based assessments as their general education peers. Moreover, as more states adopt the Common Core State Standards (CCSS; 44 states, the District of Columbia, and four territories have adopted the CCSS as of the time we wrote this chapter; http://www.corestandards.org), their students will be required to master and apply benchmark skills in English language arts (i.e., literacy) and mathematics.

In an ideal world, special education would be so effective that it would cause the consequences of disability to be insignificant—students with disabilities would benefit so much from special education that they would meet the standards for their grade and would pass the high-stakes tests in the same numbers as their non-disabled peers. As Thurlow notes in Chapter 20, however, students with disabilities do not achieve as highly or have outcomes similar to those of their peers, but we can do much to improve the outcomes of students with disabilities beyond what those outcomes would be were they to receive no special education or to receive shoddy special education.

HOW IS SPECIAL EDUCATION PRACTICED?

An answer to the question of how special education is practiced is multifaceted, but Bateman's (1971; 2007) OTTER model and our *teaching pie* provide direction for how to do it well. One of the themes that resonates through this section is that our field knows how to practice special education effectively. We have the science to plan, instruct, and evaluate. We have the tools and the processes. The authors of chapters in this section discuss some contemporary issues surrounding using these tools and implementing these processes well.

SHANNA EISNER HIRSCH'S SUGGESTIONS FOR FURTHER READING

Bruhn, A. L., Hirsch, S. E., Gorsh, J., & Hannan, C. (2014). Simple strategies for reflecting on and responding to common criticisms of PBIS. *Journal of Special Education Leadership*, 27, 13–25.

Bruhn, A. L., Lane, K. L., & Hirsch, S. E. (2013). A review of Tier 2 interventions conducted within multi-tiered models of behavioral prevention. *Journal of Emotional Behavior Disorders, 22,* 171–189. doi:10.1177/1063426613476092.

Hirsch, S. E., Ennis, R. P., & McDaniel, S. C. (2014). Student self-graphing as a strategy to increase teacher effectiveness and student motivation. *Beyond Behavior, 22*(3), 31–39.

Lane, K. L., Bruhn, A. L., Eisner, S. L., & Kalberg, J. R. (2010). Score reliability and validity of the Student Risk Screening Scale: A psychometrically-sound, feasible tool for use in urban middle schools. *Journal of Emotional and Behavioral Disorders, 18,* 211–224.

Lane, K. L., Eisner, S. L., Kretzer, J. M., Bruhn, A.L., Crnobori, M. E., Funke, L. M., . . . Casey, A. M. (2009). Outcomes of functional assessment-based interventions for students with and at risk for emotional and behavioral disorders in a job-share setting. *Education and Treatment of Children, 32,* 573–604.

Lane, K. L., Oakes, W. P., Ennis, R. P., & Hirsch, S. E. (2014). Identifying students for secondary and tertiary prevention efforts: How do we determine which students have Tier 2 and Tier 3 needs? *Preventing School Failure, 58,* 171–182.

REFERENCES

Adams, M. J. (1990). *Learning to read: Thinking and learning about print.* Cambridge, MA: MIT Press.

Alberto, P. A., & Troutman, A. C. (2012). *Applied behavior analysis for teachers* (9th ed.). Boston, MA: Pearson.

Arter, J. A., & Jenkins, J. R. (1977). Examining the benefits and prevalence of modality considerations in special education. *The Journal of Special Education, 11,* 281–298.

Arter, J. A., & Jenkins, J. R. (1979). Differential diagnosis—prescriptive teaching: A critical appraisal. *Review of Educational Research, 49,* 517–555.

Bateman, B. (1967). Three approaches to diagnosis and educational planning for children with learning disabilities. *Academic Therapy Quarterly, 2,* 215–222.

Bateman, B. D. (1971). *Essentials of teaching.* Sioux Falls, SD: Adapt Press.

Bateman, B. D. (2007). *Elements of teaching: A best practices handbook for beginning teachers.* Verona, WS: Attainment.

Becker, W. C. (1977). Teaching reading and language to the disadvantaged: What we have learned from field research. *Harvard Educational Review, 47,* 518–543.

Becker, W. C., & Carnine, D. W. (1981). Direct Instruction: A behavior theory model for comprehensive intervention with the disadvantaged. In S. W. Bijou & R. Ruiz (Eds.), *Behavior modification: Contributions to education* (pp. 145–210). Hillsdale, NJ: Erlbaum.

Becker, W. C., Engelmann, S., & Thomas, D. R. (1971). *Teaching: A course in applied psychology* (Vol. 1). Chicago: Science Research Associates.

Borman, G., Slavin, R. E., Cheung, A., Chamberlain, A., Madden, N. A., & Chambers, B. (2007). Final reading outcomes of the national randomized field trial of Success for All. *American Educational Research Journal, 44*, 701–731.

Bowman-Perrott, L., Burke, M. D., Zhang, N., & Ziani, S. (2014). Direct and collateral effects of peer tutoring on social behavioral outcomes: A meta-analysis of single-case research. *School Psychology Review, 43*, 260–285.

Bowman-Perrott, L., Davis, H., Vannest, K., Williams, L., Greenwood, C., & Parker, R. (2013). Academic benefits of peer tutoring: A meta-analytic review of single-case research. *School Psychology Review, 42*, 39–55.

Bradshaw, C., Reinke, W., Brown, L., Bevans, K., & Leaf, P. (2008). Implementation of school-wide positive behavioral interventions and supports (PBIS) in elementary schools: Observations from a randomized trial. *Education and Treatment of Children, 31*, 1–26.

Brophy, J. & Good. T. L. (1986). Teacher behavior and student achievement. In M. C. Whittrock (Ed.), *Handbook of Research on Teaching* (3rd ed.). New York: Macmillan.

Carnine, D. (1980). Relationships between stimulus variation and the formation of misconceptions. *Journal of Educational Research, 74*(2), 106–110.

Carnine, D. W. (1976). Similar sounds separation and cumulative introduction in learning letter sound correspondences. *Journal of Educational Research, 69*, 368–372.

Chall, J. C. (1967). *Learning to read: The great debate; an inquiry into the science, art, and ideology of old and new methods of teaching children to read, 1910–1965.* New York: McGraw-Hill.

Cronbach, L. J., & Snow, R. E. (1977). *Aptitudes and instructional methods.* New York: Irvington.

Cook, B. G., & Schirmer, B. R. (2003). What is special about special education? Overview and analysis. *The Journal of Special Education, 37*, 200–205.

Deno, S. L. (1985). Curriculum-based measurement: The emerging alternative. *Exceptional Children, 52*, 219–232.

Deno, S. L., & Mirkin, P. K. (1977). Developing curriculum-based measurement systems for databased special education problem solving. *Focus on Exceptional Children, 19*(8), 1–16.

Engelmann, S. (1968). The effectiveness of direct verbal instruction on IQ performance and achievement in reading and arithmetic. In J. Hellmuth (Ed.), *Disadvantaged child* (Vol. 3; pp. 339–361). New York: Brunner/Mazel.

Engelmann, S. (1979). Theory of mastery and acceleration. In J. W. Lloyd, E. J. Kameenui, & D. Chard (Eds.), *Issues in educating students with disabilities* (pp. 177–195). Mahway, NJ: Erlbaum.

Engelmann, S., & Carnine, D. (1982). *Theory of instruction: Principles and applications.* New York: Irvington.

Engelmann, S., & Carnine, D. (2011). *Could John Stuart Mill have saved our schools?* Verona, WI: Full Court.

Garrison, S. C., & Heard, M. T. (1931). An experimental study of the value of phonetics. *Peabody Journal of Education, 9*(1), 9–14.

Gersten, R., Keating, T., & Becker, W. C. (1988). The continued impact of the Direct Instruction Model: Longitudinal studies of Follow Through students. *Education & Treatment of Children, 11*, 318–327.

Greer, R. D. (1994). The measure of a teacher. In R. Gardner, D. M. Sainato, J. O. Cooper, W. L. Heward, J. Eschelman, & T. A. Grossi (Eds.), *Behavior analysis in education: Focus on measurably superior instruction* (pp. 225–248). Pacific Grove, CA: Brooks/Cole.

Greer, R. D., & McDonough, S. H. (1999). Is the learn unit a fundamental measure of pedagogy? *The Behavior Analyst, 22*, 5–16.

Hallahan, D. P., Kauffman, J. M., & Pullen, P. C. (2012). *Exceptional learners: An introduction to special education* (12th ed). Columbus, OH: Pearson.

Hirsch, S. E., Lloyd, J. W., & Kennedy, M. J. (2014) Improving behavior through instructional practices for students with high incidence disabilities: EBD, ADHD, and LD. In P. Garner, J. M. Kauffman, & J. Elliott (Eds.) *Sage handbook of emotional & behavioral difficulties* (2nd ed.; pp. 205–220). London: Sage.

Hosp, J. L. (2012). Formative evaluation: Developing a framework for using assessment data to plan instruction. *Focus on Exceptional Children, 44*(9), 1–11.

Hosp, M., Hosp, J., & Howell, K. (2007). *The ABCs of CBM: A practical guide to curriculum-based measurement.* New York: Guilford Press.

Kauffman, J. M., Mostert, M. P., Trent, S. C., & Pullen, P. L. (2006). *Identifying behavior problems. Managing classroom behavior: A reflective case-based approach* (4th ed.). Upper Saddle River, NJ: Pearson.

Kavale, K. A., & Forness, S. R. (1987). Substance over style: A quantitative synthesis assessing the efficacy of modality testing and teaching. *Exceptional Children, 54*, 228–234.

Landrum, T., & Landrum, K. M. (2014). Learning styles. *Current Practice Alerts*, 21, 1–5. Retrieved from http://TeachingLD.org/alerts.

Lane, K. L., Menzies, H. M, Oakes, W. P., & Kalberg, J. R. (2012). *Systematic screenings of behavior to support instruction: From preschool to high school.* New York: Guilford Press.

Linn, R., & Baker, E. (1996). Can performance-based student assessments be psychometrically sound? In J. B. Baron & D. P. Wolf (Eds.), *Performance-based student assessment: Challenges and possibilities. Ninety-fifth yearbook of the National Society for the Study of Education* (pp. 84–103). Chicago: University of Chicago Press.

Lloyd, J. W. (1984). How shall we individualize instruction—or should we? *Remedial and Special Education, 5*(1), 7–15.

Lloyd, J. W., & Hallahan, D. P. (2005). Going forward: How the field of learning disabilities has and will contribute to education. *Learning Disability Quarterly, 28*, 133–136.

Mann, L. (1971). Psychometric phrenology and the new faculty psychology: The case against ability assessment and training. *The Journal of Special Education, 5*, 3–14.

Marchand-Martella, N. E., Slocum, T. A., & Martella, R. C. (2004). *Introduction to Direct Instruction.* Boston: Pearson.

Murawski, W. W., & Spencer, S. A. (2011). *Collaborate, communicate, and differentiate! How to do it all in today's k-12 inclusive classroom.* Thousand Oaks, CA: Corwin.

National Institute of Child Health and Human Development (2000). Report of the National Reading Panel: Teaching children to read: An evidenced based assessment of the scientific research literature on reading and its implications for instruction. Washing DC: National Institute of Child Health and Human Development. Retrieved from http://www.nichd.nih.gov/publications/pubs/nrp/pages/smallbook.aspx.

O'Leary, K. D., & Becker, W. C. (1968). The effects of the intensity of a teacher's reprimands on children's behavior. *Journal of School Psychology, 7*, 8–11.

Pashler, H., McDaniel, M., Rohrer, D., & Bjork, R. (2008). Learning styles: Concepts and evidence. *Psychological Science in the Public Interest, 9*, 106–119.

Przychodzin-Havis, A. M., Marchand-Martella, N. E., Martella, R. C., Miller, D. A., Warner, L., Leonard, B., & Chapman, S. (2005). An analysis of Corrective Reading research. *Journal of Direct Instruction, 5*, 37–65.

Roberts, G., Torgesen, J. K., Boardman, A., & Scammacca, N. (2008). Evidenced-based strategies for reading instruction of older students with LD or risk for LD. *Learning Disabilities Research & Practice, 44*, 439–454.

Rosenshine, B., & Stevens, R. (1986). Teaching functions. In M. C. Whittrock (Ed.), *Handbook of research on teaching* (3rd ed.). New York: Macmillan.

Slavin, R. E., Madden, N.A., Dolan, L. J., Wasik, B. A., Ross, S., Smith, L., & Dianda, M. (1996). Success for All: A summary of research. *Journal of Education for Students Placed at Risk, 1*, 41–76.

Slavin, R. E., & Stevens, R. J. (1991). Cooperative learning and mainstreaming. In J. W. Lloyd, N. N. Singh, & A. C. Repp (Eds.), *The regular education initiative: Alternative perspectives on concepts, issues, and models* (pp. 177–191). Sycamore, IL: Sycamore.

Smith, T. (2001). Discrete trial training in the treatment of autism. *Focus on Autism and Other Developmental Disabilities, 16*, 86–92.

Stein, M., Carnine, D., & Dixon, R. (1998). Direct instruction: Integrating curriculum design and effective teaching practice. *Intervention in School and Clinic, 33*, 227–234.

Torgesen, J. K., & Miller, D. H. (2009). *Assessments to guide adolescent literacy instruction.* Portsmouth, NH: RMC Research Corporation, Center on Instruction.

Williams, J., & Ackerman. M. (1971). Simultaneous and successive discrimination of similar letters. *Journal of Educational Psychology, 62*, 132–137.

Wilson, M., & Sloane, K. (2000). From principles to practice: An embedded assessment system. *Applied Measurement in Education, 13*, 181–208.

Ysseldyke, J. (1973). Diagnostic-prescriptive teaching: The search for aptitude-treatment interactions. In L. Mann & D. A. Sabatino (Eds.), *First review of special education* (Vol. 1, pp. 3–31). New York: Grune & Stratton.

Getting to Know Bryan G. Cook

When I went to college (UC Santa Barbara), I had no idea what I wanted to do professionally. I studied philosophy because those classes interested me the most. Toward the end of my junior year, it dawned on me that I was virtually unemployable. After a few twists and turns, I volunteered at a local residential facility and ended up working there for years. I worked with individuals who ranged from young children to adolescents and young adults; who had disabilities ranging from very mild to very severe; and in classroom, residential, and community settings. I had the good fortune to be invited to be involved with a research grant that my mentors—Drs. Mel Semmel and Michael Gerber—had investigating the effects of school environments on students with disabilities. I started part-time, entering data and running factor analyses, before I really knew what it all meant, but found that I loved data, research, and scholarship, and I soon enrolled full-time as a doc student at UCSB.

Most of the special education practitioners and researchers I know feel a strong tie to a disability (e.g., learning disabilities), a content area (e.g., reading), or both. Maybe it's my philosophy background, or maybe I'm just afraid to commit, but I've always found myself interested in "big ideas" that cut across disability and content areas. Evidence-based practice is one of these big ideas. It addresses core issues in research and practice—How do we know what works? How can research and practice inform one another? How do we translate research to practice? How does one determine credible research, both within and across studies? These questions defy simple answers, which can make working in the area of evidence-based practice frustrating at times; but it also makes it interesting.

17

HOW SHOULD EVIDENCE-BASED PRACTICES BE DETERMINED?

Bryan G. Cook

Evidence-based practices (EBPs) represent an appealing and logical approach for improving the outcomes of students with disabilities. The EBP movement is the latest approach for identifying and prioritizing the most effective instructional practices. EBPs differ from previous attempts to identify effective practices in that they require support from multiple, high-quality research studies. Such support provides educators considerable confidence in their general effectiveness. As Slavin (2002) suggested, identifying and pervasively implementing the most effective practices in schools—as opposed to the all-too-common scenario of ineffective instruction being used while effective practices are eschewed or misapplied—has the potential to revolutionize education. The prospect of EBPs positively impacting student outcomes is probably greatest in special education, as children and youth with disabilities typically require the most effective instruction to achieve desired outcomes (see Dammann & Vaughn, 2001). Yet, despite the considerable potential of EBPs, they are commonly misunderstood and frequently ignored in special education.

As is true for many things in education, the devil of EBPs is in the details (Odom et al., 2005). As I discuss in this chapter, EBPs raise a host of vexing issues; and people often ignore and mistrust what they do not understand. Moreover, when it comes to determining what works in their classrooms and with their students, many teachers are understandably dubious of the claims of researchers who have typically not taught in a classroom in many years. Accordingly, although few special educators are against the concept of using practices shown by bodies of high-quality research to be effective, many don't really understand or trust EBPs—and therefore tend to ignore them.

The primary focus in the chapter is to explore issues related to EBPs, especially how EBPs are identified, so that readers better understand EBPs and why they should be prioritized in policy and practice. To contextualize the identification of EBPs, I first discuss (a) what EBPs are and (b) why they are important. Then, after discussing issues regarding how EBPs are identified, I end the chapter by exploring some important issues regarding consideration and use of EBPs.

WHAT ARE EVIDENCE-BASED PRACTICES?

Confusion and disagreement exist regarding many aspects of EBPs, even as to what the term means. At issue are (a) whether the term EBP refers to specific instructional practices or a general approach to teaching and (b) what standards must be met for a practice to be considered evidence-based?

Terminology

When I talk to special educators about EBPs, I hear the term EBP being used in at least three different, albeit related, ways: (a) specific instructional practices supported as effective by credible, external sources, (b) specific instructional practices supported by a body of research that meets prescribed standards of rigor—which is how I use the term, and (c) an approach to teaching that incorporates practices supported by research.

Since I started working in special education in the late 1980s, I've heard and used a variety of terms— such as best practices, recommended practices, research-based practices, and now EBPs—to refer to practices believed to work. Unfortunately these

> "The prospect of EBPs positively impacting student outcomes is probably the greatest in special education, as children and youth with disabilities typically require the most effective instruction to achieve desired outcomes."

terms have been used indiscriminately, leading to confusion as to what they mean. For example, no criteria exist for identifying best practices; that is, anyone can call something a best practice for virtually any reason (e.g., expert opinion, tradition, personal experience; Cook & Cook, 2013). Indeed, best and recommended practices often refer to instructional approaches without substantive research support (Peters & Heron, 1993). Similarly, although the phrase research-based practice clearly connotes that a practice is supported by research, a low-quality study can be found (e.g., on the internet) to support virtually any practice. In a sense, then, many ineffective practices might be considered to be research-based. Although I believe it is an incorrect use of the term, it is important to recognize that when many special educators talk about EBPs, they are using it as the most recent "phrase de jour" for preferred instructional practice—synonymous with best, recommended, and research-based practices—that may or may not actually be effective.

Another aspect of confusion regarding EBP is whether the term refers to (a) a particular instructional practice (e.g., "I used an evidence-based practice in class today") or (b) a general approach to teaching that incorporates these practices (e.g., "I engage in evidence-based practice")—what Eddy (2005) referred to as evidence-based decision making. EBP is commonly used both ways and I believe that either use is defensible. The latter use of EBP (i.e., evidence-based decision making) has the advantage of considering the broader context and multiple dimensions of instructional decision making beyond research support. Indeed, many of the foundational works regarding EBP emphasize an instructional approach that integrates research evidence with professional wisdom/ expertise and cultural values (e.g., Sackett, Rosenberg, Gray, Haynes, & Richardson, 1996; Whitehurst, 2002). However, this definition of EBP begs the question of how to determine which practices are supported by sufficient research evidence to use. For the sake of clarity, I recommend using EBP to refer to specific practices supported by trustworthy bodies of research, and phrases such as "evidence-based special education" to refer to a broader instructional approach that emphasizes these practices.

My colleagues and I have suggested that EBPs refer to specific instructional practices identified as effective on the basis of four aspects of the supporting research base: research design, quantity, quality, and effect size (e.g., Cook, Tankersley, Cook, & Landrum, 2008). These principles are consistent with how EBPs are identified in special (Gersten et al., 2005; Horner et al., 2005) and general (see What Works Clearinghouse [WWC], 2011) education.

Dimensions of EBPs

Although it is beyond the scope of this chapter to explore each dimension of EBPs in depth, it is important that readers understand why research design, quantity, quality, and effect size of supporting research are important for trusting that a practice is generally effective.

> "I recommend using EBP to refer to specific practices supported by trustworthy bodies of research, and phrases such as 'evidence-based special education' to refer to a broader instructional approach that emphasizes these practices."

How a research study is designed determines what type of information it produces and what types of questions it addresses. For example, observational and correlational research help special educators understand what occurs in classrooms, how teachers and other stakeholders feel about issues and practices, and how different variables (e.g., gender and incidence of behavioral disorders) relate to one another. However, these research approaches are not designed to determine whether a practice causes changes in student outcomes (see Cook & Cook, 2008; McDuffy & Scruggs, 2008). Design features of group experiments (e.g., comparing performance of a group who receives an intervention to that of a group of similar participants who are taught under the same conditions with the exception of the intervention) and single-subject research (e.g., examining changes in the performance of individuals over time as the researcher systematically introduces and withdraws the intervention) provide research consumers confidence that any observed changes in student performance are caused by the practice (Cook et al., 2008). Therefore, it is generally agreed that group experiments (with participants randomly assigned to groups), group quasi-experiments (with groups assigned non-randomly), and single-subject research should be used to identify EBPs (e.g., Gersten et al., 2005; Horner et al., 2005). Note that throughout this chapter, I will refer to studies using these designs collectively as experimental research.

The quality and quantity of supporting research are critical considerations when identifying EBPs. Although rigorous, trustworthy studies are conducted and disseminated regularly in special education, it is important to recognize that (a) many studies are not trustworthy and (b) no study is perfect. In fact, Ioannidis (2005) has shown that many studies likely produce false findings. One of the primary factors related to the accuracy of a study's findings is its methodological quality (e.g., Simmerman & Swanson, 2001). That is, high-quality studies are more trustworthy. Moreover, because no study—at least so far as I can imagine—is perfect, special educators should not make up their minds regarding the effectiveness of a practice on the basis of a single study, regardless of study quality. As such, decisions regarding what works (i.e., identification of EBPs) should be made on the basis of multiple, high-quality (experimental) studies.

Finally, EBPs should have meaningful, positive effects on student outcomes, not trivial or (obviously) negative effects. Although different approaches exist for gauging whether the effect of a practice across multiple studies (e.g., meta-analysis of effect sizes, counting the number of studies showing positive effects) is sufficient for the practice to be considered an EBP, the underlying intent is the same—to ensure that EBPs positively and meaningfully impact student performance.

In this chapter, then, EBPs mean specific instructional practices supported by multiple, high-quality, experimental studies as having meaningfully positive effects on learner outcomes. Now that we have a handle on what EBPs mean, let's turn to why EBPs are important.

WHY ARE EBPs IMPORTANT?

Although student outcomes are influenced by myriad factors, the instructional practices with which they are taught clearly play an important role in student learning. Unfortunately, a significant research-to-practice gap exists in special education (e.g., Carnine, 1997), in which ineffective practices are used regularly yet many practices shown to be effective are used incorrectly if at all. One of the factors underlying the research-to-practice gap is the lack of a common and clear understanding of which practices really work.

As Benjamin Bloom eloquently opined:

In education, . . . myth and reality are not clearly differentiated, and we frequently prefer the former to the latter . . . If I could have one wish for education . . . it would be the systematic ordering of our basic knowledge in such a way that what is known and true can be acted on, while what is superstition, fad, and myth can be recognized as such and used when there is nothing else to support us in our frustration and despair.
(as cited in Sloane, 2008, p. 42)

In the absence of commonly accepted guidelines for determining what works, special educators without the time and expertise to analyze the research literature for each instructional decision they face have been unable to consistently distinguish valid from bogus instructional recommendations. The advent of the internet and its explosion of readily accessible information, although initially seen as a boon for educators, may actually serve to further confuse and exasperate most teachers. Just as the ancient mariner in Coleridge's (1817) poem lamented being surrounded by an ocean of water that he could not drink ("water, water everywhere, nor any drop to drink"), special educators find themselves with access to a sea of information that provides little reliable guidance for improving the effectiveness of their instruction.

This is the niche that the EBP movement fills—it reliably and transparently identifies practices as effective (and ineffective) on the basis of multiple, high-quality, experimental research studies. The EBP movement, which originated in the field of medication (Sackett et al., 1996) in response to the gap between practice and research findings in that field, is based on the premise that scientific research—not expert opinion, personal experience, or tradition—should be the primary gauge of effectiveness. EBPs, then, represent a more rigorous approach for identifying effective practices for special educators than had previously existed. And knowing what really works is a prerequisite for providing optimally effective teaching.

Although EBPs have the potential to improve the performance of all students, they may be of particular importance in special education for at least two reasons. First, special education appears to be particularly vulnerable to "silver bullet fads" because of the fervent and heartfelt desires of family members and educators to successfully remediate the effects of disabilities. Without a reliable framework for determining what really works (i.e., EBPs), considerable expense, time, and hope can be squandered on fads and snake oil cures. Second, whereas students without disabilities will often succeed despite less-than-effective instruction, students with disabilities typically require the most effective instruction (i.e., EBPs) to succeed (Dammann & Vaughn, 2001).

> "One of the factors underlying the research-to-practice gap is the lack of common and clear understanding of which practices really work."

It is important to recognize that science is imperfect, and invalid and misleading studies are not uncommon (Ioannidis, 2005). In fact, some educators feel that science, and EBPs based on scientific research, should not hold a privileged status and may actually do more harm than good (e.g., Hammersley, 2005). Nevertheless, scientific research is generally recognized as an unparalleled tool for determining what works and is responsible for amazing progress in any number of fields (Kauffman, 1999; Slavin, 2002). One of the many strengths of science is that research studies are considered collectively and knowledge and theory are adjusted as findings accrue, enabling the correct findings to be recognized in the long run (Shermer, 2002). The existence of flawed scientific research is not unexpected and, rather than providing a reason to abandon science as a guide to knowledge, it suggests the importance of (a) conducting more and better scientific research and (b) making decisions based on multiple, high-quality research (i.e., by identifying EBPs).

Despite my enthusiasm for the role of science and research and determining what works, I concur with Whitehurst (2002) and other advocates of EBPs that science and EBPs should not be the sole factor considered when teachers determine what practices to use with their students. For example, if a teacher does not feel able to use a practice appropriately, knows from experience that a practice is not a good match for a particular student, or does not need to target the outcome promoted by the practice, that practice should not be used—regardless of whether it is an EBP. EBPs are simply tools that educators can use as guides for generally effective practices; they are not prescriptions that must be followed indiscriminately.

To make a fully informed decision regarding the role EBPs should play in determining what is taught in special education, special educators need to understand a variety of issues regarding what EBPs are and how they are identified.

How Should EBPs Be Identified?

EBPs are identified through an evidence-based review, a time-consuming process typically conducted by a team of scholars. In an evidence-based review, scholars

- Delineate the practice to be reviewed (e.g., repeated reading), the targeted outcome (e.g., reading comprehension), and the population of focus (e.g., students with learning disabilities)
- Conduct an exhaustive search of the literature for relevant research studies
- Review identified studies to select only those that (a) use an appropriate research design and (b) are of high methodological quality, which is typically determined by evaluating studies using a checklist of "quality indicators" (see Gersten et al., 2005 and Horner et al., 2005 for lists of quality indicators in special education)

- Apply standards regarding the quantity of research and effect sizes to determine if the practice is an EBP

As evidence-based reviews are a relatively new phenomenon in general and special education, it is perhaps not surprising that a number of issues remain to be resolved as to how EBPs are identified in special education.

What is a Practice in EBPs?

Cook and Cook (2013) noted that, "broad policies (e.g., inclusion, transition), instructional frame-works (e.g., universal design for learning), and educational philosophies (constructivism, behaviorism)" (p. 76) should not be considered as foci of an evidence-based review because they are not defined by concrete, operationalized instructional procedures. That is, to meaningfully determine whether a practice is effective across multiple high-quality studies, it is necessary that the same practice is being investigated across the studies (Horner, Sugai, & Anderson, 2010). Policies, frameworks, and philosophies tend to vary considerably in different settings and in different studies. For example, inclusion should not be considered a practice, because it is difficult to define and is implemented in different ways across studies. However, instructional practices or programs that are based on a policy, instructional framework, or educational philosophy can be the target of an evidence-based review, so long as the practice is defined by a set of concrete, operationalized instructional procedures.

Educators may also hear the phrase evidence-based programs used more or less synonymously with evidence-based practice. Programs generally refer to curricula or manualized instructional approaches that prescribe materials and instructional procedures. Programs tend to be the primary focus of EBPs in general education—probably because of general educators' focus on classrooms of students. In contrast, discrete, specific practices that can be used somewhat flexibly within programs (e.g., mnemonics, self-monitoring) receive more attention in special education, probably because of special educators' focus on adapting instruction to the needs of individual children. EBPs, then, can and do refer to both evidence-based programs and practices, which does not present a problem so long as the program or practice has a defined set of instructional procedures.

How High Should the Bar be Set?

The stringency of criteria related to research design, quality of studies, quantity of studies, and effect size is among the most critical and vexing issues in identifying EBPs. On one hand, a fundamental purpose of EBPs is to avoid considering practices as effective when they really are not (e.g., a Type I error), which argues for setting a high bar. However, setting the bar too high runs the risk of not identifying practices as EBPs that are actually effective—a Type II error. How high the bar should be set for supporting evidence should be a function of one's primary purpose. If one's goal is to identify all potentially effective practices, then a low bar that avoids Type II errors is appropriate. In contrast, I believe the primary purpose of the EBP movement is to provide educators with a trustworthy guide to practices that truly work, and thus should conservatively set a high bar that greatly reduces Type I errors. Although I feel that the bar for EBP criteria should be set high, this begs the question of "how high?" Issues related to how high the bar should be set exist along each of the four primary dimensions of EBPs (i.e., research design, quality, quantity, effect).

Research design. Because the essential question addressed in evidence-based reviews is, "does the practice cause meaningful gains in student outcomes?" only research designs from which causality can be inferred are considered. So far as I know, all approaches for identifying EBPs consider true group experiments, in which participants are randomly assigned to either the experimental group (which receives the intervention) or the control group (which receives typical instruction). These true experiments (or randomized controlled trials) are generally considered to be the strongest research design in terms of establishing causality (e.g., Harris et al., 2001). Should other research designs designed to establish causality, such as quasi-experimental group studies and single-subject research studies, but which are subject to more threats to validity than true experiments also be considered in evidence-based reviews?

> "The primary purpose of the EBP movement is to provide educators with a trustworthy guide to practices that truly work, and thus should conservatively set a high bar that greatly reduces Type I errors."

Because individuals are not randomly assigned to groups in quasi-experimental group studies, any differences in student performance observed between groups may be due to pre-existing differences in the groups, not because of the practice. As such, quasi-experimental studies are typically required to show that groups are meaningfully equivalent to be considered in an EBP review, and more group quasi-experiments may be required in support of EBPs than true experiments (e.g., Gersten et al., 2005). Well-designed and well-conducted group quasi-experiments (e.g., participants in groups matched on relevant variables, differences between groups assessed and statistically adjusted for) have been shown to generally yield findings similar to true experiments (Slavin, 2008). As such, it seems reasonable to me to include high quality group quasi-experimental studies when identifying EBPs, especially because results must be replicated across multiple studies.

Single-subject research studies establish causality using intra-individual comparison (e.g., comparing an individual's outcomes in the presence and absence of the intervention over time; Kazdin, 2011). However, because single-subject research studies typically involve a small number of individuals (e.g., three), they are not considered by some approaches for identifying EBPs in general education. Special educators have a long tradition of using single-subject research to investigate the effects of a practice on individual students. As such, it is not surprising that single-subject studies are considered when identifying EBPs in special education (e.g., Horner et al., 2005). A larger number of high-quality single-subject studies (e.g., five) supporting a practice is usually required for identification of an EBP due to the low number of individuals typically involved in these studies, which seems perfectly reasonable to me.

Scholars generally agree that qualitative research is not designed to establish causality (see McDuffy & Scruggs, 2008). For example, teachers might report that a practice is effective, and observations might also indicate that students are learning more after the practice was implemented. However, qualitative research is not designed to address the possibility that another factor (e.g., change in scheduling) was responsible for change in student performance, or that student performance would have improved just as much (or more) without the practice. Therefore, in my opinion, qualitative research clearly should not be used to identify EBPs. However, most approaches for identifying EBPs do not examine whether EBPs are generally acceptable to teachers or have been implemented with fidelity (i.e., as designed) under typical and varied conditions. Thus, qualitative research can play an important role in the EBP movement by generating knowledge about how teachers and other stakeholders feel about specific EBPs, which EBPs have been implemented successfully over time and which tend to be abandoned (and why), and how special educators have adapted EBPs successfully to meet the unique needs of their students.

Quality. Low-quality studies are prone to both Type I and Type II errors. For example, high attrition in a group experimental study might artificially inflate or deflate results, depending on who leaves the study. In essence, "rigor matters" (Confrey, 2006, p. 200) when evaluating the validity of study findings. In evidence-based reviews, quality of research studies typically is assessed by evaluating the presence of "quality indicators" that researchers believe are important for a study to be trustworthy.

Considerable agreement exists among researchers regarding some central tenets of high-quality research—for example, control and experimental groups must be comparable in group comparison studies, the baseline must consist of multiple points that show a consistent trend in single-subject research, and the practice must be implemented with fidelity. However, less conformity exists regarding whether and which additional quality indicators must be addressed for a study to be truly trustworthy (e.g., outcome measures are reliable and valid, interventionists are comparable across conditions, a minimum number of participants are involved, the practice is implemented for a minimum length of time). EBP reviews should not require so many quality indicators that researchers must conduct perfect (or nearly perfect) studies. Conducting perfect studies is neither likely nor necessary; sound but imperfect research can yield meaningful findings. Nonetheless, it is important that sufficient quality indicators be required so that EBPs are identified on the basis of truly trustworthy studies.

Quality indicators typically are established by a group of prominent researchers in a field. Despite the focus on high-quality research in the EBP movement, empirical evidence is seldom the basis on which quality indicators are established. In my opinion, rather than be based on the opinions of experts (which are often right, but sometimes wrong), quality indicators ideally should be demonstrably associated with study effects. For example, in their review of intervention research in the field of learning disabilities, Simmerman and Swanson (2001) reported that studies that did not report the reliability and validity of their outcome measures tended to report larger effect sizes. This suggests that trustworthy studies should be required to report adequate reliability and validity of their outcome measures. Hopefully, future meta-analytic research will provide empirical guidance regarding which aspects of research studies are reliably associated with effect sizes and should therefore be required as quality indicators.

In addition to determining which quality indicators to require, approaches for identifying EBPs must also specify whether all, or just some, of the quality indicators must be addressed. No study is perfect and if the bar is set too high, few or no studies will be deemed sufficiently trustworthy to support EBPs, resulting in few or no practices identified as EBPs. Accordingly, Gersten et al. (2005) allowed high-quality group experimental studies to not meet one essential quality indicator. Similarly, colleagues have suggested to me that it may be sufficient to require that a high-quality study address a certain proportion of quality indicators (e.g., 80 percent) or only the most important quality indicators. These are all reasonable solutions. However, if quality indicators are selected judiciously and truly represent elements of a study that are critical for trustworthy findings, these approaches open the door to the possibility of EBPs being identified on less than trustworthy studies. In my mind, quality indicators should be relatively few in number, restricted to those aspects of a research study that are truly critical for producing valid results, and should all be required; thereby ensuring that EBPs are supported by only the most trustworthy research.

Quantity. A fundamental tenet of science holds that the more often findings are replicated by independent research, the more confidence research consumers can have in them. How many supporting studies are sufficient for a practice to be considered an EBP? One is clearly insufficient, and although 10 or 15 supporting studies would provide educators with considerable confidence in the effectiveness of a practice, these numbers seem unnecessarily high and would relegate many effective practices with substantial research support to be deemed non-EBPs. Gersten et al. (2005) required that two high-quality group experiments (with random assignment) or four high-quality group quasi-experiments (without random assignment) support an EBP; and Horner et al. (2005) required that five single-subject studies support an EBP. These numbers seem reasonable to me. There is no perfect number of studies. If groups want to be very sure that EBPs are effective, they might require more; if the goal is to identify many practices that are promising, fewer studies might be required. Regardless of how many studies are required, it is important that educators are aware of how many studies (a) are required for an EBP and (b) actually support a particular practice, so that they can make informed decisions about how much to trust practices identified as EBPs.

> "Quality indicators should be relatively few in number, restricted to those aspects of a research study that are truly critical for producing valid results, and should all be required; thereby ensuring that EBPs are supported by on the most trustworthy research."

Approaches for identifying EBPs should also consider the number of studies showing neutral or negative effects of a practice (e.g., WWC, 2011). Focusing solely on the number of high-quality studies showing positive effects for a practice ignores the possibility that some high-quality studies might also show that the practice doesn't work or even does harm. Should one high-quality study showing that the practice does harm prohibit a practice from being identified as an EBP? This is the approach taken by the WWC. How many high-quality studies showing that the practice has no meaningful impact on student outcomes should be allowed for EBPs? Answers to these questions should be guided by the values and needs of a field. In my mind, it is important that no trustworthy evidence exists showing that EBPs do harm, and that the preponderance of high-quality studies show that EBPs have positive rather than neutral effects (perhaps at a ratio of at least 3:1).

Magnitude of effect. In group experimental research, effects of an intervention are commonly described using effect sizes. Cohen's d, which represents differences between groups in units of standard deviation, is probably the most frequently used effect size in group experiments. How much of an effect is necessary for an EBP? Gersten et al. (2005) recommended that any effect size significantly greater than zero is sufficient for an EBP. In contrast, on the basis of his analysis of over 800 meta-analyses in education, Hattie (2009) suggested that a d of 0.40 should be used to indicate meaningful effects, as this is the average effect of practices. He reasoned that truly effective practices should have at least an average effect, and that lower effects can be achieved primarily through time and typical instruction. The WWC (2011) takes a moderate position and requires $d > 0.25$ for substantively important positive effects.

Meaningful evaluation of effect sizes depends on a variety of factors, making a single criterion applied across and even within fields problematic (Cohen, 1988). Small changes in some outcomes (e.g., self-injurious behavior) might not be meaningful, whereas seemingly minor improvements in other outcomes (e.g., pre-reading skills) can be important. Similarly, larger effects should be expected when outcomes are measured directly after the intervention, as opposed to months or years later; and when using broad standardized, as opposed to specific, measures of achievement (Hill, Bloom, Black, & Lipsey, 2007). I harbor some trepidation about EBP reviewers setting their own criteria for positive effects, as reviewers might set inappropriately high or low standards. However, because of the vagaries associated with interpreting effect sizes, it seems that EBP reviewers should a priori determine, justify, and publicize their effect size criteria in light of the specific outcome measure and population targeted in their review.

Although different approaches can be used to calculate effect sizes for single-subject research (e.g., non-overlapping data between phases, regression models, multilevel models; see Parker, Vannest, & Davis, 2011), most approaches for identifying EBPs instead use visual analysis to gauge practice effects (e.g., Horner et al., 2005; WWC, 2011). Visual analysis involves holistically examining the graph(s) of participants' performance to determine whether the intervention (or practice) has experimental control over the outcome measure. Because experimental control does not necessarily require a particular degree or amount of change in outcomes, Horner et al. (2005) established a separate quality indicator to require that change in the outcome measure is "socially important" (p. 174). Conceptually, this makes sense, but it begs the question of what constitutes socially important change. Accordingly, I recommend that this quality indicator require that studies document socially important change using accepted procedures in single-subject research such as social comparison and subjective evaluation.

Evidence-based for Whom and Where?

The most effective practices tend to be generally effective, with positive effects that cut across a variety of student (e.g., age, gender, ethnicity, disability, language status) and environmental (e.g., classroom setting, community setting) characteristics. Nonetheless, one cannot assume that EBPs are effective for all types of learners in all types of settings. For example, a practice designed to work for infants with severe intellectual disabilities will not likely be equally effective, and may be inappropriate, for high school students with learning disabilities. Specifying the target population and setting for an evidence-based review helps guard against (a) overgeneralization of review findings and (b) errors in the review caused by including studies involving disparate populations and/or settings for which the practice has variable effects.

So, how wide a net should be cast in evidence-based reviews in terms of target population and setting? Cook, Tankersley, and Landrum (2009) recommended using common sense—that is, avoiding overly broad (e.g., all students with disabilities in any setting) and overly narrow (e.g., third grade, Hispanic girls with ADHD, predominantly inattentive type, in resource room settings) parameters—and empirical findings (e.g., an evidence-based review should be disability specific if research findings indicate that its effects vary by disability type) to guide parameters for evidence-based reviews. Typically, evidence-based reviews in special education are specific to a disability category (and/or at-risk status) and often include age-group parameters (see Cook et al., 2009), which seems reasonable in the absence of a compelling reason for setting more specific parameters (e.g., the practice is designed specifically for use with English learners).

When an evidence-based review uses specific participant and/or setting character-istics parameters, inclusion criteria for studies to be reviewed must be established. For example, in an evidence-based review regarding the effects of a practice on students with learning disabilities, should an experimental study be included in the review if only 35 of 50 participants had learning disabilities? Not including the study might result in disregarding relevant information, but it seems to me problematic to base EBP iden-tification on findings involving students (or settings) different from that targeted by the review. If findings are disaggregated for the target population and/or settings (e.g., results reported separately just for the participants with learning disabilities), then the review should include just the relevant, disaggregated findings. If findings are not disag-gregated, reviewers must establish criteria for including studies in their review. I suggest that the required proportion of participants (or settings) that align with the focus of the review should be very high (e.g., > 90 percent), so that the influence on study findings of participants from other populations/in other settings is minimized.

Should the Presence of Quality Indicators be Rated?

Typically, evidence-based reviewers evaluate quality indicators as being present or absent in a study (e.g., Gersten et al., 2005; Horner et al., 2005). However, in reality, many stud-ies partially meet a quality indicator. For example, a single-subject study might collect data showing adequate implementation fidelity, but only collects this data sporadically. It doesn't seem right to say that the study fully met or completely failed to address the quality indicator. Rating the presence of quality indicators on a 3- (e.g., met, partially met, not met) or 4-point (e.g., completely addressed, adequately addressed, minimally addressed, not addressed at all) scale allows reviewers to meaningfully evaluate studies that partially address quality indicators (see Baker, Chard, Ketterlin-Geller, Apichatabu-tra, & Doabler, 2009; Chard, Ketterlin-Geller, Baker, Doabler, & Apichatabutra, 2009; and Jitendra, Burgess, & Gajria, 2011 for examples of this approach in special education).

However, Cook et al. (2009) reported that inter-rater reliability for quality indicator ratings was markedly lower in reviews using 4-point rating scales as opposed to a dichot-omous "met/not met" approach (although Jitendra et al., 2009, reported adequate inter-rater reliability for ratings of quality indicators on a 3-point scale). It may be difficult for reviewers to "split hairs" reliably between ratings when using 4-point scales. Moreover, if it is required that each quality indicator be addressed meaningfully for a study to be considered in an evidence-based review, evaluating quality indicators appears to be a yes/no matter. Additional information provided by a multi-point rating scale of quality indicators is not particularly useful in an evidence-based review. That is, let us assume that a rating of 3 or 4 indicates that the quality indicator is adequately addressed and a rating of 1 or 2 means that it is not; we are really just complicating a yes/no decision by making two levels of yes and two levels of no, and running the risk of decreasing inter-rater reliability by doing so.

How Flexible Should Quality Indicators be?

To avoid subjective and erroneous decisions about what works, approaches for iden-tifying EBPs utilize specific quality indicators and standards to objectively determine which studies provide trustworthy findings. It would seem, then, that quality indicators should be clearly prescribed and applied rigidly (i.e., as written, without interpretation or exception). Although such an approach minimizes concerns about reviewer bias, it is likely impractical. Educational research is such a diverse enterprise, with studies varying along any number of dimensions, that no single set of quality indicators can meaningfully capture the quality of every study without some flexibility. For example, quality indicators typically require that relevant demographic information of intervention agents such as years of experience, gender, and professional licensure be described. However, special educators might want to conduct an evidence-based review on the effectiveness of a computer instructional package. In this case, the computer program is the interventionist—there are no years of experience, gender, or licensure status to report. It seems unfair for a study to not meet a quality indicator if it does not apply.

So I believe that evidence-based reviewers must have the flexibility to adapt quality indicators as necessary. Of course, this runs the risk of reviewers adapting quality indicators frequently and markedly, allowing them to manipulate the identification of EBPs. To guard against this, I recommend that evidence-based reviewers only adapt EBPs when absolutely necessary, and that they must thoroughly describe and justify any changes in quality indicators when disseminating the findings of the review. Ideally, organizations that engage in identifying EBPs have some sort of an expert advisory board, comprised of expert researchers in the field, who review and approve any adaptations to quality indicators—further guarding against unwarranted modifications in the prescribed standards.

Should Older Studies be Treated Differently?

Standards for high-quality research evolve, corresponding with changes in theory and empirical findings. For example, although now widely agreed as critical, implementation fidelity was not typically considered an important element of research in special education until recently, and therefore was assessed and reported in few older studies (e.g., Mooney, Epstein, Reid, & Nelson, 2003). Thus, requiring that all studies assess and report adequate implementation fidelity entails that the vast majority of older studies will not be considered when identifying EBPs. Holding past research to standards that didn't exist when the study was conducted (i.e., retrofitting quality indicators; Cook & Tankersley, 2007) seems unfair and runs the risk of disregarding sound research. However, if quality indicators are truly critical for trustworthy research, as I believe they should be, then they should be required no matter when a study was conducted. For example, just because implementation fidelity was not commonly assessed in research studies in the 1980s, that does not mean reviewers can safely assume that the intervention was implemented as designed in a study of that era. One possible compromise is to "grandparent in" older studies (i.e., allow them not to address certain quality indicators), but to weight those studies less than studies that address all quality indicators.

How Should the Evidence Base of Practices be Categorized?

Detrich (2008) identified two primary approaches for categorizing the evidence base of practice: threshold and hierarchical. In the threshold approach, a practice is identified as an EBP when standards (e.g., a minimum number of high-quality, experimental studies supporting a practice) are met by a body of research. If the supporting research-base for a practice does not meet the standard or threshold, it is not considered an EBP. The threshold approach for categorizing EBPs aligns well with the primary, yes/no question that the EBP movement was designed to address: "does this practice really work?" Horner et al.

(2005) take a threshold approach for determining EBPs in special education on the basis of single-subject research. Gersten et al. (2005) use a modified threshold approach in that they specify standards for two categories of practices: evidence-based practices and promising practices, the latter of which is slightly less stringent.

Because the threshold approach only differentiates between EBPs and "non-EBPs," no distinction is made between the many types of practices that are not classified as EBPs. Non-EBPs may (a) have some meaningful evidence supporting them but not quite enough to meet the rigorous standards for an EBP, (b) be shown by high-quality research to do harm, (c) have little or no high-quality research to determine whether the practice works, or (d) have been shown by some high-quality studies to work and by others to not work. A hierarchical approach to categorizing EBPs specifies a number of different types and levels of research support, typically considering the number of high-quality studies showing positive, neutral, and negative effects for a practice. For example, the WWC (2011) categorizes practices as having positive effects, potentially positive effects, mixed effects, no discernible effects, potentially negative effects, and negative effects. I recommend using the hierarchical approach, as knowing whether a non-EBP has potentially positive effects as opposed to negative effects can be very useful for educators.

How Many Groups Should Identify EBPs?

The number of groups that conduct evidence-based reviews and identify EBPs in education is growing (see Cook & Cook, 2013). On one hand, I think this is a very positive development. It shows that leading organizations in general and special education are interested in identifying and implementing EBPs. It also means that organizations focusing on particular populations (e.g., children with autism) or outcomes (e.g., transition to work and post-secondary education) will conduct evidence-based reviews specific to their interests using criteria that reflect the values and traditions of their field. Having the greatest amount of reliable information about what works for the greatest number of groups and outcomes should be the goal of the EBP movement; so in this sense, lots of different groups identifying EBPs is a good thing.

But there is a downside to so many groups being in the EBP business. Although the various approaches or identifying EBPs in special education overlap in many ways, they also differ along every aspect of EBPs. At minimum, the diversity in approaches for identifying EBPs may prove confusing for many educational stakeholders, which might make them less likely to implement EBPs. Moreover, different organizations will at times generate contrasting findings regarding the EBP status of certain practices. Such disagreements, I fear, will generate considerable mistrust of EBPs and potentially undermine the primary purpose of the EBP movement in education—to provide educators with clear answers about what works. Accordingly, I would like to see organizations that conduct evidence-based reviews coordinate with one another to standardize their quality indicators and criteria to the maximum extent feasible.

WHAT ARE IMPORTANT LIMITATIONS OF EBPs?

As special educators think about EBPs and how to use them in their teaching, educators should recognize a number of important limitations such as the existence of non-responders; matching EBPs with learner, teacher, and environmental characteristics; the importance of effective instruction; balancing implementation fidelity with adaptation; and the need to support implementation.

No single practice is going to be effective for all learners, especially given the diverse learning needs of children and youth with disabilities. EBPs are shown by research to be generally effective, not universally effective. Non-responders or treatment resistors, for whom the practice is not effective, can be found in any large study. However, high-quality research has shown that there are relatively few non-responders for EBPs. As such, although special educators can trust that EBPs are generally effective, they should monitor the progress of students even when an EBP is being used, and be ready to adapt or discontinue an EBP if and when students are not responding to it.

> "No single practice is going to be effective for all learners, especially given the diverse learning needs of children and youth with disabilities. EBPs are shown by research to be generally effective, not universally effective."

EBPs are validated by research to work for specific populations for specific outcome measures. Special educators should not expect an EBP to work for everyone or for all outcomes. Even when special educators are working with a population and have targeted an outcome for which an EBP has been validated, it is important that they use common sense to make sure that the EBP meets the learning needs of their students, is realistic to implement in their classroom (e.g., does not require resources or time that is not available), and matches their instructional capabilities and philosophies. EBPs are merely practices that should be prioritized because of their general effectiveness (see Torres, Farley, & Cook, 2012). Special educators need to use their common sense, instructional expertise, and insights regarding their students to choose the best EBP or to decide not to use an EBP in some situations.

Although EBPs have been shown to be generally effective, good teaching is still the key to learning. An EBP can be ineffective if taught poorly, and a great teacher can promote learning even given a mediocre lesson plan. EBPs will have their greatest effect when delivered in the context of generally effective teaching. For example, effective teachers show "withitness" (be aware of what is happening throughout their classroom), use pacing that is not too fast or too slow, monitor student performance, are enthusiastic, and provide students wait time after questions (see Brophy & Good, 1986; Doyle, 1986). Teachers who use these and other tricks of the trade while implementing EBPs provide their students with the greatest chance of success.

Implementation fidelity is not important just as a quality indicator in studies, but also because practitioners hoping to replicate the effectiveness of EBPs shown in research need to implement the practice as designed. Thus, when implementing an EBP, practitioners should not only be guided by a list of its critical elements but also regularly assess the degree to which the practice is being implemented with fidelity. Fidelity, however, is a complex issue (Harn, Parisi, & Stoolmiller, 2013; Johnson & McMaster, 2013). Very high levels of fidelity are associated with lower outcomes (Durlak & DuPre, 2008). It seems that rigid emphasis on fidelity leads to a cookbook approach to teaching in which instructors do not come to "own" the practice or adapt it to fit the unique needs of their students. When implementing EBPs, then, special educators need to walk a fine line between fidelity and adaptation, ensuring that critical elements are not fundamentally changed but also making sure that their students' unique learning needs are addressed.

Finally, as important as the identification of EBPs may be, it is critical to realize that it is just a first step toward improved student outcomes; without broad and sustained implementation, the potential benefits of EBPs will go largely unrealized. Schools tend to resist change, making educational reform difficult (Fixsen, Blase, Horner, & Sugai, 2009). Without significant support from multiple levels, individual teachers will find it difficult to maintain their use of EBPs over time. The emerging field of implementation science is beginning to identify supports associated with sustained implementation of EBPs such as resources and personnel allocation at the state level, supportive administrative leadership, mentorship and coaching, systematic scaling up of EBPs, and sustained professional development (Cook & Odom, 2013).

CONCLUSION

EBPs are practices shown to be generally effective by bodies of high-quality, experimental research. They fulfill an essential need for special educators, providing reliable guidance as to what works for different groups of exceptional learners. Identifying EBPs involves a myriad difficult decisions on which organizations that identify EBPs vary. Consequently, not all EBPs are equal (i.e., some are identified using less stringent standards). When considering EBPs special educators should, then, be aware of the procedures and criteria used when identifying the practice as an EBP. Improved understanding of what EBPs are and how they are identified will, I hope, result in heightened adoption of EBPs, which in turn will result in improved learning outcomes for children and youth with disabilities.

Discussion Questions

1. Why is the matter of using evidence-based practices considered especially important for students with disabilities?
2. What do people mean when they talk about a "research-to-practice gap?"
3. Do you think there is a research-to-practice gap? If yes, why? What can be done to close this gap?
4. Describe the difference between an evidenced-based practice versus an evidence-based program.
5. Do you think the EBP quality indicators should be flexible?
6. To what does the term "fidelity" refer in the discussion of using evidence-based practices and programs? Why is it important in the discussion?

BRYAN G. COOK'S SUGGESTIONS FOR FURTHER READING

Cook, B. G., & Cook, S. C. (2013). Unraveling evidence-based practices in special education. *The Journal of Special Education, 47*, 71–82.

Cook, B. G., Cook, L. H., & Landrum, T. J. (2013). Moving research into practice: Can we make dissemination stick? *Exceptional Children, 79*, 163–180.

Cook, B. G., & Odom, S. L. (2013). Evidence-based practices and implementation science in special education. *Exceptional Children, 79*, 135–144.

Cook, B. G., & Smith, G. J. (2012). Leadership and instruction: Evidence-based practices in special education. In J. B. Crockett, B. S. Billingsley, & M. L. Boscardin (Eds.), *Handbook of leadership in special education* (pp. 281–296). London: Routledge.

Cook, B. G., Smith, G. J., & Tankersley, M. (2012). Evidence-based practices in education. In K. R. Harris, S. Graham, & T. Urdan (Eds.), *APA educational psychology handbook* (vol. 1; pp. 495–528). Washington, DC: American Psychological Association.

Cook, B. G., Tankersley, M., & Landrum, T. J. (2009). Determining evidence-based practices in special education. *Exceptional Children, 75,* 365–383.

REFERENCES

Baker, S. K., Chard, D. J., Ketterlin-Geller, L. R., Apichatabutra, C., & Doabler, C. (2009). The basis of evidence for Self-Regulated Strategy Development for students with or at risk for learning disabilities. *Exceptional Children, 75,* 303–318.

Brophy, J., & Good, T. L. (1986). Teacher behavior and student achievement. In M. C. Wittrock (Ed.), *Handbook of research on teaching* (3rd ed., pp. 328–375). New York, NY: Macmillan.

Carnine, D. (1997). Bridging the research-to-practice gap. *Exceptional Children, 63,* 513–521.

Chard, D. J., Ketterlin-Geller, L. R., Baker, S. K., Doabler, C., & Apichatabutra, C. (2009). Repeated reading interventions for students with learning disabilities: Status of the evidence. *Exceptional Children, 75,* 263–284.

Cohen, J. (1988). *Statistical power analysis for the behavioral sciences* (2nd ed.). Hillsdale, NJ: Erlbaum.

Coleridge, S. T. (1817). *The rime of the ancient mariner.* Retrieved from http://en.wikisource.org/wiki/The_Rime_of_the_Ancient_Mariner_(1817).

Confrey, J. (2006). Comparing and contrasting the National Research Council report on evaluating curricular effectiveness with the What Works Clearinghouse approach. *Educational Evaluation and Policy Analysis, 28,* 195–213.

Cook, B. G., & Cook, L. H. (2008). Nonexperimental quantitative research and its role in guiding instruction. *Intervention in School and Clinic, 44,* 98–104.

Cook, B. G., & Cook, S. C. (2013). Unraveling evidence-based practices in special education. *The Journal of Special Education, 47,* 71–82. doi: 10.1177/0022466911420877.

Cook, B. G., & Odom, S. L. (Eds.) (2013). Evidence-based practices and implementation science in special education [special issue]. *Exceptional Children, 79*(2).

Cook, B. G., & Tankersley, M. (2007). A preliminary examination to identify the presence of quality indicators in experimental research in special education. In J. B. Crockett, M. M. Gerber, and T. J. Landrum (Eds.), *Achieving the radical reform of special education: Essays in honor of James M. Kauffman* (pp. 189–212). Mahwah, NJ: Lawrence Erlbaum Associates.

Cook, B. G., Tankersley, M., Cook, L., & Landrum, T. J. (2008). Evidence-based practices in special education: Some practical considerations. *Intervention in School & Clinic, 44*(2), 69–75.

Cook, B. G., Tankersley, M., & Landrum, T. J. (2009). Determining evidence-based practices in special education. *Exceptional Children, 75,* 365–383.

Dammann, J. E., & Vaughn, S. (2001). Science and sanity in special education. *Behavioral Disorders, 27,* 21–29.

Detrich, R. (2008). Evidence-based, empirically supported, or best practice? A guide for the scientist-practitioner. In J. K. Luiselli, D. C. Russo, W. P. Christian, & S. M. Wilczynski (Eds.), *Effective practices for children with autism* (pp. 3–25). Oxford, UK: Oxford University Press.

Doyle, W. (1986). Classroom organization and management. In M. C. Wittrock (Ed.), *Handbook of research on teaching* (3rd ed., pp. 392–431). New York, NY: Macmillan.

Durlak, J. A., & DuPre, E. P. (2008). Implementation matters: A review of research on the influence of implementation on program outcomes and the factors affecting implementation. *American Journal of Community Psychology, 41,* 327–350.

Eddy, D. M. (2005). Evidence-based medicine: A unified approach. *Health Affairs, 24,* 9–17.

Fixsen, D., Blase, K., Horner, R., & Sugai, G. (2009). *Concept paper: Developing the capacity for scaling up the effective use of evidence-based programs in state departments of education.* Retrieved from http://www.fpg.unc.edu/sisep/docs/Concept_Paper_SISEP_0409_WEB.pdf.

Gersten, R., Fuchs, L. S., Compton, D., Coyne, M., Greenwood, C., & Innocenti, M. S. (2005). Quality indicators for group experimental and quasi-experimental research in special education. *Exceptional Children, 71,* 149–164.

Hammersley, M. (2005). Is the evidence-based practice movement doing more good than harm? Reflections on Iain Chalmers' case for research-based policy making and practice. *Evidence & Policy, 1,* 85–100.

Harn, B., Parisi, D., & Stoolmiller, M. (2013). Balancing fidelity with flexibility and fit: What do we really know about fidelity of implementation in schools? *Exceptional Children, 79*, 181–193.

Harris, R. P., Helfand, M., Woolf, S. H., Lohr, K. N., Mulrow, C.D., Teutsch, S.M., & Atkins, D. (2001). Current methods of the US Preventive Services Task Force: A review of the process. *American Journal of Preventive Medicine, 20*(3, Supplement 1), 21–35.

Hattie, J. C. (2009). *Visible learning: A synthesis of over 800 meta-analyses relating to achievement.* New York, NY: Routledge.

Hill, C. J., Bloom, H. S., Black, A. R., & Lipsey, M. W. (2007). Empirical benchmarks for interpreting effect sizes in research. *Child Development Perspectives, 2*, 172–177.

Horner, R. H., Carr, E. G., Halle, J., Mcgee, G., Odom, S., & Wolery, M. (2005). The use of single-subject research to identify evidence-based practices in special education. *Exceptional Children, 71*, 165–171.

Horner, R. H., Sugai, G., & Anderson, C. M. (2010). Examining the evidence base for School-wide Positive Behavior Support. *Focus on Exceptional Children, 42*(8), 1–14.

Ioannidis, J. P. A. (2005). Why most published research findings are false. *PLoS Medicine, 2*, 696–701. DOI: 10.1371/journal.pmed.0020124.

Jitendra, A. K., Burgess, C., & Gajria, M. (2011). Cognitive strategy instruction for improving expository text comprehension of students with learning disabilities: The quality of evidence. *Exceptional Children, 77*, 135–159.

Johnson, L. D., & McMaster, K. L. (2013). Adapting research-based practices with fidelity: Flexibility by design. In B. G. Cook, M. Tankersley, & T. J. Landrum (Eds.), *Advances in learning and behavioral disabilities* (volume 26) (pp. 65–91). London: Emerald.

Kauffman, J. M. (1999). How we prevent the prevention of emotional and behavioral disorders. *Exceptional Children, 65*, 448–468.

Kazdin, A. E. (2011). *Single-case research designs: Methods for clinical and applied settings* (2nd ed.). New York: Oxford University Press.

McDuffy, K. A., & Scruggs, T. E. (2008). The contributions of qualitative research to discussions of evidence-based practice in special education. *Intervention in School and Clinic, 44*, 91–97.

Mooney, P., Epstein M., Reid, R., & Nelson, J. R. (2003). Status and trends in academic intervention research for students with emotional disturbance. *Remedial and Special Education, 24*, 273–287.

Odom, S. L., Brantlinger, E., Gersten, R. Horner, R. H., Thompson, B., & Harris, K. R. (2005). Research in special education: Scientific methods and evidence-based practices. *Exceptional Children, 71*, 137–148.

Parker, R. I., Vannest, K. J., & Davis, J. L. (2011). Effect size in single-case research: A review of nine nonoverlap techniques. *Behavior Modification, 35*, 303–322.

Peters, M. T., & Heron, T. E. (1993). When the best is not good enough: An examination of best practice. *The Journal of Special Education, 26*, 371–385.

Sackett, D. L., Rosenberg, W. M., Gray, J. A., Haynes, R. B., & Richardson, W. S. (1996). Evidence based medicine: What it is and what it isn't. *British Medical Journal, 312*, 71–72.

Shermer, M. (2002). *Why people believe weird things: Pseudoscience, superstition, and other confusions of our time.* New York, NY: Holt.

Simmerman, S., & Swanson, H. L. (2001). Treatment outcomes for students with learning disabilities: How important are internal and external validity? *Journal of Learning Disabilities, 34*, 221–236.

Slavin, R. E. (2002). Evidence-based education policies: Transforming educational practice and research. *Educational Researcher, 31*, 15–21.

Slavin, R. E. (2008). What works? Issues in synthesizing educational program evaluations. *Educational Researcher, 37*, 5–14.

Sloane, F. (2008). Comments on Slavin: Through the looking glass: Experiments, quasi-experiments, and the medical model. *Educational Researcher, 37*, 41–46.

Torres, C., Farley, C. A., & Cook, B. G. (2012). A special educator's guide to successfully implementing evidence-based practices. *Teaching Exceptional Children, 45*(1), 64–73.

What Works Clearinghouse. (2011). Procedures and standards handbook (version 2.1). Retrieved from http://ies.ed.gov/ncee/wwc/DocumentSum.aspx?sid=19.

Whitehurst, G. J. (2002). *Evidence-based education.* Powerpoint presentation at Student Achievement and School Accountability conference. Retrieved from ies.ed.gov/director/pdf/2002_10.pdf.

Getting to know Kathleen Lynne Lane

 My Grandpa Frank and I decided I would be a professor when I was in elementary school, as he said I was a life-long learner and school was where I was happiest. But, it was a middle school girl named Tamekia that focused my efforts on special education. A friend of mine who was a principal asked me to cover for two days in a self-contained middle-school class in a community challenged by poverty while she located a "real" teacher. At the time I was enrolled in a Masters' program pursuing a Marriage, Family and Child Counselor license and I thought it would be fun to cover this class. Although I had substituted before, I had never had my own classroom. That two-day period turned into two weeks. When I told the students I had to get back to my "real" life and that they would find a new teacher shortly, Tamekia said, "Girlfriend, you're doing a really good job—I think you should stay." And, with that I withdrew from my current program and enrolled in a teacher preparation program to pursue dual certification in general and special education. Tamekia changed my life course, and I feel like my life work has been very clear ever since.

Getting to know Hill M. Walker

I was inspired to enter the field of education by my mother who was an elementary teacher in rural Virginia for four decades. She was a natural born teacher in everything she did—inside and outside the classroom. She raised four children largely alone, of whom two earned Ph.D.s and one became an oral surgeon. In college, I majored in English and trained to become a middle school teacher. But after a year of middle school, I realized the need for more training and skills so I returned to graduate school and entered a program focused on school-related behavior disorders. Finishing my graduate work in 1967, I accepted a position in the University of Oregon College of Education and have been here ever since. I had important mentors along the way who shaped my research interests and opened numerous doors for me that led to a productive, satisfying career.

18

THE CONNECTION BETWEEN ASSESSMENT AND INTERVENTION: HOW CAN SCREENING LEAD TO BETTER INTERVENTIONS?

Kathleen Lynne Lane & Hill M. Walker

EBP

Few practitioners and researchers would argue against the view that students with emotional and behavioral disorders (EBD) are amongst some of the most difficult-to-teach students. Across the K–12 grade span, these students are well-recognized for their behavioral and social excesses and deficits in addition to their pronounced academic deficits (Crick, Grotpeter, & Bigbee, 2002; Walker, Ramsey, & Gresham, 2004). For example, students with EBD include students with externalizing behavior patterns such as verbal and physical aggression, delinquent acts, and coercive interactions with others (Achenbach, 1991). In addition, students with EBD also include those with internalizing behavior patterns such as depression, anxiety, social withdraw, and somatic complaints (Costello, Erkanli, & Angold, 2006; Kessler, Berglund, Demler, Jin, & Walters, 2005).

Not surprisingly, the challenges associated with externalizing, internalizing, and comorbid conditions lead to impaired interpersonal relationships with peers and adults (Walker, Irvin, Noell, & Singer, 1992). And, although most often noted for these behavioral and social difficulties, students with EBD also struggle academically as evidenced by low rates of academic engagement, poor work completion, deficient academic performance in content areas (e.g., reading, math, written expression), high rates of grade retention due to school failure, and ultimately school dropout (Mattison, Hooper, & Glassberg, 2002; Nelson, Benner, Lane, & Smith, 2004; Rapport, Denney, Chung, & Hustace, 2001; Reid, Gonzalez, Nordness, Trout, & Epstein, 2004). In short, students with EBD struggle in multiple domains: behaviorally, socially, and academically, posing significant costs (emotional, financial, and otherwise) for these students, their peers, their families, the educational community, and society as a whole (Walker, 2003).

Although some individuals are under the erroneous belief that students with EBD are the responsibility of special education, this is actually not the case. Recent prevalence estimates suggest approximately 12 percent of the K–12 population have moderate-to-severe forms of EBD (Forness, Freeman, Paparella, Kauffman, & Walker, 2012), with less than 1 percent of these school-age youth receiving services for emotional disturbance (ED) as defined in the Individuals with Disabilities Education Improvement Act (2004).

When coupling this discrepancy between prevalence rates of students with EBD and ED with the current emphasis on inclusive programming for all students, it becomes clear the general education community is largely responsible for identifying and supporting students with EBD.

In our work as practitioners and as researchers focused on school-based intervention, we wanted to make it clear that it is important to empower all teachers to support all students all the time. In other words, we wanted to support schools in developing graduated continua of supports to allow general and special education teachers to work together effectively to meet students' academic, behavior, and social needs. In 1996, Hill and his Oregon colleagues collaborated on a commentary piece that made the case for adapting the three-tiered Institute of Medicine prevention framework for use in schools (Walker et al., 1996). As it turned out, this framework was a perfect fit and aligned seamlessly with the challenges educators faced in allocating resources efficiently and fairly to serve the needs of students at differing levels of behavioral severity and need. The past two decades offer extensive testimony of the positive impact of this reconceptualization regarding how to address the needs of all students.

SUPPORTING STUDENTS WITH EBD IN MULTI-TIERED SYSTEMS OF SUPPORTS

Fortunately, many school-site and district-level teams have moved away from using reactive approaches when attempting to address the challenge of serving these students. Instead, such schools have constructed multi-tiered systems of support to better meet the academic, behavioral, and social needs of all students. These approaches hold particular benefit for students with EBD, as they shift away from wait-to-fail models and are more intentional with respect to the concepts of prevention and search-and-serve.

"When coupling this discrepancy between prevalence rates of students with EBD and ED with the current emphasis on inclusive education programming for all students, it becomes clear the general education community is largely responsible for identifying and supporting students with EBD."

The range of models currently available for implementation, such as response to intervention (RTI; Fuchs & Fuchs, 2006; mainly emphasizing academic performance, positive behavior intervention and supports (PBIS; Sugai & Horner, 2002; mainly emphasizing behavioral performance); and blended models such as comprehensive, integrated, three-tiered (CI3T; Lane, Oakes, & Menzies, 2010) models addressing academic, behavioral, and social performance. Each model contains graduated levels of prevention ranging from primary prevention (Tier 1) for all students, secondary prevention (Tier 2) for some students, and tertiary prevention (Tier 3) reserved for a few students. Essentially, multi-tiered systems of support offer an efficient, effective method for (a) preventing learning and behavioral challenges from developing and becoming elaborated through Tier 1 efforts and (b) responding with Tier 2 and Tier 3 efforts at the first indication of concern for students requiring more intensive supports (Lane, Kalberg, & Menzies, 2009).

These problem-solving models offer teachers, support staff, administrators, and parents a framework for coordinating a continuum of planned supports according to students' needs. Non-responsiveness is not viewed as a crisis in such models, but an expected occurrence for a certain percentage of students in the school building as primary prevention programs are not expected to meet all students' needs. In these frameworks, school-site faculty and staff provide research-based strategies and practices at each level of prevention at the earliest possible juncture when students are most amenable to intervention efforts and before gaps in academic, behavioral, and/or social performance become pronounced (Cook & Tankersley, 2013).

In our collective work, we realized the importance of accurate decision making regarding which students required assistance beyond primary prevention efforts. Namely, we needed an efficient, effective method for benchmarking students' progress—academic, behavioral, and socially so we could swiftly determine their needs and offer relevant supports. Rather than waiting for students to fail to a large enough degree or implementing an intervention that may or may not be what a student needs, we focused instead on the importance of early detection of students' challenges and support needs. Our work with the universal proactive screening and identification of at risk students, along with the development of key tools and methods for doing so, made it much more feasible to mount early intervention and prevention programs rather than relying upon the traditional "Wait to Fail" model that puts challenged students at such a disadvantage.

THE CORNERSTONE: RELIABLE DETECTION

At the heart of these models is reliable detection of students requiring Tier 2 and Tier 3 supports and sensitive monitoring of the effectiveness of additional supports (Lane, Menzies, Oakes, & Kalberg, 2012; Levitt, Saka, Romanelli, & Hoagwood, 2007). In essence, researchers and practitioners need psychometrically sound tools to (a) detect students for whom primary prevention efforts are insufficient (screening); (b) obtain a clear indication of strengths and areas of concern in order to make appropriate instructional decisions for students needing secondary and tertiary supports (program planning); and (c) monitor core aspects of each level of prevention, including treatment integrity to ensure supports are implemented as intended by the interventionist and accessed as planned by student participants, reliability of the measures used to assess students' progress, and social validity to use stakeholders' views to inform plan revision and future efforts (monitor). In short, tools are needed for screening, program planning, and monitoring—the focus of this chapter.

As we seek to better understand the connection between assessment and intervention, we emphasize the importance of screening as an essential step to delivering better interventions for all students—including those with EBD. Simply stated: supports and services cannot be enlisted until a concern is noticed. Externalizing behavior patterns are often easily recognized by even the most novice teachers as they disrupt the classroom environment and make it challenging for teachers and students to engage in the business of teaching and learning (Bradshaw, Buckley, & Ialongo, 2008). Internalizing behaviors, in contrast, are not as easily detected, resulting in these students being less likely than those with externalizing behavior problems to receive needed supports and services. This is extremely unfortunate as both these major disorders of childhood predict negative academic and post-school outcomes (Masten et al., 2005; McEvoy &Welker, 2002; Rapport et al., 2001).

> "As we seek to better understand the connection between assessment and intervention, we emphasize the importance of screening as an essential step to delivering better interventions for all students—including those with EBD."

While some teachers may contend their primary responsibility is to support students' academic learning, viewing behavioral and social skills supports as secondary considerations, this is not the case. Studies by Caprara, Barbaranelli, Pastorelli, Bandura, and Zimbardo (2000) and Malecki and Elliott (2002) suggest poor social skills may actually predict negative long-term academic achievement. As such, the educational community needs to marshal balanced expertise in academic, behavioral, and social domains.

Empirical studies have established that teachers are an "excellent test" of which students need additional assistance academically, behaviorally, and otherwise (Lane, 2007; MacMillan, Gresham, & Bocian, 1998). However, teachers are stretched to the upper limits given their multiple task demands and increased class sizes (Michelson & Harvey, 2000). Conducting screenings actually requires teachers to evaluate the behavioral and social performances of all students consistently and accurately in addition to examining academic performance (Lane et al., 2012). Systematic screenings help students as well as teachers by affording students equal access to supports while protecting teachers from overlooking students for whom primary prevention efforts are insufficient (false negatives). Yet, as noted by Walker, Small, Severson, Seeley, and Feil (2014), "careful work is needed to align available screening and assessment methods with each of the three tiers . . . So far, satisfactory achievement of this goal remains elusive as to feasibility and efficacy" (p. 34).

Conducting systematic screening on a regular basis (ideally in fall, winter, and spring) is a key first step in addressing the problem of underservice of students with EBD in the general education setting. However, screening in and of itself is insufficient. It is imperative that schools have a clearly articulated method of decision making for providing services to students with identified needs. As part of these program planning efforts for Tier 2 and Tier 3 supports, additional information is often required such as data provided by scales such as the Social Skills Improvement System—Rating Scales (SSiS-RS; Gresham & Elliott, 2008) which link students with needed (and available) supports. Still other tools are needed to monitor implementation and student progress.

PURPOSE

As we reflect back on the goal of better meeting students' multiple needs, we applaud the attention devoted to designing and testing interventions. Yet, until recently an often understudied area is assessment as it relates to intervention. The valuable connection between assessment and intervention is a commonly repeated mantra in our field but there is much variation in how the two are connected. If at all possible, there should be a proximal, intimate association between them rather than a more distal one as is often the case. In many instances, we put the cart before the horse by developing an intervention first and then the necessary assessment tools are created after the interventional plan as opposed to (a) investigating a problem area, (b) learning how to assess it well using multiple types of assessment tools, and (c) then developing an intervention approach that *specifically* addresses identified deficits that define or make up the problem area as revealed by our assessment processes.

In this chapter we discuss the important connection between assessment and intervention, explaining how screening and other forms of assessment lead to better interventions. We will illustrate how intervention is informed—sharpened, aimed, guided, and refined—by assessment, attending to these three areas: screening, program planning, and monitoring. While we focus on students with EBD as a case example, we emphasize that this logic could be applied to other student groups (e.g., students with specific learning disabilities) as well.

FACETS TO CONSIDER

Screening

As explained in the introduction, systematic behavior screening tools—as with academic screening tools—are a seminal component of three-tiered models of prevention. Walker et al. (2014) delineate several applications for systematic screening tools within the context of these models. First, data gleaned from screening tools provide a benchmark of performance offering teachers a reliable, valid method of determining if the behavioral and social performance of a particular student is on par with respect to normative patterns. Students scoring outside the parameters of normative behavior can be identified for Tier 2 and Tier 3 supports. Second, screenings can be used as one assessment to monitor performance within tiers and determine when students require a different level of prevention. Third, screening data can be one source of information for designing interventions specific to students' individual needs. Fourth, information from screenings can be used to inform professional development offerings to provide teachers with the knowledge, confidence, and skills to offer specific behavior supports to address targeted concerns (e.g., increase engagement, decrease disruption). Finally, data can be used to assess overall school-wide outcomes by examining shifts in the percentage of students with low, moderate, and high levels of risk across time. Thus, screening tools can serve a diverse set of functions within multi-tiered systems of support.

Available tools. There are a number of behavior screening tools available such as the Systematic Screening for Behavior Disorders (SSBD; Walker & Severson, 201...); Student Risk Screening Scale (SRSS; Drummond, 1994); Strengths and Difficulties Questionnaire (SDQ; Goodman, 1997); Social Skills Improvement System Performance Screening Guide (SSiS-PSG; Elliott & Gresham, 2007b), and the BASC–2 behavioral and Emotional Screening System (BASC2-BESS; Kamphaus & Reynolds, 2007). These tools vary in terms of the age range(s) served (e.g., elementary, middle, and/or high school), specific behavior patterns detected (e.g., internalizing, externalizing, hyperactivity/inattention, prosocial behavior, motivation-to-learn), methods of completion (e.g., online, paper and pencil techniques, etc.), raters (e.g., teachers, parents, and/or students), and associated costs (e.g., free access, nominal costs, and greater investments). For example, the SSBD has multiple gating procedures developed for use in the elementary grades and is available at a nominal cost of less than 150 dollars per school. The SDQ and SRSS are free-access screening tools, with evidence to support use across the K–12 continuum. The SSiS-PSG and BASC2-BESS are screening tools available as part of respective families of tools and intervention materials offering a coordinated system of screening, assessment, and intervention. We encourage interested readers to read more detailed descriptions of each screening tool available in their respective technical manuals and summative works (e.g., Lane et al., 2012) as there are a number of tool-specific features to consider prior to selecting a screening tool in addition to more general considerations discussed in the follow section.

Practices and considerations. When adopted as part of regular school practices, universal screenings typically take place three times a year: in fall, approximately 4–6 weeks after the academic year begins, in winter, prior to or immediately following winter break, and in spring, approximately 4–6 weeks prior to the end of the academic year. Screening outcome data are analyzed in conjunction with other data such as academic performance (e.g., curriculum-based measures, benchmarks, and course grades), attendance, and office discipline referrals (ODRs) to make decisions regarding responsiveness—a point we discuss more fully in subsequent sections.

In selecting which screening tool to adopt, school-site teams must consider issues such as psychometric rigor and feasibility. For example, in prevention research, errors are not uncommon. In some instances, students will be identified as having behavior concerns warranting additional assistance, when in fact they *do not* actually have the behavior concern of interest (e.g., internalizing disorder). These are referred to as false positives. In other instances, students who have a behavior concern or disorder are overlooked when they *do* actually manifest the behavior concern of interest. These are referred to as false negatives. In prevention research, the latter is the more serious error—missing a student who could potentially benefit from supplemental research-based strategies and practices. From a psychometric perspective, consumers must evaluate each tool to determine its rigor (e.g., positive predictive power, negative predictive power, sensitive and specificity—see American Educational Research Association, American Psychological Association, & National Council for Measurement in Education, 1999). In addition, consumers also need to be cognizant of feasibility concerns. Logistical considerations such as how much time and expertise are needed to prepare, administer, score, interpret, and utilize data from a given screening tool should be considered when selecting it. No matter how psychometrically sound a tool may appear to be, it is unlikely to be conducted with fidelity if it is too burdensome (Lane et al., 2010). Thus, the process of selecting a screening tool is important, warranting careful consideration.

Benefits and challenges. Finally, there are a number of benefits and challenges associated with conducting systematic screenings. As we discussed previously, systematic screenings provide benefits to students by ensuring equal consideration for additional supports. Furthermore, teachers are protected from inadvertently overlooking students (particularly those with internalizing issues) whose behavior challenges may require supplemental assistance. Teachers are not trained as school psychologists or behavior specialists, but they do have a wealth of information about how students perform when confronted with a number of task demands and in a range of social circumstances within the school context. Screening tools enable this information to be quantified in a way that allows teachers to determine if there are higher than average types of concerns relative to a student's age, developmental level, and/or gender. Information from behavior screenings also can be used in conjunction with other data to inform educational programming. For example, the student struggling with hyperactivity or inattention can be provided with behavioral supports such as self-monitoring strategies or differential reinforcement of higher rates of behavior (engagement) to help them access instruction offered (Cooper, Heron, & Heward, 2007). Similarly, students with anxiety issues who fear being called on in classes can be offered a behavioral support option in which they self-select to participate in discussions a pre-determined number of times,

> "Teachers require reliable, valid, brief, low-resource intensive screening tools to detect students for whom primary prevention efforts are insufficient, yielding the necessary information to quickly inform program planning."

with the understanding the teacher will not call on them unexpectedly (Lane, Weisenbach, Little, Phillips, & Wehby, 2006).

In addition to these benefits, there are also challenges warranting consideration. First, screening requires due diligence. Before screening, school-site leadership teams need to review federal, state, and local guidelines for determining what is permissible. For example, it is recommended they read IDEA regulations 300.301 through 300.311 (Assistance to States for the Education of Children with Disabilities and Preschool Grants for Children with Disabilities, 2006) and the Protection of Pupil Rights Amendment of 1978 (Kamphaus & Reynolds, 2007). For example, in some states, parental consent is required before conducting any screenings, with some requiring active consent (a letter signed by parents providing their express written permission for their child to participate in the screening process) rather than passive consent (a letter sent home informing parents screening will occur, giving them the option to let the school know if they do not want their child to participate in the screening process). In either case, if school-site personnel consider additional secondary or tertiary supports, parents will need to be informed—and in some cases permission obtained. In addition to these challenges, there are others: (a) time and other resources (e.g., money) need to be allocated to support screening efforts, (b) professional development is needed to support all stages of the process, including learning evidence-based practices and strategies to support students at each level of prevention (Cook & Tankersley, 2013), and (c) school-site leadership teams must be prepared to support students identified as needing additional assistance.

In essence, screening is a rigorous task. We are encouraged to see the influx of screening efforts by the research and teaching communities, as people seek tools to detect and support students believed to have behavioral challenges. Leadership teams are clear on the fact the question should be "Which behavior screening tools should we adopt?" rather than "Should we adopt behavior screening tools?" Yet, it is also equally clear practitioners are resistant to time- and labor-intensive screening tools. Teachers simply do not have the time to complete checklists or rating scales with 100+ items (Walker & Severson, 2014). Teachers require reliable, valid, brief, low-resource intensive screening tools to detect students for whom primary prevention efforts are insufficient, yielding the necessary information to quickly inform program planning.

Program Planning at Tier 2 and 3

Screening is an important precursor to intervention. Yet, as we have noted, screening alone is insufficient to support intervention efforts. There must be a mechanism for reliably determining appropriate supports for students at Tier 2 or Tier 3, specific to their individual needs. The intent is to ensure equal access to supports as well as wise resource allocations. As part of the program-planning process, we encourage school-site teams to develop an explicit, transparent method of connecting students to supports available in a school, making certain to involve parents in the planning process. One suggestion for meeting this charge is to develop a blueprint for Tier 2 and Tier 3 supports, referred to as secondary and tertiary intervention grids (see Lane, Kalberg, & Menzies, 2009 and Lane et al., 2012 for examples).

Assessment schedule. Because this is a data-driven model, outcome data from (a) screening tools and procedures are used to detect who needs additional supports,

(b) screenings as well as more detailed assessments (e.g., behavior ratings scales) can connect students to specific interventions, and (c) progress monitoring tools can determine students' progress over time (e.g., Daily Progress Reports [DPR]; Kilgus, Chafouleas, Riley-Tillman, & Welsh, 2012) and also interpret how they respond. Given the pivotal role of data within these processes, a logical starting point is to construct an assessment schedule depicting when each measure is to be administered over the course of the academic year. For example, the schedule might show AIMSweb reading and math scores are administered in October, December, and March; attendance and ODR data are collected daily and analyzed monthly; treatment integrity data of primary prevention efforts are collected and analyzed quarterly to determine the extent to which Tier 1 supports are implemented as planned, and social validity data are collected at the beginning and end of each year to examine stakeholders' (teachers, parents, and students) perspectives. This assessment schedule provides a starting point for determining which types of information are available to monitor performance and inform intervention efforts (see examples in Lane et al., 2012).

Intervention grids. Next, we recommend making a master list of all practices, interventions, and/or supports in a given school categorized as Tier 1 (for all), Tier 2 (for some), and Tier 3 (for a few), focusing at this stage on Tier 2 and 3 supports. This list can be used to construct secondary and tertiary intervention grids to make the features of each support type transparent for all stakeholders by including columns for each intervention depicting the following: (a) a description of the intervention, including logistical considerations (e.g., who does what to whom, and under what condition); (b) entry criteria operationalized using specific inclusion and exclusion criteria according to school-wide data to determine for whom this intervention is intended; (c) more sensitive data (e.g., from behavior rating scales) to inform detailed aspects of the intervention and monitor student progress (e.g., DPR or direct observation data), serving as student outcome measures, and (d) determine exit criteria, which include more global (e.g., screening scores) and sensitive (e.g., progress monitoring data) measures to guide decisions as to how to move students through the levels of prevention.

For example, consider the SSiS. A school-site team using SSiS products may proceed as follows to support students with social skills deficits. Fall SSiS-PSG scores may indicate five sixth-grade boys receiving a score of 2 or 3 (yellow band) in the prosocial domain despite participating in monthly school-wide social skills lessons using the Classwide Intervention Program (SSiS-CIP; Elliott & Gresham, 2007a). This curricular program addresses topics such as how to listen to others, following the rules, and getting along with others. After securing parent permission, teachers, parents, and students complete the respective versions of the SSiS Rating Scales, which are diagnostic tools yielding more detailed information about students' acquisition (can't do problems) and performance deficits (won't do problems). Information from these three perspectives for all five students are used to determine which lessons from the Social Skills Improvement System Intervention Guide (SSiS-IG; Elliott & Gresham, 2008) should be taught as part of the Tier 2, small group social skills interventions explicitly focusing on students' acquisition deficits. These lessons could be taught by a guidance counselor, behavior specialist, or school psychologist during study hall or intervention block, following the *tell, show, do, practice, monitor progress, and generalize* format provided by the SSiS-IG. Student progress could be monitored according to shifts in teacher, parent, and/or student ratings as well as the direct observations of specific skills taught. Determinations of when to conclude the small groups and continue solely with participation in the school-wide monthly lessons (Tier 1) or move on to more intensive supports (e.g., individualized instruction; Tier 3), could be determined according to Winter screening results on the SSiS-PSG and results of weekly or daily progress monitoring information.

This is one illustration of Tier 2 support—social skills groups for students with acquisition deficits. This same information would be coordinated and made explicit for each Tier 2 (e.g., self-monitoring to improve engagement in small reading groups, behavior contracts to facilitate homework completion) and Tier 3 (e.g., functional assessment-based interventions) set of supports available within the school. Although initially time consuming to develop this blueprint, it provides a valuable framework for coordinating all available supports within a school, which can be then used at each screening time point to connect students to supports.

> "As new strategies and practices are developed, with sufficient scientific evidence to suggest they are effective, teachers will need both the time and professional development opportunities to adopt these new innovations as part of the school-site plan."

Considerations. As part of this program planning process, we emphasize two additional points. First, it is also important to identify other research-based practices adopted to meet the academic, behavioral, and/or social needs of students not currently addressed according to available Tier 2 and 3 supports. Again, professional development will need to be provided to operationalize this process and continue knowledge and skills development for strategies and practices developed by the research community (Cook & Tankersley, 2013). Teachers will need time to review data from multiple sources (e.g., academic and behavior screening data, attendance, ODRs, and the like), to use this information in conjunction with secondary and tertiary grids to link students with appropriate supplemental supports. Also, to facilitate sustainability of these processes, mechanisms must be in place to revise blueprints and the included components annually to reflect current innovations from the scientific communities. As new strategies and practices are developed, with sufficient scientific evidence to suggest they are effective, teachers will need both the time and professional development opportunities to adopt these new innovations as part of the school-site plan.

Second, before moving forward with any Tier 2 or 3 supports, it is important to ensure that non-responsiveness is not the result of a less than optimal primary prevention plan (Bruhn, Lane, & Hirsch, 2014). Moreover, when considering how best to use screening, behavior rating scales, and progress monitoring tools as part of Tier 2 and Tier 3 supports, it is important to first attend to Tier 1 efforts. A critical element of any blueprint of supports is careful attention to the primary prevention plan. The Tier 1 plan must be as transparent as the Tier 2 and 3 supports. In addition to describing and operationally defining core components of the primary plan (e.g., which reading program is to be implemented, school-wide expectations for behavior, and/or a given bully prevention program to be implemented), defining the responsibilities of all stakeholders (e.g., teachers, students, parents, and administrators), and establishing procedures for teaching and reinforcing implementation are essential. It is also important to monitor core features of the primary plan to draw accurate conclusions regarding non-responsiveness. We discuss this final facet in the following section on monitoring.

Monitoring

In considering the "how" of monitoring, we emphasize that accurate, data-based problem solving hinges on effective monitoring. Specifically, answers to questions such as "Who needs additional assistance?" "How can we best address their needs?" "How well are these extra supports working?" can be accurately answered if we monitor the following elements for Tier 1, 2, and 3 prevention efforts: treatment integrity, reliability of monitoring tools, and social validity.

Treatment integrity. For each level of prevention, it is critical for school-site teams to monitor the degree to which the intervention is implemented as planned. If treatment integrity data are not collected, it is simply not possible to draw accurate conclusions about intervention outcomes. For example, if a student is deemed non-responsive to Tier 1 efforts, but data are not collected regarding the extent to which the teacher implemented the core reading program, school-wide positive behavior support system, and/or school-wide bullying prevention program, we cannot be certain the student was not responsive to these prevention efforts or if the student did not progress simply because the components were not in place. The same is true for Tier 2 and Tier 3 supports—treatment integrity must be monitored for each step in a multi-tiered model.

When monitoring treatment integrity, we also urge for monitoring to move beyond only examining the presence or absence of teacher behavior (Lane, Oakes, Menzies, Oyer, & Jenkins, 2013). For example, consider a Tier 2 reading intervention with a self-monitoring component to support third grade students who are reading below benchmarks and who have higher than average level hyperactivity/inattention skills according to the SDQ. In addition to monitoring treatment integrity of teacher-led components of this support, it is also necessary to monitor the extent to which students are engaged in intervention components such as participating during choral reading activities, answering questions when called on by the teacher, and accurately monitoring engagement by tracking tally marks on a self-monitoring sheet. Just because a student is seated at the table and given a self-monitoring sheet does not mean the student is engaging in the intervention procedures.

"However, greater precision in measuring treatment integrity holds promise as researchers use treatment integrity as a mediating variable in statistical models to interpret patterns of responsiveness."

We encourage monitoring of expected student behaviors as well as teacher behaviors, with careful attention to quality. We understand it is more challenging to measure the quality of implementation, as reliability of measurement becomes more cumbersome as we attempt to move beyond simple presence or absence indicators. However, greater precision in measuring treatment integrity holds promise as researchers use treatment integrity as a mediating variable in statistical models to interpret patterns of responsiveness. For example, it may be that students show greater slope changes in reading performance over the course of an intervention implemented by the teacher with high levels of integrity and when accessed more fully by students.

Reliability of monitoring tools. In addition to monitoring treatment integrity, it is also important to monitor student progress using reliable, valid measures for each level of prevention. To the maximum extent possible, researchers and practitioners need to employ measures such as behavior rating scales, progress monitoring tools, and direct observation techniques that limit measurement error. Researchers and practitioners need to be confident that changes in scores are due to intervention outcomes, rather than measurement error. For example, if student engagement during independent seat work in mathematics is being measured using direct observation techniques as part of a Tier 3 functional assessment-based intervention and data indicate high rates of engagement during the intervention condition relative to baseline conditions, we need to be certain these changes are a function of the introduction of the intervention and not observer drift or some other error in measurement.

To avoid these types of errors, we encourage school-site leadership teams to select behavior rating scales and other standardized measures with attention to psychometrics. Namely, it is important to review reliability estimates typically available in technical manuals to ensure measures are reliable and valid for monitoring intervention outcomes. When using progress monitoring tools such as DPR, conducting direct observations of behavior, or using curriculum-based measures to assess academic performance, it is equally important to adhere to the training procedures and monitor reliability of data collection, again with a goal of ensuring accurate measurement.

Social validity. Finally, we encourage school-site teams to assess social validity from multiple stakeholders' perspectives: teachers, students, and parents. Social validity measures the social significance of intervention goals, the social acceptability of intervention procedures, and the social importance of effects (Wolf, 1978). Social validity can be assessed before implementing and after completing an intervention.

In terms of assessing social validity before conducting an intervention, this information can be used to predict the likelihood the intervention will be implemented as designed with integrity (Noell & Gresham, 1993; Reimers, Wacker, & Koeppl, 1987). Ideally, if stakeholders view the intervention as targeting meaningful goals, requiring manageable procedures, and likely to produce desired outcomes, they may be more likely to implement the intervention with integrity resulting in meaningful, lasting changes. In a study of 617 teachers representing eleven elementary, three middle, and five high schools, there was a positive relationship between social validity and treatment integrity of the primary plan when examining school-level data. Specifically, of the 14 schools that went on to implement a school-wide plan after completing a year-long training series, social validity scores as measured according to the Primary Intervention Rating Scale (PIRS, an adapted version of the Intervention Rating Scale-15; Witt & Elliott, 1985) prior to plan implementation predicted treatment integrity (composite scores for teacher-completed intervention ratings between 4 and 10 times per year) during the first year ($r = .71$, $p = 0.005$; Lane, Kalberg, Bruhn, Driscoll, Wehby, & Elliott, 2009). Although additional inquiry is needed to replicate these findings, this information may be useful in modifying plan revisions. In instances where social validity scores are low, this information may be used to inform plan revision to promote buy in, with a goal of increasing the treatment integrity of plan implementation and ultimately sustainability. Revising Tier 1, 2, and 3 supports prior to implementation using feedback from consumers may enable school-site teams to save valuable resources and set the stage for high levels of integrity (Lane et al., 2009).

In addition, pre- and post-implementation social validity scores can be compared to determine if the intervention met, exceeded, or fell short of initial expectations for those involved. In each case, this information can be used to inform subsequent intervention efforts. For example, if these comparisons suggest procedures were too cumbersome (e.g., required too much teacher time or materials not typically found in a classroom), these aspects could be revised when implemented with other students or with other teachers. In essence, social validity data may hold currently untapped potential when working in the context of multi-tiered systems of supports. It may predict implementation, be used to inform intervention revisions, and ultimately help to develop feasible, effective three-tiered models of prevention.

To learn more about issues of monitoring and measurement, we refer the interested reader to the special issue of *Exceptional Children* (2005) focusing on core quality indicators for research. The articles included in this special issue provide detailed guidelines and considerations for attaining reliable and valid measurement as well as other dimensions of intervention research using single case (Horner et al., 2005) and group (Gersten et al., 2005) methodologies.

FUTURE CONSIDERATIONS

As we look to the future of education for all students—particularly those with EBD, we strongly encourage practitioners and researchers to keep a clear focus on the connection between assessment and intervention. We believe sensitive assessments have the ability to maximize the power of many existing interventions. Social skills programs provide a relevant example here. As a common practice, a core social skills curriculum is often used to teach small groups of students wherein all students are taught the same skills in the same manner and in the same sequence. While the students being instructed (as a collective group) will no doubt share some social skills deficits, it is also the case that individual students in the group will likely benefit from additional, more individualized and intensive instruction on the specific skills in which they are *each* deficit. However, one can only know this from implementing sensitive measures of each student's status on each of the skills contained in the curricular content and using that information as a guide in maximizing such instruction.

In this chapter we have highlighted the relation between assessment and intervention, discussing how screening and other forms of assessments such as more detailed behavior rating scales and progress monitoring tools can inform—and ideally improve—interventions implemented within the context of multi-tiered systems of supports. It is truly encouraging to see school-site leaders and researchers shift to systems-levels approaches for all students, including those with EBD. Such approaches require strong reliance on data-based decision making to support each facet of these problem-solving models: screening, program planning, and monitoring. This in turn requires a comprehensive set of tools. First, the field needs screening tools which serve a number of functions, including reliable detection of students for whom primary prevention efforts (when implemented with fidelity) are not sufficient. Next, a host of tools are needed to construct, revise, and evaluate multi-tiered systems of supports, including an accurate picture of students' strengths as well as skills in need of improvement to inform instructional decisions for secondary and tertiary supports. Finally, additional tools are needed to reliably monitor treatment integrity, student progress, and social validity at each level of prevention.

As we consider the recursive process of how screening and other assessment tools are used to construct, evaluate, and improve multi-tiered systems of supports, we would like to praise the individuals, research teams, and school-site teams for their work to date. In just the past five years, we have seen a number of advances in systematic screening tools. For example, there are now web-based systems such as the BASC-2 BESS, the SSiS–PGS, and most recently the SSBD. Furthermore, there is new inquiry into progress monitoring tools for behavior to parallel those currently available in the academic area such as the Direct Behavior Rating Scales (Kilgus et al., 2012), some of which include

> "At each turn as we work through this iterative process of using screening and other assessment tools to inform intervention efforts, it is imperative to remember teachers and other school personnel are often over-extended in terms of task demands, accountability, and the like—all the while receiving normal pay for what is arguably one of the most important jobs—educating our youth.

web-based approaches such as the Progress Monitoring Tool (PMT; Marquez & Yeaton, in press).

We expect other new tools, procedures, and technology will continue to advance in the coming five years. In anticipation of these advances, we offer a few final thoughts for future considerations. First, given the fact that students with internalizing issues are particularly difficult to detect, we strongly encourage increased attention to improving early detection of these students. We recognize screening efforts with this population are more challenging due to the nature of these concerns, but the work is essential given the poor outcomes for this group (Costello et al., 2006; Kessler et al., 2005).

Second, we support continued attention to progress monitoring tools, with particular attention to securing information from multiple sources. For example, the work of Gresham et al. (2010) appears to be particularly promising. In their work they have blended teacher perceptions with progress monitoring of students' social behaviors that impact academic performance as well as social skills. Given the costs associated with direct observations and narrow sampling of such behaviors, it may be better to look for progress from a different venue using the work of Gresham and colleagues as an example.

Third, we encourage teams to continue to explore new methods of creating transparent, clearly defined multi-tiered systems of support with explicit plans addressing the issue of *how*. *How* will students be detected who need Tier 2 and 3 supports? *How* will they be linked with appropriate interventions? *How* will these interventions be monitored to ensure effective implementation? *How* will student progress be assessed in a reliable and feasible manner? *How* will decisions be made about when to conclude (return to Tier 1) or supplement (move to another Tier 2 or Tier 3) support? *How* will consumer feedback be assessed and used to inform intervention efforts within the context of these models? (see Lane, Kalberg, & Menzies, 2009 for examples).

Finally, we recommend careful attention to issues of feasibility. At each turn as we work through this iterative process of using screening and other assessment tools to inform intervention efforts, it is imperative to remember teachers and other school personnel are often over extended in terms of task demands, accountability, and the like—all the while receiving nominal pay for what is arguably one of the most important jobs—educating our youth (Michelson & Harvey, 2000). We are hopeful that technical advancements and innovation in assessment and intervention domains maintain the necessary rigor, but also consider issues of efficiency, resources, and acceptability (Walker et al., 2014).

In Box 18.1, we provide the interested reader with recommended readings to help continue these important lines of inquiry. We look forward to future advances to better align screening and assessment methods within multi-tiered systems of support.

Box 18.1 Resources

Screening tools

Drummond, T. (1994). *The student risk screening scale (SRSS)*. Grants Pass, OR: Josephine County Mental Health Program.

Elliott, S. N., & Gresham, F. M. (2007b). *Social Skills Improvement System: Performance Screening Guides*. Bloomington, MN: Pearson Assessments.

Goodman, R. (1997). The Strengths and Difficulties Questionnaire: A research note. *Journal of Child Psychology and Psychiatry*, *38*, 581–586.

Kamphaus, R. W. & Reynolds, C. R. (2007). *BASC-2 behavior and emotional screening system (BASC-2 BESS)*. San Antonio, TX: Pearson.

Walker, H. M., & Severson, H. H. (2014). *Systematic screening for behavior disorders (SSBD)*; 2nd Edition., Eugene, OR: Pacific Northwest Publishing Co.

Walker, H., Severson, H., & Feil, E. (1994). *The Early Screening Project*. Longmont, CO: Sopris West, Inc.

Books and book chapters

Cook, B. G., & Tankersley, M. (Eds.). (2013). *Research-based practices in special education*. Boston, MA: Pearson.

Lane, K. L., Menzies, H. M, Oakes, W. P., & Kalberg, J. R. (2012). *Systematic screenings of behavior to support instruction: From preschool to high school*. New York: Guilford Press.

Marquez, B. & Yeaton, P. (in press). Progress monitoring methods and tools for behavioral performance. In H. Walker & F. Gresham (Eds.), *Handbook of Research in Emotional and Behavioral Disorders*. New York: Guilford, Inc.

Walker, H., Severson, H., & Seeley, J. (2010). Universal, school-based screening for the early detection of behavioral problems contributing to later destructive outcomes. In M. Shinn & H. Walker (Eds.), *Interventions for Achievement and Behavior Problem in a Three-Tier Model Including RTI* (pp. 677–702). Bethesda, MD: National Association of School Psychologists.

Walker, H. M., Ramsey, E., & Gresham, F. M. (2004). *Antisocial behavior in school: Evidence-based practices*. Belmont, CA: Wadsworth.

Discussion Questions

1) Why do you think there is such a large discrepancy between the number of students with EBD and those who receive special education services under the ED label?
2) In addition to screening, what other forms of assessment are important in education of students with learning and behavior problems?
3) What steps do you think a school would need to consider when adopting behavior screening practices?
4) What are the similarities in the practices described by Lane and Walker and those described by Lembke (Chapter 9)? How do they differ?
5) Discuss various ways that treatment integrity can be recorded in Tiers 1, 2, and 3.
6) What is the appropriate role for special education in a multi-tiered system?

KATHLEEN LYNNE LANE'S AND HILL M. WALKER'S SUGGESTIONS FOR FURTHER READING

Barton, E. & Harn, B. (2012). *Educating young children with autism spectrum disorders.* Bethesda, MD: National Association of School Psychologists and Corwin Press.

Dunlap, G., Wilson, W., Strain, P., & Lee, J. (2013). *Prevent-teach-reinforce for young children: The early childhood model of individualized positive behavior support.* Baltimore: Paul Brookes, Inc.

Lane, K. L., Kalberg, J. R., & Menzies, H. M. (2009). *Developing schoolwide programs to prevent and manage problem behaviors: A step-by-step approach.* New York, NY: Guilford Press.

Lane, K. L., Menzies, H., Bruhn, A., & Crnobori, M. (2011). *Managing challenging behaviors in schools: Research-based strategies that work.* New York, NY: Guilford Press.

Lane, K. L., Menzies, H. M, Oakes, W. P., & Kalberg, J. R. (2012). *Systematic screenings of behavior to support instruction: From preschool to high school.* New York, NY: Guilford Press.

Walker, H. M. & Gresham, F. M. (2014). *Handbook of evidence-based practices for emotional and behavioral disorders: Applications in schools.* New York: Guilford, Inc.

Walker, H. M., Ramsey, E,, & Gresham, F. M. (2004). *Antisocial behavior in school: Evidence-based practices* (2nd ed.). Belmont, CA: Wadsworth.

REFERENCES

Achenbach, T. M. (1991). *Manual for the child behavior checklist/4-18 and 1991 profile.* Burlington: University of Vermont, Department of Psychiatry.

American Educational Research Association, American Psychological Association, & National Council for Measurement in Education. (1999). *Standards for educational and psychological testing.* Washington, DC: American Educational Research Association.

Bradshaw, C. P., Buckley, J., & Ialongo, N. (2008). School-based service utilization among urban children with early-onset educational and mental health problems: The squeaky wheel phenomenon. *School Psychology Quarterly, 23,* 169–186.

Bruhn, A., Lane, K. L., & Hirsch, S. (2014). A review of secondary interventions conducted within multi-tiered models of behavioral prevention. *Journal of Emotional and Behavioral Disorders,* March.

Caprara, G. V., Barbaranelli, C. Pastorelli, C., Bandura, A., & Zimbardo, P. G. (2000). Prosocial foundations of children's academic achievement. *Psychological Science, 11,* 302–306.

Cook, B. G., & Tankersley, M. (Eds.), (2013). *Research-based practices in special education.* Boston, MA: Pearson.

Cooper, J. O., Heron, T. E., & Heward, W. L. (2007). *Applied behavior analysis.* Upper Saddle River, N.J.: Pearson Education, Inc.

Costello, E. J., Erkanli, A., & Angold, A. (2006). Is there an epidemic of child or adolescent depression? *Journal of Child Psychology and Psychiatry, 47,* 1263–1271.

Crick, N., Grotpeter, J., & Bigbee, M. (2002). Relationally and physically aggressive children's intent attributions and feelings of distress for relational and instrumental peer provocations. *Child Development, 73,* 1134–1142.

Drummond, T. (1994). *The student risk screening scale (SRSS).* Grants Pass, OR: Josephine County Mental Health Program.

Elliott, S. N., & Gresham, F. M. (2007a). *Social Skills Improvement System: Classwide intervention program guide.* Bloomington, MN: Pearson Assessments.

Elliott, S. N., & Gresham, F. M. (2007b). *Social Skills Improvement System: Performance Screening Guides.* Bloomington, MN: Pearson Assessments.

Elliott, S. N., & Gresham, F. M. (2008). *Social Skills Improvement System: Intervention guide.* Bloomington, MN: Pearson Assessments.

Forness, S. R., Freeman, S. F. N., Paparella, T., Kauffman, J. M., & Walker, H. M. (2012). Special education implications of point and cumulative prevalence for children with emotional or behavioral disorders. *Journal of Emotional and Behavioral Disorders, 20,* 4–18.

Fuchs, D., & Fuchs, L. (2006). Introduction to response to intervention: What, why, and how valid is it? *Reading Research Quarterly, 41,* 93–99.

Gersten, R., Fuchs, L. S., Compton, D., Coyne, M., Greenwood, C., & Innocenti, M. S. (2005). Quality indicators for group experimental and quasi-experimental research in special education. *Exceptional Children, 71,* 149–164.

Goodman, R. (1997). The Strengths and Difficulties Questionnaire: A research note. *Journal of Child Psychology and Psychiatry, 38*, 581–586.

Gresham, F., Cook, C., Collins, T., Dart, E., Rasetshwane, K., Truelson, E., & Grant, S. (2010). Developing a change-sensitive brief behavior rating scale as a progress monitoring tool for social behavior: An example using the Social Skills Rating System—Teacher Form. *School Psychology Review, 39*, 364–379.

Gresham, F. M., & Elliott, S. N. (2008). *Social Skills Improvement System: Rating Scales.* Bloomington, MN: Pearson Assessments.

Horner, R. H., Carr, E. C., Halle, J., McGee, G., Odom, S., & Wolery, M. (2005). The use of single-subject research to identify evidence-based practice in special education, *Exceptional Children, 71*, 165–179.

Individuals with Disabilities Education Improvement Act of 2004, 20 U.S.C. 1400 *et esq.* (2004) (reauthorization of Individuals with Disabilities Act 1990).

Kamphaus, R. W. & Reynolds, C. R. (2007). *BASC-2 behavior and emotional screening system (BASC-2 BESS).* San Antonio, TX: Pearson.

Kessler, R. C., Berglund, P. A., Demler, O., Jin, R., & Walters, E. E. (2005). Lifetime prevalence and age-of-onset distributions of DSM-IV disorders in the National Comorbidity Survey Replication (NCS-R). *Archives of General Psychiatry, 62*, 593–602.

Kilgus, S., Riley-Tillman, Chafouleas, S., & Welsh, M. (2012). Direct behavior rating scales as screeners: A preliminary investigation of diagnostic accuracy in elementary school. *School Psychology Quarterly, 27*(1), 41–50.

Lane, K. L. (2007). Identifying and supporting students at risk for emotional and behavioral disorders within multi-level models: Data driven approaches to conducting secondary interventions with an academic emphasis. *Education and Treatment of Children, 30*, 135–164.

Lane, K. L., Kalberg, J. R., Bruhn, A. L., Driscoll, S. A., Wehby, J. H., & Elliott, S. (2009). Assessing social validity of school-wide positive behavior support plans: Evidence for the reliability and structure of the Primary Intervention Rating Scale. *School Psychology Review, 38*, 135–144.

Lane, K. L., Kalberg, J. R., & Menzies, H. M. (2009). *Developing schoolwide programs to prevent and manage problem behaviors: A step-by-step approach.* New York: Guilford Press.

Lane, K. L., Menzies, H. M, Oakes, W. P., & Kalberg, J. R. (2012). *Systematic screenings of behavior to support instruction: From preschool to high school.* New York: Guilford Press.

Lane, K. L., Oakes, W. P., & Menzies, H. M. (2010). Systematic screenings to prevent the development of learning and behavior problems: Considerations for practitioners, researchers, and policy makers. *Journal of Disabilities Policy Studies, 21*, 160–172.

Lane, K. L., Oakes, W. P., Menzies, H. M., Oyer, J., & Jenkins, A. (2013). Working within the context of three-tiered models of prevention: Using school wide data to identify high school students for targeted supports. *Journal of Applied School Psychology, 29*, 203–229.

Lane, K. L., Weisenbach, J. L., Little, M. A., Phillips, A., & Wehby, J. (2006). Illustrations of function-based interventions implemented by general education teachers: Building capacity at the school site. *Education and Treatment of Children, 29*, 549–671.

Levitt, J., Saka, N., Romanelli, L., & Hoagwood, K. (2007). Early identification of mental health problems in schools: The status of instrumentation. *Journal of School Psychology, 45*, 163–191.

MacMillan, D. L., Gresham, F. M., & Bocian, K. (1998). Discrepancy between definitions of learning disabilities and what schools use: An empirical investigation. *Journal of Learning Disabilities, 31*, 314–326.

Malecki, C. K., & Elliott, S. N. (2002). Children's social behaviors as predictors of academic achievement: A longitudinal analysis. *School Psychology Quarterly, 17*, 1–23.

Marquez, B., & Yeaton, P. (in press). Progress monitoring methods and tools for behavioral performance. In H. Walker & F. Gresham (Eds.), *Handbook of Research in Emotional and Behavioral Disorders.* New York: Guilford, Inc.

Masten, A. S., Roisman, G. I., Long, J. D., Burt, K. B., Obradovic, J., Riley, J. R.,...Tellegen, A. (2005). Developmental cascades: Linking academic achievement and externalizing and internalizing symptoms over 20 years. *Developmental Psychology, 41*, 733–746.

Mattison, R. E., Hooper, S. R., & Glassberg, L. A. (2002). Three-year course of learning disorders in special education students classified as behavioral disorder. *Journal of the American Academy of Child & Adolescent Psychiatry, 41*, 1454–1461.

McEvoy, A., & Welker, R. (2002). Antisocial behavior, academic failure, and school climate: A critical review. *Journal of Emotional and Behavioral Disorders, 8*, 130–140.

Michelson, M., & Harvey, A. S. (2000). Is teachers' work never done? Time-use and subjective outcomes. *Radical Pedagogy, 2*(1).

Nelson, J. R., Benner, G. J., Lane, K., & Smith, B. W. (2004). An investigation of the academic achievement of K-12 students with emotional and behavioral disorders in public school settings. *Exceptional Children, 71*, 59–73.

Noell, G. H., & Gresham, F. M. (1993). Functional outcome analysis: Do the benefits of consultation and prereferral interventions justify the costs? *School Psychology Quarterly, 8,* 200–226.

Rapport, M. D., Denney, C. B., Chung, K. M., & Hustace, K. (2001). Internalizing behavior problems and scholastic achievement in children: Cognitive and behavioral pathways as mediators of outcome. *Journal of Clinical Child Psychology, 30,* 536–551.

Reid, R., Gonzalez, J., Nordness, P., Trout, A., & Epstein, M. (2004). A meta-analysis of the academic status with emotional/behavior disturbances. *The Journal of Special Education, 38,* 130–143.

Reimers, T. M., Wacker, D. P., & Koeppl, G. (1987). Acceptability of behavioral treatments: A review of the literature. *School Psychology Review, 15,* 212–227.

Sugai, G. & Horner, R. H. (2002). Introduction to the special series on positive behavior supports in schools. *Journal of Emotional and Behavioral Disorders, 10,* 130–135.

Walker, H. M. (2003, February 20). *Comments on accepting the Outstanding Leadership Award from the Midwest Symposium for Leadership in Behavior Disorders.* Kansas City, KS: Author.

Walker, H.M., Horner, R.H., Sugai, G., Bullis, M., Sprague, J., Bricker, D., & Kaufman, M. (1996). Integrated approaches to preventing antisocial behavior patterns among school-age children and youth. *Journal of Emotional and Behavioral Disorders, 4,* 193–216.

Walker, H. M., Irvin, L. K., Noell, J., & Singer, G. H. S. (1992). A construct score approach to the assessment of social competence: Rationale, technological considerations, and anticipated outcomes. *Behavior Modification, 16,* 448–474.

Walker, H. M., Ramsey, E., & Gresham, F. M. (2004). *Antisocial behavior in school: Evidence-based practices.* Belmont, CA: Wadsworth.

Walker, H. M., & Severson, H. H. (2014). *Systematic screening for behavior disorders : SSBD* (2nd Ed.). Eugene, OR: Pacific Northwest Publishing Co.

Walker, H., Small, J., Severson, H. H., Seeley, J. R., & Feil, E. G. (2014). Multiple-gating approaches in universal screening within school and community settings: Practice and methodological considerations. In R. J. Kettler, T. A. Golver, C. A. Albergs, & K. Feeney-Kettler (Eds.), *Universal screening in educational settings: Identification, implementation, and interpretation* (pp. 47–75). Division 16 Practitioners' Series, American Psychological Association.

Witt, J. C., & Elliott, S. N. (1985). Acceptability of classroom intervention strategies. In T. R. Kratochwill (Ed.), *Advances in school psychology* (Vol. 4, pp. 251–288). Mahwah, NJ: Earlbaum.

Wolf, M. M. (1978). Social validity: The case for subjective measurement or how applied behavior analysis is finding its heart. *Journal of Applied Behavior Analysis, 11,* 203–214.

Getting to Know Charles R. Greenwood

I come from a line of educators. My grandfather was a principal, and my aunts and uncles were teachers, a school librarian, and a PE teacher. They were great role models. My big break came with an opportunity to be a summer volunteer working in a program for children with moderate to severe behavior and emotional problems. Thereafter, I was inspired to pursue this work in my graduate program and professionally.

Those early days were exciting times. The elementary-aged children I served as classroom teacher were of every sort, and each was challenged with some "edgy" behaviors. Many would come to class but not remove their coats, because they intended to leave later when they felt like it. Yet, when we made their classroom experience more interesting than truancy, they turned around and started to learn to read. For example, making and flying paper airplanes from our second floor classroom with a ground crew outside to mark flight time and distance was hard to resist.

What I learned helped me later to raise a daughter with a developmental disability and contribute to the parent-driven independent living program for young adults where she now lives. Thanks to the IDEA and the professional contributions of the folks in this volume (among others), we now have a generation of 30-somethings who had access to a free, public education alongside peers. Although they are still challenged, they are talented and capable individuals. The prior generation of these Americans did not have an education and most were institutionalized. The difference between these two groups of adults is vast. Many in the IDEA generation can communicate, care for their personal needs, read, compute, enjoy sports, and use their social skills. They hold jobs and are an asset to the communities where they live. We can only imagine what the next generation can do.

19

HOW SHOULD LEARNING ENVIRONMENTS (SCHOOLS AND CLASSROOMS) BE STRUCTURED FOR BEST LEARNER OUTCOMES?

Charles R. Greenwood

WHAT IS LEARNING ANYWAY? AND, WHY IS IT SO DIFFICULT TO AGREE ON WHAT IT IS?

My views on learning were formed at university by at least three groundbreaking experiences. I learned that (a) pigeons could be taught to do really amazing things, (b) instruction could be made explicit and programmed to become vastly more effective than implicit or incidental instruction, and (c) teaching young children with challenging behavior and emotional disorders in schools could also be highly effective. Because I had a semester course in experimental psychology, I studied operant learning theory through both lecture and lab experiences. In a nutshell, operant learning theory states that learning, or a change in performance, is a function of changes in the environment and corresponding student response to these changes. New behaviors are learned because environmental events that evoke them lead to consequences for responding that are valued by the learner. Most interestingly, I learned that operant learning principles apply equally well to animals and humans.

That semester I was assigned care of a pigeon in the department's animal laboratory, my very first student. As a matter of the course requirements, I was required to teach the bird new skills by applying operant learning principles taught in the course. My bird's classroom was a highly structured, operant learning environment (a small chamber) (Skinner, 1953; 1972). The chamber was a small box with a built-in grain feeder for providing the bird edible consequences for responding and a number of eye-level, programmable stimulus buttons (with and without colored lighting) for use in arranging environment events and stimuli (http://www.youtube.com/watch?v=ymkT_C_NWXw).

In completing my lab assignments, I taught my bird simple behaviors like pecking the disk to produce brief access to the grain feeder. More complex skills followed, such as walking to the left corner of the chamber or even in circles in the presence of the disk with light on and then in right circles with the disk light off, as well as waiting for periods of time without movement prior to pecking the disk to access the grain feeder. These grand achievements with the pigeon were possible because of the earlier discoveries by behavioral scientists that advanced our understanding of shaping new behavior by using small steps, schedules of reinforcement, discrimination of responding in the presence of different events and different reinforcement, and cessation of behavior through extinction and the lack of reinforcing consequences. Using knowledge learned in the course, I was successful at teaching my bird how to acquire new behaviors, to make them more frequent, and to reduce them in favor of teaching other new behaviors. The new behaviors I taught the bird were at first nonexistent in its repertoire, then tentative and awkward as a result of reinforcing approximations to the desired response, and later rapid and fluent due to experiencing schedules of reinforcement, and then persistent in the face of no reinforcement.

Seeing my student grow in skill week to week, and knowing that these newly acquired skills were the result of my efforts, was exciting and eye opening. My bird was learning to do the things I planned in advance and then taught him by making changes in the stimulus disks and consequences to responding. I realized that my teaching made a clear difference in what the bird was able to do. For many teachers working with students in real classrooms, examples of student learning with this kind of clarity, I suspect, are not common—but they should be. This undergraduate course led me to become an undergraduate psychology major and prepared me for additional foundational lessons.

A subsequent course in programmed instruction was another eye-opener. Behavioral and educational psychologists in the 1970s were busy learning how to apply Skinner's ideas and principles of learning to the creation of really effective instruction. Some of the learning principles used to program instruction included: a focus on the individual learner rather than the class, identification of specific learner outcomes, building in opportunities for the learner to respond and practice using multiple exemplars, providing feedback and error correction as needed for the desired learning outcome, and progressing at one's own rate based on successful mastery of small learning units on the path toward the desired outcomes. Instruction was purposely sequenced so that students first learned the precursor skills needed to successfully learn the next step prior to the next new skill. The result of sequencing and mastery required to move ahead was that learning error rates were reduced. Students were taught new concepts first, followed by discriminations programmed to help students accurately identify positive from negative examples of the concept. Because the instruction was mediated through programmed materials (prior to computers at this time!), students could learn at their own pace, and did not have to wait for others.

Another key aspect of developing program instruction was its modification based on observing differences in learners' errors and rates of progress within and across sequential lessons. By tracking the errors learners made, it was possible to redevelop a lesson iteratively, such that subsequent learners experienced fewer errors and required less correction, thereby resulting in more effective instruction. Instruction was improved based on the learner's performance in the program.

"Seeing my student grow in skill week to week, and knowing that these newly acquired skills were the result of my efforts was exciting and eye opening."

This course brought me face-to-face with designing the details of instruction. Once again, learning was directly observable through data, and I could see my teaching was making a difference in learning outcomes. Both these early lessons about teaching making a difference in what students actually learned in the late 1960s and early 1970s were in stark contrast to the fact that it was not until 1986 that leaders in the profession of education actually stated that what teachers did in the classroom had an influence on what their students learned (Brophy, 1986)!

While a graduate student, I extended these lessons as a teaching-assistant (TA) in a psychology course designed around the same learning principles; in this situation I structured the learning environment of undergraduate students. This Introduction to Behavior Analysis course was structured in a design plan known as Personalized Systems of Instruction (PSI). Today, PSI is a common design framework used in online and distance instruction (Grant & Spencer, 2003). The course was yet another application reliant on selected small units of material that contained aspects of programmed instruction. Students studied the assigned units in order and took mastery quizzes over each unit. My role as the TA, a role I was qualified for because I had passed the course with an A in a prior semester, was to correct their quizzes by providing them face-to-face, on-the-spot correction, feedback, and redirection for review and re-study based on errors they made. My contribution helped students improve the accuracy of their answers, but because they had to engage me in conversation about their answers with explanation, they also became conversant in the course content. Students could move through the course at their own rate and could complete the course early in the semester by passing the minimum number of required units. Attendance at course lectures was not required of students, rather, it was voluntary. The lectures were designed to be of high interest often including select topics and guest speakers, considered to be reinforcing experiences.

I guess it is no surprise that I brought these lessons with me to my subsequent elementary teaching. My first position was as a teacher of students receiving special education services for challenging behavior and emotional problems. The most challenging leap for me was how to translate what I had learned to a classroom environment serving 20 plus students—all selected for their dislike of school and teachers and their high degree of non-responsiveness—if not outright resistance to classroom instruction!

With this new challenge, I began with a focus on identifying clearly what the desired skills and outcomes were expected of these students. Next was to structure the learning environment to support learning of these skills, and I incorporated teaching procedures based on learning principles. In preparing for the school year, it was clear to me that the pathway to any academic learning of all these individuals had to be through teaching them the precursors: appropriate classroom social skills. Accomplishing this, as it turned out, put the students in the position of engaging with academic instruction and in tolerating each other, such that learning of academic skills in the classroom became possible.

To this end, my co-teacher and I established a class-wide token reinforcement system that enabled us to teach appropriate classroom social conduct, reduce inappropriate behavior, and engage the students in curriculum and instruction. To monitor progress, we implemented a behavioral observation system to provide feedback on how well we reduced problem behavior and increased attention and academic engagement. We also used mastery monitoring to provide feedback on what students were learning. To differentiate instruction to meet the diverse academic needs of this group of students, we used a variety of techniques. We used small groups and learning centers to help focus and intensify teacher-directed instruction, early Direct Instruction materials in reading, and peer supervision techniques with small groups of students working in different levels of programmed math instruction (Greenwood, Sloane, & Baskin, 1974). To further improve social skills and broaden social opportunities, we sold school jobs to students in our token economy as back-up consequences. Students loved earning these jobs in return for points received for desired behavior and daily academic accomplishment including time outside of class helping the janitor on these duties, or working in the office. We sold in-classroom jobs as well, such as cleaning up materials after lessons, being the hall monitor, being the math peer manager, etc. Students asked for more selections as well as suggested others that we would include.

While this teaching assignment was at first a daunting experience, as weeks went by we were increasingly able to see learning happening in the data and in the children, as less disruption, more time on task, and mastery of learning units resulted from our efforts to structure the classroom in these ways. Most importantly, this approach to restructuring the classroom led to greatly improved social and academic outcomes for these students.

So, what is learning? Why is it so difficult to see it occurring? And why can't we agree on what it is? Learning is behavior that is changing moment-to-moment with experience, instruction, consequences, and time. It is particularly difficult to see up close because we have so few controlled opportunities for observing it. As a result, many of us aren't sure what it is. Fortunately, I had at least three controlled opportunities that allowed this observation; from each, it was possible to see learning occurring because of direct observation and the data collected over time as an indicator of progress and change. These experiences in the laboratory, in development of programmed instructional materials and curriculum, in college teaching, and in elementary classroom instruction greatly influenced my approach to structuring effective teaching.

I have long thought that similar controlled opportunities in contemporary teacher preparation and professional development programs could be created if trainees were assigned projects that require them to document that their efforts actually produce measurably clear changes in what an individual student knows and can do (Greenwood & Maheady, 1997).

WHAT IS NECESSARY FOR LEARNING TO OCCUR IN CLASSROOMS AND SCHOOLS?

For the main discussion of this chapter, I turn to answering how learning environments should be structured for achieving the best learner outcomes. However, before launching into that discussion, I digress briefly to introduce another big idea and a framework that helps us organize the answer. The first digression deals with the important difference between the structure and function of classroom instruction, and the second considers measures for evaluating function in terms of classroom structure.

The Structure versus Function Distinction

Structure refers to how we plan to organize the learning environment, and how we actually implement that plan in the effort to promote students' learning. Structure refers to the arrangement of classroom settings in terms of setting events that become the experiences that we teachers and educators provide as active ingredients in our teaching. Examples include daily subject matter foci as they are nested in a schedule of what, when, and how long; the materials and curriculum used in each; and the procedures, practices, and teaching behaviors we use to engage students in each learning activity.

Other examples of setting events include the architectural and physical arrangement of the classroom including the arrangement of desks and seating, centers, shared spaces, etc. They also include the numbers and kinds of teachers (e.g., aide, peer tutor) and students, including their characteristics (e.g., with and without disabilities).

A lot of what we know about the structure of school settings we owe to ecological psychologists who study the human habitat. Barker's ecological approach viewed different environmental units in terms of the number and types of behavior settings (Barker, 1968; Odom et al., 1996). According to Barker, the structure of a behavior setting determined the appropriate behaviors in that setting. His evidence was the observation that behaviors differed largely when in church, as compared to a classroom, or a theater, or when at work at the office, and so on. Additionally, he observed that the behavior of people when in these settings was more similar than compared with their behavior in different settings. I think we would all agree that student behavioral expectations during reading instruction should be different in some important ways from those in spelling or mathematics.

> "I have long thought that similar controlled opportunities in contemporary teacher preparation and professional development programs could be created if trainees were assigned projects that require them to document that their efforts actually produce measurably clear changes in what an individual student knows and can do."

To this, Bronfenbrenner (1986) contributed a multi-level system perspective by representing multiple family influences on child development. Like Barker (1968), Bronfenbrenner recognized that environments were not only structured differently, but also represented micro- to macro-levels of proximity to the child or student at any moment in time. At the micro-level, persons were in direct contact with the immediate and present environment. Classroom examples include the daily schedule and curriculum and teachers' behaviors. At the macro-level, he conceptualized concentric layers, each setting more distal from the other. In this sense, the social organization of environments at the classroom, school, district, state, and federal levels reflected, if you will, a continuum of increasingly distal social influences on the structure of the classroom environment and student at the micro-level. He further posited that these macro-levels interact in ways contributing to various positive and/or negative influences on child development at the micro-level. Negative influences on child development, for example the interaction of under-educated parents with limited family financial resources and a high-crime neighborhood, create a risk of delay in child development. Conversely, the opposite influences of highly educated parents, adequate resources, and a safe neighborhood interact in ways that promote resilience and typical rates of development.

Function, on the other hand, refers to how the student learner is actually responding to classroom-level influences. Function refers to the momentary effects on students' behavior occurring during teaching efforts. Some highly desired examples of student response to instruction are engagement in active, academic responding. These include oral and silent reading, task participation, writing, and talk-discussion about academics. Other examples include the task management behaviors needed to enable academic responding to occur. These are behaviors and conduct that the students need to help manage their learning activities; for example, attending to the teacher when the teacher is talking and raising their hands to ask or answer a question. Inappropriate classroom behaviors are those that break class rules and interfere with engagement in academic responding or task management and may include aggression, disruption, noncompliance, looking around, and inappropriate talk, among others (i.e., self-abuse).

As I think you will agree, the big idea in the structure–function distinction is simply that structuring classroom instruction does not guarantee that said structure will actually promote active academic responding in the classroom, and the experiences needed to attain better achievement outcomes. Changes in structure, like a substitute teacher, may make no change in behavioral function at all, or it may lead to increased rates of inappropriate behavior and lower engagement in academic responding, depending on differences in said structure.

Unfortunately, neither Bronfenbrenner's (1986) nor Barker's (1968) frameworks explained very well how learning actually was created at the micro-level of personal contact with the instructional environment. However, behaviorists provided an answer with their momentary, environment–behavior–environment interaction theory. They posited and demonstrated that to acquire new academic skills in response to classroom instruction (A), students' behavior (B) needed to yield them positive consequences and useful results (C). Learning interactions of this kind they called "Antecedent –Behavior–Consequence" (ABC) interactions (Bijou, Peterson, & Ault, 1968), or in classrooms and teaching as "Opportunities to Respond" (Hall, Delquadri, Greenwood, & Thurston, 1982), or as "learn units" (Greer & McDonough, 1999). When consequences are positive and useful, behavioral interaction theory tells us that the behaviors producing them will be strengthened and occur more frequently in the future. Thus, learning is the product of instructions leading to a change in behavior or performance that becomes established, maintained, and changed by its antecedents and consequences, all of which are under the control of the teacher and instructor (Morris & Midgley, 1990).

A multitude of behavior research has reported and replicated the role played by ABC interactions in changing individual behavior in classrooms and a vast range of other applied settings (e.g., homes, communities) (Catania, 2013; Vladescu & Kodak, 2010). Taken together, we now have a framework for understanding the structure of schooling at the macro-levels of events and how that structure may be evaluated in terms of function.

Measurement and Analysis of Structure and Function of Instruction

To improve our ability to evaluate and assess the structure and function of classroom instruction in research seeking to improve instructional effectiveness, my colleagues and I used these ideas in a design plan for developing observational measures (Greenwood, Carta, & Atwater, 1991; Morris & Midgley, 1990). We used the term "ecobehavioral interaction" to refer to the structure–function relationship as a basis for moving theory to empirical studies of instructional effectiveness. Ecobehavioral interaction is an accounting of what is actually happening at the macro-level of teaching as well as its momentary influences on micro-level student response. Direct observational measures were designed to capture when instruction and student behavior were influencing one another as desired, and when not. As previously discussed, when it does we have a functional relationship between the teaching structure and the student behavioral results, and learning at the micro-level is occurring. When we don't have function, learning is not occurring.

Our first ecobehavioral observational measures, the Code for Instructional Structure and Student Academic Response (CISSAR) (Greenwood & Delquadri, 1988) is seen in Table 19.1 (see Greenwood & Kim, 2012 for a current treatment). Most classroom observation instruments at the time we developed it measured either ecological events or behavioral events. CISSAR was one of the first attempts that combined recoding of the ecological events, teacher behavior, and student behavior in one instrument with the intention of analyzing student behavior as a function of its classroom ecology. The ecobehavioral framework helped us describe and understand the structural components of instruction as well as what happens within and between these components and their function, either promoting or failing to promote student engagement in learning.

CISSAR provided a rich description of classroom structure in terms of the percentage occurrence of events (e.g., reader and paper and pencil) within a category (i.e., tasks). It also provided the ability to compare the effects of tasks, for example, in terms of engagement in academic responding, task management, and inappropriate behaviors. Using CISSAR and subsequent ecobehavioral observation measures that were developed over

Table 19.1 CISSAR Ecobehavoral Taxonomy of Categories, Event Codes, and Descriptions

Ecological Categories, Events, and Descriptions

Activity: The Subject of Instruction

AC	Arts/crafts	M	Mathematics
BM	Business/management	R	Reading
CT	Can't tell	Sc	Science
FT	Free time	Ss	Social studies
H	Handwriting	S	Spelling
L	Language	Tn	Transition

Task: The Curriculum Materials or the Stimuli Set by the Teacher to Occasion Responding

FP	Fetch/put away	Rr	Readers
Ll	Listen to lecture	Tsd	Teacher–student discussion
Om	Other media	Wb	Workbook
Pp	Paper/pencil	Ws	Worksheet

Structure: Grouping and Peer Proximity During Instruction

EG	Entire Group	Sg	Small Group
I	Individual		

Teacher Position: Teacher's Position Relative to the Student and/or Group Observed

AS	Among students	IF	In front
AD	At desk	O	Out of room
BH	Behind	S	Side of Student

Teacher Behavior: Teacher's Behavior When Observed

A	Approval	OT	Other talk
D	Disapproval	T	Teaching
NR	No response		

(Continued)

Table 19.1 (Continued)

Student Behavior Categories, Events, and Descriptions

Academic Response: Specific, Active Response in Relation to Academic Tasks

AGP	Academic game play	RS	Read silent
ANS	Answer question	TA	Talk academic
ASK	Ask question	W	Write
RA	Read aloud		

Task Management: Prerequisite or Enabling Response

AT	Attention	PA	Play appropriate
LM	Look for materials	RH	Raise hand
M	Move		

Competing Responses: Responses that Compete or are Incompatible with Academic or Task-Management Behavior

DI	Disrupt	LA	Look around
IL	Inappropriate locale	TNA	Talk non-academic
IP	Inappropriate play	SS	Self-stimulation
IT	Inappropriate task		

the years (Greenwood, Carta, Kamps, Terry, & Delquadri, 1994) we were able to address empirically a range of issues including, (a) the magnitude of students' engagement in different instructional settings, (b) gaps in students' achievement outcomes, (c) effects of specific instructional interventions, (d) fidelity of intervention, and (e) identification of naturally effective instruction and interventions improving the success of next-environment transitions. We now turn to what we learned about structuring effective classroom instruction research in different schooling environments (e.g., low-income school classrooms, inclusive classrooms, dual language classrooms, preschools).

THE LOW MAGNITUDE OF STUDENTS' ENGAGEMENT IN DIFFERENT INSTRUCTIONAL SETTINGS

Preliminary work indicated that the structure of classroom instruction was often quite weak in terms of behavioral function; we observed that classroom instruction did not promote the comparable high levels of students' engagement in academic responding that one might expect it would! During reading instruction, for example, we reported seeing no student reading at all during scheduled reading instruction. We reported seeing the lowest ability reading groups meeting for less time than more advanced groups because they were held last in the morning schedule up against recess or lunch breaks. When the more advanced groups went longer than schedule, as they often did, the lowest groups were often cut short due to break time (structure). In these groups, we often observed very little student reading occurring, in favor of listening to other children read one at a time, and waiting (function), when they should have been much more directly engaged in oral and silent reading.

In our first systematic study, we collected CISSAR ecobehavioral observation data for students served in fourth grade low-income school classrooms. Findings indicated that students engaged in academic responding an average of only 62 minutes (15 percent) of a seven-hour school day compared to a mean of 73 minutes (17 percent) in suburban school classrooms in the same district (Stanley & Greenwood, 1983).

During most of this classroom time, students in low-SES schools were looking at the teacher making presentations, lacking materials to respond to, only occasionally raising their hands to answer questions, and mostly, just watching otherwise. Levels of inappropriate behavior during this core instruction were generally low. The weak function of classroom instruction with respect to engagement in high priority learning behaviors was replicated subsequently in a second longitudinal study of children in grades 1–4 (Greenwood, 1991), special education classrooms (Kamps, Greenwood, & Leonard, 1991), English-as-a-Second-Language (ESL) and bilingual classrooms, and most recently in prekindergarten classrooms with literacy goals (Greenwood et al., 2012).

Another line of research by others at the time used CISSAR to examine the differences in the function of general versus special education classroom instruction in terms of student academic engagement. Surprisingly, few differences were found. Low levels of student engagement in academic responding in both special and general education classrooms were reported (Thurlow, Ysseldyke, Graden, & Algozzine, 1984; Ysseldyke, Thurlow, Mecklenburg, Graden, & Algozzine, 1984).

In a recent prekindergarten study, we reported that the average percentage of time that students' literacy engagement (defined as writing, reading, manipulating academic tasks, academic verbal responses, or academic attention) occurred was for an average of only 22 percent ($SD = 17.8$) of time observed (Greenwood et al., 2012). This was the equivalent of only 7 out of 30 minutes of instructional time observed.

Why was this?

Teachers structured instruction with a literacy focus for only 15 percent ($SD = 15$), or 6 minutes in a 30-minute observation. Teacher literacy focus included topics like phonological awareness, alphabet/print concepts, story and other comprehension, vocabulary, and reading. The amount of teacher literacy focus ranged from a high of 26 percent (8 minutes) in prekindergarten program classrooms connected with elementary schools to a low of only 5 percent (1.5 minutes) in Head Start classrooms. While only programs with stated literacy goals were included in the study, teachers in these classrooms were at best structuring literacy topics only 26 percent of instruction time, and at worst, they were structuring literacy topics only 5 percent of the time.

The prospects of improving the function of preschool literacy instruction are very great because our findings showed that children were nearly three times more likely to engage in writing, reading, academic manipulation, academic verbal response, and academic attention when the teachers provided a focus on literacy instruction ($M = 49$ percent, $SD = 36$) compared to non-literacy instruction ($M = 17$ percent, $SD = 21$). Simply helping teachers fill available instructional time with a literacy focus, in my opinion, will lead to vastly increased academic responding and learning.

Together these findings confirmed and replicated our hypothesis that instruction is often not structured in ways that lead to high rates of student engagement in academic responding. Less implementation was observed than was scheduled, and was widely variable. The result was much less exposure to academic subjects than was planned.

Explaining gaps in students' achievement outcomes

Building on these findings, we were able to use EBA to help explain not only low levels of academic responding, but also gaps in achievement and other student outcomes. In the Stanley and Greenwood (1983) study of low versus moderate to high-SES student groups, these groups were divergent in academic achievement and in their engagement in academic responding. While the function of instruction was weak overall in terms of academic responding at 17 percent of the day, it was even weaker at 15 percent in low-SES classrooms. Students in low-SES classrooms were engaged 11 fewer minutes per day than students in moderate-high SES school classrooms. While seemingly a small amount of time per day, we estimated that low-SES students would need to attend school for as much as 1.5 extra months during summer vacation to obtain an equivalent amount of engaged academic response time as moderate to high-SES students obtained in just 1 school year (Stanley & Greenwood, 1983).

We found these gaps again in a second study with students in grades 1–4. As early as fall of first grade, students in low-SES schools were .3 grade levels lower in academic achievement moderate to high-SES students in suburban school classrooms. By the end of fifth grade, the students were 3.5 grade levels lower than their counterparts in moderate to high-SES classrooms. We also found diverging trajectories in engagement in academic responding over grades. Low-SES groups grew more slowly in academic engagement, and the gap widened over time (Greenwood, 1991).

We reported an even larger 24-minute daily difference in academic engagement favoring students in suburban over urban school classrooms. With no changes in the function of business-as-usual instruction, elementary grade students in low-SES school classrooms needed an extra 1.6 years of schooling beyond the fifth grade to attain the same cumulative amount of academic engagement experience as moderate to high-SES students attain in five years of elementary schooling (Greenwood, Hart, Walker, & Risley, 1994).

"Simply helping teachers fill available instructional time with a literacy focus, in my opinion, will lead to vastly increased academic responding and learning."

We also looked for structural differences in the instruction received to see if we could identify factors associated with lower academic responding. Teachers in low-SES classrooms spent more time lecturing and presenting lessons to large groups of students, whereas teachers in moderate to high-SES schools did less of this, spending more time on instruction in small groups, with more independent study time associated with more reading, writing, and discussion of academics.

Understanding that daily differences in time students were engaged in academic responding became large cumulative differences in each student's personal history of schooling suggested to us that engagement is at least one potentially causal variable in understanding the persistent differences in achievement and social inequities emerging in larger society. Large cumulative differences compounded out of small daily instructional experiences were sobering, particularly when considering remediation efforts. Simply asking lower achieving students to attend school longer in terms of extra months and years is not a solution to the weak function of instruction provided. Improving the function of instruction to avoid cumulative deficits is needed.

Effects of specific instructional interventions

In addressing these gaps in low-SES elementary schools, we sought to improve the function of core instruction through what became known as ClassWide Peer Tutoring (CWPT). Preliminary work indicated that engagement in academic responding was readily promoted by restructuring with one-on-one peer tutoring. We reported (Delquadri, 1978), as did many others (e.g., Bloom, 1984), that students who were not responsive to classroom instruction and receiving failing grades and test scores, could make vastly greater progress with pull-out, one-on-one peer tutoring. I also had learned that teaching individual students practices for managing student study groups was feasible, reliable over time, and effective.

With CWPT we focused on translating one-on-one peer tutoring and peer management to a class-wide format appropriate for core instruction. CWPT at this time was emerging right when students with disabilities were being "mainstreamed" to receive instruction in the general education classroom, making the diversity of learners' skill levels included in core instruction even greater. Teachers working with us also wanted a method of core instruction by which all students could be included in instruction without the stigma of always being in the low instructional group.

Unlike most peer tutoring models at that time, CWPT was designed to be reciprocal, so that all students in class served as both the tutor and the tutee during each CWPT session as they worked with the reading, spelling, or math content that the teacher had prepared for that week. Teachers developed the content to be learned each week in terms of small units derived from the curriculum. Tutees earned points from the tutor that were summed each week and winning teams announced. Thus, the structure of CWPT included both content components and increased opportunities for responding in the dual roles of tutor and tutee. It also included motivational components in the form of individual and group contingencies of reinforcement (Greenwood, 1981; Greenwood & Hops, 1981).

CWPT structured 30 minutes of core instruction during which half of the students tutored the other half in pairs for a 10–15 minutes. Halfway through, students switched roles and the tutees now became the tutors and vice versa. If an unequal number of students were present because of absences, a tutoring triad was formed. In the role of tutee, the student was either presented spelling words to spell one at a time from the weekly list, or was to read from passages in the week's reading assignment, or was to compute math facts from the week's curriculum. If the tutee made an error in response and was corrected by the tutor, the tutee practiced the correct response three times.

In the role of tutor, they were responsible for awarding their tutees 2 points for each correct response and 1 point for a completed correction. At the end of the session, students' points were summed and reported to the teacher for team summation. Tutor pairs were equally divided on two competing teams for the week's highest score. CWPT was not only effective in comparison to business as usual teacher-led instruction, but was preferred by students and liked by teachers.

The CWPT structure proved to be functional, producing vastly more time engaged in academic responding each school day and reducing the gap (Greenwood, 1991; Greenwood, Delquadri, & Hall, 1989). CWPT students talked more about academics, read and wrote more, and as an additional result were more social and better behaved. Follow-ups in middle and high school also confirmed that students maintained their advantage in achievement, and a lower percentage of students in the CWPT group had received special education services according to district records (Greenwood & Delquadri, 1995; Greenwood et al., 1989). (What Works Clearing House http://ies.ed.gov/ncee/wwc/interventionreport.aspx?sid=81).

CWPT became the basis for Peer-Assisted Learning Strategies (PALS) (e.g., Fuchs, Fuchs, Mathes, & Simmons, 1997). Successful extensions were made to Reading and Math PALS that combined the CWPT core structure and with increasing numbers of well-designed curriculum components (Fuchs et al., 1997; Rohrbeck, Ginsberg-Block, Fantuzzo, & Miller, 2003) (What Works Clearing House http://ies.ed.gov/ncee/wwc/interventionreport.aspx?sid=364). CWPT also shared greater effectiveness with other reciprocal peer and group-oriented, class-wide structures of instruction (e.g., Fantuzzo, King, & Heller, 1992; Harper & Maheady, 1999). CWPT was also extended in applications with more diverse and challenging learners during core instruction (Kamps, Barbetta, Leonard, & Delquadri, 1994; Mortweet et al., 1999).

Fidelity of intervention

Beyond confirming the function of classroom instruction with EBA data, it proved possible to use that data to confirm that teachers were actually implementing interventions like CWPT. EBA made possible comparisons between business-as-usual instructional structures (baseline) and experimental structures in terms of their ecological and behavioral differences. Whether used in educational research experiments or in professional development applications, we learned that we could use EBA to confirm differentiation of practices being implemented as previously described.

For example, we could document differences in a variety of classroom measures: student grouping, tasks and materials used, whether teacher or peers were teaching the target student, the proximity of teacher, teachers' use of approval, etc. This was possible because the EBA taxonomy enabled standard structural comparisons between alternative instructional practices yielding differences in how classroom events are arranged, and what the teacher was doing while teaching. We termed these structure comparisons as profiles, footprints, or templates, each reflecting different ecobehavioral patterns associated with the different practices (e.g., Cone, Bourland, & Wood-Shuman, 1986; Cone & Hoier, 1986). Template items in this case consisted of the ecological and behavioral items defined by the CISSAR or ESCAPE taxonomies. Differences between templates were considered to be potential intervention targets or deviations between well-implemented and poorly implemented programs. In addition to visual comparisons, statistics were available to test the similarity (and dissimilarity) of two profiles or templates.

Identification of naturally effective instruction

We used EBA template matching to identify the structure of naturally effective classroom instruction and promote its wider use by other teachers in the same school. We first sought to identify teachers producing the highest and lowest achieving students. We then sought to identify the practices, including the structure of the instruction the teachers of high achieving students were using (Greenwood, Arreaga-Mayer, & Carta, 1994). Once identified, we sought to teach teachers of low-achieving students in the same school to implement these identified practices and assess effects on student learning. We reported that these naturally effective procedures did indeed produce better student outcomes when implemented well by other teachers (Greenwood, Carta, Arreaga-Mayer, & Rager, 1991). In addition to taking advantage of old

"CWPT students talked more about academics, and read and wrote more, and as an additional result were more social and better behaved. Follow-ups in middle and high school also confirmed that students maintained their advantage in achievement, and a lower percentage of students in the CWPT group had received special education services according to district records."

lessons learned about the structure and function of instruction, the approach was consistent with building-based approaches to program improvement through professional development, teacher coaching, and the implementation of effective practices.

Preparation of students for the next environment

Another application of EBA template matching focused on students making next environment transitions from special to general education. Students, particularly those with developmental delays and disabilities served in special education at the time, faced often glaring differences in how the preschool and kindergarten environments were arranged. This included differences in teachers and teacher behaviors as well as the behaviors/skills expected of children in kindergarten. This work sought to make transition programming more successful (Carta, Atwater, Schwartz, & Miller, 1990). While such issues may seem obsolete today because of inclusion, IDEA, and other educational rights policies planning for and preparing students for next environment transitions, was another instructive example of how EBA templates can be used to design and implement more effective instruction.

The goal was to make environment transitions more manageable using information about the next environment (kindergarten) to align the sending preschool environment's structure and function so that students experienced a greater match between what they could do versus what would be expected in the future.

Carta and colleagues using the *Ecobehavioral System for the Complex Assessment of Preschool Environments* (ESCAPE) (Carta et al., 1990), reported that special preschoolers spent significantly more time than regular kindergartners in play while regular kindergartners spent more time in transition between activities, classroom business, and music/dance/recitation. Children in the two settings spent roughly equivalent amounts in time in preacademics, fine motor, and story activities. Children in special preschools were more likely to spend time at tables but children in regular kindergarten spent roughly equivalent amounts of time on the floor and at tables. Children in regular kindergartens were also much more likely to be standing in line than were children in the special preschool. Children in special preschool classrooms were much more likely to be observed in small groups of five or fewer children (75 percent of the time); compared to children in regular kindergartens in instructional groups of larger than five (75 percent of their time).

The most common instructional arrangement during class business in kindergarten was the children sitting on the floor in large groups (i.e., more than five children) attending to no materials and the teacher providing a verbal prompt. This arrangement was in place for 10 percent of all class business times. This same arrangement was never observed in the special preschool during class business. The implication for transition is that although the "opening circle" time is a standard activity in both the special preschool and regular kindergarten, the common ecological arrangements during this activity are vastly different in the two settings. Obviously, this is one of many adjustments that children with disabilities must make in adapting to a regular kindergarten class.

Agar and Shapiro (1995), used the template approach to align actual identified differences between instructional environments in sending and receiving classes through to intervention development and evaluation. First, ESCAPE data was used to profile the differences in structure and function. The profiles or templates were graphed to reveal side-by-side differences. An intervention focusing on some of the major differences found between the environments was developed in collaboration with the preschool staff and implemented for eight weeks in the preschool.

"In addition to taking advantage of old lessons learned about the structure and function of instruction, the approach was consistent with building-based approaches to program improvement through professional development, teacher coaching, and the implementation of effective practices."

The intervention was successful in making the preschool environment look and feel more like kindergarten, including the teacher behaviors, with those reflected in the kindergarten data. Follow-up results of preschool students that received the intervention when in kindergarten indicated fewer competing behaviors and they also were the recipients of fewer individual prompts during independent work tasks. Somewhat similar procedures and findings using template match were reported for children in the elementary grades (Hoier, McConnell, & Pallay, 1987).

Summary

Based on our use of EBA we have learned that the risk is high that the structure of typical instruction, whether general, special, bilingual, or prekindergarten literacy, is weak in terms of its student behavioral function. Typical instruction was observed to produce low levels of engagement in academic responding. We learned that gaps in student's engagement in academic responding help account for observed gaps in academic achievement, and that using more effective instructional practices removed these gaps over time and produced better academic outcomes. We learned that reforms, interventions, and practices that restructure the function of instruction to promote academic responding likely boost academic achievement. It appeared to us that engagement in academic responding was a dimension of instructional intensity. Additionally, it was possible and feasible to identify the superior effects of naturally effective instruction practices in some classrooms, and replicate them in others. These practices led to better outcomes. We learned that it was possible to more closely align the structure of sending and receiving instructional environments, making transitions more successful. The science behind this is our improved ability to differentiate instruction environments using EBA in terms of their structure and function. This information is useful in creating, implementing, and maintaining effective instruction for individuals and groups of students.

HOW THEN SHOULD WE STRUCTURE HIGHLY EFFECTIVE LEARNING ENVIRONMENTS IN SCHOOLS?

School-level Perspectives

School-level influences on classroom instruction and student learning are well-recognized and may have systematic effects on classroom structure and function, as previously discussed. Recent school-level reforms to support earlier intervening with struggling learners are one relevant example (Greenwood & Kim, 2012). Instead of a "wait to fail" approach to providing students special education supports, early intervening provides to students additional learning supports as soon as needs are recognized. The goal of early intervening is to prevent early learning difficulties and behavior problems from becoming disabilities later (Berkeley, Bender, Peaster, & Saunders, 2009; Shinn & Walker, 2010). Perhaps the most cogent example we have on the effectiveness of a school-wide practice is School-Wide Positive Behavior Support (SWPBS).

Early intervening requires that the school is organized to provide Multiple Tiers of Support (MTS). MTS refers to a means of differentiating the instruction of individual learners not making progress in the core curriculum (Tier 1). Learners in this approach who are not making expected rates of progress are provided extra supplemental instruction (Tier 2) in addition to Tier 1 as a means of accelerating their progress. Similarly, learners who are not succeeding with Tier 2 supports are provided additional and more intensive experiences (Tier 3). Detailed treatment of MTS is beyond the scope of this discussion, however, the ideas of differentiating instruction through exposure to more intensive instruction are highly relevant. EBA applied to the implementation and improvement of school-wide MTS can provide useful, objective information on the structure and function of these supports, as well as the fidelity of implementation and professional development provided to the teachers implementing tiers of support.

A question one may ask is what makes Tier 2 and 3 supports more intensive than Tier 1? The answer is that they need to be structured to effectively promote academic responding. Steps in this direction include reducing student–teacher ratio by using small groups, adding more opportunities to respond, and using highly focused materials and procedures. Another is designing explicit instruction to increase intensity. An example of Tier 2 language and literacy instruction in preschool is the use of storybooks containing embedded instruction. Students identified with weak skills are provided three lessons per book per week, with new books and new vocabulary to be learned in a series of 18 story books in all (Spencer et al., 2013).

> "We learned that reforms, interventions, and practices that restructure the function of instruction to promote academic responding likely boost academic achievement. It appeared to us that engagement in academic responding was a dimension of instructional intensity."

Similarly, what makes Tier 3 instruction even more intensive than Tier 2 is providing Tier 3 instruction one-on-one or in very small group arrangements with more explicit or programmed instruction focused on the target skill of greatest need for an individual student. I believe an ecobehavioral assessment of students' access to additional Tier 2 and/or Tier 3 instruction would confirm these assertions in terms of structural differences and behavioral function.

Other Tier 2 and Tier 3 methods and techniques could reasonably include uses of peer tutoring and/or electronic technology combined with well-designed instruction to reduce direct teacher time and cost. For example, taking advantage of what we know about peer-tutoring, including both its academic benefits to both learners (tutees) and teachers (tutors), is a wise and generally low cost solution to providing services. A number of RTI reports in the literature use across-age tutors in which older secondary students tutor elementary students (Greenwood, Seals, & Kamps, 2010). We also know that peers can manage small groups of students working in programmed instruction or group projects of an academic nature (Greenwood, Seals, & Kamps, 2010).

In continuing to address disparities in students' schooling outcomes in our low income community schools at greatest risk, how then should we organize schools to meet the challenge? One relatively untapped area is prekindergarten education, where we still don't have universal schooling provided to all students prior to kindergarten! Consistent with recent reports of the beneficial impacts of prekindergarten on children's later life outcomes (Reynolds, Temple, Ou, Arteaga, & White, 2011), providing all students with two years of schooling in prekindergarten (ages 3–5), will add significantly to the national educational product. Doing so will also provide an economic benefit to society for this investment (Heckman, 2006; Heckman & Masterov, 2007).

The national data on school progress suggests that progress rates are slow for older students in middle and high school when compared to elementary school students. Why is this, and is there an instructional explanation and solution? The EBA approach could be useful in addressing these questions as it has been in the schooling of younger students. Work is needed to strengthen the function of classroom instruction in these schools, to accelerate academic growth and create better outcomes. Year-to-year improvement in secondary education and in the future will be advanced by my earlier points: through implementing Pre-K universally in the USA, and employing prevention using MTS or similar models and practices.

To the extent that we are successful improving the function of classroom instruction in multiple schools and districts in states, the more we will broaden and maintain impact nationally.

District-level Perspectives

District-level policies have powerful influences on school-level influences that impact what happens in the classroom. One example of such policies is the selection and adoption of the models and practices at the district level to be used in district schools. Models provide the frameworks for service provision, and districts (and their boards of education and parent stakeholders) are responsible for deciding what the major goals and outcomes will be, including whether or not individual district schools will adopt similar models and practices, and if not, what latitude schools will have in their selection. The MTSS prevention model is one example and its use in all of a district's schools is another.

Another example is the selection and adoption of practices to be used in district models including practice standards in schools, or whether or not the schools will be responsible for their own practices and standards. Yet one more is the support and effort put into quality implementation and maintenance of model/practices in district schools over time. Implementation science tells us that implementation of evidence-based practices in schools, as in other professions, is a matter of using procedures and methods capable of achieving and maintaining fidelity of intervention through changes in organizational structure, staff expectations, and professional development (Fixsen, Naoom, Blase, Friedman, & Wallace, 2006). At the district level, EBA can play a role in documenting what is actually being implemented in schools at the classroom level and whether or not said implementation is consistent with or at variance with what is intended.

SUMMARY/IMPLICATIONS/CONCLUSION

The purpose of this chapter has been to discuss some personal lessons learned over the years about teaching and learning, and how to structure and design classroom instructional environments to best influence the learning of all students, including those with disabilities. A key question addressed was how multiple influences (micro and macro to the learner) combine to create exceptional learning environments and evidence that supports this view.

My personal view is that highly effective learning environments are organized using practices that structure the delivery of instruction in ways that promote high levels of desired academic responding. As discussed, these practices include: specifying objectively what the learner needs to know and do in alignment with appropriate standards, providing instruction focused on these skills that is explicit, providing multiple opportunities to respond using a mix of teacher- and peer-led lesson formats and materials that keep things interesting, differentiating instruction based on learners' response to instruction, and arranging useful consequences for correct responding and appropriate classroom conduct. We also need to use locally collected data for decision making and make fidelity of implementation in classrooms and schools "best" practice. Lastly, we need to make these practices the expectation at the school and district levels of influence.

I would hope that teachers and educators realize that exceptional instruction is that which promotes and maintains high levels of daily academic responding. The accumulation of these experiences over years in school is an important driver in what students will know, and what they will be able to do during and after their education. Assuring that structure leads to function is the evidence we need to keep learning on track.

Discussion Questions

1. Greenwood described the Personalized Systems of Instruction (PSI). How do you think this framework can be integrated into today's flipped classroom model? What challenges do you foresee?
2. How do you think ClassWide Peer Tutoring (CWPT) would need to be modified so that it could be used with learners of different ages and disability categories?
3. How could the EBA template be used to transition students from elementary to secondary settings?
4. How would you create an instructional environment that promotes academic engagement and successful transitions?
5. Describe the differences between Tier 2 and Tier 3 supports. Discuss the similarities and differences among these tiers as Greenwood describes them and as Lane and Walker and Lembke describe them.

CHARLES R. GREENWOOD'S SUGGESTIONS FOR FURTHER READING

Carta, J. J., Greenwood, C. R., Walker, D., & Buzhardt, J. (2010). *Using IGDIs: Monitoring progress and improving intervention results for infants and young children.* Baltimore, MD: Brookes.

Greenwood, C. R., Carta, J. J., Baggett, K., Buzhardt, J., Walker, D., & Terry, B. (2008). Best practices in integrating progress monitoring and response-to-intervention concepts into early childhood systems. In A. Thomas & J. Grimes (Eds.), *Best practices in school psychology V* (pp. 535–548). Washington DC: National Association of School Psychology.

Greenwood, C. R., Delquadri, J., & Hall, R. V. (1984). Opportunity to respond and student academic performance. In W. Heward, T. Heron, D. Hill & J. Trap-Porter (Eds.), *Behavior analysis in education* (pp. 58–88). Columbus, OH: Merrill.

Greenwood, C. R., Hops, H., Delquadri, J., & Guild, J. (1974). Group contingencies for group consequences: A further analysis. *Journal of Applied Behavior Analysis, 7*, 413–425.

Greenwood, C. R., Kratchowill, T., & Clements, M. (2008). *School-wide prevention models: Lessons learned in elementary schools.* New York: Guilford.

Greenwood, C. R., Terry, B., Utley, C. A., Montagna, D., & Walker, D. (1993). Achievement placement and services: Middle school benefits of ClassWide Peer Tutoring used at the elementary school. *School Psychology Review, 22*(3), 497–516.

REFERENCES

Agar, C. L., & Shapiro, E. (1995). Template matching as a strategy for assessment of and intervention for preschool children with disabilities. *Topics in Early Childhood Special Education, 15,* 187–218.

Barker, R. G. (1968). *Ecological psychology: Concepts and methods for studying the environment of human behavior.* Stanford, CA: Stanford University Press.

Berkeley, S., Bender, W. N., Peaster, L. G., & Saunders, L. (2009). Implementation of response to intervention: A snapshot of progress. *Journal of Learning Disabilities, 42*, 85–95.

Bijou, S. W., Peterson, R. F., & Ault, M. H. (1968). A method to integrate descriptive and experimental field studies at the level of data and empirical concepts. *Journal of Applied Behavior Analysis, 1*, 175–191.

Bloom, B. S. (1984). The 2 sigma problem: The search for methods of group instruction as effective as one-to-one tutoring. *Educational Researcher, 13*, 4–16.

Bronfenbrenner, U. (1986). Ecology of the family as a context for human development. *Developmental Psychology, 22*, 723–742.

Brophy, J. (1986). Teacher influences on student achievement. *American Psychologist, 41*, 1069–1077.

Carta, J. J., Atwater, J. B., Schwartz, I. S., & Miller, P. A. (1990). Applications of ecobehavioral analysis to the study of transitions across early education. *Education and Treatment of Children, 13*, 298–315.

Catania, A. C. (2013). *Learning (5th ed.)*. Cornwall-on-Hudson, NY: Sloan.

Cone, J. D., Bourland, G., & Wood-Shuman, S. (1986). Template matching: An objective approach to placing clients in appropriate residential services. *Journal of the Association for Persons with Severe Handicaps, 11*, 110–117.

Cone, J. D., & Hoier, P. (1986). Assessing children: The radical behavioral perspective. In R. J. Prinz (Ed.), *Advances in behavioral assessment of children and families* (Vol. 2, pp. 1–27). Greenwich, CT: JAI Press.

Delquadri, J. (1978). An analysis of the generalization effects of four tutoring procedures on the oral reading responses of eight learning disability children. Doctoral Dissertation, University of Kansas, Lawrence, KS.

Fantuzzo, J. W., King, J. A., & Heller, L. R. (1992). Effects of reciprocal peer tutoring on mathematics and school adjustment: A component analysis. *Journal of Educational Psychology, 84*, 331–339.

Fixsen, D. L., Naoom, S. F., Blase, K. A., Friedman, R. M., & Wallace, F. (2006). *Implementation research: A synthesis of the literature*. Tampa, FL: National Implementation Research Network, University of South Florida.

Fuchs, D., Fuchs, L. S., Mathes, P., & Simmons, D. C. (1997). Peer-assisted learning strategies: Making classrooms more responsive to diversity. *American Educational Research Journal, 34*, 174–206.

Grant, L. K., & Spencer, R. E. (2003). The Personalized System of Instruction: Review and applications to distance education http://www.irrodl.org/index.php/irrodl/article/view/152/233. *The International Review of Research in Open and Distance Education, 4*(2).

Greenwood, C. R. (1981). Peer-oriented technology and ethical issues. In P. Strain (Ed.), *The utilization of classroom peers as behavior change agents* (pp. 327–360). New York: Plenum.

Greenwood, C. R. (1991). Longitudinal analysis of time engagement and academic achievement in at-risk and non-risk students. *Exceptional Children, 57*, 521–535.

Greenwood, C. R., Arreaga-Mayer, C., & Carta, J. J. (1994). Identification and translation of effective teacher-developed instructional procedures for general practice. *Remedial and Special Education, 15*, 140–151.

Greenwood, C. R., Carta, J. J., Arreaga-Mayer, C., & Rager, A. (1991). The behavior analyst consulting model: Identifying and validating naturally effective instructional models. *Journal of Behavioral Education, 1*, 165–191.

Greenwood, C. R., Carta, J. J., & Atwater, J. J. (1991). Ecobehavioral analysis in the classroom: Review and implications. *Journal of Behavioral Education, 1*, 59–77.

Greenwood, C. R., Carta, J. J., Atwater, J., Goldstein, H., Kaminski, R., & McConnell, S. R. (2012). Is a response to intervention (RTI) approach to preschool language and early literacy instruction needed? *Topics in Early Childhood Special Education, 33*(1), 48–64.

Greenwood, C. R., Carta, J. J., Kamps, D., Terry, B., & Delquadri, J. (1994). Development and validation of standard classroom observation systems for school practitioners: Ecobehavioral assessment systems software EBASS. *Exceptional Children, 61*, 197–210.

Greenwood, C. R., & Delquadri, J. (1988). Code for instructional structure and student academic response: CIS-SAR. In M. Hersen & A. S. Bellack (Eds.), *Dictionary of behavioral assessment techniques* (pp. 120–122). New York: Pergamon.

Greenwood, C. R., & Delquadri, J. (1995). ClassWide Peer Tutoring and the prevention of school failure. *Preventing School Failure, 39*(4), 21–25.

Greenwood, C. R., Delquadri, J., & Hall, R. V. (1989). Longitudinal effects of classwide peer tutoring. *Journal of Educational Psychology, 81*, 371–383.

Greenwood, C. R., Hart, B., Walker, D., & Risley, T. R. (1994). The opportunity to respond revisited: A behavioral theory of developmental retardation and its prevention. In R. Gardner, D. M. Sainato, J. O. Cooper, T. E. Heron, W. L. Heward, J. W. Eshleman & T. A. Grossi (Eds.), *Behavior analysis in education: Focus on measurably superior instruction* (pp. 213–223). Pacific Grove, CA: Brooks/Cole.

Greenwood, C. R., & Hops, H. (1981). Group contingencies and peer behavior change. In P. Strain (Ed.), *The utilization of classroom peers as behavior change agents* (pp. 189–259). New York: Plenum.

Greenwood, C. R., & Kim, J. M. (2012). Response to intervention (RTI) services: An ecobehavioral perspective. *Journal of Education and Psychology Consultation, 22*, 1–27.

Greenwood, C. R., & Maheady, L. (1997). Measurable change in student performance: Forgotten standard in teacher preparation? *Teacher Education and Special Education, 20,* 265–275.

Greenwood, C. R., Seals, K. & Kamps, D. (2010). Peer teaching for multiple levels of support. In M. R. Shinn & H. M. Walker (Eds.), *Interventions for achievement and behavior problems in a three-tier model including RTI,* (pp. 633–674), Bethesda: NASP.

Greenwood, C. R., Sloane, H., & Baskin, A. (1974). Training elementary-aged peer behavior managers to control small group programmed mathematics. *Journal of Applied Behavior Analysis, 7,* 103–114.

Greer, R. D., & McDonough, S. H. (1999). Is the learn unit a fundamental measure of pedagogy? *The Behavior Analyst, 22* (1), 5–16.

Hall, R. V., Delquadri, J., Greenwood, C. R., & Thurston, L. (1982). The importance of opportunity to respond to children's academic success. In E. Edgar, N. Haring, J. Jenkins & C. Pious (Eds.), *Serving young handicapped children: Issues and research* (pp. 107–140). Baltimore, MA: University Park Press.

Harper, G. F., & Maheady, L. (1999). Classwide Student Tutoring Teams: Aligning course objectives, student practice, and testing. *Proven Practice: Prevention and Remediation of School Problems, 1,* 55–59.

Heckman, J. J. (2006). Skill formation and the economics of investing in disadvantaged children. *Science, 312*(5782), 1900–1902.

Heckman, J. J., & Masterov, D. V. (2007). The productivity argument for investing in young children. *Review of Agricultural Economics, 29*(3), 446–493.

Hoier, T. S., McConnell, S., & Pallay, A. G. (1987). Observational assessment for planning and evaluating educational transitions: An initial analysis of template matching. *Behavioral Assessment, 9,* 5–19.

Kamps, D., Barbetta, P. M., Leonard, B. R., & Delquadri, J. (1994). Classwide peer tutoring: An integration strategy to improve and promote peer interactions among students with autism and general education peers. *Journal of Applied Behavior Analysis, 27*(1), 49–61.

Kamps, D., Greenwood, C. R., & Leonard, B. (1991). Ecobehavioral assessment in classrooms serving children with autism and developmental disabilities. In R. J. Prinz (Ed.), *Advances in behavioral assessment of children and families* (pp. 203–237). New York: Jessica Kingsley.

Morris, E. K., & Midgley, B. D. (1990). Some historical and conceptual foundations of ecobehavioral analysis. In S. Schroeder (Ed.), *Ecobehavioral analysis and developmental disabilities: The twenty-first century* (pp. 1–32). New York: Springer-Verlag.

Mortweet, S. L., Utley, C. A., Walker, D., Dawson, H. L., Delquadri, J. C., Reddy, S. S., . . . Ledford, D. (1999). Classwide peer tutoring: Teaching students with mild mental retardation in inclusive classrooms. *Exceptional Children, 65*(4), 425–536.

Odom, S. L., Peck, C. A., Hanson, M. J., Kaiser, A. P., Lieber, J., Horn, E., . . . Schwartz, I. (1996). Inclusion of preschool children with disabilities: An ecological systems perspective. *SRCD Social Policy Report, 10*(2–3), 18–30.

Reynolds, A. J., Temple, J. A., Ou, S. R., Arteaga, I. A., & White, B. A. B. (2011). School-based early childhood education and age-28 well-being: Effects by timing, dosage, and subgroups. *Science, 333*(6040), 360–364.

Rohrbeck, C. A., Ginsberg-Block, M. D., Fantuzzo, J. W., & Miller, T. R. (2003). Peer-assisted learning interventions with elementary school students: A meta-analytic review. *Journal of Educational Psychology, 95,* 240–257.

Shinn, M. R., & Walker, H. M. (Eds.). (2010). *Interventions for achievement and behavior problems in a three-tier model including RTI.* Washington, DC: National Association of School Psychologists.

Skinner, B. F. (1953). *Science and Human Behavior.* NY: Free Press.

Skinner, B. F. (1972). *Cumulative record: A selection of papers* (3rd ed.). New York: Appleton-Century-Crofts.

Spencer, E. J., Goldstein, H., Sherman, A., Noe, S., Tabbah, R., Ziolkowski, R., & Schneider, N. (2013). Effects of an automated vocabulary and comprehension intervention: An early efficacy study. *Journal of Early Intervention, 14*(1), 195–221.

Stanley, S. O., & Greenwood, C. R. (1983). Assessing opportunity to respond in classroom environments through direct observation: How much opportunity to respond does the minority disadvantaged student receive in school? *Exceptional Children, 49,* 370–373.

Thurlow, M. L., Ysseldyke, J. E., Graden, J., & Algozzine, B. (1984). Opportunity to learn for LD students receiving different levels of special education services. *Learning Disability Quarterly, 7,* 55–67.

Vladescu, J. C., & Kodak, T. (2010). A review of recent studies on differential reinforcement during skill acquisition in early intervention. *Journal of Applied Behavior Analysis, 43,* 351–355.

Ysseldyke, J. E., Thurlow, M. L., Mecklenburg, C., Graden, J., & Algozzine, B. (1984). Changes in academic engaged time as a function of assessment and special education intervention. *Special Services in the Schools, 1*(2), 31–43.

Getting to Know Martha L. Thurlow

My connection to special education started in high school in the mid-1960s, and then blossomed before I entered graduate school. Each experience I had with individuals with disabilities made me wonder why their experiences were so different from mine.

During high school, I volunteered to help staff at an institution for individuals with severe intellectual disabilities. After earning my Bachelor's degree in psychology, I volunteered at a different institution. These volunteer experiences were eye-opening for me because each time I was struck by the realization that the children and adults in these settings were not that different from me. I could not understand why they were there, in stark buildings with no stimulation except TVs tuned to some channel that they did not select. They were learning in the same way that I was learning—when someone expected them to learn and took the time to teach them.

I am happy to say that institutions no longer exist in the state in which I had volunteered. Still, my experiences in them led me to my core beliefs in the value of high expectations and access to high-quality instructional experiences. These values guided me my entire career as I moved from a focus on small-scale interventions for students with cognitive disabilities, to a focus on assessment issues for young children with disabilities and students with learning disabilities, then dropout prevention, and finally a focus on policy and its implications for universal design, accessible assessments, and increased expectations and opportunities for students with disabilities.

20

HOW SHOULD WE EVALUATE WHETHER SPECIAL EDUCATION WORKS?

Martha L. Thurlow

Evaluate the effectiveness of special education? This topic has been around for decades—how effective is special education for students with disabilities who need special education services? Investigators have taken several approaches to addressing this question, including focusing on the variables that seem to be related to teacher effectiveness and student outcomes, and focusing on the measures of effectiveness themselves (e.g., Hocutt, 1996; Marston, 1988; Tindal, 1985). With the passage of the Elementary and Secondary Education Act in 2001 (also known as No Child Left Behind) and the subsequent alignment of the Individuals with Disabilities Education Act to it in 2004, the conversation has shifted to the importance of the academic achievement of students with disabilities (see for example, President's Commission on Excellence in Special Education, 2002), and more recently to the readiness of students with disabilities for college and careers (Thurlow, 2012) and various indicators of post-school outcomes, such as employment and participation in postsecondary education programs (Bureau of Labor Statistics, 2012; Wagner, Newman, Cameto, Garza, & Levine, 2005).

Having worked on the inclusion of students with disabilities in assessment and accountability systems for much of my career, I recognize the importance of academic achievement measures for all students, including those with disabilities. Some of the major changes in the academic achievement outcomes of students with disabilities, including those with the most significant cognitive disabilities, have come about because of the emphasis that has been placed on the inclusion of students with disabilities in assessments of reading, writing, mathematics, and other content, and in holding schools accountable for the performance of students with disabilities on these measures. Although it would be inaccurate to say that academic achievement is the only measure that we need to examine to evaluate whether special education works, it is a very important one, and one that has improved dramatically over time.

To address the question of how special education should be evaluated, I would like to take a bit of a historical tour through my career. Doing so covers a variety of topics, which I lump into two areas: (a) what the important outcomes of special education are, and (b) measuring the academic outcomes of education for students with disabilities.

I then discuss the latest iteration of examining the effectiveness of special education, an approach that focuses on evaluating educator effectiveness. I conclude with my perceptions of the future of evaluating the effects of special education.

WHAT ARE THE IMPORTANT OUTCOMES OF SPECIAL EDUCATION?

When I started my career in special education more than four decades ago, I had the opportunity to work on a number of projects that covered such topics as learning strategies, curriculum development, learning disabilities, academic engaged time, and early childhood assessment practices. I was privileged to work with great mentors and thinkers at the University of Minnesota—James Turnure, Maynard Reynolds, Robert Bruininks, Stanley Deno, James Ysseldyke, and many others too numerous to mention, as well as educators and researchers across the country. At the University of Minnesota, we were fortunate to be supported in our work through several large federal grants, including the Research and Development Center in the Education of Handicapped Children (1969–1976), the Institute for Research on Learning Disabilities (1977–1983), and the Rehabilitation Research and Training Center (1988–1993), as well as numerous other projects examining normalization, follow-up of students with mild, moderate, and severe intellectual disabilities, and dropout prevention and intervention projects.

> "Although it would be inaccurate to say that academic achievement is the only measure that we need to examine to evaluate whether special education works, it is a very important one, and one that has improved dramatically over time."

Among my earliest research were studies designed to examine the extent to which students with intellectual disabilities could use mediation techniques to learn pairs of words or symbols (paired-associate learning). The findings of this early work, which took place before the passage of the Education of All Handicapped Children Act (the early version of the Individuals with Disabilities Education Act) were exciting—students with intellectual disabilities could learn the same things as other students (Taylor, Thurlow, & Turnure, 1977; Thurlow & Turnure, 1972; Turnure, Buium, & Thurlow, 1976; Turnure, Larsen, & Thurlow, 1973; Turnure & Thurlow, 1973, 1975, 1976)! (I am embarrassed to write this now, but it was a "finding" in the early 1970s.) I worked with colleagues on using the same types of techniques that we had used in experimental studies to actually teach concepts to students with intellectual impairments in classrooms (e.g., Thurlow & Turnure, 1977).

Despite the success of much of this early work, I noticed how relatively narrow it was in its impact, and how it tended not to endure over time. At the same time, I grew in my awareness of the policy world, and the effectiveness of some policies in changing practice. Prompted by some dramatic changes that began to occur after the enactment of the Education for All Handicapped Children Act in 1975, my interest in the effects of special education (and education in general) for students with disabilities grew.

With the funding of the National Center on Educational Outcomes (NCEO) in 1990, my focus narrowed in some ways and expanded in other ways. One of the first questions that was addressed by NCEO in the early 1990s was "What are the important outcomes of special education?" (Ysseldyke & Thurlow, 1994). In identifying and tracing critical issues in special education, Ysseldyke, Algozzine, and Thurlow (2000) noted the following in relation to the important outcomes for students with disabilities:

> At that time [prior to the 1990s], the lists of important outcomes for students with disabilities often were different from those for students in general education. Even though there were many areas of overlap (e.g., achievement, school participation, post-secondary experiences/status), some of those identified for students with disabilities were not identified as important for students in general education (e.g., quality of life, work readiness). Similarly, some of the outcomes identified for general education were not included in lists for students with disabilities (e.g., creative thinking/problem solving, interpersonal/organizational skills).
>
> (p. 354)

NCEO brought together stakeholders from diverse perspectives, including representatives from the American Federation of Teachers (AFT), the National Educational Association (NEA), the National Association of State Directors of Special Education (NASDSE), the Council for Exceptional Children (CEC), and many other organizations, along with individuals representing various disabilities (e.g., deaf-hard of hearing, learning disabilities, attention disabilities) and educational entities (school administrators, teacher trainers, state departments of education, state boards of education, special schools). Across the age and grade spans for which stakeholders were brought together (preschool age 3, preschool age 6, grade 4, grade 8, high school, postschool), there was the consistent message that the important outcomes for students with disabilities were the same as the important outcomes for students without disabilities (Shriner, Ysseldyke, Thurlow, & Honetschlager, 1994; Ysseldyke & Thurlow, 1995; Ysseldyke, Thurlow, & Bruininks, 1992; Ysseldyke, Thurlow, & Shriner, 1992). Also, the message was clear that there were many things that contributed to reaching desired outcomes (see Conceptual Model for grade 4 outcomes in Figure 20.1).

As evident in Figure 20.1, the stakeholder groups identified sets of outcomes for each age and grade level (Ysseldyke, Thurlow, & Erickson, 1994a, 1994b; Ysseldyke, Thurlow, & Gilman, 1993a, 1993b, 1993c, 1993d). For each outcome domain, several outcomes were identified, and for each outcome, specific indicators were suggested (see Figure 20.2 for grade 4 outcomes and indicators for the academic and functional literacy domain; see Figure 20.3 for the outcomes and indicators at the same grade for the personal and social adjustment domain). School age outcomes included the following domains of outcomes (NCEO, no date):

- *Academic and Functional Literacy*–the use of information to function in society, to achieve goals, and to develop knowledge
- *Presence and Participation*[1]–opportunities for physical presence as well as active and meaningful participation in school and the community by all individuals
- *Family Involvement/Accommodation and Adaptation*[2] –the extent to which students have and use adjustments, adaptive technologies, or compensatory strategies that are necessary for individuals to achieve outcomes, and the presence of family support
- *Physical Health*–the extent to which the individual demonstrates or receives support to engage in healthy behavior, attitudes, and knowledge related to physical well-being

326 • Thurlow

**Conceptual Model of Outcomes
Grade 4**

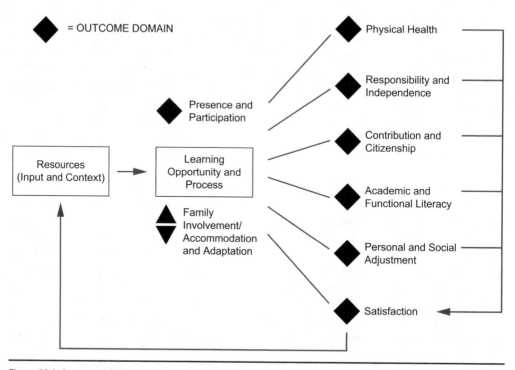

Figure 20.1 Conceptual Model of Outcomes for Grade 4

Ysseldyke, Thurlow, and Erickson (1994a), p. 2. Reprinted with permission from Martha Thurlow.

- *Responsibility and Independence*–the extent to which the individual's behavior reflects the ability to function independently or interdependently, and to assume responsibility for oneself
- *Contribution and Citizenship*–the extent to which the individual gives something back to society or participates as a citizen in society
- *Personal and Social Adjustment*–the extent to which the individual demonstrates socially acceptable and healthy behaviors, attitudes, and knowledge regarding mental well-being, either alone or with guidance and support
- *Satisfaction*–the degree to which a favorable attitude is held toward education

Generally, the same outcome domains were reflected across the age and grade ranges, although the specific indicators varied (see Ysseldyke, Krentz, Elliott, Thurlow, Erickson, & Moore, 1998; Ysseldyke, Krentz, Elliott, Thurlow, Thompson, & Moore, 1998).

A host of data sources were identified for each of these outcome domains (see, for example, for grade four, Ysseldyke, Thurlow, & Erickson, 1995). Box 20.1 shows the list of possible data sources that was generated for the school-age indicators in the academic and functional literacy domain. Despite general agreement on the important outcomes, data on these outcomes for students with disabilities were almost nonexistent (see Bruininks,

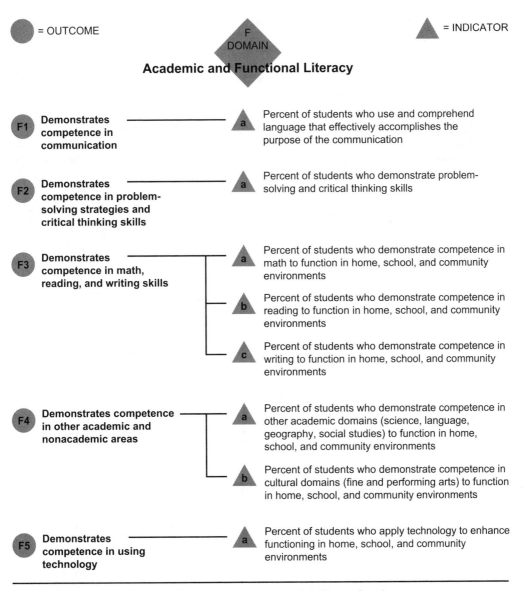

● = OUTCOME

▲ = INDICATOR

F DOMAIN

Academic and Functional Literacy

F1 Demonstrates competence in communication —————— **a** Percent of students who use and comprehend language that effectively accomplishes the purpose of the communication

F2 Demonstrates competence in problem-solving strategies and critical thinking skills —————— **a** Percent of students who demonstrate problem-solving and critical thinking skills

F3 Demonstrates competence in math, reading, and writing skills —————— **a** Percent of students who demonstrate competence in math to function in home, school, and community environments

b Percent of students who demonstrate competence in reading to function in home, school, and community environments

c Percent of students who demonstrate competence in writing to function in home, school, and community environments

F4 Demonstrates competence in other academic and nonacademic areas —————— **a** Percent of students who demonstrate competence in other academic domains (science, language, geography, social studies) to function in home, school, and community environments

b Percent of students who demonstrate competence in cultural domains (fine and performing arts) to function in home, school, and community environments

F5 Demonstrates competence in using technology —————— **a** Percent of students who apply technology to enhance functioning in home, school, and community environments

Figure 20.2 Outcomes and Indicators for Grade 4 Academic and Functional Literacy Domain

Ysseldyke, Thurlow, and Erickson (1994a), p. 13. Reprinted with permission from Martha Thurlow.

Thurlow, & Ysseldyke, 1992; McGrew, Thurlow, & Spiegel, 1993; McGrew, Algozzine, Ysseldyke, Thurlow, & Spiegel, 1995; Vanderwood, McGrew, & Ysseldyke, 1998). Two of the possible data sources (school or district results from statewide assessment program; selected items from the National Center for Education Statistics' National Assessment of Educational Progress–NAEP) were ones that were reacted to with alarm–why were students who could and should participate in these assessments *not* doing so (Kantrowitz & Springen, 1997; Zlatos, 1994). Despite attempts to broaden the focus to other educational outcomes, the field seemed to believe, as suggested by Shriner (1994) that "the

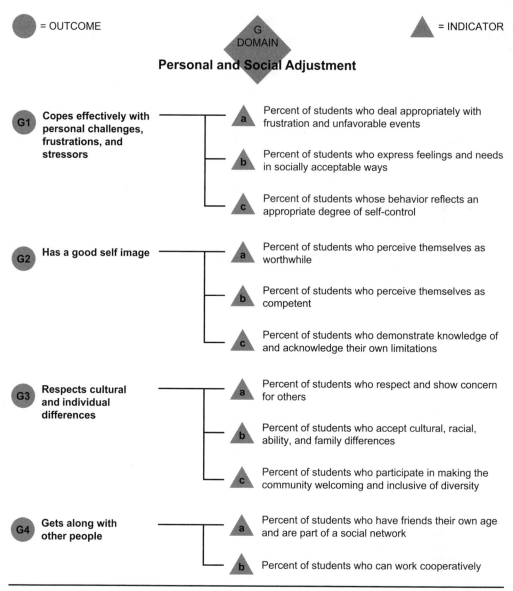

Figure 20.3 Outcomes and Indicators for Grade 4 Personal and Social Adjustment Domain

Ysseldyke, Krentz, Elliott, Thurlow, Erickson, & Moore (1998), p. 58. Reprinted with permission from Martha Thurlow.

belief is that schools should stick to academics because a well-educated student body will take care of personal, social, community, and environmental interactions . . ." (p. 153).

Many other efforts were underway in educational reform in general, and many of these efforts were also focused on identifying the outcomes of education that needed to be tracked to ensure that students in U.S. schools were making progress and reaching desired outcomes. After waves of reports on the poor performance of students in the U.S. and the need for reform, including *A Nation at Risk* (National Commission

---

Box 20.1 Possible Sources of Data for School-age Indicators

- Teacher observations of student in academic environments.
- Student contracts, portfolios, or performance records.
- Parent/guardian survey or interview.
- Teacher survey or interview.
- Teacher ratings.
- Student survey or interview.
- Peer survey or interview.
- School or district results from statewide assessment program.
- Performance on language, mathematics, reading or writing tests.
- Performance-based assessment results.
- Results of speech or language assessments (for students receiving services).
- Selected items from U.S. census on percentage of students who are "linguistically isolated" (living in a household where no one over age 14 speaks English fluently or as their only language).
- Observations of student performance and scaling responses using rubrics from existing problem-solving and critical thinking skills materials.
- School or district participation records in speech, debate, or theater.
- Selected items from the National Center for Education Statistics' *National Assessment of Educational Progress.*
- Comparison of performance on tasks to the U.S. Department of Education's *Youth Indicators 1993: Trends in the Well-Being of American Youth.*
- Analysis of teaching plans.
- Inventory of technology available to school populations in the school or district.
- Ratings of success after six months in next environment.
- Reports by the U.S. Office of Technology Assessment (OTA).

Source: Ysseldyke, Krentz, Elliott, Thurlow, Erickson, & Moore (1998), p. 58.

---

on Excellence in Education, 1983), *Time for Results* (National Governors' Association, 1986), *America's Shame, America's Hope* (Carnegie Council on Adolescent Development, 1989), *Transforming Education* (National Governors' Association, 1993), and *A Nation Still at Risk* (Center for Education Reform, 1998), all of the governors met to agree on eight national goals for education (see Box 20.2). A quick glance at the goals confirms that none of these goals was met. They disappeared, and policymakers tried to refocus the attention of the nation on educational outcomes.

"With the enactment of the 1997 Individuals with Disabilities Education Act, which required the participation of students with disabilities in state and district assessments and the 2001 No Child Left Behind Act, which focused attention on reading, mathematics, and science, the 'important' outcomes were defined for the country."

Box 20.2 Eight National Goals Identified by the Nation's Governors

- Goal 1: By the year 2000, all children in America will start school ready to learn.
- Goal 2: By the year 2000, the high school graduation rate will increase to at least 90 percent.
- Goal 3: By the year 2000, American students will leave grades 4, 8, and 12 having demonstrated competency over challenging subject matter including English, mathematics, science, foreign languages, civics and government, economics, history, and geography; and every school in America will ensure that all students learn to use their minds well, so that they may be prepared for responsible citizenship, further learning, and productive employment in our nation's modern economy.
- Goal 4: By the year 2000, the nation's teaching force will have access to programs for the continued improvement of their professional skills and the opportunity to acquire the knowledge and skills needed to instruct and prepare all American students for the next century.
- Goal 5: By the year 2000, United States students will be first in the world in science and mathematics.
- Goal 6: By the year 2000, every adult American will be literate and will possess the knowledge and skills necessary to compete in a global economy and exercise the rights and responsibilities of citizenship.
- Goal 7: By the year 2000, every school in the United States will be free of drugs, violence, and the unauthorized presence of firearms and alcohol and will offer a disciplined environment conducive to learning.
- Goal 8: By the year 2000, every school will promote partnerships that will increase parental involvement and participation in promoting the social–emotional, and academic growth of children.

The lack of success in making progress on the eight national education goals contributed to a new focus on standards, assessments, and accountability. The Education Commission of the States (1998) directed attention to accountability systems: "*accountability* systems collect, evaluate, and use data about students and schools to hold educators and others responsible for results" (p. 19). The National Research Council (Elmore & Rothman, 1999) laid out a conceptual model for standards-based reform, and also supported a study of the inclusion of students with disabilities in standards-based reform (McDonnell, McLaughlin, & Morison, 1997). These and numerous other forces resulted in a narrowing of focus to academic outcomes not seen since the Sputnik scare.

With the enactment of the 1997 Individuals with Disabilities Education Act (IDEA), which required the participation of students with disabilities in state and district-wide assessments, and the 2001 No Child Left Behind Act (NCLB), which focused attention on reading, mathematics, and science, the "important" outcomes were defined for the country. Everything else—behavioral and social adjustment, family involvement, and so on—took a back seat to measuring and reporting on the performance of students—including students with disabilities—in academic achievement assessments based on educational standards.

MEASURING THE ACADEMIC ACHIEVEMENT OUTCOMES OF STUDENTS WITH DISABILITIES

Many educators and parents have commented on the *sea change* brought about in the education of students with disabilities as a result of requirements that they be included in state assessments of academic achievement and that their results be reported publicly in the same way as the results were presented for other students. Increased transparency for the academic results of these students brought a new level of attention to what was happening for them instructionally and to the nature of the assessments used to measure their performance.

My work since the mid-1990s focused almost entirely on the nature of large-scale assessments used to measure the academic achievement of students with disabilities. This work reflected the IDEA approach—most students with disabilities should participate in the same state and district assessments as students without disabilities, with accommodations if needed; for those students unable to participate in the same assessments, states and districts needed to develop alternate assessments. Clarification about who the students were who were unable to participate in regular state assessments came via ESEA through regulation in 2003, when it clarified that only those students with the most significant cognitive disabilities should participate in alternate assessments based on alternate achievement standards (AA-AAS), and that for accountability purposes, only up to 1 percent of the total population of students could be counted for NCLB Adequate Yearly Progress (AYP) accountability by showing proficient performance on the AA-AAS.

By 2000 when, according to IDEA 97, states were to have developed the AA-AAS, the attention to students with disabilities and their participation in state and district assessments—as well as in NAEP—was in high fervor! Several topics had to be addressed at the same time, including accommodations, universally designed assessments, reporting results, and development of AA-AAS.

Although the field generally agreed that most students with disabilities should participate in the same assessments as other students, not all believed that the same assessments were adequate. In addition to the AA-AAS, educators pushed for an alternate assessment based on modified achievement standards (AA-MAS). The opportunity for states to develop this type of assessment became a reality in 2007 through regulation, but was actively being removed from policy by 2011 (Lazarus, Thurlow, Ysseldyke, & Edwards, 2013). Despite its decline, the AA-MAS taught the field much about ways to improve assessments so that they more accurately reflected the knowledge and skills of all students, not just those with disabilities (Thurlow, Lazarus, & Bechard, 2012). These changes reflected what were considered by many to be universal design principles for assessments (see Thompson, Thurlow, & Malouf, 2004; Thurlow et al., 2009). Tremendous changes occurred between the early 2000s, when the notion of applying universal design principles to assessments first emerged, to the late 2010s, when nearly every state indicated that it incorporated the principles of universal design into the development of its assessments (Altman et al., 2008) and when new consortia of states were formed to develop Race-to-the-Top assessment systems.

Despite the push to make assessments more appropriate for students with disabilities from the beginning, it was recognized that accommodations were still an important aspect of the participation of students with disabilities in assessments (NCEO, 2011). Accommodations and the policies that surround them have been a challenge for the educational system, not only for assessments but for instruction (Thurlow, 2013, 2014; Thurlow, Lazarus, & Christensen, 2013), yet in many ways they have been one of the major areas of change that have occurred with the increased emphasis on outcomes and including students with disabilities in standards-based educational assessments.

There has been a flurry of research undertaken to evaluate whether accommodations produce valid results, or whether they unfairly advantage students with disabilities (see Thurlow, 2014). At the same time, policymakers are aggressively exploring ways to incorporate what previously would have been called "accommodations" into the design of technology-based assessments (Russell, 2011; Russell, Hoffman, & Higgins, 2009a, 2009b). There are many fruitful efforts underway that may very likely result in dramatic improvements in assessment, and hopefully in instruction, as technology provides avenues of access that were unimaginable before.

> "There are many fruitful efforts underway that may very likely result in dramatic improvements in assessment, and hopefully in instruction, as technology provides avenues of access that were unimaginable before."

Perhaps even more dramatic changes have occurred in the academic instruction and assessments for students with significant cognitive disabilities (Quenemoen, 2008). The requirement that state and district academic assessments be developed for these students meant that there needed to be: (a) creative thinking and design work on how to assess students with very significant disabilities, including most often those with intellectual disabilities, multiple disabilities, and significant autism, (b) dramatic changes in the instruction for these students, who rarely received academic instruction, and (c) significant professional development for those educators who worked with the students in the AA-AAS.

The AA-AAS continues to be the subject of controversy, with some arguing that students with significant cognitive disabilities do not need to spend their time on academics, but rather need to focus on other important functional skills. Although this argument still rages, more and more educators are recognizing that teaching academics to students with significant cognitive disabilities does not mean that all other instruction disappears, and that in fact, an academic focus more often helps these students interact with their peers and potentially be more ready for future work placements and post-secondary training opportunities (Kearns et al., 2010).

Going Full Circle—Outcomes to Academics to College and Career Ready

The individuals and organizations identifying important outcomes of education for students with disabilities in the early 1990s were thinking about the eventual outcomes for these students—were they employed, were they good citizens, were they able to function independently and take responsibility for themselves? Essentially, they were thinking about the post-school lives of individuals with disabilities.

Although outcomes have improved in the past decade, we continue to see evidence that individuals with disabilities have poorer outcomes when it comes to employment and post-secondary training (Bureau of Labor Statistics, 2012; Wagner et al., 2005). With the new policy emphasis on common core academic standards and college and career readiness, concerns about the outcomes of students with disabilities are raised to a new level, even as the opportunities are recognized (Thurlow, 2012). The Common Core State Standards developed by the National Governors' Association and the Council of Chief State School Officers have brought renewed attention to the focus on instruction for students with disabilities, and to the ways in which we assess all students, including those with disabilities (Thurlow, Quenemoen, & Lazarus, 2011).

It should not be a surprise that students with disabilities tend, on average, to have poorer outcomes than other students. Since their inclusion in state and district assessments, students with disabilities have performed at significantly lower levels than students without disabilities (Thurlow, Bremer, & Albus, 2011). Although increases have been noted for both state assessments (Thurlow, Quenemoen, Altman, & Cuthbert, 2007) and NAEP assessments (see Cortiella, 2007), the improvements have not been dramatic enough to significantly narrow gaps. In some states, the gaps have not narrowed at all.

The poor performance of students with disabilities is not universal. Several studies have demonstrated that there are places where the performance of students with disabilities is more like that of their peers than it is different (Cortiella & Burnette, 2009; Donahue Institute, 2004). A concerted effort to find districts that are improving the performance of students with disabilities was undertaken in 2011 in collaboration with NCEO (Telfer, 2011). Common practices across the districts were: (a) use data well; (b) focus your goals; (c) select and implement shared instructional practices; (d) implement deeply; (e) monitor and provide feedback and support; (f) inquire and learn. This successful effort to identify districts and their practices spawned a host of materials to support districts in their efforts to narrow their achievement gaps, including those evident for their students with disabilities. These materials include a district self-assessment guide (Telfer & Glasgow, 2012), a parent/family companion guide (Cortiella, 2012), and higher-education materials (e.g., Howley & Howley, 2012).

THE FUTURE OF EVALUATING THE EFFECTS OF SPECIAL EDUCATION

Policy pushes have increased in intensity in the past several years, most of them directed toward increasing the academic content standards to which K–12 students are held. The standards are benchmarked to international standards and are viewed as more rigorous than previous standards set for students (Kober & Rentner, 2012; Porter, McMaken, Hwang, & Yang, 2011). These new standards promote the importance of being college and career ready. Although researchers in the area of college readiness focus on outcomes beyond academics (Conley, 2010), the standards and assessments continue to focus on academics.

> "One of the major challenges has been the fact that special education students rarely have a single educator working with them."

In 2011, the U.S. Department of Education provided states with the opportunity to apply for flexibility from the No Child Left Behind AYP requirements and consequences. To do so, states had to consult with diverse groups on an alternative approach to accountability, and meet three principles: (I) college and career ready expectations for all students; (II) state-developed differentiated recognition, accountability, and supports; and (III) supporting effective instruction and leadership (U.S. Department of Education, 2011). Principle III has represented a big change for most states, especially as they attempt to include all of their educators in a system of educator effectiveness evaluation. The specific directions to states about the third principle were:

> To receive this flexibility, an SEA and each LEA must commit to develop, adopt, pilot, and implement, with the involvement of teachers and principals, teacher and principal evaluation and support systems that: (1) will be used for continual improvement of instruction; (2) meaningfully differentiate performance using at least three performance levels; (3) use multiple valid measures in determining performance levels, including as

a significant factor data on student growth for all students (including English Learners and students with disabilities), and other measures of professional practice (which may be gathered through multiple formats and sources, such as observations based on rigorous teacher performance standards, teacher portfolios, and student and parent surveys); (4) evaluate teachers and principals on a regular basis; (5) provide clear, timely, and useful feedback, including feedback that identifies needs and guides professional development; and (6) will be used to inform personnel decisions. (p. 6)

Including special educators and special education students in educator effectiveness evaluation systems has been particularly challenging. One of the major challenges has been the fact that special education students rarely have a single educator working with them. Questions about how to divide up the responsibility for the student are among the challenges (Holdheide, Goe, Craft, & Reschly, 2010; Warren et al., 2012).

Most states applying for flexibility have approached the inclusion of students with disabilities and special education teachers by devising a different system for them. It is common to see that for special education teachers (similar to teachers of "non-tested grades"), student learning objectives (SLOs) are identified and each student's progress toward those goals is used to evaluate the educator's effectiveness. Advocates are concerned about this approach because it harkens back to the time when the Individualized Education Program (IEP) was the only accountability mechanism for students with disabilities, a time that most agree did not serve students with disabilities well (Espin, Deno, & Albayrak-Kaymak, 1998; McDonnell et al., 1997; McLaughlin & Thurlow, 2003; Yell, Shriner, & Katsiyannis, 2006).

The Office of Special Education Programs in the U.S. Department of Education has for years identified indicators of special education services that it monitors to ensure that students with disabilities receive a Free and Appropriate Public Education (FAPE) and benefit from that education. Within the past couple years, OSEP has started to explore ways to include the educational outcomes of students with disabilities in its program of monitoring and providing technical assistance to states, which in turn will influence the monitoring and technical assistance provided to districts by states. OSEP's efforts started through an exploration of how it could include the results from state assessment systems in its review and technical assistance efforts (see NCEO, 2012). This step toward holding special education units in schools, districts, and schools accountable for the educational outcomes of students with disabilities is consistent with those outcomes valued for general education students. It is an important step forward.

MY PERSPECTIVE

Academic performance clearly is not all that special education is about, but it should be a big part of what it is about. The academic preparation of students with disabilities is a critical part of their being ready to leave the K–12 system and enter the worlds of work and post-secondary education. My long history of working on state and district assessment systems probably gives a hint that I would view them as a critical part of evaluating whether special education works. These assessments are now much better than they have been in the past (not to suggest that there is not still room for improvement).

"The academic preparation of students with disabilities is a critical part of their being ready to leave the K–12 system and enter the worlds of work and post-secondary education."

The emphasis on academics over the past couple decades has been good for students who receive special education services, at least when those responsible for their education do not focus all their efforts on test preparation or "drill-and-kill" on basic skills. The findings from successful districts, which emphasize a comprehensive and data-based approach to the education of all of their students, demonstrate that for students to succeed in academics, including students with disabilities, they need to participate in an educational system that is targeted on academic success.

The focus of the measurement system used to address whether special education works should not be the sole focus of instruction. And, it does not define what we measure in the future. For example, graduation rates are another important indicator of whether special education works, but this measure needs to be supported by measures that address successful progress through the grades, based on achieving expected outcomes for each grade. And, certainly social adjustment, independence, and responsibility are all important. There are many aspects that could be considered in evaluating whether special education works, but if we include all of them from the beginning, we run the real risk of not focusing on anything.

Discussion Questions

1. Thurlow's early research sparked stakeholders to address several outcomes for students with and without disabilities. Do these outcomes hold true to this day?
2. Why do you think that none of the goals featured in Box 20.2 were met?
3. Although NCLB included students with disabilities in its focus on academic outcomes, there was not a comparable focus on behavioral and social outcomes in detail. Why do you think this was the case? How are behavioral and social outcomes being addressed today?
4. Describe the types of technology improvements you have observed for assessing students with disabilities.
5. What special problems arise when evaluating the effectiveness of special education teachers? What do you think should be the focus of special education teacher effectiveness?

NOTES

1. This outcome is aligned with the learning opportunity and process aspect of the conceptual model of outcomes, and at one point was called an "enabling outcome."
2. This outcome is aligned with the learning opportunity and process aspect of the conceptual model of outcomes; and at one point was called an "enabling outcome."

MARTHA L. THURLOW'S SUGGESTIONS FOR FURTHER READING

Thurlow, M. L. (Nov 2000). Standards-based reform and students with disabilities: Reflections on a decade of change. *Focus on Exceptional Children, 33*(3), 1–16.

Thurlow, M. L. (2002). Positive educational results for all students: The promise of standards-based reform. *Remedial and Special Education, 23*(4), 195–202.

Thurlow, M. L. (2004). Biting the bullet: Including special-needs students in accountability systems. In S. H. Fuhrman & R. F. Elmore (Eds.), *Redesigning accountability systems for education* (pp. 115–137). New York: Teachers College Press.

Thurlow, M. L. (2005, December). Educating students with disabilities: Do you pass the test? *Principal Leadership*, 6(4), 12–15.

Thurlow, M. L., & Johnson, D. R. (2010, August). From high school to success: Implications of diploma options for the future. *The State Education Standard*, 11(2) 34–39.

Thurlow, M. L., & Quenemoen, R. F. (2011). Standards-based reform and students with disabilities. In J. M. Kauffman & D. P. Hallahan (Eds.), *Handbook of special education* (pp. 134–146). New York: Routledge.

REFERENCES

Allinder, R. M. (1994). The relationship between efficacy and the instructional practices of special education teachers and consultants. *Teacher Education and Special Education*, 17(2), 86–95.

Altman, J. R., Lazarus, S. L., Thurlow, M. L., Quenemoen, R. F., Cuthbert, M., & Cormier, D. C. (2008). *2007 survey of states: Activities, changes, and challenges for special education.* Minneapolis, MN: University of Minnesota, National Center on Educational Outcomes.

Bruininks, R., Thurlow, M. L., & Ysseldyke, J. E. (1992). Assessing the right outcomes: Prospects for improving education for youth with disabilities. *Education and Training in Mental Retardation*, 27(2), 93–100.

Bureau of Labor Statistics. (2012). *Persons with a disability: Labor force characteristics–2011* (USDL-12-1125). Available at www.bls.gov/news.release/pdf/disabl.pdf.

Conley, D.T. (2010). *College and career ready: Helping all students succeed beyond high school.* San Francisco: Jossey-Bass.

Cortiella, C. (2007). *Rewards & roadblocks: How special education students are faring under No Child Left Behind.* New York: National Center for Learning Disabilities.

Cortiella, C. (2012). *Parent/family companion guide: Using assessment and accountability to increase performance for students with disabilities as part of district-wide improvement.* Minneapolis, MN: University of Minnesota, National Center on Educational Outcomes.

Cortiella, C., & Burnette, J. (2009). *Challenging change: How schools and districts are improving the performance of special education students.* New York: National Center for Learning Disabilities.

Donahue Institute. (2004). *A study of MCAS achievement and promising practices in urban special education: Data analysis and site selection methodology.* Amherst, MA: University of Massachusetts.

Education Commission of the States. (1998). *The progress of education reform: 1997.* Denver, CO: Author.

Elmore, R.F., & Rothman, R. (Eds.) (1999). *Testing, teaching, and learning: A guide for states and school districts.* Washington, DC: National Academy Press.

Espin, C.A., Deno, S.L., & Albayrak-Kaymak, D. (1998). Individualized Education Programs in resource and inclusive settings: How "individualized" are they? *Journal of Special Education*, 32(3), 164–74.

Heward, W. L. (2003). Ten faulty notions about teaching and learning that hinder the effectiveness of special education. *The Journal of Special Education*, 36(4), 186–205.

Hocutt, A. M. (1996). Effectiveness of special education: Is placement the critical factor? *The Future of Children*, 6(1), 77–102.

Holdheide, L. R., Goe, L., Craft, A., & Reschly, D. J. (2010). *Challenges in evaluating special education teachers and English language learning specialists* (TQ Research Policy Brief). Washington, DC: National Comprehensive Center for Teacher Quality.

Howley, A., & Howley, M. (2012). *Administrator preparation guide: Using assessment and accountability to increase performance for students with disabilities as part of district-wide improvement.* Minneapolis, MN: University of Minnesota, National Center on Educational Outcomes.

Kantrowitz, B., & Springen, K. (1997, Oct 6). "Why Johnny Stayed Home." *Newsweek*, p. 60.

Kearns, J., Kleinert, H., Harrison, B., Sheppard-Jones, K., Hall, M., & Jones, M. (2010). *What does "College and Career Ready" mean for students with significant cognitive disabilities?* Lexington: University of Kentucky.

Lazarus, S.S., Thurlow, M.L., Ysseldyke, J. E., & Edwards, L.M. (2013). An analysis of the rise and fall of the AA-MAS policy. *Journal of Special Education*. Online First: January 29.

Kober, N., & Rentner, D. S. (2012). *Year two of implementing the Common Core State Standards: States' progress and challenges.* Washington, DC: Center on Education Policy.

Marston, D. (1988). The effectiveness of special education: A time series analysis of reading performance in regular and special education settings. *The Journal of Special Education*, 21(4), 13–26.

McDonnell, L. M., McLaughlin, M. J., & Morison, P. (Eds), *Educating one & all: Students with disabilities and standards-based reform.* Washington, DC: National Academy Press, 1997.

McGrew, K. S., Algozzine, B., Ysseldyke, J. E., Thurlow, M. L., & Spiegel, A. N. (1995). The identification of individuals with disabilities in national databases: Creating a failure to communicate. *Journal of Special Education, 28*(4), 472–487.

McGrew, K. S., Thurlow, M. L., & Spiegel, A. N. (1993). An investigation of the exclusion of students with disabilities in national data collection programs. *Educational Evaluation and Policy Analysis, 15*(3), 339–352.

McLaughlin, M. J., & Thurlow, M. (2003). Educational accountability and students with disabilities: Issues and challenges. *Educational Policy, 17*(4), 431–451.

National Commission on Excellence in Education. (1983). *A nation at risk: The imperative for educational reform.* Washington, DC: U.S. Government Printing Office.

NCEO. (no date). *Foundations for NCEO's Outcomes & Indicators Series.* Minneapolis, MN: University of Minnesota, National Center on Educational Outcomes.

NCEO. (2011). *Don't forget accommodations: Five questions to ask when moving to technology-based assessments* (NCEO Brief #1). Minneapolis, MN: University of Minnesota, National Center on Educational Outcomes.

NCEO. (2012). *Using assessment data as part of a results-driven accountability system: Input from the NCEO Core Team.* Minneapolis, MN: University of Minnesota, National Center on Educational Outcomes.

Porter, A., McMaken, J., Hwang, J., & Yang, R. (2011). Common core standards: The new U.S. intended curriculum. *Educational Researcher, 40*(3), 103–116.

President's Commission on Excellence in Special Education. (2002). *A new era: Revitalizing special education for children and their families.* Washington, DC: U.S. Department of Education.

Quenemoen, R. (2008). *A brief history of alternate assessments based on alternate achievement standards* (Synthesis Report 68). Minneapolis, MN: University of Minnesota, National Center on Educational Outcomes.

Russell, M. (2011). *Digital test delivery: Empowering accessible test design to increase test validity for all students.* Washington, DC: Arabella Advisors.

Russell, M., Hoffman, R., & Higgins, J. (2009a). Nimble Tools: A universally designed test delivery system. *Teaching Exceptional Children, 42*(2), 6–12.

Russell, M., Hoffmann, T., & Higgins, J. (2009b). Meeting the needs of all students: A universal design approach to computer-based testing. *Innovate: Journal of Online Education, 5*(4).

Shriner, J. G. (1994). Broadening educational outcomes beyond academics. In J. E. Ysseldyke & M. L. Thurlow (Eds.), *Educational outcomes for students with disabilities* (pp. 139–154). New York: Haworth Press.

Shriner, J. G., Ysseldyke, J. E., Thurlow, M. L., & Honetschlager, D. (1994). "All" means "all": Including students with disabilities in performance-based systems. *Educational Leadership, 51*(6), 38–42.

Taylor, A. M., Thurlow, M. L., & Turnure, J. E. (1977). Vocabulary development of educable retarded children. *Exceptional Children, 43*, 444–450.

Telfer, D.M. (2011). *Moving your numbers: Five districts share how they used assessment and accountability to increase performance for students with disabilities as part of district-wide improvement.* Minneapolis, MN: University of Minnesota, National Center on Educational Outcomes.

Telfer, D.M., & Glasgow, A. (2012). *District self-assessment guide for moving your numbers: Using assessment and accountability to increase performance of students with disabilities as part of district-wide improvement.* Minneapolis, MN: University of Minnesota, National Center on Educational Outcomes.

Thompson, S. J., Thurlow, M. L., & Malouf, D. (2004, May). Creating better tests for everyone through universally designed assessments. *Journal of Applied Testing Technology, 10*(2). See *http://www.testpublishers.org/atp.journal.htm.*

Thurlow, M. L. (2012). Common Core State Standards: The promise and the peril for students with disabilities. *The Special EDge, 25*(3), 1, 6–8.

Thurlow, M. L. (2013). Accommodation for challenge, diversity, and variance in human characteristics (Occasional Paper). New York: Gordon Commission.

Thurlow, M.L. (2014). Instructional and assessment accommodations in the 21st century. In L. Florian (Ed.), *The Sage handbook of special education* (2nd ed., pp. 597–631). Thousand Oaks, CA: Sage.

Thurlow, M. L., Bremer, C., & Albus, D. (2011). *2008–09 publicly reported assessment results for students with disabilities and ELLs with disabilities* (Technical Report 59). Minneapolis, MN: University of Minnesota, National Center on Educational Outcomes.

Thurlow, M. L., Lazarus, S. S., & Bechard, S. (2012). *Lessons learned in federally funded projects that can improve the instruction and assessment of low performing students with disabilities.* Minneapolis, MN: University of Minnesota, National Center on Educational Outcomes.

Thurlow, M. L., Lazarus, S. S., & Christensen, L. L. (2013). Accommodations for assessment. In B. Cook & M. Tankersley (Eds.), *Effective practices in special education* (pp. 311–327). Iowa City: Pearson.

Thurlow, M. L., Laitusis, C. C., Dillon, D. R., Cook, L. L., Moen, R. E., Abedi, J., & O'Brien, D. G. (2009). *Accessibility principles for reading assessments.* Minneapolis, MN: National Accessible Reading Assessment Projects.

Thurlow, M., Quenemoen, R., Altman, J., & Cuthbert, M. (2007). *Trends in the participation and performance of students with disabilities* (Technical Report 50). Minneapolis, MN: University of Minnesota, National Center on Educational Outcomes.

Thurlow, M. L., Quenemoen, R. F., & Lazarus, S. S. (2011). *Meeting the needs of special education students: Recommendations for the Race to the Top consortia and states.* Washington, DC: Arabella Advisors.

Thurlow, M. L., & Turnure, J. E. (1972). Elaboration structure and list length effects on verbal elaboration phenomena. *Journal of Experimental Child Psychology, 14,* 184–195.

Thurlow, M. L., & Turnure, J. E. (1977). Children's knowledge of time and money: Effective instruction for the mentally retarded. *Education and Training of the Mentally Retarded, 12,* 203–212.

Tindal, G. (1985). Investigating the effectiveness of special education: An analysis of methodology. *Journal of Learning Disabilities, 18*(2), 101–112.

Turnure, J. E., Buium, N., & Thurlow, M. L. (1976). The effectiveness of interrogatives for promoting verbal elaboration productivity in young children. *Child Development, 128,* 851–855.

Turnure, J. E., Larsen, S. N., & Thurlow, M. L. (1973). Effects of brain-injury and other subject characteristics on paired-associate performance under paragraph elaboration. *American Journal of Mental Deficiency, 78,* 70–76.

Turnure, J. E., & Thurlow, M. L. (1973). Verbal elaboration and the promotion of transfer of training in educable mentally retarded children. *Journal of Experimental Child Psychology, 15,* 137–148.

Turnure, J. E., & Thurlow, M. L. (1975). The effects of structural variations in elaborations on learning by EMR and non-retarded children. *American Journal of Mental Deficiency, 79,* 632–639.

Turnure, J. E., & Thurlow, M. L. (1976) Acquisition and reversal of paired-associates by young children under extended verbal discourse. *Journal of Genetic Psychology, 128,* 251–261.

U.S. Department of Education. (2011). *ESEA flexibility.* Available at www.ed.gov/esea/flexibility.

Vanderwood, M., McGrew, K., & Ysseldyke, J. (1998). Why we can't say much about students with disabilities during educational reform. *Exceptional Children, 64,* 359–370.

Wagner, M., Newman, L., Cameto, R., Garza, N., & Levine, P. (2005). *After high school: A first look at the postschool experiences of youth with disabilities: A report from the National Longitudinal Transition Study-2.* Menlo Park, CA: SRI International.

Warren, S., Thurlow, M., & Others. (2012). *Forum on evaluating educator effectiveness: Critical considerations for including students with disabilities.* Minneapolis, MN: University of Minnesota, National Center on Educational Outcomes.

Yell, M. L., Shriner, J. G., & Katsiyannis, A. (2006). Individuals with Disabilities Education Improvement Act of 2004: Implications for educators, administrators, and teacher trainers. *Focus on Exceptional Children, 39*(1), 1–24.

Ysseldyke, J.E., Algozzine, B.A., & Thurlow, M.L. (2000). *Critical issues in special education.* Boston: Houghton Mifflin.

Ysseldyke, J., Krentz, J., Elliott, J., Thurlow, M. L., Erickson, R., & Moore, M. L. (1998). *NCEO framework for educational accountability.* Minneapolis, MN: University of Minnesota, National Center on Educational Outcomes.

Ysseldyke, J., Krentz, J., Elliott, J., Thurlow, M. L., Thompson, S., & Moore, M. L. (1998). *NCEO framework for educational accountability: Post-school outcomes.* Minneapolis, MN: University of Minnesota, National Center on Educational Outcomes.

Ysseldyke, J. E., & Thurlow, M. L. (1994). What results should be measured to decide whether instruction is working for students with disabilities? In J. E. Ysseldyke & M. L. Thurlow (Eds.), *Educational outcomes for students with disabilities* (pp. 39–49). New York: Haworth Press.

Ysseldyke, J. E., & Thurlow, M. L. (1995). What results should be measured to decide whether instruction is working for students with disabilities? In J. E. Ysseldyke & M. L. Thurlow (Eds.), *Educational outcomes for students with disabilities* (pp. 39–49). New York: Haworth Press.

Ysseldyke, J. E., & Thurlow, M. L., & Bruininks, R. H. (1992). Expected educational outcomes for students with disabilities. *Remedial and Special Education, 13*(6), 19–30.

Ysseldyke, J. E., Thurlow, M. L., & Erickson, R. N. (1994a). *Educational Outcomes and indicators for grade 4.* Minneapolis, MN: University of Minnesota, National Center on Educational Outcomes.

Ysseldyke, J. E., Thurlow, M. L., & Erickson, R. N. (1994b). *Educational Outcomes and indicators for grade 8.* Minneapolis, MN: University of Minnesota, National Center on Educational Outcomes.

Ysseldyke, J. E., Thurlow, M. L. & Erickson, R. N. (1995). *Possible sources of data for grade 4 indicators.* Minneapolis, MN: University of Minnesota, National Center on Educational Outcomes.

Ysseldyke, J. E., Thurlow, M. L., & Gilman, C. J. (1993a). *Educational outcomes and indicators for early childhood (age 3).* Minneapolis, MN: University of Minnesota, National Center on Educational Outcomes.

Ysseldyke, J. E., Thurlow, M. L., & Gilman, C. J. (1993b). *Educational outcomes and indicators for early childhood (age 6)*. Minneapolis, MN: University of Minnesota, National Center on Educational Outcomes.

Ysseldyke, J. E., Thurlow, M. L., & Gilman, C. J. (1993c). *Educational outcomes and indicators for individuals at the post-school level*. Minneapolis, MN: University of Minnesota, National Center on Educational Outcomes.

Ysseldyke, J. E., Thurlow, M. L., & Gilman, C. J. (1993d). *Educational outcomes and indicators for students completing school*. Minneapolis, MN: University of Minnesota, National Center on Educational Outcomes.

Ysseldyke, J. E., Thurlow, M. L., & Shriner, J. G. (1992). Outcomes are for special educators too. *Teaching Exceptional Children, 25*(1), 36–50.

Zlatos, B. (1994). Don't test, don't tell: Is "academic red-shirting" skewing the way we rank our schools? *American School Board Journal, 181*(11), 24–28.

Section V
WHEN SHOULD SPECIAL EDUCATION BEGIN AND END?

Are there limits to special education? The answer is, "Of course!" Some of them are temporal. In the U.S., even babies may receive special education, and youths may continue to receive special education until they "age out" when they reach their 22nd birthday. There are other limits, too, though they may be less clearly marked. Special education sometimes extends into families' homes and into communities. But should it? What are the appropriate limits for special education? In this section, we examine questions about *when* special education occurs.

- When should special education begin?
- When should special education end?
- Should special education only occur in schools or should it also extend to playgrounds, parks, and other public areas?
- Should special education provide services for families or is that the domain of other public or private organizations?
- Does special education, by its very nature, saddle individuals with disabilities with a stigma that is never-ending?

Getting to Know Sarah E. Dillon

In the sixth grade, my math class was located next to a self-contained class of about eight students. I noticed that they did not follow the same schedule as other students. I remember asking a friend why those kids always had the same teacher and the response was, "They are the bad kids." Naturally, I was interested in what it must be like to be a student in that class. What was it like to be that teacher? These same questions motivated me later in life to pursue an undergraduate degree in psychology, followed by a graduate degree in special education, both from the University of Virginia. I wanted to teach students with disabilities— specifically students whose behaviors negatively affected their education.

After college, I was hired as a resource and collaborative teacher. Immediately I learned that no two students' needs are the same, and that no year would mirror the previous one. Strong behavior management is essential to ensure order and to promote a safe and successful learning environment. To aid in this skill, I have embedded numerous research-based practices into my teaching, and sought the advice of professionals in the field. After years of reaching out in efforts to bring in new methods for the instruction of special education students, I returned to the University of Virginia. Currently, I am enrolled in a Ph.D. program in special education, and plan to focus on the implementation and effect of school-wide positive behavioral support plans in reducing problem behavior.

21

WHEN SHOULD SPECIAL EDUCATION START AND END?

Barbara Bateman, John Wills Lloyd, Melody Tankersley, & Sarah E. Dillon

The easy answer to when students who have a disability should be identified and served is "as soon as possible." That is what people who care about children with disabilities—parents, many teachers, administrators, advocates, and others—want. However, as with many easy answers, it is neither complete nor completely accurate. There are constraints.

Which children with disabilities should be identified early? How do we know that they have disabilities? How early can we identify them? Does identifying some children as having disabilities when they are very young actually do them harm rather than helping them?

And there are a host of other questions, too. Should special education continue to be provided even past the usual years of schooling? How about special education during summer school, so that students with disabilities do not lose what they may have gained during the nine-month school year? There are so many *when* questions, too many to be addressed in this section of the book. However, there are some important perspectives brought to the fore for those who read these chapters.

WHEN DOES SPECIAL EDUCATION START?

Young children's brains are still developing rapidly and thus interventions with them when they are young have the greatest potential impact (Ellison & Semrud-Clikeman, 2007). Early interventions can reduce the likelihood of a child's future need for special education (Casto & Mastropieri, 1986). Further good news is that unlike some areas of special education, early interventions have been the subject of much federally funded research over many years. We have a wealth of information about effective practices for use in early childhood settings (Marshall, Brown, Conroy, & Knopf, 2011; Odom & Wolery, 2003).

Research has determined that effective interventions include: (a) activities in which the child is an active participant; (b) activities focused on the child's interests; (c) adults who respond to and interact with the child; (d) activities conducted in natural learning environments; and (e) practices which increase the family's capacity for dealing with the child and with professionals (Dunst, 2011). However, when the focus is on enhancing school readiness and beginning academics, research supports other principles, as we discuss later.

Unfortunately, there is less-than-perfect correspondence between what we know is effective in early intervention and what we actually do (Gersten, Vaughn, Deshler, & Shiller 1997). From 2000 to 2010, the numbers of infants, toddlers, and preschoolers being served under IDEA has increased dramatically (see, e.g., U.S. Department of Education, Office of Special Education and Rehabilitation Services, Office of Special Education Programs, 2011). However, many of the services they receive are not always consistent with effective, evidence-based practices. Even worse than using ineffective practices, in at least one state the prekindergarten program, which serves over 75,000 children and costs about $2 billion annually, "has been beset by rising costs, conflicts of interest and outright fraud in private companies providing these services" (*New York Times*, July 16, 2012). Oversight of these private program providers has clearly been inadequate and undoubtedly the program content has been affected negatively by such practices.

Why is there this disconnect between research and practice? A bit of history may help explain this. In 1986, the same year Part C of IDEA was established for toddlers (birth to 3 years old), the National Association for the Education of Young Children promulgated its developmentally appropriate practices (DAP; Bradekamp, 1986). That paper both reflected and shaped then-current practices in the field of early childhood education. The DAP position highlighted a focus on children's play as the primary vehicle for development. The teacher's role was that of guide or facilitator and the curriculum focus was play—child-initiated, child- directed, and teacher-supported.

In the meantime, since the early 1960s, research on interventions based on operant learning theory has been ongoing. Instructional approaches based on behavioral principles were developed and their effectiveness established. This research was embraced by much of special education and over the last 50 years the research culminated in direct instruction and positive behavioral supports—both highly effective (Becker & Carnine, 1981; Marshall et al., 2011). As the accountability-in-education movement urges educators to adopt only those educational practices that are evidence-based, such data will become more important.

At one time the developmental approach preferred by the early childhood field contrasted sharply with the growing acceptance of behavioral approaches in special education. This could be seen in the terms "early childhood" and "early intervention." Implied in Carta's discussion, often in special education the focus was on deliberately changing the behavior or skill level of the child, typically a child with a disability or from a disadvantaged background. For this reason "early intervention" was frequently used by special educators, while "early childhood" usually referred to child-centered, developmental practices and philosophy of the DAP 1986 position paper.

In the early 1980s some efforts were made to integrate the developmental approach of the early childhood camp with the approaches of special education, although they were widely considered incompatible at the time. The influence of research in the adoption of evidence-based practices can be seen in the DAP position paper in 2009, almost a quarter of a century after the 1986 paper. The focus on "children's play" changed to "intentional teaching and high-quality play." The teacher changed from being a "guide or facilitator" to being "intentional and responsive." Similarly, the curriculum moved from "child initiated, child-directed and teacher-supported" to "planned."

The efforts to combine and integrate these disparate philosophies and theoretical frameworks resulted in calls for practices that meet evidence standards and also fit into what is familiar to early childhood educators. Similarly, some have advocated a conceptual framework that combines evidence-based and values-based practices. Exactly what this means is not always clear. What if there is a conflict between evidence-based and values-based practices? Isn't this exactly what happened when direct instruction was rejected by most early childhood educators on the grounds they didn't believe it was good for children, in spite of the undeniable and overwhelming evidence from Project Follow Through that it was highly effective in promoting academic growth and self-concept?

IDEA Part C has been heavily criticized in the past for not keeping up with advances in theory, assessment, and interventions. It often emphasized services that have little support in evidence over experiences and opportunities that have been shown to be effective. However, in recent years, this has changed significantly. IDEA now requires that "IFSPs [Individual Family Service Plans, which are similar to IEPs, but for younger children] contain a statement of specific early intervention services based on peer-reviewed research, to the extent practicable, necessary to meet the unique needs of the infant or toddler and the family, including the frequency, intensity, and method of delivering services." The Office of Special Education (OSEP) has now said that when peer-reviewed research indicates that the frequency and intensity of a service is integral to its effectiveness, the IFSP must reflect and incorporate that frequency and intensity (*Letter to Kane, 55 IDELR 203* [OSEP, 2010]).

Another question and one about which we have relatively little hard evidence is whether or the extent to which the process of identifying a disability or labeling a person as having a disability is possibly detrimental to the child. Attitudes toward disabilities are related to culture, to one's knowledge about disabilities and the amount of contact one has had with persons who have disabilities. Another factor that has a major role in affecting attitudes is whether the disability is visible or hidden. When we talk about the effects of labeling we must try to separate the effect of the label from the effect of the disability itself. If a child was born with major limb deformities, then adding the IDEA label of orthopedically impaired probably has little negative effect. On the other hand, if a child who has been seen by all as a typically developing child until he starts third grade unable to read is suddenly labeled "learning disabled," negative effects may well result. Under these circumstances the label can become a self-fulfilling prophecy, can unduly lower expectations and can negatively affect self-concept and self-esteem.

The most problematic labels for school age and older children are probably "emotionally disturbed" and "learning disabled." The newest term for mental retardation is "intellectually disabled." It remains to be seen when and if "intellectual disability" acquires the negative connotations that prompted the banishing of "mental retardation." Even if there is a possible downside to the earliest possible identification and labeling, how do we weigh that risk against the possible benefits? This concern could lead one to advocate a combination of caution when we are uncertain about the existence of a disability and careful monitoring of the child, combined with a willingness to identify and serve the child if and when that is indicated. In an abundance of caution, one might fantasize that it is possible to provide services without labeling (Biklen, 1992; cf Kauffman, 2011).

A good label is one that helps more than it hurts. How can a label help? What are the likely benefits of labels? Could these benefits be obtained without the labels? Do you see any commonalities among the characteristics of learning disability, emotional

346 • Bateman, Lloyd, Tankersley, & Dillon

disturbance, and intellectual disability that might make them more problematic than other labels such as "blind" or "other health impaired?"

WHEN DOES SPECIAL EDUCATION END?

When does special education end? Should special education reach outside the traditional school day, traditional school age span, the school year, the curriculum or the physical environment?

To ask these questions is to ask whether IDEA should be significantly changed. The current boundaries of special education are in the ages covered and in the services offered to the eligible children. By law, we know that children with disabilities are covered from birth to age 22 (in contrast to the traditional 12-year span) or to graduation from high school with a regular diploma. In a few cases, compensatory education has been awarded beyond age 22, as Wehmeyer notes briefly in his chapter. The services to be provided during these ages are special education and related services. Remember from our earlier chapter that special education is defined as specially designed instruction to meet the unique needs of the individual with a disability. Presently, related services under IDEA are defined as transportation and such developmental, corrective, and other supportive services as are required to assist a child to benefit from special education.

One of the common related services is an extended school year (ESY) which can vary from a few weeks of summer school to a 24-hour placement in a residential facility for 365 days a year, an after-school program, or a weekend tutoring session to any other time extension for either special education or other related services. Often a related service is provided off the school premises, e.g., a trained aide to accompany a student on a school or public bus, to field trips or to provide door-to-door transport between home and school. Extracurricular activities such as a swim meet at a community pool, an away-from-home ball game, a chess tournament, or a dance class must be made available if they are available to students who do not have a disability.

In every instance of providing a related service, IDEA requires that the IEP team first must determine that the activity or support service is necessary to assist the child to benefit from special education and then include the service on the IEP. (Note that this is not the same as asking whether the child can benefit from the related service, which is a different and erroneous question to ask.) IDEA's list of possible related services is very extensive, including a few that are seldom provided such as recreation (including therapeutic recreation), medical services for diagnostic or evaluation purposes, and parent counseling and training. Furthermore, the list is not exhaustive. Other services must be provided if necessary to assist the child to benefit from special education and if it is not one of the excluded medical services such as an implanted device. The boundaries of special education and related services are very flexible as to time and space. The only fixed boundaries are the needs of individual children who have disabilities.

Perhaps the question is not where are the boundaries of special education, but where do we believe they should be? Some believe one simple, effective, and appropriate way to rein in the boundaries is to identify and serve fewer children with fewer services. A New Jersey school superintendent said special education "is completely out of control.... Everything else has a finite limit. Special education ... is similar to the universe. It has no end" (Scull & Winkler, 2011, p. 2). The process of closing the IDEA door to some previously eligible students began in the mid-1970s when mild or educable mental retardation

(EMR) was defined out of IDEA—or at least we thought that had happened—by low-ering the IQ required to fit the category of mental retardation. However, the drop in numbers of children labeled mentally retarded was all but matched by increases in those labeled as having a specific learning disability (SLD).

What about, however, extending special education to other parts of an individual's life? Is it appropriate to help individuals with disabilities learn how to get along socially with others in settings outside of school? Could this come under the heading of "gener-alization training" and actually benefit in-school behavior? If we extend special educa-tion to help individuals with disabilities gain more effective social skills, would it make it easier for others to change the way they view individuals with special needs? As Weh-meyer discusses, the answer to when special education will end is dependant upon how society views disabilities.

It now appears to some that an increase of the use of Response to Intervention (RTI) may be resulting in lowered numbers of children being identified as IDEA eligible. How-ever, it is also possible the two factors are merely correlated and that the cause of the decrease in special education numbers is something else. A factor that might be behind the marked decrease in specific learning disabilities (a drop from 2.9 million to 2.4 million over the past decade), in mental retardation (from 624,000 to 480,000) and emotional disturbance (480,000 to 407,000) is better identification. Of course, better identification is probably responsible to some extent for the quadruple increase in autism spectrum disorders from 93,000 to 378,000. It seems somewhat unlikely that better identification would result, even partially, in such a huge increase in one disability and decreases in the others. Diagnostic substitution—that one classification (high functioning autism, for example) is used in place of another (e.g., learning disabilities) has been found to be the likely source for some of these changes (e.g., Coo et al., 2008). This is a topic to which we shall return in our final chapter.

Another factor that may be implicated in the overall decrease in numbers of special education students from their peak in 2004–5 (13.8 percent of the total school pop-ulation) to 2009–10 (13.1 percent) is increased motivation to reduce the numbers by whatever means seem appropriate. Budgetary concerns are huge in almost every school district. Forty percent of all increases in education funding between 1996 and 2005 went to special education even though the special education population increased far less than that—from about 12.5 percent to 13.8 percent (Scull & Winkler, 2011).

In sum, as Carta clearly shows, there are legitimate reasons to provide special educa-tion as early as possible without unduly risking the downside of identifying a child as disabled when she or he is not so, in fact. At the present time, the scope of special edu-cation and related services is undeniably broad and far-reaching. Also, it is undeniably expensive due to the scope of the services (such as residential placement in a specialized facility plus many therapies), the number of children receiving them, and the time span over which they must be provided. As IDEA is currently written, the only legitimate way to reduce the expenditures for special education is to reduce the numbers of children served, the services provided, the time span over which they are provided, or combina-tions of these.

A very provocative approach to limiting services to children under IDEA is currently being taken by one of the five largest school districts in the United States. The district has publicly and proudly declared that in-home applied behavior analysis (ABA) inter-vention for young children who have autism is not part of FAPE and thus none of the

IDEA procedural safeguards or protections apply to the evaluation of these children for the services or to the provision of the services (Harley & Redmond, 2010). After a student has been found to be IDEA-eligible due to autism, the student may (or may not) be evaluated by a member of a unit called the Low Incidence Deliberation Team (LIDT) and that assessment will determine if—and if so, how much—ABA in-home intervention the child will receive. The district maintains that FAPE is always and only provided in its in-school program and that, therefore, to be eligible for consideration for in-home ABA the child must be enrolled full time in the district's preschool program. This applies to all the children who have autism, regardless of their individual needs, abilities, or readiness for a full-time school program. If the LIDT finds the child is eligible for in-home ABA and the IEP team concurs, then the parents must locate, contract with, and pay the ABA provider up-front and then may seek reimbursement from the district. One can only hope that by the time you are reading this, appropriate legal action has resulted in young children who have autism receiving what might be their only ticket to a "normal life."

To date (late 2012), the most visible and apparent efforts to reduce expenditures have appeared in the reduced numbers of children eligible to receive special education and related services. The eligibility criteria of IDEA have not changed. But something has. What is that? No one in public schools can be oblivious to the budgetary pressures that have affected all school districts in her or his state. This awareness, consciously or not, cannot help but lead teachers to hesitate to refer children for a special education evaluation and equally aware and concerned evaluation teams to find the student does not meet the IDEA eligibility requirements. This especially applies to the requirement that the student must, to be IDEA eligible, need special education and related services. Even though a student has not made adequate or significant progress in the regular education program, it may be easy to suggest he or she could do so if only appropriate services in regular education were provided.

The underlying issues in this discussion are whether and why we should or should not provide and pay for these services for the fraction of the population of the school population that has a disability. This question most obviously jumps out at us when we contemplate the cost and scope of special education and related services. In the earlier section of this book on the topic of WHY have special education, we addressed why we should or should not expend as much as we do for children who have disabilities. Do you think we spend enough, not enough, or too much for special education?

As you read the chapters in this section, you will have the opportunity to learn the view of some of special education's foremost experts on topics we have discussed in this brief introduction. Judy Carta and Michael Wehmeyer are eminent scholars who have contributed greatly to special education. We asked Professor Carta to discuss her knowledge about prevention, early identification, early intervention, and the transition young children make when they enter schooling. In Professor Wehmeyer's case, we solicited his views because of his work on self-determination and the transitions that people make when they move into adulthood.

SARAH DILLON'S SUGGESTIONS FOR FURTHER READING

Bradshaw, C., Reinke, W., Brown, L., Bevans, K., & Leaf, P. (2008). Implementation of school-wide positive behavioral interventions and supports (PBIS) in elementary schools: Observations from a randomized trial. *Education and Treatment of Children, 31*, 1–26.

Hirsch, S. E., Lloyd, J. W., & Kennedy, M. J. (2014). Improving behavior through instructional practices for students with high-incidence disabilities: EBD, ADHD, and LD. In P. Garner, J. M. Kauffman, & J. Elliot (Eds.), *Handbook of emotional & behavioral difficulties* (2nd ed.; pp. 205–220). London: Sage.

Kazdin, A. E., & Weisz, J. R. (Eds.) (2003). *Evidence-based psychotherapies for children and Adolescents.* New York: Guilford Press.

Walker, H. M., Ramsey, E., & Gresham, F. M. (2004). *Antisocial behavior in school: evidence-based practices* (2nd ed.). Belmont, CA: Thomson/Wadsworth.

Walker, H. M., & Sprague, J. R. (2007). Early, evidence-based intervention with school-related behavior disorders: Key issues, continuing challenges, and promising practices. In J. B. Crockett, M. M. Gerber, & T. J. Landrum (Eds.), *Achieving the radical reform of special education: Essays in honor of James M. Kauffman* (pp. 37–58). Hillsdale, NJ: Erlbaum.

REFERENCES

Becker, W. C., & Carnine, D. W. (1981). Direct Instruction: A behavior theory model for comprehensive educational intervention with the disadvantaged. In S. W. Bijou & R. Ruiz (Eds.), *Behavior modification: Contributions to education* (pp. 145–210). Hillsdale, NJ: Erlbaum.

Biklen, D. (1992). *Schooling without labels: Parents, educators, and inclusive education.* Philadelphia, PA: Temple University Press.

Bradekamp, S. (Ed.). (1986). *Developmentally appropriate practice.* Washington, DC: National Association for the Education of Young Children.

Casto, G., & Mastropieri, M. A. (1986). The efficacy of early intervention programs: A meta-analysis. *Exceptional Children, 52,* 417–424.

Coo, H., Ouellette-Kuntz, H., Lloyd, J. E. V., Kasmara, L., Holden, J. J. A., & Lewis, M. E. S. (2008). Trends in autism prevalence: Diagnostic substitution revisited. *Journal of Autism and Developmental Disorders, 38,* 1036–1046.

Dunst, C. (2011). Advances in theory, assessment, and intervention with infants and toddlers with disabilities. In J. M. Kauffman & D. P. Hallahan (Eds.), *Handbook of special education* (pp. 687–702). New York: Routledge.

Ellison, P. A., & Semrud-Clikeman, M. (2007). *Child Neuropsychology.* New York: Springer.

Gersten, R., Vaughn, S., Deshler, D., & Shiller, E. (1997). What we know about using research findings: Implications for improving special education practice. *Journal of Learning Disabilities, 30,* 466–476.

Harley, M. S., & Redmond, P. V. (2010, August). *What educators need to know about autism.* Paper presented at Utah Law Conference, Ogden, UT. Downloaded from http://www.schools.utah.gov/sars/DOCS/disability/edautism.aspx.

Kauffman, J. M. (2011). *Toward a science of education: The battle between rogue and real science.* Verona, WI: Attainment.

Letter to Kane, 55 *IDELR 203* (OSEP, 2010).

Marshall, K. J., Brown, W. H., Conroy, M. A., & Knopf, H. (2011). Early intervention and prevention of disability: Preschoolers. In J. M. Kauffman & D. P. Hallahan (Eds.), *Handbook of special education* (pp. 703–715). New York: Routledge.

Odom, S. L., Brantlinger, E., Gersten, R., Horner, R. H., Thompson, B., & Harris, K. R. (2005). Research in special education: Scientific methods and evidence-based practices. *Exceptional Children, 71,* 137–148.

Odom, S. L., & Wolery, M. (2003). A unified theory of practice in early intervention/early childhood special education: Evidence-based practices. *The Journal of Special Education, 37,* 164–173.

Scull, J., & Winkler, A. M. (2011). *Shifting trends in special education.* Retrieved from http://edexcellence.net/publications/shifting-trends-in-special.html.

Shaywitz, S. (2004). *Overcoming dyslexia.* New York: Alfred A. Knopf.

U.S. Department of Education, Office of Special Education and Rehabilitation Services, Office of Special Education Programs. (2011). *30th annual report to Congress on the implementation of the Individuals with Disabilities Education Act, 2008.* Washington, DC: Author. Retrieved from http://http://www2.ed.gov/about/reports/annual/osep/2008/parts-b-c/30th-idea-arc.pdf.

Getting to Know Judith J. Carta

 I think I really began to appreciate the power of teaching when I was still in high school and participated in a tutoring program for inner-city children. It was 1968—one of the most violent years in our country. My high school colleagues and I would be bussed into one of the toughest neighborhoods in Chicago and we would be instructed to run into the buildings because it wasn't safe to walk. But once inside, we gathered in a recreation center that was an urban oasis of positive energy. There I had the opportunity to work one-on-one each week with a third grader and not only tutor her but to learn about her family and what it was like to grow up in that setting. That experience opened my eyes and taught me about the power of individualized instruction and attention by a mentor. That early experience helped me realize how the many risks that children are exposed to in their early lives are powerful forces in shaping their development but that education and relationships can counter those adverse effects. I have focused most of my career in understanding how we can help children from those environments "beat the odds" of growing up there. Some 45 years after my high school experience, children are still growing up in those neighborhoods and facing those same risks. My hope is that we have developed effective ways of finding the children who need help and better ways of meeting their needs through research-based instruction, engaging their families, and providing excellent training for their teachers.

22

CHILDREN SHOULD BE IDENTIFIED AND RECEIVE SPECIAL EDUCATION SERVICES IN EARLY CHILDHOOD

Judith J. Carta

The question of when to begin special education services intersects with many other separate questions. Is early intervention an effective and efficient way of improving children's lifelong outcomes? Is it worthwhile to identify young children who may have delays in development before they enter school? When we *do* identify children in the early years, does providing early intervention make a difference in their later educational and social achievement? Does it change their developmental trajectories? How do we know what to do in those early intervention programs? What is the best way to intervene; what practices are most effective? What features of these practices are critical to their effectiveness? For whom are they effective? In what contexts should intervention occur? How can we ensure that children receive high-quality intervention across these contexts?

These are questions I have attempted to answer in my 30-plus years in the field of early intervention wearing the hats of preschool teacher, program director, researcher, and parent of a daughter with autism. Although I wish that wearing multiple hats had afforded me more wisdom, I think it has only allowed me to view the questions from multiple vantage points.

THE QUESTION OF "WHEN SHOULD INTERVENTION BEGIN?"

One of the most critical questions is "When should intervention begin? How soon should children be identified in order to receive special services? Are there benefits to identifying children early? Are there drawbacks? When I began my career in early childhood special education in the mid-1970s, these questions had no clear answers. Individuals around the country were just beginning to test special education techniques that had been successful with older children to see if they would improve outcomes for children younger than school age.

Although today there is general consensus that the earlier we begin providing special education and other therapies to children with special needs the more beneficial it is, this perspective has not always been widely accepted. In the mid-1970s, the idea of bringing preschool-aged children with disabilities into classrooms was rejected by many parents and policymakers alike. Many thought that the best place for young children was at home, and few thought that the years before kindergarten could be anything besides "nursery school." Thus, a prevailing view was that the early identification of young children with special needs in the years before school seemed warrantless. In that era, parents who thought that their child might be showing some delays in development were advised to wait and see if their child would "grow out of it." Physicians often advised parents with infants with clearly identifiable disabilities such as Down syndrome to just "take them home and love them" and offered no course of intervention to enhance their development or improve their life outcomes. When I visited my daughter in her child care program with all typically developing children, I would observe her continually walking around the edges of the playground, oblivious to the fun her peers were experiencing with each other. Today, we realize the importance of the earliest years of development for learning and that we can't stand back and watch as children with disabilities fail to engage in instruction and opportunities for social interaction and friendship with their peers. We have learned the importance of identifying and beginning early intervention to minimize the long-term effects of developmental problems and to prevent delays whenever possible in the years before school.

As I reflect on the question, "when should intervention begin?" I look back on what we've learned about the impact of early intervention for children with developmental concerns and what the repercussions may be for these children in the absence of quality education and treatment. My overwhelming response to the question of when to begin is: "Now—we can't wait!" And before I discuss what we've learned about early intervention, there are at least three reasons I would point to as reasons why we can't wait to begin intervention once we know a child has a disability. First, we know that the negative impact of disabilities on children's development increases as children get older. We know, for example, that the gap between children with and without disabilities increases as children age and this results in children with developmental delays becoming more discrepant from their typically developing peers. These growing discrepancies are more likely to lead to greater stigmatization and social isolation and less acceptance by their peers and less participation in activities with other children their age.

Second, children's disabilities often prevent them or greatly interfere with their capabilities for learning from their environments and from peers and adults in their everyday contexts. For example, although typically developing children learn through observing and imitating others, some children with disabilities fail to do this and so they are deprived of this important avenue of learning. Another example is the fact that many children with disabilities have limited play skills. Although many young children learn about their environments through their explorations and manipulations of toys and other materials, children with special needs often show a restricted range of behaviors in these types of interactions. Therefore, in this area also, until they are specifically taught how to play and interact with peers, children with disabilities often miss out on important opportunities to learn about their world.

"My overwhelming response to the question of when to begin is: 'Now—we can't wait!'"

Finally, disabilities in one area of development if untreated oftentimes will lead to secondary disabilities or delays in other areas of development. For example, it is not uncommon for children with communication disorders to develop challenging behaviors because of their frustration in being unable to communicate effectively. Therefore, the reasons for beginning to provide intervention that will minimize the effects of disabilities and allow children with special needs to avail themselves of *all* possible avenues of learning to minimize the gaps with typically developing children are many.

DOES EARLY INTERVENTION MAKE A DIFFERENCE?

Some of the earliest research on early intervention sought to answer whether early intervention could make a difference in the lives of very young children. In this "first generation" of early intervention research (Guralnick, 1997), a number of small experimental studies were carried out to study the long-term development of young children with developmental problems who received special early intervention. For example, in a very early study, Skeels and Dye (1939) selected 13 1- to 2-year-old children who were classified with mental retardation and removed them from the unstimulating environment of an orphanage, and then placed them in the care of teenage girls who lived in the same institution. These teenagers learned specific skills for providing cognitive stimulation to these infants simply by talking with them, attending to them, and holding and feeding these children. A comparison group of infants and toddlers who also had mental retardation remained in the orphanage and received adequate health and medical attention but no additional enriching interaction as the other group had with the teenage girls. When both groups of children were tested two years later, the IQs of children receiving intervention in the form of extra stimulation increased by more than 25 points (so that many of them were no longer considered to have intellectual disabilities), and most were deemed eligible for adoption. IQs of the contrast group, on the other hand, decreased by 26 points. Also, in a remarkable follow-up of these individuals 25 years later, Skeels (1966) located all the participants from both groups who were in the original study. Almost all the children who had been in the intervention group had married and they had a median education of twelfth grade. Many worked in professional or business jobs or were homemakers. Children who had remained in the orphanage had a median level of education of third grade and were either still institutionalized or working as unskilled laborers. This landmark study provided some of the first evidence that intelligence was not "fixed" and that early intervention in the form of responsive interacting and caring adults could make a significant difference in the life trajectories of individuals with intellectual disabilities.

Other studies in those early years demonstrated the effects of preschool intervention or the benefits of teaching mothers with very low IQ how to interact with their children in ways that would stimulate children's early cognitive development (Garber & Heber, 1973; Kirk, 1958). In each case, children receiving early intervention demonstrated gains in IQ over those children who were in control groups without the specialized early instruction. Each of these early studies drove home the possibility that children's intelligence and learning abilities could be enhanced by special training in the early years of life.

"Disabilities in one area of development if untreated oftentimes will lead to secondary disabilities or delays in other areas of development."

One additional large-scale study, the Abecedarian Project that began in the 1970s, has had a profound impact on our understanding of the importance of early intervention (Ramey & Campbell, 1984). It has long been known that many children who grow up in poverty experience long-term adverse effects, most notably in school achievement and cognitive development (Duncan, Brooks-Gunn, & Klebanov, 1994). Analyses attempting to unravel exactly how poverty exacts its toll on children have determined that although nutrition and toxic substances in poor environments have some causal link to these later adverse effects, the primary mechanism affecting children growing up in poverty is the home environment. These settings for children from low-income families too often provide children with reduced cognitive stimulation and their interactions with adults often offer more limited exposure to language and enriching experiences.

The Abecedarian Project was designed specifically to test whether (what we then called) mental retardation due to social-environmental causes could be prevented by intensive early education (Ramey & Campbell, 1984). Infants who came from low socioeconomic backgrounds were randomly assigned to either an intensive early intervention program consisting of a high-quality child-care program and a comprehensive cognitive stimulation program that occurred 5 days per week and 50 weeks per year *or* to a control condition that included supplemental medical, nutrition, and social services but no daily early education services. Compared to control group children, children in the intervention group made positive IQ gains, were 50 percent less likely to fail a grade in school and obtained higher IQ, reading, and mathematics scores when they were 12 years old. Long-term follow-up of these two groups has indicated that children who received early intervention were still outperforming their control group peers at age 21 in reading, math, and overall IQ scores? In addition, they were much more likely to attend college and be engaged in skilled jobs, and much less likely to become a teenage parent (Campbell, Ramey, Pungello, Sparling, & Miller-Johnson, 2002). This and other studies like it have been important in documenting not only that early intervention can make a long-term difference in life outcomes, but also that when children who receive early intervention grow up to lead more productive lives and require fewer special services, this results in a long-term economic benefit to society (Karoly et al., 1998; Masse, & Barnett, 2002).

Today, besides having results from long-term studies of the advantages of early intervention for children, we also have the benefit of knowing more about early brain development and how children's early experiences provide a foundation for future learning. We know that a substantial amount of the brain's circuitry is developed in the first few years of life and that this is influenced by a child's early experiences and supportive, stimulating interactions with caring adults (Shonkoff & Phillips, 2000). However, when a child's earliest years are in impoverished, neglectful or abusive environments, the result can be a future of increased risk for learning, behavior, and health-related problems (Center on the Developing Child at Harvard University, 2007). So, with converging evidence of the importance of a threshold of quality in children's early environment to stimulate brain development as a foundation of later development, and the results of long-term studies showing the positive outcomes resulting from early intervention, we now have a fairly strong research base to indicate that investments in children in the earliest years of life can pay off over the lifespan (Heckman, 2011).

DESIGNING INTERVENTION PROGRAMS FOR YOUNG CHILDREN WITH SPECIAL NEEDS

Answering the question about whether early intervention is effective was only the first step to figuring out whether early intervention programs could be established in communities across the U.S. for children with special needs to make a difference in their lives and the lives of their families. The story of how programs such as these began can be traced back to the early 1970s. With the first evidence that starting intervention for children in the years before school could help improve children's outcomes, the federal government established some policies to fund educational programs for young children with special needs. In 1975, the U.S. Congress enacted the Individual with Disabilities Education Act (P.L. 94–142). Although this law mandated a free appropriate public education for all school-aged children, it also provided incentives to states to begin establishing preschool programs for children with disabilities. Early research had bolstered the idea that early intervention could make a difference for children who were at risk for developmental problems, and a number of small-scale experimental programs around the country that demonstrated a variety of approaches for teaching young children with developmental delays. So, at this point, the focus of research shifted from *whether* early intervention could make a difference to demonstrations of *how early intervention should best be structured* to enhance children's skills. In the early 1970s at the Experimental Education Unit at the University of Washington, for example, infants with Down syndrome who lived at home were enrolled in an infant development program soon after birth that focused on teaching their parents the skills they would need to promote their children's social, communication, cognitive, self-help, and motor behaviors (Hayden & Haring, 1976). Early results from that study indicated that those children who received early intervention from infancy approximated the development of typical children. We were discovering as a field that we could change the trajectories of children's development— especially if we started as early as possible in children's lives.

At the same time around the country, many demonstration programs were developed through funding by the Handicapped Children's Education Program (HCEEP) of the U.S. Bureau of Education for the Handicapped (later the Office of Special Education Programs) (Gallagher, 2000). The object of this funding was to provide models of services to young children with disabilities that could be replicated in local communities. Thus, in many communities, demonstration programs began exploring the possibilities of educating preschool children with disabilities (Hebbeler, Smith, & Black, 1991).

At other universities, researchers were exploring how best to minimize the effects of developmental delays and disabilities in the years before school. Many individuals began examining the effects of integrating young children without disabilities into preschool programs for children with special needs (Allen, Benning, & Drummond, 1972; Bricker & Bricker, 1976). In their programs, they studied the effects of integration or "reverse mainstreaming" of children without disabilities into special demonstration programs for children with disabilities and found advantages for both groups. Children with disabilities were found to make developmental progress that was at least equivalent to children with disabilities who were in settings serving exclusively children with special needs (Odom & McEvoy, 1988) and in some instances, children with disabilities outperformed those children with special needs in segregated settings (Hoyson, Jamieson, & Strain, 1984). In addition, in these reverse-mainstreaming settings, children without disabilities experienced no adverse effects of being included in a learning environment with children with developmental problems.

> "We know that a substantial amount of the brain's circuitry is developed in the first few years of life and that this is influenced by a child's early experiences and supportive, stimulating interactions with caring adults."

In my own career journey at the time, I was a research assistant and joined a group of colleagues at the University of Oregon who were developing an integrated program for young children and we, like many others in the country, engaged in another type of research, one that focused on examining the effectiveness of specific techniques for improving the outcomes of young children with disabilities across a wide variety of areas such as language, social competence, and cognitive development. We and other colleagues around the country began a second generation of research on early intervention focusing on how to do early intervention. This work was substantially enhanced when, in 1977, OSEP began funding Early Childhood Research Institutes to develop and test new methods and approaches for promoting the early learning of young children with special needs (U.S. Department of Health, Education, and Welfare, 1977). These institutes became the engines of innovations that generated the content that should be taught to children with special needs in the years before kindergarten and the instructional techniques for teaching those skills.

Developing Curricula: Identifying What Should Be Taught

The study of the content or curriculum for early intervention programs has taken various shapes over the years. Certainly, the content for young children is very different from what one would expect to see in the elementary grades. Most often, in programs for infants, toddlers, and preschool-aged children, the focus is on communication, social, cognitive, motor, and adaptive development (Bricker, 1989; Thurman & Widerstrom, 1990). A common approach for organizing the content in these areas in early childhood programs is following a developmental model. When curriculum follows a developmental approach, children are taught skills across domains in a sequence that follows the order in which typically developing children acquire these skills. The theory behind this approach to organizing curriculum content in early intervention programs is that young children with developmental problems acquire skills in sequences that mirror those of children without disabilities but their rate of acquiring these skills is slower than the typical rate (Bennett-Gates & Zigler, 1998).

A somewhat different view of what should be taught to preschoolers with disabilities is the functional perspective. This approach identifies content of the curriculum based on the skills children may need to function more successfully in a variety of community settings. This perspective reinforces the idea that curriculum should be adapted to meet the child's needs, and there should be a clear reason why each skill is being taught. When this approach is employed, the skills that children require to be successful in a variety of real-world settings (such as in their homes, child care settings, or classrooms) become the focus of the children's learning goals and objectives.

A third perspective on curriculum focuses on skills needed in future settings. Over the years much research and development has focused on identifying the types of skills children in early intervention programs will need to be successful in their future environments. Although some attention in this regard has been on preparing infants and toddlers for the transition to preschool programs, the primary focus of this teaching for the next environment has taken place in preschool settings. Here, some curriculum content focuses on the pre-academic and the social survival skills that will help children succeed in inclusive kindergarten settings (Chandler, 1992).

"When curriculum follows a developmental approach, children are taught skills across domains in a sequence that follows the order in which typically developing children acquire these skills."

Early childhood programs have not always embraced the teaching of pre-academic skills when children were still in preschool. Child development experts once theorized that young children were incapable of learning early academic and pre-literacy skills and that exposure to academic concepts could even be harmful (Bowman, Donovan, & Burns, 2000). More recent research has demonstrated that young children are capable of learning far more complex skills and concepts than previously believed, and so early literacy, mathematics, science, and other pre-academic skills are part of many programs that teach typically developing children as well as children with special needs (Carta & Driscoll, 2012).

Besides pre-academic skills, another set of skills that are often included in the curriculum for preschoolers with special needs are the survival skills children may need to be successful in future inclusive settings. These are skills such as: following classroom routines, completing tasks in the absence of teacher direction, and making transitions from one classroom activity to another. Research we completed on survival skills indicated that children with special needs who had received training on skills were rated as having fewer behavior challenges not only in preschool but in their early elementary school years as well (Carta, Atwater, & Schwartz, 1991). These findings strengthened the notion that curriculum design should attend to the skills that will help children be successful both in their present environments as well as in the future settings.

Designing Instruction: Figuring Out How to Instruct

Identifying the content of early intervention programs was one of the major tasks in developing effective programs for young children. An even bigger challenge has been determining the most effective instructional approaches or determining how best to teach young children with disabilities. In the early years of this research, many of these techniques grew out of the behavioral tradition (c.f. Strain et al., 1992) and were centered on ways to manipulate the environment in purposeful ways that would allow children to acquire and use new behaviors and skills (Wolery & Fleming, 1993). Researchers carried out studies to determine how best to arrange or manipulate both the physical and social environment in classroom and home environments to promote children's skill acquisition and use of practice of newly acquired behaviors. Researchers learned, for example, that manipulating specific aspects of the environment such as the amount and types of materials made available to a group of preschoolers or the number and characteristics of peers and adults present would change children's level of engagement, their level of social interaction with peers, and their vocalizations (Lawry, Danko, & Strain, 1999; Lelaurin & Risley, 1972; Noonan & McCormick, 2006). Critical to each of these various environmental manipulations was that they were specifically designed to set the occasion for, to deliberately teach specific skills, and to promote their more generalized use. This notion of how to design educational experiences for young children with special needs was more than providing high-quality enriching and supportive caregiving environments and hoping that they would naturally learn as most typically developing children do. Thus, a key difference between early intervention aimed at children with special needs and early education for the general population of children is that for the former, instruction must be provided in intentional ways to help children acquire skills, learn to use them at natural rates (fluency), keep using them once specific instruction has ended (maintenance), and learn to use the skills when and where they are needed (generalization) (Wolery & Fleming, 1993).

With intentional instruction, teachers (or home-based interventionists) structure the classroom environment (or for home-based programs, help parents and family members arrange the home setting) in various ways to promote learning and support children's development. Through the use of precise and consistent techniques such as prompting, shaping, and reinforcing, teachers or early interventionists address children's learning objectives, monitor progress through frequent data collection, and modify instructional plans based on progress data. A critically important point, however, is that although these specialized approaches to instruction are essential to promote the learning of children with developmental delays and disabilities, they need not occur within specialized or segregated settings serving only children with special needs. In fact, there is considerable evidence of the benefits that children with disabilities receive when they are educated in inclusive settings (Odom, Buysse, and Soukakou, 2011).

Over the years, especially as young children with special needs began receiving instruction in inclusive early education settings, there has been some tension about the degree of direct teaching that should occur in the early years. Many early education programs have endorsed a strictly child-centered approach for fostering children's development depending on the child to take the lead in exploring and engaging their learning environment. As a result, the direct teaching approaches advocated by early childhood special educators have often been less than enthusiastically embraced by the general early education community. This tension came to a head in 1987, with the publication of the principles of Developmentally Appropriate Practice by the National Association for the Education of Young Children (NAEYC), the principal professional organization of early educators (Bredekamp, 1987). The DAP guidelines suggested that highly structured, adult-directed classroom activities were counterproductive to young learners, that many programs were pushing children too hard, and that early childhood instruction should take place during child-initiated play activities. The guidelines also suggested that extrinsic motivation systems (e.g., tokens, stickers, or high rates of teacher praise) were unnecessary and disruptive to the early childhood learning environment. The DAP guidelines suggested that young children are intrinsically motivated to learn based on their desire to understand their environment and that preschool environments should emphasize exploratory play activities rather than formal instruction.

Some individuals from the early childhood special education community expressed concerns that the original NAEYC DAP guidelines published in 1987 were not sufficient for promoting optimal development for young children with disabilities and did not adequately address the issue of individualizing the types of instruction needed by children across children who might be functioning at different developmental levels (Carta, Atwater, Schwartz, & McConnell, 1991). A more recent NAEYC document outlining the principles of DAP now emphasizes both developmental appropriateness as well as individual appropriateness of instruction that takes into consideration the unique features of each individual child (Bredekamp & Copple, 1997). Discovering what works best for all children requires knowledge of each child, knowledge of how children learn, and specific learning objectives for each child.

"There is considerable evidence of the benefits that children with disabilities receive when they are educated in inclusive settings."

The field of early childhood special education continues to struggle with the level of structure that might be appropriate for young children with disabilities. Although naturalistic approaches are used with greater frequency in current practice, they are in contrast to the more structured and teacher-driven instructional procedures advocated in the early years of this field, when researchers were first determining whether they could design instructional procedures that made a difference in children's learning. Recent thinking about how to deliver instruction on a specific outcome to a young child with special needs recognizes that instructional intensity and the level of teacher-directedness must be determined for each child and for each learning objective. What is necessary is a determination of the level of support that each child needs to give the child the opportunity to acquire, generalize, and maintain the behavior or skill of interest. Least intensive are those based on environmental arrangement (Davis & Fox, 1999) and most intense or structured often use specific stimulus modification and response prompting techniques in a one-to-one format (Bailey & Wolery, 1992). Although each type of instruction has potential legitimacy for use with young children with disabilities, the prevailing opinion is that teachers should use the level of intensity and structure that is most "normalized" as well as effective for each child. What follows is a description of the continuum of instructional supports that form the array of options for individualizing instruction that are currently the primary ways in which learning is promoted for children with special needs from birth through kindergarten: arranging the environment, specialized procedures, and integrated approaches.

Arranging the environment. At the least intrusive level of intervention, changing various aspects of the environment may provide opportunities for children to learn or practice learning goals or objectives. These are deliberate manipulations made by teachers in specific aspects of the child's learning environment such as: (a) the amount and types of materials made available, (b) the amount or arrangement of space, (c) the types and schedule of activities available, and (d) the number and characteristics of peers and adults present. For example, we know that in general, children with disabilities exhibit higher levels of social interactions in a smaller space as compared to a larger space, when engaged with social toys versus isolate toys, when involved in socially designed learning centers versus more isolate areas, and in integrated rather than segregated settings (Hemmeter & Ostrosky, 2003). We also have learned through research that we can engineer classrooms to evoke higher levels of engagement, play behaviors, compliance, and vocalizations (Lawry, Danko, & Strain, 1999; Noonan & McCormick, 2006; Sainato & Carta, 1992). These types of environmental manipulations are minimally intrusive, and although they have been shown to promote certain behaviors, they will often not be sufficient for children with more significant delays in development or who have greater challenges. For these children, progress on some specific learning objectives may be difficult to attain without more direct intervention (Goldstein & Kaczmarek, 1992). For example, for children with significant delays in communication, just putting them in a carefully defined play area with adequate toys may not necessarily result in increases in their social interaction (Kohler & Strain, 1999). Instead, adult prompting of conversations using some of the specialized procedures described below might be necessary to increase the frequency and complexity of their talk with other peers (e.g., Filla, Wolery, & Anthony, 1999).

Specialized procedures. A second level of intervention strategies to teach children's goals/objectives includes a set of more direct intervention strategies. These can be grouped into the following categories: (1) responsive interaction strategies, (2) naturalistic or milieu teaching strategies, and (3) reinforcement-based procedures. Although the research on these procedures is not new, they are the foundation for some of the more complex and comprehensive interventions that have been developed more recently.

Responsive interaction procedures are a set of strategies aimed at promoting communication between a child and adults in a conversational context within the child's natural environment. These procedures are especially useful when the goal is to promote children's attempts at communicating their wants and needs, to learn cause-and-effect relationships, and to learn how to explore their environments (Dunst et al., 1987). Responsive interaction strategies include: following the child's lead (i.e., interacting with the child about the things in which he/she shows an interest), responding contingently to the child's behavior with animated expressions, and taking turns in interactions with the child. An extensive literature documents not only that responsive interaction strategies are effective for promoting communication (e.g., Yoder et al., 1995) but that parents and other caregivers can learn to implement these strategies and embed them into natural routines in homes and classrooms (see Dunst & Kassow, 2004 for a review).

Naturalistic or milieu teaching strategies are a set of procedures based on responsive interactions but that go one step further. These procedures are based on the notion that when parents talk with non-disabled children, they typically talk about objects and events that attract their children's attention, they imitate and expand on their children's attempts at communication, and they repeat and clarify words that their children do not seem to understand (Hart & Risley, 1975). Naturalistic teaching strategies based on this style of interaction are called enhanced milieu teaching procedures and are called: (1) the mand-model procedure, (2) naturalistic time delay, and (3) incidental teaching (Kaiser & Trent, 2007). Although these procedures were developed and initially implemented for use in promoting communication skills, they have been shown to be effective in teaching social and other skills (e.g., Brown, McEvoy, & Bishop, 1991) and for teaching children in settings that range from classrooms to homes and child care settings (Noonan & McCormick, 2006).

Finally, among the most frequently used reinforcement-based procedures are strategies called differential reinforcement, response shaping, behavioral momentum (e.g., Davis & Brady, 1993), and correspondence training (Wolery & Sainato, 2005). These procedures are often useful for increasing the complexity and frequency of children's interactions, promoting more engagement and play, and encouraging appropriate behavior. One example of these is behavior momentum, in which the teacher quickly asks the child to respond to a number of simple requests, and then follows these with a request that is the real target of teaching which has a low probability of an appropriate child response. Procedures like these are used to teach children social skills, to engage in specific types of communication behaviors, respond to indirect questions and comments, and to increase their use of augmentative communication devices (e.g., Davis & Reichle, 1996).

Integrated approaches. Most recent trends in instructional approaches for preschoolers with disabilities focus on methods that integrate multiple types of intervention procedures and attempt to individualize instruction within the context of classroom teaching. One approach, called Activity-Based Instruction (ABI) (Pretti-Frontczak & Bricker, 2004), is characterized by its method of individualizing instruction by integrating a variety of intervention approaches and embedding them in the course of natural interactions across the classroom day. ABI is considered a naturalistic child-directed approach to intervention because of the emphasis on following the child's interests and actions. Key features of ABI include: embedding a child's individual goals or objectives in routine, planned, or child-initiated activities, selecting functional target skills, and using logically occurring antecedents and consequences to teach children new behaviors. Recent studies suggest that activity-based interventions are more effective than didactic procedures in promoting skill generalization (e.g., Losardo & Bricker, 1994).

A second integrated approach to intervention recently being implemented in programs for young children is the use of multi-tiered systems of support or tiered models of instruction. This approach, sometimes referred to as the Response to Intervention (RTI) model, is being widely used with school-aged children as means of preventing and intervening in learning disabilities or serious behavior problems. This model is based on three components: (1) High-quality instruction matched to student need that has been demonstrated through research to produce high rates of learning, (2) measurement of student's growth and level of learning and behavior, and (3) the availability of multiple tiers of intervention varying in intensity and determination of students' level of intensity based on data about their response to intervention (NASDSE, 2006).

"Discovering what works best for all children requires knowledge of each child, knowledge of how children learn, and specific learning objectives for each child."

Examples of three-tiered models have begun to be applied to programs for children younger than school-age (Greenwood et al., 2011). Fox and her colleagues (Fox, Dunlap, Hemmeter, Joseph, & Strain, 2003) have developed a model of prevention and intervention called the Pyramid Model that outlines the early education practices needed to promote social–emotional development and behavior of all children. Their model borrows some of the same features of the three-tiered models but lays them out into a four-level hierarchy that includes: (1) Promoting positive relationships with children, families, and colleagues; (2) Implementation of classroom preventive practices; (3) Utilization of social–emotional teaching strategies; and (4) Use of positive behavior support. Although research on the use of the entire model is just emerging, each level of the hierarchy is based on a set of evidence-based practices. The Pyramid Model has been scaled up and is available to practitioners in early intervention, early education, and community-based child care settings across the U.S. in several countries (Fox & Hemmeter, 2011).

EPILOGUE

We certainly have more evidence today than we did back in the 1970s that we need to identify and begin to provide services to young children with disabilities as soon as we can. We know that early intervention makes a difference in children's lives in their early years—they are more likely to learn social as well as pre-academic skills that can help narrow the gap in educational performance. We know much more about what to teach children and effective procedures for teaching them. We have become much more astute in understanding that approaches for teaching need to be individualized so that children receive the intensity of instruction that is most effective to help them reach their individual goals across domains. One of the biggest challenges that lie ahead is how to be sure that children receive the high-quality instructional and educational experiences that they require. Although research continues to expand the range of evidence-based practices available to teachers of children with special needs, one of the biggest challenges is the high fidelity implementation of these practices on a frequent basis in the variety of environments (classrooms, childcare settings, homes, and other community settings) where young children with special needs spend their days. Young children with disabilities typically receive instruction from a number of different "teachers." In past decades, early intervention to preschoolers with disabilities was delivered by an early childhood special educator and occasionally from a range of therapists. Although these persons are still instrumental in educating these young children, their roles are changing as more young children with disabilities receive instruction and care in inclusive, community-based settings. The role of the interventionist becomes one of instructing adults in these settings on how to help the children with disabilities in their charge.

Thus, research is needed in how to translate effective instructional practices to individuals with a range (and oftentimes limited) of background knowledge and training. There is a growing acknowledgment that to close the gap between available evidence-based strategies and their actual implementation, new and creative approaches to dissemination are needed. We need a clearer identification of these practices and an "on demand" training and technical assistance system that helps this range of teachers obtain the best available information about evidence-based practices and focused, effective professional development delivered in ways that makes it easier, and much more likely, that these effective procedures will be adopted in various settings. Our focus in the coming decade must be on ways to ensure the high-fidelity implementation of known-effective interventions in ways that contribute directly to improved outcomes so that early identification will be the first step to obtaining life-improving intervention for all children with disabilities throughout the country.

Discussion Questions

1. How has the question of "when should intervention begin" changed over time?
2. What are the similarities and differences between the developmentally appropriate and intentional instruction approaches to early childhood education? How have these changed over the years?
3. What are potential consequences or risks for children who do not receive early interventions? Which factors make a child more or less likely to receive early intervention?
4. How do young children with disabilities typically differ from children without disabilities? What strategies are often used by interventionists to help bridge the gap between these two populations?
5. Multi-tiered approaches to intervention, such as RTI, are widely used and accepted in prevention and intervention of disabilities in school-aged children and younger. How are these multi-tiered models structured, and what makes them so effective?

JUDITH J. CARTA'S SUGGESTIONS FOR FURTHER READING

Carta, J. J. (1994). Developmentally appropriate practice: Shifting the emphasis to individual appropriateness. *Journal of Early Intervention, 18,* 342–343.

Carta, J. J., Atwater, J. B., Greenwood, C. R., McConnell, S. R., McEvoy, M., & Williams, R. (2001). Effects of cumulative prenatal substance exposure and environmental risks on children's developmental trajectories. *Journal of Clinical Child Psychology, 30,* 327–337.

Carta, J., Greenwood, C., Walker, D., & Buzhardt, J. (Eds.). (2010). *Individual Growth and Developmental Indicators: Tools for monitoring progress and measuring growth in young children* (pp. 421–431). Baltimore: Paul H. Brookes.

Carta, J., Greenwood, C., Baggett, K., Buzhardt, J., & Walker, D. (2012). Research-based approaches for individualizing caregiving and educational interventions for infants and toddlers in poverty. In S. Odom, E. Pungello, & N. Gardner-Neblett (Eds.), *Re-visioning the Beginning: The implications of developmental and health science for infant/toddler care and poverty* (pp. 333–349). New York: Guilford Press.

Carta, J., & Greenwood, C. (2013). Promising future research directions in response to intervention in early childhood. In V. Buysse & E. Peisner-Feinberg, E. (Eds.), *Handbook of response to intervention in early childhood* (pp. 421–432). Baltimore: Paul H. Brookes.

Carta, J. J. & Kong, N. Y. (2007). Trends and issues in interventions for preschoolers with developmental disabilities. In S. L. Odom, R. H. Horner, M. Snell and J. Blacher (Eds.), *Handbook on developmental disabilities* (pp. 181–198). New York: Guilford Press.

REFERENCES

Allen, K. E., Benning, P. M. & Drummond, W. T. (1972). Integration of normal and handicapped children in a behavior modification preschool: A case study in G. Semb (Ed.), *Behavior analysis and education.* Lawrence, KS: University of Kansas Support and Development Center.

Bailey, D. B., & Wolery, M. (1992). *Teaching infants and preschoolers with disabilities.* (2nd ed.). New York: Macmillan.

Bennett-Gates, D., & Zigler, E. (1998). Resolving the developmental-difference debate: An evaluation of the triarchic and systems theory models. In J. A. Burack, R. M., Hodapp, & E. Zigler (Eds.), *Handbook of mental retardation and development* (pp. 115–131). New York: Cambridge University Press.

Bowman, B. T., Donovan, M. S., & Burns, M. S., (Eds.) (2000). *Eager to learn: Educating our preschoolers.* Washington, DC: National Academy Press.

Bredekamp, S. (1987). *Developmentally appropriate practice in early childhood programs serving children from birth through age 8.* Expanded edition. Washington, DC: NAEYC.

Bredekamp, S., & Copple, C. (1997). *Developmentally appropriate practice in early childhood programs* (Rev. ed.). Washington, DC: National Association for the Education of Young Children.

Bricker, D. (1989). *Early intervention for at-risk and handicapped infants, toddlers, and preschool children.* Palo Alto, CA: VORT.

Bricker, W. A., & Bricker, D. D. (1976). The infant, toddler, and preschool research and intervention project. In T. D. Tjossem (Ed.), *Intervention strategies for high risk infants and young children* (pp. 545–572). Baltimore: University Park Press.

Brooks-Gunn, J., Duncan, G. J., Klebanov, P. K., & Sealand, N. (1993). Do neighborhoods influence child and adolescent behavior? *American Journal of Sociology, 99*, 335–395.

Brown, W. H., McEvoy, M. A., & Bishop, N. (1991). Incidental teaching of social behavior. *Teaching Exceptional Children, 24*(1), 35–38.

Campbell, F. A., Ramey, C. A., Pungello, E., Sparling, J., & Miller-Johnson, S. (2002). Early childhood education: Young adult outcomes from the Abecedarian Project. *Applied Developmental Science, 6*, 42–57.

Carta, J. J., Atwater, J. B., & Schwartz, I. S. (1991, April). The Effects of Classroom Survival Skills Intervention on Young Children with Disabilities: Results of a Two-year Follow-up. Presentation at the Biennial Meeting of the Society for Research in Child Development, Seattle, WA.

Carta, J. J., Atwater, J. B., Schwartz, I. S., & McConnell, S. R. (1991). Developmentally appropriate practice: Appraising its usefulness for young children with disabilities. *Topics in Early Childhood Special Education, 11*(1), 1–20.

Carta, J., & Driscoll, C. (2012). Early literacy interventions for young children with special needs. In T. Shanahan & C. Lonigan (Eds.), *Literacy in preschool and kindergarten children: The National Early Literacy Panel and beyond* (pp. 233–253). Baltimore: Paul H. Brookes.

Center on the Developing Child at Harvard University (2007). *A Science-Based Framework for Early Childhood Policy: Using Evidence to Improve Outcomes in Learning, Behavior, and Health for Vulnerable Children.* http://www.developingchild.harvard.edu.

Chandler, L. K. (1992). Promoting children's social/survival skills as a strategy for transition to mainstreamed kindergarten programs. In S. L. Odom, S. R. McConnell, & M. A. McEvoy (Eds.), *Social competence of young children with disabilities: Issues and strategies for intervention* (pp. 245–276). Baltimore: Paul H. Brookes.

Davis, C. A., & Brady, M. P. (1993). Expanding the utility of behavioral momentum with young children: Where we've been, where we need to go. *Journal of Early Intervention, 17*, 211–223.

Davis, C. A., & Fox, J. (1999). Evaluating environmental arrangement as setting events: Review and implications for measurement. *Journal of Behavioral Education, 9*, 77–96.

Davis, C. A., & Reichle, J. (1996). Variant and invariant high-probability requests: Increasing appropriate behaviors in children with emotional-behavioral disorders. *Journal of Applied Behavior Analysis, 19*, 471–482.

Duncan, G. J., Brooks-Gunn, J., & Klebanov, P. K. (1994). Economic deprivation and early-childhood development. *Child Development 65*, 296–318.

Dunst, C. J., & Kassow, D. Z. (2004). Characteristics of interventions promoting parental sensitivity to child behavior. *Bridges* [on-line], *3*(3), 1–17. Available: http://www.researchtopractice.info/products.php#bridges.

Dunst, C. J., Lesko, J. J., Holbert, K. A., Wilson, I.I., Sharpe, K. L., & Liles, R. F. (1987). A systematic approach to infant intervention. *Topics in Early Childhood Special Education, 7*(2), 19–37.

Filla, A., Wolery, M., & Anthony, L. (1999). Promoting children's conversations during play with adult prompts. *Journal of Early Intervention, 22*, 93–108.

Fox, L., Dunlap, G., Hemmeter, M. I., Joseph, G., & Strain, P. (2003). The teaching pyramid: A model for supporting social competence and preventing challenging behavior in young children. *Young Children, 58*(4), 48–52.

Fox, L., & Hemmeter, M. L. (2011). Coaching early educators to implement effective practices: Using the Pyramid Model to promote social-emotional development. *Zero to Three, 32*(2), 18–24.

Gallagher, J. J. (2000). The beginnings of federal help for young children with disabilities. *Topics in Early Childhood Special Education, 20*, 3–6.

Garber, H., & Heber, R. (1973). *Early intervention as a technique to prevent mental retardation.* (Technical paper). Storrs: University of Connecticut.

Goldstein, H. & Kaczmarek, L. (1992) Promoting communicative interaction among children in integrated intervention setting. In S. F. Warren & J. Reichle (Series Eds.), & S. F. Warren & J. Reichle (Vol. Eds.), *Communication and language intervention series: Vol. 1: Causes and effects in communication and language intervention* (pp. 81–111). Baltimore: Paul H. Brookes.

Greenwood, C. R., Bradfield, T., Kaminski, R., Linas, M., Carta, J. & Nylander, D. (2011). The response to intervention approach in early childhood. *Focus on Exceptional Children, 43*(9), 1–22.

Guralnick, M. J. (Ed.). (1997) *The effectiveness of early intervention.* Baltimore, MD: Paul H. Brookes.

Hart, B., & Risley, T. (1975). Incidental teaching of language in the preschool. *Journal of Applied Behavior Analysis, 8*, 411–420.

Hayden, A., & Haring, N. G. (1976). Early intervention for high risk infants and young children: Programs for Down's syndrome children. In T. D. Tjossem (Ed.). *Intervention strategies for high risk infants and young children* (pp. 573–608). Baltimore: University Park Press.

Hebbeler, K., Smith, B., & Black, T. (1991). Federal early childhood special education policy: A model for the improvement of services for children with disabilities. *Exceptional Children, 58*, 104–112.

Heckman, J. J. (2011). The economics of inequality. *American Educator, 31*–47.

Hemmeter, M. L., & Ostrosky, M. (2003). Executive summary: Classroom preventative practices. In G. Dunlap, M. Conroy, L. Kern, G. DuPaul, J. VanBrakle, P. Strain, et al. (Eds.), *Research synthesis on effective intervention procedures.* Tampa, FL: University of South Florida, Center for Evidence-Based Practice: Young Children with Challenging Behavior.

Hoyson, M., Jamieson, B., & Strain, P. S. (1984). Individualized group instruction of normally developing and autistic-like children: The LEAP curriculum model. *Journal of the Division for Early Childhood, 8*, 157–172.

Kaiser, A. P., & Trent, J. A. (2007). Communication intervention for young children with disabilities: Naturalistic approaches to promoting development. In S.L. Odom, R. H. Horner, M. Snell and J. Blacher (Eds.), *Handbook on developmental disabilities* (pp. 224–248). New York: Guilford.

Karoly, L.A., Greenwood, P. W., Everingham, S. S., Houbé, J., Kilburn, M.R., Rydell, P., Sanders, M., & Chiesa, J. (1998). *Investing in Our Children: What We Know and Don't Know About the Costs and Benefits of Early Childhood Interventions.* Retrieved from http://www.rand.org/pubs/monograph_reports/MR898.html.

Kirk, S. A. (1958). *Early education of the mentally retarded: An experimental study.* Urbana, IL: University of Illinois.

Kohler, F. W., & Strain, P. S. (1999). Maximizing peer-mediated resources in integrated preschool classrooms. *Topics in Early Childhood Special Education, 19*, 319–345.

Lawry, J., Danko, C., & Strain, P. (1999). Examining the role of the classroom environment in the prevention of problem behaviors. In S. Sandall & M. Ostrosky (Eds.), *Young exceptional children: Practical ideas for addressing challenging behaviors* (pp. 49–62). Longmont, CO: Sopris West and Denver, CO: DEC.

Lelaurin, K., & Risley, T. R. (1972). The organization of day-care environments: "Zone" versus "man-to-man" staff assignments. *Journal of Applied Behavior Analysis, 5*, 225–232.

Losardo, A., & Bricker, D. (1994). Activity-based intervention and direct instruction: A comparison study. *American Journal on Mental Retardation, 98*, 744–765.

Masse, L. N., & Barnett, W. S. (2002). A Benefit-Cost Analysis of the Abecedarian Early Childhood Intervention, New Brunswick, N.J.: National Institute for Early Education Research. Retrieved from http://nieer.org/resources/research/AbecedarianStudy.pdf.

McConnell, S. R. (1994). Social context, social validity, and program outcome in early intervention. In R. Gardner, D. M., Sainato, J. O. Cooper, T E. Heron, W. L., Heward, J., Eshleman, & T. A. Grossi (Eds.), *Behavior analysis in education: Focus on Measurably Superior Instruction* (pp. 75–86). Belmont, CA: Wadsworth Publishing.

NASDSE (2006). Response to intervention: NASDSE and CASE White Paper on RTI. Retrieved from: http://www.nasdse.org/Portals/0/Documents/Download%20Publications/RTIAnAdministratorsPerspective1-06.pdf.

Noonan, M. J., and McCormick, L. (2006). *Young children with disabilities in natural environments.* Baltimore: Paul H. Brookes.

Odom, S. L., Buysse, V., & Soukakou, E. (2011). Inclusion for young children with disabilities: A quarter century of research perspectives. *Journal of Early Intervention, 33*, 344–356.

Odom, S. L., & McEvoy, M. A. (1988). Integration of young children with handicaps and normally developing children. In S. L. Odom & M. B. Karnes (Eds.), *Early intervention for infants and children with handicaps: An empirical base* (pp. 241–267). Baltimore: Paul H. Brookes.

Odom, S. L., & Strain, P. S. (1984). Classroom-based social skills instruction for severely handicapped preschool children. *Topics in Early Childhood Special Education, 4*, 97–116.

Pretti-Frontczak, K., & Bricker, D. (2004). *An activity-based approach to early intervention* (3rd Ed.). Baltimore: Paul H. Brookes.

Ramey, C. T., & Campbell, F. A. (1984). Preventive education for high-risk children: Cognitive consequences of the Carolina Abecedarian Project. *American Journal of Mental Deficiency, 88*, 515–523.

Sainato, D. M., & Carta, J. J. (1992). Classroom influences on the development and social competence in young children with disabilities. In S. L. Odom, S. R. McConnell, & M. A. McEvoy (Eds.), *Social competence of young children with disabilities: Issues and strategies for intervention* (pp. 93–109). Baltimore: Paul H. Brookes.

Shonkoff, J.P. & Phillips, D.A. (Eds), (2000). From *Neurons to Neighborhoods: The science of early child development.* Washington DC: National Academy Press.

Skeels, H. M., (1966). Adult status of children with contrasting early life experiences. *Monograph of the Society for Research in Child Development, 31*(3) 1–65.

Skeels, H. M., & Dye, H.B. (1939). A study of the effects of differential stimulation on mentally retarded children. *Convention Proceedings: American Association on Mental Deficiency, 44*, 114–136.

Strain, P., McConnell, S. R., Carta, J. J., Fowler, S., A., Neisworth, J. T., & Wolery, M. (1992). Behaviorism in early intervention. *Topics in Early Childhood Special Education, 12*, 121–141.

Thurman, S. K., & Widerstrom, A. H. (1990). *Infants and children with special needs: A developmental and ecological approach* (2nd ed.). Baltimore: Paul H. Brookes.

U.S. Department of Health, Education, and Welfare. Office of Education (1977). Request for proposal (RFP No. 77–18). Washington, DC: Author.

Warren, S. F., & Kaiser, A. P. (1988). Research in early language intervention. In S. L. Odom & M.B. Karnes (Eds.), *Early intervention for infants and children with handicaps: An empirical base* (pp. 89–108). Baltimore: Paul H. Brookes.

Wolery, M., & Fleming, L. A. (1993). Implementing individualized curricula in integrated settings. In C. A. Peck, S. A. Odom, & D. D. Bricker, (Eds.), *Integrating young children with disabilities in to community programs: Ecological perspectives on research and implementation* (pp. 109–132). Baltimore: Paul H. Brookes.

Wolery, M., & Sainato, D. M. (2005). General curriculum and intervention strategies. In S. L. Odom &M. McLean (Eds.), *Recommended practices in early intervention* (pp. 125–158). Austin, TX: Pro-Ed.

Yoder, P., Kaiser, A., Goldstein, H. Alpert, C., Mousetis, L., Kaczmarek, L., et al. (1995). An exploratory comparison of milieu teaching and responsive interaction in classroom applications. *Journal of Early Intervention, 19*, 218–242.

Getting to Know Michael Wehmeyer

 I entered the field of special education in 1980 with the first wave of teachers hired under the then-new Public Law 94-142. I had not intended to teach students with more extensive support needs (referred to as Severely and Profoundly Handicapped students then), but the hiring director saw that I was over 6 feet tall and could do some heavy lifting, literally, and told me she had just the class for me. I talk a lot about self-determination in my writing, but sometimes life just hands things to you, and that was the case with my career focus on severe disabilities. At the time, students with extensive support needs were still educated, primarily, outside of typical school campuses, so I taught in a United Way agency (and had to work in that agency's sheltered workshop after the school bus left) before landing a job in the public schools.

As long as the students I taught were not creating problems, I was given pretty much free rein on what I wanted to do. After seven years, though, I had a sense that I had gone as far as I could go in creating meaningful changes. I still hear from the families of some of my students from those days, and, on most days, I think of myself as more of a special education teacher than a researcher.

I had been taking courses toward my doctorate while I taught, and in the late 1980s had the wonderful opportunity to serve as a Rotary Teacher of the Handicapped Fellow to the University of Sussex, in Brighton, England, so I left the classroom. When I returned and finished my dissertation, I took a job as a psychologist in an institution for people with "mental retardation" because, when I asked the Chief Psychologist what his goals for the next five years were, he said "to close the place down." The year I spent in that setting profoundly influenced my opinions about how to support people with intellectual and developmental disabilities. In 1990, fate again threw me a softball, and I had the opportunity to direct a funded project to promote the self-determination of adolescents with "mental retardation." There are few times in life when one knows that one's passions and purposes intersect, but I recognized immediately this should become my life's work, and it's been a great ride!

23

WHEN DOES SPECIAL EDUCATION END?

Michael Wehmeyer

In most states, some students with disabilities—most frequently students with more severe disabilities—are eligible for IDEA-mandated special education and related services through the age of 21 years. IDEA actually leaves it up to states to determine age-related eligibility parameters, so the age at which special education and related services cease to be available varies somewhat state-by-state. The majority of states use 21 as the cutoff point, though a few have, over the years, ended eligibility at 18 and a few more have extended eligibility through the age of 26. The rationale for providing, on average, three more years of public education for students whose IEP teams determine they need it is that . . . well, that because of the nature and severity of their disability, these students need the additional three years to successfully transition to adulthood. Specifically, these so-called 18–21 services were intended to provide a concentrated period of time in which educators could focus on providing students with the instructional and experiential activities that enable students to transition to work, independent living, community inclusion, post-secondary education, and so forth. My colleagues and I have articulated a list of indicators of high-quality 18–21 services and supports:

1. Educational services for students with intellectual and developmental disabilities ages 18–21 are provided in age-appropriate environments allowing for social interaction and promoting community inclusion.
2. High-quality educational services are ecologically valid and community-based.
3. High-quality services are outcome-oriented.
4. Academic instruction in quality programs is functional and focused on outcomes.
5. Quality services emphasize person-centered planning and active family involvement.
6. Quality services involve active participation of adult service providers in planning and implementation.
7. Quality services implement best practice in transition.
8. Quality services foster active student involvement and promote self-determination.

(Wehmeyer, Garner, Yeager, Lawrence, & Davis, 2006)

Theoretically, or perhaps hypothetically, these final three years would provide the extra push necessary to launch students with disabilities into the rest of their lives. Anecdotally, and somewhat tangentially, there is little evidence that this really occurs. I say anecdotally because the limited number of existing published studies of 18-21 services tend to be studies of those services that meet most, if not all, of the quality indicators listed above. To my knowledge, there has been no nationwide study of the quality and impact of 18-21 services. There are in the neighborhood of 15,000 public school districts in the United States. Each must provide special education services according to their respective state's plan, and thus the majority of these will provide 18–21 services of some shape or form. The studies of exemplary programs have, at most, 100 participating districts. It is my personal experience working with school districts across the United States for two decades or more on these 18–21 services, that most districts provide such services in the student's home high school and, by and large, the 18–21 program looks no different than the preceding three years in which the student was "officially" in high school. The unfortunate reality, in my opinion, is that in most cases the extra three years simply perpetuate the questionable quality secondary experience had by too many students with severe disabilities; experiences that are marked by segregated programs focused on life skills in settings that would rarely generalize to real life. The light at the end of the tunnel for special education services beyond the age of 18 involves a recent trend toward the establishment of postsecondary education programs for students with intellectual and developmental disabilities in two- and four-year colleges and universities (Hart, Mele-McCarthy, Pasternack, Zimbrich, & Parker, 2004).

> "The light at the end of the tunnel for special education services beyond the age of 18 involves a recent trend toward the establishment of postsecondary education programs for students with intellectual and developmental disabilities in two- and four-year colleges and universities (Hart, Mele-McCarthy, Pasternack, Zimbrich, & Parker, 2004)."

To return, however, to the central question I was asked to address, the technical answer to the question "When does special education end?" is at the end of high school for students who are not eligible for 18–21 services, and, for those students who are eligible for such services, typically at the age of 21. I should note that although most of the students receiving 18–21 services have severe disabilities, about one-third of the students receiving such services have learning disabilities, autism, or emotional/behavioral disorders (Gaumer, Morningstar, & Clark, 2004).

AN ALTERNATIVE QUESTION

That answer is, of course, both less interesting and fails to capture the essence of what I think the question is really asking. Had the question posed to me been "When do students lose eligibility to receive special education services?" then my chapter would end here. But, that wasn't the question . . . the question was "When does special education end?" By now I'm sure you've read the chapter by Barbara Bateman, John Lloyd, and Melody Tankersley titled "What is Special Education?" and you'll recall from that chapter that IDEA defines "special education" as "specially designed instruction." Specially designed instruction refers to instructional strategies that are necessary for students with disabilities to reasonably benefit from their educational program. But, if I answer the question "When does special education end?" with reference to the provision of specially designed instruction, it brings me to a point that is similar to where I am if I answer the question as if it referred to eligibility for special education services. I say similar because, as discussed, the eligibility for specially designed instruction ends at the ages of 18 or 21 in the vast majority of states. The need for supports that enable these now-young-adults to be successful post-high school (or post-18 to 21) continue, however . . . and one can reasonably presume that as young adults, most students who received special education services will continue to need some level of "specially designed" something, be it instruction or non-teaching supports, through the rest of their lives to be successful.

Still, if I answer the question "When does specially designed instruction end?" I'm still near the end of what I would have to say. If that were the question I was addressing, I would discuss the current trend toward a supports paradigm for adults with disabilities (and I will, eventually), and be done with it. Obviously, most young adults who needed specially designed instruction when they were in school will need ongoing supports to be successful in adulthood.

But, that's not the question I chose to answer here either. I want to take a step beyond special education eligibility or specially designed instruction and answer the question "When does special education end?" by discussing when the stigma and stereotypes that the term "special education" brings to the minds of most people, particularly the public, ends and, so as not to run the risk of writing a complete rant, discuss how current trends in understanding disability emphasizing self-determination, community inclusion, and empowerment can move us away from such stereotypes.

Technically, special education is a noun, referring to a particular type of education. For much of the history of our field, though, "special education" has been used as an adjective, to describe a student (she's a special education student) or a place (he goes to special education). Mention "special education" to your Average Joe or Jolene, and I believe that is what they think of; *special ed* as a place where *special ed* students go. The most socially conscious of these Average Joes or Jolenes just think of the young people who "go" to special education as "special"—special being, of course, a synonym for disabled. This understanding is perpetuated in adulthood. There are "special" Boy Scout troops that allow adults with intellectual disability to participate; there are special camps and special sports and special shopping days and special this's and special that's. To the less socially conscious Average Joe or Jolene, "special ed student" is just a politically correct term for "retarded student "or "handicapped student" or "crippled student." If you think I'm overstating this, just check out whatever the latest media sensation is in which the term "retarded" has been applied to a person as a pejorative—I'm sure there will be one. Or, look back and see how many terms were originally introduced as labels for conditions like intellectual disability, but are now just insults; idiot, imbecile, moron, and retard come to mind. I'm reminded of a story that I think illustrates my point. In the late 1980s, the then-named Canadian Association for the Mentally Retarded released a one-minute public service announcement (PSA) featuring the then immensely popular hockey star, Wayne Gretzky, and a young man named Joey who worked as the locker room attendant for the team on which Gretzky played, the Edmonton Oilers. The PSA was intended to make the point that people with Down syndrome were valued community members. Joey had Down syndrome and Gretzky came to know him while he was dating Joey's older sister and, subsequently, helped Joey get the job as the Oilers' locker room attendant.

The PSA shows Gretzky and Joey in the aforementioned Oilers' locker room, with shots of Joey stacking hockey sticks, taking out towels, and lacing skates, while Gretzky talks about the many things that Joey, and other people with Down syndrome, can achieve if given an opportunity.

"Every day, Joey works hard in the Oilers dressing room, preparing things for our team," says Gretzky. "I've found that people who are mentally handicapped, like Joey, can really surprise you with all the things they can do by simply being part of our lives."

Accepting that terms like handicapped were simply part of nomenclature of that era, it's really a touching message showing a young man who clearly has a lot of skills and abilities, not the least of which is the ability to get people to like him, achieving beyond what society expects of him.

The PSA closes with Gretzky saying: "Open up your life. Let people who are mentally handicapped be a part of your community." Gretzky points at the camera and then he and Joey turn to look at one another. All of a sudden, Gretzky raises his hand and scratches the side of his head (or sort of waves his hand behind his ear, the gesture is difficult to distinguish). This is obviously a game that he has developed with Joey, who immediately imitates the action and says "Gretzky!" with evident joy, followed by a laugh and hand clap. Gretzky laughs as well, puts his arm over Joey's shoulder, and the PSA closes.

Because of his Down syndrome, Joey's attempt to say "Gretzky" is garbled . . . if you know that's what he's saying, as you do in the context of this PSA, you recognize it, otherwise you'd be hard pressed to identify what it was that Joey had said.

What was the lasting cultural impact from this heartfelt video? I'm sure many people were touched. Perhaps someone actually let someone who was "mentally handicapped" be a part of his or her community. Hard to tell. What wasn't hard to tell was that for a period of time, children and young people would scream "Gretzky" in a garbled way and wave behind their ears as an insult to suggest that a friend was "retarded." Further, the term "Joey" began to be used to refer to all people with Down syndrome, as in "he's a Joey." Stigma and stereotypes.

So, to begin with, I want to answer the question as if it asked "When does the stigma associated with special education end?" When do people with disabilities who receive special education services quit being treated based upon others' understanding of their disability? Answering this question is, I think, at the heart of any attempt to answer a broader question referencing what types of "specially designed whatever" do people need to succeed as an adult. I should note that my perspective on these issues is shaped by my years of work with people with intellectual and developmental disabilities, and the experiences of people with other types of disabilities certainly varies. I've heard many people with learning disabilities say that they simply walked away from the label once they graduated, walking away from the stigma associated with it. I suspect that is what most people do, if they can. I've also heard, though, the same people talking about their struggles through adulthood with the hidden disability, and I suspect if they could disassociate the stigma associated with the label with the benefits of supports to overcome limitations inherent with the disability, many people would do so. Further, I'm fairly convinced that even people who can walk away from the label continue to think about themselves in ways that reflect how they were treated in school, and thus can never really walk away. But, if it is obvious, physically or otherwise, that you have a disability, you certainly can't simply leave it behind.

So, let's ask ourselves, when does the stigma associated with special education end? The truth is, for many people, it doesn't. Why? In large measure, because we have established a separate and, I would argue, inherently unequal, system that looks more like special ed as an adjective than special education as a noun. The special education system set up in the immediate aftermath of the passage of Public Law 94-142, the Education for All Handicapped Children Act, mirrored a 100-year legacy of completely separate services provided through residential placement of people with disabilities (Thompson & Wehmeyer, 2008). That is, generalizing from our nation's prior history of providing services in institutions, special education services were founded on the rationale that separate

"When do people with disabilities who receive special education services quit being treated based upon others' understanding of their disability?"

schools and classrooms would be more feasible, efficient, and effective for meeting student needs (Jackson, Ryndak, & Wehmeyer, 2010). To a significant degree, for students with more severe disabilities, not much has changed in the 35 years since P.L. 94-142's passage, and they move from a largely segregated public school experience to a largely segregated adult world; sheltered workshops, group homes, special arts and recreation programs, and so forth. Even the requirements of an annual meeting in which others decide what to do to the person (active treatment) continue ad nauseam throughout the person's life.

Lest the reader despair that this chapter will simply be a lamentation over the purportedly miserable state of affairs for people with disabilities, let me turn toward what is happening that provides hope that we can think about the notion of "special education" into adulthood differently than we have to this point. I have written recently about a third wave of the disability movement that is predicated on a new way of understanding disability (Wehmeyer, 2014), and I would like to present my major points from that publication to describe where I see the field moving over the next decade.

We need to begin, though, with considering how disability has been understood historically, and how that led us to believe that the services needed in school and adulthood should be as I have described them. That is, historically, *disability* has been understood as an extension of a medical model that conceived health as an *interiorized state* of functioning and health problems as an individual pathology: as a problem *within* the person. Within such a context, disability was understood to be medical in nature and a characteristic of a person; as residing within that person. The person was, as such, viewed as in some way broken. The language of the professions that emerged to create programs for people with disability reflect that conceptualization; people with disability were described, depending upon the profession, as diseased, pathological, atypical, or aberrant (Wehmeyer et al., 2008).

Let me more fully articulate my thesis with regard to why we set up special education as we did in the mid-1970s; that is, how disability is understood determines how people with disability are treated, both in the sense of the nature and structure of services provided to them and in the sense of how others, including the public, respond to that person. If, as has been the case for much of history, we see people with disabilities as broken, aberrant, atypical, diseased, or deficient; our response to them is to fix or cure them. If that is not possible, the historical responses have ranged from magnanimous attempts focused on segregated learning or living environments, to decidedly less magnanimous attempts to isolate, sterilize, and separate people (Smith & Wehmeyer, 2012).

I suspect that many people see statements such as the above as simply climbing aboard the bandwagon bashing the medical model, and, perhaps, creating a straw man argument. I will respectfully disagree. I hear people point out that the percentage of students with disabilities who receive most of their education in the general education curriculum has climbed impressively in the last decade. And, assuredly, there have been substantial gains in this area. Data from the Institute for Educational Sciences show that 59 percent of children with disabilities spend most of their day (more than 80 percent) in the general education setting. That's up from only 33 percent a decade earlier. Except . . . check those percentages for students served under the intellectual disability category or the multiple disability category; 17 percent and 13 percent respectively. Self-contained classrooms remain, overwhelmingly, the primary educational setting for this population.

I would also deny jumping on the bash-the-medical-model bandwagon because the description of how disability was historically understood was from a medical body itself . . . the World Health Organization. Be that as it may, however, I'm of the firmly held opinion that if we understand disability as an interiorized state of pathology and as residing within the person, there is not much to be hopeful about in the future. We will continue to isolate and segregate students and then, when they leave school, they will continue to be segregated and isolated.

Over the past half century, however, forces have conspired to move us beyond this historical understanding of disability. The parent movement of the mid-twentieth century resulted in a community focus for intervention and resulted in the right to a free, appropriate public education. The self-advocacy and self-determination movement of the latter decades of the twentieth century resulted in greater civil protections (the ADA prominent among them), and has resulted in a reconsideration of how disability is understood.

The catalyst for the changing conceptualization of disability is the same body that originally defined disability as an interiorized state; the World Health Organization. In the context of health care, it became apparent by the late 1970s that individual pathology models offered a far too narrow perspective for effectively describing, understanding, and addressing the problems of people experiencing *chronic* or *pervasive health issues*, including disability. Consequently, in 1980, the World Health Organization introduced the International Classification of Impairments, Disabilities, and Handicaps (ICIDH) (World Health Organization, 1980; Wood, 1989). Essentially, the ICIDH proposed different perspectives or planes of experience for looking at human functioning and for describing the consequences of diseases. Within this perspective, human functioning refers to all the life activities of a person. The ICIDH perspectives for describing the impact of a pathology on human functioning were: (1) the "exteriorization of a pathology" in body anatomy and functions, (2) "objectified pathology" as expressed in the person's activities (e.g. adaptive behavior skills), and (3) the "social consequences of pathology" (e.g. participation in social life domains) (World Health Organization, 1980, p. 30). Later, it was recognized that besides the impact of pathology, contextual factors are of pivotal importance for the understanding of human functioning. Contextual

"We will continue to isolate and segregate students and then, when they leave school, they will continue to be segregated and isolated."

factors are "environmental factors" and "personal factors.". It was also understood that problems in human functioning are not necessarily linear or causal consequences of a pathology, but that human functioning should be conceived as multiple interactive processes where each factor can influence each other factor either directly or indirectly. By adding "environmental factors" and "personal factors," a broader descriptive model of human functioning was created in the ICIDH successor, the International Classification of Functioning, Disability, and Health (ICF; World Health Organization, 2001).

The ICF offers clear definitions of each dimension of human functioning and of the factors described in the model (World Health Organization, 2001):

- *Functioning* is an umbrella term for all life activities of an individual and encompasses body structures and functions, personal activities, and participation areas. Problems or limitations in functioning are labeled a "disability." Disability can result from any problem in one or more of the three dimensions of human functioning [body structures and functions, personal activities, participation]. The origin of such a problem should be situated in the interaction of health and functioning.
  - *Body structures* are anatomical parts of the body; *body functions* are the physiological and psychological functions of body systems. Problems in body functions and structures are called "impairments."
  - *Activity* is the execution of a task or action by an individual. Activities refer to skills and abilities of the individual that allow him to adapt to the demands and expectations of the environment. Problems in this dimension are referred to as "activity limitations."
  - *Participation* is defined as "involvement in a life situation." Participation is related to the functioning of the individual in society. It refers to roles and interactions in the areas of home living, work, education, leisure, spiritual and cultural activities. Problems an individual may experience in involvement in life situations are called "participation restrictions" (Wehmeyer et al., 2008).
- The *health condition* of an individual can affect his functioning directly or indirectly in each or all of the three dimensions. Health condition problems are "disorders," "diseases" or "injuries,"etc. as classified in the International Statistical Classification of Diseases and Related Health Problems (ICD-10) (WHO, 1999). The ICD-10 provides an etiological framework for health conditions affecting human functioning.

Finally, the ICD-10 identified *Contextual Factors* that include (a) environmental factors and (b) personal factors and that represent the complete background of an individual's life. They may have an impact on the individual's functioning and must also be considered in the evaluation of human functioning.

- *Environmental factors* make up the physical, social, and attitudinal environment in which people live and conduct their lives. Environmental factors sometimes act as facilitators when, in interaction with personal factors, they contribute to the accomplishment of adapted behavior. For example, positive employees' attitudes and accessibility ramps act as facilitators when contributing to an adapted behavior such as working. On the other hand, the absence of such facilitators or presence of other environmental factors such as negative attitudes or inaccessible buildings can hinder the accomplishment of adapted behaviors such as working. Under these circumstances, environmental factors are referred to as "barriers."

- *Personal factors* are characteristics of a person such as gender, race, age, other health conditions, fitness, lifestyle, habits, upbringing, coping styles, social background, education, profession, past and current experience (past life events and concurrent events), character style, individual psychological assets, and other characteristics, all or any of which may play a role in disability at any level. They are composed of features of the person that are not part of a health condition or health state (Wehmeyer et al., 2008).

Thus, within ICD-10, *disability* serves as an umbrella term for problems in human functioning, including impairments (e.g., problems in body structures or function), activity limitations, or participation restrictions. Activity limitations are difficulties an individual may have in executing activities. Participation restrictions are problems an individual may experience in involvement in life situations.

CONSIDER A PERSON–ENVIRONMENT VIEW

Why such a detailed description of the WHO conceptualizations of disability? Quite simply, it is because I believe such conceptualizations are, fundamentally, game changers in the way in which we respond to disability in the lives of people with disability. How? First, the ICD-10 conceptualizes disability only in the context of typical human functioning. Disability is not apart from typical human functioning, but a part of typical human functioning. Second, disability is an exteriorized state, not an interiorized pathology; that is a function of the relationship between personal characteristics and their impact on activity and participation. The ICF/ICD-10 model is one of a rising number of person–environment interaction models introduced to explain complex human behavior. Person–environment interaction models date back to the earliest years of the twentieth century in psychology (Chartrand, 1991; Neufeld et al., 2006). Many aspects of human behavior can be explained by these interactive processes, and a number of examples exist in the literature of the application of such person–environment interaction models to disability and other contexts. Currently, the U.S. Department of Health and Human Services' Center for Disease Control incorporates a social–ecological model to address public health issues.

How does a person–environment interaction model (also sometimes referred to as social–ecological models or person–environment fit models) become a game changer for people with disabilities? First, such models shift from a deficits focus to a strengths focus. Of interest is the degree to which a person's capacities enable him or her to function, successfully, in typical environments or contexts, be they work, school, or community. Second, the emphasis in intervention shifts from programs to remediate deficits to supports to close the gap between personal capacity and the demands of the environment. This (e.g., closing the gap between personal capacity and the demands of the environment) can be achieved by either increasing personal capacity or by modifying aspects of the environment or context to enable successful functioning. Third, these models presume competence, not incompetence. The assumption is that we can either enhance capacity sufficiently or modify the environment sufficiently to narrow the gap between the two to such an extent that disability doesn't really matter.

Think about some examples of the potential of these models using now readily available or ubiquitous technologies. Twenty years ago, to work as a cashier, you had to possess a host of skills related to math (calculating totals, making change, etc.). Today, you have to be able to scan a bar code over a laser and the computer that is now a cash register tells you how much change to provide and, sometimes, distributes the change needed. Put the same person behind the counter in these two eras, and while nothing about the person would have changed, their capacity to function successfully would have changed dramatically. Or, for another example that looks at emerging technologies; like most Americans who live in the Midwest, I don't have the necessity to parallel park all that often, and when I do, I'm adequate, but not great. On a recent trip to England, I was in an automobile with a friend who needed to parallel park. Of course, everything is smaller, narrower, and more difficult to navigate in England, and the parking spot into which my friend was trying to parallel park was only slightly longer than his automobile. Frankly, I would have never even attempted to pull in, but not my friend. He aligned his car with the car in front of the open spot and proceeded to perform a perfect parallel park. About halfway through, I glanced over and noticed that he wasn't touching the steering wheel. In fact, this automobile had the newly developed automatic parking system allowing the vehicle to park itself. I'd heard on the news about cars that drive themselves, but all of a sudden, I was sitting in one and it became less futuristic. In a not-too-distant future, automobiles will, in fact, drive themselves and whether you are a good driver or a poor driver will become irrelevant.

> "Closing the gap between personal capacity and the demands of the environment can be achieved by either increasing personal capacity or by modifying aspects of the environment or context to enable successful functioning."

Now, let's say your disability manifested such that you were, previously, unable to drive. In this extreme example, the advent of cars that drive themselves means that you can successfully use an automobile to solve the transportation problems that have limited your access to work or community inclusion. Your disability doesn't disappear, necessarily; it just doesn't matter any longer in this context.

The United States has been relatively slow to adopt the ICF/ICD-10, but in the rest of the world, this model of disability is well understood and is driving practice, and it is beginning to be so in the U.S. as well. How? Well, first, as I've mentioned, the focus of such models shift from efforts to quantify deficits to efforts identifying and expanding strengths. Think about the energy we, as a field, expend in diagnosis and quantifying deficits. Of course, not all such activities are unnecessary or harmful, but now think about the energy put into quantifying strengths. Not really equivalent, is it? This is particularly important for adulthood, where the focus should be on maximizing a person's strengths to enable him or her to be more successful. Second, these person–environment interaction models require that we focus attention on narrowing the gap between the person's capacities and the demands of the environment by providing supports that enable them to function successfully.

This notion of supports, and a supports paradigm, is an important one that is slowly making its way into practice in the U.S. Historically, the response to disability has been to create "programs" that are, in some way, linked to the type or severity of the person's disability. The segregated service system is built upon such programs; when I began teaching students with intellectual disability, students with "moderate levels" of impairment were sent to the "Trainable" program where they received a curriculum largely predicated on the severity of their disability. It remains almost pro forma to presume that adults with intellectual disability "belong" in a sheltered workshop or work activities center. This is despite the fact that we have more than 25 years of experience showing that people with severe disabilities can be supported to work in typical, competitive work settings through models such as supported employment, customized employment, or self-employment. I am always astonished to hear people in the adult services field express bafflement that people with severe disabilities don't "need" sheltered work.

SUPPORTS RATHER THAN PROGRAMS

If not programs, then what? The movement toward person–environment fit models has introduced a supports paradigm to the field. The 1992 American Association on Mental Retardation (now American Association on Intellectual and Developmental Disabilities) Terminology and Classification manual defined supports as:

> Resources and strategies that promote the interests and causes of individuals with or without disabilities; that enable them to access resources, information and relationships inherent within integrated work and living environments; and that result in their enhanced interdependence, productivity, community integration, and satisfaction.
> (Luckasson, et al., 1992; p. 101)

What are supports and what characteristics of "providing supports" differentiate this intervention approach from traditional models of programs and service delivery? There are several aspects of a supports model that do so. First, there are the three "key aspects of supports" identified in the above definition: (1) they pertain to resources and strategies; (2) they enable individuals to access other resources, information, and relationships within integrated environments; and (3) their use results in increased integration and enhanced personal growth and development. In other words, supports have the unambiguous intent to enhance community integration and inclusion by enabling people to access a wide array of resources, information, and relationships. Second, supports are individually designed and determined, with the active involvement of key stakeholders in the process, particularly the person benefiting from that support. Traditional service delivery models have too often been designed primarily in a top-down process.

Finally, Luckasson and Spitalnik (1994) suggested that "supports refer to an array, not a continuum, of services, individuals, and settings that match the person's needs" (p. 88). Luckasson and Spitalnik refer to a "constellation" of supports needed by people with disability where the person is in the center, and types of supports range from self-directed and self-mediated supports, like the person, his or her family and friends and non-paid supports, like coworkers or neighbors, to generic supports (those that everyone uses) and specialized supports, like those provided in a disability service system.

"It remains almost pro forma to presume that adults with intellectual disability 'belong' in a sheltered workshop or work activities center."

The notion of supports is more than just reframing programs or services. As noted, supports are resources and strategies that enhance human functioning (Luckasson et al., 2002), thus aligning the notion with ICD-10/ICF understandings of disability within a broader frame of typical human functioning. We all use supports, we live in an interdependent world in which each of us needs a variety of supports to function successfully (Thompson et al., 2009). People with disabilities are no different, but can be understood to require extraordinary supports to function successfully when compared to people without disability. The need for extraordinary supports provides a means to measure what is referred to as support needs. *Support needs* is a psychological construct referring to the pattern and intensity of support a person requires to participate in activities associated with normative human functioning (Thompson et al., 2009, p. 236). The American Association on Intellectual and Developmental Disabilities (AAIDD) has pioneered the measurement of support needs as a function of person-centered planning and resource allocation. The Supports Intensity Scale-Adult version (Thompson, Bryant et al., 2013) is the latest iteration of a tool designed to measure the relative intensity of support that each person with intellectual disability and related developmental disabilities (ID/DD) needs to fully participate in community life. The Supports Intensity Scale-Children's version (SIS-A; Thompson, Wehmeyer et al., 2013) is a similar tool for use with school-age children with intellectual and developmental disabilities (SIS-C) that is currently being normed.

Both versions of the SIS are measures of support need; the type, intensity, and duration a person needs to function successfully in typical environments. Contrast this with widely used assessments, such as intelligence tests or adaptive behavior measures. Both of the latter are measures of personal competence; or, if you don't do well on them, personal incompetence. The SIS versions are measures of support needs, not personal incompetence. Intelligence and adaptive behavior tests are widely used to diagnose and determine eligibility for services and programs, but I would argue that they are relics of hopefully-soon-antiquated ways of thinking about disability. For one thing, these are imperfect indicators of the types of supports a person really needs. Line ten people up who have an IQ score of 65. Now, consider whether the supports needed for each person to function successfully are the same? Making resource allocation or "program" decisions based upon IQ score suggests they are. But, what if one person engages in particularly challenging behavior? Doesn't that person need more support than another person with the same IQ score who doesn't? For that matter, doesn't someone with severe behavioral issues who has a higher IQ score probably need supports of a different type, intensity, or duration than someone with a lower IQ score who does not engage in problem behavior? What if one person is prone to suicidal ideation? What if another person has need for seizure management? What if one person is particularly good at a task suited for a job? Measures of support needs can determine these variable needs better than static proxy measures of deficits. This ensures not only better information for intervention planning, but more equitable distribution of scarce resources, like disability-related funding. Currently, almost 20 U.S. states and Canadian provinces, as well as numerous European countries, use the SIS-A to determine resource needs.

ADDITIONAL IMPLICATIONS

This new "disability paradigm" also leads us in a few other directions. As I've stated, this paradigm abandons old notions of disability as residing within or being a characteristic of a person. It instead focuses on the interaction between the person, his or her personal characteristics, including competencies, and the environment or context in which that person must function. This emphasis on functioning requires that interventions focus less on fixing or curing the individual and more on designing and implementing supports that address the "fit" between the person and the context in which he or she must function. Second, the culmination of the independent living, deinstitutionalization, and normalization movements of the late twentieth century is that the place in which we must provide this array of supports is the community. Third, accordingly, the rights focus of the independent living and civil rights movements that emerged in the late twentieth century and are ongoing, have resulted in a focus on legislative and civil protections and assurances of equal opportunity and access and the emergence of a new disability movement, what I would call the self-advocacy/self-determination movement. This movement focuses on the person as the "most natural" support, consumer controlled and directed services, and empowerment (Wehmeyer, 2014).

This latter point is important to consider when addressing the question "When does special education end?" if we're considering issues of stigma and stereotypes. The new disability paradigm places the person at the center of efforts to provide supports. At the heart of such efforts is a focus on self-determination. Research has linked higher self-determination to more positive school (Shogren, Palmer, Wehmeyer, Williams-Diehm, & Little, 2012) and adult outcomes, including employment and independent living, for youth with disabilities (Shogren, Wehmeyer, Palmer, Rifenbark, & Little, 2015; Wehmeyer & Palmer 2003; Wehmeyer & Schwartz 1997), as well as to a higher quality of life (Lachapelle et al., 2005; Nota, Ferrrari, Soresi, & Wehmeyer, 2007; Wehmeyer & Schwartz 1998).

Within adult-support models, promoting self-determination becomes central in supporting adults with disabilities to achieve more positive life outcomes. Walker and colleagues (2011) have proposed a "social-ecological" model to promote self-determination that (1) adopts the person–environment interaction model of disability, emphasizing both capacity enhancement and modifications to environments and contexts; (2) proposes that efforts to achieve meaningful adult outcomes (e.g., employment, community inclusion, independent living, etc.) for adults with disabilities must recognize principles of adult learning, particularly that adults learn in more self-directed, self-guided fashions; and (3) uses efforts to promote self-determination as a "gateway" to achieving meaningful adult outcomes. The model recognizes that learning in adulthood is complex, and involves mediating and moderating factors, like gender or cultural contexts, that must be taken into account when supporting people with severe disabilities to achieve outcomes like employment or independent living. The social–ecological model emphasizes the importance of social networks and social capital on achieving meaningful outcomes for adults with disabilities.

I will use employment models to illustrate the application of person–environment interaction models, such as the Walker et al. model, on efforts to support adults with disabilities because intervention models consistent with such practices already exist. Supported employment is the most obvious of these. For literally decades now, we have known that people with severe disabilities can work competitively through strategies used in supported employment, such as job carving or job sharing, as well as in innovative employment models such as customized employment or self-employment. These outcomes are achieved by, of course, supports that enable the worker to gain as many skills needed for the job as possible, and then modifications to the job description, job tasks, or workplace environment that further reduce the gap between the person's capacities and his or her success on the job (Wehman, 2011).

WHEN DOES SPECIAL EDUCATION END?

So, finally, let me return to make a concentrated effort to answer the question "When does special education end?" taking into account the various meanings of that question and the just completed discussion of a new paradigm of disability. Support needs are personal characteristics that remain relatively stable over a person's life, one assumes (though this remains to be tested empirically). A person with intellectual disability or a more severe disability will, likely, require extraordinary supports to function successfully in typical environments for the duration of his or her life. Certainly, skill acquisition can reduce support need, but over time, the need for supports will remain stable. We can state, though, that the need for supports does not end without running into the problem introduced by asking the question when "special ed" as associated with stigma, ends. All people need supports. Supports are resources and strategies that promote typical human functioning. My smartphone has become a tool that not only supports my capacity to function, but in fact, extends that capacity. That some people need more support than others is a matter of quantity, not a qualitative difference. Supports that successfully bridge the gap between personal capacity and the demands of an environment or context make disability irrelevant. This is true whether one's disability is hidden or not.

> "When does special education end? Quite simply, when we choose to change the way we think about disability itself."

When does special education end? Quite simply, when we choose to change the way we think about disability itself. There are examples aplenty that people with all types of disabilities can live, learn, work, and play successfully, if they are supported to do so. I believe it is a matter of will that, for example, we continue to propagate sheltered workshops or congregate living settings as in some way required by people with disabilities, and not a matter of what the people relegated to those environments might be able to achieve if afforded adequate supports (Wehmeyer, 2011). If we, as a society, had the will to do so, we could change this immediately. That we haven't already done so simply speaks to the fact that the answer to the question about when the stigma association with *special ed* will end is, unfortunately, not soon.

Discussion Questions

1. Why do you think that different states have different ages at which students officially no longer qualify for special education services?
2. Why is Wehmeyer not interested in talking about the age at which services end as the focus of his chapter?
3. What are the indicators of high-quality 18–21 services and supports for individuals with intellectual disabilities?
4. Technically, the term "special education" is a noun used to reference a type of education. Describe how the term has been used historically as an adjective. What stigma and stereotypes are associated with special education even after students leave the educational system?
5. Under the Education for All Handicapped Children Act, how were special education services originally designed and provided to individuals with

intellectual disabilities? Has the special education system evolved in years past for individuals with severe disabilities? Would you consider modern day services for these individuals to be primarily separate or inclusion based within the educational setting, and into adulthood within the community? Be sure to include specifics to support your claim.
6. Explain how person–environment interaction models strive to close the gap between personal capacity and the demands of the environment.
7. How are "supports" different from programs and services designed to help individuals with disabilities?

MICHAEL WEHMEYER'S SUGGESTIONS FOR FURTHER READING

Shogren, K., Palmer, S., Wehmeyer, M. L., Williams-Diehm, K., & Little, T. (2012). Effect of intervention with the *Self-Determined Learning Model of Instruction* on access and goal attainment. *Remedial and Special Education, 33*, 320–330.

Smith, J. D., & Wehmeyer, M. L. (2012). *Good blood, bad blood: Science, nature and the myth of the Kallikaks.* Washington, DC: American Association on Intellectual and Developmental Disabilities.

Wehmeyer, M. L. (Ed.), (2013). *The story of intellectual disability: An evolution of meaning, understanding, and public perception.* Baltimore: Paul H. Brookes.

Wehmeyer, M. L. (Ed.), (2013). *Handbook of positive psychology and disability.* Oxford, UK: Oxford University Press.

Wehmeyer, M. L. Buntinx, W. E., Lachapelle, Y., Luckasson, R., Schalock, R., Verdugo-Alonzo, M. . . . Yeager, M. (2008). The intellectual disability construct and its relationship to human functioning. *Intellectual and Developmental Disabilities, 46*, 311–318.

Wehmeyer, M. L., Palmer, S., Shogren, K., Williams-Diehm, K., & Soukup, J. (2013). Establishing a causal relationship between interventions to promote self-determination and enhanced student self-determination. *The Journal of Special Education, 46*, 195–210.

Wehmeyer, M. L., Shogren, K., Palmer, S., Williams-Diehm, K., Little, T., & Boulton, A. (2012). The impact of the *Self-Determined Learning Model of Instruction* on student self-determination. *Exceptional Children, 78*, 135–153.

REFERENCES

Chartrand, J. M. (1991). The evolution of trait-and-factor career counseling: A person x environment fit approach. *Journal of Counseling & Development, 69*, 518–524.

Gaumer, A.S., Morningstar, M.E., & Clark, G. M. (2004). Status of community-based transition programs: A national database. *Career Development for Exceptional Individuals, 27*(2), 131–149.

Hart, D., Mele-McCarthy,J., Pasternack, R. H., Zimbrich, K., & Parker, D. R. (2004). Community college: A pathway to success for youth with learning, cognitive, and intellectual disabilities in secondary settings. *Education and Training in Developmental Disabilities, 39*, 54–66.

Jackson, L.B., Ryndak, D.L., & Wehmeyer, M.L. (2010). The dynamic relationship between context, curriculum, and student learning: A case for inclusive education as a research-based practice. *Research and Practice for Persons with Severe Disabilities, 33*(4), 175–195.

Lachapelle, Y., Wehmeyer, M.L., Haelewyck, M.C., Courbois, Y., Keith, K.D., Schalock, R. . . . Walsh, P.N. (2005). The relationship between quality of life and self-determination: An international study. *Journal of Intellectual Disability Research, 49*, 740–744.

Luckasson, R., Borthwick-Duffy, S., Buntix, W.H.E., Coulter, D.L., Craig, E.M., Reeve, A. . . . Tasse, M. (2002). *Mental retardation: Definition, classification, and systems of supports* (10th Ed.). Washington, DC: American Association on Mental Retardation.

Luckasson, R., Coulter, D. L., Polloway, E. A., Reiss, S., Schalock, R. L., Snell, M. E. . . . Stark, J. A. (1992). *Mental retardation: Definition, classification, and systems of supports* (9th Edition). Washington, DC: American Association on Mental Retardation.

Luckasson, R., & Spitalnik, D. M. (1994). Political and programmatic shifts of the 1992 AAMR definition of mental retardation. In V. Bradley, J. W. Ashbaugh, & B. C. Blaney (Eds.), *Creating individual supports for people with developmental disabilities: A mandate for change at many levels* (pp. 81–96). Baltimore: Paul H. Brookes.

Neufeld, J., Rasmussen, H., Lopez, S., Ryder, J., Magyar-Moe, J., Ford, A., Edwards, L., & Bouwkamp, J. (2006). The engagement model of person-environment interaction. *The Counseling Psychologist, 34*(2), 245–259.

Nota, L., Ferrrari, L., Soresi, S., & Wehmeyer, M.L. (2007). Self-determination, social abilities, and the quality of life of people with intellectual disabilities. *Journal of Intellectual Disability Research, 51,* 850–865.

Shogren, K., Palmer, S., Wehmeyer, M.L., Williams-Diehm, K., & Little, T. (2012). Effect of intervention with the *Self-Determined Learning Model of Instruction* on access and goal attainment. *Remedial and Special Education, 33*(5), 320–330.

Shogren, K., Wehmeyer, M.L., Palmer, S.B., Rifenbark, G., & Little, T. (2015). Relationships between self-determination and postschool outcomes for youth with disabilities. *Journal of Special Education, 48,* 256–267.

Smith, J.D., & Wehmeyer, M.L. (2012). *Good blood, bad blood: Science, nature, and the myth of the Kallikaks.* Washington DC: American Association on Intellectual and Developmental Disabilities.

Thompson, J. R., Bryant, B. R., Schalock, R. L., Shogren, K. A., Tassé, M. J., Wehmeyer, M. L. . . . Silverman, W. P. (2013). *Supports Intensity Scale-Adult (SIS-A).* American Association on Intellectual and Developmental Disabilities: Washington, DC.

Thompson, J.R., Buntinx, W., Schalock, R.L., Shogren, K.A., Snell, M.E., Wehmeyer, M.L. . . . Yeager, M.H. (2009). Conceptualizing supports and the support needs of people with intellectual disability. *Intellectual and Developmental Disabilities, 47,* 135–146.

Thompson. J. E.. &. Wehmeyer, M. L (2008). Historical and legal issues in developmental disabilities. In H. P. Parette & G.R. Peterson-Karlan (Eds.), *Research based practices in developmental disabilities* (2nd ed., pp. 13–42). Austin, TX: ProEd.

Thompson, J. R., Wehmeyer, M.L., Copeland, S.R., Little, T.D., Patton, J.R., Polloway, J.R. . . . Tassé, M. J. (2013). *Supports Intensity Scale-Children's version (SIS-C) Field test version.* American Association on Intellectual and Developmental Disabilities: Washington, DC.

Walker, H.M., Calkins, C., Wehmeyer, M., Walker, L., Bacon, A., Palmer, S. . . . Johnson, D. (2011). A social-ecological approach to promote self-determination. *Exceptionality, 19,* 6–18.

Wehman, P. (2011). JVR 20th anniversary—Editor's introduction. *Journal of Vocational Rehabilitation, 35*(3), 143.

Wehmeyer, M.L. (2014). Disability in the 21st century: Seeking a future of equity and full participation. In M. Agran, F. Brown, C. Hughes, C. Quirk, & D. Ryndak (Eds.), *21st century issues for individuals with severe disabilities: ensuring quality services and supports in challenging times* (pp. 3–23). Baltimore: Paul H. Brookes.

Wehmeyer, M.L. (2011). What is next in the transition and employment movement? *Journal of Vocational Rehabilitation, 35*(3), 153–356.

Wehmeyer, M.L. Buntinx, W.E., Lachapelle, Y., Luckasson, R., Schalock, R., Verdugo-Alonzo, M. . . . Yeager, M. (2008). The intellectual disability construct and its relationship to human functioning. *Intellectual and Developmental Disabilities, 46*(4), 311–318.

Wehmeyer, M.L., Garner, N., Yeager, D., Lawrence, M., & Davis, A.K. (2006). Infusing self-determination into 18–21 services for Students with Intellectual or Developmental Disabilities: A multi-stage, multiple component model. *Education and Training in Developmental Disabilities, 41,* 3–13.

Wehmeyer, M. L., & Palmer, S. B. (2003). Adult outcomes from students with cognitive disabilities three years after high school: The impact of self-determination. *Education and Training in Developmental Disabilities, 38,* 131–144.

Wehmeyer, M. L., & Schwartz, M. (1997). Self-determination and positive adult outcomes: A follow up study of youth with mental retardation or learning disabilities. *Exceptional Children, 63,* 245–255.

Wehmeyer, M. L., & Schwartz, M. (1998). The relationship between self-determination and quality of life for adults with mental retardation. *Education and Training in Mental Retardation and Developmental Disabilities, 33,* 3–12.

Wood, P.H.N. (1989). Measuring the consequences of illness. *World Health Statistics Quarterly, 42,* 115–121.

World Health Organization. (1980). *International classification of impairments, disabilities, and handicaps. A manual of classification relating to the consequences of disease.* Geneva: Author.

World Health Organization. (1999). ICD-10: *International statistical classification of diseases and related health problems* (10th ed., Vols. 1–3). Geneva: Author.

World Health Organization. (2001). *International classification of functioning, disability, and health (ICF).* Geneva: Author.

Section VI
WHY DO WE HAVE SPECIAL EDUCATION?

Special education is supposed to provide a free and appropriate education for students with disabilities that is designed to meet their unique educational needs. People might emphasize different reasons for providing special education, with some stressing a moral obligation and others underscoring an economic rationale. However, some might see more sinister reasons for the existence of special education: Is it a costly way to shuffle problem students aside so that they do not disrupt the functions of the larger school system? This section examines *why* we have special education. Consider some of these questions as you read these chapters.

- What are the moral-ethical reasons for having special education?
- What are the economic reasons for having special education?
- Why can't education be special for all students?
- Why is it easier to see the need for special education for students with sensory or severe disabilities than it is for students with learning disabilities or emotional or behavioral disorders?
- Are the reasons for having special education the same regardless of the kind of disability students may have?

24

WHY SHOULD WE HAVE SPECIAL EDUCATION?

John Wills Lloyd, Melody Tankersley, & Barbara Bateman

Asking why a society should have special education raises both narrower practical questions and broader social questions. On the broader dimension, the question might provoke some to speak about concerns regarding equity: Why should some children receive education and others not? What are the economic and political benefits of having special education? Does society benefit in some ways from educating individuals with disabilities?

At a more practical level, one might wonder whether special education provides benefits for the educational system, making it function more smoothly for everyone by differentiating services for those who have disabilities. Others might argue that special education harms the system by consuming too many resources. Still others might say that the mixture of special education and ethnic and linguistic diversity has been so problematic as to invalidate special education's benefits.

In the next few parts of this introduction to the *why* section, we shall present an over-view of some of these issues and note the connections between them and the chapters in this section. We discuss reasons for providing special education including arguments based on equity, economic and social benefits, and the law.

EQUITY CONCERNS

Education in America has a long and rich history with roots that reach to colonial times (Urban & Waggoner, 2009). Compulsory education—the requirement that "all" children attend school also has colonial roots, but it was not until the early 1900s that all states legally required that children attend, and enforcement of that law came even later.

Although states had compulsory education laws, there were exceptions. Some states permitted extended absences for particular purposes such as farming, and the U.S. Supreme Court recognized an exception on the basis of religious doctrine—the famous *Yoder* decision (Katz, 1976).

There were also exceptions made for individuals with disabilities, as shown in Box 24.1. As one can understand from reading the rationale of people about 100 years ago, the question of why—or why not—to provide education for students with disabilities is not new. That question came to the fore in the early 1970s in the U.S.

**Box 24.1 An Example of How a Student with a Disability
was Excluded from School 100 Years Ago**

Later, in 1919, the Wisconsin Supreme Court upheld a school's exclusion of a thirteen-year-old crippled child named Merritt. Merritt had been crippled since birth. His paralysis affected his entire physical and nervous system so that he did not have normal control of his voice, hands, feet, and body. He had a high, rasping tone of voice, and would make uncontrolled facial contortions. On these facts the court made the following statement:

> It is claimed, on the part of the school board, that his physical condition and ailment produces a depressing and nauseating effect upon the teachers and school children; that by reason of his physical condition he takes up an undue portion of the teacher's time and attention, distracts the attention of other pupils and interferes generally with the discipline and progress of the school.

Source: Surer, A. D. (2013). Placing the ball in Congress' court: A critical analysis of the Supreme Court's Decision in Arlington Central School District Board of Education v. Murphy, 126 S. Ct. 2455 (2006). *Journal of the National Association of Administrative Law Judiciary, 27*, 547–602.

Author's note: The first paragraph is a direct quote from p. 554 of Surer's article; the indented quote is from page 154 of a case she quoted: Beattie v. Bd. of Educ., 172 N.W. 153 (Wis. 1919).

Prior to the 1970s many shameful circumstances for children with disabilities existed. Children who were considered uneducable or unmanageable lived in institutions with scores or hundreds of other similar children (see, for example, *Christmas in Purgatory*, Blatt & Kaplan, 1966; *Willowbrook Photo Essay*, Minnesota Governor's Council on Developmental Disabilities, no date). Concern, and even outrage, about the conditions depicted in the exposés as well as legal developments (the *PARC* and *Mills* cases; see Wright & Wright, 2006) led the U.S. Congress to conduct hearings about the condition of special education.

Access

Hearings held prior to the passage of P. L. 94-142 showed that that between 4 and 5 million children of school age with disabilities were receiving no education or an education that was not appropriate to their needs. Although states had special education programs, some states were educating as few as a fifth or a third of their students with disabilities and only 17 states were educating a half or more of those students (Martin, 2013; Surer, 2013; Zettel & Ballard, 1979). The United States constitution does not create or acknowledge a right to education. Instead, state constitutions typically require that the state provide public education to all children in the state. Since the early 1970s courts have held that all 'all' children includes those with disabilities. Prior to these cases children with disabilities had no legal right to an education, but some states wisely chose to provide education anyway.

IDEA now provides children with disabilities a federal right to a free and appropriate public education if the state in which they live accepts federal IDEA funds, and all 50 U.S. states do.

Appropriateness

Many individuals with disabilities have unique educational needs. Some few individuals with disabilities actually do not require special education, because their disabilities do not interfere with their learning, their achievement in school, or their social–behavioral adjustment. And for some individuals with disabilities, appropriate special education can be provided very simply. Consider a young student who only needs a specially inclined desk to allow her to work for extended periods on writing and keyboarding tasks.

For the vast majority of students with disabilities, however, it is each individual's *unique educational needs* that defines the appropriateness of special education. In U.S. law, Congress created a mechanism for ensuring that each individual's unique educational needs would be addressed so that he would receive an appropriate education. That mechanism is the Individualized Education Program (IEP). Bateman and Linden (2012) contend that IEPs are at the center of the law.

IEPs are important because they describe how *special* education will be provided to students with disabilities. Special education, as many of the authors in this book have noted (but see the chapters in this book by Scruggs and Mastropieri and by Pullen and Hallahan, especially), is different from general education. It requires instructional practices and procedures that have *special* features (e.g., are more detailed, explicit, and systematic; Kame'enui, this volume) and are delivered in *special* ways (e.g., with more persistence, precision, and monitoring) than would be usually seen in general education (Kauffman & Hallahan, 2005). Kauffman also explains why special instruction is one of the key reasons for special education in a chapter in this section.

Cost

Providing free and appropriate public education for students with disabilities obviously costs the educational system. Providing special seating for students who cannot sit up in a regular chair, braille or other reading devices for those who cannot access print, small-group instruction for those who need additional practice opportunities to reach mastery, or any of the other myriad services that students with disabilities might require as a part of their education simply costs extra money. Someone has to pay for the special chair, the reading devices, or the supplemental instructional materials, and the highly trained personnel to deliver that instruction. To address this concern in the U.S., the federal legislature proposed to provide supplemental funding as a part of laws mandating special education services.

The U.S. Congress proposed to pass through to the states 40 percent of the average per-pupil cost of providing special education services for students with disabilities. In the years since the passage of the legislation, that level of funding has never been reached. As discussed by Parrish and Harr-Robins (2011) and Parrish in a chapter in this section, fiscal policy has had profound effects on the funding of special education. Indeed, for many reasons (including the possibility that funding of special education might be creating a perverse incentive for schools to identify children as having disabilities), Congress modified the funding procedures in 1997. Still, the 40 percent funding level has remained a target for many in special education (e.g., Council for Exceptional Children, 2014).

What would it take to reach the 40 percent level of funding? A by-partisan group of U.S. Representatives introduced a bill providing a plan to do so by increasing appropriations gradually over 10 years (IDEA Full Funding Act, H. R. 4136, 2014). Figure 24.1 shows the costs and the change in the percentage of "full funding" that the bill recommended.

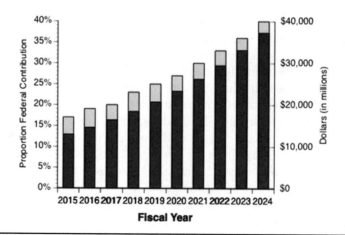

Figure 24.1 Projected expenditures for reaching "full funding" of the federal share of 40 percent of the average per-pupil cost. Lighter bars show percentage of full funding, culminating at 40 percent in 2024. Darker bars show cost in millions of dollars. (Data from IDEA Full Funding Act, H. R. 4361, 2014).

Federal expenditures would have to increase by more than double—$21 billion—to meet the goal. Clearly this is a substantial investment.

Some advocates object to the cost of special education. They say that special education is simply too expensive. There are many versions of this argument, often based on an example that seems outrageous, such as the one illustrated in Box 24.2. Readers will likely hold their own perspectives about appropriateness of funding for related services; IDEA requires the IEP team to determine what services are required to assist a student to benefit from special education services. One basic view is that government should spend the same amount on each student, regardless of the individual student's needs. Another is that some students are inherently more valuable to society than others and therefore deserve more resources. Yet a third view is that those who have the most substantial needs deserve the most resources. These three positions—which, in the galvanizing terms that are common in early twenty-first-century rhetoric, might be characterized as (a) equal for all, (b) invest in the best, and (c) save the weakest—are readily available in the comments on discussion boards of blogs and comments sections of news articles. However, there is an entirely different concern about the economics of *why* we have special education; it has to do with the financial benefits of educating students with disabilities.

Box 24.2 How Much Should Schools Pay for Special Education?

The following paragraph describes an example of an especially expensive use of funds for special education services. It is one illustration of many that one can find. However, one must be careful to check the facts about such cases. Are the facts accurate? Are they explained in an unbiased way?

The trouble is that the law pits the single interest of every disabled child against the broader interest of the school and arms his parents with a legal right to a "free and appropriate public education" in "least restrictive environment." Needless to say, the vagueness of these words is a recipe for litigation. A whole cottage industry of lawyers and advocates has grown up to help parents get what they want out of the school system. Furthermore, school districts must pay parents' court fees if they lose. Overburdened, underfunded, and without the expert legal advice parents can draw on, schools tend to give in rather than face a case that could bankrupt them. "Districts will provide services they don't think are appropriate because they can't afford to go to court," says April Port. One southern California school district pays for a severely brain-damaged boy to attend a specialized school in Massachussetts [sic], and to fly his parents and sister out for regular visits, at an annual cost of roughly $254,000. The superintendent only balked when the family demanded extra visits for the boy's sister.

(Worth, 1999, no page number)

Detractors of special education sometimes use examples such as this to criticize the cost of special education. As Jay P. Greene, who writes often about education finance and policy, says, they blame special education for the financial problems of education by pointing to the cost of special education and saying that it drains resources from the budgets of education and local governments. Mr. Greene, however, noted that the costs of these sorts of cases are miniscule.

Without calling Mr. Worth's reporting into question, it is worth considering this case. Is it fair to spend so much money on supporting one student? Could the local education agency find a way to provide a free and appropriate education for the student at his local school or at least one that is closer to his home? What are some other questions you would like to ask about this situation?

ECONOMIC AND SOCIETAL BENEFITS

After one has seen sheer joy illuminate the face of a child when a teacher shows him how he can use two skills that he already knows to resolve a previously unconquered problem, it seems mundane to talk about the economic benefits of education. Recall the case studies that Janette Klingner and her colleagues (Chapter 8) presented and how the authors, their students, and their students' families delighted in the new skills that Gerardo, Ameena, Maria, Darnell, Ashley, and the others acquired—new skills that provided access to communication, reading, independence, peers, and dignity. Those economic or societal benefits are an important reason for educating students, regardless of whether the students have disabilities.

Preschool programs not only provide children with a boost going into the early grades, but they also help with later outcomes. As Judy Carta documented in Chapter 22 of this volume, programs such as the Abecedarian Project have lasting benefits for children. In addition to better schooling results, other high-quality preschool programs also lead to lower chances of becoming involved with the juvenile justice system and dropping out of school (Karoly & Bigelow, 2005; Reynolds, Temple, Roberson, & Mann, 2002).

Completing high school is an important outcome for economic and social success. Although it is easy to find the example of an individual entrepreneur who succeeded despite having dropped out of high school, such cases are rare—perhaps 1 in a 1,000,000 or rarer—when dropping out is common—more than 1,300,000 students drop out of U.S. school every year (Alliance for Excellence in Education, 2010). Households led by high school graduates have 10 times more assets (over $250,000 across a usual career) than those headed by dropouts, and these assets give those households greater access to health care, opportunities for the children in the household, and so similar advantages (Alliance for Excellence in Education, 2007).

All of these same factors apply just as well, if not more so, to students with disabilities. Newman, Wagner, Cameto, and Knokey (2009) provided a thorough analysis of the experiences of students with disabilities during their early adulthood. Although there are many important results from this study that merit consideration, some of those that are especially relevant to this discussion concern the benefits that accrue to students with disabilities who graduate from high school. Newman et al. found that students with disabilities who completed high school by one of several different markers (e.g., graduated, received a certificate of completion, passed a general education diploma exam) had more positive outcomes in all the following ways in comparison to their peers who did not complete high school. As we paraphrase the summary by Newman and colleages (Newman et al., 2009, paraphrased from p. xxi), students who completed high school:

- Were three times more likely to have enrolled in a postsecondary school (51 percent vs. 17 percent);
- Were more likely to use financial tools, such as savings (60 percent vs. 35 percent) or checking accounts (53 percent vs. 13 percent) or credit cards (32 percent vs. 8 percent);
- Were more likely to take part in some form of community activity (55 percent vs. 20 percent) and in extracurricular classes specifically (26 percent vs. 4 percent); and
- Were less likely to have been involved with the criminal justice system, including being stopped by police other than for a traffic violation (73 percent vs. 48 percent), arrested (49 percent vs. 22 percent), and put in jail overnight (33 percent vs. 11 percent).

Thus, there appear to be real benefits for students—both those with and without disabilities—of crossing the high school graduation stage. Students who reach this specific marker of success simply have better lives later.

Not everything is rosy for individuals with disabilities when they finish high school, to be sure. Individuals with disabilities are often unemployed or underemployed—for example, Kelly (2013), found that only 39 percent of a nationally representative sample of U.S. adults with visual impairments participated in the work force—and adult outcomes for individuals with disabilities usually lag behind those of their non-disabled peers (Blackorby & Wagner, 1996). What is more, as adults they still require costly services, such as help with vocational rehabilitation (e.g., Cimera & Cowan, 2009).

Greater Contributions by Well-educated Citizens

A society reaps benefits when students with disabilities get an education, however. Democratic nations have long appreciated the positive consequences of having a well-educated citizenry. Thomas Jefferson wrote to his mentor, George Wyeth, that he thought the most important legislation of all would be "for the diffusion of knowledge among the people. No other sure foundation can be devised, for the preservation of freedom and happiness" (Boyd et al., 1950, p. 244). In his *Notes on the State of Virginia*, Jefferson recommended a bill promoting universal education, a radical idea at that time because it went beyond education for the male gentry and proposed basic literacy instruction for children regardless of background and additional instruction for those who were especially successful at the initial levels of learning (Urban & Waggoner, 2009). He presented an elaborate plan by which top students would receive what amounted to state-supported scholarships; some would be selected to go on to higher education studies while others would become future teachers. Although we have no evidence that he referred specifically to children with disabilities, the language of Jefferson's declaration foreshadows contemporary calls for education to serve students regardless of their ability: "The general objects of this law are to provide an education adapted to the years, to the capacity, and the condition of every one, and directed to their freedom and happiness" (Jefferson, 1787, p. 272).

Spreading education among people, regardless of their disabilities, helps society, not just because it helps the individuals, but also because it helps society as a whole. This is a two-pointed argument: Educated individuals with disabilities cost less for society and they contribute more.

Ill-educated individuals, including those with disabilities, exert a drag on society. Society often must ante-up social services to sustain them with dignity. The better job educators can do in equipping individuals to sustain themselves with some dignity, the less society has to contribute to supporting them. Some individuals with disabilities may not become completely self-sustaining, but every increase in self-sufficiency requires fewer social services. Not only does society spend fewer resources in social services, but it also gains a member who can function more independently and it has a happier camper.

And the flip side is that those educated individuals with disabilities are more likely to contribute to society. Some will contribute in spectacular ways, an idea to which we return in the following section, but many will contribute just as most ordinary citizens do. Many early adults with disabilities will become productively engaged in their communities (Newman et al., 2009), 85 percent will take jobs, they will spend their earnings (essentially employing others), they will pay taxes, and so forth. That is, they will contribute to society. That is quite a reversal from exerting a drag on society.

So, why do we have special education? One answer would be that we want citizens with disabilities to be able to contribute to society, just like any other citizens.

Unleashing the Contributions of Individuals with Disabilities

The benefit of educating students with disabilities goes beyond relieving society of the costs of caring for those individuals after their school years. The second part of the two-pointed argument to which we alluded earlier is that some individuals with disabilities make unusually valuable contributions to society. We might even say that these individuals, despite their disabilities, were unusually *gifted* or *talented*.

It is very challenging to identify individuals as having disabilities based on historical information. First, the diagnostic data are often not available, and we are reduced to depending on anecdotal reports ("Jim got Ds and Fs in reading, but now he's a superstar").

Second, the individuals whom people often refer to when discussing historic figures who might have disabilities (Albert Einstein, for example) lived under such different social, economic, and political—to say nothing of *educational*—conditions that we must be cautious in judging those anecdotal data. Nevertheless, even if we put less weight on the cases of disabilities of some of the historical figures, as illustrated in Box 24.3, there are many people with disabilities who have made remarkable contributions to society.

Box 24.3 High Flyers Who Have Disabilities

Natalie Du Toit

Natalie Du Toit is a world-class swimmer who has a disability that might surprise many people: Her left leg was amputated at the knee after an accident. Many people know that the Special Olympics (SpecialOlympics.org) provide opportunities for individuals with intellectual disabilities to participate in Olympic-like sporting events. Many also know that the Paralympic Games (Paralympic.org) provide opportunities for individual athletes, who may have any of 10 different classifications of impairments, to compete against others who have similar impairments.

Ms. Du Toit, who swam competitively before the accident, lost her leg when she was 17 years old (Hawthorne, 2006). Not only was she a Paralympics champion—at the 2004, 2008, and 2012 games she won 17 medals, 15 of which were gold[1]—she also swam in competitions with able-bodied individuals. She was strong enough that she sometimes won those races outright. In 2008, she qualified for and competed in the able-bodied 10K-meter swim at the Beijing Olympics, finishing 16th (Du Toit, n. d.).

David Boies

As do other successful people—Charles Schwab, who founded a stock brokerage firm and used the proceeds to endow many philanthropic projects; Paul Orfalea, the business leader who founded and built the Kinkos line of copying stores that Fedex bought; or Keira Knightley, the actress who must memorize lines for her parts in stage and screen productions—David Boies has dyslexia. According to interviews with Malcolm Gladwell (2013), he did not begin to read until third grade and has never read for pleasure. Yet Mr. Boies has been remarkably successful in a demanding profession.

Mr. Boies is an attorney who is one of the founders of the law firm Boies, Schiller, and Flexner. He is widely known for having represented important clients in many high-profile cases. For example, he was the attorney for the U. S. Department of Justice in the antitrust case, *United States v. Microsoft* at the end of the 1990s. He also represented former U. S. vice-president Al Gore in the famous challenge over the count of votes in Florida that ultimately decided the presidential election of 2000. More recently, Mr. Boies led legal efforts to secure a constitutional right for gay and lesbian citizens to marry their partners.

Christy Brown

When one thinks about someone writing his autobiography in the 1950s, the visual image probably includes a typewriter that does not even have electric power. That is just the image one needs to have when thinking of Christy Brown typing the manuscript for his book, except that he had been born with cerebral palsy and could only control one part of his body well enough to use it to type—the little toe of his left foot (Fraser, 1981). His book, *My Left Foot* (Brown, 1955), became a best seller and he wrote other books of fiction and poems (e.g., Brown, 1970; Brown, 1971).

How did Mr. Brown learn to read and write as a child with cerebral palsy in the 1930s? His mother taught him. He reported in his autobiography (Brown, 1955) that when he was five years old, with many members of his family watching, he held a piece of yellow chalk between his toes and copied the letter "A" that his mother had printed on a slate. And he was encouraged by a physician and author (Hambleton, 2007). Obviously, there was a lot of talent in that little foot, though. After Mr. Brown died in the early 1980s, *My Left Foot* was produced as a movie and two actors—Daniel Day-Lewis and Brenda Fricker as Christy Brown and his mother, respectively—earned Academy Awards for their performances. You might want to watch that movie.

Stevie Wonder

The iconic singer Stevie Wonder grew up blind, the likely result of either prematurity (retinopathy of prematurity, or "ROP") or exposure to oxygen during the early days of his life (premature babies were often put in oxygen-rich environments after birth on the hypothesis that this would help them; c.f., Haskins & Benson, 1978; Lanman, Guy, & Dancis, 1954). He also grew up in front of audiences performing music and, after release of a few other recordings, at age 12 his release of "Fingertips, Pt. 2" became a sensation. One of his record albums appeared in 1963 with the title, "*Little Stevie Wonder: The Twelve-Year-Old Genius.*"

An interviewer asked Mr. Wonder whether his blindness and race have seemed like disadvantages (handicaps) to him. His answer is instructive:

> "Do you know, it's funny," he starts, "but I never thought of being blind as a disadvantage, and I never thought of being black as a disadvantage. I am what I am. I love me! And I don't mean that egotistically—I love that God has allowed me to take whatever it was that I had and to make something out of it."
>
> (Lester, 2012, no page number)

Mr. Wonder, who reads braille (King, 2010), attended the Michigan School for the Blind (Haskins & Benson, 1978). In 1995, after 115 years of providing education for students such as Mr. Wonder, the Michigan School for the Blind closed. Why? Because there were not enough blind students to sustain its programs. After enrolling 250–300 students in Mr. Wonder's era, the Michigan legislature required it to enroll at least 25 students in 1995 or else merge with the Michigan School for the Deaf. It enrolled 19 that year so, despite objections from some parents, the two schools for students with sensory disabilities were combined (School for the blind in Lansing closes; lack of students is cause, 1995).

Do you think that this is a sensible outcome? Special education is a substantial financial burden for communities, as you will learn from later chapters if you have not already thought about it. How much should schools spend on a few individuals? What if those individuals might go on to make incredible contributions to society?

Special education should help people such as those identified here to be able to succeed. However, when interviewed, many people with, for example, learning disabilities report that they experienced lifetimes of doubt, disappointment, and struggle (Gerber & Reiff, 1991; Rodis, Garrod, & Boscardin, 2001). Indeed, David Boies (whom we feature in Box 24.3) continues to have struggles. In his popular book, *David and Goliath: Underdogs, Misfits, and the Art of Battling Giants*, Malcolm Gladwell (2013) described some of Mr. Boies's continuing difficulties with literacy:

> Even today, he might read one book a year, if that. He watches television—anything, he says with a laugh, "that moves and is in color." His speaking vocabulary is limited. He uses small words and short sentences. Sometimes if he's reading something out loud and runs into a word he doesn't know, he will stop and spell it out slowly. "My wife gave me an iPad a year and a half ago, which was my first computer-like device, and one of the things that was interesting is that my attempt to spell many words is not close enough for spell-check to find the correct spelling," Boies says. "I can't tell you how many times I get the little message that says, 'No spelling suggestions.'"
>
> (Gladwell, 2013, pp. 107–108)

Neither society in general nor educators especially, would want education to be the reason that an individual such as one of the people described in Box 24.3 could not achieve well. Some rare individuals might, with the help of parents and others and with lots of dedication (as our examples show), be able to succeed with little or no special education. But these people would probably be the exception. Furthermore, we selected special examples because of their noteworthy successes.

Our successful individuals may not represent the millions of individuals with disabilities, but they do show that individuals with disabilities can succeed. Why do we have special education? Another answer would be that we want citizens with disabilities to be able to pursue their unique passions that may allow them to experience great success. For millions of others with disabilities, the successes may not include Olympic-caliber swimming, arguing important legal ideas that change the course of history, and similar achievements, but special education allows many of them a much greater opportunity to attain personal successes than they would have had without it.

SUMMARY

We provide special education for reasons of equity and economic and social benefits, as we have described. From the perspective of some, however, the reasons for special education are much more menacing. Rather than providing ways to help students with difficulties succeed, they see special education as providing ways to remove students who are different from the broader, accepted social system of schools. Among other concerns, they point to the use of segregated classrooms, the number of males and minority students who are identified for special education purposes, and students' lack of movement out of special education as evidence of a duplicitous enterprise. For them, perhaps, the answer is to dismantle special education. Because it is not a perfect system, we should not use it.

In contrast to the arguments that special education is a mistake stand people who argue that special education benefits schooling by helping to expose students who do not have disabilities to their peers who have disabilities, thereby promoting greater under-standing of differences among people. Special education provides a continuum of ser-vices and service delivery options that provide access to educational programming that benefits the greatest number of students. Disabilities are lifelong considerations for those who have them and many students will need services over the entire course of their edu-cational experience and beyond. We believe that science has provided us good evidence of the effectiveness of special education and that science will continue to provide direc-tion as special educators and our allies (physicians, speech pathologists, school psycholo-gist, and others) continue to advance the research and practice received by students with disabilities.

Why do we have special education? Another answer would be that we want citizens with disabilities to be treated equitably and to have their unique educational needs met. As it happens, in the U.S. and a growing number of countries around the world, elected representatives of the people have agreed with that desire and codified it in law. But this law represents many of the ideas on which we have touched as we have introduced this section of the book: Concerns about justice, costs, and even prickly research.

In the next few chapters, well-known experts examine many of these ideas, too. Kauff-man squarely confronts historical, administrative, and scientific issues (among others) as he argues strongly about the value of special education. Parrish provides a close look at the data about—and explains the benefits and some of the problems inherent in—how special education is funded. And Landrum presents the case for why research should guide the efforts of special educators as they decide how to address issues in special education.

NOTE

1. Source: http://www.paralympic.org/ipc_results.

REFERENCES

Alliance for Excellence in Education. (2007). *Hidden benefit: The impact of high school graduation on household wealth*. Washington, DC: Author.

Alliance for Excellence in Education. (2010). *High school dropouts in America*. Washington, DC: Author.

Bateman, B. D., & Linden, M. A. (2012). *Better IEPs: How to develop legally correct and educational useful programs* (5th ed.). Verona, WI: Attainment.

Blackorby, J., & Wagner, M. (1996). Longitudinal postschool outcomes of youth with disabilities: Findings from the National Longitudinal Transition Study. *Exceptional Children, 62*, 399–413.

Blatt, B., & Kaplan, F. (1966). *Christmas in purgatory*. Boston, MA: Allyn & Bacon.

Boyd, J. P., Cullen, C. T., Catanzariti, J., Oberg, B. B., et al., (Eds.) (1950). *The papers of Thomas Jefferson* (vol. 10). Princeton, NJ: Princeton University Press.

Brown, C. (1955). *My left foot*. New York: Simon and Schuster.

Brown, C. (1970). *Down all these days*. New York: Stein and Day.

Brown, C. (1971). *The poems of Christy Brown*. New York: Stein and Day.

Cimera, R. E., & Cowan, R. J. (2009). The costs of services and employment outcomes achieved by adults with autism in the US. *Autism, 13*, 285–302.

Council for Exceptional Children (2014, 10 March). CEC-endorsed legislation introduced to fully fund IDEA. [Web log message]. *CEC Policyinsider*. http://www.policyinsider.org/2014/03/cec-endorsed-legislation-introduced-to-fully-fund-idea.html

Du Toit, N. (n.d.). *Natalie Du Toit – BIO – Beijing 2008*. Retrieved from http://www.nataliedutoit.co.za/category/bio

Fraser, C. G. (1981, 8 September). Christy Brown, author, died; crippled, he wrote with toe. *New York Times*. http://www.nytimes.com/1981/09/08/obituaries/christy-brown-author-dies-crippled-he-wrote-with-toe.html.

Gerber, P. J., & Reiff, H. B. (Eds.), (1991). *Speaking for themselves: Ethnographic interviews with adults with learning disabilities*. Ann Arbor, MI: University of Michigan Press.

Gladwell, M. (2013). *David and Goliath: Underdogs, misfits, and the art of battling giants*. New York: Little, Bown.

Greene, J. P. (2009, January 4). Blaming special ed [Web log message]. Retrieved from http://jaypgreene.com/2009/01/04/blaming-special-ed,

Hambleton, G. L. (2007). *Christy Brown: The life that inspired My Left Foot*. Edinburgh: Mainstream.

Haskins, J., & Benson, K. (1978). *The Stevie Wonder scrapbook*. New York: Grossett & Dunlop.

Hawthorne, T. (2006). *Natalie du Toit: Tumble turn*. Philadelphia: Oshun.

IDEA Full Funding Act of 2014, H. R. 4136, 113th Cong. (2014).

Jefferson, T. (1787). *Notes on the state of Virginia*. Richmond, VA: J. W. Randolf. https://archive.org/details/notesonstateofvi01jeff and http://etext.virginia.edu/etcbin/toccer-new2?id=JefVirg.sgm&data=/texts/english/modeng/parsed&tag=public&part=all.

Karoly, L. A., & Bigelow, J. H. (2005). *The economics of investing in universal preschool education in California*. Santa Monica, CA: RAND Corporation.

Katz, M. S. (1976). *A history of compulsory education laws*. Bloomington, IL: Phi Delta Kappa.

Kauffman, J. M., & Hallahan, D. P. (2005). *What is special education and why do we need it?* Englewood Cliffs, NJ: Prentice Hall.

Kelly, S. M. (2013). Labor force participation rates among working-age individuals with visual impairments. *Journal of Visual Impairment & Blindness, 107*, 509–513.

King, L. (2010, 5 December). CNN Larry King live: Interview with Stevie Wonder.

Lanman J. T., Guy, L. P., & Dancis, J. (1954). Retrolental firbroplasia and oxygen therapy. *Journal of the American Medical Associationa, 155*, 223–226.

Lester, G. (2012, 30 August). Stevie Wonder: "I never thought of being blind and black as a disadvantage." *The Guardian*, retrieved from http://www.theguardian.com/music/2012/aug/30/stevie-wonder-blind-black-disadvantage

Martin, E. W. (2013). *Breakthrough: Federal special education legislation 1965–1981*. Sarasota, FL: Bardoff.

Mills v. Bd. of Educ. of D.C., 348 F. Supp. 866 (D.D.C. 1972).

Minnesota Governor's Council on Developmental Disabilities. (no date). *Willowbrook photo essay*. http://mn.gov/mnddc/extra/wbrook/willowbrook.html.

Newman, L., Wagner, M., Cameto, R., & Knokey, A. (2009). *The post-high school outcomes of youth with disabilities up to 4 years after high school: A report from the National Longitudinal Transition Study-2 (NLTS2)*. Washington, DC: US Department of Education Institute of Education Studies.

PARC Pa. Association for Retarded Children v. Pennsylvania, 334 F. Supp. 1257 (E.D. Pa. 1972).

Parrish, T., & Harr-Robins, J. (2011). Fiscal policy and funding for special education. In J. M. Kauffman & D. P. Hallahan (Eds.), *Handbook of special education* (pp. 363–377). New York: Routledge.

Reynolds, A. J., Temple, J. A., Roberson, D. L., & Mann, E. A. (2002). Age 21 cost-benefit analysis of the Title I Chicago child-parent centers. *Educational Evaluation and Policy Analysis, 24*(4).

Rodis, P., Garrod, W., & Boscardin, M. L. (Eds.). (2001). *Learning disabilities and life stories*. Boston: Allyn & Bacon.

School for the blind in Lansing closes; lack of students is cause. (1995, 30 September). *Ludington Daily News*. Retrieved from http://news.google.com/newspapers?nid=110&dat=19950930&id=_DRQAAAAIBAJ&sjid=pVUDAAAAIBAJ&pg=5274,8662108.

Surer, A. D. (2013). Placing the ball in Congress' court: A critical analysis of the Supreme Court's Decision in Arlington Central School District Board of Education v. Murphy, 126 S. Ct. 2455 (2006). *Journal of the National Association of Administrative Law Judiciary, 27*, 547–602.

Urban, W. J., & Waggoner, J. W., Jr. (2009). *American education: A history* (4th ed.). New York: Routledge.

Walker, H. M., Stieber, S., & Bullis, M. (1997). Longitudinal correlates of arrest status among males at-risk for antisocial behaviors. *Journal of Child and Family Studies, 6*, 289–309.

Winters, M., & Greene, J. P. (2007) Debunking a special education myth: Don't blame private options for rising costs. *Education Next, 7*(2). Retrieved from http://educationnext.org/debunking-a-special-education-myth/.

Worth, R. (1999). The scandal of special-ed: It wastes money and hurts the poor. *The Washington Monthly Online, 31*(6). Retrieved from http://www.washingtonmonthly.com/features/1999/9906.worth.scandal.html.

Wright, P. W. D., & Wright, P. D. (2006). *Special education law* (2nd ed.). Hartfield, VA: Harbor House.

Zettel, J. J., & Ballard, J. (1979). The Education for All Handicapped Children Act of 1975 (P.L. 94-142): Its history, origins, and concepts. *Journal of Education, 161*(3), 5–22.

Getting to Know James M. Kauffman

I started teaching grades 5–6 (doing some teaching of seventh and eighth graders as well) in a little country school in Indiana in the middle of the 1961–62 school year (I'd just completed a degree in elementary education at Goshen College). Then, as a conscientious objector to war, I went to Kansas to teach emotionally disturbed kids at the Southard School, the children's division of the Menninger Clinic, as an alternative to military service. My teaching at Southard was my introduction to special education.

After teaching at Southard for two years, then teaching emotionally disturbed kids for a year in a public school, then teaching regular elementary grades in northeast Kansas for a couple of years, I went to graduate school at the University of Kansas. I received my Ed.D. in special education from the University of Kansas in 1969, where Dick Whelan was my advisor.

I'm now Professor Emeritus of Education at the University of Virginia, where I joined the faculty in 1970. At U.Va., I taught mainly graduate students, usually courses in behavior management, characteristics of emotionally disturbed students, and doctoral seminars. I have been fortunate to have had great mentors, fine students, and wonderful colleagues. I've authored or co-authored numerous journal articles, book chapters, and text books in special education and co-edited some. Two books I wrote by myself are *Toward a Science of Education: The Battle Between Rogue and Real Science* (2011) and *The Tragicomedy of Public Education: Laughing and Crying, Thinking and Fixing* (2010). I have been fully retired since 2006, although I do manage to stay active in the field of special education.

25

WHY WE SHOULD HAVE SPECIAL EDUCATION

James M. Kauffman

We have become so accustomed to thinking of special education as a part of schooling that we may need to remind ourselves of its nature and origins. It is easy to forget what special education—indeed, education in general—is and is not. In fact, we may need to remind ourselves that special education is a human creation, not a natural phenomenon. That is, it is not something discovered but something invented, like universal public education. In asking why we should have special education in the twenty-first century, we need to think about why special education was invented, most obviously in the twentieth century. Important things to consider are the conditions that gave rise to special education and the extent to which these conditions have changed.

Perhaps John Lewis stated most succinctly the problem of public schooling that special education was designed to address. In his prefatory comments to a book that was perhaps the first special education textbook to be published, he observed that the problem "is found in the fact of variability among children to be educated" (Horn, 1924, pp. 6–7). Even before all children without obvious disabilities were required to attend school (i.e., before school attendance was mandatory in all states for children without disabilities), educators noticed the extreme variability among students. Educators saw the folly in expecting the teacher of a general education class to provide sufficient differentiation in instruction to meet the needs of all students. As more students with disabilities were brought into the public education system, the problem became more extreme, and in 1975 federal law mandated appropriate education for all children with disabilities (see Martin, 2013). Special education was an invention designed to address the fact of variability among students by reducing it to a reasonably manageable level in a given classroom. The variability among students remains a problem, because "The public schools, although 'modern' in many senses, are fundamentally the same as . . . in 1900" (Gerber, 2011, p. 13).

Some people argue for a dramatic restructuring of public education because, they correctly note, the basic structure of education—schools in buildings, students in classrooms, teachers of groups of students, school administrators, public or "government" schools, an academic year, and so on—has not changed much for more than a century. The issue of school structure aside, however, the issue of variability among students remains, and the question of what to do about it remains a key question for special education (Gerber, 2011; Kauffman, 2010, 2011; Kauffman & Hallahan, 2005). Thus, grouping for instruction always will be an issue as long as schooling involves aggregating students, regardless how else the structure may change. If students are no longer instructed in groups, then the variability among students is only a problem of designing appropriate instruction for individuals. For purposes of socialization and efficiency in the use of the resources allocated to education, it seems highly unlikely that instruction of groups of students will be abandoned for some system of total individualization in which students are simply not aggregated for teaching. Even with technology allowing individualization of instruction for all students and with universal design for learning, aggregation for academic instruction seems probable. Furthermore, should students be aggregated for socialization alone, not instruction in academics, two problems remain: (1) teaching social skills needed in aggregates of human beings and (2) gravitation of students themselves toward others who share their capabilities and interests, along with the inevitable comparisons, social hierarchies, and social stigma.

> "Special Education was an invention designed to address the fact of variability among students by reducing it to a reasonably manageable level in a given classroom."

In short, in any imaginable future or restructuring of schooling the problem of human variation remains. One might argue that such diversity should be embraced, but this does nothing to address the lives of those whose abilities compare unfavorably to the average, and the assumption that such comparisons should not or will not be made is denialism of the rankest kind (see Specter, 2009). The question for educators and other social service providers is really what to do to help those who compare unfavorably, especially those whose unfavorable comparison is greater than a stated criterion.

Frequent objections to special education are that it separates those who need special help from those who do not, that the decision to separate a student is arbitrary and often based on unreliable judgment, and that some of those who need special help are not found eligible for it. But the nature of any special program is that it must do this kind of sorting, a line must be drawn, and some individuals will be on or very near whatever criterion is set. Typically, the criterion is arbitrary, in that it can be changed at will, but the simple fact is that if no line is drawn then the special program cannot exist, and the reality is that there will be ambiguity about the side of the line on which some cases fall (see Kauffman & Lloyd, 2011). This is a basic truth for many social functions and programs, including special education. It is true of tax brackets, housing assistance, financial aid for students, and so on.

The "solutions" often proposed are making all children "special," offering individualized instruction for all students, or otherwise pretending that either all students or no child should be identified as having special educational needs. But, again, this is the most obvious sort of denialism, which we easily detect in the pretense that we need not separate those who are poor or homeless from those who are not in designing a program of special economic or social assistance. If we want a special program for any purpose, then we must draw a line that defines eligibility for it. The proposal to provide special education (or its equivalent) to *all* students is merely a prescription for making sure that students with disabilities are not considered special. Bottom line: no line-drawing means no special program.

The two primary reasons that we should have special education are administrative and instructional. One of these is not likely to be effective without the other. Both are issues that special and general education reforms proposed since the 1980s have not addressed. Neither is an issue for which the most popular proposed reforms have support in empirical studies or rational analyses. Rather, both are problems for which popular proposals are both ideological and illogical (see Kauffman & Badar, 2014). Before thinking about the two primary reasons for having special education, the important role of science should be considered.

THE ROLE OF SCIENCE IN ANSWERING QUESTIONS

It would be wonderful if experimental studies comparing special and general education (i.e., comparing special education to no special education for comparable groups of students) were available and indicated clearly the benefits of special education, including economic benefits. Unfortunately, these studies do not now and may never exist. However, this fact does not mean that there is no relevant scientific evidence, nor does it mean that in the absence of direct experiments demonstrating special education's value we should abandon rationality or logical thinking about the data we do have. It simply means that we should pose the scientific questions for which we can conduct good experiments and use logical thinking about the data we do have and the observations we make.

"The question for educators and other social service providers is really what to do to help those who compare unfavorably, especially those whose unfavorable comparison is greater than a stated criterion."

Science is not only about obtaining reliable data; it is also about careful, logical, linear thinking about data, even if they are data related only by analogy to the problem at hand (Kauffman, 2011, 2014a, 2014b). We should rely on direct scientific evidence whenever we can and use our best critical thinking when direct scientific evidence regarding a problem is not available. A scientist does not approach a problem by assuming that no reasoned guess can be made about what will happen. Scientists' reasoned guesses are known as hypotheses. When possible, experiments are designed to test hypotheses. But in some sciences some questions cannot be answered by direct experiments, simply because controlled experiments are impossible. Geologists and astronomers, for example, often cannot conduct direct experiments to test how geological features were formed or how stars are formed. They must rely on observation and rational thinking about what they observe, interpreting their observations in the light of related experimental evidence and rational thinking about phenomena.

The two primary reasons for having special education are not the result of direct experimental evidence. Rather, they are the outcomes of rational thinking about the nature of the problems of administrative reality and instructional heterogeneity that are inevitably encountered in universal education. They are also based on rational thinking about experience, including conclusions reached by others about administration and teaching, sometimes on the basis of trials or experiments.

Scientists find general principles, not just specific results. For example, the rate at which objects fall in a vacuum can be stated as a general principle. Knowing the general principle is terribly important in addition to understanding caveats involving such things as air resistance (e.g., a feather will fall more slowly than an iron ball in ordinary atmospheric conditions, although both will fall at the same rate in a vacuum). The point most relevant here is that once a general principle is established, it is not important from a scientific point of view to test the principle with every conceivable object. For example, it will not be important to check whether the carcasses of a cow, a pig, and a chicken will fall at the same rate. Of course, it may be important to note that a pig carcass may fall more slowly if it has a parachute than if it doesn't. Sometimes questions that appear to be scientific are trivial or mere distractions, such as whether an educational procedure that has been found effective with one group will be effective with another when the distinctions are irrelevant to teaching (e.g., whether an instructional procedure will be effective for children with one skin hue but not with children having a different skin hue). True, teachers must keep contextual variables in mind and take into account students' particular learning histories. However, in education, it is important to understand that some questions are tantamount to asking whether cow carcasses fall at a faster rate than chicken carcasses.

Of course, there are those who will suggest that education cannot be scientific in the sense of finding general principles. That is, they will argue that every situation is different, that general principles cannot be found or are trivial. But this leaves teachers without any tools, only improvisations. Only through noticing samenesses can anyone make sense of the world, including the social world (see Engelmann & Carnine, 1982, 2011). We need special education because we observe samenesses and differences in the way children respond to instruction.

ADMINISTRATIVE REASONS FOR HAVING SPECIAL EDUCATION

Kauffman and Hallahan (1993) explained in considerable detail why special and general education simply cannot be integrated or merged if special education is to function effectively. Briefly, if a program is to flourish, then it must have visibility, status, budget, and personnel dedicated to it. These are the things that give a program borders and identity. Without them, any program inevitably becomes increasingly derelict.

We accept this premise readily in thinking of most government functions. At the federal level, we can easily see why there are certain Presidential Cabinet level departments. Elevation of something to departmental level means we think it is critically important; elimination or downsizing a department or merging it with another is advocated only by those who believe that the department does not deserve such visibility, status, budget, and personnel. In short, when we believe that something is really important, it has its own administrative line, and when we think it is not terribly important we recommend that it be merged with something else. This is not a great mystery, simply a fact of how administrative processes work.

> "We need special education because we observe samenesses and differences in the way children respond to instruction."

In education, something similar to the notion of merging or integrating special and general education was proposed for teacher education. The idea was that all of higher education was so important to teacher education that teacher education should not be considered a separate and distinct entity—there should be no teacher education program as such, as teachers needed training and support from all aspects of higher education, hence the education of teachers should simply be considered a function of every department and every class in a university. The consequence of this kind of thinking and the rhetoric resulting from such assumptions was a disastrous neglect of teacher education. Goodlad (1990) stated these conclusions about integrating teacher education into higher education:

> First, the farther down in a university's organizational structure teacher education finds itself, the less chance it has to obtain the conditions necessary to a healthy, dynamic existence. Second, the farther down in the hierarchy teacher education finds itself, the less likely it is that it will enjoy the tender loving care of those tenure-line faculty members universities strive so hard to recruit. Who, then, speaks for teacher education? Who speaks for those who would become teachers?
>
> (p. 277)

Special education might be substituted for teacher education in this statement with the same cautions. The basic idea here is how to make sure that a function does not get lost in an administrative organization. If one wants to make sure that a function, such as the preparation of special educators, fits comfortably into higher education, then the following appear to be essential:

1. A school or center of pedagogy with a sole commitment to special education.
2. A separate budget protected from competing interests.
3. Authority and responsibility for student selection and personnel.
4. A full complement of faculty.
5. Control ever specification of prerequisites for admission (see Goodlad, 1990, p. 278 for these points related to teacher education).

Although Goodlad argued these points for teacher education, we might surmise that such minimum essentials apply also to the administration of special education in a system of schooling at primary and secondary levels. Those who propose the assimilation of special education into general education or the merging of special and general education cannot be both aware of the realities of educational administration and concerned for special education's viability.

As is true of teacher education or any enterprise with which one is concerned, the project must have adequate and protected resources. As Goodlad (1990) put it regarding the needed resources for teacher education:

> And these resources must be made secure for the purposes intended. That is, they must be earmarked for and assigned to a unit with clear borders, a specified number of students with a common purpose, and a roster of largely full-time faculty requisite to the formal and informal socialization of these students into teaching. Put negatively, these resources must not go to the larger, multipurpose unit of which teacher education is a part: there they run the danger of being impounded by entrepreneurial program heads and faculty members.
>
> (p. 152)

A clear focus, an unambiguous identity, and ultimate authority are required in an administration for any program to flourish. As Goodlad put it, without these things teacher education remains "an orphan, dependent on charity and goodwill" (1990, p. 153). The same can be said of the administration of special education in universities and K–12 schools.

In the early twenty-first century, two interests are competing most obviously for special education's resources. First, the concern for underachieving students in general and, second, pursuit of higher performance standards for all students. Both are legitimate concerns, but both are dangers to special education if it loses focus, identity, and authority in organizational structure and program administration.

The thinking that is most dangerous to special education is often cast in very positive terms. An obvious, frontal assault on special education is quite unlikely, as it probably would be seen immediately as distasteful and immoral. Rather, ideas that undermine special education will be presented as concern for *all* children. People will argue that the integration of general and special education is egalitarian and that the civil rights of students with disabilities can be assured only by such integration, even as these arguments misrepresent the issues of fairness and civil rights of students with disabilities in schooling (see Kauffman & Landrum, 2009). They will argue that special education does not address the special needs of students who are low achievers but do not meet the criteria for identification as having a disability. These arguments will have enormous appeal to those who do not understand or do not care about their ultimate consequences. Perhaps the most effective way to circumvent or destroy special education is to propose scintillating alternatives to it that lose their shimmer after it is too late to save it.

The difference between integrating special education into thinking about public education (i.e., recognizing it as an important part of public education) and integrating it administratively with general education is enormous. Kauffman and Hallahan (1993) concluded:

> After a long period of struggle, special education has finally achieved the status of a normal part of public general education, and been integrated into the fabric of our thinking about students' special needs. It has done so only by recognizing the realities of which Goodlad speaks [see prior statements by him], and it will remain such only if it is successful in fending off the entrepreneurial interests and irresponsible attacks that threaten its hard-won position.
>
> (p. 98)

Gerber (2011) has said, "It is easy to see that contemporary opposition to special education sometimes appears in the guise of a kind of advocacy expressed by 'moral' arguments for its re-integration into the common experiences and academic expectations of everyday schooling" (p. 13). It is easy to be persuaded by these false arguments, to fail to see the sham they represent, to see how they could lead to the opposite of advocacy for appropriate education, to understand that they lead ultimately to the demise of special education. Not only are arguments for integrating special and general education built on false premises about morality, civil rights, and fairness in education, but they deny special education the focus, identity, and authority it must have.

INSTRUCTIONAL REASONS FOR HAVING SPECIAL EDUCATION

As Lewis (in Horn, 1924) suggested, special education is designed to address the variability among students—variability in learning, not variability of other kinds, but differences in what students know and need to learn. Kauffman and Hallahan (2005),

"Not only are arguments for integrating special and general education built on false premises about morality, civil rights, and fairness in education, but they deny special education the focus, identity, and authority it must have."

Zigmond, Kloo, and Volonino (2009) and Zigmond and Kloo (2011) have discussed how such variability in instruction requires special education.

The question for special education is how much heterogeneity of learning among students a teacher can handle effectively. Some people suggest that a teacher should be able to offer differentiated learning experiences for all students, such that all students are given tasks and opportunities to respond that are appropriate for them. Of course, differentiation of instruction is required in teaching any class, as there will always be some level of heterogeneity among learners, but the important instructional question is just how much differentiation a teacher can manage and still teach effectively. Zigmond and Kloo (2011) put it this way:

> The disgrace is not that general education teachers are not adequately prepared to deliver a special education to the students with disabilities in their large and diverse classrooms. The disgrace is that we have come to believe that special education is so *not-special* that it can be delivered by a generalist, busy teaching 25 other students a curriculum that was generated at the school board, or state, or federal level.
>
> (p. 70)

The ability of any teacher to accommodate learners through differentiation of instruction is limited, and regardless of their training few teachers have the ability to provide the most effective instruction to students with disabilities in the context of a general education classroom. That is, no matter how good the teacher, greater heterogeneity makes the task of teaching more difficult, and every teacher is limited in the amount of heterogeneity she or he can manage effectively. This is not a condemnation of teachers or their training, merely a realistic observation.

Teacher preparation and education policy and administration too often founder because of one or both of two major errors: (1) assuming that all teachers are capable of handling the same level of heterogeneity as the best teacher can handle and (2) misunderstanding the nature of the most effective instruction. Both errors are avoidable, the first most obviously by having special education and the second by insisting upon the most effective instruction in special education.

The first error sets unrealistic, unreachable expectations for most teachers, who simply cannot instruct extremely heterogeneous groups effectively. The larger the group and the greater the heterogeneity of instructional needs, the greater the difficulty any teacher is going to have in providing effective instruction for all of the students in the class (see Grossen, 1993; Kauffman, 2011 for a discussion of homogeneous and heterogeneous grouping for instruction). Special education is needed to reduce the heterogeneity of both general and special classes.

The second error involves the assumption that instruction other than explicit, direct instruction will be sufficiently effective (see Engelmann & Carnine, 1982, 2011 for explanations of Direct Instruction). Arguments about the nature of good and poor instruction might be perpetual. However, research on teaching clearly supports the idea of teacher-directed, systematic instruction (see Snider, 2006). This kind of direct and systematic instruction has been shown repeatedly to produce superior results to alternatives (see

Bateman, 2004; Engelmann, 2007; Engelmann, Bateman, & Lloyd, 2007; Engelmann & Carnine, 2011; Rosenshine, 2008). However, the question at hand is the kind of grouping that facilitates or is essential to that kind of direct teaching. Educational researcher Siegfried Engelmann provided four criteria for appropriate grouping for direct instruction based on his research, as follows:

1. The child's performance should be 70% correct the first time on the material that is being taught.
2. The child should be at least 90% correct the first time on material that's been taught previously and is assumed to have been mastered.
3. The child should be able to go through a lesson in the anticipated amount of time and should not require great amounts of additional practice.
4. At the end of each lesson, the child should be virtually 100% correct on everything present in the lesson.

(Engelmann, 1997, p. 183)

Simply put, in the absence of special education, such instruction is extremely unlikely for two reasons. First, explicit instruction and monitoring of responses (the kind of differentiation needed by most, if not all, students with disabilities) is antithetical to what is often described as good instruction in general education. Second, the typical teacher is not able to manage such instruction for students with disabilities while teaching the rest of the general education class, even if such instruction is seen as desirable for all.

CONCLUSION

We need special education for a variety of reasons, most obviously for administrative and instructional reasons. Special education is influenced by many factors, and it may be weakened by a variety of social and economic currents. Among these is pressure for reforming general education, especially for increasing academic achievement standards and obtaining better average outcomes for nondisabled children without increasing the expenditure of public funds. Certainly, market forces, especially short-term entrepreneurial objectives, are consistent with the view that special education is a sink-hole of public education funds and the assumption that vouchers and charter schools are preferable to spending more money to improve the education of children with disabilities in special classes and schools (see Anastasiou & Kauffman, 2009).

Popular ideas would make special education an invisible, seamless, universal part of general education. But is it is neither reasonable nor feasible to assume that a vibrant, effective special education will be subsumed under the administration of general education. There, its focus, identity, and authority are inevitably diluted, and it becomes easy prey for competing interests. Regarding instruction, Kauffman and Hallahan (2005) concluded:

Simply put, it is neither reasonable nor feasible to provide special education for every student. Special implies something atypical, unusual, and different from the norm. First of all, by definition, not all education can be special education. Second, the extraordinary effort demanded for special education is not reasonable to expect for all students or for all who teach them. The education of all students can be and should be good, but it cannot be special for all students.

(p. 64)

We might be skeptical, too, of the rhetorical argument that special education as it has been practiced has been a failure because it is a separate system, but that special education will be a success if all children with disabilities are included in general education classrooms. The emphasis on the location of students with disabilities in general education rather than on their effective instruction and the emphasis on integration of general and special education rather than on the focus, identity, and authority of special education are, indeed, disappointing and pernicious developments in American public education. This disappointing and pernicious advocacy, which puts the place of education ahead of the effectiveness of instruction, has become all too common in education in many developed nations (see Kauffman & Badar, 2014; Kauffman & Hung, 2009; Kauffman, Ward, & Badar, in press; Warnock, 2005).

Perhaps even more ominous are the destructive consequences for special education in many developing nations of the world, in which education resources are few and the class size in general education is great—sometimes double or more the typical class size in the USA, with several students sharing a book. The United Nations' Convention on the Rights of Persons with Disabilities, which appears to have widespread support, including that of the International Council for Exceptional Children, is particularly troubling (see http://www.un.org/disabilities/convention/conventionfull.shtml or search for Convention on the Rights of Persons with Disabilities). Note especially its Article 24 – Education, which reflects misunderstanding of the practical and civil rights issues involving the education of students with disabilities. The right to an appropriate education simply cannot be achieved by the same means as other desirable rights of persons with disabilities in any society. Notwithstanding its vaunted moral appeal, Article 24 is a certain prescription for the failure of many students with disabilities to learn all they can and for special education to become an afterthought.

Discussion Questions

1. Kauffman posits that "grouping for instruction will be an issue as long as schooling involves aggregating students." What are the implications of this statement for students in general and for students who require differentiated instruction to meet their potential? What are the implications for schools and for training teachers?

2. Kauffman points out that social functions or programs demand a "sorting" of those who get something from those who do not. He goes on to point out that if such sorting does not occur, nothing *special* can happen. What programs or services other than education require such sorting?

3. What would be lost administratively if special education merged with general education? How would those lost administrative duties evidentially diminish the educational services that learners with disabilities receive? Or would it?

4. How does Kauffman's description of the type of instruction needed for effective special education line up with what other authors in this volume put forth as needed? What conclusions can you draw from the sum of the chapters about effective special education?

5. Kauffman concludes by discussing special education in developing nations. How is he answering "Why Special Education?" by ending this way?

JAMES M. KAUFFMAN'S SUGGESTIONS FOR FURTHER READING

Anastasiou, D., & Kauffman, J. M. (2011). A social constructionist approach to disability: Implications for special education. *Exceptional Children, 77,* 367–384.

Forness, S. R., Freeman, S. F. N., Paparella, T., Kauffman, J. M., & Walker, H. M. (2012). Special education implications of point and cumulative prevalence for children with emotional or behavioral disorders. *Journal of Emotional and Behavioral Disorders, 20,* 1–14.

Kauffman, J. M. (2012). Science and the education of teachers. In R. Detrich, R. Keyworth, & J. States (Eds.), *Advances in evidence-based education, Volume 2. Education at the crossroads: The state of teacher education* (pp. 47–64). Oakland, CA: Wing Institute.

Kauffman, J. M. (2013). Labeling and categorizing children and youth with emotional and behavioral disorders in the USA: Current practices and conceptual problems. In T. Cole, H. Daniels, & J. Visser (Eds.), *The Routledge international handbook of emotional and behavioural difficulties* (pp. 15–21). London: Routledge.

Kauffman, J. M., & Hallahan, D. P. (Eds.), (2011). *Handbook of special education.* New York: Taylor & Francis.

Kauffman, J. M., & Landrum, T. J. (2006). *Children and youth with emotional and behavioral disorders: A history of their education.* Austin, TX: Pro-Ed.

REFERENCES

Anastasiou, D., & Kauffman, J. M. (2009). When special education goes to the marketplace: The case of vouchers. *Exceptionality, 17,* 205–222.

Bateman, B. D. (2004). *Elements of successful teaching: A best practices handbook for beginning teachers.* Verona, WI: Attainment.

Engelmann, S. (1997). Theory of mastery and acceleration. In J. W. Lloyd, E. J. Kame'enui, & D. Chard (Eds.), *Issues in educating students with disabilities* (pp. 177–195). Mahwah, NJ: Erlbaum.

Engelmann, S. (2007). *Teaching needy kids in our backward system: 42 years of trying.* Eugene, OR: ADI Press.

Engelmann, S., Bateman, B. D., & Lloyd, J. W. (2007). *Educational logic and illogic.* Eugene, OR: Association for Direct Instruction.

Engelmann, S., & Carnine, D. (1982). *Theory of instruction: Principles and applications.* New York: Irvington.

Engelmann, S., & Carnine, D. (2011). *Could John Stuart Mill have saved U. S. education?* Verona, WI: Attainment.

Gerber, M. M. (2011). A history of special education. In J. M. Kauffman & D. P. Hallahan (Eds.), *Handbook of special education* (pp 3–14). New York: Routledge.

Goodlad, J. I. (1990). *Teachers for our nation's schools.* San Francisco: Jossey-Bass.

Grossen, B. (Ed.). (1993). Focus: Heterogeneous versus homogeneous grouping. *Effective School Practices, 12*(1), Whole Issue.

Horn, J. L. (1924). *The education of exceptional children: A consideration of public school problems and policies in the field of differential education.* New York: Century.

Kauffman, J. M. (2010). *The tragicomedy of public education: Laughing and crying, thinking and fixing.* Verona, WI: Attainment.

Kauffman, J. M. (2011). *Toward a science of education: The battle between rogue and real science.* Verona, WI: Attainment.

Kauffman, J. M. (2014a). Prologue: On following the scientific evidence. In H. M. Walker & F. M. Gresham (Eds.), *Handbook of evidence-based practices for emotional and behavioral disorders: Applications in schools* (pp. 1–5). New York: Guilford.

Kauffman, J. M. (2014b). Epilogue: Science, a harsh mistress. In H. M. Walker & F. M. Gresham (Eds.), *Handbook of evidence-based practices for emotional and behavioral disorders: Applications in schools* (pp. 583–585). New York: Guilford.

Kauffman, J. M., & Badar, J. (2014). Instruction, not inclusion, should be the central issue in special education: An alternative view from the USA. *Journal of International Special Needs Education, 17,* 13–20.

Kauffman, J. M., & Hallahan, D. P. (1993). Toward a comprehensive delivery system for special education. In J. I. Goodlad & T. C. Lovitt (Eds.), *Integrating general and special education* (pp. 73–102). Columbus, OH: Merrill/Macmillan.

Kauffman, J. M. & Hallahan, D. P. (2005). *Special education: What it is and why we need it.* Boston: Allyn & Bacon.

Kauffman, J. M., & Hung, L. Y. (2009). Special education for intellectual disability: Current trends and perspectives. *Current Opinion in Psychiatry, 22,* 452–456.

Kauffman, J. M., & Landrum, T. J. (2009). Politics, civil rights, and disproportional identification of students with emotional and behavioral disorders. *Exceptionality, 17,* 177–188.

Kauffman, J. M., & Lloyd, J. W. (2011). Statistics, data, and special education decisions: Basic links to realities (pp. 27–36). In J. M. Kauffman & D. P. Hallahan (Eds.), *Handbook of special education.* New York: Routledge.

Kauffman, J. M., Ward, D. M., & Badar, J. (in press). The delusion of full inclusion. In R. M. Foxx & J. A. Mulick (Eds.), *Controversial therapies for autism and intellectual disabilities* (2nd ed.). New York: Taylor & Francis.

Martin, E. W., Jr. (2013). *Breakthrough: Federal special education legislation 1965–1981*. Sarasota, FL: Bardolf.

Rosenshine, B. (2008). Systematic instruction. In T. L. Good (Ed.), *21st Century education: A reference handbook: Vol. 1* (pp. 235–243). Thousand Oaks, CA: Sage.

Snider, V. E. (2006). *Myths and misconceptions about teaching: What really happens in the classroom*. Lanham, MD: Rowman & Littlefield.

Specter, M. (2009). *Denialism: How irrational thinking hinders scientific progress, harms the planet, and threatens our lives*. New York: Penguin.

Warnock, M. (2005). *Special educational needs: A new look*. Impact No. 11. London: Philosophy of Education Society of Great Britain.

Zigmond, N., & Kloo, A. (2011). General and special education are (and should be) different. In J. M. Kauffman & D. P. Hallahan (Eds.), *Handbook of special education* (pp. 160–172). New York: Routledge.

Zigmond, N., Kloo, A., & Volonino, V. (2009). What, where, and how? Special education in the climate of full inclusion. *Exceptionality, 17*, 189–204.

Getting to Know Thomas Parrish

My education career began teaching elementary grades in a public school in Arizona and a private school in Belgium. There were only semblances of special education programs at that time and I had diverse learners in all my classes. During my doctoral studies, research exposure to special education came through education adequacy studies in Illinois and Alaska, which included meetings of special educators from across the state determining the resources needed (e.g., numbers and types of teachers, specialists, administrators, etc.) to provide "quality programming" statewide. These interactions were invaluable for their multiple and sometimes conflicting perspectives. Next, I had prominent roles in two national studies sponsored by the U.S. Department of Education on special education, which produced a broad array of cost data. My dissertation was primarily a cost comparison of special education services in public and private settings in California. However, as costs are linked to resources, these analyses delved deeply into the state's special education funding system. I was struck by its incoherence, inequities and inefficiencies. Also, special education appeared sufficiently mysterious to fiscal policy types and fiscal policies to program providers, that very few statewide had a clear grasp on the state's special education funding system. This initiated a long-standing interest in special education fiscal policy and its effects on programming and provision. For 10 years I co-directed the national Center of Special Education Finance. My research in special education has led to a fairly wide array of written materials as well as studies and consultations in about one-half of the states, as well as engagements in Canada, England, Germany, Belgium, and Russia. My most recent interests are in the area of special education efficiency with the goal of increasing the benefits derived from special education provision in terms of educational progress and life outcomes.

26

HOW SHOULD WE PAY FOR SPECIAL EDUCATION?

Thomas Parrish

After 30 years of studying, writing about, and making policy recommendations concerning fiscal issues related to special education, the appeal of adding one more chapter on this topic is the opportunity to speak directly concerning my views. When conducting studies for governmental entities, you are almost always addressing someone else's research questions and are bound by what has come before, the current policy climate, and what appear to be the predominant local concerns. I have no complaints about these prior constraints and have chosen a career in contract research primarily because I enjoy and believe work to be most useful when conducted in real-world situations, with real clients, and the ever-present policy constraints. However, after 30 years, it is refreshing to be asked to write a short chapter largely based on what I have concluded from this extensive experience.

I have broken this assignment into several sub-questions. The first is how we should consider special education finance. In response, I provide a conceptual framework in an attempt to provide a larger backdrop for some of the more limited questions that are often raised. These include how much is being spent on special education? Are we spending enough, or too much? What are the best formulas to use for distributing special education funds? What is fair, sufficient, and avoids fiscal incentives for certain practices that policymakers may wish to discourage?

The second question for this chapter is what do we know about current provision? Addressing this question provides important background for considering how we should pay for these services in the future.

To provide a sense of my views on what "should" be done, however, I will start with a single concept, "productivity." Thus, the third question addressed by this chapter is how we might raise productivity, which includes a section providing examples of what I believe are highly productive districts in regard to special education provision.

Within this larger context, the last question to be more specifically addressed in the chapter is how we should fund special education. I believe recommendations regarding proper financing of special education require a laser-like focus on what is being produced. Funds for special education, or any other service, will always by finite. Given limited resources, we need to ensure the provision of educational services to all students that lead to high-quality outcomes. If the outcomes are not at the level we have a right to expect, then these services by definition are not of high quality. In addition, this last section also focuses on the related concepts of recognizing and rewarding success, creating a level playing field of funding and provision, the merits of weighted student funding, and an argument for continuing the local, state, and federal partnership in support of this program.

A CONCEPTUAL FRAMEWORK FOR FINANCING AND PROVIDING EDUCATION

Figure 26.1 provides a fairly simple framework for considering education finance issues. It is based on ideas presented by Henry Levin of Teachers College. It is made up of four boxes (a) the dollars allocated for education, which are used to acquire; (b) educational resources and services, which are designed to produce; (c) educational outcomes, which are valuable because they lead to enhanced (d) life outcomes, which are the ultimate goal of education efforts.

Each box leads to the next, providing a simple overview for the consideration of what can be a very complex set of questions. For example, the first box includes such questions as how many dollars, what constitutes an equitable distribution of funds, and how many funds are enough? The second box raises questions about the nature of the resources and services needed, i.e., in what quantity and of what quality to produce enhanced

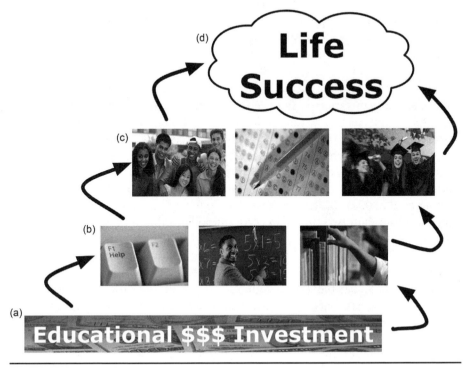

Figure 26.1 A depiction of how education funding provides educational services that affect school outcomes, which in turn promote life outcomes

educational outcomes? The box on educational outcomes includes which outcomes, how they are best measured, and how these measures may vary by type of student. The last box, however, is the most important. It reminds us that the literacy, numeracy, and social skills resulting from education are not ends in themselves. As a society, we invest in students' acquisition of those competencies because they result in enhanced life outcomes such as self-sufficiency, responsible membership in society, and the capacity for informed participation in a democratic society.

Although the question of how we should fund special education seems to focus primarily on the first box, it is only with the last box in mind that we can fully consider this question. We should fund special education in a manner that produces the life outcomes needed for students to prosper as members of society.

Thus, although a reader might expect this chapter to focus narrowly on fiscal policies and how they affect such practices as special education identification and inclusion, I believe all of these questions need to be framed in a larger context. Given the ultimate goal of enhanced life outcomes, our focus needs to be on fiscal policies and practices that lead to strong academic, social, and emotional outcomes. In my experience, special education fiscal policy has grossly under-stated the importance of academic outcomes and has paid even less attention to enhancing social and emotional learning, which is so important to short and long-term success in life.

WHAT DO WE KNOW ABOUT THE CURRENT PROVISION OF SPECIAL EDUCATION?

In alignment with the conceptual framework I presented in the introduction, it is important to ask what we know about spending for special education and about the provision of services for special education. I discuss these topics in this section.

What Do We Know About Special Education Spending?

Nationally, special education is financed through a complex combination of federal, state, and local funds using a variety of formulas. Although the federal government does not systematically collect data on special education spending due to the wide range of accounting and reporting procedures used by individual states, there have been several federally funded attempts to collect such data.

Unfortunately, the last of these is now quite old, i.e., for the 1999–2000 school year (Chambers et al., 2002). Based on these data, per pupil special education spending is estimated as more than two times (in constant dollars) that of the late 1960s when this measure was first calculated.

"We should fund special education in a manner that produces the life outcomes needed for students to prosper as members of society."

However, this study also showed that the average expenditure per student in general education had doubled. As a result, the ratio of spending per student in special education as compared to a student in general education remained fairly constant over time (at a ratio of about two to one).

Despite this constant ratio, however, special education spending has increased as a percentage of total education spending. This is due to the long prevalent trend of increasing percentages of students in special education. This goes back to the passage of the IDEA and the first collection of data in the late 1970s, with the percentage of children in special education rising steadily for in excess of 25 years[1]. This persistent national trend, however, began to reverse in 2004 and has now begun to decline somewhat every year since.

This is important because the percentage of students identified for special education services is the most predominant factor affecting special education spending overall and as a percentage of total K-12 spending. The percentage of students identified for special education varies considerably across states. For example, while Rhode Island tops the country at 18 percent, Texas, at 9 percent, is at the bottom. The average percentage across all states is 13 percent.

Special education services are financed through state and federal funding sources with the remaining costs offset by local sources. Although current data are not available to estimate the percentage share across these three sectors, prior data show state revenues as the primary source of special education support, followed by local sources, with federal funds coming in third.

Four types of funding formulas are predominantly used as the basis for allocating special education within and across states: pupil-weighted, census-based, resource-based, and percentage reimbursement. A list of the states using each of these formula types as well as language describing each state's special education funding formula can be found in Ahearn (2010). For this chapter, we will limit the discussion to the two most prevalent types of formulas.

Pupil-weighted funding allocates dollars per student based on specified criteria such as category of disability and placement. One benefit cited for this type of formula is that it accounts for differences in the cost of services across districts. A possible disadvantage is that higher funding weights may create incentives for over-identification in some categories of disability or for placement of students in higher cost (and possibly more restrictive) settings.

Census-based funding assumes a fixed cost for the average student in special education and a fairly even concentration of students with disabilities across districts. It allocates a set amount per student (counting all students both in special education and non-special education). The primary cited advantage is that because it is detached from any count of students in special education, needs, or services, it eliminates or reduces fiscal incentives for identifying more students. Disadvantages are that census-based funding does not account for the differential special education costs districts may experience and creates a fiscal incentive for reduced identification and scaled-back services. Federal special education funding is now primarily based on a census formula.

What Do We Know About Special Education Service Provision?

The second box pertains to the conversion of dollars into educational resources and services. What is known at a macro-level about how this varies across states in terms of the quantity and nature of what is provided?

Given the importance of special education services and the concerns sometimes expressed about their cost, we might expect more thorough and current information on special education spending. However, such data are not federally collected. Even in states with fairly detailed special education expenditure tracking systems there are no federal accounting guidelines to ensure comparable estimates.

Lacking expenditure data, one way to estimate the relative level of special education resources across states is to use allocations of special education staff to special education enrollments.[2] Multiplying nationally standardized salary estimates by the number of special education staff reported by each state, which is federally required annually, provides a standardized cost estimate based on these counts of personnel. Dividing this amount by the number of students in special education in the state provides a standardized special education personnel cost estimate per student in special education.

Comparing these state-level cost estimates to the national average produces a personnel-based special education expenditure index. As salaries account for approximately 85 percent of special education costs, this may provide the best available proxy measure of relative special education resource allocations by state.

Because the base is the national average, each of the index amounts shown by state can be compared to a national average index value of 1.00. These index values reveal vast differences across states in the average level of personnel-based services provided the average student in special education. These index values range from 1.77 in New York to .56 in Mississippi.

These data suggest that the special education personnel resources allocated to the average student in special education in New York is more than triple that received in Mississippi. These variances exist under the same federal law, guidelines, and provisions. They are also unaffected by salary differences across states, as standardized salary estimates are used in these calculations.

Another important macro-statistic known about special education services across the nation is where students in special education primarily receive services. These data assist the federal government, as well as individual states, to monitor the degree to which students are served in the least restrictive environment (LRE) appropriate to their needs as required by federal law.[3]

One category of placement for which these data are collected is for students spending "80 percent time or more in a regular education classroom."[4] This is considered the "least restrictive" among the placement categories because it allows for the greatest degree of integration into general education settings. Nationally, placement in this "least restrictive" setting has risen over the past decade from 50 percent of all students in special education to slightly above 60 percent in 2008.

Of even greater interest, I think, is the degree to which this fundamental component of special education service provision varies by state. For example, although Alabama reports 83 percent of its students in special education as served in this least restrictive setting, Hawai'i reports only 21 percent. These data seem to indicate broadly varying interpretation of this fundamental component of special education law across states.

What do We Know About Special Education Outcomes?

There was a time not too long ago when the information most vital to the effective management of special education was extremely lacking. That is, we had fairly little information on what we were spending or producing. However, the requirements under the federal "No Child Left Behind" law have resulted in much better information within states regarding how their students in special education are performing overall and by district and school within a given state.[5]

However, the National Assessment Educational Progress (NAEP) is the only assessment that allows special education academic achievement comparisons across states.[6] Based on these results, 38 percent of students with disabilities nationwide show basic or advanced status across fourth and eighth grade reading and mathematics. Across the states, comparable measures range from 59 percent in Massachusetts to 19 percent in Hawai'i.

Across the conceptual framework presented above, these data show broad state-level variation across what is invested in special education, how these services are provided, and what is produced. This base of information is instrumental to consideration of how we should pay for special education. Prior to moving to this specifically, however, let us consider what is known regarding the last box from the conceptual framework.

What do We Know About Life Outcomes for Students in Special Education?

The best, most current source of information regarding life outcomes for students in special education is the National Longitudinal Transition Study-2 (NLTS2) funded by the U.S. Department of Education (Newman et al., 2011). This study was designed to "help in developing an understanding of the experiences of secondary school students with disabilities nationally as they go through their early adult years."[7]

Of interest to this chapter are the categories used to define these post-secondary experiences. These provide guidance as to what may constitute "life outcomes" within the conceptual framework for this chapter. The NLTS2 includes the categories continuing education, employment, productive engagement in the community, household circumstances, and social and community involvement. These can be used to provide a working definition of the life outcomes we are attempting to favorably affect through the funding of special education. How these services are funded should be informed with these outcomes in mind.

"In my experience, special education fiscal policy has grossly under-stated the importance of academic outcomes and has paid even less attention to enhancing social and emotional learning, which is so important to short and long-term success in life."

What do we know about the relationship among the components of the framework, i.e. spending, service provision, and outcomes?

Overall performance data by school and by district have clearly become a matter of public record, appearing annually in local newspapers and through other venues, often to great fanfare or consternation depending on the results. Too often, a school or district fails to show progress for students in special education and as a result may be identified for improvement under NCLB.

Given the challenges that students in special education face, some may believe that low performance is inevitable. However, the cross-state comparisons shown above indicate otherwise. Also, an analysis of key district characteristics and outcomes for students in special education in two states–California (Parrish, 2012) and Illinois (Parrish, 2010)– show striking within-state disparities, ranging from quite poor to fairly strong academic performance. This suggests that lower performance for this population is not a given. Districts in both states range in the percentage of students in special education scoring proficient in English language arts (ELA), from 15 to 80 percent in Illinois (2008) and from about 5 to 50 percent across California (2007).[8]

A fair amount of the variation reported above is negatively correlated with district poverty (defined as the percentage of students eligible for free or reduced priced lunch). That is, greater district-level poverty is associated with lower academic performance for students in special education.

Table 26.1 Relationship between ELA proficiency of students in special education and poverty, spending, identification, and educational placement in California and Illinois

	California		Illinois	
	Coefficient	p-Value	Coefficient	p-Value
Percentage of Students Eligible for Free or Reduced Price Lunch	−0.30	0.00	−0.33	0.00
Per-Student Special Education Expenditure (in increments of $100)	0.01	0.03	0.02	0.15
Percentage of Students in Special Education with Specific Learning Disability or Speech/Language Impairment	−0.14	0.07	0.06	0.39
Percentage of Students in Special Education in General Education Class 80% or More	0.10	0.05	0.29	0.00
Percentage of Students in Special Education in General Education Class Less than 40%	0.01	0.82	−0.01	0.89
Percentage of Students in Special Education in a Separate Facility	−0.05	0.71	−0.54	0.00
Constant	38.44	0.00	35.15	0.00

Thus, these studies included analyses holding poverty, which is outside local control, constant. They also include other variables that are, at least to some degree, within local control. These include the average per pupil special education expenditure, educational placement, and the percentage of students in special education designated as having a specific learning disability or a speech-language impairment.

Table 26.1 summarizes these results for both states. Of most interest to a discussion on productivity are the results for spending and educational placement. Although the coefficients associated with these variables are fairly small, the possible policy implications of these findings seem of interest and worthy of further exploration. In Illinois, the analyses show no academic gains associated with added spending, and in California the impact is shown to be quite small.

Among the variables listed in this equation, those over which districts may have the most control are the percentages of students in special education in various educational placements. In both California and Illinois, the percentage of students spending 80 percent or more time in the general education class shows a strong statistical relationship (holding other variables shown in the equation constant) with ELA proficiency.

This relationship was also found in an examination of special education provision in Massachusetts (Hehir, Grindal, & Eidelman, 2012). The authors reported that the "degree to which students with disabilities are included in classrooms with their non-disabled peers is substantially related to Massachusetts Comprehensive Assessment System performance, controlling for a host of relevant variables such as income, race and English language proficiency" (p. 1).

In addition, although fairly small, the placement effect is shown to be much larger and easier to obtain than increases in spending. For example, for every 10-point increase in the percentage of students spending 80 percent or more time in a general education setting, the students in special education scoring proficient in ELA statewide would be predicted to increase by nearly three percent. This would not only improve compliance with IDEA in regard to least restrictive placements (Illinois and California report special education placement data that are among the most restrictive in the nation (Parrish, 2010; Parrish, 2012), but also could be important in improving the academic performance of students in special education.

However, the question is sometimes raised as to whether including students in special education in general education classes may be detrimental to the learning of other students. Analyses of the degree of inclusion for students with disabilities and the academic outcomes of all students show no relationship based on California data for the 2009–10 year (Parrish, 2012). Thus, these data show a positive academic association from inclusion for students with disabilities accompanied by no negative academic association for other students.

In addition, this variable is of particular interest to this discussion due to its potential contribution to successful life outcomes. It may be one of the best measures available as to the extent to which students with disabilities (and all students) are receiving the social benefits associated with interacting with a diverse student enrollment.

The inclusion variable is also of interest because it is something districts can, to a large degree, control. For example, unified districts in California range from 9 percent to 91 percent of students in special education in this most inclusive setting, and in Illinois this ranges from 11 percent to 100 percent.

Last, the percentage of students with disabilities placed predominantly in general education classrooms seems relevant to the question of special education funding in that this type of placement does not appear to have special education spending implications, indicating that the cost side of the productivity equation is unaffected. For example, no statistically significant association is shown between the degree of spending per student and type of placement in either California or Illinois (Parrish, 2010; Parrish, 2012).

However, these data should not be interpreted as providing evidence that increased inclusion will automatically result in higher academic outcomes for students with disabilities. The positive relationships noted for Illinois, California and Massachusetts should be seen as correlational and not causal.

For example, analyses in these states clearly revealed individual districts showing relatively high rates of inclusion and low outcomes for students with disabilities. In fact, plotting all districts using axes of the percentage academically proficient or above and the percentage in inclusive settings shows that virtually all of the highest performing districts also tend to be high inclusion. However, some of the lowest performing districts also show high inclusion. On average, however, we see an overall positive relationship between these two variables in all three states.

This seems to suggest that inserting students with disabilities into general education classrooms without appropriate professional development and support can be one of the worst things that can be done. However, when students are included with appropriate support this may be an important element to enhanced academic results for students with disabilities, and social outcomes for all students.

HOW MIGHT WE INCREASE SPECIAL EDUCATION PRODUCTIVITY?

Even in these austere times, where spending on public education in most states is substantially in check or even declining, educators across the nation face considerable pressure to improve educational results. Federal and state education accountability systems are designed to enforce sanctions on public schools not showing continuous academic improvement.

Thus, virtually all districts are faced with the daunting challenge of doing more with less. Coupled with this, however, are opportunities. Programs such as Response to Intervention (RTI), which is designed to identify students who appear to be struggling academically early and to introduce interventions (often outside of special education), may be especially effective in increasing outcomes for students while reducing costs when implemented well.

It should be noted, however, that RTI alone is not necessarily a panacea. Information on the full range of activities districts across the nation are doing under the name of RTI is generally lacking as are studies of the relative costs and benefits of this program on a large scale. Also, it should be noted that the primary purpose of RTI is not to lower the percentage of students in special education, but rather to provide systematic interventions that benefit all students in a data driven and accountable way. However, when early intervention is successfully employed, reductions in the number of children ultimately referred to special education may result.

Thus, the use of approaches like RTI, which is designed to intervene early with children showing signs of additional education needs, when well implemented, may improve outcomes for students. They may also lead to a reduction in the number of referrals to special education, which are costly, as well as precluding the need for these services for some students.

"This seems to suggest that inserting students with disabilities into general education classrooms without appropriate professional development and support can be one of the worst things that can be done."

Serving students effectively outside of special education is likely to be cost-effective because of the relatively high cost of procedures associated with eligibility determination. Also, the data show that once children are identified as eligible for special education they tend to continue to receive these services throughout their school career. Thus, strategic investments designed to help students succeed academically as soon as a need is determined may be cost-effective.

For the students for whom it is determined that special education services are needed, careful compliance with federal provisions requiring the placement of these students in the least restrictive environment appropriate to their needs also appears cost-effective. Rising costs do not appear related to such placements although there is evidence of a relationship between enhanced academic results and the enhanced potential of social benefits through interaction with a diverse set of peers accruing to all children.

Examples of "High Productivity Districts"

Is it possible to control special education spending while improving educational outcomes for students, including those with disabilities? A report released by the California Comprehensive Center at WestEd analyzed data from the 2005–06 through 2008–09 school years in an attempt to identify California school districts with substantially higher-than-statistically-predicted achievement for students with disabilities on state-wide performance measures (Huberman et al., 2012). Publicly available data from the Academic Performance Index (API), Annual Yearly Progress (AYP), CSTs, and California High School Exit Exam (CAHSEE) databases, as well as district demographic data for ethnicity, poverty, the proportion of English learners (ELs), and the proportion of students with disability were included in these analyses.[9]

Some strong sites emerged from these analyses, and four districts where students in special education substantially outperformed other districts with similar characteristics across the state were specifically featured. Two of these districts are discussed below. Each includes a summary of how district respondents reported producing substantially more in terms of student outcomes for students in special education as well as the cost implications of these strategies.

Sanger Unified School District. This district is in the heart of California's Central Valley where the child poverty rate is two to three times the national average. Despite this, the district has made great academic strides. In 2004, seven of the district's schools were designated as Program Improvement (PI) sites under NCLB. Today, five are State Distinguished Schools, and two have been recognized as National Blue Ribbon Schools. Sanger employees have received local and national recognition, such as the National Superintendent of the Year Award, the Bell Award for Outstanding School Leadership, and Fresno County Administrator and Teacher of the Year.

As described by Sanger's former superintendent, Marcus Johnson, special education was one of the first populations on which the district focused at the onset of his tenure there.[10] One reason he cited was it provided a clear opportunity for a "quick win." This population had been largely separated from mainstream instruction and therefore it was not surprising that they did not perform well on state tests based on this material. Reorienting the way students in special education were served in the district produced relatively quick gains on standardized tests. As this population constituted approximately 10 percent of Sanger's students at that time and were among its lowest performers, gains for the special education population had an important impact on the district's overall performance.

Over time, Sanger introduced more comprehensive reforms. One example is RTI. As described by the district's former director of special education, Matt Navo,[11] the district realized it needed a strong RTI model due to its large percentage of English learners and students qualifying for special services.[12] Combined with decreasing budgets, district service providers were stretched to deal with the needs of an increasing special population of students who were already far behind benchmark goals.

Mr. Navo describes RTI as an approach that brought the general and special education staff together to implement and ensure success. RTI allowed Sanger schools to begin addressing its special education needs and its general education challenges. Through the use of RTI and other interventions, the percentage of students receiving special education services in the district is now 7 percent, compared to the state-wide average of 10 percent, and a national average of over 13 percent.

Despite the fact that reduced identification means that its special education program is focused only on students with the most severe needs, Sanger's students in special education perform better than the state average and substantially better than other districts with similar demographics. In the 2008–09 school year, based on the AYP calculation of percent proficient, 49 percent of Sanger's students in special education scored proficient or above in mathematics and 38 percent in ELA, compared to 33 percent and 32 percent for students in special education state-wide, and 28 percent and 26 percent in districts with comparable student poverty.

Mr. Navo cites the combination of Sanger's commitment to fully include as many children as possible in the general education setting, its RTI philosophy to meet students' exceptional needs through the use of Explicit Direct Instruction (EDI),[13] and collaboration through professional learning community teams as its recipe for success.

However, the question of cost remains. Did Sanger's implementation of the interventions described above and its substantially improved student outcomes for students with disabilities (and all students) require a substantial added investment in special education?

Based on data from the California Department of Education, Sanger's reported special education expenditure per student is $7,808 compared to the state average of $13,625. As their state and federal special education revenues per student are very close to the state average ($8,575 versus $8,523), Sanger is one of 84 districts state-wide (out of over 950 districts included in these analyses) for which CDE data show special education revenues exceeding spending. Thus, Sanger shows much stronger than statistically predicted academic outcomes for students with disabilities (and for all students) while holding special education spending well under control.

These data showing Sanger's special education revenues exceeding spending are not surprising. Sanger identifies one of the lowest percentages of students in special education within the state. Because the state's census-based special education funding system allocates special education revenues on the basis of total enrollment, districts with low identification rates receive larger allocations of state and federal aid per identified student.

Val Verde Unified School District. Val Verde district is relatively large with an enrollment of approximately 20,000 students. About three quarters of the district's students are eligible for free or reduced-price lunch, and more than one quarter are ELs. In the 2008–09 school year, 37 percent of Val Verde's students in special education scored proficient or above in mathematics for AYP while 33 percent scored proficient or above in ELA.

However, this relatively high level of performance for students in special education is fairly new to the district. For example, Troy Knudsvig, a district special education coordinator, described state academic growth for the district's elementary school students in special education as rising from a California Academic Index of 488 in 2007 to 706 in 2010.[14]

How did they realize such large gains? As described by the district's director of special education, students in special education are performing well partly because all students in the district are performing well. The philosophy in the district is that special education is not separate from general education. Also, special education is deliberately located in the curriculum and instruction department to bridge the gap between general and special education.

He also mentioned the use of RTI strategies, which allowed them to identify and provide services for at-risk students while keeping their special education population low at about 9 percent. In addition, Mr. Knudsvig discussed greater inclusion of students with disabilities in general education classes as a way of improving outcomes, reducing the need for special education identification, and reducing costs.

Because the vast majority of their students in special education are served in general education classrooms, special education professionals are in these classes working closely with the general education teacher. This includes working with small groups containing students at risk, which may allow their needs to be remediated prior to referral for special education.

Moving most special education services to general education classes also helped Val Verde "get rid of alternative special education curricula." All students are now focused on the same core curriculum, which relates to the standards on which students will be tested. Mr. Knudsvig described this alignment of instruction to the standards on which students are tested as key.

In addition to improving results, according to Mr. Knudsvig these changes have resulted in savings. Like Sanger, Val Verde identifies students for special education at a rate that is lower than the state average (9 percent), which reduces special education costs but not revenues given the state's census-based funding. One source of savings comes from students with disabilities increasingly attending their neighborhood schools. This provides social benefits of allowing students to attend school with their siblings, friends, and neighbors. In addition, Mr. Knudsvig estimates their annual transportation cost to be $50,000 per bus route. Thus, moving large numbers of students to neighborhood schools improves outcomes and reduces costs.

Conclusion Related to Increased Special Education Productivity

Because Sanger and Val Verde districts have realized these results does not mean that all districts can. However, both districts appeared as unlikely candidates for these accomplishments a decade ago. With relatively high rates of poverty and English learners, one could argue that if these districts can do this others can as well. At the least, it would appear that the kinds of practices employed in districts where students are performing higher than statistically predicted at a reasonable cost should serve as basis for dissemination and training statewide.

In pointing to Sanger and Val Verde as examples of efficiency, I am aware that some special education advocates and others may argue that they should not be commended for using RTI to reduce their special education rates of identification. When this notion was posed to Sanger's current Director of Special Education, Kimberly Salomonson, she agreed that RTI is not a reason to postpone assessment for special education eligibility and should never be used as such. She noted the importance of tight timelines for data reviews and decisions regarding a student's response to intervention, and if failure occurs that a prompt referral for special education eligibility assessment is appropriate.

However, regarding Sanger's low special education identification rate, she argues that the use of RTI has allowed them to identify at a rate more appropriate to their district's true need for special education services. She explains that special education operates under a discrepancy model, which is largely designed to wait until children fail prior to intervening.

"Using RTI properly, we can remediate some students through early intervention. When students can be remediated in this way to learn the skills needed to access core instruction and maintain grade level success, they are not special education and should not be labeled as such." Based on this, she argues that Sanger's rate is not low but is actually closer to true special education incidence than the statewide average of somewhat less than 11 percent.

HOW SHOULD WE FUND SPECIAL EDUCATION?

How we fund special education is important due to the size of investment, estimated to be $50 billion per year in 1999–2000 (Chambers et al., 2002). However, its greatest significance lies in its promise of enhanced lifetime outcomes for participants, who may be especially at risk in areas of employment, productive community engagement, and social involvement.

How special education is funded is also important because of its effect on program provision. For example, when fiscal resources are allocated on the basis of certain student characteristics—such as the student's special education status, disability category, or educational placement—questions may be raised as to whether these provisions may lead to increased placement in these categories or in more restrictive environments.

Concerns have been raised about whether any funding provisions based on allocations per student in special education may lead to over-identification. Such concerns were articulated in the 1997 reauthorization of the IDEA when the federal formula was altered from providing funding based on the number of students in special education due to concerns about over-identification. For example, although the House and Senate reports for the 1997 reauthorization conceded that "it is unlikely that individual educators ever identify children for the additional funding that such identification brings," it noted that fiscal incentives may decrease checks on the special education referral process (Apling, 2001). Furthermore, during the same reauthorization cycle, the IDEA included a requirement that states allocating state funding based on the type of educational setting must ensure that this does not result in placements that violate LRE.

"How special education is funded is also important because of its effect on program provision."

These types of concerns are the impetus for studies of the relationship between state special education funding formulas and practice (Greene & Forster, 2002; Kane & Johnson, 1993; Mahitivanichcha & Parrish, 2005a, 2005b). Overall, these studies indicate, and I have observed through 30 years of special education fiscal policy consultations, that fiscal policy clearly can affect practice, although often in subtle ways.

Even when there is no statistical evidence of a causal effect of fiscal incentives, formulas can send powerful messages about a state's priorities and expectations and may affect the ways in which services are provided. Given this opportunity, why not clearly place the emphasis on what is most important for students with disabilities, i.e., fostering best practices that lead to enhanced educational outcomes and life opportunities?

With these ideas in mind, I suggest the following features in answer to the question of how we should fund special education. These include recognize and reward success, create a level playing field for the funding and provision of services, consider weighted student funding formulas, and fund special education based on a local, state, and federal partnership.

Recognize and Reward Success.

Although all funding formulas contain incentives of one type or another, I am not aware of any that create incentives for strong performance. In the policies I have reviewed over the past 30 years, I have found virtually no overt reference to identifying and rewarding districts showing strong academic performance for students with disabilities (or other desired outcome measures) or to shoring up districts with unusually weak performance.

Once a system is in place for clearly identifying strong performing districts,[15] supplemental funds might be allocated based on their willingness to guide and assist others. Although I know of no examples of such an approach, I believe we can no longer continue to fund chronic failure on an ongoing basis without providing program assistance. Also, the best source of useful assistance seems most likely to come from academic leaders and service providers in similar districts that have been able to consistently produce much stronger results with like student populations.

As we have identified such districts through projects such as described in Huberman et al. (2012), I have sometimes discussed district leaders potential interest in dissemination. I have generally heard a very warm reception, with some school leaders describing how they are already supporting such dissemination activities using their own resources.

Enhancing the academic performance and life outcomes for students with disabilities would seem to be of the highest priority for states and other governmental entities funding special education services. Given this, why not allocate some relatively small portion of these funds to leverage the educational excellence found across the state?

Foster a Level Playing Field For the Funding and Provision of Special Education Services.

A major concern I have observed through the many years I have worked in this field is substantial inequities in funding across districts and service sectors. This is a problem in its own right and also leads to substantial inefficiencies in service.

Many states have extremely complex special education funding provisions. For example, Illinois has six separate components to its formula and entirely separate provisions for Chicago Public Schools, which enrolls 13 percent of all students in special education statewide. Although each component has some relatively reasonable rationale as it stands alone, including the one for Chicago, in the aggregate the formula is a confusing and sometimes conflicting mass of provisions which results in vast inequities and inefficiencies in the allocation of special education funds statewide (Parrish, 2010).

This formula also contains substantial fiscal incentives for districts to place students in private special education schools such that over 10 percent of all state funds allocated for special education services go to the support of such institutions. As another example, special education funding and service provisions for special education in the District of Columbia have led to nearly 20 percent of their students in special education being placed in private schools (FY 2008) (Parrish, et al., 2007).

Substantial funding inequities have also been found in studies in Oregon (Parrish and Harr, 2007), California (Parrish, 2012), Wyoming (Parrish, et al., 2002), North Dakota (Parrish and Harr, 2006), Nevada (Parrish, et al., 2008), Georgia (Parrish and Harr, 2005), and Alberta, Canada (Parrish, 2009). Although I have not examined special education funding provisions across all states in detail, I have seen enough to believe this to be an important problem.

In California, the formula is quite simple in theory, i.e., a census-based formula where allocations are based on total enrollment. However, because of historic inequities that were supposed to have been phased out over time and other provisions, considerable inequities in funding across districts persist (Parrish, 2012).

When the state funds allocated to students in special education are more governed by zip code than student needs, we have an inequitable system that is also highly inefficient because scarce resources are not allocated to where they are most needed.

When states create substantial fiscal incentives to place students in separate, highly segregated, schools, as is the case for virtually all private special education institutions, they are promoting the provision of these types of services for students who may not require them. This not only violates the LRE provisions of federal law, but also is inefficient in that these services may be more costly than is needed and also limit student access to non-disabled peers and mainstream instruction in ways that may negatively affect academic and life outcomes.

Some students may require access to special services that in some states only private special education schools provide. However, these placements should be fully driven by student need and not on the basis of substantial fiscal favoritism toward this sector of service.

Special education should be funded on an equitable and transparent basis. Although funding differences per student may be justified based on student need or other clearly defined cost factors, differences in funding that are not based on clear criteria are unfair to all and stand in the way of the most efficient use of scarce special education resources.

Consider Weighted Student Funding Formulas.

I have been reluctant to recommend a single type of funding system in the past as all have advantages and disadvantages. For example, student funding weights are generally differentiated based on category of disability, category of placement, or some combination of the two. Disadvantages relate to concerns of fiscal incentives to place students in certain categories of disabilities or placements (or both).

"When the state funds allocated to student in special education are more governed by zip code than student needs, we have an inequitable system that is also highly inefficient because scarce resources are not allocated to where they are most needed."

However, the ability to create incentives for certain practices under a weighting system can also be an advantage. For example, states may wish to create incentives for more inclusive categories of placement. Thus, funding weights may be based on some combination of category of disability and category of placement such that greater funding is associated with what have been shown to be more costly categories of disability and with more inclusive placements.

This type of system could be tied to the recommendation above to recognize and reward success. For example, weighting premiums could be granted to districts showing substantially stronger academic success for students in special education than statistically predicted. Such districts might also be allowed to retain a base level of overall funding even as their identified special education percentage declines when their remaining students in special education, as well as all students, are performing at a higher than predicted level.

To avoid possible incentives, identification caps might be placed by category of disability in regard to funding with the option of allowing districts to appeal and receive a program audit if they believe their true incidence is beyond the specified limits to claim funding.

Another reason for advocating pupil weighted funding is that we have entered an era with substantially more student choice among schools and schooling systems. For example, a census-based approach may make sense if students are largely locked into the enrollment area where they reside and the incidence of disability is fairly evenly distributed across the state. However, increasingly, students and parents have a choice among schools, districts, and type of school, e.g. charter versus non. With such mobility, census-based approaches create an incentive for discouraging the enrollment of students in special education.

However, in a more mobile education environment, it seems especially important that the funding system encourage the recruitment and acceptance of students with disabilities. A major example of this concern is with the growing number of charter schools, which are sometimes said to not enroll students with disabilities in commensurate numbers as non-charter schools.

One reason for this may be the difficulty of establishing programs to serve the full range of students with disabilities. These challenges are further exacerbated by provisions where special education funding does not follow the student. It would seem especially important that larger weights and greater fiscal incentives be associated with students with more severe disabilities.

Fund Special Education Based on a Local, State, and Federal Partnership.
I believe that special education should continue to be funded through a three-way partnership. In some states, quite a bit of concern is expressed about the fact that state and federal sources of support for special education services are insufficient. In California, for example, local support for special education is often referred to as "encroachment." Given its dictionary definition, "to enter by gradual steps or by stealth into the possessions or rights of another," the use of this term does not foster friendly cooperation between general and special education.

Wyoming addresses this concern by fully funding special education through state reimbursements. However, to reinforce the notion that all students, including those in special education, are students first, I believe a three-way partnership best demonstrates the importance of full cooperation and collaboration. For example, if other states and the federal government were to fully fund special education, would this encourage increased identification into this category of service and create incentives for the provision of virtually all services to this population by special educators?

If we want to encourage shared responsibility for educational and life outcomes of students in special education, a broad base of financial support for these services is important. This approach should also encourage efficiencies in special education provision, as the more cost-effective they are the lower the impact on local sources of support.

CONCLUSION

How should we fund special education? As indicated at the onset of this chapter, I believe special education productivity to be of foremost importance in considering this question. How do we get the maximum effect from every dollar available for these services to improve life outcomes for students. In a recently released volume, Levenson (2012) describes this well. In addition, in a recent personal communication with the author of this chapter, he commented, "Right now, there is enormous pressure from (maintenance of effort provisions) to make sure districts spend enough. I would rather put pressure on districts to make sure students learn enough."[16]

Discussion Questions
1. Different funding formulas have unique advantages and disadvantages. What do you think should weigh heaviest in determining the state formula—how it might limit resources or how it might be misused in identification?
2. If schools were over-identifying students for increased funding, what other costs will they assume?
3. Parrish concludes that the data regarding percentage of students served 80 percent of the time or more in a regular education classroom are an indicator of the state's use of the least restrictive environment as a placement. Do you think Zigmond (Chapter 13) would interpret this differently?
4. Parrish states that "once children are identified as eligible for special education they tend to continue to receive these services throughout their school career. Thus, strategic investments designed to help students succeed academically as soon as a need is determined may be cost-effective." How could you use this information to convince a school to invest more in prevention efforts or preschool programming?

NOTES

1. About 7.5 percent of students were identified as special education in 1975–76 rising over time to about 14 percent in 2004–2005.
2. Every state must report numbers of full-time special education teachers, therapists and aides serving students in special education as well as the numbers of students in special education being served. According to the 2009–10 Part B data collection instructions, these counts are also supposed to include all staff, contracted or employed, including those in separate schools and facilities.
3. "To the maximum extent appropriate, children with disabilities, including children in public or private institutions or other care facilities, are educated with children who are not disabled, and special classes, separate schooling, or other removal of children with disabilities from the regular educational environment occurs only when the nature or severity of the disability of a child is such that education in regular classes with the use of supplementary aids and services cannot be achieved satisfactorily" (20 U.S.C. 1412(a)(5)(B)).
4. The federal educational environments for children served under IDEA are: 80 percent or more time spent inside a regular classroom; between 40 percent-79 percent of time spent in a regular classroom; less than 40 percent of time spent in a regular classroom; and external placements, which include special schools, residential facilities, parentally placed in private schools, correctional facilities, and home/hospital environments.
5. The 2001 reauthorization of the ESEA, known as the *No Child Left Behind (NCLB) Act,* specifies that schools be held accountable for the adequate yearly progress (AYP) of all students. It also specifically requires the disaggregation and reporting of data for specified subgroups, including students with disabilities.
6. NAEP is designed such that sub-population samples are of sufficient size and composition to support ranked comparisons across states.
7. Findings can be found at: http://www.nlts2.org/reports/2011_09_02/nlts2_report_2011_09_02_execsum.pdf.
8. It is important to note that assessments and results are not comparable across states and that cross-state comparisons of proficiency should be interpreted with caution. The lower performance in California relative to Illinois may be due to a variety of factors, such as more stringent state standards, less adequate academic preparation for students in special education, or due to smaller percentage of students identified for special education in California, which may mean that their education needs, on average, are greater.
9. Scores on the California Modified Assessment (CMA) or the California Alternate Performance Assessment (CAPA) were not considered, as the majority of students in special education take the CST with or without accommodations.
10. This description and corresponding data were presented by Mr. Johnson at the state-wide "On the Right Track 6" Conference held in Burlingame on September 29, 2008.
11. Mr. Navo continues to serve at Sanger and has responsibilities for children in special education. The current district Director of Special Education, Kimberly Salomonson, is quoted later in this paper.
12. These observations by Mr. Navo are taken from the California Comprehensive Center report cited above.
13. Explicit Direct Instruction (EDI) focuses on the use of (a) instructional grouping (using flexible skill grouping as opposed to "tracking"), (b) increased instructional time (increasing academic learning time—the time students are successfully engaged), and (c) continuous assessment (providing ongoing in-program assessments to inform instructional practice). EDI is mostly used at the K–8 level, with weekly monitoring by school and district administrators to ensure consistent implementation.
14. This is based on the Academic Performance Index (API) from California's *Public Schools Accountability Act of 1999,* which measures the academic performance and growth of schools on a variety of measures.
15. See Huberman et al. (2012) for one example as to how such districts were identified based on state data in California.
16. Personal conversation with the author on October 23, 2014.

TOM PARRISH'S SUGGESTIONS
FOR FURTHER READING

Ahearn, E. (2010). *Financing special education: State funding formulas.* Alexandria, VA: Project Forum, National Association of State Directors of Special Education (NASDSE).

Chambers, J., Parrish, T., & Harr, J. J. (2002). *What are we spending on special education services in the United States, 1999–2000? Special Education Expenditure Project (SEEP).* Palo Alto, CA: American Institutes for Research, Center for Special Education Finance.

Harr, J. J., Parrish, T., & Chambers, J. (2008). Special education. In H. F. Ladd & E. B. Fiske (Eds.), *Handbook of research in education finance and policy* (pp. 573–590). New York: Routledge.

Huberman, M., Navo, M., & Parrish, T. (2011). *Lessons from California districts showing unusually strong academic performance for students in special education.* Palo Alto, CA: American Institutes for Research.

Levenson, N. (2012). *Boosting the quality and efficiency of special education*. Washington, DC: Thomas Fordham Institute.

Parrish, T. (2012). *Special education expenditures, revenues and provision in California*. San Mateo, CA: American Institutes for Research.

REFERENCES

Ahearn, E. (2010). *Financing special education: State funding formulas*. Alexandria, VA: Project Forum, National Association of State Directors of Special Education (NASDSE).

Apling, R.N. (2001). Individuals with Disabilities Education Act (IDEA): Issues regarding "Full Funding" of Part B Grants to States. *Congressional Research Service Report* Number: RL30810 *Washington, DC:* Congressional Research Service, Library of Congress. Available: http://digital.library.unt.edu/govdocs/crs/permalink/meta-crs-1604.

Chambers, J., Parrish, T., & Harr, J. J. (2002). *What are we spending on special education services in the United States, 1999–2000?* Special Education Expenditure Project (SEEP). Palo Alto, CA: American Institutes for Research, Center for Special Education Finance.

Greene, J.P., & Forster, G.F. (2002). *Effects of funding incentives on special education enrollment* (Civic Report No. 32). New York: Manhattan Institute, Center for Civic Innovation.

Hehir, T., Grindal, T., & Eidelman, H. (2012). *Review of special education in the Commonwealth of Massachusetts*. Boston, Massachusetts.

Huberman, M., Navo, M., & Parrish, T. (2012). Lessons from California districts showing unusually strong academic performance for students in special education. *Journal of Special Education Leadership*.

Kane, D., & Johnson, P. (1993). *Vermont's Act 230: A new response to meeting the demands of diversity*. Montpelier, VT: Vermont Department of Education.

Lapp, D. (2009). DRAFT: State survey of special education funding formulas. Education Law Center of Pennsylvania. Available at: http://reformspecialedfunding.org/wp-content/uploads/2009/07/DRAFT.HowStatesFundSpecEd.pdf.

Levenson, N. (2012). *Boosting the quality and efficiency of special education*. Thomas Fordham Institute, Washington, DC.

Mahitivanichcha, K., & Parrish, T. (2005a). Do non-census funding systems encourage special education identification? Reconsidering Greene and Forster. *Journal of Special Education Leadership, 18*(1), 38–46.

Mahitivanichcha, K., & Parrish, T. (2005b). The implications of fiscal incentives on identification rates and placement in special education: Formulas for influencing best practice. *Journal of Education Finance, 31*(1), 1–22.

Newman, L., Wagner, M., Knokey, A.-M., Marder, C., Nagle, K., Shaver, D., ... Schwarting, M. (2011). *The post-high school outcomes of young adults with disabilities up to 8 Years after high school*. A Report From the National Longitudinal Transition Study-2 (NLTS2) (NCSER 2011–3005). Menlo Park, CA: SRI International.

Parrish, T. (2008) *Special education funding in Nevada*, before the Nevada Department of Education, Carson City, NV.

Parrish, T. (2009) *Presentation on funding and accountability*, at the Setting the Direction Minister's Forum, Edmonton, Canada.

Parrish, T. (2010). *Policy alternatives for special education funding in Illinois*, Palo Alto, CA: American Institutes for Research.

Parrish, T. (2012). *Special education expenditures, revenues and provision in California*. San Mateo, CA: American Institutes for Research.

Parrish, T., & Harr, J. (2005). *Reconsidering special education funding in Georgia*. Palo Alto, CA: American Institutes for Research.

Parrish, T., & Harr, J. (2006). *Special education funding in North Dakota: An assessment of current practice and recommendations for the future*. Palo Alto, CA: American Institutes for Research, Center for Special Education Finance.

Parrish, T. B., & Harr, J. J. (2007). *Special education funding in Oregon: An assessment of current practice with preliminary recommendations*. Palo Alto, CA: American Institutes for Research.

Parrish, T., Harr, J., Perez, M., Esra, P., Brock, L., & Shkolnik, J. (2002). *Wyoming special education expenditure project and cost based funding model: Final Report*. Palo Alto, CA: American Institutes for Research.

Parrish, T, Harr, J. J., Poirier, J., Madsen, S., & Yonker, S. (2007). *Special education financing study for the District of Columbia*. Palo Alto, CA: American Institutes for Research.

Getting to Know Timothy J. Landrum

 My orientation to special education and my deep appreciation of the science behind it developed hand in hand, shaped by several experiences. My entry into the field was prompted by an introductory class in special education I took on a whim as an undecided, undeclared undergraduate. I remember only two experiences from that class: field hours working with adults with intellectual disabilities in a recreation program and being intrigued by snippets from some "Lovaas" video tapes showing something I had never heard of—*applied behavior analysis*. That course prompted me to major in special education, where a behavior management course furthered my grasp of applied behavior analysis (ABA), and to take my first job at a residential school for children with autism, where ABA dominated our approach to instruction. Despite having limited training and experience, I loved the precision, logic, and elegant simplicity of ABA, and found it to be effective and rewarding.

Four years later, during my second semester in graduate school, I took a single-subject research design course from the same professor (John Wills Lloyd) who had taught the undergraduate behavior management class. This course broadened my perspective dramatically; I learned to think logically and analytically about how learning occurs and how relationships between variables can be analyzed systematically. My immersion was quick; John and I implemented a study of self-recording the very next semester, which was published in the *Journal of Applied Behavior Analysis.*

For more than 20 years now I have worked with pre-service and practicing teachers and taught graduate courses in special education. Most of my work centers on emotional and behavioral disorders, classroom and behavior management, and issues around evidence-based practice in special education. I believe the title of a recent piece captures a theme of most of my work in schools: Classroom misbehavior is predictable and preventable.

27

SCIENCE MATTERS IN SPECIAL EDUCATION
Timothy J. Landrum

Science is far from the perfect instrument of knowledge; it's just the best we have. (Sagan, 1996, p. 27)

Carl Sagan's assessment of the place and value of science and scientific thinking in American culture painted a bleak picture of the prospects for progress in many spheres, not the least of which is education. His analysis of strongly held beliefs in things decidedly untrue (e.g., that aliens regularly abduct humans or create elaborate artwork in grain fields in the form of crop circles) seemed to imply as much a criticism of the logic of individuals who hold to such fanciful notions as it did a stinging critique of an American education system that produces such utterly illogical thinkers. As many writers have noted, illogic in fact pervades education, particularly at the level of policy initiatives and reform efforts. Kauffman (2012), for example, noted the patent absurdity of simple mathematical impossibilities that are centerpieces of specific legislation and policy, most notably the No Child Left Behind Act, which included a goal of 100 percent proficiency in basic academic skills. The "retreat from inquiry and knowledge" described by Sasso (2001) has come to characterize not only education, but special education specifically (Kauffman, 2011; Landrum & Tankersley, 2004). I submit that if special education is to produce the best outcomes for students with disabilities, then Sagan's recommendation about science providing the most-trustworthy guide for practice must be taken to heart. In particular, in this chapter I suggest that teaching can be viewed as an ongoing series of decisions, and that logic and science are clearly the foundations of the most effective decision-making of which humans are capable. Importantly, I concede that logic and science neither result in perfect decision-making nor provide answers for all of education's most vexing problems. But I conclude, as did Sagan, that among the tools for sound decision-making, science—despite its limitations—is indeed the best we have.

DECISIONS IN THE CLASSROOM

Teaching involves making decisions. Lots of them. It is not an exaggeration to suggest that teachers make decisions on an almost continuous basis in the course of their school day. Some decisions are made in advance of teaching, as teachers prepare to teach. They decide what chunks of material to cover in a particular lesson, what examples to use to convey particular concepts, how to group students for instruction, and what specific tasks to present or questions to ask of students in what order, to name only a few. A dramatically greater proportion of decisions are probably those made on the fly, as teachers respond to student (and environmental) inputs—in other words *as they teach*. The variety and combination of inputs teachers must juggle and react to mean that teaching is an enormously complex undertaking. Teachers are simply faced with a prodigious number and fluid constellation of instructional variables that must be taken into account and addressed by specific decisions, many of them split-second decisions that do not allow time for typical, conscious decision-making.

"As many writers have noted, illogic in fact pervades education, particularly at the level of policy initiatives and reform efforts."

Suppose in a simple example a teacher plans to present a demonstration of how to solve a particular type of mathematical problem, and then to walk and talk students though an example with guided practice. She or he selects an exemplar that can be used to model the key steps in the problem-solving process, plans out specific questions to ask as the lesson progresses, makes notes about the nature of feedback to provide for correct responses as well as incorrect responses, and maps out a backup set of examples to use in case the first examples leave students confused or uncertain. She or he further develops a series of additional and more varied examples for students to work on independently, with the assumption that students who appear to be mastering the concept can move ahead while others work in a smaller group with the teacher for a dose of more in-depth, concrete instruction. The teacher believes this level of planning will help the lesson run more smoothly. Upon implementing the lesson, however, the plan is met immediately with complications: as soon as the first example is presented, one student calls out loudly in an exasperated tone, "we already did this yesterday!" The teacher forges ahead with the planned instruction, but the examples are met with dazed looks and incorrect responses from most students. Several note loudly enough to be heard, "I don't get this." As the teacher elicits more responses from the class, it becomes clear that more answers than not are incorrect, so the likelihood of independent practice being useful is small. As the teacher prepares to abandon entirely the lesson as planned and move to an ill-defined plan B, class is interrupted by a call from the front office requesting that "Kevin" be sent down, which elicits howls from several students. As Kevin leaves the room, the teacher notices that the two most capable students in class have their heads down on their desks; they appear to be asleep.

Although similar scenarios probably play out with some regularity in U.S. schools, a reasonably skilled teacher, even one in training, could probably analyze this case and note multiple examples of decisions the teacher made—or failed to make—in both planning and implementing instruction that contributed to a poorly executed lesson. Most obviously, few if any of the complications that occurred were anticipated and planned for. Heath and Heath (2008), borrowing from the military adage attributed to Helmuth von Moltke that "no battle plan survives contact with the enemy," suggested that applied to education, this axiom might be "no lesson plan survives contact with teenagers." The complexity and unpredictability of adolescent learners would appear to be among Heath and Heath's main points, but it may be instructive to consider as well just how complex classroom teaching can be. For example, what learner factors do teachers really control? A student's genetic predispositions, socio-economic background, dominant language, home life, nutrition, and physical and mental health are largely, if not wholly, beyond the control of the individual teacher. Environmental variables also come into play—how clean, orderly, and safe are school grounds? Are school routines structured in ways that increase opportunities for engaged instructional time (a known correlate of achievement), and minimize instructionally irrelevant disruptions and distractions? The exponential complexity brought on by the interplay among school, community, child, and family variables cannot be overstated. For example, did a given student leave a chaotic home this morning? How many hours did the student sleep last night? What kind of food—if any—did the student eat this morning? Was the student harassed or bullied on the way to school? Can the student read instructional material at a level of comprehension that allows them to keep pace with instruction? Did the student master basic factoring when she or he took Algebra I two years ago? Indeed is it even possible to know—let alone control or account for—all of the potential school, community, child, and family variables that might affect a child and which carry potentially significant implications for their education?

In the case described earlier, the teacher clearly did not anticipate *all* possible scenarios, and in truth it is clearly impossible to do so. Pilot Chesley ("Sully") Sullenberger, credited with safely landing an Airbus A320 aircraft on the Hudson River in 2009 following catastrophic engine failures, famously reported that he did nothing heroic or out of the ordinary. Rather, he matter-of-factly ascribed his cool demeanor and calm handling of an extraordinarily complex, stressful, and potentially fatal situation to years of experience and training, which of course included a checklist of steps to take in the event of engine failure (though he further noted in one interview that in the 208 seconds between engine failure and his airplane hitting the water, he and his crew completed only 1 page of their 3-page checklist). But despite having logged 20,000 flight hours and countless hours of additional training (not to mention having a three-page checklist to follow), Sullenberger further reported that he had *never* practiced nor even prepared for the specific circumstances he encountered that day. So what allowed him to be successful?

The complexity and unpredictability of learners will probably never compare to a bird strike and double engine failure on a fully loaded 50-ton aircraft, and the importance of an Algebra lesson pales in comparison to the need to guide a powerless aircraft with more than 150 people on board to some relatively safe landing spot amidst the most densely populated city in the United States. Still, something about Sullenberger's decision-making seems worth knowing when we consider the vast number of decisions teachers must make in rapid succession, often with distractions swirling around them. How did Sullenberger make the decisions he made? Did he have time to think about or ponder options? If, as he has suggested, he had literally never prepared for these specific circumstances, how did he carry off a reportedly flawless set of decisions that probably represented the only possible way he and his passengers could have survived?

It may be worth noting that despite being almost universally hailed as a national hero, Sullenberger was not uniformly praised as a pilot of any particularly exceptional skill. Langewiesche (2009), for example, noted that although the captain certainly showed extraordinary concentration and focus under duress, there was nothing particularly noteworthy about his *piloting* skills—nothing, according to Langewiesche, that any equally experienced pilot with similar training would not have done. Charges of hero-bashing aside, this observation makes the point all the more compelling—how is such concentration and decision-making under extreme distress possible? Moreover, if Langewiesche is correct, such well-developed decision-making is not only possible but common among pilots. The question for special educators is this: are well-trained and experienced teachers also able to make good decisions on a regular basis in the context of a rapidly changing, potentially chaotic classroom environments?

Heath and Heath (2008) continued their "battle-plan" metaphor by further suggesting that in the case of the military, something called *commander's intent* drives the successful altering of plans once resistance is encountered and original plans seem doomed to fail. That is, missions are not simply scrapped altogether when plans fall apart; rather, successful leaders (or pilots, or teachers) maintain focus on achieving the desired objective—the commander's intent, in military parlance—regardless of how plans must be altered in order to do so. The driving factor here is keeping the objective or desired outcome in mind, or more specifically on maintaining a focus on what needs to happen to achieve the desired outcome, rather than becoming consumed with fixing a doomed plan. In the case of Captain Sullenberger, it was true that significant effort was devoted to restarting the stalled engines, but this was done as a matter of course (according to the checklist), and carried out by a co-pilot; the captain himself focused his attention on achieving the key objective: getting the plane safely to the ground (or as it turned out, to the water).

In the reminder of this chapter, I first consider the notion of teaching as decision-making in special education, and argue that teachers can indeed become adept at making multiple critical decisions in rapid succession in the context of classrooms. How they reach this level of decision-making proficiency remains elusive, but I suggest that science and logic are solid guideposts. Next, I discuss two key reasons that science and logic are not viewed as helpful by huge numbers of important stakeholders in education: (a) science does not really answer education's most vexing questions, and (b) science does not really answer questions at all, but only speaks to probabilities.

TEACHER AS DECISION-MAKER

In the case described previously, the teacher developed many aspects of a plan, with an apparent objective in mind: teaching students how to solve a particular type of math problem. The teacher further thought through several aspects or components of the planned lesson, believing that these additional plans would come in handy if certain events came to pass as predicted. Some of this planning even showed foresight in that the teacher predicted some of the most likely outcomes (e. g., confusion at the first demonstration; some students mastering content quickly; some students needing additional, more intensive instruction), and developed specific plans to address them (e.g., preparing additional backup examples; planning independent practice examples for those who were successful; planning for intensive doses of instruction for those who struggled).

But what about two key aspects of the process: (a) the plans for reacting to some of the specific inputs he or she did not anticipate (an interruption from the office; more students than anticipated struggling with this lesson; capable students being bored to sleep), and perhaps more importantly, (b) how to maintain focus on the objective. Without belaboring the example, some obvious fixes may have included a quick review of previous learning to make sure students had mastered and understood the skills upon which they would be building in this lesson, or perhaps pre-assessing the skill to be taught (and its prerequisite sub-skills) at the very beginning of this lesson in order to group students in advance and to better differentiate instruction.

> "The question for special educators is this: are well-trained and experienced teachers also able to make good decisions on a regular basis in the context of a rapidly changing, potentially chaotic classroom environments?"

Perhaps a larger consideration here is simply experience and practice. Would a veteran teacher be as likely to make the mistakes seen here in planning and implementing instruction? A simple view of teacher decision-making might suggest that teachers are better able to make on-the-fly, heat-of-battle decisions when they have practiced their craft repeatedly; when their responses to various instructional stimuli have become routinized. Learning the most common scenarios and practicing responses to them again and again would seem essential. Including in pre-service teachers' practice (practicum and student teaching experiences) a variety of problem scenarios and modifications to routines they might make in response to these complications seem particularly logical. Automaticity is the goal. It is what we ask of students as they learn the building blocks of more complex skills; a classic example is beginning reading. To read fluently with comprehension, a child cannot pause over each letter to think about its name, what sound it makes, or how to blend that sound with another. But in terms of teaching, is automaticity enough, and is it even possible? Recall that Sully Sullenberger had accumulated more than 20,000 hours of flight experience in addition to his specific pilot training. Based on a teacher's workday involving a very generous estimate of 6 hours of instruction, Captain Sullenberger's cockpit experience alone equates to approximately 18 years of teaching experience. But recall too that he had never prepared for nor practiced the scenario he encountered over the Hudson River. Can teachers practice and prepare for all of the possible classroom scenarios they will encounter?

Klein (1998) described what he calls "recognition-primed" decision-making, which in truth is not decision-making at all, at least not in the sense that options present themselves and are evaluated, and an individual chooses a course of action based on some judgment about likely outcomes. Wishing to study how decisions are made in high-stress or high-pressure contexts, Klein analyzed the decision-making of firefighters and nurses particularly, and was surprised to learn that many such professionals reported a similar sentiment: they seldom made decisions at all— *they don't have time*. Firefighters in particular reported that they rarely, if ever, had time to consciously consider or weigh options, but rather had to simply react, almost instantly, to the situations that presented themselves. What most had developed, according to Klein, was the ability to recognize patterns or key characteristics of the problem scenarios they encountered, which were then associated with a particular course of action. In the case of firefighters, variables such as the cause of the fire if known, precise location(s) of the fire, the nature and intensity of a fire, and the structure and layout of a home or building, are key elements of the patterns. Recognition-primed decision-making, it would seem, is precisely what Captain Sullenberger did in guiding his aircraft to a safe water landing. He perceived the problem almost instantly—his aircraft had no power. He further perceived, again, almost instantly, that at low altitude and with little air speed, this lack of power meant that seeking a conventional landing spot (i.e., another airport) was not an option. Thus, his only decision was where within an extraordinarily limited space he might even attempt to "land" the plane.

To carry Klein's (1998) analysis of decision-making under duress further, the notion of commander's intent described by Heath and Heath (2008) seems particularly relevant. Firefighters approach their job with several key priorities in mind, and even when situations deteriorate and plans change, these driving objectives remain central to their every move and decision (i.e., saving lives of occupants; keeping firefighters themselves from harm; preventing property loss and spread of the fire). That is, their plan to battle a fire may change, sometimes dramatically, but their objectives *never* change, no matter how many wrenches are thrown into a situation or how dire circumstances become. For example, no firefighter would risk the life of a civilian occupant of a home to save an empty, adjacent building.

What's a Teacher to Do?

The concepts of recognition-primed decision-making described by Klein (1998) and commander's intent described by Heath and Heath (2008) would seem to have at least some direct relevance to teaching. But these concepts are not likely to translate well to teaching unless certain conditions are apparent. First, it would seem that teachers must be clear on their intent for any given lesson or activity. Is it to maintain a quiet, orderly classroom with no disruptions or disrespect? To cover the required state standards or a particular section of the textbook in a certain class period? To have all students demonstrate mastery of a given concept by engaging in a minimum number of correct responses with 80 percent accuracy? Such intent would seem to be the essential foundation of effective instruction. Everything the teacher does in the context of a lesson—every decision they make—must be driven by how a given action or decision will allow them to accomplish their stated intent for that lesson. Heath and Heath describe an example of this intense focus on intent from the business world. In the early years of its existence, Southwest Airlines established a mantra (and thus intent) of becoming "*the* low-fare airline," and their CEO legendarily demanded that any decision made by him or any other employee should be focused on achieving that goal. When members of his staff brought him suggestions on improving any aspect of the airline, from baggage handling to flight schedules to food service, he was insistent on knowing how any proposed improvement would help Southwest become *the* low-fare airline. Even good suggestions for improving the airline were dismissed if they did not meet the stated intent. He did not wish to be known as the on-time airline, the airline with the best food, or the airline with the most flights to a given city. Their focus was clear, and all decisions had to move them toward that goal. Teachers, it would seem, need to be as committed to their goals, though perhaps settling

> "Everything the teacher does in the context of a lesson—every decision they make-- must be driven by how a given action or decision will allow them to accomplish their stated intent for that lesson."

on attainable goals that states, districts, administrators, parents, and teachers themselves all agree on as *the* priority may be the larger hurdle.

Even if suitable goals are established, teachers probably need better-developed skills in decision-making of the sort Klein (1998) described (the recognition-primed decision-making model). I alluded earlier to the concept of rehearsal and repeated practice perhaps leading to automaticity. For teachers, this means seeing a scenario and being able to react to all of the variables in play—essentially without thinking—although maintaining focus on their instructional intent. Success in developing automatic teaching skills that move teachers toward their stated intent is surely an elusive goal, and is complicated by at least two factors. The first has to do with whether such automaticity is even possible with regard to teaching. In terms of piloting aircraft, there is no doubt whatsoever that the immediate consequences of decisions are enormous. These are literally life-and-death decisions, and the stress under which decisions are made in these professions cannot be underestimated. But it may also be the case that although specific scenarios pilots encounter are innumerable, the ways in which these scenarios vary are generally (though certainly not totally) confined to measurable variables— altitude, speed, fuel, power, type and weight of aircraft, weather conditions, distance from potential landing areas, etc. Although the combinations of these variables can create an overwhelming array of possibilities, I would submit that patterns might still be discernible (e.g., having x power at y altitude and z amount of fuel on board xx miles from the airport). Classroom interactions might produce an even more dizzying array of inputs and outputs. Twenty or more generally unpredictable students with extraordinarily varied backgrounds and background knowledge in a classroom, each of whom may react differently to any given input, plus the idea of transactional influence, in which each person's behavior in turn affects the behavior or others, would seem to make the idea of pattern recognition significantly less useful (as I note later, however, this remains an empirical question).

The complexity of classrooms is but the first concern with regard to automaticity in teaching. Malcolm Gladwell (2008) earned notoriety for his assessment that 10,000 hours of practice is probably necessary to become world-class, or an expert, in any field of endeavor. There has been much debate about what Gladwell actually wrote and what he meant by it (all of which is beyond the scope and beside the point of this chapter), but suffice it to say that his concepts were probably generally accurate: (a) a massive amounts of practice are probably necessary to become expert in something; (b) this "practice" is not just repetitive engagement in the activity, but *dedicated practice*, driven by a desire to get better, and designed specifically to improve performance (see Ericsson, Krampe, & Tesch-Romer, 1993); and (c) there is nowhere near a perfect correlation, and an even less clear causal connection, between practice and world-class expertise. To this latter point, one cannot simply decide to become world-class in something, and then put in 10,000 hours of practice as a means of achieving superstardom. Indeed, Gladwell's 10,000 hour rule drew heavily from the work of psychologist K. Anders Ericsson, and in particular from a single study (Ericsson et al.) in which the authors noted the general disparities in practice hours put in by the most accomplished violinists at the Music Academy of West Berlin. The point is equally well made when one considers all teachers with 30 or more years of experience; some are incredibly skilled, facile with instruction, flexible, adaptable, and effective. Others are decidedly less so. What matters is the type of experiences (practice) they have had, and whether they were driven to improve.

SCIENCE DOES NOT ANSWER EDUCATION'S MOST VEXING QUESTIONS

Science can certainly be thought of correctly as the search for answers, but this simple characterization carries extraordinary danger of gross misinterpretation. Science does not answer policy questions, or budget questions. It does not provide particular guidance on moral or ethical dilemmas. As physicist Richard Feynman (1998) noted, any decision about a course of action really involves two questions: (a) if we do this, what will happen? and (b) *should* we do this? Questions like (a) are generally answerable by science; questions like (b) clearly are not. Consider questions school boards often grapple with when choosing among competing priorities for dwindling funds. Are drug awareness programs, afterschool programs, or remedial summer reading programs for middle schoolers the "best" way to spend money? Note that there are answerable questions embedded in each of these; for example, we can study the impact of a drug awareness program on students' attitudes toward drug use, and even their reported use or abuse of substances over time (i.e., addressing the question: if we do this, what will happen?). In fact this has been done repeatedly (see Rosenbaum & Hanson, 1998). But ultimately, someone must make a judgment as to what course of action to recommend, and although the decision can be informed by science, the call to be made requires ethics, morality, a gut feeling or instinct, or something else decidedly unscientific. Suppose we knew, for example, that Program A results in a 16 percent decrease in middle schoolers' reported drug use after one year, although Program B can result in a mean increase of 8 percentile points on a standardized assessment of children's reading ability. Which program represents the better way to allocate our resources?

Although Feynman's analysis distinguishes scientific from nonscientific questions, a greater problem may be that even when scientific questions are answered, the answers do not satisfy the layperson, practitioner, or policy-maker. The incremental nature of science is doubtless a main culprit; each answer (e.g., results of a single scientific study) generally only inches scientists closer to understanding the phenomenon under study. In addition to answering only very small parts of our questions incrementally, a second frustration may be that we seldom get a definitive answer at all. Rather, much of science results in little more than probability statements about the likely relationship between two variables.

SCIENCE DOES NOT ANSWER QUESTIONS; SCIENCE SPEAKS TO PROBABILITY

Perhaps most troubling to those who would eschew science as a guide to decision-making is the observation that science does not result in perfect decisions. Consider what is likely the most common reply by any social scientist (and indeed many in the hard sciences as well) to any question about whether a cause-and-effect relationship is observed between any two events or variables: "it depends." This uncertainty surely contributes to a distrust of, if not disdain for scientific thought, but more importantly reflects what Sagan (1996) lamented was a fundamental misunderstanding of what science is and is not. Most fundamentally, science is about prediction; scientists study relationships between variables with an eye toward discovering and describing the nature and strength of those relationships. It is exceedingly rare that any such relationship is perfect (i.e., that a correlation between two variables is 1.0). In medicine, for example, penicillin remains the recommended first course of treatment for cases of *streptococcal pharyngitis* (strep throat) (National Institutes of Health, 2012), even though up to 10 percent of the population may have adverse reactions to penicillin (see Salkind, Cuddy, & Foxworth, 2001), and the rates of streptococcal infections that are resistant to penicillin continues to climb (McCormick et al., 2003; U. S. Food & Drug Administration, 2011). In other words, penicillin will not cure 100 percent of strep throat cases, but it works in most cases, and generally works better than any other currently available treatment. In public safety, according to the National Highway Traffic Safety Administration (NHTSA), seat belt usage reduces the likelihood of fatality in an automobile crash by approximately 50 percent (2009). Note that seat belt use does not prevent all fatalities; it merely doubles the odds of survival, which makes seat belts the best currently available means of preventing automobile related fatalities.

"Most fundamentally, science is about prediction; scientists study relationships between variables with an eye toward discovering and describing the nature and strength of those relationships."

It is troubling that education decision-makers do not play the odds science allows as readily as do medicine and other disciplines. Gallagher (1998) has been among the most vocal in denigrating the utility of a positivist tradition to guide decision-making in special education. Among her arguments, it seems, was that even when interventions show positive effects for some majority of students, we can never be certain why they were less than 100 percent effective. That is, for the percentage of students for whom no improvements were observed, was the intervention poorly implemented? Or are these students cases in point of the intervention's ineffectiveness? Conversely, might some of the students who benefitted from the intervention have improved their performance without it, or performed equally well with some other intervention? Left with this uncertainty, Gallagher argued, teachers cannot know how to plan and proceed with instruction. Landrum and Tankersley (2004) reasoned that this is a false conundrum, however. When instruction fails, they argued, a skilled special educator can do much to analyze instructional sequences and students' performance, and then develop and test hypotheses about potential modifications to such elements as the specific teaching routines, materials, or feedback schedules used.

More importantly is that Gallagher (1998) and other critics have simply missed the point as to what science is all about: *prediction*. Should drivers not wear seat belts because data suggest that one might still die in an automobile crash while wearing such a restraint? Does a physician choose not to prescribe an antibiotic for strep throat because she knows that in some percentage of cases, it will simply not work? In this sense, medical jargon seems particularly apt for special education interventions. Medical professionals follow recommended *first courses* of treatment for illnesses precisely because they have been shown to be the most efficacious options. In virtually all cases, there are second (and often third and fourth) courses of treatment as well; what to try if Plan A fails, and what to try if Plan B fails, etc. For streptococcal infections, penicillin remains the preferred first course of treatment, followed by cephalosporins (Casey & Pichichero,

2004). There are certainly symptoms or complications associated with the individual case that may cause a physician to try one versus another treatment for a given patient (perhaps prescribing a cephalosporin first, instead of trying penicillin), but two facts remain. First, there are clearly preferred courses of treatment. Second, if one diverges from these indicated treatments, it is generally because of scientific reasoning (e.g., the patient has other conditions that contraindicate the typical first course; has a known drug allergy; or had a previous adverse reaction to similar drugs, and a similar side effect can be anticipated). Responsible prescribing off list is seldom because of personal choice, gut instincts, or the fact that the physician was trained in only one form of treatment and not aware of other options. Why are educators not as forceful in stating that we too have first courses of treatment? For example, we can make a number of evidence-informed statements about professionally responsible first courses of treatment for early reading failure (e.g., Torgesen, 2004), for early signs of antisocial behavior (e.g., Walker et al., 1998), or for struggles with written expression (e.g., Graham & Harris, 2003). If the field of education at large, or even the individual teacher, does not adhere to prescribed courses of treatments—treatments that have some measure of validation based on science—it seems incumbent upon educators to at least explain and justify to parents and other stakeholders the reasoning that goes into decisions about curricular, instructional, and disciplinary interventions.

CONCLUSION

Credible scientists have never claimed that science deals in absolutes, but this very fact seems to have left science by the roadside simply for its failure to achieve perfect prediction. But prediction that results in better decisions is precisely what science offers. Accumulated data allow better predictions than chance, and better predictions than choosing paths based on financial exigency, public opinion, or political will. Whether educators can embrace this notion remains to be seen. Policy-makers seem particularly unable to do so, and thus the relationship between education policy and scientific thinking remains on shaky ground (Landrum & Tankersley, 2004). At the level of the individual teacher, day-to-day practice is about decision-making, and we must become better at understanding how teachers make decisions, particularly amidst the rapidly changing array of student, classroom, and environmental variables that fly at them during the course of instruction. Complicating their task even more are increasing pressures on their performance and that of their students. We know some things about how decisions are made in stressful or pressurized situations (Klein, 1998) and we have theories about how plans change and objectives might still be achieved when complications arise (Heath & Heath, 2008), as well as theories about the amount of practice that might result in either automaticity or high levels of expertise and proficiency. The interplay of these concepts might represent particularly fruitful lines of future research. For example, can constellations of classroom variables, which I have suggested can be overwhelming, truly be distilled into patterns that teachers can come to recognize instantly as Klein's model suggests (and which Chesley Sullenberger did over the Hudson River in 2009)? Moreover, can this result in instantaneous decisions on the part of teachers as to courses of action to take? The notion of dedicated practice was also raised, and future research is clearly needed on both (a) whether teachers can indeed adopt a model similar to Klein's recognition-primed decision-making, and if so, (b) whether they can consistently implement *evidence-based* decisions. Simply making decisions quickly is of no particular use if the decisions are haphazard or unlikely to meet with success. Finally, just how much practice, and of what type, will be needed if we expect teachers to truly gain a high level of facility in implementing effective instruction, not to mention the ability to not only recognize the need for adaptation but to seamlessly adapt instruction on the fly?

> "It is troubling that education decision-makers do not play the odds science allows as readily as do medicine and other disciplines."

Carl Sagan's (1996) treatment of the devaluation of science and scientific thinking was certainly not directed toward special education, but his messages seem to resonate sharply within our field more than a decade later. To be sure, there are many unresolved issues with regard to precisely how to follow science in translating research into practice; simply stating that we should use science to guide our thinking in education is woefully naïve. Cook and others (see Cook, Cook, & Landrum, 2013; Cook, Tankersley, & Landrum, 2009) have written extensively about the challenges in defining "evidence" in education research, and more specifically about how to translate that research into practice. Special education scholars have much work to do grappling in earnest with a set of concepts around determining what works. But in the meantime, science has laid a foundation for effective practice, and more importantly a foundation for the framework in which decisions are made, practices are implemented, their effects monitored, and instruction altered as needed. Sagan lamented that U.S. schools and American schooling have not prepared particularly logical thinkers, nor skeptics who question supposed facts and test out hypotheses in systematic ways. He marveled at the widespread acceptance of fanciful notions completely devoid of data or even any logical basis in fact (e.g., alien abductions). Perhaps more troubling than unfounded beliefs that sasquatches roam the Pacific Northwest are concerns about the more subtle errors in judgment and illogical decision-making that seem to pervade the human experience, particularly as they impact education. We generally trust our physicians and pilots to make sound decisions. Why we would expect less of educators seems especially illogical.

Discussion Questions

1. What arguments might some people put forth *against* using science as the guide for determining which practices special education should employ?
2. Landrum illustrates the number of decisions teachers may make during an instructional event. He also makes the point that automaticity of decision-making is important. How do we educate teachers to use science automatically to make decisions?
3. What should the relationship between use of a practice and outcome be in order to endorse it? Should it double the student's chances of learning a skill or is having a 10 percent likelihood of being successful a good enough reason for a teacher to use that practice?
4. Landrum asks, "Why are educators not as forceful [as medical experts] in stating that we too have first courses of treatment?" What do you think?

TIMOTHY J. LANDRUM'S SUGGESTIONS
FOR FURTHER READING

Landrum, T. J., Cook, B. G., Tankersley, M., & Fitzgerald, S. (2002). Teachers' perceptions of the trustworthiness, useability, and accessibility of information from different sources. *Remedial and Special Education, 23(1)*, 42–48.

Landrum, T. J., & Kauffman, J. M. (2006). Behavioral approaches to classroom management. In C. M. Evertson & C. S. Weinstein (Eds.), *Handbook of classroom management: Research, practice, and contemporary issues* (pp. 47–71). Mahwah, NJ: Erlbaum.

Landrum, T. J., Scott, T. M., & Lingo, A. S. (2011). Classroom misbehavior is predictable and preventable. *Kappan, 93(2)*, 30–34.

Landrum, T. J., & Tankersley, M. (1999). Emotional and behavioral disorders in the new millennium: The future is now. *Behavioral Disorders, 24*, 319–330.

Landrum, T. J., & Tankersley, M. (2004). Science in the schoolhouse: An uninvited guest. *Journal of Learning Disabilities, 37*, 207–212.

Landrum, T. J., Tankersley, M., & Kauffman, J. M. (2003). What's special about special education for students with emotional or behavioral disorders? *The Journal of Special Education, 37*, 148–156.

REFERENCES

Casey, J. R., & Pichichero, M. E. (2004). Meta-analysis of cephalosporin versus penicillin treatment of group A streptococcal tonsillopharyngitis in children. *Pediatrics, 113*, 866–882.

Cook, B. G., Cook, L. H., & Landrum, T. J. (2013). Moving research into practice: Can we make dissemination stick? *Exceptional Children, 79*, 163–180.

Cook, B. G., Tankersley, M., & Landrum, T. J. (2009) Determining evidence-based practices in special education. *Exceptional Children, 75*, 365–383.

Ericsson, K. A., Krampe, R., & Tesch-Romer, C. (1993). The role of deliberate practice in the acquisition of expert performance. *Psychological Review, 100*, 363–406.

Feynman, R. P. (1998). *The meaning of it all: Thoughts of a citizen-scientist.* Reading, MA: Perseus Books.

Gallagher, D. (1998). The scientific knowledge base of special education: Do we know what we think we know? *Exceptional Children, 64*, 493–502.

Gladwell, M. (2008). *Outliers: The story of success.* New York: Little, Brown and Company.

Graham, S., & Harris, K. R. (2003). Students with learning disabilities and the process of writing: A meta-analysis of SRSD studies. In H. L. Swanson, K. R. Harris, & S. Graham (Eds.), *Handbook of learning disabilities* (pp. 323–344). New York: Guilford.

Heath, C., & Heath, D. (2008). *Made to stick: Why some ideas survive and others die.* New York: Random House.

Kauffman, J. M. (2011). *Toward a science of education: The battle between rogue and real science.* Verona, WI: Attainment.

Kauffman, J. M. (2012). Science and the education of teachers. In R. Detrich, R. Keyworth, & J. States (Eds.), *Advances in evidence-based education. Volume 2. Education at the crossroads: The state of teacher preparation* (pp. 47–64). Oakland, CA: The Wing Institute

Klein, G. (1998). *Sources of power: How people make decisions.* Cambridge, MA: The MIT Press.

Landrum, T. J., & Tankersley, M. (2004). Science in the schoolhouse: The uninvited guest. *Journal of Learning Disabilities, 37*, 207–212.

Langewiesche, W. (2009). *Fly by wire: The geese, the glide, the miracle on the Hudson.* New York: Farrar, Straus, & Giroux.

McCormick, A. W., Whitney, C. G., Farley, M. M., Lynfield, R., Harrison, L. H., Bennett, N. M., et al. (2003). Geographic diversity and temporal trends of antimicrobial resistance in Streptococcus pneumoniae in the United States. *Nature Medicine, 9*, 424–430.

Rosenbaum, D. P., & Hanson, G. S. (1998). Assessing the effects of school-based drug education: A six-year multilevel analysis of Project D.A.R.E. *Journal of Research in Crime and Delinquency, 35*, 381–412.

Sagan, C. (1996). *The demon-haunted world: Science as a candle in the dark.* New York: Random House.

Salkind, A. R., Cuddy, P. G., & Foxworth, J. W. (2001). Is this patient allergic to penicillin? An evidence-based analysis of the likelihood of penicillin allergy. *Journal of the American Medical Association, 285*, 2498–2505.

Sasso, G. M. (2001). The retreat from inquiry and knowledge in special education. *Journal of Special Education, 34*, 178–193.

Torgesen, J. K. (2004). Lessons learned from research on interventions for students who have difficulty learning to read. In P. McCardle & V. Chhabra (Eds.), *The voice of evidence in reading research* (pp. 355–382). Baltimore, MD: Paul H. Brookes.

U. S. Food and Drug Administration (2011). *Combating antibiotic resistance.* Retrieved from http://www.fda.gov/downloads/ForConsumers/ConsumerUpdates/UCM143470.pdf.

Walker, H. M., Severson, H. H., Feil, E. G., Stiller, B., & Golly, A. (1998). First Step to Success: Intervening at the point of school entry to prevent antisocial behavior patterns. *Psychology in the Schools, 35*, 259–269.

Section VII

WHITHER SPECIAL EDUCATION?

In what directions will special education go in the future? What issues will future special educators confront? Given today's reforms, restructuring, and redistribution of funding, might special education simply become one form of general education? Should it?

- Will it ever be possible to provide *special* education without being planned, intense, relentless, purposeful, and goal-driven teaching that is essential for individualized instruction?
- Will technology make it possible to eliminate the need for most special education?
- Where should we turn for the answers to the who, what, where, when, why, and how of special education?
- Who will solve the future issues in special education?

Getting to Know Christine Balan

When I was in high school, working as a lifeguard during the summers, I was *volunteered* to be the teacher in an experimental adapted aquatics class for children with disabilities. Honestly, I was a little more than apprehensive as I began, but soon found that I really enjoyed the students and the challenges of my new position.

The more I worked with children with disabilities, the more I wanted to and I quickly began a graduate assistantship with the Kent State University Motor and Leisure Skills Program (MLSP). I was in charge of a group of 3–5 year olds, with and without disabilities, in a recreation setting. In this position, I learned the importance and relative ease with which skills could be adapted so that every child in the group could participate.

This knowledge translated to my work with adults, as well. After completing my Master's degree in motor development, I began a position as a Qualified Mental Retardation Professional (Q.M.R.P., using the parlance of the times) in a residential treatment center, even though I neither felt qualified, nor professional. In many respects, I think my uneasiness with my title actually helped me do a better job as a Q.M.R.P. I didn't have preconceived notions about what skills men aged 18–72, who were diagnosed with moderate to severe mental retardation, emotional disorders, and severe behavioral disorders could and, more importantly, couldn't learn. While the lack of specialized training often brought me into conflict with the administration at the facility, I was undeterred in my quest to get my clients out into the community, off of unnecessary medication, and making choices about daily living tasks. This position brought with it a quick baptism into the world of behavioral interventions and raised questions about the effectiveness of pharmacological interventions. I had to know more.

In my doctoral program, I focused on applied behavior analysis, and the use of positive behavioral interventions to prevent problem behaviors. Additionally, I focused on pharmacological interventions—the drugs that were administered to each one of my residents in an attempt to reduce or eliminate dramatic aggressive, self-injurious, or stereotypic behaviors. I was convinced that, like behavioral interventions, there was a way to evaluate the effectiveness of pharmacological interventions and to reduce or eliminate the ones that were not effective.

I have translated these foci into a career as a faculty member in the Special Education program at Kent State University and as consultant to school districts and nursing homes. I believe that the more teachers and service providers can approach their students, clients, or residents and see possibility, the more willing we are to look for and implement positive and effective interventions.

Getting to Know Patricia A. Lloyd

I had no intention of becoming a teacher. After 12 years of being taught by nuns, the prospect of emulating them did not appeal to me. So it was serendipity that brought the goodness of young children into my life. That, and of course, sitting on a bench at Cal State L.A. with John Lloyd, as a group of skipping children passed us. We followed them down to a basement classroom (even then special education students were in the basement) and the rest is history.

My life, fortunately, continued to be involved with the goodness of those very special children—from teaching in private schools, to being a foster parent (see John Lloyd's entry), to working in a group home for adults with severe impairments, to directing the Child Development Center at the University of Virginia, to being a school administrator and reading teacher (probably my favorite, as using an evidence-based Direct Instruction program helped the students to grow by leaps and bounds, much to the amazement of fellow teachers, who espoused the notion that "those kids can't learn").

After retirement (I'm still waiting for John to join me), I've had the opportunity to supervise student teachers and coach teachers in the field, to throw around ideas related to special education, effective instruction, and just what it is that makes a good teacher (is it an art or a science?) with John and other colleagues.

As I reflect back on my career, it's been more about learning from those children than anything I may have imparted to them. I'm also amazed that both John and I started our careers with little formal training in teaching or special education. It would be polite to say that we "were flying by the seat of our pants." The children were patient with us and allowed us to grow in wisdom and grace under their good tutelage (and fine mentors, including Barb Bateman, Zig Engelmann, Hill Walker, and Adelle Renzaglia, to name only a few). I shall always be grateful.

28

WHITHER SPECIAL EDUCATION?

John Wills Lloyd, Melody Tankersley, Barbara Bateman,
Christine Balan, & Patricia A. Lloyd

Although we organized the story of special education using the familiar five Ws and an H, we took some liberties with that structure. For example, the sections of this book do not occur in the order in which one usually encounters the six questions. However, the questions, in whatever order, still help to structure the discussion. The outstanding contributors to this volume explained many important ideas regarding issues in their areas of expertise related to these topics.

However, the chapters in this book do not cover all the issues in special education. To exhaust the controversies in special education would require a multi-volume treatise, perhaps one for each of the six areas we used here and a seventh for topics that did not fit neatly into those six. In this chapter, we shall provide (a) a recap of the concepts, (b) a précis of some omitted issues, and (c) a discussion about some issues we anticipate will arise as readers of this book progress through their careers. As will become apparent, those topics we address in the last two sections actually still fit the structure you have followed so far.

REVIEW

At the beginning of this text, we challenged readers to think about the provision of services to students with disabilities and educators' positions in relation to some of the most substantial questions in the field of special education. In this section we briefly revisit what Kipling called "six honest serving-men" for a quick summary of the main topics covered by the authors of the previous chapters.

What is Special Education?

Special education is, as many authors in this volume noted, specially designed instruction that should meet the unique needs of learners who have disabilities and require such instruction. Scruggs and Mastropieri (Chapter 3) clearly enumerated the instructional necessities of special education—the *things* that make special education special and different from other forms of education. Specifically, they discussed how special education teaches things that are not commonly part of the general education curriculum; teaches things that are not directly taught in the general education curriculum, but are things that students need to know to be successful in school; teaches things that must be learned differently; and teaches using a different pace and intensity of instruction than is found (and different than is necessary) in a general education curriculum. Pullen and Hallahan (Chapter 4) and Kame'enui (Chapter 6) echoed these areas of difference and concluded that the characteristics of instruction unique to special education, indeed its very architecture, are that its structure and form and its theory-based content is communicated explicitly and systematically, with intensity, and focused on providing frequent corrective feedback and reinforcement.

Browder (Chapter 5) gave us the example upon which we can pull these instructional *things* together by asking us to consider the notion of specialized, individualized instruction of academic skills to learners with moderate and severe disabilities. This idea is so fundamental to thinking about special education in the U.S. that it is codified into law: "specially designed instruction . . . to meet the unique needs of a child who has a disability." Special education requires carefully planned and faithfully executed instruction that goes beyond regular education.

Who Should Receive and Provide Special Education?

As Pullen and Hallahan (Chapter 4) noted in their discussion of *What*, it seems unreasonable to expect that a general education teacher could provide the vast array of services that students with disabilities require in the general education classroom. In the *Who* section, Klingner and her colleagues (Chapter 8), Lembke (Chapter 9), Weiss (Chapter 10), and Rock and Billingsley (Chapter 11) discussed diverse topics related to the people involved in special education. Of course, we know that there are students, teachers (including future teachers), co-teachers, and parents involved but, thanks to other authors, it is clear that there are many others engaged in the enterprise of special education, too. From Cook (Chapter 17) and Landrum (Chapter 27), to name only two, it is clear that there are many researchers who contribute to the fabric of special education. Parrish (Chapter 26) referred to data that illustrate the importance of considering administrators' and policy makers' roles in special education and Huefner (Chapter 14) provided an overview of the legislative rule-makers' critical importance in the process. Certainly, special education requires many individuals from many different vantage points to ensure that we provide appropriate access, instruction, and services to students with disabilities.

Lembke (Chapter 9) walked us through the process of determining *Who* is identified and how making decisions using data and evidence-based practices are critical components to the on-going process of determining who receives special education. Rock and Billingsley (Chapter 11) pointed out that knowing who receives special education is one part of the equation of delivering special education; who teaches students with disabilities requires capable, caring, and committed teachers who were prepared through intensive pre-service programs to be able to provide the relentless, intensive, and individualized instruction that our *What* authors (Scruggs and Mastropieri, Chapter 3; Pullen and Hallahan, Chapter 4; Browder, Chapter 5; and Kame'enui, Chapter 6) described. However, as Weiss (Chapter 10) pointed out, not every teacher is able to do this. And not every teacher will fit the criteria needed to work effectively in a co-teaching arrangement. As educators consider *Who* provides special education, the teachers and the arrangements through which they teach, they also need to ensure that the tenets of *What* constitutes special education can be provided effectively.

Where Should Special Education Take Place?

It is interesting to us that where special education should take place has been and remains such a hot-button issue. However, considering Wiley's (Chapter 15) discussion on moral judgments and given the social complexities surrounding it, perhaps we should not be surprised that issues related to where specialized instruction occurs remain relevant today.

As Zigmond (Chapter 13) described, the question of *Who* delivers *specialized instruction* to students with disabilities is inextricably tied to the question of *Where* these services are delivered. In the past few decades, the question of *Where* seemed to dominate the field of special education. Where special education takes place is very important to the implementation of special education practice (the *How*), but we do have strong guidance from IDEA, as Huefner (Chapter 14) explained. *Where* students with disabilities receive specialized instruction must allow those students access to students without disabilities to the greatest extent possible, but it must do so without compromising their *appropriate, individualized* education. Certainly, where students with disabilities receive specialized instruction is closely linked to questions of what special education is and how it is practiced. Zigmond advanced one unequivocal position in relation to *Where*: Place doesn't matter if educators are not providing appropriate, specialized instruction. The place *Where* instruction occurs must provide the elements of special education discussed in the *What* section and provide the foundations for effective instruction presented in the *How* section.

How is Special Education Practiced?

Certainly, the question of how educators practice special education—or more critically, how special educators practice special education well—is very important. As we discussed in the opening chapter to the *How* section, the issues of practice are at both a macro-level and micro-level of concern. The authors of chapters in the *How* section discussed contemporary issues, some of which have already been raised in previous chapters. For example, Lembke (Chapter 9) discussed the use of multi-tiered methods for identifying who receives special education services in that previous section of the text. The multi-tiered model that became popular during the 2000s has also become a structure for *How* special education is practiced. Lane and Walker (Chapter 18) discussed using this structure and the assessments that are engrained within it to provide an accurate and up-to-date picture of students' strengths and weaknesses to guide instructional decisions. Similarly, Greenwood (Chapter 19) provided evidence for structuring the learning environment to improve students' levels of responding—the basic building block of effective instruction. The delivery of special education practice is a micro-level issue of substantial importance to researchers and practitioners alike.

Cook's topic (Chapter 17), evidence-based practices, was implicitly considered by many of the previous authors, but he focused us on what they are and the importance of identifying and using them. Because of the diverse and specialized needs of students with disabilities, special educators must use practices that provide the best likelihood of effective instruction and beneficial outcomes. In line with Cook's plea for use of evidence-based practices, Thurlow (Chapter 20) reminded readers of the importance of evaluating how special education is implemented, focusing on both personal and social outcomes as well as academic achievement outcomes of students with disabilities.

When Should Students be Identified and Receive Services?

There are many answers to the questions about when special education happens, because there are many questions about that issue. Is the question about when society should begin to provide special education services? Or at what age should society stop providing special education? Does special education only pertain to schooling, not the training in children's homes and other environments (e.g., parks, stores, work environments) where they need to apply skills they are learning?

Answers to these questions depend on many factors, such as our view of disability and services as Wehmeyer (Chapter 23) explained, or on the needs of the child as Carta (Chapter 22) discussed. In essence, Carta said special education should begin as early as possible and Wehmeyer said that he hoped supports would come without stigma some see as associated with the provision of special education for most students. As their colleagues said in the previous sections, students need intentional, individualized, and specialized instruction in as natural a setting as it is possible to deliver it effectively from entry until exit and points beyond.

Why Should We have Special Education?

The social and practical implications of special education evoke very different, but related concerns. Should our society provide appropriate education to all of its children? If we don't, who does not receive it? What are the economic and political benefits of providing it and not providing it?

Kauffman (Chapter 25) tackled the question of *Why* from the perspective of human variation and the administrative and instructional considerations devoted to the delivery of special education programs, while Parrish (Chapter 26) approached the question from a fiscal perspective. Both Kauffman and Parrish discussed the importance of maintaining a unique identity and resources associated with it, as well as the importance of advancing strong outcomes of instruction. Landrum (Chapter 27) encouraged us to keep science at the center of our decision making regarding questions of why we should have special education. The three different chapters focused on three different considerations regarding *Why*, but they agreed on the importance of using evidence to guide our practice.

RECURRING THEMES

As readers probably noticed, across the sections in this book there are themes that recurred. Among these are three on which we shall focus briefly: (a) the importance of good teaching; (b) the value of reason and science in advancing special education, and (c) the importance of connecting research and practice. These themes are summarized in a quotation from a 1990s book on issues in special education (Lloyd, Kame'enui, & Chard, 1997) that honored Bateman on her retirement from full-time teaching; in that chapter, special education was aptly characterized as "first and foremost, instruction focused on individual need. It is carefully planned. It is intensive, urgent, relentless, and goal directed. It is empirically supported practice, drawn from research" (pp. 384–385). In the following subsections, we briefly recapture these ideas with references back to some of the chapter authors' expressions of these themes.

Good Teaching is Important

Perhaps readers will have heard other themes more strongly, but we think that the authors of the chapters in this book emphasized the importance of good teaching more than any other idea. It is, of course, no surprise that the authors of the chapters in the *What* section focused on the importance of teaching. Among others, Scruggs and Mastropieri (Chapter 3), Pullen and Hallahan (Chapter 4), Browder (Chapter 5), and Kame'enui (Chapter 6) all considered instruction to be a central part of special education. They argued articulately, clearly, and powerfully that the outcomes of students with disabilities are affected substantially by how well they are taught.

Those authors were not alone in their advocacy for instruction, however. Rock and Billingsley (Chapter 11) made the axiomatic claim that students who receive instruction from more effective teachers will make greater gains than those who are taught by less effective teachers. Zigmond (Chapter 13) harbored the same opinion regarding the chief importance of instruction and explained that she considered *What* is happening in different education settings—the instruction—to be a more important issue in special education than *Where* it is happening. Wiley (Chapter 15) then echoed Zigmond's view, asserting that place has a smaller effect than instruction on students' outcomes. In the *How* section, Cook (Chapter 17) contended that good teaching is essential for learning, and Greenwood (Chapter 19) placed teachers in control of instruction and gave instruction a leading role in affecting learning outcomes.

Based on sheer volume, the case is strong that good teaching is necessary for special education. But is good teaching sufficient? No. Although he decries failures to employ good instructional practices, Kauffman (Chapter 25) makes clear why sometimes general educators or even special educators operating in general education settings cannot provide levels of good teaching that will be sufficient to help students with disabilities. When you follow Kauffman's argument, you realize that special education requires a combination of the excellent instruction our authors have described and the unique circumstances that allow them to provide that instruction.

Special educators must remember that good instruction matters. What is more, as we develop in the next section, good instruction cannot be something that educators create anew from imagination. It must be informed by reason and science.

Reason and Science as Guides

Among publications for special educators one will encounter many articles, chapters, and books with appealing titles extolling their practical content. They often mix numbers, catchy adjectives (e.g., "surefire," "useful," "practical," and even "evidence-based"), and contemporary buzzwords ("collaboration," "cooperative," "differentiation," "inclusion," and so forth) to form a title that promises easy access to useful methods. The result is titles such as "100 Surefire Tips for Differentiation in the Inclusive Classroom" or "Inclusion for Every Day, Every School, Every Student: Practical, Evidence-based Procedures."[1]

Occasionally, a book with such a title lives up to its promise (e.g., *The Teacher's Encyclopedia of Behavior Management: 100 Problems/500 Plans for Grades K-9*; Sprick & Howard, 1995), but that is rare. More often, such books are compendia of tips and techniques that have what one might call "cosmetic-cardiac-belt appeal": They look good on their face, feel good to the heart, and appeal to the gut. They are often cast as practical, because they are based on the author's clinical experiences. However, upon careful examination, the recommendations often fail to pass logical tests and have tenuous evidentiary support; they simply do not meet standards of reason and science (Kauffman, 2011).

Another recurring theme sounded by the authors of these chapters is that reason and science should trump personal experience. Zigmond (Chapter 13) explained that passion and principle are important in debate, but resolution of questions will require that educators bring reason and rationality into those debates as well. In the same way, Landrum (Chapter 27), in discussing how teaching requires teachers to make frequent decisions, explained that reason and science should be the foundation for making those decisions effectively. Indeed, Wiley (Chapter 15) noted that groups—including groups of researchers—may make mistakes; however, as he clarified, the solution to the problem of mistakes in research is not to abandon research, but to conduct additional studies using more rigorous scientific methods. In fact, Cook (Chapter 17) may have been even more direct as he championed reason and evidence in discussing how scientific research rather than personal experience or traditions—or even expert opinion—should be the foremost measure or gauge of effectiveness. Other authors confirmed these ideas in their chapters, too.

Research Matters for Practice

Although reason and evidence must be educators' guides to practice, it is not always possible to test everything. Indeed, special education itself has not been tested rigorously; doing so would present quite a challenge, as indicated in Box 28.1. We shall develop this idea further in a later section, but here we note that sometimes reason—logical thinking—is the primary guide for resolving issues. Kauffman (Chapter 25) described such a case when he explained that the two primary explanations (one administrative and one instructional) for why we have special education have not been tested experimentally. Still, research findings provide critically important foundations for the practice of special education.

Box 28.1 A Special Education Thought Experiment

Suppose that scientists were asked to test the effectiveness of special education in an experimental way. That is, imagine that the people who condemn special education as a dead-end trap, something that does more harm than good (Colvin & Helfand, 1999; Hettleman, 2004; Rudin, 2010; Worth, 1999), were to be able to evaluate their claim that no special education is better than special education.

Although this experiment would be subject to many of the problems of most experiments, and it probably would be very difficult to conduct it in the real world, let's suppose that it can be conducted and be done with the utmost care and precision.

How would we design this experiment? If we want to test the effectiveness of special education, we need to think about special education broadly. As Carta (Chapter 22) explained, sometimes it is important to begin special education at birth. So, our imaginary study will have to begin tracking children then. Also, if we are going to test special education's effects, we would want to test it for the many different types of disabilities that come under the umbrella of IDEA. Some of those disabilities occur with greater frequency than others, and because some occur infrequently, we would have to follow a lot of babies just to catch one child who was deaf. What is more, so that we would have enough children with any given low-incidence disability that we could get trustworthy statistical data, we would need to follow even more babies; for example, although actual prevalence is difficult to determine, the number of children who have traumatic brain injury (TBI) probably is no more than 3 in 1000 (Hawley, Ward, Long, Owen, & Magnay, 2003; McKinlay, Grace, Horwood, Fergusson, Ridder, & MacFarlane, 2008), so to have 60 individuals who might acquire TBI we would probably have to follow at least 20,000 babies, and probably 30,000 would be safer.

Following 30,000 babies would provide enough participating children for one of the experimental conditions. In an experiment, one needs at least an "experimental" and a "control" group. Let's imagine that any children with disabilities of any sort in one group of 30,000 babies will not receive any form of special education (even though this would be illegal under the laws of many countries, including the U.S.'s IDEA, and also morally untenable); we can call this the experimental group.

In the control group, however, if an individual has a disability, she or he will receive special education services. Moreover, let us stipulate that the special education will be of the sort implied in the chapters of this book. If an infant, toddler, or very young child shows the need for special education services, instruction consistent with the recommendations by Carta (Chapter 22) and Greenwood (Chapter 19) will be provided. For those children who are identified and placed using reasonable procedures as discussed by Huefner (Chapter 14), their teachers will deliver powerful instruction such as described by Scruggs and Mastropieri (Chapter 3), Pullen and Hallahan (Chapter 4), and Browder (Chapter 5). Assessments will be conducted consistently throughout schooling in ways described by Lembke (Chapter 9), Lane and Walker (Chapter 18), and Thurlow (Chapter 20) and appropriate adjustments will be made for those students who need modifications in their academic and social-behavioral instruction.

As in any good experiment, we would need to measure outcomes carefully. Let's suppose that we could have lots of reasonable measures, so we could have a broad, conceptual measure for each outcome as well as more specific measures for certain outcomes (e.g., reading braille). And, remember, because we are likely to have enough participants with each disability (even though those in the experimental group will not ever have been formally identified), we should be able ask specific questions on a disability-by-disability basis.

- In which group will there be fewer dropouts?
- In which group will there be more school completers among students with Down syndrome?
- Which group of parents will be happier with their children's educational progress?
- In which group will students with disabilities have more friends who do not have disabilities?
- In which group will students with autism average higher scores on state tests?

There are many other questions that can be added. Make up some!

Different kinds of research provide different kinds of direction for practice, and some of those kinds of research provide relatively more informative and powerful direction than other kinds (Grossen, 1998; Lloyd, Pullen, Tankersley, & Lloyd, 2006). Whereas descriptive research (e.g., case studies) can be engaging and helpful, they are open to many possible interpretations and, therefore, cannot yield the explicit directions about which practices benefit students that can be gleaned from true experiments (including single-case methods). Similarly, *basic* research such as studies of child development may show that children behave in certain ways at particular ages (i.e., "stages"), but to help educators understand how to create instructional environments that accelerate children's progress in mastering concepts or operations that are acquired in those stages at those ages we have to conduct experiments that test one method compared to another method. Only experimental research can provide those sorts of results (Lloyd et al., 2006).

The authors of chapters in this volume have explained the importance of powerful evidence repeatedly. For example, Browder (Chapter 5) discussed how important it is for teachers to have templates, commercially available products, models of blended practices, and academic instructional procedures, and community-referenced instructional practices that have been tested. Cook (Chapter 17) explained why it is important for teachers to know what works, why that knowledge is a prerequisite for providing optimally effective instruction. And Carta (Chapter 22) argued that one of the most important challenges for professional educators in contemporary early-childhood education—and we think it applies across age levels—is helping teachers who have a wide range of background knowledge, experience, and preparation to learn about and employ evidence-based practice and employ them with a high levels of fidelity.

Bringing research into practice has been a recurring theme in special education. Science, as Landrum and Tankersley (2004) aptly noted, too often seems like an uninvited guest in schoolhouses. Teachers apparently do not depend on reports in journals when seeking information about teaching procedures (Landrum, Cook, Tankersley, & Fitzgerald, 2002) and some educators even seem to embrace anti-scientific slogans and reject evidence (Kauffman, 2010).

Carnine (1997) identified critical impediments to the use of research by educators. Some of these problems lie with the research and researchers and others lie with the research consumers and their application of research. On the research side, Carnine identified three features of research that merited improvement: *trustworthiness* (how much teachers can readily depend on research to provide them guidance), *usability* (how practical and applicable the results of research are for practicing educators), and *accessibility* (how easy it is for practicing educators to understand the often arcane and impenetrable language and methods of research).

On the consumer side, Carnine (1997) called on professional organizations, legislators, business groups, and others to promote and support the adoption of evidence-based procedures. He recommended collaboration among the various stakeholders, meeting as organizations and individuals with shared interests, to pursue a common goal. More recently, after additional review and analyses, other notable experts in special education (e.g., Greenwood & Abbott, 2001) have recommended similar actions. To date, a bridge between research and practice has not been built. When it is built, we expect that it will need to be a two-way span, running both from research to practice and practice to research (Carnine, 1997; Cook & Odom, 2013; Sugai Horner, & Sprague, 1999).

Researchers will learn a great deal from practices in the field both about what to study and what it takes to make things work regularly at scale.

Without an increasingly close relationship between research and practice, however, children and youths with disabilities will be shortchanged. They will not have the benefits of receiving the most effective practices implemented in ways that have been tested and shown to be more helpful than alternatives. Given that students in special education require special education (i.e., *extra*ordinary teaching), we cannot simply offer them general education, even if it is good general education. Providing special instruction requires that we identify and implement—with fidelity—the most efficient and effective practices known. The authors of many of the chapters presented here repeatedly noted that:

- Instruction must be planned, intense, purposeful, and relentless.
- Instruction must be specially designed and based on the individualized needs of the learner, and it must be provided where the teacher can provide it and learner can access it.
- Services must be grounded in science and in the law.
- Data-based decisions are required for administration, funding, identification, implementation, evaluation, and every action in-between those.

Whither special education goeth, it should go with these basic tenets at its foundation.

THE MISSING

Some topics that have been hot button issues in education have not been extensively addressed in the foregoing pages, however. For example, the debate about educationally explicit and systematic approaches versus discovery methods, described by Carta (Chapter 22), has only light coverage in this book; the evidence is stronger for the effectiveness of explicit and systematic approaches, yet debates persist. The absence of such hot button issues does not indicate that they are insignificant. It is simply a consequence of the structure of the book, the foci of the contributors, and the current emphases of the time when this volume was assembled. To provide direction for further study, however, we briefly catalog some other topics that are often discussed but not yet settled.

Gifted Education

One of the most substantial omissions in this treatment of special education is that there is virtually no discussion of giftedness. Education for students who have unusual gifts and talents is just as contentious as any other area of special education. As with most other categories of disabilities, gifted education suffers from stereotypes. For example, among the common myths that Hallahan, Kauffman, and Pullen list for individuals who are gifted are that they "are physically weak, socially inept, narrow in interest, and prone to emotional instability"; "mentally unstable"; and [can] "do everything well" (2012, p. 428). As Hallahan et al. explain, these generalizations are not accurate. Consistent with our emphasis on reasoning carefully, it is clear that some students who are gifted may have one or more of these attributes, but it is a mistake to generalize from a case to the population of students who are gifted. Just because one or a few members of a group fits a pattern does not mean that all members of the group fit that pattern.

The problems of definition, identification (especially of children from different cultural and linguistic backgrounds, as discussed by Klingner et al. (in Chapter 8), and comorbidity (who), grouping (where), and programming (how) are common topics in analyses of the literature on gifted education (e.g., Callahan, 2011). Readers might be surprised to learn that issues about high-stakes assessments, as discussed by Thurlow (Chapter 20), also arise for students identified as gifted; for example, instead of differentiating instruction in ways that would help students who are gifted, they are more likely to revert to a "one-size-fits-all" approach when preparing for state testing programs (Moon, Brighton, & Callahan, 2003). Similarly, as authors have noted repeatedly in their discussions (e.g., Cook, Chapter 17), there is substantial emphasis on evidence-based practices in special education, and that emphasis is also evident in gifted education (e.g., Robinson, Shore, & Enerson, 2007).

Thus, although one of the limitations of this text is the absence of a thorough discussion of issues in gifted education, readers should understand that many of the issues about which they learned from the authors in these chapters resonate in the sub-discipline of gifted education, too. One can learn a great deal by perusing resources available from professional organizations such as The Association for the Gifted (http://www.csectag.org) and the National Association for Gifted Children (http://nagc.org).

Labeling

Concern about identifying students with disabilities according to categorical labels has long been a recurring issue in special education. Some educators would rather see a non-categorical approach to offering special education to students who need it (e.g., Smith, Peters, Sanders, & Witz, 2010). Because many students, especially those with high-incidence disabilities of LD, EBD, and mild ID, share many learning and behavioral characteristics (Hallahan & Kauffman, 1977; phenotype-genotype), it is tempting to argue that there is no need to categorize them separately. Still, as current U.S. law is structured, students must have a disability and need special education to be eligible for special education services; once they are found eligible, then they are to receive an *individualized education plan*, not a categorical plan (not an LD, a CP, or an OHI plan). The categories are for the purposes of getting access to the services.

Most of the benefits to labels can be interpreted as having corresponding negative considerations. For example, where some (e.g., Kauffman, 2007) argue that labels have benefits in that they promote clear communication, enable more scientific classification, and so forth, others fear that the labels might lead people to perceive students in different ways. Research on this issue began years ago (see, e.g., Algozzine, Mercer, & Countermine, 1977; Severance & Gasstrom, 1977) and has been extensive. According to contemporary labeling theory, assigning a label such as "student with learning disabilities" to individuals actually causes lower outcomes by lowering teachers' and parents' expectations (e.g., Shifrer, 2013). Also, questions about labeling often are mixed with concerns about whether students of some groups, especially cultural and linguistic groups, are over-represented among some categories of special education. Although this issue was mentioned previously, we note it again here to remind readers of its importance (e.g., Trent & Artiles, 1995). For example, disproportionally fewer African-American than Caucasian children are identified as having ADHD and more identified as having EBD (Mandell, Davis, Bevans, & Guevara, 2008); disproportionally fewer Asian-American and Pacific-Islander children are identified as having intellectual disabilities or emotional and behavioral disorders than their Caucasian peers (Oswald, Coutinho, Best, & Singh, 1999). Because of issues such as these, detractors of special education will see the harm of labeling as having more weight than supporters of special education.

Technology

Applications of technology to the problems faced by individuals with disabilities is a contemporary topic in special education where controversies abound. There are many and they range from concerns about hearing to instruction. We shall take up only two as illustrations.

Cochlear implants as a cultural issue. Although there are many issues in deaf education—there are entire books on the topic (e.g., Gregory, Knight, McCrackle, Powers, & Watson, 1998)—one that has been especially controversial is the use of a technology called cochlear implants to enable deaf individuals to hear. People who have cochlear implants have surgery to place a small, electronic receiver on the side of the head near the ear; the receiver is connected to an array of electrodes that distribute impulses to different parts of the auditory nerve. They wear an external device composed of a microphone that picks up sound and a miniature speech processor that organizes the sound; these parts then send the processed sound to the receiver and, hence, on to the auditory nerves. In essence, a cochlear implant bypasses the damaged parts of the deaf person's hearing system (National Institute on Deafness and Other Communication Disorders, 2013). Although cochlear implants do not permit people to have the same level of hearing that they would if their auditory systems were intact, the implants permit them to hear well enough to recognize alarms and even to carry on conversations. Of course, children will require instruction to learn to speak, but research reveals that receiving the implant at a younger age improves outcomes (Connor, Craig, Raudenbush, Heavner, & Zwolan, 2006; Geers, Moog, Biedenstein, Breener, Hayes, 2009).

To many people, cochlear implants seem like a wonderful technology, but they are not considered desirable by some. Some individuals oppose implants because they consider them to be an attempt to fix something that the advocates do not consider a disability. Although this idea might seem foreign, allow some opponents of cochlear implants to explain:

> Conventional wisdom in medicine assumes that deaf children have a serious sensory impairment that gives rise to a disability and to social, educational, and linguistic handicaps. From that perspective, childhood deafness should be mitigated or corrected as far as possible. However, the disability construction of deafness has been challenged by deaf communities in the U.S. and abroad for more than a century (Lane, 1984).
>
> (Lane & Grodin, 1997, p. 231)

Because they challenge the conventional wisdom about deafness, Lane and Grodin strongly object to the cochlear implants. They argue that the deaf individuals form a unique sub-culture—they call it "DEAF-WORLD" and usually capitalize the word "deaf"—that is much like the culture of ethnic minorities and that "being DEAF is highly valued in DEAF culture" (p. 233). Lane and Grodin go on to discuss cochlear implants under a heading referring to eugenics and refer to questions about whether children should have cochlear implants as a dispute between deaf and hearing cultures.

> The underlying reason, we submit, that doctors and parents want cochlear prostheses for DEAF children is that their construction of those children's reality is based on disability.

The underlying reason that the DEAF-WORLD is at odds with them is that its cultural construction of the reality of DEAF children is based on the children's potential for sharing the language and culture of the DEAF-WORLD and identifying with it (Lane 1992, 1995 . . .). It follows from the disability construction that being DEAF is not a good thing and that efforts will be undertaken not only to eradicate the underpinning physical difference in the individual child with prosthetic surgery but also to prevent more children with that disability from being born through genetic counseling and genetic engineering. (Lane & Grodin, 1997, p. 242)

Here we have technology mediating the clash of cultures. The questions become complex. Do the decisions of hearing parents that their children should have cochlear implants count as eugenics or do they count as compassionate efforts to help their offspring? Reasonable people may differ. And evidence about the effects of the practice, albeit growing, will be debated. For example, although research about the social experiences of individuals who grew up with cochlear implants (e.g., Moog, Geers, Gustus, & Brenner, 2011; Percy-Smith, Cayé-Thomasen, Gudman, Jensen, & Thomsen, 2008) shows that they have friends in both the deaf and hearing communities, school experiences similar to their peers, normal self-concepts, and report good social adjustment, people will spin those results lots of different ways.

The controversy of cochlear implants underscores an important concern in understanding issues in special education. There must be a balance between people's fundamental presumptions—biases, if you will—and their accommodation of evidence. Each of us must find that fulcrum. Where is the balance between a cultural group's autonomy and a family's concern about a child? Which matters more? Perhaps some people would say that there is not any such thing as the DEAF-WORLD. Would they say that same thing about African-American culture? These are issues that merit considerate, calm discussion among caring people.

Technology and teaching and testing. Applications of technology in special education have a lengthy and broad history (Woodward & Rieth, 1997). Educators have known for a long time that simply putting computer technology in proximity to students with disabilities is not likely to engender improvements in their outcomes (Sapona, Lloyd, & Wissick, 1986). As Thurlow (Chapter 20) discussed, technologies are becoming part of assessment and they have become deeply entrenched in instruction, but they must be used intelligently (Wissick & Gardner, 2011). Some educators welcome and even applaud these developments, but they are sometimes controversial (Pitoniak, & Royer, 2001; Sireci, Scarpati, & Li, 2005).

Teachers can resolve most questions about using technology accommodations for testing the same way they can with just about any accommodation. They can simply ascertain whether a student would be allowed to use the accommodation during regular instruction. If an accommodation is allowed on a large-scale assessment and it is consistent with a student's IEP, then it should be appropriate (Edgemon, Jablonski, & Lloyd, 2006).

Universal design for learning (UDL) represents the highest-profile example of technology applied to special education (Edyburn, 2010). Its promise is that by providing multiple means of representing material, multiple means of action and expression, and multiple means of engagement, students will be able to learn and demonstrate what they have learned without being handicapped by their disabilities. Table 28.1 elaborates on these principles.

Table 28.1 The Basics of UDL

Name of the Principle:	Multiple Means of Representation	Multiple Means of Action and Expression	Multiple Means of Engagement
Explanation	Provide alternatives that overcome perceptual, language, and cognitive barriers.	Provide alternative ways that learners can navigate the environment, express what they know, and so forth.	Provide alternative ways for learners to participate in learning activities.
Examples of Usual Mechanisms	• Printed material may be inaccessible for some learners.	• Turning book pages may be impossible for some learners. • Writing essays may be difficult for some learners.	• Having structured class periods. • Having unstructured class periods.
UDL Alternatives	• Provide comparable content through different modalities (larger print; amplified sounds). • Hyperlink novel vocabulary words to video representations explaining them.	• Employ special software that "knows" when the readers' eyes reach the end of a page. • Use speech-to-text software.	• Recruit students' interest. • Have students sustain effort. • Develop students' self-regulation.

UDL principles have a lot of appeal. They have the gloss of modality-based modifications. At the extremes (e.g., blindness) it makes absolute sense to presume that instructional approaches cannot depend on visual modalities; in the big picture, teachers must be prepared to have alternatives available for students who have visual impairments. UDL advocates expand this obvious point to "the print impaired," including anyone who might not decode well. If a student has a visual problem, meaning she does not decode well, then educators should provide her with alternative representations of the material she cannot decode. Let her hear it. Have a device read it for her.

Does UDL work? Let's hope so. It has been touted in the halls of the U.S. Congress (see Hehir, 2009). In fact, a re-authorization of the U.S. special education law (IDEA, 2004) explicitly mentioned UDL in a section on National Instructional Materials Accessibility Standard. But, few data are available to establish its effectiveness. As even the advocates for UDL note, research examining the effects of it "is still in its early stages and much more will be needed" (Rose, Gravel, & Gordon, 2013, p. 485) and the Center for Applied Special Technology does not publish a list of scientific studies on the center's Web site (http://cast.org).

Rao, Ok, and Bryant (2014) searched the literature and found few research studies about UDL. They located only 13 studies overall, and five of those addressed UDL applications at the post-secondary level. Of those addressing K–12 students, many either (a) reported students' or teachers' opinions about UDL activities rather than their outcomes (e.g., Kortering, McClannon, & Braziel, 2008) or, (b) if they did report effects on students' outcomes, did not use rigorous research methods (e.g., Leiber, Horn, Palmer, & Fleming, 2008). One strong demonstration of effects on the performance of students in K–12 was in a study by Browder, Mims, Spooner, Ahlgrim-Delzell, and Lee (2008); they found that three students responded more frequently on their own when a UDL condition was introduced. In another example of a reasonable study, Proctor et al. (2011) found effects on vocabulary for English language learners; they did not study students with disabilities. Some studies have illustrated how UDL principles can mix with guidance from other instructional models to produce beneficial outcomes (e.g., Coyne, Pisha, Dalton, Zeph, & Smith, 2012; Kennedy, Thomas, Meyer, Alves, & Lloyd, 2014).

In sum, then, UDL sounds appealing. It has the cache of high technology and the authority that goes with being associated with U.S. law. It has not yet, however, demonstrated the level of scientific evidence required for endorsement as an evidence-based practice.

Whither special education situates, it must continue to work toward settling issues such as those related to gifted education, labeling, and the use of technology, as well as others that are evident in the field and that will arise over time.

THE FUTURE

Special education has changed dramatically since the 1950s, 1960s and 1970s, and 1980s and 1990s when we (BB; JWL and PAL; MT; and CB, respectively) began watching it. Some of us worked with children living in state hospitals before laws ensuring their right to attend public schools existed. Having seen those conditions, we share a reluctance to return to those days and are glad to have witnessed the deinstitutionalization movement. Other children with disabilities may not have lived in institutions, but they still did not receive systematic schooling or, if they were in schools, their needs often were not met, because there were no laws protecting them or guaranteeing access to school.

Securing children's access to schools and getting them out of sometimes-wretched environments were big issues "back in the day." But, what about the future of special education? What concerns might special educators encounter as the pressing issues in coming decades? In the next sections we discuss just two: the possible dilution of special education and international developments.

The Dilution of Special Education

In the 2004 re-authorization of IDEA, Congress added special language that permitted local education agencies to use their special education funds for "early intervening services." This was a departure from the way special education funds had been spent since 1975. Beginning in 2005, when the rules went into effect, schools could spend up to 15 percent of their special education monies on K–12 (but especially K–3) children who had "not been identified as needing special education or related services but who need additional academic and behavioral support to succeed in a general education environment" (Individuals with Disabilities Education Improvement Act of 2004, 613(f)(1)).

Twenty years earlier, Stainback and Stainback had proposed "the merger of special and regular education into a unified system structured to meet the unique needs of all students" (1984, p. 102). The 2004 change in the funding rules—providing special education funding for students not identified with a disability—breached the financial wall between the two systems. But that is only one of the ways that special education is being diluted.

Early intervening services are closely related to the response-to-instruction (RTI) movement, and RTI appears to be a factor that is contributing to the dilution of special education in its own way. Fuchs, Fuchs, and Stecker (2010) described two different perspectives on RTI and suggested that one of them was having the effect of blurring the differences between general and special education. According to their interpretation, supporters of an RTI approach predicated on a problem-solving model that is account-ability driven do not believe special education really works; they believe that full inclu-sion is a good idea, that special education funds would be better spent in other ways, and that school psychologists' efforts would be better devoted to tasks other than con-ducting eligibility assessments. When one listens to some advocates of RTI (and other general education reform efforts such as Positive Behavior Interventions and Supports), one often hears that a measure of their success is reductions in the numbers of students referred for special education. Is this the right measure of success? Is special education such a bad thing that schools should want to keep students from getting it?

As Thurlow (Chapter 20) discussed, another way that special education is being weak-ened is by the increasingly important role that standards are playing in accountability in special education. McLaughlin (2010) argued that one of the effects of standards-driven accountability—which was supposed to help close the achievement gap between students with disabilities and their non-disabled peers, but may not have done so in her estimation—has been to blur the distinction between special and general education. She speculated that as more students with disabilities are required to meet general educa-tion standards, then only the few who are held to alternative or modified standards will become recognized as "special education students."

Not only are the methods of accountability, funding, and identification for services con-tributing to the dilution of special education, instructional arrangements that involve spe-cial education teachers in differential roles in the classroom, does as well. Weiss (Chapter 10) explained some of the problems with co-teaching and presented the literature that places co-teaching, itself, as a practice that eliminates special education for many students. Special educators too often are delegated as co-teachers in classrooms where beneficial co-teaching models have not been clearly established. Should people with masters degrees and the very specialized knowledge accompanying that preparation be willing to sit still when they see ineffective practices (i.e., those that are contradicted by scientific evidence) employed with students whom they know they could teach better (cf. Tankersley, Niesz, Cook, & Woods, 2007)? How can *special* education that is planned, intense, purposeful, and relentless—the basic tenants of special education as described repeatedly by the scholars in this volume—be delivered in an individualized manner if the special education teacher is not actively engaged in the instructional process? Good general education is not *special* education; and *special* education cannot be delivered without the knowledge of practices that are grounded in science and the opportunity to provide them in an individualized manner.

As students with mild to moderate disabilities are receiving more of their instruction from general education teachers, paraprofessionals are assigned to assist students who need greater disability-related services (Cameron, Cook, & Tankersley, 2012; Giangreco, 2010). We see assigning paraprofessionals to individual students with substantial dis-abilities with the intent that those students can participate in general education classes as another consequence of the inclusion movement (Suter & Giangreco, 2009). We wonder whether this adequately constitutes special education. Should special education consist of having an un-credentialed adult serving as a full-time assistant and accompanying a student so that she can be close to her age mates? Does that align with the U.S. definition of special education in 34 C. F. R. 300.39?

It seems clear to us that special education is being diluted in its authorization, its avail-ability, and its delivery. Funds are taken from services for special education students—those who have been identified with a disability—and provided to other programs and students.

Practices encourage the reduction of numbers of students identified for special education, regardless of the need. As we hold students with disabilities to the same standards as their nondisabled peers, we teach them more often in general education classrooms with general education teachers and general education practices. Or, we provide them a well-meaning adult to sit with them. These realities do not constitute special education to us.

We would prefer—and hope that we all demand—that students with disabilities are quickly identified for special education services and receive evidence-based instruction focused on increasing their academic and social competence. Their education should be one designed and monitored by certified special educators who understand the sense and sensibility of Zigmond's characterization of special education instruction, that is "intensive, urgent, relentless, and goal directed . . . empirically supported practice, drawn from research" (1997, pp. 384–385). We are concerned about a future of special education if it turns away from a focus on the very instruction that has been one of its best heritages (Lloyd & Lloyd, in press).

Whither special education? We must ensure that special education continues and that it is not diluted in its scope or its delivery.

International Developments

In our consideration of the future of special education, another important development has been an increase in international concern about the education of children and youths with disabilities. Since their founding in the later 20th century, international organizations such as the Division for International Special Education Services (1990) and the International Association for Research in Learning Disabilities (1976), among others, have had increasing international membership and impact. In a broader realm, the United Nations (2006) promoted the Convention on the Rights of Persons with Disabilities (CRPD), one part of which addressed education and emphasized inclusion.

Inclusion (*Where*) has become an increasingly contentious concern during our careers here in the U.S. Following the deinstitutionalization movement, inclusion burst forth as "the regular education initiative" in the 1980s (Hallahan, Keller, McKinney, Lloyd, & Bryan, 1988; Lloyd, Singh, & Repp, 1991) and then it became a juggernaut sometimes with unintended consequences (e.g., Tankersley et al., 2007). With the international developments, we wonder whether it will continue to be an issue in the remaining years of this decade and the next. Might there be a reversal of the pendulum or backlash coming?

Seen from an international perspective, inclusion has a strong social justice flavor and is less concerned about practical matters such as instruction than in the U.S. For example, four organizations in Great Britain —the Alliance for Inclusive Education (ALLFIE), Disabled People Against Cuts, Equal Lives, and Inclusion London—issued a manifesto founded on 12 foundational pillars including such matters as access to information, transportation, the environment, housing, employment, and income. The pillar about education included a strong statement endorsing the right of individuals with disabilities to receive education in "one fully inclusive mainstream education system" (UK Disabled People's Manifesto: Reclaiming Our Futures, 2013, p. 4).

Although the bulk of the CRPD is devoted to broad and general matters such as equity, justice, access, freedom from torture, and so forth, one part specifically addressed education. Article 24 of the CRPD is devoted to education and it includes two references to "inclusive" education and one reference to "full inclusion": "Effective individualized support measures are provided in environments that maximize academic and social development, consistent with the goal of full inclusion" (Article 24.2.e).

A careful reading of the sentence comprising Article 24.2.e reveals support for both full inclusion and individualized education, which sounds essentially contradictory. Suppose that "full inclusion" means "the inclusion of *all* students in the mainstream of regular education classes and school activities with their age peers from the same community" (Stainback & Stainback, 1991, p. 225; emphasis in original) and "effective individualized support" requires meeting the individual educational needs of each student with a disability. If the unique needs of just one or a few of those students with disabilities required that they receive some of their education in a separate setting so they can benefit academically and socially, then there is a conflict in these goals. Which direction does one go? Should one favor the goal of inclusion or the goal of better outcomes for students?

The international inclusive schools movement seems to be substantially predicated on gaining access to education for students with sensory and physical disabilities (cf. Reiser, 2013). Those advocates in the U.S. who lived through the times when it was necessary to seek redress of grievances in the courts to gain access to schooling for children and youths with disabilities recognize that these are important efforts, and gains in these areas merit extraordinary efforts.

Still, educators in the U.S. objected to the emphasis on inclusion in the CRPD. For example, Kauffman and Badar argued that "sometimes . . . exclusion on the basis of disability is necessary to provide an appropriate education and to achieve substantive social justice" (2014, p. 14). What is more, when ratification of the CRPD was debated in the U.S. Senate, senators discussed their votes on ratification using references to abortion rights, states' rights, home-schooling, and the like (Pecquet, 2012).

"Inclusion," and especially "full inclusion," appears to mean something very different in U.S. schools than it does in international parlance. The choice of words is very important, as educators know from long experience. "Inclusion" and "inclusive" may some day be seen as restrictive, to be replaced by some other phrase with different shadings of meaning, just as "mental retardation" was replaced by "intellectual disability." In 1921, C. McFie Campbell warned as much when he talked about the history of the treatment of emotional and behavioral disorders at McLean Hospital in Waverley, Massachusetts:

> The physician of the twenty-first century may . . . look back on our halting arrangements in a maturely critical way. He may even criticize the language of the times and may find that some of our words have become as offensive to him as the term lunatic has become offensive to us. He may shudder when he reads that a sick man was 'confined in an institution' when the patient was really admitted to a hospital.
>
> (1921, p. 538)

WHITHER SPECIAL EDUCATION?

The purpose of this text was to provide readers answers to the most significant and enduring questions in the field—who, what, where, when, why, and how. The answers to these questions, answers provided by influential scholars in our field, consistently referred to the importance of good teaching, reason and science, and connecting research and practice. It seems to us that the scholars were unified in advocating that special education must remain special in order to meet the unique needs of each individual student. They were unified in the position that special education must remain intensive and focused on delivering services that are different from what is available in general education. They were unified in their insistence that the practice of special education must be based on empirical evidence. Whither special education? The readers of this text will be among those who will shape its direction and purpose. We hope they will be vigilant in considering what special education is and why they are doing it; who gets it and gives its; how and how well it is done; and when and where it is provided. Most importantly, we hope that they make sure it really is *special* education.

NOTE

1. We hasten to note that one of us (JWL) created these titles on the fly. We hope they bear no close resemblance to any actual publications, just that they are catchy enough that readers will recognize the genre when they next peruse a shelf of popular education books or search the offerings of an online bookseller in the section on special education teaching.

CHRISTINE BALAN'S SUGGESTIONS FOR FURTHER READING

Alberto, P. A., & Troutman, A. C. (2012). *Applied behavior analysis for teachers.* Boston: Pearson.
Julien, R. M., Advokat, C. D., & Comaty, J. E. (2011). *A primer of drug action.* New York: Worth Publishers.
Kauffman, J. M., & Hallahan, D. P. (2005). *Special education: What it is and why we need it.* Boston: Allyn & Bacon.
Lane, K. L., Cook, B. G., & Tankersley, M. (2012). *Research-based strategies for improving outcomes in behavior.* Boston: Pearson.
Rhode, G., Jenson, W. R., & Reavis, H. K. (2010). *The tough kid book.* Eugene: OR: Pacific Northwest Publishing.

PATRICIA LLOYD'S RECOMMENDATIONS FOR ADDITIONAL STUDY

Bateman, B. D. (2004). *Elements of conceptual teaching: General and special education students.* Verona, WI: IEP Resources.
Carnine, D. W. (2000). *Why education experts resist effective practices (and what it would take to make education more like medicine).* Washington, DC: Thomas B. Fordham Institute. Available from http://edex.s3-us-west-2.amazonaws.com/publication/pdfs/carnine_9.pdf.
Coyne, M., Kame'enui, E. J., & Carnine, D. W. (2007). *Effective teaching strategies that accommodate diverse learners.* Upper Saddle River, NJ: Pearson.
Engelmann, S. (1992). *War against the schools' academic child abuse.* Portland, OR: Halcyon House.
Kidder, T. (1989). *Among school children.* Boston, MA: Houghton Mifflin.
Lloyd, J. W., Forness, S. R., & Kavale, K. A. (1998). Some methods are more effective. *Intervention in School and Clinic, 33,* 195–200.

REFERENCES

Algozzine, B., Mercer, C. D., & Countermine, T. (1977). The effects of labels and behavior on teacher expectations. *Exceptional Children, 44,* 131–132.
Browder, D. M., Mims, P. J., Spooner, F., Ahlgrim-Delzell, L., & Lee, A. (2009). Teaching elementary students with multiple disabilities to participate in shared stories. *Research and Practice for Persons with Severe Disabilities, 33,* 3–12.
Callahan, C. M. (2011). Special gifts and talents. In J. M. Kauffman & D. P. Hallahan (Eds.), *The handbook of special education* (pp. 304–317). New York: Routledge.
Cameron, D. L., Cook, B. G., & Tankersley, M. (2012). An analysis of the different patterns of 1:1 interactions between educational professionals and their students with varying abilities in inclusive classrooms. *International Journal of Inclusive Education, 16,* 1335–1354.
Campbell, C. M. (1921). History of insanity during the past century with special reference to the Mclean Hospital. *Boston Medical and Surgical Journal, 185,* 538–544.
Carnine, D. (1997). Bridging the research-to-practice gap. *Exceptional Children, 63,* 513–521.
Colvin, R. L., & Helfand, D. (1999, December 12). Special education in state is failing on many fronts. *Los Angeles Times.* Retrieved from http://articles.latimes.com/1999/dec/12/news/mn-43238.

Connor, C. M., Craig, H. K., Raudenbush, S. W., Heavner, K., & Zwolan, T. A. (2006). The age at which young deaf children receive cochlear implants and their vocabulary and speech-production growth: Is there an added value for early implantation? *Ear and Hearing, 27*, 628–644.

Cook, B. G., & Odom, S. L. (2013). Evidence-based practices and implementation science in special education. *Exceptional Children, 79*, 135–144.

Coyne, P., Pisha B., Dalton, B., Zeph, L., & Smith, N. C. (2012). Literacy by design: A universally designed digital reading approach for young students with significant intellectual disabilities. *Remedial and Special Education, 33*, 162–172.

Edgemon, E. A., Jablonski, B. R., & Lloyd, J. W. (2006). Large-scale assessments: A teacher's guide to making decisions about accommodations. *Teaching Exceptional Children, 38*(3), 6–11.

Edyburn, D. (2010). Would you recognize universal design for learning if you saw it? Ten propositions for new directions for the second decade of UDL. *Learning Disability Quarterly, 33*, 33–41.

Fuchs, D., & Fuchs, L. S. (1994). Inclusive schools movement and the radicalization of special education reform. *Exceptional Children, 60*, 294–309.

Fuchs, D., Fuchs, L. S., & Stecker, P. M. (2010). The "blurring" of special education in a new continuum of general education placements and services. *Exceptional Children, 76*, 301–323.

Geers, A. E., Moog, J. S., Biedenstein, J., Brenner, C., & Hayes, H. (2009). Spoken language scores of children using cochlear implants compare to hearing age-mates at school entry. *Journal Deaf Studies and Deaf Education, 14*, 371–385.

Giangreco, M. F. (2010). One-to-one paraprofessionals for students with disabilities in inclusive classrooms: Is conventional wisdom wrong? *Journal Information, 48*, 1–13.

Greenwood, C. R., & Abbott, M. (2001). The research to practice gap in special education. *Teacher Education and Special Education, 24*, 276–289.

Gregory, S., Knight, P., McCracken, W., Powers, S., & Watson, L. (Eds.). (1998). *Issues in deaf education*. New York: David Fulton.

Grossen, B. (1998). What does it mean to be a research-based profession? In W. M. Evers (Ed.), *What's gone wrong with America's classrooms?* (pp. 86–98). Stanford, CA: Hoover Institution Press, Stanford University.

Hallahan, D. P., & Kauffman, J. M. (1977). Labels, categories, behaviors: ED, LD, and EMR reconsidered. *The Journal of Special Education, 11*, 139–149.

Hallahan, D., Kauffman, J. & Pullen, P. (2012). *Exceptional learners: An introduction to special education* (12th ed.). Boston: Allyn & Bacon.

Hallahan, D. P., Keller, C. E., McKinney, J. D., Lloyd, J. W., & Bryan, T. (1988). Examining the research base of the regular education initiative: Efficacy studies and the adaptive learning environments model. *Journal of Learning Disabilities, 21*, 29–35.

Hawley, C. A., Ward, A. B., Long, J., Owen, D. W., & Magnay, A. R. (2003). Prevalence of traumatic brain injury amongst children admitted to hospital in one health district: A population-based study. *Injury, 34*, 256–260.

Hehir, T. (2009). Policy foundations of universal design for learning. In D. T. Gordon, J. W. Gravel, & L. A. Schifter (Eds.), *A policy reader in universal design for learning* (pp. 35–45). Cambridge, MA: Harvard.

Hettleman, K. R. (2004). *The road to nowhere: The illusion and broken promises of special education in the Baltimore City and other public school systems*. Baltimore, MD: Abell Foundation.

Individuals with Disabilities Education Improvement Act of 2004, P.L. No. 108–446, 118 Stat. 2647 (amending 20 U.S.C. §§ 1400 et seq.).

Kauffman, J. M. (2007). Labels and the nature of special education: We need to face realities. *Learning Disabilities: A Multidisciplinary Journal, 14*, 245–248.

Kauffman, J. M. (2010). *The tragicomedy of public education: Laughing and crying, thinking and fixing*. Verona, WI: Fullcourt Press.

Kauffman, J. M. (2011). *Toward a science of education: The battle between rogue and real science*. Verona, WI: Attainment.

Kauffman, J. M., & Badar, J. (2014). Instruction, not inclusion, should be the central issue in special education: An alternative view from the USA. *Journal of International Special Needs Education, 17*(1), 13–20.

Kennedy, M. J., Thomas, C. N., Meyer, J. P., Alves, K. D., & Lloyd, J. W. (2014). Using evidence-based multimedia to improve vocabulary performance of adolescents with LD: A UDL approach. *Learning Disability Quarterly, 37*, 71–86.

Kortering, L. J., McClannon, T. W., & Braziel, P. M. (2008). Universal design for learning: A look at what algebra and biology students with and without high incidence conditions are saying. *Remedial and Special Education, 29*, 352–363.

Landrum, T. J., Cook, B. G., Tankersley, M., & Fitzgerald, S. (2002). Teacher perceptions of the trustworthiness, usability, and accessibility of information from different sources. *Remedial and Special Education, 23*, 42–48.

Landrum, T. J. & Tankersley, M. J. (2004). Science in the schoolhouse: An uninvited guest. *Journal of Learning Disabilities, 37*, 207–212.

Lane, H. (1984). *When the mind hears: A history of the deaf.* New York: Random House.

Lane, H. (1992). *The mask of benevolence: Disabling the deaf community.* New York: Alfred Knopf.

Lane, H. (1995). Constructions of deafness. *Disability and Society, 10*, 171–189.

Lane, H., & Grodin, M. (1997). Ethical issues in cochlear implant surgery: An exploration into disease, disability, and the best interests of the child. *Kennedy Institute of Ethics Journal, 7*, 231–251.

Leiber, J., Horn, E., Palmer, S., & Fleming, K. (2008). Access to the general education curriculum for preschoolers with disabilities: Children's school success. *Exceptionality, 16*, 18–32.

Lloyd, J. W., Kame'enui, E. J., & Chard, D. (Eds.), (1997). *Issues in educating students with disabilities.* Mahwah, NJ: Erlbaum.

Lloyd, J. W., & Lloyd, P. A. (in press). Reinforcing success: What special education could learn from its early accomplishments. *Remedial and Special Education.*

Lloyd, J. W. Pullen, P. L., Tankersley, M., & Lloyd, P. A. (2006). Critical dimensions of experimental studies and research syntheses that help define effective practices. In B. G. Cook & B. R. Schirmer (Eds.), *What is special about special education: Examining the role of evidence-based practices* (pp. 136–153). Austin, TX: Pro-Ed.

Lloyd, J. W., Singh, N. N., & Repp, A. C. (1991). *The regular education initiative: Alternative perspectives on concepts, issues, and models.* Sycamore, IL: Sycamore.

Mandell, D. S., Davis, J. K., Bevans, K., & Guevara, J. P. (2008). Ethnic disparities in special education labeling among children with attention deficit/hyperactivity disorder. *Journal of Emotional and Behavioral Disorders, 16*, 42–51.

McKinlay, A., Grace, R. C., Horwood, L. J., Fergusson, D. M., Ridder, E. M., & MacFarlane, M. R. (2008). Prevalence of traumatic brain injury among children, adolescents and young adults: Prospective evidence from a birth cohort. *Brain Injury, 22*, 175–181.

McLaughlin, M. J. (2010). Evolving interpretations of educational equity and students with disabilities. *Exceptional Children, 76*, 265–278.

Mesinger, J. F. (1985). Commentary on "A rationale for the merger of special and regular education": or Is it now time for the lamb to lie down with the lion? *Exceptional Children, 51*, 510–512.

Moog, J. S., Geers, A. E., Gustus, C., & Brenner, C. (2011). Psychosocial adjustment in adolescents who have used cochlear implants since preschool. *Ear and hearing, 32*(1 Suppl), 75S.

Moon, T. R., Brighton, C. M., & Callahan, C. M. (2003). State standardized testing programs: Friend or foe of gifted students? *Roeper Review: A Journal on Gifted Education, 25*(2), 49–60.

National Institute on Deafness and Other Communication Disorders. (2013). Cochlear implants. Retrieved from https://www.nidcd.nih.gov/health/hearing/pages/coch.aspx.

Oswald, D. P., Coutinho, M. J., Best, A. M., & Singh, N. N. (1999). Ethnic representation in special education: The influence of school-related economic and demographic variables. *The Journal of Special Education, 32*, 194–206.

Percy-Smith, L., Cayé-Thomasen, P., Gudman, M., Jensen, J. H., & Thomsen, J. (2008). Self-esteem and social well-being of children with cochlear implant compared to normal-hearing children. *International Journal of Pediatric Otorhinolaryngology, 72*, 1113–1120.

Pecquet, J. (2012, December 4). UN disabilities treaty expected to fail in Senate amid GOP opposition. *The Hill.* Retrieved from http://thehill.com/policy/international/270729-un-disabilities-treaty-expected-to-fail-in-senate.

Pitoniak, M. J., & Royer, J. M. (2001). Testing accommodations for examinees with disabilities: A review of psychometric, legal, and social policy issues. *Review of Educational Research, 71*, 53–104.

Proctor, C. P., Dalton, B., Uccelli, P., Biancarosa, G., Mo, E., Snow, C., & Neugebauer, S. (2011). Improving comprehension online: Effects of deep vocabulary instruction with bilingual and monolingual fifth graders. *Reading and Writing, 24*, 517–544.

Rao, K., Ok, M. W., & Bryant, B. R. (2014). A review of research on universal design educational models. *Remedial and Special Education, 35*, 153–166.

Reiser, R. (2013). Implementing inclusive education: A commonwealth guide to implementing article 24 of the UN Convention on the Rights of People with Disabilities (2nd ed.). London: Commonwealth Secretariat.

Robinson, A., Shore, B. M., & Enerson, D. L. (2007). *Best practices in gifted education: An evidence-based guide.* Waco, TX : Prufrock Press.

Rose, D. H., Gravel, J. W., & Gordon, D. T. (2013). Universal design for learning. In L. Florian (Ed.), *The Sage handbook of special education: Volume 2* (2nd. ed., pp. 475–489). Los Angeles, CA: Sage.

Rudin, A. (2010, October 7). There is nothing "special" about special education [Web log message]. http://www.huffingtonpost.com/april-rudin/spedthere-is-nothing-spec_b_749966.html.

Sapona, R. H., Lloyd, J. W., & Wissick, C. A. (1986). Microcomputer use in resource rooms with learning-disabled children. *Computers in the Schools, 2*(4), 51–59.

Severance, L. J., & Gasstrom, L. L. (1977). Effects of the label "mentally retarded" on causal explanations for success and failure outcomes. *American Journal of Mental Deficiency, 81*, 547–555.

Shifrer, D. (2013). Stigma of a label: Educational expectations for high school students labeled with learning disabilities. *Journal of Health and Social Behavior, 54*, 462–480.

Sireci, S. G., Scarpati, S. E., & Li, S. (2005). Test accommodations for students with disabilities: An analysis of the interaction hypothesis. *Review of Educational Research, 75*, 457–490.

Smith, S. L., Peters, M., Sanders, M., & Witz, K. (2010). Applying a response to intervention framework for noncategorical special education identification. *Communiqué, 38*(8), 9–11.

Sprick, R. S., & Howard, L. M. (1995). *The teacher's encyclopedia of behavior management: 100 problems/500 plans for grades K-9.* Longmont, CO: Sopris West.

Stainback, W., & Stainback, S. (1984). A rationale for the merger of special and regular education. *Exceptional Children, 51*, 102–111.

Stainback, W., & Stainback, S. (1991). A rationale for integration and restructuring: A synopsis. In J. W. Lloyd, N. N. Singh, & A. C. Repp (Eds.), *The regular education initiative: Alternative perspectives on concepts, issues, and models* (pp. 226–239). Sycamore, IL: Sycamore.

Sugai, G., Horner, R. H., & Sprague, J. (1999). Functional assessment-based behavior support planning: Research-to-practice-to-research. *Behavioral Disorders, 24*, 223–227.

Suter, J. C., & Giangreco, M. F. (2009). Numbers that count: Exploring special education and paraprofessional service delivery in inclusion-oriented schools. *The Journal of Special Education, 43*, 81–93.

Tankersley, M., Niesz, T., Cook, B. G., & Woods, W. (2007). The unintended and unexpected side effects of inclusion of students with learning disabilities: The perspectives of special education teachers. *Learning Disabilities: A Multidisciplinary Journal, 14*, 135–144.

Trent, S. C., & Artiles, A. J. (1995). Serving culturally diverse students with emotional or behavioral disorders: Broadening current perspectives. In J. M. Kauffman, J. W. Lloyd, D. P. Hallahan, & T. A. Astuto (Eds.), *Issues in educational placement: Students with emotional and behavioral disorders* (pp. 215–250). Mahwah, NJ: Erlbaum.

UK Disabled People's Manifesto: Reclaiming Our Futures. (2013). Retrieved from http://www.inclusionlondon.co.uk/domains/inclusionlondon.co.uk/local/media/downloads/UK_Disabled_People__s_Manifesto___Reclaiming_Our_Futures.pdf.

United Nations. (2006). Convention on the Rights of Persons with Disabilities. Retrieved https://www.un.org/disabilities/convention/conventionfull.shtml.

Wissick, C. A., & Gardner, J. E. (2011). Technology and academic instruction. In J. M. Kauffman & D. P. Hallahan (Eds.), *The handbook of special education* (pp. 484–500). New York: Routledge.

Woodward, J., & Rieth, H. (1997). A historical review of technology research in special education. *Review of Educational Research, 67*, 503–536.

Worth, R. (1999). The scandal of special-ed: It wastes money and hurts the poor. *Washington Monthly, 31*(6), 34–39.

Zigmond, N. (1997). Educating students with disabilities: The future of special education. In J. W. Lloyd, E. J. Kameenui, & D. Chard (Eds.), *Issues in educating students with disabilities* (pp. 325–342). Mahwah, NJ: Erlbaum.

INDEX

Page numbers in italics refer to information in figures and boxes and those in bold type refer to tables. Page numbers that refer to notes are followed by 'n' and note number.

4 point rule/scale 135, 140, 146, 276
18–21 services 367–8

AA-AAS *see* alternate assessments based on alternate assessment standards
AAIDD *see* American Association on Intellectual and Developmental Disabilities
AA-MAS *see* alternate assessment based on modified achievement standards
ABA *see* applied behavior analysis
ABC interactions *see* Antecedent-Behavior-Consequence (ABC) interactions
Abecedarian Project 353–4, 389
ABI *see* Activity-Based Instruction
academic achievement: and accountability systems 417–18; alternate assessment 53–4, 55, 66, 67–8, 331–2, 333–4; "basic psychological processes" 14–15; blurring/diluting general/special distinction 458, 459; EBA to explain achievement gap 312; ELA proficiency and inclusion 416, 417, 420; grade level goals 138–9; IDEA's adverse effect requirement 98; impact of class/group size 190; improved by assessment system 323, 335; and inclusion 13, 202–3, 206, 240; and Internalizing behaviors 287–8; and life prospects 389–91, 415; NCEO's conceptual-outcome model 323, 325, *326*, *327*, 330; in productivity analyses 411, 412, 414–17, 418–20, *419*, 422–3; research directions 67–8; as a result of co-teaching 209; societal benefits of special education 390–1; and teacher effectiveness 99–100, 172, 209
academic content: blended-practice models 55, 67, 68, 286, 451; defining "educational performance" for special education eligibility 98; in ecological curricular framework 66; experimental research 55, 66; functional academics 53, 54, 60, 65, 68; literacy/reading *see* literacy/reading; mathematics *see* mathematics; outcomes *see* academic achievement; pre-academic skills 356–7, 361; science teaching 25, 55, 60, 62–5; setting *see* inclusion; teacher expertise 100, 159, 161–2, 170–1, 172; templates/commercial resources 67, 451; *see also* curriculum
academic strategies/study skills 24–5
accommodation *see* adapted instruction
accountability: and alternative assessment 67, 331; and co-teaching 208–9; and the dilution of special education 458, 459; and eight education goal failure 329–30; flexibility from NCLB Adequate yearly progress requirements 333–4; and general education standards 54, 55, 261–2; and improved academic outcomes 323; schools sanctioned 417
active text processing 24; *see also* comprehension skills
Activity-Based Instruction (ABI) 360–1
adapted instruction: and accommodations 121, 191, 455; differentiated instruction 42, 205–6, 253–4, 404, 453; and EBP implementation fidelity 279; NCEO's conceptual-outcome model 325, *326*; programmed instruction 304; section 504 of Rehabilitation Act (1973) 224, 229; special education requires teaching things differently 25–6; *see also* assistive technology
ADHD *see* attention deficit hyperactivity disorder
administrative reasons for having special education 399, 401–3, 405, 447, 449
adults *see* post-school outcomes

adverse affect requirement 98
advocacy: as a critical component of special education 33; and the demise of special education 403; discussion question 34; self-advocacy 31, 372, 378; and the setting debate 219, 403, 406, 448; teacher confidence and expertise 160; for workforce policy reform **174**, 179–80
African Americans: *Brown v. Board of Education* ruling 199, 216; and Dr. Poplin's change of viewpoint 245; overrepresentation in special education 98–9, 110, 120, 453; stereotypes 121
Ahlgrim-Delzell, L. 456–7
AIMSweb 142, 143, 149, 292
Akers, L. xviii
Alabama 414
Alper, S. 55
alternate assessment 53–4, 55, 66, 67–8, 331–2, 333–4
alternate assessment based on modified achievement standards (AA-MAS) 331
alternate assessments based on alternate assessment standards (AA-AAS) 331
Alves, K. D. 188
American Association on Intellectual and Developmental Disabilities (AAIDD, formerly American Association on Mental Retardation) 376, 377
American Indians 98, 99
American Sign Language (ASL) 194, 219
anger, and moral judgment 241
Annamma, S. 99, 108
anorexia and obesity 242–3
Antecedent-Behavior-Consequence (ABC) interactions 308
anxiety 285, 290–1
applied behavior analysis (ABA) 53, 347–8, 428
Asian Americans 99, 119, 226, 453–4
ASL *see* American Sign Language
Asperger's Syndrome 97, 98, 220
assessment: alternate 53–4, 55, 66, 67–8, 331–2, 333–4; for community inclusion 377; gifted students 453; NCEO special education outcome definition 323, 325, *326*, *327*, 330; program implementation *see* implementation fidelity/treatment integrity; progress monitoring *see* progress monitoring; screening *see* eligibility; identification; of special education *see* accountability; use of technology 332, 455
assessment schedule 291–3
assistive technology 22, 227, 229, 325, 375, 379; *see also* Universal Design for Learning
athletics 98, 99
attention deficit hyperactivity disorder (ADHD) 98, 99, 190, 222, 224, 290, 294, 453
auditory learners/teaching 253
autism 15, 23, 97, 98, 220, 258, 332, 347–8, 363
automaticity 433, 435, 438

Baker, J. 157, 208
Balan, C. 442

Barker, R. G. 307, 308
BASC2-BESS *see* Behavioral and Emotional Screening System
"basic psychological processes" 14
Bateman, B. D. xiv, 3, 7, 75, 254, **255**, 262, 368, 387, 447
behavior: as a disorder *see* emotional and behavioral disorders; environmental structuring for learning behavior *see* environmental structuring
behavioral economics and workforce quality/efficacy 172–3, 181–2; *see also* TEAM strategic workforce renewal plan
Behavioral and Emotional Screening System (BASC2-BESS) 289, 297
behavioral momentum 360
Berlin, Isaiah 243
Berry, R. A. 111, 112
bilingual students *see* English Language Learners
Billingsley, B. 99, 159, 162, 167, 181, 445, 448
blended-practice models 55, 67, 68, 286, 451
blind/visually impaired students 12, 38, 224, 226, 227, 456
blogging 176
Bloom, Benjamin 45, 269
Boardman, A. 99, 106
Boelé, A. 99, 105
Boies, David *392*, 394
Boudah, D. J. 157
braille 12, 38, 227, 387, *393*, *450*
brain development 354
Brain Gym® 18
brain injury 12
brains 76, 234
Branson, T. A. 66
Brigham, F. J. 156–7
Britain 459
Bronfenbrenner, U. 307, 308
Browder, D. M. 15, 18, 51, 67, 258, 445, 448, *450*, 451, 456–7
Brown, Christy *392–3*
Brown, T. S. 10
Brown v. Board of Education (1954) 13, 195, 199–200, 216
Bruner, J. S. 85, 86, 87
Bryant, B. R. 456
bullying 220, 228
Bureau of Education for the Handicapped 355
Burlington School Committee v. Massachusetts Department of Education 223

Cabrera, A. F. 179
California 415, 416, 417, 418–21, 423, 425
Cameto, R. 390
Campbell, C. McFie 460
Campbell, J. 82, 83–4, 85, 86, 87, 89
Canadian Association of the Mentally Retarded public service announcement 369–70
Carnine, Douglas W. 87–9, 451

Carta, J. J. 315, 344, 347, 348, 350, 389, 447, *449, 450*, 451, 452

CBM *see* Curriculum-based measurement

census-based funding formulas 413, 420, 423, 424

Chard, D. xi

charter schools 424

Chetty, R. 99–100

Chicago 423

CISSAR *see* Code for Instructional Structure and Student Academic Response

citizenship 326, 391

civil rights xiii, 13, 81, 193, 216, 378, 403, 406

class/group size 39–40, 190, 204, 207–8, 210, 227, 312, 317

classrooms: complexity and decision-making 430–1, 433, 435, 438; *see also* setting

ClassWide Peer Tutoring (CWPT) 259, 312–14

Clyde K. v. Puyallup School District 222

cochlear implants 454–5

Cochran-Smith, M. 241, 243

Code for Instructional Structure and Student Academic Response (CISSAR) 308–10, 311, 314

Cohen, J. 274

collaboration: co-teaching *see* co-teaching; professional networks *see* social media; special/ general education teachers 119–22, 128, 133, 145; teachers and parents 113–15, 128; TEAM strategic workforce renewal plan 173, 181, 182

Collaborative Instruction Model 157

college/post-secondary education: assessing special education outcomes 68, 323, 332–3; and early intervention 100, 354; functional skills prerequisite/ double standards 65; and high school completion 389–90; postsecondary education programs 15, 368

Collins, B. C. 66

Columbia, District of 199, 216, 217, 261, 423

commander's intent 432, 434

commercial resources 67

Common Core State Standards (CSS) 65, 66, 68, 86, 171, 261, 332

communication disorders 352, 359; *see also* autism; hearing-impaired/deaf children

communication theory *see* information theory

community inclusion 369, 376, 378, 415

Compelling Conversations 141

comprehension skills: automaticity 433; for ELLs 111, 117, 127; sample fidelity checklist 145–6; systematic instruction 66; using interactive read alouds 56, 57, 59, 66

computer science *see* information theory

consequentialist rules 239–40, 245, 247n8

conservatives and liberals 237–8

content: academic strategies 24–5; determining setting 191–2; general/special education differences 12, 14–15, 23–5, 444–5; and instructional design 85, 86–9; message of specially designed instruction 81–9; *see also* academic content; functional life skills

continua, instruction on 42–4

continuum of placement: against full inclusion 44–5, 46, 192, 208, 219–20, 227–8, 232; and learner characteristics 191; and LRE 200, 217–18; in a multi-tiered system 286–7; placement percentages 226

contribution and citizenship 326, 391

Convention on the Rights of Persons with Disabilities (CRPD) *see* United Nations' Convention on the Rights of Persons with Disabilities

Cook, B. G. 209, 253, 254, 265, 275, 276, 277, 439, 445, 446, 448, 449, 451, 453

Cook, Lynne 155–6, 158, 161–2

Cook, S. C. 271

corrective feedback: as critical special education component 40–1, 256, 445; data from assessment 261; Direct/direct Instruction comparison *17*; instruction on continua 40–1, 43, 44, 46; in MTS/ RTI methods 225, 295, 297; power/success of 56, 66, 333; programmed instruction 304; prompting and feedback 56, 59, 66, 259, *260*

correspondence training 360

cost: as an argument against special education *388–9*; behavior screening tools 289; criteria shift to reduce identification 96, 347–8; evidence-based programs 17; funding deficits 119, 134, 180, 228, 387–8, *388*; market forces 405; of not educating students with disabilities 390–1; and placement 192, 193–4, 221, 222–3, 228–9, 405, 420, 423, 424; *see also* funding; productivity

co-teaching: defining 155–6; and the dilution of special education 458; implementation challenges 162–3; one-teach, one-assist model 157, 158, 160, 227; ownership and agency 159, 160–2; preferred- service-delivery model post IDEA (1997) 201; and productivity 420; and resource budgets 210; specialized instruction 31, 156, 157, 158, 159–60, 305–6; student outcomes 158, 208–9; teacher preparation/training 162

critical theory 245

CRPD *see* United Nations' Convention on the Rights of Persons with Disabilities

CSS *see* Common Core State Standards

cultural and linguistic diversity: applicability of RTI 419; and arguments in favor of inclusion 219; cochlear implant controversy 454–5; diagnosing differences rather than disabilities 93, 110, 111–13, 115–16, 126–8; as invalidation of special education's benefits 385; need to value diversity 111–13, 128; significance of family context 116–19, 122–6, 127, 128; special/general teacher collaboration 119–22, 128; teacher/parental collaboration 113–15, 128; *see also* ethnicity

cultural values 237

curriculum: access through general classroom inclusion xiii, 155, 192, 201, 203–4, 208–9, 218, 372, 420; appropriateness debate 12, 14, 15, 32, 52–6, 65, 332; in eligibility definition 98; evidence- based programs and practices 17, 66, 256, 257, 271; and functional life skills 55, 193; integration

of special and general education goals 13, 31–2, 66, 139; modifications and LRE application 192, 221; for pre-school intervention 344–5, 356–7; and RTI evidence base and implementation fidelity 140, 141, 144, 146–7, 150; social skills program 292, 296; things not commonly part of the general curriculum 23–4, 444–5; *see also* academic content; instruction
Curriculum-based measurement (CBM) 46, 135, 137, 138, 243, 261
CWPT *see* ClassWide Peer Tutoring

Daniel R.R. v State Board of Education (1989) 221
DAP (developmentally appropriate practices) guidelines 344, 358
Darling-Hammond, L. 100
data-point collection 138, 139–40, 145
DATA TO KNOWLEDGE **173**, 175
Davidson, A. O. 99, 104
deaf/hearing impaired children 113, 194, 219, 224, 226, 246n4, 454–5
DEAF-WORLD 454–5
decision-making: essential supplement to screening 288; experience/practice 431, 433–4, 435–6, 438; intent 432, 434; logic and science 429, 432, 436–8, 439, 447, 449; ; RTI as model for 97, 135–45; *see also* moral judgment
dedicated practice 435, 438
deinstitutionalization movement 13, 187, 218, 457, 459
Delpit, L. 122, 245
Demchak, M. 55
Deno, E. 7, 44, 133, 134, 145, 200
Deno, S. L. 136, 324
deontological rules 238–40, 245
descriptive research (defined) 451
Deshler, D. D. 157
Detrich, R. 277
developing countries 406
developmentally appropriate practices (DAP) guidelines 344, 358
diagnosis *see* eligibility; identification
diagnostic-remedial/prescriptive teaching 253
Diagnostic and Statistical Manual of the American Psychiatric Association (DSM-5/V) 97
diagnostic substitution 347
differential effectiveness 28–30
differential reinforcement 360
differentiated instruction 42, 205–6, 253–4, 305, 404
Dillon, S. 342
dilution of special education 405, 457–9
Direct Behavior Rating Scales 297
Direct/direct Instruction: appropriate grouping criteria 404–5, 426n13; "big DI"/ "little di" comparison *16–17*; DISTAR *16*, 116; EDI 419; and Engelmann and Carnine's theory of instructional design 87–9; as evidence-based practice 256, 344, 345; Greenwood's teaching assignment 305–6; in

multi-tiered model 257–8; as recognized practice 205, 245
Direct Instruction Systems for Teaching Arithmetic and Reading (DISTAR) 16, 116
disability: IDEA definitions of 96; as interiorized state of function/health 371–2; WHO conceptualization 372–4
discipline 25, 26, 122–6
discrepancy model 97, 135–6, 137, 143, 144
disordinal interactions 28
disproportionate representation 98–9, 110, 219
dissemination activity potential 422
DISTAR see Direct Instruction Systems for Teaching Arithmetic and Reading
Downing, J. E. 55
Down syndrome 352, 355, 369
Driver, M. K. 94
DSM-5/V (Diagnostic and Statistical Manual of the American Psychiatric Association) *see* Diagnostic and Statistical Manual of the American Psychiatric Association
Ducommon, C. E. 100
Dudley-Marling, C. 243
Dunlap, G. 361
Dunn, L. 133, 134, 145
duration and frequency 40, 138, 139–40, 143, 147, 210, 345
Du Toit, Natalie *392*
Dye, H. B. 353

early intervention: funding 198–9, 343, 355, 356, 357, 457; history of 351–2, 353–6; labeling concerns 345–6, 347; longitudinal efficacy studies 353–4, 389–90; in MTI/RTI models *see* multi-tiered systems of support; program design 317, 343–5, 354–61, 362; rationale for 352–3
EBA *see* ecobehavioral assessment
EBD *see* emotional and behavioral disorders
EBP *see* evidence-based practice
ecobehavioral assessment: application to district policies 318; CISSAR taxonomy to analyse ecobehavioral interaction 308–10, 311, 314; environmental transition planning 315–16; and the general weaknesses of classroom structure 310–11, 316; intervention fidelity measurement 314, 316; and multi-tiered systems of support 316–17, 318; and the structure-function relationship 306–8; to confirm CWPT effectiveness 312–14; to explain achievement gaps 312, 316
Ecobehavioral System for the Complex Assessment of Preschool Environments (ESCAPE) 315
ecological curricular framework 66
ecological psychology 307
economic and societal benefits (of special education) 385, 389–94
EDI *see* Explicit Direct Instruction
educational discontinuity 127
Education for All Handicapped Children Act (EHA, 1975) xiv, 78–9, 81, 134, 206, 216, 324, 371

educational performance: legal definitions 98; *see also* academic achievement

education outcomes *see* academic achievement

effect size 28, 30, 39, 157, 268, 273, 274–5

EHA *see* Education for All Handicapped Children Act

Elementary and Secondary Education Acts (ESEA): 1965 198; 2001 *see* No Child Left Behind Act; 2003 AA-AAS-based assessment 331

eligibility: and adult-support models 377, 378, 379; age-related parameters 341, 346, 367–8, 369, 447; as an enduring issue 133–4; and the ideal of special education for all 95–6, 136, 399, 403, 405; need to define 399, 453; shifting criteria 96–7, 346–7, 348; "who" questions 93; *see also* identification

Elliott, S. N. 175

ELLs *see* English Language Learners

emotional and behavioral disorders: ADHD 98, 99, 190, 222, 224, 290, 294, 453; autism 15, 23, 97, 98, 220, 258, 332, 347–8, 363; behavior measurement tools 287, 288, 289–92, 293, 294–5, 296, 297; behavior patterns 285, 287; and CWPT 259; Darnell case study 120–2; discipline 26, 122–3; houseparenting 79–80; identification decreases 347; Maria case study 122–3; mnemonics for 28; MTS models for 286–7; outcomes 285, 288, 326, **328**; and premature general classroom placement 219–20; ruled out by RTI decision-making 143; as a secondary disability 352; special education coverage of 285–6

emotional decision-making 234, 235

employment: adult outcomes 68, 332–3, 390–1, 415; in the inclusion debate 218, 241; legislative focus on readiness for 14, 15, 65, 323, *330*; and self-determination 378; supported 14, 376, 378, 379

end/stop point of special education 341, 346–8, 367–8, 447; and the need to reconceptualize disability 369–76; supports paradigm (for adults with disabilities) 369, 375–7, 378, 379

Engelmann, Siegfied 87–9, 405

English Language Learners (ELLs) 110, 111–16, 126–8, 151

environmental factors (in ICD-10) 373–4

environmental structuring 446; in "a model for how" 254, 255–6; causing intellectual disability (and early intervention for) 353–4; early (pre-school) intervention programs 357–8, 359; and EBA approach *see* ecobehavioral assessment; group size *see* group size/class size; multi-tiered systems *see* multi-tiered systems of support; operant conditioning theory 45–6, 303–4; and person-environment models of disability 374–8, 379; reinforcement *see* reinforcement

equity *see* fairness

Ericsson, K. A. 435

ESCAPE *see* Ecobehavioral System for the Complex Assessment of Preschool Environments

ESEA *see* Elementary and Secondary Education Acts

ESY *see* extended school year

ethnicity: disproportionate representation 98–9, 110, 120, 219, 453–4; and individual's functioning capacity 374; placement percentages 226; *see also* African Americans; cultural and linguistic diversity

evidence-based practice 5; adaptation and fidelity balance 279; currency/treatment of older studies 277; curricula 256; design of research 268, 272–3; EBA to monitor implementation 318; effect size 268, 273, 274–5; evidence base categories 277–8; and gifted student education 453; and "Grandmother's Brownies" fallacy 15–17; Horner's criteria for 60; importance of 254, 269–70, 446, 452, 453, 461; intentional instruction for pre-school children 344–5, 361; and logic and science 429, 432, 436–8, 439, 447, 448–9, 451; number of groups identifying EBPs 278; peer-review 15, 141, 270–1, 345; potential of 266; quality of research 268, 272, 273–4, 276–7; quantity of research 268, 274; research-to-practice gap 266, 269, 344, 451–2; and RTI core intervention 138, 140–1, 142, 143, 144, 145, 147; specifying participant and setting parameters 275–6; sustainability 280; as teacher skill 171, 172, 280; terminology 267–8, 271; and UDL 456–7; *see also* experimental research

expenditure *see* cost; productivity

experimental research: alternative research types 451; differential facilitation 30; EBA observational studies 308–16; on instructional design 89; limitations/challenges of 242, 400–1, 449–50; on literacy teaching 55–9, 66, 324; on mathematics teaching 59–60, *61*; operant learning theory 303–4; on placement 202–3; on pre-school intervention 353–4, 355, 356; on science teaching 60, 62–5; tradition of 17–18

Explicit Direct Instruction (EDI) 419

explicit instruction: in continua of critical components 42, 43, 44, 46, 47; in co-teaching classes 31, 209; defined 38; differential effectiveness 30; in DI programs 257; EDI 419; environmental structuring 303, 317, 318, 445; as evidence-based practice 254, 452; instructional intensity in MTS 317; intentional instruction for pre-school children 344–5, 357–61; and the need for specialized settings 204, 205, 208, 209, 210; organizational study skills 24–5; and the rationale for special education 404, 405; social skills interventions 292, 293; as teacher skill 159

extended school year (ESY) 346

externalizing behavior patterns 285, 287

fact errors 259, *260*

fairness: and accommodation for special education students 121, 191, 455; civil rights xiii, 13, 81, 193, 216, 378, 403, 406; as a "hard topic" 4; inclusion 13, 210–11, 218–19, 228, 232, 238–9, 241–2, 459; and institutionalization 215; pre 1975 education for disabled students 385–6; and the rationale for special education 385, 395, 403; rights of disabled students to full educational opportunity 65; in social-intuitionist model of moral judgment 237, 238

false negative and positive screening 135, 288, 290

families: cultural and linguistic context 116–19, 122–6, 127, 128; early associations 198; and effective early childhood interventions 343–4; involvement/accommodation and adaptation, as defined outcome domain 325, *326*; modern expectation of 5; *see also* parents; socio-economic background

feedback: for teachers 171, **174**, 180, 334; *see also* corrective feedback

Feng, L. 100, 168

Feynman, R. P. 81, 436

fidelity *see* implementation fidelity/treatment integrity

Figueroa, R. 99, 107, 122–3

firefighters 433–4

first courses of treatment 437–8

FLKs *see* "funny looking kids"

Florence County School District v. Carter (1993) 194, 223

formative assessment 261

Fox, L. 361

frequency and duration 40, 138, 139–40, 143, 147, 210, 345

Friedman, J. N. 99–100

Friend, Marilyn 155–6, 158, 161–2

Fuchs, D. 457–8

Fuchs, L. S. 457–8

full inclusion *see* inclusion

function: effective learning environment structuring *see* ecobehavioral assessment; and the human-functioning approach to disability 372–6, 379

functional academics 53, 54, 60, 65, 68

functional life skills: and the appropriateness of academic content 15, 52–4, 65, 332; blended-practice models 55, 67, 68, 286, 451; functional academics 53, 54, 60, 65, 68; and the goals of special education 31–2; inclusion debate 193, 195; and individualized instruction 55, 192; NCEO's conceptual-outcome model 326; pre-school children 356, 357; reading as 57, 59; and school accountability legislation 330; screening tools 288, 289, 292, 293, 297; *see also* post-school outcomes

funding: 1960s legislation 198–9; and the dilution of special education 457–8; distribution based on SIS 377; early intervention 198–9, 343, 355, 356, 357, 457; equity and transparency 423–4; federal/state/local partnership 425; formulas 412, 413, 421–2, 423, 424; HCEEP 355; need to earmark 402, and outcome relationship 425; private placements and LRE requirements 192, 193–4, 220, 223, 423; public spending challenge 228–9; special education teachers 179; underfunding 119, 134, 180, 228, 387–8, *388*; *see also* cost; productivity

"funny looking kids" (FLKs) 76

further education *see* college/post-secondary education

Gallagher, D. J. 239, 241, 246n3, 437

Garda, R. A. 98

gender: disproportions in disability categories 98, 99

general education reform 328–30

general/special education differences: blurring/dilution 457–9; content 12, 14–15, 23–5, 444–5; goals 31–3; instruction 12–14, 17, 25–31, 33, 37, 41–5, 205–6, 403–5, 452, 458; to define special education 11–12

Gersten, R. 40, 273, 274

gifted/talented students 13, *392–3*, 394, 452–3

Gladwell, M. *392*, 394, 435

Glassdoor.com **173**, 176–7

goals: 1990s general education reform 329, *330*; commander's intent 432, 434; and IEPs 13, 15, 47, 66, 113–15, 227; setting process in RTI model 138–9, 140, 142–3; of special education 31–2, 68

Goodlad, J. I. 402, 403

grade level alignment *see* academic achievement; academic content

graduation 170, *330*, 335, 346, 390

Graham, J. 238, 241, 243

Grammatical Man: Information, Entropy, Language and Life (Campbell) 82, 85

"Grandmother's Brownies" fallacy 15–17

graphic organizers 60, 67

Great Britain 459

Greenwood, C. 302, 303–6, 312, 446, 448

Greer v. Rome City School District 221

Gresham, F. 297

Grodin, M. 454–5

group/class size 39–40, 190, 204, 207–8, 210, 227, 312, 317

grouping for instruction 399, 404–5, 426n13

Haidt, J. 234–8, 243, 245

Hallahan, D. P. 18, 36, 133, 204, 255, 258, 387, 401, 403, 405, 445, 448, *450*, 452

Hall, T. A. 66

Handicapped Children's Early Education Assistance Act (1968) 198–9

Handicapped Children's Education Program (HCEEP) 355

Harbort, G. 158

Hawaii 75, 76, 414, 415

HCEEP *see* Handicapped Children's Education Program

health care costs 228–9

hearing-impaired/deaf children 194, 219, 224, 226, 246n4, 454–5

Heath, C. 430, 430–1, 432, 434

Heath, D. 430, 430–1, 432, 434

Hemmeter, M. L. 361

hidden curriculum 15, 18, 24; *see also* functional life skills

hierarchical approach to categorizing EBP evidence base 277, 278

high-stakes testing *see* accountability; eligibility; identification

Hippocrates 76

Hirsch, S. E. 252
history of special education: and concepts of disability 77, 372–3; content/curriculum 14–15, 201; family associations and early funding 198; inclusion/ segregation xiii, 12–13, 76, 195, 198–201, 215–16, 371–2, 385–6, *386*; of issues 4–5; pre-school intervention 351–2, 353–6; relevance of xiii–xiv, 5, 134
Horner, R. H. 60, 274, 275
houseparenting 79–80
"how": questions of 6, 204–5, 251, 253–4, 262, 446
Huefner, D. S. 189, 190, 191, 192, 195, 214, 445, 446, *450*
human-functioning approach to disability 372–8, 379

ICD-10/ICF model 374, 375, 376
ICD-10 (International Statistical Classification of Diseases and Related Health Problems) 373–4
ICF (International Classification of Functioning, Disability and Health) 373
ICIDH *see* International Classification of Impairments, Disabilities and Handicaps
IDEA *see* Individuals With Disabilities (IDEA) legislation
identification: behavior screening tools 287, 288, 289–92, 293, 294–5, 296, 297; and culture, language and ethnicity 93, 98–9, 110, 111–13, 115–16, 126–8; discrepancy model 97, 135–6, 137, 143, 144; gifted students 453; importance of EBP 445; over-identification 413, 422; in a paradigm for mastery 47; percentages of students in special education 412–13; possible delays using RTI 225, 226; reductions-from-RTI approach 225, 347, 418, 419, 420, 421, 458; RTI decision-making process 135–45; under identification of EBD students 28, 285–6; universal screening in an MTS framework 257; *see also* eligibility
ideology 245
IEPs *see* individualized educational programs
IES *see* Institute for Education Sciences
IFSPs *see* Individual Family Service Plans
Illinois 25, 254, 415, 416, 417, 423
impact charting **174**, 179
implementation fidelity/treatment integrity: EBA application 314, 318; home/community settings for pre-school children 361–2; identifying EBPs 277, 278, 279; in RTI decision-making 138, 140–1, 144, 147, 150; and social validity measurement 295; teacher and student behavior 294; tools for 287, 288, 292
inclusion: assistive technology 227, 229; and class/group size 207–8, 210, 227; cost/resource implications 221, 228–9, 405, 420, 424; co-teaching *see* co-teaching; court decisions 193, 220, 221, 222; and CWPT 313; and the dilution of special education 13, 458; and effective instruction 30–1,

205–6, 208, 209–10, 215, 219, 227–8, 405–6; efficacy research limitations 202–3, 240, 242; fairness/justice of 13, 210–11, 218–19, 228, 232, 238–9, 241–2; for general education curriculum xiii, 155, 192, 201, 203–4, 208–9, 218, 372, 420; history of inclusion/ segregation xiii, 12–13, 76, 195, 198–201, 215–16, 371–2, 385–6, *386*; international perspective 459–60; and LRE placement 95, 187, 192–3, 200, 217–18, 221, 222, 414, 416, 418; monitoring in OSEP annual reports 206–7; as a moral debate 189, 195, 232–4, 236–7, 238–43, 244–5, 446; placement percentages 226, 372; prekindergarten 362; and the regular education initiative xiii, 13, 201, 459; relationship to academic achievement 416, 417, 420; reverse mainstreaming for pre-school children 355; and RTI 225; and social behavior 218, 219–20, 417; society's acceptance of diversity 193, 218, 394–5
independence *see* functional life skills
Individual Family Service Plans (IFSPs) 345
individualized educational programs (IEPs): and accommodations 121, 191, 455; as accountability mechanism 334; blending curriculum/life skills 55, 68, 113–15; ecological curricular framework 66; eligibility for additional years of special education 367; and the general education curriculum 13, 15; instruction-driven placement 44, 217; methods for goal setting 138–9; outcome measures 47; in private placement 194, 223; progress tracking 261; and related service provision 224, 346; and setting 191, 203, 217–18, 227, 228; to deliver individualized instruction 37, 387, 453
individualized instruction: and academic goals 32; for all 95–6, 399, 405, 457; as continua of critical components 38–44, 47; co-teaching 31, 156, 157, 158, 159–60, 305–6; defining special education 37, 215, 452; and group/class size 190; for mastery 45–6, 47, 191, 304, 305; maximized by progress monitoring/assessment 46, 47, 296, 304; for pre-school children 360–1; rights established in case law 216; and specialized/general placement 203, 205–6, 209–10, 211, 417, 446, 448; Tier 3 in multi-tiered models 257; *see also* continuum of placement; individualized educational programs
Individuals With Disabilities (IDEA) legislation: on assistive technology 227, 456; defining what special education is 11, 12, 77–8; eligibility criteria 96, 97–8, 135, 225, 346–7, 348; end parameter of special education 346, 367, 368–9; funding 179–80, 194, 387–8, *388*, 412, 422, 457; on general curriculum access 53, 155, 192, 201, 203; IEP requirements 13, 37, 217, 346, 388; individual-based student goals 32; LRE/placement continuum 191, 192, 193, 200, 217, 416; neighborhood placement 222; OESP Annual Reports 206; peer-reviewed research 15, 171; placement trends 226; and post-school outcome focus 14; for pre-school children 344, 345, 457; and private placement 192, 194, 222–3; related services 224, 229, 346; screening 291; state student‾

assessment 330, 331; teacher qualification 170, 171; workforce issues 179
information theory 81–4, 85, 87
Institute for Education Sciences (IES) 56, 75, 178
institutionalization *see* deinstitutionalization movement; residential placement; segregation
instruction: "a model for how" (teaching pie) 254–62; blended-practice models 55, 67, 68, 286, 451; design of 81–9; general/special education differences 12–14, 17, 25–31, 33, 41–5, 205–6, 403–5, 452, 458; grouping for 399, 404–5, 426n13; learning environment characteristics 190–1; modality-based 253–4; programmed instruction 304, 305, 306; rationale for special education 399, 403–5, 447, 449; science-teaching strategies 25, 55, 60, 62–5; significance of the words "specially designed instruction" in IDEA 77–9; systematic *see* systematic instruction; tiered models of instruction *see* multi-tiered systems of support; what is an instructional approach *18–19*; *see also* adapted instruction; Direct/direct Instruction; environmental structuring; evidence-based practice; explicit instruction; individualized instruction; intensity; resources; systematic instruction
instructional reasons for having special education 399, 403–5, 447, 449
intellectual disability: fixedness of 32, 353; labels/labeling for 76, 96–7, 99, 345–6, 369–70, 453–4; person-environment reconceptualization 373–8, 379; and physical attributes 75–6; placement percentages 226
intensity: in continua of critical components 43, 44, 46, 47; duration and frequency 40, 138, 139–40, 143, 147, 210, 345; and engagement 316, 317; and group size 39–40, 190, 210, 317; IFSPs 345; MTS/RTI models 135, 142, 143, 225, 286, 292, 296, 361; pace 13–14, 23, 26–8, 39–40, 445; prekindergarten programs 359, 361; Supports Intensity Scales 377
intentional instruction for pre-school children 344–5, 357–61
interactive read alouds 55, 56, 57, *58*, 59–60, *61*, 66
internalizing behavior patterns 285, 287, 297
International Classification of Functioning, Disability and Health (ICF) 373; *see also* ICF/ICD-10 model
International Classification of Impairments, Disabilities and Handicaps (ICIDH) 372
international developments 459–60
International Statistical Classification of Diseases and Related Health Problems (ICD-10) 373–4; *see also* ICF/ICD-10 model
intervention grid 292–3
interventionist teachers 112, 128, 362
intra-individual framework of goal setting 139
intuition *see* social-intuitionist model of moral judgment
Iowa public schools 136, 137
IQ measures 44, 56, 97, 347, 353, 354, 377

Jameson, J. M. 66
Jefferson, T. 390–1
Joseph, G. 361
justice *see* fairness
juvenile justice system 389

Kame'enui, E. J. 18, 73, 75–7, 79–81, 387, 445, 448
Kauffman, J. M. 133, 204, 243, 387, 395, 397, 401, 403, 405, 429, 447, 448, 449, 452, 460
Kennedy, J. F., Panel on Mental Retardation 198, *199*
keyword method of mnemonics 29
Klein, G. 433–4, 435, 438
Klingner, J. K. 99, 102, 119, 389, 445, 453
Kloo, A. 14, 404
Knokey, A. 390
Kohlberg's stage theory of moral development 234
Kruelle v. new Castle County School District (1980) 220–1
Kurz, A. 175

labeling: adulthood stigma 369–71, 379; as deficit-driven 76, 243, 244, 371–2; effects on self-perception/confidence 120, 126, 128, 341, 345–6; and ethnicity 98–9, 110, 219, 453–4; "mental retardation" to "intellectual disability"/changing stigmatizing labels 96–7, 228, 345, 460; moral stereotyping 241–3; necessary for eligibility 399, 453; person–environment views of disability 372–6; and reduced expectations 453; social construction 242–3, 245; and the WHO reconceptualization of disability 371–4; "wrongness" and abolition of special education/full inclusion 95, 96, 239
Lakeside Middle School 119
Landrum, T. J. 209, 257, 258, 275, 395, 428, 445, 447, 448, 451
Lane, H. 454–5
Lane, K. L. 253, 257, 283, 446, *450*
Language Experience Approach 116
learning style 18, 205, 254, 360; *see also* modality-matching hypothesis
learn units 258, 308
least restrictive environment 191; and continuum of placement 192, 200; cost/funding implications 416, 418, 422, 423; and the general education curriculum 203; and inclusion 95, 187, 192–3, 200, 217–18, 221, 222, 414, 416, 418; and private placement 192, 193, 223, 423
Lee, A. 456–7
legislation: 1960s funding for educating children with disabilities 198–9; for compulsory education 385, 386; ESEA (2003) on AA-AAS-based assessment 331; historical focus on xiii; Rosa's Law 96; and special education issue evolution 5; *see also* Education for All Handicapped Children Act; Individuals With Disabilities (IDEA) legislation; No Child Left Behind Act
Lembke, E. S. 97, 132, 253, 445, 446, *450*
leprosy 76
lesson planning 256, 430, 432–3
Levin, H. 411

Lewis, J. 398, 403
liberals and conservatives 237–8
LIDT *see* Low-Incidence Deliberation Team
life-course perspective **174**, 178–9
life outcomes *see* post-school outcomes
life skills *see* functional life skills
linguistic and cultural diversity *see* cultural and
    linguistic diversity
literacy/reading: automaticity 433; Bateman's OTTER
    model **255**; braille 12, 38, 227, 387, *393*, *450*; class
    size 207; as a controversial topic 254; corrective
    feedback 40–1; EBA approach to preschool 311, 316,
    317; experimental research 55–9, 66, 324; functional
    literacy outcomes 325, *326*, *327*; group size 40;
    instruction on continua example 43–5; literacy as a
    functional skill 57, 59, 245; pre-academic skills 357,
    361; as a pre-requisite/assumed general secondary
    education skill 23–4; program development and
    "Grandmother's Brownies" fallacy 16; Project
    RAISE 56–7; read alouds 55–6, 57, *58*, 59–60, *61*, 66;
    RTI progress monitoring 143
Lloyd, J. W. xiv, 1, 13, 36, 40, 73, 74, 75, 156, 157, 254,
    259, 368, 399, 405, 428, 443, 447
Lloyd, P. 1, 443
Low Incidence Deliberation Team (LIDT) 348
LRE *see* least restrictive environment
Luckasson, R. 376

McDonnell, J. 66
McDuffie, K. A. 31, 157
McLaughlin, M. J. 458
Magiera, K. 157
Massachusetts 223, *388–9* , 415, 416, 417, 460
mastery 45–6, 47, 208, 257, 304, 305, 306
Mastropieri, M. A. 21, 22–3, 30, 31, 157, 255, 258, 387,
    444, 445, 448, *450*
mathematics: alternate assessment example 67–8;
    benefits of early intervention 354, 357; blended
    practice/as functional skill 54, 245; CISSAR
    taxonomy **309**; corrective feedback 40; effective
    teaching strategies 59–60, *61*, 66, 67, 313; in RTI
    models 33, 40; and technology 375
math stories 59, *61*, 67
Matta, D. 31, 209
Maxwell, J. 180
medical model of disability 371–2
memory: mnemonics 28–30
mentoring assistance for newly qualified teachers 171,
    173, 174, 177, 181
message: communication theory 82–4, 85; *see also*
    content
method of agreement (Mills) 87–8
milieu/naturalistic teaching strategies 359, 360
Mill, J. S. 87–8
Mills v. District of Columbia (1972) 199, 216, 386
Mims, P. 66, 456–7
Minneapolis Public Schools 136, 137
mnemonic instruction 28–30, 271
mobile technology support 181

modality-matching hypothesis 253–4; *see also*
    learning styles
modernization of recruitment **174**, 180–1
monitoring: OSEP Annual Reports 206–7, 226;
    program implementation *see* implementation
    fidelity/treatment fidelity; social validity of MTS
    interventions 292, 295–6; student progress *see*
    progress monitoring
Moore, B. 99, 103
moral foundations 237, 238
moral intuitions 234, 235, 237
moral judgment: and the crossing of moral divides
    233, 234, 244–6; how we hold place values 238–43;
    monism/pluralism 243–4; social-intuitionist model
    195, 233, 234–8, 245
moral psychology 233
Morton, Glen 247n9
motivated reasoning 235, 242
motor exercises 14, 18
MTS *see* multi-tiered systems of support
multi-tiered systems of support 253, 257, 446; early
    intervention programs (for young children) 361;
    EBA approach 316–17, 318; evolving teacher role
    160; focus on prevention 210; Pyramid Model 361;
    range of models 286–7; tools 287, 288, 289–95, 296,
    297; *see also* response-to-intervention (RTI) models
Murawski, W. W. 157, 254
Muscular Dystrophy Association 198
*My*iLogs (My Instructional Learning Opportunities
    Guidance System) **173**, 175

NAEP *see* National Center for Education Statistics'
    National Assessment of Educational Progress
NAEYC *see* National Association for the Education of
    Young Children
National Association for the Education of Young
    Children (NAEYC) 344, 358
National Center on Educational Outcomes (NCEO)
    324–5, 333
National Center for Education Statistics' National
    Assessment of Educational Progress (NAEP) 327,
    331, 333, 414
National Center on Intensive Intervention (NCII) 138, 139
National Center on RTI 141
National Longitudinal Transition Study (NLTS2) 415
National Reading Panel 254
naturalistic fallacy 234
naturalistic/milieu teaching strategies 359, 360
Navo, M. 419
NCEO *see* National Center on Educational Outcomes
NCII *see* National Center on Intensive Intervention
NCLD *see* No Child Left Behind Act
neighborhood placement 217–18, 222
neurology 76, 234
new brain/cognitive processing system 234
Newman, L. 390
NLTS2 *see* National Longitudinal Transition Study
No Child Left Behind Act (NCLB, 2001):
    accountability 54, 55, 261; alternative assessment 54,

333–4; appropriateness of general academic/grade-level goals 31–2, 55, 59, 429; data/reporting 414; and inclusion/teaching challenges 155, 170, 201; and special education focus 323, 330
nonscientific questions/thinking 429, 436, 451
normalization principle 128

obesity and anorexia 242–3
occupational therapy (OT) 223, 224
O'Connor, Sandra Day 194
Office of Special Education Programs (OSEP): Annual Reports 206–7, 226; early intervention funding 355, 356; on IFSPs 345; school accountability 334
Ok, M. W. 456
old brain/cognitive processing system 234
omission bias 240–1
one-teach, one-assist model 157, 158, 160, 227
one-to-one instruction 39, 190, 208, 210, 359
operant conditioning/learning theory 45–6, 303–4, 344
opportunities: to teach/learn (TEAM strategic workforce renewal plan) **173**, 175
opportunities to respond (OTR) *258*, 259, 304, 308
organizational skills 24–5, 31
OSEP *see* Office of Special Education Programs
OT *see* occupational therapy
OTR *see* opportunities to respond
OTTER model 254, **255**, 262
outcomes: defining special education goals 31–2, 33; differential effectiveness 28–30; and labeling 453; NCEO's conceptual-outcome model 324–30; societal and economic benefits 385, 389–94; teacher effectiveness 99–100, 168, 172, 181–2, 448; *see also* academic achievement; assessment; post-school outcomes; progress monitoring
over-identification 413, 422

pace 13–14, 23, 26–8, 39–40, 445
Pacific Islanders 75–6, 99, 226, 453
PALS *see* Peer-Assisted Learning Strategies
Panel on Mental Retardation 198, *199*
para-professionals 12, 191, 219, 220, 227, 458
PARC (Pennsylvania Association for Retarded Citizens) v. Pennsylvania (1971) 199, 216, 386
parents: choice and funding formulas 424; early family associations 198; full evaluation rights 225; pre-school implementation fidelity 361; setting/inclusion preferences 193, 194, 217, 220–3, 239; as stakeholder in MTS for EBD assessment 291, 292, 293, 295; and teacher collaboration 113–15, 128; *see also* families
Parrish, T. 387, 395, 409, 445, 447
Part D funding 180
participation and presence, NCEO's outcome model 325, *326*
pathognomic teachers 111, 128
PBIS *see* positive behavior intervention and supports
Peer-Assisted Learning Strategies (PALS) 313–14

peer-review 15, 141, 270–1, 345
peer tutoring/mediation 30, 31, 259, 312–14, 317
Pennsylvania Association for Retarded Citizens (PARC) v. Pennsylvania (1971) 199, 216, 386
perceptual-motor exercises 14, 18
performance errors 259, *260*
Personalized Systems of Instruction (PSI) 305
personal and social adjustment, NCEO's conceptual-outcome model 326, **328**
person-environment models of disability 373–8, 379
personnel-based special education expenditure index 414
persuasion 235–6
phonics 16, 254
phonological awareness 56–7, 254, 311
phrenology 75
physical health, NCEO's conceptual-outcome model 326, **328**
physical/sensory disabilities: adapting general education 25, 26; defining what is special education 38; international inclusive schools movement 460; parent-teacher collaboration case study 113–15; and setting 191; and special education goals 32
physical therapy (PT) 223, 224
P.L. 87-276 (Teachers of the Deaf Act, 1961) 198
P.L. 89-313 (State Schools Act, 1965) 198
P.L. 90-538 (Handicapped Children's Early Education Assistance Act, 1968) 198–9
P.L. 94-142 (Education for All Handicapped Children Act, EHA, 1975) xiv, 78–9, 81, 134, 206, 216, 324, 371
P.L. 111-256 (Rosa's Law, 2010) 96
placement *see* setting
planning and analysis tactics (TEAM strategic workforce renewal plan) **174**, 177–9
play skills **310**, 315, 352
policy reform advocacy **174**, 179–80
Polychronis, S. 66
Poplin, M. S. 244–5
portfolio assessment 54, *329*, 334
positive behavior intervention and supports (PBIS) 286, 458
post-hoc reasoning 235, 236, 245
postmodernism 245
post-school outcomes: in conceptual finance framework 411, 412, 415, 421, 422, 423, 425; and early intervention 100, 354; in the inclusion debate 218, 241, 423; legislative focus on readiness for 14, 15, 65, 323, *330*; measures of 68, 323, 332–3, 390, 391, 415–17; and the need to reconceptualize disability 369–76; post-secondary education programs 15, 368; and self-determination 378; sheltered/supported employment 14, 376, 378, 379; supports paradigm (for adults with disabilities) 369, 375–7, 378, 379; to evaluate special education effectiveness 323, 332–3, 335, 446
post-secondary education *see* college/post-secondary education

poverty: and academic performance 353–4, 416, 418–21; EBA applied to low SES schools 311–14, 317
power mapping **174**, 179
pre-academic skills 356–7, 361
prediction and first courses of treatment 437–8
prekindergarten/Pre-K: early intervention history 198, 351–2, 354–6; EBA approach 311, 315–16; longitudinal efficacy studies 353–4, 389–90; need for universal education 317, 318; pre-general education skills 23; program design 317, 343–5, 354–61, 362; reasons for early intervention 352–3
presence and participation, NCEO's conceptual-outcome model 325, *326*
presentation techniques 30
prevention models *see* multi-tiered systems of support
Primary Intervention Rating Scale (PIRS) 295
private placements 192, 193–4, 220, 223, 423
private program providers (prekindergarten) 344
private reflection (link in social-intuitionist model) 236, 237, 245
probability and science 436–8
productivity: a conceptual framework 410, 411–12; current provision knowledge 410, 412–17; dissemination activity potential 422–3; examples of high productivity districts 418–21; funding recommendations 421–5; link between funding formula and practices 413, 420, 421–2; RTI models 418, 419
professional development *see* teacher training/preparation
programmed instruction 304, 305, 306
program planning tools for EBD students in an MTS approach 287, 288, 291–3, 296
progress monitoring: alternate assessment 53–4; classroom structuring 305; EBD program planning/monitoring tools 287, 288, 289, 291–5, 296, 297; formative assessment 261; RTI for eligibility decision-making 135, 136, 137, 138–40, 142–3, 145, 147–9; and teaching for mastery 46, 47
Project RAISE 56–7
propaganda 237
proportionality/disproportionate representation 98–9, 110, 219
protected values 238, 239–40
PSI *see* Personalized Systems of Instruction
psychological process, basic deficits 14
PT *see* physical therapy
Pullen, P. 18, 36, 255, 256, 258, 387, 445, 448, *450*, 452
pull-out services 200–1, 202, 204–5, 206–7, 210, 217, 225, 226, 313
pupil-weighted funding formulas 413, 421–2, 424
Pyramid Model 361

quasi-experimental group studies 268, 272, 274

race *see* ethnicity
RAISE, Project 56–7
Rankin, S. W. 66

Rao, K. 456
rates of improvement measures (ROI) 138, 139, 142, 143, 149
rationalist-cognition models 234, 235
read alouds 55, 56, 57, *58*, 59–60, *61*, 66
Reading First funding 136
reading/literacy *see* literacy/reading
RealClimate 178
reasoned judgment (link in social-intuitionist model) 236, 245
reasoned persuasion (link in social-intuitionist model) 235–6
recognition-primed decision-making/practice 431, 433–4, 435–6, 438
recruitment 168, **174**, 180, 182
Regular Education Initiative xiii, 13, 201, 459
Rehabilitation Act (1973) 13, 191, 224, 229
REI *see* Regular Education Initiative
reinforcement: ADHD strategies 290; consequating responses 259–60; as instruction on continua component 41, 43, 44, 46, 47; intentional instruction for pre-school children 358, 360; and operant/environmental conditioning 41, 304, 305–6, 308, 313
related services *11*, 223–4, 346
research *see* evidence-based practice
residential placement 79–80, 206, 220–1, 346, 347, 371, 386
resource room placement 111, 200, 202, 206–7, 217, 225, 226
resources: 1950s equipment 12–13; age-appropriate reading material 120–1; argument against full inclusion 219, 228; assistive technology 22, 227, 229, 325, 375, 379; lack of in racially diverse settings 119, 120, 121; read alouds 55, 56, 57, *58*, 59–60, *61*, 66; for RTI implementation 145–50; special education textbooks 204; templates and commercial materials 67; *see also* tools/technology; Universal Design for Learning
response-shaping 360
response-to-intervention (RTI) models: academic focus of 286; as an optimal identification method 143–5; cost/resource implications 210, 418, 419–20; and the dilution of special education 457–8; for early intervention 134, 135, 137, 143, 226, 418, 421, 457; federal approval under IDEA 97; group size guidelines 40; intervention delivery 33, 136; for pre-school children 361; process of 135, 137–43, 147–50, 225; and the reduction of special education diagnoses 225, 347, 418, 419, 420, 421, 458; responding to the shift of special education to the general classroom 160, 225–6, 419, 420; and special education teacher skills 33, 170
responsibility and independence, NCEO's conceptual-outcome model 326
responsive interaction procedures 359, 360
reverse mainstreaming 355
Rhode Island 413

Riesen, T. 66
Rock, M. 159, 162, 166, 445, 448
Rockoff, J. E. 99–100
ROI *see* rates of improvement measures
Rosa's Law (P.L. 111-256, 2010) 96
Rosenshine, B. 256
Rush, B. 4
Ryndak, D. L. 55

Sachs, B. 4
sacralization 241
Sacramento City Unified School District v. Rachel H.
    (1994) 221
Sagan, C. 429, 436, 439
Sager, N. 109
Sanford, T. 179
Sanger Unified School District 419–20, 421
SASS System *see* Schools and Staffing Survey (SASS)
    System
Sass, T. 100, 168
satisfaction: NCEO's conceptual-outcome model 326;
    staff retention issues 168, 169, 172, 175, 177, 182
Schools and Staffing Survey (SASS) System
    174, 178
School-Wide Positive Behavior Support (SWPBS) 316
Schumaker, J. B. 157
science: content instruction 25, 55, 60, 62–5, 158;
    cultural-diversity case study 112; in decision-
    making 429, 432, 436–8, 439, 447, 449; and the
    rationale for special education 400–1; *see also*
    evidence-based practice
SCREAM variables 30
screening *see* eligibility; identification
Scruggs, T. E. 18, 21, 26–7, 30, 31, 157, 255, 258, 387,
    444, 445, 448, *450*
SDQ *see* Strengths and Difficulties Questionnaire
section 504 (of the 1973 Rehabilitation Act) 224, 229
segregation: history of inclusion/segregation xiii,
    12–13, 76, 195, 198–201, 215–16, 371–2, 385–6, *386*;
    sheltered/supported employment 14, 376, 378, 379;
    see also residential placement
self-advocacy 31, 372, 378
self-determination 369, 372, 378
self-monitoring 30, 31, 145–6, 257, 271, 290, 293, 294
Self Regulated Strategy Development (SRSD) 27–8
self-righteousness 236, 241
setting: activity-determined 189–91, 203–4;
    continuum of placement *see* continuum of
    placement; home (implementation fidelity)
    361–2; and the importance of instruction 203,
    205–6, 209–10, 211, 417, 446, 448; and learner
    characteristics 189, 191, 195, 203, 431; parental
    preference 193, 194, 217, 220–3, 230, 239; placement
    characteristics 190–1, 195; posing the question of
    "where" 187, 189–95, 446; private placements 192,
    193–4, 220, 223, 423; for related services 223–4; RTI
    as response to the shift to the general classroom 160,
    225–6, 419, 420; segregation *see* segregation; *see also*
    environmental structuring; inclusion

Shannon, C. 82, 83, 87
sheltered/supported employment 14, 376, 378, 379
Shriner, J.G. 327–8
sight-word instruction 53, 54, 55, 56
Simmerman, S. 273
single-subject research studies 268, 272, 273, 274, 275,
    276, 278
SIS *see* Supports Intensity Scales
situated learning (SL) **174**, 181
Skeels, H. M. 353
Skinner, B. F. 45, 304
SL *see* situated learning
slope data 138, 139, 294
SNAP *see* Student in Need of Alternative
    Programming
Snell, M. E. 53
social behavior *see* emotional and behavioral disorders
social-ecological models *see* person-environment
    models of disability
social-intuitionist model of moral judgment:
    application to full-inclusion debate 238–43; and the
    crossing of moral divides 234, 244–6; how moral
    values are held 233–4, 238–43; overview 195, 233,
    234–8
social media **173**, 176, 177, 179, 180, 181, 182
social persuasion (link in social-intuitionist model)
    235–6
Social Skills Improvement System-Performance
    Screening Guide (SSiS-PSG) 289, 292, 293, 297
Social Skills Improvement System-Rating Scales
    (SSiS-RS) 288
social validity of MTS interventions 292, 295–6
societal and economic benefits (of special education)
    385, 389–94
socio-economic background: and classroom
    structuring 311–14, 317; poverty/intellectual
    disability link 353–4
special education: definitions 11–19, 23–6, 37, 42–5,
    77–8, 81; dilution of 405, 457–9; history of *see*
    history of special education
speech therapy *11*, 12, 198, 224
Spencer, S. A. 254
Spitalnik, D. M. 376
Spooner, F. 456–7
SRSD strategy *see* Self Regulated Strategy
    Development (SRSD)
SRSS *see* Student Risk Screening Scale
SSBD *see* Systematic Screening for Behavior Disorders
SSiS-PSG *see* Social Skills Improvement
    System-Performance Screening Guide
SSiS-RS *see* Social Skills Improvement System-Rating
    Scales
staff retention/satisfaction issues 168, 169, 172, 175,
    177, 182
Stainback, S. 239, 457, 460
Stainback, W. 239, 457, 460
Stanley, S. O. 312
starting point of special education 6, 343–6, 351–3,
    447; *see also* early intervention

State Schools Act (1965) 198
Stecker, P. M. 457–8
stereotypes/stereotyping: African Americans 121; moral 241–3; and stigmatization *see* labeling
Stevens, R. 256
stigmatization *see* labeling; supports paradigm (for adults with disabilities)
Strain, P. 361
strategy instruction 28–30, 31, 271
Strengths and Difficulties Questionnaire (SDQ) 289
structured instruction *see* systematic instruction
structuring the learning environment *see* environmental structuring
Student in need of Alternative Programming (SNAP) 136
Student Risk Screening Scale (SRSS) 289
study skills/academic strategies 24–5
Success for All program 256, 257
Sullenberger, Chesley ("Sully") 431, 432, 433, 434, 438
Sullivan, A. 12
summer school 346
supported/sheltered employment 14, 376, 378, 379
Supports Intensity Scales 377
supports paradigm (for adults with disabilities) 369, 375–7, 378, 379
Supreme Court 13, 98, 199, 216, 222–3, 385, *386*
Sutherland, R. 173
Swanson, H. L. 157, 273
SWPBS *see* School-Wide Positive Behavior Support
systematic instruction: in continua of critical components 42, 43, 44, 46, 47; defined 38–9; and discovery method debate 452; intentional instruction for pre-school children 344–5, 357–61; in OTTER approach 255, 256–7; prompting and feedback 56, 59, 66, 259, *260*; in RTI first intervention 225; sequencing 39, 46, 256, 304, 305, 361; as special education critical component 12, 47, 205, 404, 445; as teacher skill 160; templates and commercial resources 67
Systematic Screening for Behavior Disorders (SSBD) 289, 297

talented/gifted students 13, *392–3*, 394, 452–3
Tankersley, M. xiv, 2, 275, 368, 437, 451
teachers: collaboration *see* collaboration; content expertise 100, 159, 161–2, 170–1, 172; decision-making 429, 430–6, 438–9; and EBD screening tools/identification 287–8, 289, 290, 291, 293; effectiveness/evaluation 66, 99–100, 140, 144, 168, 227, 324, 333–4, 404, 448; and evidence-based practice 171, 172, 280; interventionist 112, 128; need to understand the full context/family background 116–19, 122–6, 127, 128; pathognomonic 111, 128; personnel-based special education expenditure index 414; prekindergarten 362; Sanger district awards 419; shortage of/retention issues 100, 168–9, 170, 172, 177, 228; special education in a general education classroom 33, 46, 80, 93, 227–8, 404,

445; student ratio *see* group/class size; time use 171–2, **173**, 175–6; workforce renewal *see* workforce renewal plan; *see also* implementation fidelity/treatment integrity; instruction; teacher training/preparation
Teachers of the Deaf Act (1961) 198
teacher training/preparation: and administrative reasons for special education 401–2; co-teaching 162; fast track/alternative certification programs 100, 168, 169, 170; mid twentieth century legislation 198; need for teacher support 228; in TEAM workforce renewal plan **173, 174**, 177, 180–1; as a "who" question 93, 445
teaching pie: based on Bateman's OTTER approach 254, **255**; curricula 256; environment/classroom culture 255–6; evaluating 261–2; general teaching procedures 256–7; individual task instruction 258–60; planning 257–8
TEAM strategic workforce renewal plan: advocate for policy reform **174**, 179–80; collaboration/interdisciplinarity 173, 181, 182; planning and analysis tactics **174**, 177–9; recruitment, preparation/training and induction modernization **174**, 180–1; transforming workforce conditions **173**, 175–7
technology *see* tools/technology
templates: ecobehavioral *see* ecobehavioral assessment; teaching plans 67, 451
Texas 413
text summary 57, *58*
Theory of Instruction (Engelmann and Carnine) 87–9
Thomas, L. B. 141, 144
Thompson, Hunter S. 74–5
thought experiment *449–50*
threshold approach to categorizing EBP evidence base 277–8
Thurlow, M. L. 253, 262, 322, 324, 325, 446, *450*, 453, 455, 458
tiered models of instruction *see* multi-tiered systems of support
tools/technology: for assessment 332, 455; assistive 22, 227, 229, 325, 375, 379; behavior measurement 287, 288, 289–92, 293, 294–5, 296, 297; CBM 46, 135, 137, 138, 243, 261; cochlear implants 454–5; and group instruction 399; science as 270, 429; for the supports paradigm 377; workforce renewal **173, 174**, 175–7, 178, 179, 180–1 *see also* Universal Design for Learning
training/preparation *see* teacher training/preparation
treatment integrity/implementation fidelity *see* implementation fidelity/treatment integrity
Trela, K. 67
trend-line rule 135, 137, 140, 143, 144
Twain, Mark 79
Type I errors 271, 273
Type II errors 271, 273

UDL *see* Universal Design for Learning
United Cerebral Palsy Association 198

United Nations' Convention on the Rights of Persons with Disabilities (CRPD) 406, 459
Universal Design for Learning (UDL) 455–7

Val Verde Unified School District 420, 421
Vasile, C. 176
verbal reasoning 234, 235
visual learners 253
visually impaired students 12, 38, 224, 226, 227, 456
vocabulary 16, 29, 56, 66, 208, 254, 311, 317, **456**, 457
Volonino, V. 14, 404

Wagner, M. 390
Walker, H. M. 253, 257, 284, 289, 378, 446, *450*
web-based teacher support **173**, 176, 177, 179, 180–1
Weerts, D. J. 179
Wehmeyer, M. 346, 347, 348, 366, 447
weight 242–3
Weintraub, F. 37, 44
Weiss, M. P. 154, 156–7, 171, 209, 445, 458
Weller, M. 178
" what", questions of 6, 9, 11–19, 203–4, 444–5
What Works Clearinghouse (WWC) 181, 268, 274, 278, 313, 314
"when", questions of 6, 341, 343–8, 447
"where", questions of 6, 187, 189–95, 203–5, 446
"whither": special education 6–7, 441, 452

WHO *see* World Health Organization's conceptualizations of disability
"who", questions of 6, 93, 95–100, 203, 445
"why", questions of 6, 383, 385–95, 447
Wiley, A. L. 189, 195, 231, 446, 448, 449
Willis, T. 76
Will, M. 201
Wonder, Stevie *393*
workforce renewal plan 172–3; advocate for policy reform **174**, 179–80; collaboration/ interdisciplinarity 173, 181, 182; planning and analysis tactics **174**, 177–9; recruitment, preparation/training and induction modernization **174**, 180–1; transforming workforce conditions **173**, 175–7
workload studies (TEAM strategic workforce renewal plan) **173**, 176
World Health Organization's conceptualizations of disability 372–4
writing, as fun 74–5
WWC *see* What Works Clearinghouse
Wyoming 423, 425

young children *see* prekindergarten
Ysseldyke, J. E. 28, 325

Zigmond, N. P. 14, 31, 157, 189, 190, 191, 192, 195, 197, 404, 446, 448, 449, 459
Zirkel, P. A. 141, 144